The Birds of Gloucestershire

The Birds of Gloucestershire

Gordon Kirk and John Phillips
for the Gloucestershire Ornithological Co-ordinating Committee

Liverpool University Press

First published 2013 by
Liverpool University Press
4 Cambridge Street
Liverpool L69 7ZU

Copyright © 2013 Gordon Kirk and John Phillips for the Gloucestershire Ornithological Co-ordinating Committee

The authors' rights have been asserted in accordance with the Copyright, Designs and Patents Act, 1988.

All rights reserved. No part of this book may be reproduced, stored in a retrieval system, or transmitted, in any form or by any means, electronic, mechanical, photocopying, recording, or otherwise, without the prior written permission of the publisher.

British Library Cataloguing-in-Publication data
A British Library CIP record is available

ISBN 978-1-84631-808-5

Designed and typeset by BBR (www.bbr.uk.com)

Cover illustrations by Terence Lambert

Printed and bound by Gutenberg Press, Malta
Gutenberg Press prints for BirdLife Malta

Contents

vii	Foreword by HRH the Prince of Wales
viii	Abbreviations
ix	Acknowledgements
1	An outline of Gloucestershire and its birdlife
38	A brief history of bird watching, recording and conservation in Gloucestershire
42	The 2007–11 Bird Atlas project
48	Bird surveys in Gloucestershire

Species accounts

52	Introduction
58	The main accounts
431	Exotics and escapes
433	Appendix 1: Square stewards and fieldworkers
437	Appendix 2: Scientific names of non-bird species
438	Appendix 3: A checklist of the birds of Gloucestershire
442	References
446	Index to scientific names of birds
449	Index to English names of birds

ILLUSTRATION: LITTLE TERN BY KEITH SHACKLETON

CLARENCE HOUSE

When I can find time to retreat to my home at Highgrove, in Gloucestershire, one of the greatest joys that I look forward to is being able to see and hear the birds that live there and which, over the last thirty-two years, I have done my best to encourage and sustain. From my study window I can see the birds I feed during the Winter – among others, various tits, finches and thrushes, not to mention woodpeckers and nuthatches. In Summer, swallows and house martins nest among the outbuildings, while owls of various kinds, including barn owls, add ornithological interest during the night hours.

While my casual observations give a general impression of those species present and, relatively speaking, how common or scarce they are, I am acutely aware that what can be noticed by a single person is never enough to ascertain the whole picture. That is why I was delighted to hear that volunteer birdwatchers working with the British Trust for Ornithology, or B.T.O., would between 2007 and 2011 be making regular visits to Highgrove to gather data on which birds were there, how many of them there were and how their numbers changed from year to year.

I was all the more impressed to learn that not only were there to be systematic surveys of Highgrove, but also of the whole county of Gloucestershire – and, indeed, the whole British Isles – so as to compile a new countrywide Atlas. One result of all this hard work is the book you have in your hand. It contains a summary of the information collected for Gloucestershire and is by far the most up-to-date and comprehensive summary of birds in our county.

With information gathered by members of the B.T.O., it has been possible to put together accurate detailed maps revealing the distribution of our many different species of birds – and, in the process, creating a marvellous book that will be of general interest to anyone with even the faintest interest in birds – while at the same time producing a science-based tool that will be invaluable in the years ahead, not least in conserving the birds that we so often take for granted.

No part of the world will escape the effects of major global changes that are already underway, especially as a result of ever-more extreme shifts in climate, and the more we know about how things are changing at the level of individual species, and in different geographical areas, the more likely we will succeed in conserving our rich and precious wildlife. The fine detail gathered in this book will certainly contribute to that process.

I greatly admire the productivity of the amateur naturalists who diligently document the natural world around us and will therefore treasure my copy of "The Birds of Gloucestershire".

Abbreviations

BBS	BTO/JNCC/RSPB Breeding Bird Survey
BBRC	British Birds Rarities Committee
BTO	British Trust for Ornithology
BOU	British Ornithologists' Union
BWP	*Birds of the Western Palearctic* (Cramp *et al.* 1977–94; Snow & Perrins 1998)
CDNS	Cheltenham & District Naturalists' Society
CNFC	Cotteswold Naturalists' Field Club
DBPS	Dursley Birdwatching and Preservation Society
GBR	*Gloucestershire Bird Report*
GNS	Gloucestershire Naturalists' Society
GOCC	Gloucestershire Ornithological Co-ordinating Committee
GWT	Gloucestershire Wildlife Trust
IOC	International Ornithological Committee
JNCC	Joint Nature Conservation Committee
NA	Natural Area
NCOS	North Cotswold Ornithological Society
RBBP	Rare Breeding Birds Panel (for use as an academic reference, see p. 53)
RSPB	Royal Society for the Protection of Birds
SEGG	Severn Estuary Gull Group
SSSI	Site of Special Scientific Interest
TTV	Timed Tetrad Visit
WeBS	BTO Wetland Bird Survey
WWT	Wildfowl & Wetlands Trust

1875–1900 Atlas	*The Historical Atlas of Breeding Birds in Britain and Ireland* (Holloway 1996)
1968–72 Breeding Atlas	*The Atlas of Breeding Birds in Britain and Ireland* (Sharrock 1976)
1981–84 Wintering Atlas	*The Atlas of Wintering Birds in Britain and Ireland* (Lack 1986)
1988–91 Breeding Atlas	*The New Atlas of Breeding Birds in Britain and Ireland* (Gibbons *et al.* 1993)
1983–87 (or 'first') Cotswolds Atlas	*An Atlas of Cotswold Breeding Birds* (Wright *et al.* 1990)
2003–07 (or 'second') Cotswolds Atlas	*Birds of the Cotswolds: a new breeding atlas* (Main *et al.* 2009)

Acknowledgements

The production of this book has been possible only through the hard work and dedication of hundreds of individuals and the invaluable input of many different organisations, and here we do our best to acknowledge those who have contributed. We apologise wholeheartedly if anyone has been inadvertently omitted.

The 2007–11 Bird Atlas project

Atlas committee

The committee that was set up to organise the national atlas project at the county level consisted of Richard Baatsen, Phil Davis, David Evans, Mike King, Gordon Kirk, Andy Lewis, John Phillips, Mike Smart, Neil Smart and Michael Sutcliffe. Members of this committee provided unwavering support and good counsel throughout the project and happily took on any tasks they were asked to perform.

In particular, David Evans offered much invaluable advice, drawing on his 11-year stint as editor of the *Gloucestershire Bird Report* (GBR).

Fieldwork

Most of our knowledge of Gloucestershire's birdlife is ultimately derived from records provided by individual observers. In particular, the maps that appear in the species accounts are based on records submitted during the 2007–11 national atlas project, and the names of all those who took part in atlas fieldwork in the county are listed in Appendix 1 (p. 433). These observers were ably supported and cajoled by the 'square stewards', also listed in Appendix 1, who made sure the fieldwork was completed on time and according to the correct methodology, and also played an important role in checking the data for 'their' squares. We are grateful to the county's bird clubs, the Gloucestershire Naturalists' Society (GNS) and the Gloucestershire Wildlife Trust (GWT) for the part they played in supporting and publicising the project and encouraging their members to get involved.

In addition to the results of this important survey, we have drawn on information dating back to the nineteenth century and beyond to document the changing fortunes of Gloucestershire's birds, and we are indebted to all the county's birdwatchers and ornithologists, past and present. We particularly acknowledge all those contributors, too numerous to mention here by name, who since 1947 have submitted their records to the annual GBRs.

Records and data analysis

This project could not have been undertaken without the tremendous support provided by the national atlas team at the British Trust for Ornithology (BTO), notably Dawn Balmer and Simon Gillings, who have answered our many queries promptly and patiently, and spent a great deal of time providing detailed county-level data.

Richard Baatsen, the county bird recorder, has played a central role throughout the project, checking records on the county bird database and answering many questions about records old and new. Both he and Phil Davis devoted considerable time and effort to producing many lists, summaries and tables.

The 'Birds of Gloucestershire' project

Developing the text

Each of the 330 bird species accounts in this book results from the collaboration of two or more writers, rather than being the work of a single author. The species were initially divided up and allocated to a total of ten writers, who produced first drafts of the text. These drafts were then reviewed and revised by the two editors with the original writers and, in a few cases, they were also shown to additional reviewers for comment. For some species, by the time the final account was produced, the initial draft had been subjected to ten or more revisions by various contributors and in such cases the end product is, not surprisingly, significantly different from the original.

With this in mind, it would be misleading to credit species accounts to individual authors. However, it remains true that the writers to whom the species were originally allocated did the bulk of the background research and the collation of information, and their hard work is warmly acknowledged as follows:

- David Evans: 59 species, particularly wildfowl, gamebirds and rarities
- Andy Lewis: 20 species, particularly thrushes and finches
- Andrew Jayne: 17 species, notably raptors, waders, crakes and pigeons
- John Sanders: Black-headed, Lesser Black-backed, Herring, Yellow-legged, Caspian, Iceland, Glaucous, Great Black-backed and Glaucous-winged Gulls
- Mike Smart: Grey Heron, Little Egret, Snipe, Curlew, Lapwing and Redshank
- Jerry Lewis: Goshawk and Hawfinch
- Frank Lander: Pied Flycatcher
- Ivan Proctor: Nightjar

The remaining 215 species accounts were initially drafted by the two editors, although these too were substantially revised.

Neither of the editors of this book was 'born and bred' in Gloucestershire, and we would not have been able to complete the task without drawing on the knowledge and experience of local birdwatchers and experts in their field. The following provided valuable comments and input for various sections of the book, including the introductory and background chapters as well as the species accounts:

Gareth Harris (Cotswold Water Park Trust), Richard Hearn (Wildfowl & Wetlands Trust (WWT)), Andrew Jayne, Jenny Kirk, Heather Lilley (Forestry Commission), Ben MacDonald, Paul Masters, Martin McGill (WWT), Hannah Morton (RSPB), Julia Newth (WWT), Dave Pearce, Viv Phillips, Vic Polley, Ivan Proctor, Ian Ralphs and Mike Smart.

Andrew Bluett provided a great deal of very useful and interesting background material relating to the history of ornithology in the county and to species which have become extinct as breeding birds here.

Special mention and thanks are due to Peter Rock and John Sanders, not only for their dedication to monitoring gulls, but also for their willingness to share their data, knowledge and expertise. Similarly, Frank Lander helped us with essential background about Pied Flycatchers in the Forest of Dean.

Jacquie Clark and Dorian Moss of the BTO were very helpful in responding to queries about ringing records.

Keith Naylor provided information about historical rarities.

A number of local birders, notably Andrew Jayne and Mike Smart, gave us much useful information about birds and birding in the county, especially at the Severn Estuary. Information on other, more specific bird-related points came from Gordon Avery, Roy Bircher, Terry Fenton, John Overfield and Dave Pearce.

Early in the project we occasionally sought advice from our counterparts in other counties where similar books had already been produced. In particular, Peter Cranswick, one of the co-authors of *Birds of Wiltshire* (Wiltshire Ornithological Society 2007) provided valuable guidance in the initial stages. Members of the NCOS editorial committee for *Birds of the Cotswolds* (Main et al. 2009), especially Iain Main and Peter Dymott, also provided very useful support and advice.

Finally, as our writing task was drawing to a close, we were delighted when HRH the Prince of Wales agreed to provide a foreword for the book.

Generating the maps

Almost all the dot maps in this book were produced by Phil Davis using DMAP for Windows v7.3a, a huge and complex task which Phil undertook with great skill and enthusiasm. The exceptions are those on p. 3, which were created by Dave Pearce. We also gratefully acknowledge Dr Alan Morton, the creator of DMAP, for his excellent support.

Bob Hubbard provided invaluable advice to help ensure that the dot maps were clear to colour-blind readers.

The background map used in the species accounts and the general map of the county on p. xii were produced by Geoinnovations Ltd. They contain public sector information licensed under the Open Government Licence v1.0.

The water features map on p. 2 (courtesy of BTO) was produced by Neil Calbrade and contains Ordnance Survey data. © Crown copyright and database right (2012).

The Natural Areas map on p. 3 was produced by Esther Collis of Gloucestershire County Council. © Crown copyright and database right (2012), Ordnance Survey 100019134.

Linda Moore of the Gloucestershire Centre for Environmental Records provided advice on maps and mapping on several occasions.

Artwork

It was decided at an early stage that this book should have artwork as well as photographs to accompany the species accounts. Paul Walkden did a splendid job as art editor in acquiring the magnificent illustrations in this book which draw on the talents of some of the best bird artists in the country, including a number who sadly are no longer with us. Sir Peter Scott, for example, simply had to appear: he is internationally recognised as 'The Father of Conservation', and he lived at Slimbridge for some 40 years as founder and Honorary Director of WWT and co-founder of the World Wide Fund for Nature. We are particularly grateful to Dafila Scott for permission to use her father's work in this volume.

Terence Lambert, Peter Partington and Jackie Garner merit special mention as they took time out of their busy schedules to produce much of the artwork. Terence also painted the pictures for the cover. However, giving these major contributors a special mention is in no way to detract from the part played by all of the artists, either in producing new work or for allowing existing material to have another airing. In this respect special thanks are due to Terance James Bond, Keith Shackleton, Robert Gillmor and Thelma Sykes. Moss Taylor kindly gave permission for us to use artwork by R. A. Richardson in his possession. Some of the illustrations have already appeared elsewhere, but a greater number have been specially created for this volume. They were all provided at no cost and we thank you all for your enthusiasm, kindness and commitment to this project.

Artists: Richard Baatsen, Terance James Bond, Basil Ede, Andrew Forkner, Jackie Garner, Robert Gillmor, Tim Hayward, Terence Lambert, Jonathan Latimer, Martin McGill, Rodger McPhail, Julian Novorol, Peter Partington, Bruce Pearson, Darren Rees, Chris Rose, Richard A. Richardson, Peter Scott, Keith Shackleton, Trevor Smith, Thelma Sykes, Archibald Thorburn, Simon Trinder, Ian Wallace, Mike Warren and Owen Williams.

Photographs

The county's bird photographers were generous in making many images available, again free of charge, and the process of gathering, cataloguing and selecting them was ably co-ordinated by Andy Lewis. All the bird photographs were taken by local birders, and the vast majority were taken in the county. However there are a few exceptions, notably Red-breasted Merganser (p. 105), Arctic Tern (p. 237), auks (pp. 242-43), Lesser Whitethroat (p. 330), Marsh Warbler (p. 340), White's Thrush (p. 355) and rarer finches (pp. 420-21).

Landscape photography by Terry Fenton, Gordon Kirk, James S. Lees, Andy Lewis, John Phillips, John Sanders, Lewis Thomson and Colin Twissell.

Bird photography by Phil and Chris Andrews, Gavin Black, Andrew Bluett, Paul Bowerman, Mike Boyes, Rob Brookes, Mark Dowie, Gareth Harris/Cotswold Water Park Trust, Dave Pearce, Mark Hope, Malcolm Hopkins, Gordon Kirk, James S. Lees, Helen Mugridge, Peter Rock, John Sanders, Lewis Thomson, Richard Tyler and Graham Watson.

Robert Bewley donated his valuable time to take the aerial photographs which appear in 'An outline of Gloucestershire and its birdlife' and on p. 42.

The main satellite image of the county which appears on the end-papers was produced by Cosmographics Ltd, © PlanetObserver (www.planetobserver.com), all rights reserved.

The detailed satellite images in 'An outline of Gloucestershire and its birdlife' and on p. 50 are by Infoterra RGB Aerial Photography © GeoPerspectives (courtesy of Gloucestershire Centre for Environmental Records).

Book production

We wish to express our sincere thanks to Anthony Cond and the team at Liverpool University Press for their support throughout this project, and also to Chris Reed and Amanda Thompson at BBR, who have done such a great job in turning everybody's work into the book you are reading. Their patience and professionalism have been outstanding.

Finance

Most importantly, the whole project would not have been possible without adequate funding. The GNS acted as bankers for the project and also stood as the legal entity which signed contracts, official documents and the like. The GNS also provided by far the largest single financial contribution to this book, donating £10,000 at the beginning of the project, and the support provided by the GNS executive committee and officers is gratefully acknowledged. Lynne Garner and Patrick Wise provided invaluable assistance by devising a fundraising strategy and helping to carry it through such that more than £13,000 in additional funding was raised from various sources. The Trefoil Trust and the Jack Lane Charitable Trust each gave £500 and the Langtree Trust, £300. The county's bird clubs donated a total of £2,100. Around £6,000 (including Gift Aid) was raised by species sponsorship, mainly from atlas volunteers; another splendid response by them. The sum of £1,750 came from a service level agreement with the Gloucestershire Centre for Environmental Records concerning use of the atlas data, and a successful bid for £1,640 was made to the Natural History Museum's Open Air Laboratories (OPAL) Fund, which distributes money from the Big Lottery Fund. Finally, around £600 came from consultancy work carried out by the county bird recorder. All these contributions are very gratefully acknowledged.

Last, but by no means least, we thank our wives, Jenny Kirk and Viv Phillips, for all their support and encouragement during this very time-consuming project.

Figure 1. The county of Gloucestershire, showing relief, principal roads and the main settlements.

An outline of Gloucestershire and its birdlife

The earliest surviving written reference to 'Gloucestershire' appears to be in the *Anglo-Saxon Chronicle* for the year 1016, in connection with a meeting at Alney, 'by Deerhurst' between King Cnut (Canute) and King Edmund. It seems that the county at that time comprised two former 'shires' governed from Gloucester and Cirencester, together with the then 'small town' of Bristol. Shortly afterwards much of the Forest of Dean was incorporated, along with another 'shire' based on Winchcombe, which was then an important administrative and commercial centre although these days it is only a small Cotswold town. Thus, the approximate shape of modern Gloucestershire was created (Figure 1).

Over the years, however, the county boundary has undergone some quite radical changes, especially during the nineteenth and twentieth centuries. Previously very intricate convolutions or 'wiggles' in the border have been smoothed out in a number of areas, and some completely detached portions of Gloucestershire and its neighbours have been reassigned to different counties to create more logical, easily administered territories. A number of these former complexities still survive in the boundaries of the Watsonian vice-counties, which were devised in the mid-nineteenth century and continue to be used for some biological recording purposes; Gloucestershire broadly corresponds to vice-counties 33 and 34. However, for recording birds the modern county boundary is used.

A more recent and significant change took place when the Local Government Act (1972) came into effect on April 1st 1974. On this date a substantial area of south-west Gloucestershire, east of the Severn, was transferred to the newly created county of Avon, which subsequently established its own bird recording scheme. In 1996 Avon was abolished and its former Gloucestershire component was transformed into the new Unitary Local Authority of South Gloucestershire, which remains administratively separate from the rest of the county. For the sake of continuity it was decided to retain the existing Avon bird recording area in its entirety and, accordingly, no records from what is now South Gloucestershire are included in this book.

In common with all counties, Gloucestershire is a highly artificial entity in biogeographical terms. It is located at the meeting point of four broadly defined regions of the country, namely the South Midlands, the Welsh Marches, South Wales and the South-west Peninsula, and its landscapes and wildlife show affinities with each of these regions. In addition, and very significantly, Gloucestershire is deeply penetrated in the south-west by the upper Severn Estuary, linking it with the Bristol Channel and thence the open sea. This imparts a decidedly maritime aspect to what is, conversely, a county whose most interior parts are as far from the sea as anywhere in England. Figure 2 (overleaf) shows the Gloucestershire boundary with its neighbouring counties, and also gives an indication of relief together with the principal urban areas and the main rivers and lakes (this image is also used as the background for the maps shown in the species accounts). Figure 3 shows the county's water features in more detail, including canals and ditches as well as rivers and lakes.

Gloucestershire is very much an average-sized rural English county, measuring some 70 km from east to west and 45 km north to south, with a boundary approximately 400 km long. Its surface area is about 2,700 km^2, close to the mean of 3,200 km^2 for the 33 current non-metropolitan English counties; it ranks seventeenth out of these 33 in terms of area. There are quite extensive tracts of land in the Severn Vale that are not much above sea level, but there are also some substantial areas of relatively high ground. At 330 m (just over 1,000 ft) Cleeve Hill, on the edge of the Cotswold scarp just north-west of Cheltenham, is the highest point in the county and indeed in the whole of the Cotswolds; May Hill, a prominent feature close to the Herefordshire border near Newent, reaches 296 m, and parts of the Forest of Dean plateau are almost as high.

Most of the county's inhabitants are concentrated in the main towns of Gloucester, Cheltenham, Stroud and Cirencester, and overall Gloucestershire is a comparatively thinly populated county. In 2010 it had about 593,500 residents, an average density of 188 people per square kilometre, rather below the mean of about 250

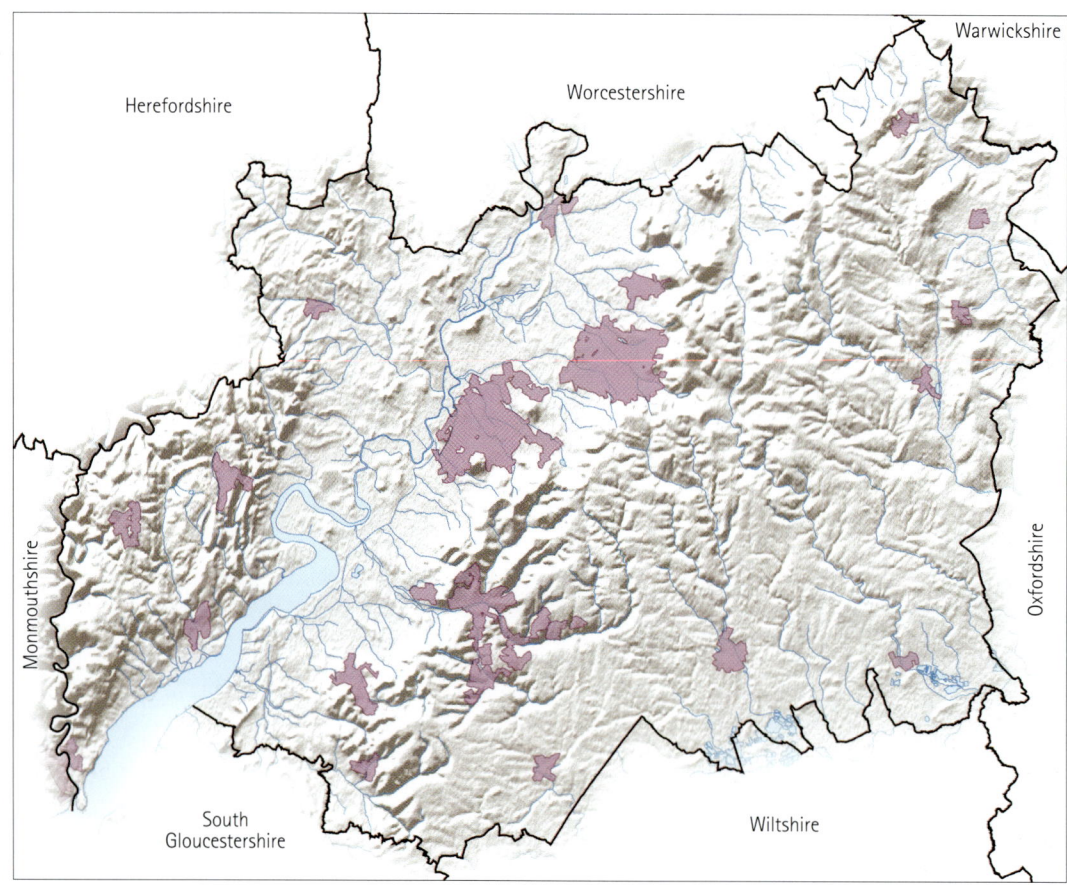

Figure 2. Gloucestershire and its neighbouring counties, showing relief, the principal urban areas (in purple) and the main rivers and lakes.

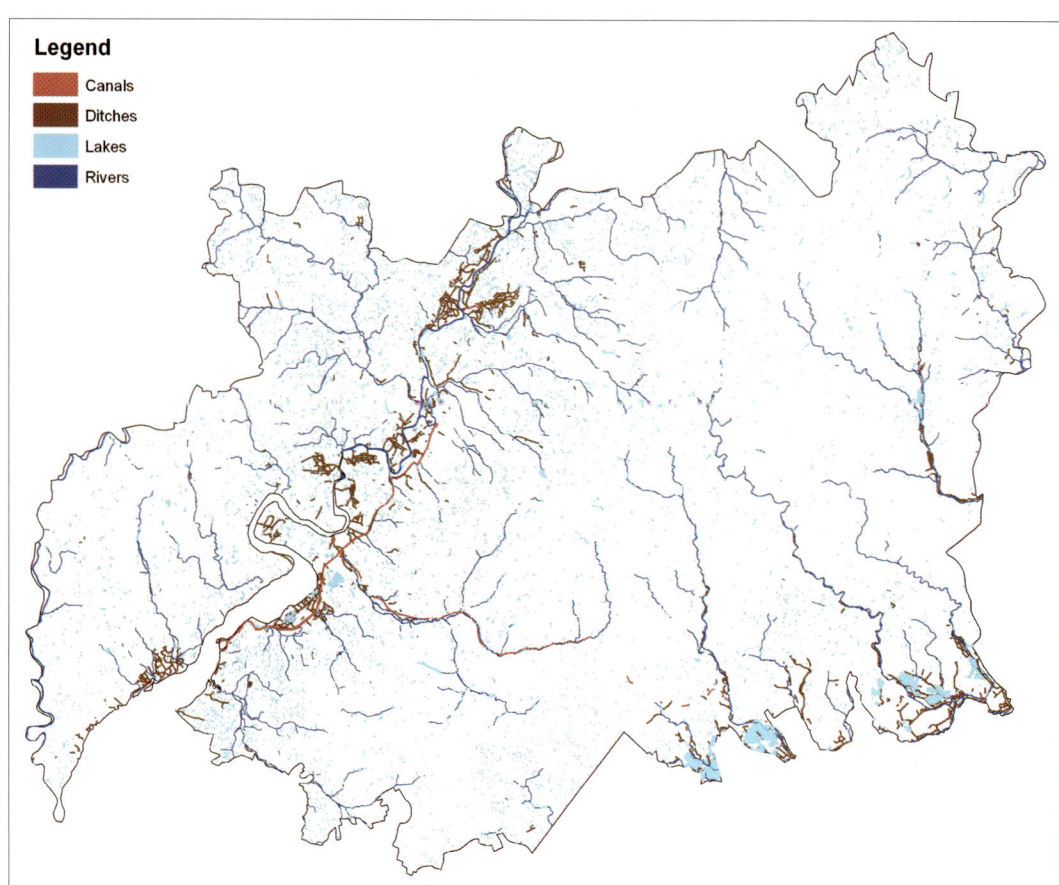

Figure 3. The county's water features in more detail, including canals and main ditches as well as rivers and lakes.

An outline of Gloucestershire and its birdlife

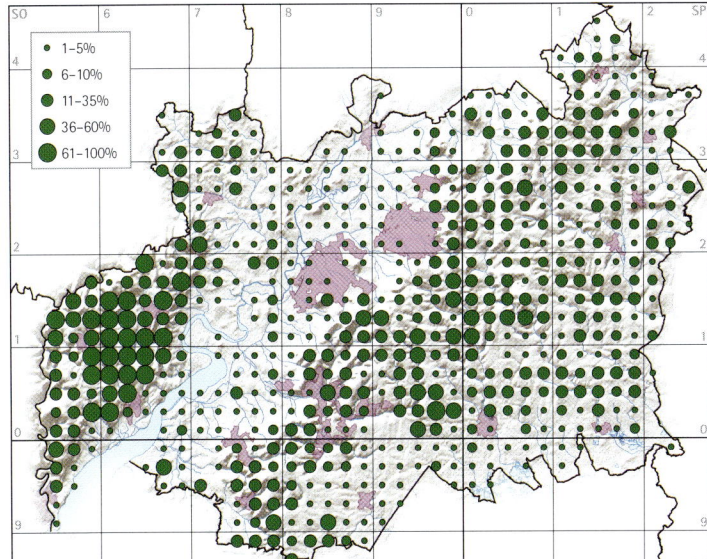

Figure 4. The approximate distribution of woodland in Gloucestershire, mapped by tetrad.

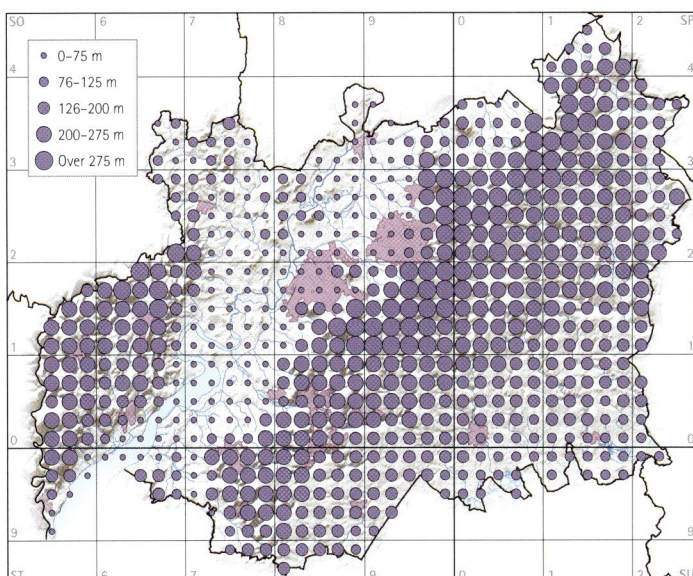

Figure 5. The estimated maximum altitude of each tetrad in Gloucestershire.

per square kilometre for the 33 rural English counties and making it twentieth out of these 33 counties in decreasing order of population density.

Overall this is one of the warmer English counties, but the climate varies quite considerably between different districts. At Gloucester city in the Severn Vale the mean maximum temperature in January is 8°C and the mean minimum is 3°C; in July the figures are 23°C and 13°C respectively. Mean annual rainfall there is about 738 mm (29 ins). Compared with the Vale, the Forest of Dean plateau receives significantly more rain, up to 1,000 mm or even higher in the west. Rainfall amounts in most of the Cotswolds are intermediate between the two, and this is the part of the county with the most markedly 'continental' climate, experiencing higher summer and lower winter temperatures than elsewhere. The highest and most open parts of the Cotswolds in particular can be forbiddingly bleak and exposed during cold winter weather. Quite frequently the higher areas of the Dean and most notably the high Cotswolds experience fairly heavy snowfalls, which lower in the Vale fall as rain. Especially during south-westerly gales, the wind can be a noticeable feature of the weather, particularly in the Vale, where the high land of the Dean on the one side and the Cotswolds on the other tend to create a funnelling effect.

Figures 4 and 5 show the county's woodland cover and relief on a tetrad basis, using dots in a similar way to the maps in the species accounts. In Figure 4 the size of the dot indicates what percentage of the tetrad is woodland, and in Figure 5 the size of the dot is proportional to the maximum altitude in the tetrad. These features are mapped on the basis of subjective assessments, so these maps are not completely precise at tetrad level, but they do give an overall picture and, together with Figures 2 and 3, may be used alongside the species maps to assess whether a given species is associated with these broad habitat features.

For the purposes of describing the landscapes, habitats and the birds that they support, it is useful to refer to the system of Natural Areas (NAs), instigated in 1993 by what was then English Nature (currently Natural England). These have been formally defined as 'biogeographic zones which reflect the geological foundation, the natural systems and processes and the wildlife in different parts of England and provide a framework for setting objectives for nature conservation divisions'. Rather than being determined by artificial, political boundaries, NAs are based on geomorphology, landscape types, land use and other large-scale human impacts, and wildlife. As Figure 6 shows, Gloucestershire contains parts of eight different NAs but, as three of these barely extend into the county, for bird recording purposes they are included in their larger, neighbouring NAs. Each of the NAs are described in turn below, progressing from west to east across the county.

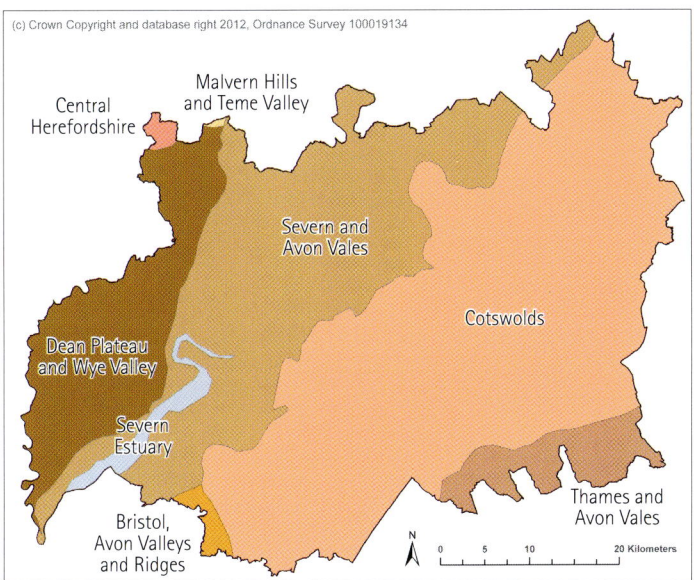

Figure 6. Gloucestershire's eight Natural Areas.

JOHN PHILLIPS

Dean Plateau and Wye Valley (NA G1)

The boundary of this NA in Gloucestershire is defined in the west by the border with Monmouthshire and Herefordshire, and in the east and south by the western limit of the low-lying Severn Vale. In the far north it borders two other NAs, namely the Malvern Hills and Teme Valley NA, and the Central Herefordshire NA, both of which extend only marginally into Gloucestershire.

Within the county, the NA comprises three distinct zones: the valley of the river Wye itself, the Forest of Dean plateau, and the 'wild daffodil country' of Over Severn, which straddles the Gloucestershire–Herefordshire border. The river valley and part of the Dean plateau are included in the Wye Valley Area of Outstanding Natural Beauty, as designated in 1971.

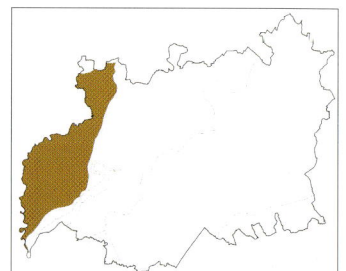

River Wye

Apart from two minor deviations the Wye runs along the Gloucestershire border for some 55 km, from the northern foot of the Forest of Dean plateau to its confluence with the Severn at Beachley Point near Chepstow. For much of this distance the river winds its way along a steep-sided, wooded valley through Devonian Old Red Sandstone, where any cultivation tends to be along the narrow band of low-lying land

An outline of Gloucestershire and its birdlife

adjacent to the river itself. In its lower reaches the river runs swiftly through deep and, by British standards at least, spectacular gorges, cut through Carboniferous Limestone. The Wye is always visibly tidal for several kilometres upstream from the Severn confluence, and occasionally as far as Redbrook, about 30 km upriver from Beachley.

The Wye Valley has extensive areas of ancient semi-natural woodland: much is of international ecological significance and there are some parts, especially on the steeper slopes, that are thought to have changed little since the days when most of Britain was covered by ancient 'wildwood'. These Wye woods are among the most natural woodlands in England, and are very species-rich. Although there is a long history of active management including coppicing, cessation of such traditional practices has resulted in a large proportion of the woods being unmanaged for the last 50 to 100 years.

On the river itself there are nesting Kingfishers and Grey Wagtails, and a number of small colonies of Sand Martins. The Wye also supports increasing numbers of Goosanders and Cormorants, particularly during winter. The cliffs overlooking the river provide nesting sites for Buzzards and Ravens, and one of the best-known places in the whole country for Peregrines is the viewing point at Symonds Yat Rock, from where the local pair is watched by thousands of visitors every year. A wide range of other species also feed or breed along the river-banks.

The sandstone of the Wye gorge near Symonds Yat. Kingfishers and other waterbirds share the river with human activities such as canoeing and fishing.

A satellite image of a meander in the lower Wye at Lancaut, taken early in the morning and showing the shadows cast by the steep cliffs, some of the few natural cliffs in the county. The waterbody in the bottom right corner is a flooded former quarry, now the home of the National Dive and Activity Centre.

Forest of Dean

The present-day Forest of Dean mostly lies in a saucer-shaped depression in a fairly high (150–200 m), steep-sided plateau. The whole is underlain by Coal Measures and surrounded by a narrow band of sandstones, with limestone becoming more predominant towards the Wye.

Within the central plateau the Dean takes the form of a parallel series of steep valleys and intervening ridges, running approximately north–south. In these valleys the watercourses are lined with wet woodland, particularly of alder and willow, and they have been dammed in places to form artificial ponds or minor lakes, including Soudley Ponds, Cannop Ponds and the lakes at Mallard's Pike. In addition, the lake at Woorgreens near Cinderford was created by flooding an open-cast coal site after mining ended there in 1981.

An abundance of coal and metal ores, together with large quantities of timber, has meant that the Dean has been heavily industrialised at certain periods. Iron and other metals were widely mined, especially during Roman times and also in the seventeenth and eighteenth centuries. Similarly, the Coal Measures have been extensively worked, with coal still being mined in the area, albeit on a very small scale. Stone for building and for the production of lime has also been extracted over many years and there are still a number of active quarries, some of which, such as those near Stowe and near Drybrook, are quite large operations. Relics of this industrial history are visible today in the form of variously overgrown spoil heaps, disused lime kilns, mine reservoirs and old railway trackways, many of the latter having been converted into footpaths and cycle routes. Since the mid-twentieth century, forestry and increasingly tourism

The lake at Woorgreens resulted from opencast mining and is an unusual habitat in the Dean area. It is jointly managed by the Forestry Commission and the GWT.

Cannop Ponds: part of the wetland habitat here is a GWT reserve.

An outline of Gloucestershire and its birdlife

A disused railway near Cannop. The central Forest of Dean is criss-crossed by a network of disused goods lines.

have been the main industries, and the Forest has developed the rural, tranquil character we see today. This belies the fact that the Dean is fairly densely populated, with villages and small towns intermingled with the wooded areas. Farming is mostly concentrated around the west and south-west edges of the central plateau where the land, though high and exposed, is flatter and more easily cultivated. Some traditional haymaking and grazing still takes place on the poorer soils around the periphery of the Forest, as well as on the steeper slopes of the Wye Valley. Elsewhere, richer soils support a mixture of intensively managed pasture and arable land, with some orchards, especially around the eastern and northern edges of the Dean plateau.

It is as a large block of wooded countryside that the Forest of Dean is most important for birds and other wildlife. The Dean was given Royal Forest status in the eleventh century, meaning that dwellings and grazing animals were largely prohibited. This, together with the district's isolation and topography, goes a long way towards explaining the continuous presence of woodland. In 1668 the Dean Forest (Reafforestation) Act was passed with the aim of replenishing the stocks of trees that had been much depleted by the removal of mature timber for shipbuilding. Many of the broad-leaved plantations, particularly of sessile oak and beech, that were established in this era now have a mature, 'semi-natural'

Ruardean, on the northern edge of the Dean plateau, looking into Wales. Here the landscape opens out into pasture and small blocks of woodland.

An outline of Gloucestershire and its birdlife

A satellite image of woodland at Nagshead, near Coleford, showing the contrast between the more recent plantations on the left and the older, natural woodland, including the Nagshead RSPB reserve, on the right. Part of Cannop Ponds can be seen at the top right.

A clear-fell area at New Fancy View; sites like this can provide habitat for Nightjars and Tree Pipits.

Heath restoration at Edge Hills near Cinderford.

character. Of the NA as a whole, about one-sixth (over 14,000 ha) has been identified as ancient woodland, that is, woodland present since approximately 1600. Much of this is now very different in character from its original state, particularly because of the planting of non-native conifers, although current Forestry Commission policy means that the area occupied by native broad-leaved species is increasing again.

Since Saxon times the understorey in the Forest has been browsed by sheep, producing a generally open structure. Sheep grazing is still quite widespread, though at a lower level since the outbreak of foot-and-mouth disease in 2001. The Dean now also harbours rapidly increasing populations of deer (mostly fallow but with recent sightings of roe and muntjac) and also wild boar. Along with the ubiquitous and very numerous grey squirrels, these herbivores seem certain to have profound effects on the structure and composition of the Dean woodlands in years to come.

Whilst much of the Forest is occupied by woodland and plantations there are also some fairly extensive open areas of grassland and scrub, for example around settlements and on former industrial areas, where poor soils or continued grazing have suppressed the growth of trees. There is also a shifting mosaic, amounting to a significant total area, of temporary grassland and scrub which develop in the years immediately following the harvesting of timber by clear-felling. In years gone by, heath was widespread on the Dean plateau, and the vegetation that appears in some clear-fell areas has a distinct heathland character, including plants such as heather, gorse and bilberry. Very often these areas have been restocked with trees, but increasingly heath restoration is being undertaken, for example at the Park and Poor's Allotment near Tidenham, Wigpool Common near Mitcheldean, and Crabtree Hill and Edge Hills near Cinderford.

The characteristic birds of the Dean's broad-leaved woodlands are those that prefer open-structured western oak woods: Redstarts, Pied Flycatchers and Wood Warblers. Other Dean specialities include Lesser Spotted Woodpeckers and Hawfinches, both of which have undergone severe national declines in recent years. A few pairs of similarly threatened Turtle Doves and Willow Tits can also still be found.

Some conifer plantations now contain stands of old trees that are of value for conservation and provide nesting habitat for an increasing population of Goshawks, as well as Crossbills, Siskins and small numbers of Firecrests. The newly restored areas of heath have already attracted some birds typical of this habitat, including Stonechats and Linnets, with indications that other, rarer species might also follow. Clear-fells at different stages of regrowth provide ideal nesting habitat for Tree Pipits and Nightjars as well as commoner species such as Willow Warblers and Whitethroats.

Many of the Dean's woodland birds can be seen at the Nagshead reserve operated by the Royal Society for the Protection of Birds (RSPB), which contains a good mix of recent plantations and older, more natural woodland.

Dippers can be found on some of the streams, although not in such high numbers as in parts of the Cotswolds. The larger waterbodies provide habitat for a healthy breeding population of Mandarin Ducks, which have become a Forest of Dean speciality and, despite their exotic origins, seem to coexist peacefully with the local Mute Swans, feral Canada and Greylag Geese, Mallard, Moorhens, and a few pairs of Coots. The artificial cliffs created by quarrying are used as nest sites for species such as Kestrels, Jackdaws and Stock Doves.

Outside the Forest, in the strict woodland sense, the area of mixed farmland on the plateau around Bream and St Briavels still supports a few Tree Sparrows, Lapwings and also Yellowhammers, which are otherwise scarce in this part of the county. One or two pairs of Curlews are present most years in the St Briavels area.

Over Severn

An area of gently undulating country, this accounts for approximately 100 km^2 of Gloucestershire and lies to the north-east of the Forest of Dean in the area around Newent and Dymock. It is characterised by its extensive areas of unimproved or semi-improved neutral grasslands with abundant wild daffodils, which have been attracting visitors for many years. There is also a significant proportion of parkland and orchards. The area is of less interest from the ornithological point of view than the Dean itself and the Wye Valley but, as the maps in the species accounts show, this varied and comparatively unintensively farmed region does support a fairly wide range of species.

Marginal Natural Areas adjacent to Dean and Wye

Malvern Hills and Teme Valley (NA 57)
This NA accounts for only around 5 km^2 of Gloucestershire at the southern end of the Malvern Hills. While the landscape is noticeably different, with sandstone predominating, the area involved is so small as to be insignificant here from an ornithological point of view.

Central Herefordshire (NA 59)
This NA accounts for about 10 km^2 of Gloucestershire, south-west of Ledbury. It merges into the Over Severn part of the Dean and Wye NA around Dymock and is very similar in general appearance and birdlife.

The Over Severn area is a flatter and more low-lying district than the rest of the NA. This is near Dymock, with May Hill in the background and wild daffodils in the foreground.

ANDY LEWIS

Severn and Avon Vales (NA 56)

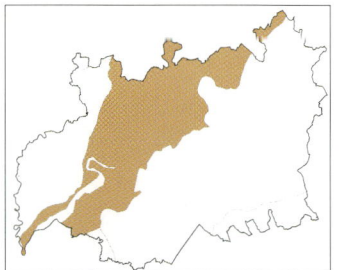

As a whole, this NA consists essentially of a gently undulating plain, lying mostly in Worcestershire and Gloucestershire, through which flow the Severn, the Warwickshire Avon and their tributaries. The Gloucestershire part of the NA comprises the low-lying ground, mainly less than 50 m above sea level (but in many places much lower), between the Forest of Dean plateau to the west and the Cotswolds to the east. At its broadest point near Cheltenham this Vale is about 25 km wide. In the north the NA extends over the county boundary into Worcestershire, and in the south-west it grades into the Severn Estuary Maritime NA. The river Avon joins the Severn at Tewkesbury after flowing for only about 7 km along the Gloucestershire–Worcestershire boundary so, although this Avon stretch is undoubtedly ornithologically important, the NA is usually referred to by birdwatchers in the county as 'the Severn Vale' or even simply 'the Vale', and this terminology is also used in this book.

The river Severn flows through the county for about 85 km of its total 350 km length, from just north-west of Tewkesbury, via Gloucester, to its confluence with the Wye at Beachley Point. Unlike the Wye, the Gloucestershire part of the Severn is a typical lowland river, winding its way slowly through a broad, gently undulating floodplain. A number of relatively minor tributaries (the rivers Swilgate, Chelt, Frome, Cam and Little Avon) flow in from the direction of the Cotswolds, the river Leadon drains

An outline of Gloucestershire and its birdlife

a fairly wide area of land around Dymock and Newent and joins the Severn just above Gloucester, and a series of streams run down from the Forest of Dean plateau. Historically the Severn was tidal as far upriver as Worcester and beyond, and this influence is still reflected in the botany of the riverside meadows. However, a series of locks and weirs were built, mainly in the nineteenth century, to aid navigation and nowadays the tide can be detected only as far as Lower Lode, close to the county boundary near Tewkesbury. Nevertheless, during high spring tides (above 8 m) the river still overtops the weir at Maisemore, just above Gloucester.

The Severn Vale is underlain by soft rocks, mostly consisting of Keuper Marls and Liassic Clays, with some Triassic sandstone mainly west of the Severn, giving rise to fertile but heavy, loam or clay soils. Although the Severn Vale was well wooded until the early Middle Ages, by the early fourteenth century it had been largely cleared to create pasture. These days the landscape is generally open, with the remaining woods tending to be small and sparsely distributed. Exceptions include Michaelwood on the border with South Gloucestershire, and Highnam Woods west of Gloucester, much of which is now an RSPB reserve. In recent years a relatively large area of plantation woodland (nearly a square kilometre) has been created at Nebrow Hill, between Frampton on Severn and Slimbridge. There is also some wet woodland along the river valleys, and a number of areas of lowland wood pasture and parkland, for example at Whitcliff Park near Berkeley.

For the most part the NA is fairly intensively farmed, with both arable crops and livestock. Horticulture and fruit growing are also major land uses, although the proportion of land occupied by orchards, particularly those under traditional management, has declined markedly in recent decades. A feature of the local orchards is the abundance of mistletoe; Gloucestershire and its neighbouring counties constitute a national stronghold for this much-loved plant.

Much of the floodplain of the Severn would once have been wetland for at least part of the year, but land drainage, river engineering and reclamation over the centuries have reduced the area of wetland to a fraction of its former extent. Water levels in the river are now controlled by upper catchment impoundments and a series of locks and weirs, and much of the land adjoining the river is protected by man-made embankments. However, partly as a consequence of this artificial hydrological regime, widespread flooding still frequently occurs, particularly upriver of Gloucester, either as a result of local streams being unable to discharge into the Severn and 'backing up' to cause local flooding, or through the Severn breaking its banks, especially as a result of heavy rain higher in the catchment in Wales. If significant flooding occurs in summer, as happens perhaps once every 40 years, it causes much greater damage to properties and crops, and can have a severe impact on wildlife, as was experienced most recently and catastrophically in June–July 2007 and September 2008. Winter flooding is still a regular event at a number of sites in the Vale, resulting in washlands of high

Hasfield and Ashleworth Hams, north of Gloucester in August 2012. 'Ham' is a Gloucestershire word for an area of pasture close to the Severn that is expected to flood in winter. The uncultivated, wet areas of the Ashleworth Ham GWT reserve can be seen in the lower right hand quarter.

Water levels in drainage ditches are sometimes controlled by sluices or 'stanks'. Reed and Sedge Warblers benefit from the bankside vegetation.

Floods at Walmore Common near Westbury-on-Severn, May 2012. Such out-of-season deluges can be catastrophic for nesting waders.

The reed-beds near the '100 Acre' at Frampton on Severn. This is a rare but important habitat in the Vale.

An outline of Gloucestershire and its birdlife

conservation interest. Examples of such seasonally or intermittently flooded grassland include Hasfield and Ashleworth Hams and the recently restored Coombe Hill Meadows upriver of Gloucester (which are owned and managed by the GWT), and Minsterworth Ham, Walmore Common and Wilmer Common downriver.

Many of these flood meadows are simply grazed seasonally by cattle, but in some places ancient 'Lammas Meadows' survive. These are fields, divided according to the medieval strip system, which are cut for hay and then grazed after 'Lammas Day' on August 1st by livestock belonging to people with commoners' rights. The best known example is at Upham Meadow and Summer Leasow (better known locally as the Great Hay Meadow) by the Avon near Twyning. In recent years many of these fields, some of which had been ploughed up, have reverted to grassland under the Higher Level Stewardship scheme of the Department for Environment, Food and Rural Affairs. These areas of semi-natural grassland have become increasingly important in the national context as 95% of traditional hay meadows have been lost in recent decades.

In addition, in places along the edge of the Severn Estuary there are some fairy extensive residual areas of relatively undisturbed salt-marsh grassland. The principal sites are in the Frampton–Slimbridge area on the left bank of the estuary and between Lydney and Chepstow, in particular at Aylburton Warth, on the right bank.

Away from the river, most of the permanent bodies of still water in the NA are ornamental, or the result of industrial activity: for example, former gravel workings at Frampton and old claypits just north of Gloucester. In addition there is one reservoir in the NA, at Witcombe, very close to the Cotswolds scarp. These sites can all attract migrants, especially Frampton Pools which sometimes host huge numbers of hirundines and Swifts and constitute the county's most reliable site for Black Terns and Little Gulls. At the WWT reserve at Slimbridge, a system of specially designed wetlands has been created including freshwater ponds and scrapes, and brackish pools behind the sea wall, all of which attract a wealth of birdlife throughout the year.

In summer, the flood meadows and 'Hams' still provide habitat for nesting waders such as Lapwing, Redshank and Curlew, though Snipe probably no longer breed in the county and numbers of the other species have declined catastrophically in recent decades. Redshank and Lapwing also still breed at some of the remaining areas of salt-marsh, and Oystercatchers have become more common in recent years.

None of the reed-beds along the Severn are particularly large, but they are valuable nesting sites nevertheless for birds such as Reed Buntings and Reed Warblers, which nest in even the smallest patches of reed all the way along the river and upper estuary. Another characteristic feature of this NA is the osier or withy beds that are still numerous in places, especially along the Severn above Gloucester and by the Avon. These small plantations of fast-growing willows of various species were managed to produce stems or wands of various ages and strengths for making fences, baskets, eel-traps and traditional 'putchers' for catching salmon. They were the favoured habitat of the now extinct population of Marsh Warblers in Gloucestershire and Worcestershire. Nowadays they are largely abandoned, overgrown and dank, but continue to provide insect food and habitat for woodpeckers, warblers, tits and buntings.

Frampton Pools attract wildfowl in both summer and winter, and the sailing lake (shown here) is the most reliable site in the county for Black Terns on passage.

The wetlands bordering the Severn Estuary are well known as important sites for wildfowl in winter. Three areas are designated as Ramsar sites and Special Protection Areas for this reason: Walmore Common, Severn Estuary and Upper Severn Estuary. The last two are also proposed as Special Areas of Conservation under the European Commission's Habitats and Species Directive. The best known estuary site for birds is, of course, Slimbridge, famous for its wintering Bewick's Swans and White-fronted Geese, which feed on specially managed semi-improved grasslands as well as on the more natural salt-marsh vegetation.

The relatively few areas of woodland in this NA are generally of lesser significance for birds, although Nightingales still nest at Highnam Woods and Frampton. Lesser Spotted Woodpeckers and Hawfinches are present in low numbers, especially closer to the Forest of Dean and where the woodland habitat is augmented by traditional orchards.

Barn Owl, Quail, Grey Partridge, Tree Sparrow and Corn Bunting are all birds that were formerly very much characteristic of the farmland of this NA but have suffered moderate to severe declines both here and throughout Britain in recent decades, due largely to the intensification of agriculture. A few pairs of Yellow Wagtails still breed in the Vale, some in what used to be their characteristic damp grassland habitat, although in recent years arable crops have become increasingly favoured.

The GWT reserve at Coombe Hill, north of Gloucester. The large photograph (right) looks west: the disused Coombe Hill Canal, which linked the Severn to Cheltenham, runs through the centre and the Severn itself can be seen in the distance. The reserve wetlands are also visible; this photograph was taken in August 2012 after a period of summer flooding. The mixed farmland typical of the Vale contains less woodland than elsewhere in the county.

The smaller photograph (above) looks east. The diagonal line marks the disused canal, and the prominent semi-circular copse (a former withy bed) in the centre can also be seen bottom-centre in the large photograph. This smaller photograph was taken in August 2007 following the unprecedented flooding of that summer. The invertebrate fauna suffered badly from weeks of standing water, and consequently so did nestlings in this area.

An outline of Gloucestershire and its birdlife

JAMES S LEES

Severn Estuary Maritime Natural Area (NA 116)

Gloucestershire has been described as 'inland but maritime', and it is the deep penetration of the Severn Estuary into the county that gives it this dual character.

The Severn Estuary Maritime NA includes both sides of the river, between the Wye confluence near Chepstow on the right bank and Brean Down (Somerset) on the left, upstream as far as about Frampton on Severn. The transition between this NA and the Severn and Avon Vales NA is indistinct, the boundary being approximately defined by the band of regularly flooded salt-marsh habitats between the muds and sands of the estuary itself and the grassland above high water. The upper salt-marsh zone in particular may be considered as common to both NAs. These saline or brackish wetlands contribute to the classification of several sites as internationally important for wintering wildfowl.

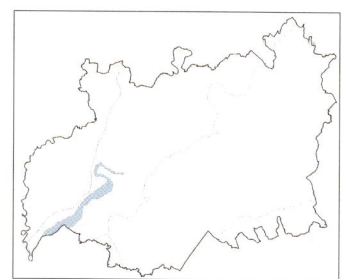

Having rounded the major horseshoe-shaped bend of the Arlingham peninsula, the river Severn abruptly broadens out to a width of over 2 km at the Noose, at the level of Slimbridge. After narrowing briefly in the Sharpness–Lydney section, it then gradually opens out again to a width of nearly 4 km as it approaches Beachley Point; here the estuary is shared between Gloucestershire and South Gloucestershire. The whole of this stretch of 30 km or so from Arlingham to Beachley is characterised by vast areas of deposited mud and sand, much of it exposed at low tide and some not covered except

An outline of Gloucestershire and its birdlife

by high spring tides. Largely due to the estuary's long funnel shape, the tidal range here is the second highest in the world, after the Bay of Fundy in North America. It is this shape, compounded by embankments built to prevent flooding, that produces the famous Severn Bore, a spectacular surge wave caused by millions of cubic metres of tidal water sweeping upriver over a period of only an hour or so. The very mobile, active tidal regime results in high turbidity and wide areas of scoured sand and rock, restricting the opportunities for colonisation by invertebrates. The density of birds is correspondingly lower than for many less dynamic estuaries in the British Isles. For example, Knot, which congregate in thousands at some sites, are only encountered in dozens here. Similarly, fewer Bar-tailed Godwits occur here, and indeed in the whole of the Bristol Channel area, than might be expected. However, the Severn's large size means that the total numbers of many species are nevertheless of international importance; particularly in winter, it provides habitat for a substantial proportion of the world populations of a wide variety of waders and wildfowl. The estuary, as a whole or in part, has been designated as a conservation site under a wide range of different headings: Site of Special Scientific Interest (SSSI), National Nature Reserve, Ramsar Site, Special Protection Area and potential Special Area of Conservation.

The WWT reserve at Slimbridge is a magnet for waders and wintering wildfowl – and for birders: a huge number of roving records came from this area.

An incoming tide on the Severn Estuary, which is regularly scoured by the very active tidal regime. The vast areas of mud and sand exposed at low tide create feeding habitat for shorebirds at all seasons.

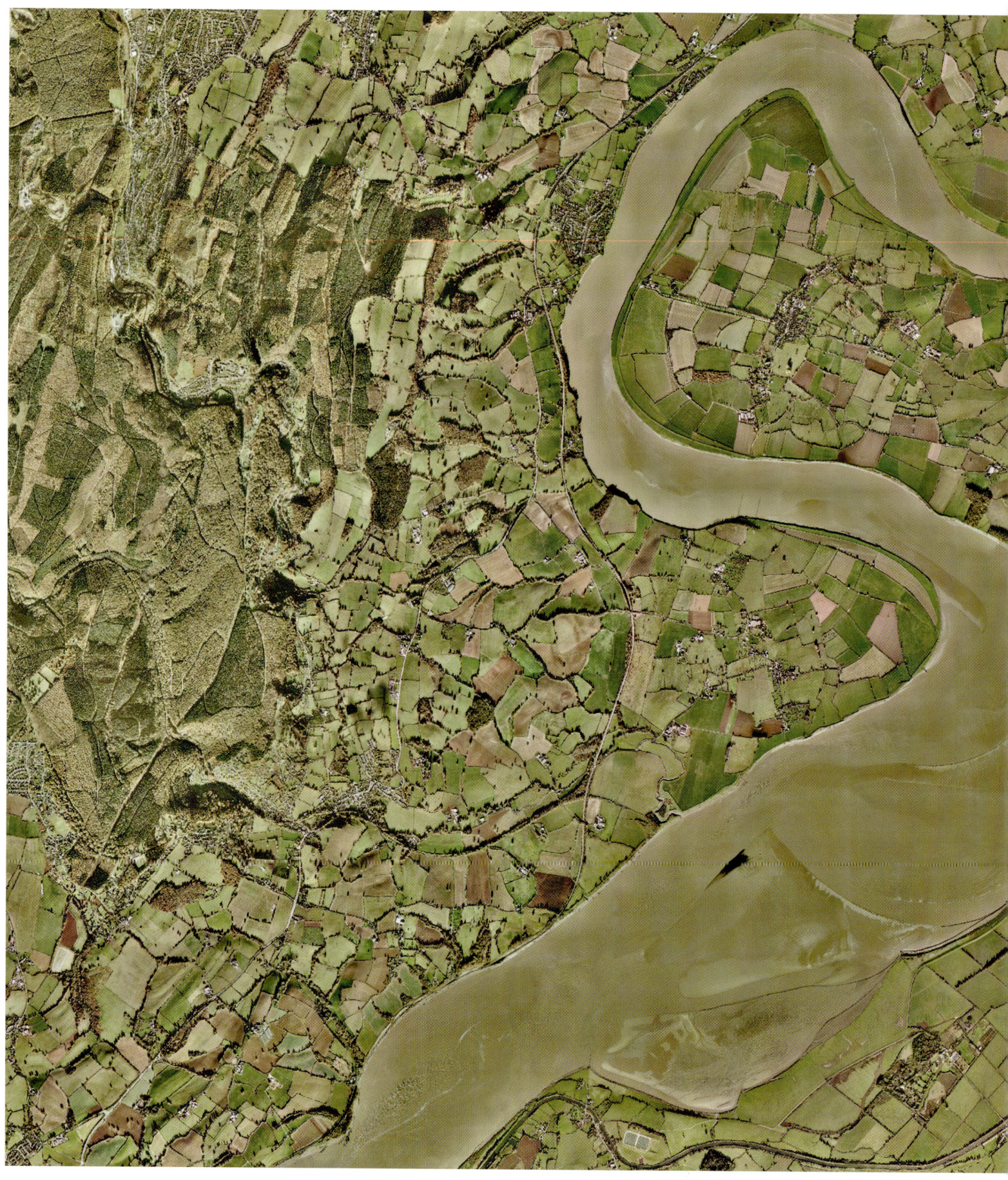

An outline of Gloucestershire and its birdlife

A satellite view showing the part of the Severn estuary known as 'The Noose' and the Arlingham peninsula, upstream of Slimbridge, at low tide. On the left is the eastern fringe of the Forest of Dean with Cinderford at the top and part of Lydney visible in the bottom left-hand corner. Running north-east to south-west, the dark line to the right of the river is the Gloucester and Sharpness Canal, and the lighter lines further right are the A38 and M5. Note the almost complete lack of woodland of any significance to the east of the river.

WWT Slimbridge from the air, looking north. The Severn (at high tide) can be seen in the top left, and below it part of the famous 'Dumbles', home to wintering swans and geese and many a rare wader.

Birdwatching at the estuary can be a demanding and frustrating activity: the distances are vast, the light is often poor, and even on quite cool days the action of the sun's warmth on dry sand, mud and water can create a surprisingly troublesome heat 'shimmer'. Furthermore the birds are often quite localised, and in many areas the first impression can be of wide expanses of more or less birdless mud and sandflats. However, once the favoured spots are known, and especially with the aid of a good telescope, the importance of the estuary for so many species can be appreciated. At times the mudflats swarm with Curlews, Dunlin and Shelducks, in particular in the Noose area off Slimbridge and downriver of Lydney Harbour. Gulls are also nearly always conspicuous, whether 'loafing', feeding on the incoming or outgoing tide, or especially flying in to roost. Downriver of Slimbridge, the main gull roost near Purton can hold many thousands of birds and, apart from the county's landfill sites, the estuary is the best place to find Glaucous and Iceland Gulls, especially in late winter.

Nowadays most records of birds on the estuary come from around Slimbridge and Frampton on Severn, with fairly regular

Sedbury Cliffs, on the western side of the estuary, close to Beachley Point and the Severn Bridge.

An outline of Gloucestershire and its birdlife

The eastern shore of the estuary at Severn House Farm, south of Berkeley. Note the variety of foreshore habitats.

reports from the Berkeley Shore area. The section near Guscar Rocks and Aylburton Warth, on the right bank of the river south of Lydney, also used to produce many records, but reports from here have decreased in more recent years. This could be due in part to a decline in the number of observers visiting the area, but also quite possibly to changes in the structure of the estuary at that point as a result of erosion, and also perhaps to increased human disturbance. There is also the complicating fact that recent habitat improvements due to conservation management in the Slimbridge area may well have attracted some birds away from their former haunts.

As a major inlet of the sea extending well inland, the estuary provides a well-used route for migrating water birds, which can be seen in spring flying up the estuary and continuing on overland, or in autumn flying downstream, presumably having flown overland across the country from the east coast. Various species frequently fly straight through without stopping: in spring, Dunlin, Ringed Plovers, Bar-tailed Godwits and Whimbrel can often be observed in flocks of dozens or more, with lower numbers of other species such as Grey Plovers, Turnstones and Sanderlings. There is also a regular upriver passage of Kittiwakes and terns, notably Arctic. In autumn the downriver movements of shorebirds and terns are less well defined but still regular, whilst Arctic Skuas can also seen in small numbers at both seasons. These movements are hard to predict and no doubt depend partly on weather conditions elsewhere but, in any event, they are most often seen at high tide.

In addition, seabirds are frequently driven up the estuary, more or less against their will, by south-westerly gales. It is here where most county birdwatchers see their Leach's Petrels, Fulmars, Gannets and Great Skuas, and where the occasional really rare seabird (in the Gloucestershire context) is discovered – a Sabine's Gull or a

Sharpness Docks seems an unpromising location, but it is the county's most reliable site for wintering Black Redstarts.

Storm Petrel, for example. Favoured 'seawatching' sites include Saul Warth upriver of Frampton, the Holden Tower and Middle Point at Slimbridge, Sharpness and, on the opposite side of the estuary, at Lydney Harbour and the end of the Awre peninsula near Newnham. Beachley Point has proved to be very productive at times, but its position relatively far from the main population centres means that it has not been visited so regularly by the county's birders.

TERRY FENTON

Cotswolds (NA 55)

The Cotswold Hills escarpment is situated on a band of Jurassic oolitic limestone that extends from Warwickshire to Somerset. It is this honey-coloured and easily worked stone which is still quarried in a few places, that gives Cotswold buildings their characteristic mellow appearance. The area is well known for its picturesque villages and attractive landscape and, in recognition of this, the Cotswolds Area of Outstanding Natural Beauty was designated in 1966.

This NA accounts for nearly half of the surface area of Gloucestershire. The Cotswold scarp more or less cuts the county in half diagonally, running from south-west to north-east. At its foot the Severn Vale lies to the west, and the 'high wold' on the top gives way to the dip-slope, which falls gradually to the east. In the north-east of the county the steep slopes of the scarp form a sharp boundary with the Severn and Avon Vales NA, whilst further south and west between Stroud and Wotton-under-Edge the scarp is less abrupt and altogether more complex and meandering, so that the boundary with the Bristol, Avon Valleys and Ridges NA is correspondingly less well-defined. To the south-east, the gentle Cotswold dip-slope merges gradually with the low-lying Thames and Avon Vales NA.

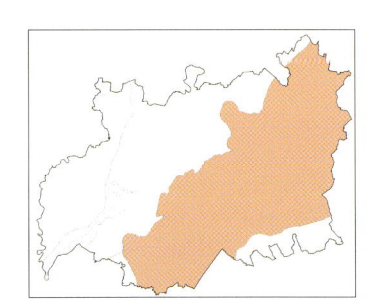

In common with much of lowland Britain the Cotswolds would have been well wooded up to the arrival of Neolithic people, but most of the trees had probably been removed by about 3,500 years ago, creating today's largely open landscapes. However, the present-day Cotswolds still have some significant areas of woodland, especially along the scarp, along the valleys of streams and rivers, and wherever there are parks and large estates. Woodland is more scattered in the North Cotswolds and on the eastern dip-slope, but even within a landscape of predominantly arable fields such as this, there is a scattering of small copses and plantations that have largely been created or retained for rearing game birds for shooting. Similar areas were also retained as fox coverts, for the benefit of the hunt. In an area dominated by farmland these sites can provide valuable habitat for woodland birds, even though they are not necessarily managed with nature conservation in mind.

Although dry-stone walls are often thought of as the typical Cotswold field boundary, hedges are also a widespread feature, and are particularly characteristic of the scarp, the southern Gloucestershire Cotswolds and the area around Moreton-in-Marsh, where they contribute to the impression of a fairly well-wooded landscape.

Over the centuries the predominant agriculture in the Cotswolds has alternated between sheep-rearing and arable farming. This was a very important wool-producing region during the five centuries or so up to about 1900, with its own local breed of sheep. More recently there has been a resurgence of arable, and at present the farming is probably as 'mixed' as it has ever been, with arable crops

Compton Abdale, between Cheltenham and Northleach. The wolds consist of a patchwork of arable land and pasture, with dry-stone walls and small copses and coverts.

Quenington, near Fairford. The habitat in and around villages is usually more varied than in the surrounding farmland, and village edges can be rich in birdlife.

The Cotswold scarp gives way to a line of outlying hills rising out of the Severn Vale. Crickley Hill (foreground) and Churchdown Hill (background) attract migrants such as Wheatears and Whinchats.

accounting for over half of the farmland in this NA as a whole, and permanent pasture and long-term grass ley amounting to about one-third. The Gloucestershire part of the dip-slope has a higher proportion of arable land than the parts outside the county.

In recent years a significant aspect of the farming in the Cotswolds has been the quite high rate of uptake of government agri-environment schemes such as Higher Level Stewardship, especially on the poorer soils. This has resulted in, for example, wide margins around field boundaries, fallow plots (useful for ground-nesting birds) and areas planted with wild bird seed and nectar mixtures. Together with the planting of game crops for shooting, these measures should be benefiting farmland birds

For bird recording in Gloucestershire, the Cotswolds NA is often divided into the three zones: scarp, high wold and dip-slope.

Scarp

The semi-natural and relatively 'wild' character of this zone results largely from the steepness of the terrain, which makes it unsuitable for cultivation and difficult to manage. This is exacerbated to some extent by the comparatively high altitudes at the top of the scarp, with substantial areas above 250m. As a result the land cover here is predominantly woodland, interspersed with varying amounts of permanent pasture. Whilst the woods are mainly beech-dominated south of Cheltenham, they are more mixed to the north. A number of the beech 'hangers' are considered to be internationally important and some of those near Painswick form part of the Cotswolds Commons and Beechwoods National Nature Reserve. Midger Wood SSSI, further south on the county boundary near Wotton-under-Edge, is a good example of ancient woodland (in this case dominated by ash) in a very steep-sided valley cut into limestone grassland. Despite the steepness of the slopes, natural rock outcrops are practically absent, and most areas of exposed rock are the legacy of quarrying. A few relatively minor watercourses run through the scarp itself: the river Isbourne joins the Worcestershire Avon at Evesham, and the Chelt and the Frome run into the Severn via Cheltenham and Stroud respectively; further south, the Cam flows into the Severn via the Gloucester and Sharpness Canal, and a number of small streams run down the scarp to form the Little Avon, which also joins the Severn near Berkeley. The Frome and its tributaries in particular are heavily wooded along much of their length and arable farming is sparse.

Typical breeding birds of the scarp include a wide range of woodland species, nesting Buzzards and Ravens and, especially in the more southern areas, a substantial population of Dippers.

High Wold

This zone corresponds to the highest part of the dip-slope, immediately behind (i.e. generally to the east) of the scarp. The ground is gently undulating and the landscape is largely one of open fields interspersed with blocks of woodland, plantations and shelter belts,

An outline of Gloucestershire and its birdlife

Permanent pasture on the high wold in the North Cotswolds.

Typical high wold east of Cheltenham, with cereals and fairly young plantations.

The Washpool is part of the Cleeve Hill SSSI. Ring Ouzels can be found here in both migration periods, and Meadow Pipits are ever-present.

with walls and farm buildings of local stone. Soils here are well drained and light and, although this was prime sheep country in years gone by, these days large-scale arable farming predominates. However, there are still areas where sheep (and also cattle) are grazed, notably on the large expanse of unimproved limestone grassland at Cleeve Hill, which has survived largely due to its ancient Common status, and also similar areas above Stroud, in particular Minchinhampton and Rodborough Commons, which are managed by the National Trust. Where there is no active management, similar areas of permanent grassland elsewhere are tending to become overgrown with scrub, a process which has been exacerbated by the decline in rabbit numbers following the introduction of myxomatosis in the 1950s. In places, such grasslands are being restored using grazing animals, notably Belted Galloway cattle. Nowadays there is a great deal of casual human disturbance on most of these areas and this has a negative impact on wildlife in general and ground-nesting birds in particular. Skylarks are still present in some numbers, but both Tree and Meadow Pipits are very restricted now; scarcer species including Stonechat, Grasshopper Warbler and Redstart breed in a few areas. Cleeve Hill in particular is a good site for migrating landbirds, and is the only really reliable place in the county for passage Ring Ouzels.

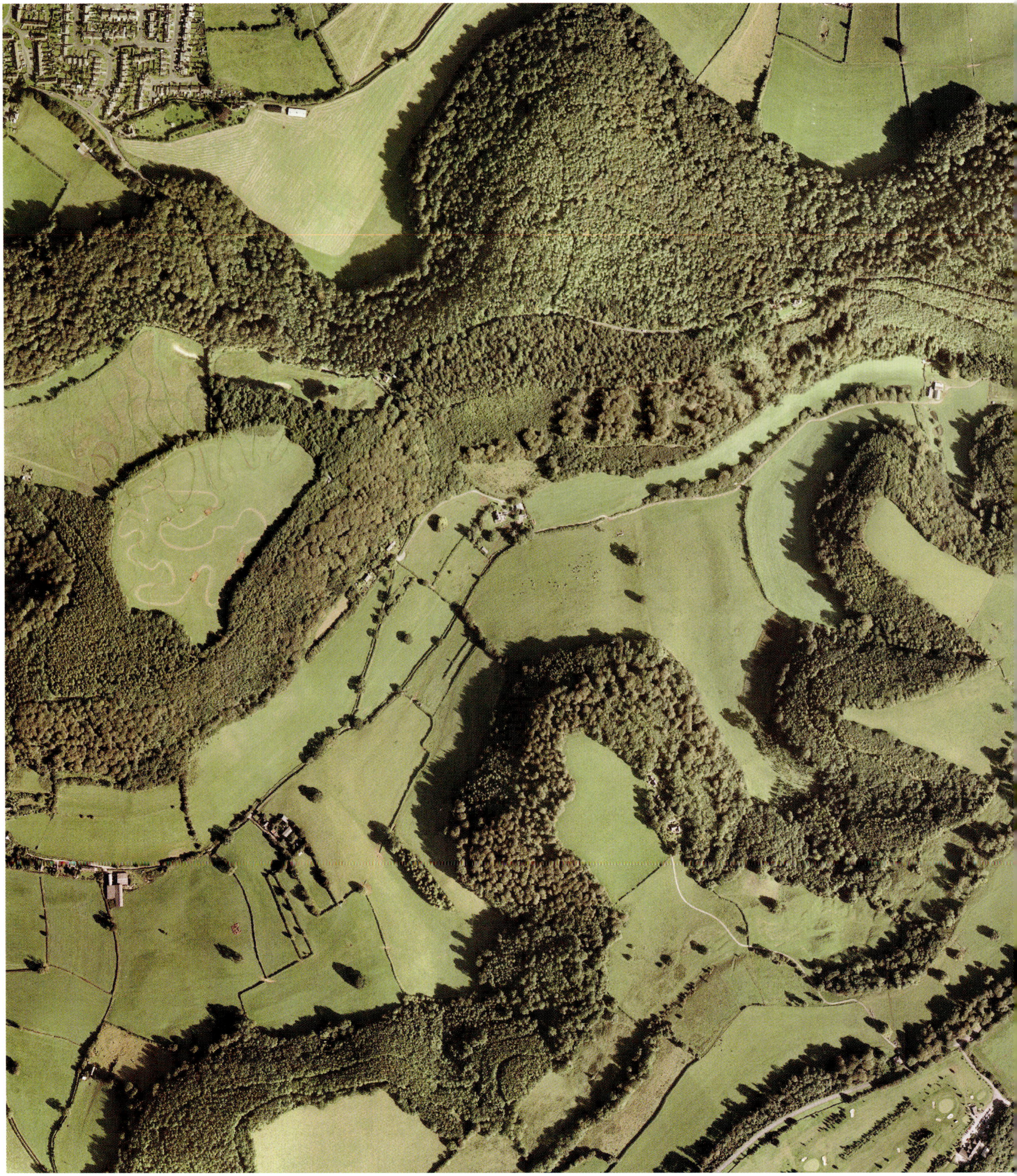

An outline of Gloucestershire and its birdlife

A satellite view of the area south-east of Dursley, centred on Waterley Bottom. In the south of the county the scarp edge is very indented in places, and the steep slopes are heavily wooded.

Dip-slope

In general this zone presents a gently undulating appearance, with characteristic wide-open Cotswolds views across large, mostly arable fields bounded by stone walls or hedges and interspersed with blocks of woodland or plantations. The gradient of the land along the dip-slope is scarcely perceptible on the ground, but most of that part of Gloucestershire south and east of a line between Cirencester and Stow-on-the-Wold varies between 100 and 200 m in altitude. The rolling dip-slope plateau is dissected by many small dry valleys or 'bottoms', whose sides are too steep for cultivation and where grazing by sheep and cattle maintains flower-rich limestone grassland. In addition there are a number of rivers, flowing into the Thames: the Churn, Coln, Leach and Windrush. These watercourses are fast-flowing in their upper reaches, where they may dry out completely in summer, but they soon become slow and meandering as the slope of the land decreases downstream. Near the north-east corner of the county, on the edge of the Cotswolds near Moreton-in-Marsh, the river Evenlode meanders through its broad clay valley before leaving Gloucestershire near Stow-on-the-Wold.

Many of the valley bottoms are devoted to permanent pasture, mostly 'improved', with arable farming on the more gentle slopes. However, some of the river valleys are very well wooded and there

Unlike other Cotswold valleys, that of the river Evenlode is broad and low-lying, and partly given over to pasture, producing scenes like this reminiscent of the Severn Vale.

A satellite view showing open arable fields around Leighterton, west of Tetbury, and the block of woodland containing the well-known Westonbirt arboretum. This woodland includes Silk Wood, one of the largest ancient woods on the Cotswold plateau and partly a GWT reserve.

The disused gravel-pits at Bourton-on-the-Water are a good site for wildfowl, especially in winter.

are also some substantial blocks of woodland elsewhere, of which three are worthy of note: Chedworth and Withington Woods consist of a large area of mixed largely mature woodland and plantation with old conifers; the Cirencester Park complex encompasses about 12 km^2 of actively managed but largely undisturbed maturing plantations, west of Cirencester; and Silk Wood at Westonbirt, which adjoins the Forestry Commission's well-known and much-visited National Arboretum, is one of the largest ancient woodlands on the Cotswold plateau.

In the south-east, the land becomes less undulating, stone walls give way completely to hedges, and the characteristic high, windswept Cotswold landscape blends into the lowland arable farmland of the Thames and Avon Vales.

The dip-slope is the Gloucestershire stronghold of a number of farmland birds whose populations have declined severely in Britain as a whole: whilst Skylarks and Yellowhammers are still common and there is a fairly healthy Corn Bunting population, Lapwings and Tree Sparrows have become much scarcer and Grey Partridges seem to be heading for extinction. Quail are annual visitors in very variable numbers and Yellow Wagtails nest patchily in arable fields, particularly bean crops. Dippers still breed in a few places, despite large declines, while active and disused quarries provide sites for cliff-nesting species such as Kestrels and Stock Doves. Goshawks occur in small numbers, whilst Crossbills and sometimes Hawfinches visit, mainly in winter but occasionally in summer, raising hopes that they might one day breed. In winter, flocks of Golden Plovers mingle with the gulls, especially Common Gulls, in the fields, although they have tended to decline here lately, preferring the Severn Vale, particularly Slimbridge. Short-eared Owls winter at a few favoured sites and in recent years small numbers of Hen Harriers have also appeared at this season. Last but not least, Red Kites have become almost a commonplace sight, particularly in the east of the region, following their rapid increase and spread.

In general, the impression obtained by the casual visitor to the Gloucestershire Cotswolds is of a region with few standing waterbodies, and there are indeed extensive areas with no significant ponds or lakes. However, one-fifth of tetrads in the 13 10 km squares making up the NCOS recording area contain waterbodies with a surface area of around a hectare or greater (Main *et al.* 2009). Most notable are Dowdeswell reservoir, in a valley cutting into the scarp near Cheltenham, and the disused gravel-pits at Bourton-on-the-Water. These isolated waterbodies attract terns and waders on passage and wintering wildfowl, as well as some breeding wetland species.

Marginal Natural Area adjacent to the Cotswolds

Bristol, Avon Valleys and Ridges (NA 62)

This NA occupies just a few square kilometres of the county, on the South Gloucestershire border near Charfield. Bird records from here are included with those from the Cotswolds NA.

Thames and Avon Vales (NA 63)

This NA forms the central section of an extensive belt of low-lying countryside running through south and central England from Somerset to Lincolnshire. It is broadly defined by the lower catchment areas of the Thames and the Bristol Avon. Only about 100 km² of Gloucestershire falls within the NA; to the south and east it extends across the county border into Wiltshire and Oxfordshire, whilst in the north it blends into the gently rising foothills of the Cotswolds. Geologically, the Gloucestershire part of the NA mostly overlies Jurassic Oxford clays, with extensive deposits of Quaternary gravels, and lies at a very uniform altitude of 70–80 m above sea level. Wet woodland dominated by willows, alder and ash would have been a common feature in the distant past but, as with much of lowland England, very little of this habitat remains following clearance for agriculture, and the modern landscape is one of farmland with scattered small woods. In the context of southern England, human population density is relatively low.

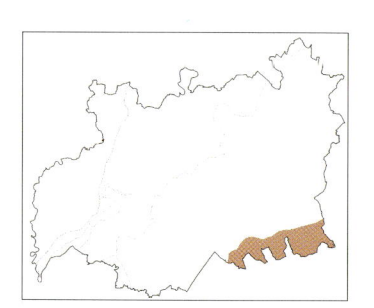

Although this NA accounts for only a small proportion of Gloucestershire, it is nevertheless ornithologically significant because it contains the wetlands of the Cotswold Water Park, which as a whole extends over about 100 km². Sand and gravel have been extracted here continuously for more than 50 years, and extraction may continue for up to another 50 years depending upon the economic growth and development of the region. Once the minerals are removed, the resulting pits are flooded to produce lakes and large ponds (already 151 distinct waterbodies at the time of writing) and, increasingly, areas of reed-bed, grassland and woodland. This process of extraction followed by restoration creates a complex and rapidly changing ecosystem. Some of the restored pits are managed for water sports and angling, some have been incorporated into waterside housing developments, whilst others have been created and managed with wildlife in mind. Many of the waterbodies have been given names by their owners, but for bird recording the original pit numbers are more often used.

Until recently there have been two separate sections of the Water Park: south of Cirencester there is the 'western' section, which is mainly in Gloucestershire but extends into Wiltshire, and near Fairford there is the 'eastern' section, which is entirely within the county. In the mid-2000s the process of joining together the eastern and western sections began, with the initiation of mineral extraction in the 'central' section. This is set to become a key nature conservation area as much of the post-extraction restoration will be carried out with habitat creation in mind, including large areas of reed-bed. In addition, several farms in this vicinity have entered into agri-environment schemes, with the focus on wet grassland and farmland birds.

As the water of the former pits is often very alkaline and with low levels of pollutants, a number of the lakes are developing into marl lakes (i.e. with a calcareous clay substrate), which support a wide range of often specialised aquatic plants and associated

Lakes in the Cotswold Water Park may progress to a range of habitats. This reed-bed is part of the Edward Richardson–Phyllis Amey reserve, maintained by the GWT.

A recently worked-out pit near Shorncote in the western section of the Cotswold Water Park. Active extraction means the area's habitat and geography can change rapidly.

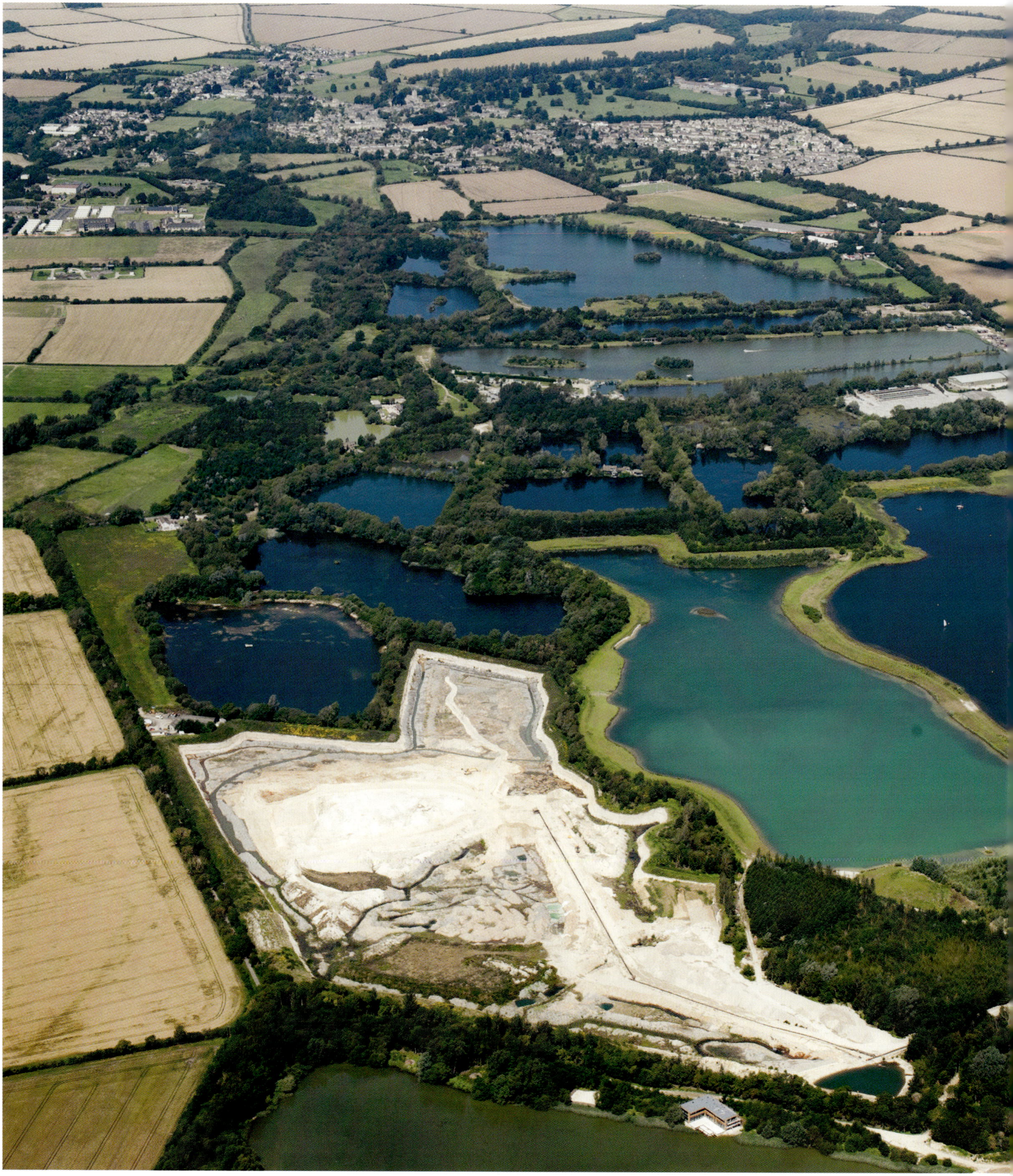

ROBERT BEWLEY

An outline of Gloucestershire and its birdlife

Looking north over part of the western section of the Cotswold Water Park, showing recently built lakeside housing and with Somerford Keynes visible in the distance. The extensive vegetation surrounding the 'undeveloped' lakes provides habitat for a range of species, notably Nightingales.

Cotswold Water Park, looking west over part of the eastern section, with Fairford in the distance. The various stages of lake development can be seen, with active gravel extraction in the foreground, the early stages of reinstatement in the turquoise lake, and the more mature lakes showing darker blue. These are used in various ways: those on the right are for recreation (in this case sailing), while the two on the left in the foreground are the GWT's Whelford Pools reserve. The Water Park as a whole is a very important site for wintering wildfowl.

invertebrates. This is a scarce habitat nationally and the Water Park is the most extensive marl lake system in Britain. The Cotswold Water Park SSSI comprises ten units (lakes) designated for aquatic plants, and particularly stoneworts (Charophytes) for which the Water Park is of European importance, supporting a wide variety and great abundance. It is also a hot spot for dragonflies, supporting over half of the species found in Britain, some in large numbers.

The Water Park is nationally important for wintering wildfowl, including Coot, Gadwall, Tufted Duck, Pochard and, in some years, Shoveler and Smew. It is also nationally important for breeding species including Mute Swan, Coot, Great Crested Grebe, Gadwall and Little Ringed Plover, whilst at the county scale it supports most of Gloucestershire's breeding Black-headed Gulls, Common Terns and Sand Martins as well as sizeable populations of Reed and Sedge Warblers and Reed Buntings. Oystercatchers, Redshank and Shelduck also breed here, and this is one of the few areas of the county that still supports Nightingales. Groups of up to 30 Hobbies have gathered here on passage in recent springs, whilst adults can be seen throughout the summer, attracted by the abundant dragonflies and hirundines over the lakes. The Water Park is also interesting for its Red-crested Pochards, hosting up to 80% of the national breeding population, and during the winter more than 21,000 gulls come to roost; this is an internationally important site for wintering Lesser Black-backed Gulls.

As might be expected, the Water Park is a popular birdwatching site and rare migrants are frequently found, thanks to the dedication of the local birders who are faced with the challenging task of covering this huge and correspondingly hard-to-watch area.

The lakes and wetlands of the Water Park are set within a series of river corridors of the Thames and its tributaries; the associated

The Thames is not easily navigable above Lechlade, giving sanctuary to shyer water birds such as Water Rail and Little Grebe.

An outline of Gloucestershire and its birdlife

Arable land near Fairford hosts a declining population of Tree Sparrows, as well as Yellowhammers and Skylarks.

Damp areas with scrub and hedgerows provide habitat for Reed Buntings and Sedge Warblers.

network of species-rich meadows and wet grassland creates an abundance of habitat for riverine birds throughout the year. The gravel-bottomed Cotswold tributaries such as the Windrush, Churn, Coln and Leach support numerous Kingfishers and Grey Wagtails, with riverside nesting habitat for Mute Swans, Moorhens, Reed Warblers and Reed Buntings. Although rare, Curlew and Redshank may just be hanging on. During winter the flooded meadows provide extensive wetland for feeding waterfowl, notably large flocks of Wigeon, Mallard and Teal, and occasional Bewick's and Whooper Swans.

Aside from the wetland areas, the landscape in this NA within the county is largely open, mixed farmland with a few small woods; the fields tend to be small and bounded by tall hedges. Up to the late 1960s, English elms were a prominent feature, but following the devastating outbreak of Dutch elm disease the hedgerows are now dominated by other species, notably crack willow, many of which are pollarded. A large population of the native black poplar, Britain's rarest timber tree, survives here. Perhaps the most significant farmland bird in this area of the county at present is the remnant population of Tree Sparrows, which still clings on in the Fairford area. Yellow Wagtails are also regular breeders and Barn Owls breed here at quite high densities in Gloucestershire terms, presumably benefiting from good hunting opportunities along the river corridors.

A brief history of bird watching, recording and conservation in Gloucestershire

The early days

According to Swaine (1982), the earliest written county bird record probably dates from as long ago as January 1683, when at 'Hosbury Bridge', four miles from Gloucester (thought to be the present-day Horseferry Bridge at Witcombe), a 'strange bird' was killed by one Thomas Stevenson. It is clear from the remarkably detailed account that the bird involved was a Waxwing. Sadly, this model description was the exception rather than the rule in those days; in general the available early information is fragmentary and derives from all kinds of sources not specifically devoted to bird recording. Moreover, the major British bird books from the late eighteenth century and much of the nineteenth make little or no mention of Gloucestershire.

The first formal organisation devoted to the study of wildlife in the county was inaugurated on May 9th 1829. The Gloucester Natural History Society resolved to form a museum and library, and voted that members should pay a subscription of one guinea. It held a number of meetings at which lecturers addressed the members on a variety of topics. However, the society's finances were never firmly established and its final meeting took place on March 6th 1834.

Around fifty years later, the fate of the Stroud Natural History and Philosophical Society followed a similar pattern to its Gloucester counterpart. It was founded in 1876 and its members also resolved to form a museum, but it was not long-lived. However, in 1880 Charles Witchell took over as president and around that time Edward Evans' avifauna was produced (see the section on books below).

Meanwhile, on July 7th 1846 the Cotteswold Naturalists' Field Club (CNFC) had been formed at the Black Horse Inn, Birdlip, with stated interests in agriculture, natural history, geology and archaeology. This was the first club of its kind in England and it is still active today. Although it very soon became clear that geology rather than natural history would be the main focus of the CNFC, which is still the case today, it did publish an outline of the birds of Siddington near Cirencester (Bowly 1860). In addition, between 1925 and 1947, it produced the first *Gloucestershire Bird Notes*, essentially an embryonic bird report restricted to a few species and areas and edited by Herbert E. Norris. An ornithological section of the CNFC was established by Guy Charteris and Arthur Whitaker in 1947. Whitaker edited the bird report for 1947 and became county bird recorder in 1948, but he died shortly afterwards, obliging Charteris to step in and replace him.

The Gloucestershire Naturalists' Society and the start of systematic recording

In 1948 the Cheltenham & District Naturalists' Society (CDNS) was established, complete with an ornithological section; its aim was to promote an interest in the varied wildlife of the county, and at the same time it assumed the task of recording Gloucestershire's flora and fauna. The society's name was changed in 1956 to the North Gloucestershire Naturalists' Society and again in 1974 to its present form, the GNS. It still appoints and supports county recorders for many types of wildlife – birds, mammals, insects and flowering plants for example – and organises lectures and field meetings.

From the outset, the precursors of the GNS provided a platform for Charteris, Whitaker and others to publish regular and consistent notes on the birds of Gloucestershire. Their bird report for 1948–50 was welcomed as a 'first step towards filling one of the important remaining gaps in the series of county reports' (Wood 1952). From 1950 to 1962 these Gloucestershire bird reports were in effect published jointly by CDNS and CNFC, in order to cover as wide an area of the county as possible, but even so, most early issues lack records from west of the Severn. In addition, up to the end of 1962 'Gloucestershire' for bird recording purposes extended south only to an arbitrary line between Tetbury and Slimbridge, whilst further south of this was the territory of the Bristol Naturalists' Society, which had been founded in 1862. Then in 1963 a County

Records Committee was set up for the whole of Gloucestershire, which included all of this southern region until 1974, when it was absorbed first into 'Avon' and then South Gloucestershire.

The first annual bird report for the whole county covered 1963, so the series has now been running for 50 years. The GBR is still published by the GNS, which also produces the journal *The Gloucestershire Naturalist*, containing more scientific articles on the county's wildlife, as well as a quarterly newsletter. The GNS has in addition made a vital contribution to the publication of this book, having provided significant financial backing and organisational support.

Other organisations

In December 1945, Peter Scott and some friends drove through Slimbridge village, crossed the canal and went down a muddy drive to a wartime pillbox overlooking the Severn. In what Scott later described as a 'spine-tingling' moment, they discovered two Lesser White-fronted Geese – only the third and fourth ever recorded in Britain. Remarkably, they also found Barnacle, Bean, Brent, Greylag, and Pink-footed Geese among the 2,000 or so European White-fronts, and Scott decided that this was the place to site the organisation he was planning for the scientific study and conservation of wildfowl (Walkden 2009). The reserve area was established the following year, providing a safe haven for the geese.

The Severn Wildfowl Trust (now the WWT) quickly became a national concern, with an international reputation to match that of another organisation Scott helped to establish in 1961, the World Wildlife Fund (now the World Wide Fund for Nature). With professional ornithologists working at Slimbridge, Gloucestershire's profile in the bird world was spectacularly enhanced, and the location of the centre (and Peter Scott) is said to have played no small part in the BBC's decision to choose Bristol as the site for its Natural History Unit when it was set up in 1957. Scott was appointed CBE in 1953 for his work with the Severn Wildfowl Trust, and in 1973 he was knighted – the first time such an honour had been awarded for services to conservation. Now with an educational remit to match its research and conservation functions, Slimbridge continues to draw both visitors and interesting birds to the county.

Rather than a single county-wide ornithological society or bird club, Gloucestershire has several, more locally based organisations, devoted to the study and enjoyment of birds. All offer their members local programmes of indoor and field meetings, and some organise trips further afield; most have websites giving details of their activities.

The Dursley Birdwatching and Preservation Society (DBPS) was formed in 1953. Membership reached 100 in 1976 and 300 by 1998, and charity status was awarded in 1991. At first its 'home patch' remained within a ten-mile radius of Dursley Parish Church, but in 1980 it was extended to 16 10 km squares, as the Society was increasingly taking part in national surveys. Dursley's geographical position less than 10 km from Slimbridge has resulted in close ties between the DPBS and the WWT. In 1978, it instigated a Garden Bird Feeding Survey and in 1982 became more involved in active conservation work by restoring the lake and erecting nest-boxes at Newark Park, a National Trust property near Wotton-under-Edge. DBPS celebrated a significant anniversary with the publication in 1993 of *Forty Years On* by Maurice Bullen, a book that not only reviewed the society's activities over that period but also included a wide range of articles and information about conservation in the county.

In addition to his work at Slimbridge, Peter Scott was also active in helping to set up the GWT, which started life in 1961 as the Gloucestershire Trust for Nature Conservation. This is a thriving organisation, with over 26,000 members and 500 active volunteers as of 2012. It owns or manages more than 60 nature reserves totalling around 800 ha throughout the county, including extensive areas of wetland at the Severn Hams. It aims to preserve habitats, species and landscapes, to make them accessible to the public and to promote awareness of the need for conservation. It is the leading partner of the Gloucestershire Centre for Environmental Records which, at the time of writing, holds over two million county wildlife records.

In 1973 the RSPB Gloucestershire Local Group was founded to provide a service for RSPB members in the county, to raise awareness of the Society and to assist with projects, recruitment and fundraising. The Group was instrumental in the RSPB's purchase in 1987 of Highnam Woods; at the official opening the Bishop of Tewkesbury was accompanied by a singing Nightingale! The Group contributed significant funds towards the visitor centre at Nagshead, the other county bird reserve managed by the RSPB, which was opened in 2003.

Statue of Sir Peter Scott at Slimbridge.

A fine heritage of art, inspired by nature

Birdwatchers are not the only enthusiasts to be captivated by the variety and splendour of the avain world. Over the years, artists too have found inspiration in birdlife, and Gloucestershire is fortunate to be home to Nature in Art (www.nature-in-art.org.uk), the world's first museum and art gallery dedicated to fine, decorative and applied art inspired by the natural world. Located at Wallsworth Hall, a Georgian mansion just outside Gloucester, it holds a significant and growing collection of work by over 600 wildlife artists, including Archibald Thorburn and Peter Scott, as well as many of the other illustrators featured in this book.

Thorburn, who lived from 1860 to 1935, is of particular note. By adding an artistic sensibility to his sketches and paintings, he broke away from the fashion of treating bird illustrations as 'merely scientific maps of plumage'. His minutely detailed work would become an inspiration to Peter Scott amongst others, and earn him the title of Britain's greatest ever painter of birdlife.

Peregrine by Archibald Thorburn.
Reproduced by kind permission of Paul Walkden.

The North Cotswold Ornithological Society (NCOS) was formed in February 1983 with the aim of carrying out more systematic, quantitative recording in this hitherto underwatched area. Fieldwork carried out between 1983 and 1987 led to the publication of an atlas of breeding birds in the Cotswolds (Wright *et al.* 1990) and, as NCOS moved towards its twentieth anniversary, the exercise was repeated with a second atlas based on fieldwork carried out from 2003 to 2007 (Main *et al.* 2009). NCOS continues to carry out long-term and species-specific studies in winter and summer.

The Cheltenham Bird Club came into being in 1980, with its origins in a series of adult education evening classes in birdwatching. It now has over 100 members, and as well as a programme of indoor and outdoor meetings, it also arranges field trips abroad in most years.

Launched in 1999, the Painswick Bird Club is the youngest and smallest in the county but is no less active for that, and has a close involvement with many sections of the Painswick community, both young and old.

A significant event in 1985 was the formation of the Gloucestershire Ornithological Co-ordinating Committee (GOCC), which was established to provide an umbrella under which the various county bird groups could combine forces to improve the recording and reporting of the county's birdlife. GOCC took on the responsibility for compiling the annual GBR from records submitted to the county bird recorder; all groups and individuals are encouraged to send in their records. The County Records Committee, which assesses reports of scarce species in Gloucestershire, is a subcommittee of GOCC, and the production of this book naturally also took place under the aegis of GOCC.

When formal annual bird reports were first produced in the late 1940s the key individuals involved were Arthur Whitaker, L. W. Hayward and Guy Charteris, who each acted as county recorder or report editor, or both, at various times. In the early days, the recorder was called 'Honorary Secretary to the County Records Committee'. Charteris kept records in a more or less unofficial capacity until 1953, and Christopher Swaine took over in 1954 and continued until 1978, aided in the last ten of those years by Malcolm Ogilvie. Subsequent recorders have been John Sanders, Rick Goater, Gordon Avery, Andrew Jayne and, from 2002 to the present, Richard Baatsen. It was Richard who established a standardised records database for the county, which greatly facilitated much of the data analysis for this book.

Until the end of the 1980s it was usually the county recorder who edited the GBR but, as the numbers of records being submitted have grown and processing the data has become more complex, the roles have been split and since 1990 the editors have been Richard ffrench, John Sanders, Martin McGill, Paul Marshall and David Evans – the latter from 2001 onwards, and hence throughout the atlas period.

For further details of the history of ornithology in Gloucestershire, please see Bluett (2012).

Present-day bird surveying and recording

Volunteer birdwatchers in the county undertake a good deal of survey work, much of which contributes to the national monitoring programmes organised by the BTO. Over 50 1 km squares and several stretches of waterway are surveyed each year for the Breeding Bird

A Nightingale, held by a ringer. Ringing birds provides valuable information about movements, survival and productivity.

Survey (BBS) schemes, and significant contributions are made to the Garden Bird Survey, the Wetland Bird Survey (WeBS), the Nest Record Scheme, the RSPB's Volunteer and Farming Alliance, and various single-species surveys (see p. 48 for the results of two county surveys).

Gloucestershire is also relatively well provided with bird-ringers and over 10,000 birds are currently ringed each year in the county. The Severn Vale Ringing Group was very active from 1966 to 2009 and many former members continue to operate as individuals. The Severn Estuary Gull Group (SEGG) was formed in 1988 to study the vast numbers of gulls, believed to exceed 300,000 at peak times, which were then roosting on the Gloucestershire parts of the Severn Estuary and feeding at local landfill sites. Cannon netting, plus the ringing of nestlings in urban rooftop colonies, ensured for example that Gloucestershire accounted for 75% of all Lesser Black-backed Gulls ringed in Britain and Ireland between 1986 and 1995 (Bullen 1998). In 2003 the Cotswold Water Park Ringing Group was formed to ensure co-ordination of efforts at this large site, which extends across the county boundary into Wiltshire. It works in partnership with the Cotswold Water Park Trust (formerly the Cotswold Water Park Society), which aims to provide education, conservation, recreation and leisure in the area. WWT staff at Slimbridge carry out other bird-ringing activities, as do a number of individual ringers operating independently in the county, some of whom concentrate on particular species such as the raptors that have returned to breed here in recent decades and the Pied Flycatchers at Nagshead RSPB reserve.

Plain and simple birdwatching in the county received a huge boost in August 2000 when Mike King set up the 'Gloster Birder' website (www.birder.pwp.blueyonder.co.uk). Interest and records grew very quickly, as did the number of visits to the site, passing the one million mark on 28 July 2011 – and still marching on.

Gloucestershire bird books

Despite the advances of the electronic age, books have not yet been superseded, and this one is the first to show the current distribution and relative abundance of species in the county in both summer and winter, while also reviewing historical records and including passage migrants and rarer visitors to complete the picture. As such it is the most comprehensive county bird book to date, but it draws on information from a number of previous publications.

An early avifauna of sorts was 'The Birds of Gloucestershire' (Evans 1880), based on a talk given to the Stroud Natural History and Philosophical Society in 1879. It included an appended list of 170 species, but it was incomplete and inaccurate in many respects. Then in 1892 Charles Adolphus Witchell and William Bishop Strugnell published their *Fauna and Flora of Gloucestershire*, based on contributions from landowners, naturalists and sportsmen from both inside and outside the county. The accounts are by no means comprehensive, often because particular areas lacked interested contributors, and the commoner species are treated only very briefly. Although the work might be considered 'anecdotal', it is nevertheless a valuable resource and it does set a benchmark for comparison with later records.

The first book devoted specifically to Gloucestershire's birds was W. L. Mellersh's *A Treatise on the Birds of Gloucestershire*, published in 1902. Again, some species are dealt with less than comprehensively and the coverage of the county is not entirely complete, but present-day readers would recognise this work as a serious attempt to catalogue the county's birdlife. The next attempt at a county bird book came much later, as one of a series of brief guides in pamphlet format (Webster & Wood 1976). It followed the style of an annual bird report and also included much information from Mellersh.

In 1982, Christopher M. Swaine's *Birds of Gloucestershire* was published, the first significant county bird book for 80 years and based largely on records that had been previously published in the GBR. Swaine managed to pack a wealth of information on the status and history of the county's birds, their conservation and habitats, into what is by today's standards a very slim volume.

So now, more than 30 years on, after huge advances in the abilities of birdwatchers, in our knowledge of the birds and in the collation of records, the time is right for a new appraisal of the birds of Gloucestershire.

The 2007–11 Bird Atlas project

The maps and much of the other information presented in this book are derived from the results of the 2007–11 Bird Atlas project for the whole of the British Isles (Balmer *et al.* 2013), organised by the BTO in partnership with the Scottish Ornithologists' Club and Birdwatch Ireland. The fieldwork for this survey was carried out between November 1st 2007 and July 31st 2011.

This chapter describes the organisation of the atlas fieldwork, the methodology used and the nature of the records collected by the observers, and presents some general results.

Fieldwork organisation

The national survey was organised and managed at the county level, taking advantage of the long-standing ornithological infrastructure. However, because birds were to be mapped in the national atlas on the basis of the 10 km squares (hectads) of the Ordnance Survey national grid, county boundaries were adjusted for the purposes of the survey to bring them into line with the boundaries of these 10 km squares. Each 'atlas county' therefore consisted of an exact number of whole 10 km squares, a total of 26 in the case of Gloucestershire, referred to as the 'core' squares (those contained within the bold outline in Figure 1). This means that teams in some of our neighbouring counties were responsible for organising and supervising the fieldwork in parts of our county and vice versa, and in writing this book a certain amount of data swapping between 'atlas counties' was necessary. In Gloucestershire, each 10 km square was allocated a 'square steward' whose job it was to ensure the smooth running of the survey at the local level and liaise closely with the county atlas organiser.

At both national and local levels, the basic *recording unit* was the *tetrad*. This is a specific 2 km × 2 km square located within a 10 km square, so each 10 km square contains 25 tetrads, identified by letters as shown in Figures 1 and 2. For the national survey, the *mapping unit* was the *10 km square*. Tetrad-level records were used to obtain information about the abundance of birds within these 10 km squares (see below). However for Gloucestershire, it was

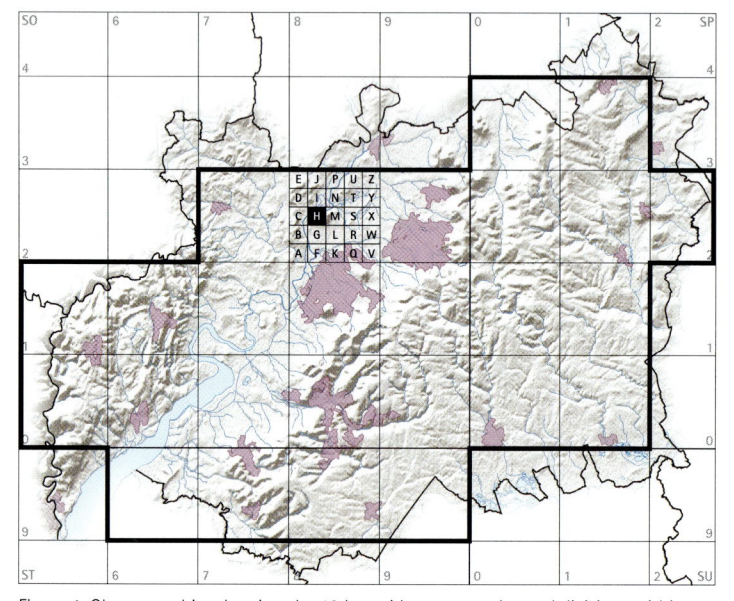

Figure 1. Gloucestershire showing the 10 km grid squares and tetrad divisions within a single 10 km square. The highlighted tetrad is SO82H, north of Gloucester.

Figure 2. An aerial view showing the extent of tetrad SO82H, highlighted in Figure 1.

The 2007–11 Bird Atlas project

decided to map as well as to record at the *tetrad* level, to give a more detailed picture and at a finer scale, of the distribution and abundance of birds in our comparatively small survey area.

There are of course many tetrads which straddle the real county border, but for mapping purposes it was decided that any tetrad with more than 50% of its area in Gloucestershire would be treated as a 'Gloucestershire tetrad'. The basis for this decision was that, if all counties took the same approach, there would be no gaps and no duplication in the tetrads covered. Under this 'more than 50%' rule, Gloucestershire consists of 683 tetrads (compared with 650 tetrads in the 26 core 10 km squares).

For our purposes it was clearly important to establish whether birds, particularly less common species, were actually in Gloucestershire and not just in tetrads with more than 50% of their area inside the county, so all observers surveying these border tetrads were asked to make a note of the county in which any particularly unusual sightings took place. In the event, such sightings were few and far between.

Survey methods

Two field survey methods were used, with different but complementary aims:

Timed Tetrad Visits

During a Timed Tetrad Visit (TTV) the observer spent a fixed time in a pre-allocated tetrad and *counted* all the birds of every species encountered. A TTV could last for either one or two hours. During two-hour visits, the birds counted in the first and second hours were recorded separately in order to make it possible to compare the results with those from previous national atlases, for which one-hour visits had been used. Observers were asked to visit all the major habitat types in the tetrad during the TTV and where possible to apportion their time to reflect those habitat types, so if a tetrad was 75% woodland the observer should ideally have spent 75% of the time in woodland.

Each tetrad received TTVs twice during winter: once in either November or December, and once in either January or February. Similarly in the breeding season, one TTV took place in either April or May and another in either June or July. Only four TTVs were undertaken in each tetrad during the four years of fieldwork; they were not repeated every year.

The purpose of TTVs was to provide data to compare the *abundance* of birds in different parts of the survey area, whether county or country. The abundance maps in this book are based entirely on the TTV data obtained during the atlas survey period.

Roving records

The data produced by the TTVs was supplemented by records from various other sources, collectively known as 'roving records':

- Individual observers' sightings as submitted to the atlas recording scheme specifically for atlas purposes.
- General birding records sent to county recorders by individuals and bird clubs.
- The BTO 'BirdTrack' online reporting system.
- The BTO Nest Record Scheme.
- The BTO Ringing Scheme.
- The birders' website, BirdGuides.com.

In addition, records were imported into the database from various national surveys, notably the BBS and WeBS.

The purpose of roving records was to produce extra information so as to obtain as comprehensive an idea as possible of the overall *distribution* of each species. Counts of birds could be submitted as roving records for general recording purposes, but for atlas purposes it was only a species' *presence* that was registered. The distribution maps in this book are based on all available tetrad-level records from the four-year atlas period.

Local aspects of the methodology

In Gloucestershire the national methodology was adopted in its entirety, so that county records could contribute to the national atlas and vice versa. However, particular emphasis was placed on some optional aspects of the fieldwork as described below, and it can be seen that the response from observers in the county to those additional features was truly excellent.

Timed Tetrad Visits

The national atlas methodology stipulated that ideally a minimum of eight of the 25 tetrads in each 10 km square should receive TTVs, to provide a good basis for calculating the *average* numbers of birds seen per hour in that 10 km square. In Gloucestershire it was agreed that all 683 tetrads in the county should be surveyed, except for two by the Severn Estuary (ST59Y and ST69J) as they include hardly any dry land. Observers were also asked to survey for two hours if at all possible, to improve the reliability of the abundance estimates.

In the event, not only did all 681 eligible tetrads receive their full complement of four TTVs over the four-year period, but 98% of TTVs lasted two hours; the complete set of data from TTVs represents some 5,385 hours of systematic, quantified field observations in the county.

Fieldworkers headed in all directions in the course of their surveying.

Breeding codes

Whether carrying out TTVs or submitting roving records, observers were encouraged to use the standard BTO codes to indicate breeding activity. These codes are based on bird behaviour that can be observed in the field, and they are grouped into four main categories which can reasonably be deduced from those types of behaviour, as shown in the table below.

Although the 'breeding season' for atlas surveying was between April 1st and July 31st, coded breeding records from outside these months were welcomed as they often provided extra evidence for early or late nesters, such as Goshawks displaying in March or Yellowhammers feeding young in August.

'Non-breeding'	
F	Flying over
M	Migrant
U	Summering non-breeder
'Possible breeding'	
H	Observed in suitable nesting habitat
S	Singing male
'Probable breeding'	
P	Pair in suitable nesting habitat
T	Permanent territory (defended over at least a week)
D	Courtship and display
N	Visiting probable nest site
A	Agitated behaviour
I	Brood patch of incubating bird (from bird in hand)
B	Nest building or excavating nest-hole
'Confirmed breeding'	
DD	Distraction display or injury feigning
UN	Used nest or eggshells from the current season
FL	Recently fledged young or downy young
ON	Adults entering or leaving nest site in circumstances indicating occupied nest
FF	Adult carrying faecal sac or food for young
NE	Nest containing eggs
NY	Nest with young seen or heard

A singing Cuckoo is recorded as 'possible' breeding.

A pair of Mandarin Ducks is recorded as 'probable' breeding.

An active Reed Bunting nest is recorded as 'confirmed' breeding.

Roving records

For national purposes, where mapping was to be at the 10 km level, submission of roving records with this degree of precision was acceptable. However for Gloucestershire, where tetrad-scale mapping was planned, observers were asked to submit roving records at the tetrad level wherever possible. Overall, 96% of all such records for the county were submitted at the tetrad level. The few exceptions were mainly from birding sites encompassing more than one tetrad, where it would not be practicable for observers to split their sightings into separate tetrads. These included almost all the records from BirdGuides.com for the county, which were mostly from 'Slimbridge', and some WeBS sites. In addition, there were a few cases where observers very understandably chose not to divulge precise locations of rarer breeding birds.

Additional visits

In order to achieve coverage that was as complete as possible, observers were encouraged to make additional visits to Gloucestershire tetrads in which they had carried out TTVs. In the final year of the project in particular, special efforts were made to survey in those tetrads which had received no visits apart from TTVs. This was achieved for all but a single tetrad, and this extra effort resulted in many more dots on the distribution maps and significantly improved breeding evidence for many species.

Weather conditions during the survey

The weather can have a significant effect not only on birds, but also on how easy (or otherwise) it is to survey them. Probably the most notable feature of the atlas period in this respect was that three out of the four winters were unusually cold by present-day standards. In January and February in both 2009 and 2010, there were extended periods of subzero temperatures and also heavy snow, which was

The 2007–11 Bird Atlas project

long-lasting on higher ground. In 2010, the country suffered its coldest December since 1890, although this cold spell was not as sustained as in the previous two winters.

Overall, the weather in the first three breeding seasons (2008, 2009 and 2010) is perhaps best described as average, whereas in 2011 it was good with a warm, dry, settled spring. Rainfall across the whole four-year period was significantly below average.

Two events that took place just outside the atlas recording period are so significant as to warrant a mention. In June and July 2007 the biggest summer flood ever recorded had severe impacts on parts of the Severn Vale, with negative effects on breeding habitats continuing into subsequent years, and there was a similar though smaller flood in September 2008.

More detailed accounts of the weather during the survey period can be found in the newsletters of the GNS and in the annual GBR.

Potential biases in the data

The results of experiments or fieldwork often have the potential to be biased or misleading, and it is important to be aware of this before trying to draw conclusions from the data. In this project it is considered that the following two factors are the most likely to have given rise to bias:

Uneven effort

All tetrads had the same amount of time expended on them during TTVs, so the TTV data (and hence the abundance maps) do not suffer from uneven effort. The same is not true for roving records and hence for the distribution maps, since observers could make 'roving' visits to any sites they wished and there was no limit to the amount of time they could spend recording. This might mean that more thinly distributed species and less frequent visitors are more likely to have been located in favoured areas such as well-known birding hot spots, nature reserves, birders' gardens and regular local 'patches'. This will have been redressed to some degree by the successful efforts to ensure that every tetrad received at least one visit over and above its required TTVs in both seasons.

Variable skills

All observers worked to the standardised BTO fieldwork instructions and guidelines, but of course observers have different abilities as well as varying levels of enthusiasm and confidence, and guidelines can be interpreted in different ways, especially those regarding breeding codes. It is inevitable that the maps in this book will reflect those variations to some extent. However with so many observers involved (about 650) and with so many tetrads surveyed, it is very unlikely that these differences will be anything other than randomly distributed across the county, and the overall large-scale patterns of distribution and abundance of birds in different areas should not be significantly affected.

Overview of the results

About 366,000 records were submitted for the county over the atlas fieldwork period, divided more or less evenly between the breeding season (48%) and winter (52%).

Figure 3 shows the breakdown of records, 61% of which came from fieldwork specific to the atlas. Of the rest, 62% were records sent to the county recorder, 33% were received via BirdTrack, and the remaining 5% were imported from other surveys such as BBS and WeBS and from ringing and nest records. Of all TTV and roving records submitted for the breeding season, 72% included a breeding code.

Excluding exotics, escapes, domestic wildfowl, hybrids and birds recorded only as 'flying over', 249 species were recorded in total (224 during the breeding season and 203 in winter). The 25 species that were seen only in winter, and the 46 recorded only in the breeding season, included a high proportion of rarities and off-season migrants as well as species that are specifically seasonal visitors to Gloucestershire.

The number of tetrads in which individual species were recorded ranged from one to 682 in the breeding season and from one to 683 in winter, out of a total of 683 tetrads. Table 1 shows how many species were widespread, sparsely distributed or 'middling' at each season, and it can be seen that the proportions are similar in winter and in the breeding season.

Table 2 shows the most widespread 20 species for each of the two seasons, together with the number of tetrads (out of a total of 683) in which they were recorded. At the other end of the scale, 21 species were seen only in one tetrad in the breeding season (mostly rarities, but also one or two lingering winter visitors including

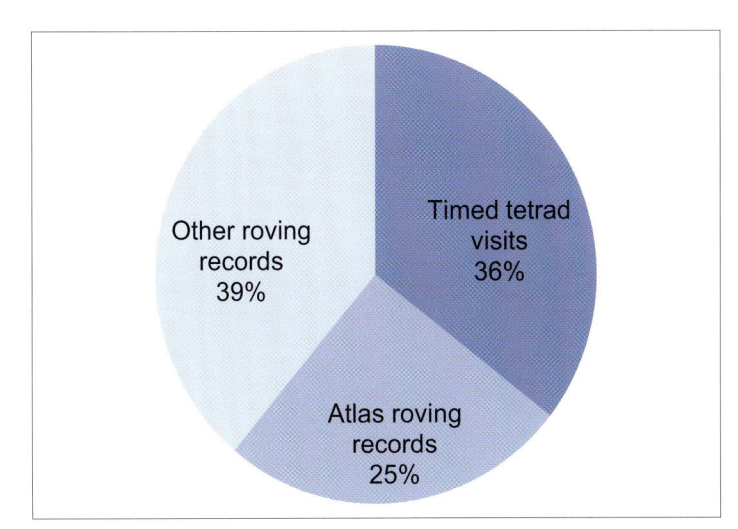

Figure 3. The proportions of different types of records submitted in the survey.

	Percentage of species recorded in			
	< 1% of tetrads	1–10% of tetrads	10–50% of tetrads	> 50% of tetrads
Breeding season (n=224)	28%	31%	20%	22%
Winter (n=203)	31%	30%	15%	25%

Table 1. Patterns of species distribution in each season in the survey.

Waxwing and Great Grey Shrike), and 23 were only found in one tetrad in winter (again predominantly rarities, but including some lingering summer visitors such as House Martin and Sedge Warbler). The mean number of apparently occupied tetrads per species in the breeding season was 170 (median 34), and in winter was 174 (median 35); the discrepancy between the mean and median figures reflects the fact that so many species, at both seasons, were found in few tetrads (about 60% of species recorded in 10% of tetrads or fewer, see Table 1).

Some idea of the overall abundance of a given species at either season can be obtained by identifying the higher of the two TTV counts (i.e. early or late visit) for each tetrad, and then adding these figures together to give a total count for the species for the whole county. This does not of course give an estimate of the total population, and it should be remembered that the numbers for different species will be heavily influenced by how easy, or otherwise, they are to detect during the fieldwork. On the other hand the calculation has the advantage of being repeatable in future surveys, allowing any declines or increases to be quantified to a

Breeding season	Tetrads
Blackbird	682
Blue Tit	682
Chaffinch	682
Great Tit	682
Robin	682
Woodpigeon	682
Wren	682
Carrion Crow	681
Blackcap	680
Dunnock	680
Chiffchaff	679
Song Thrush	678
Goldfinch	676
Buzzard	675
Swallow	675
Greenfinch	671
Jackdaw	660
Great Spotted Woodpecker	646
Pheasant	643
Whitethroat	643

Winter	Tetrads
Carrion Crow	683
Blackbird	682
Woodpigeon	682
Blue Tit	681
Chaffinch	681
Great Tit	681
Robin	681
Wren	681
Buzzard	676
Dunnock	676
Goldfinch	668
Redwing	667
Magpie	665
Song Thrush	665
Jackdaw	664
Long-tailed Tit	664
Fieldfare	663
Great Spotted Woodpecker	651
Greenfinch	645
Starling	643

Table 2. The most widespread 20 species in the two seasons.

Breeding season	Counts
Woodpigeon	24,345
Rook	19,189
Jackdaw	16,394
Blackbird	13,974
Chaffinch	11,022
House Sparrow	10,707
Carrion Crow	8,808
Robin	8,339
Wren	8,132
Blue Tit	8,117
Swallow	7,717
Great Tit	6,525
Goldfinch	5,803
Starling	5,787
House Martin	5,487
Greenfinch	4,471
Pheasant	4,135
Dunnock	3,972
Chiffchaff	3,914
Skylark	3,828

Winter	Counts
Woodpigeon	79,234
Starling	50,086
Fieldfare	43,525
Rook	32,062
Jackdaw	31,219
Redwing	28,871
Chaffinch	23,103
Black-headed Gull	22,012
Blackbird	17,329
Lapwing	15,121
Carrion Crow	14,831
Common Gull	13,099
Blue Tit	12,256
Lesser Black-backed Gull	11,178
House Sparrow	10,188
Robin	9,684
Pheasant	9,520
Golden Plover	9,319
Great Tit	9,316
Herring Gull	8,458

Table 3. The most abundant 20 species in the two seasons.

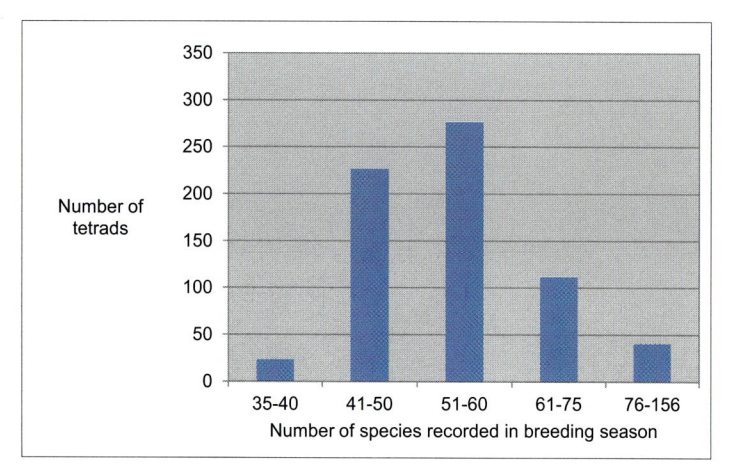

Figure 4. The number of species in tetrads in the breeding season.

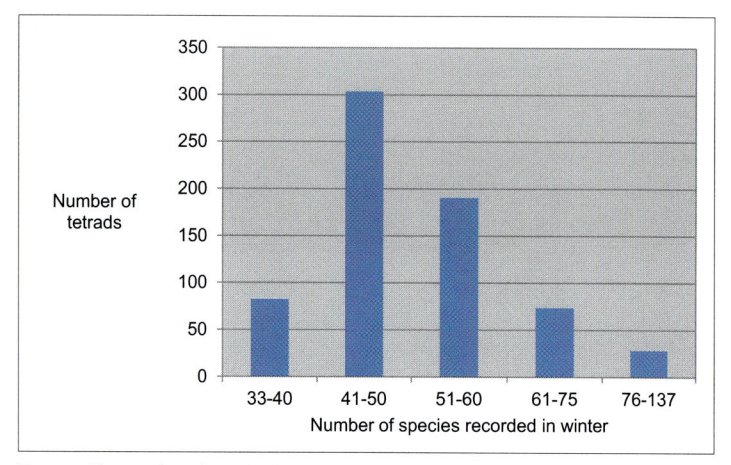

Figure 5. The number of species in tetrads in winter.

The 2007-11 Bird Atlas project

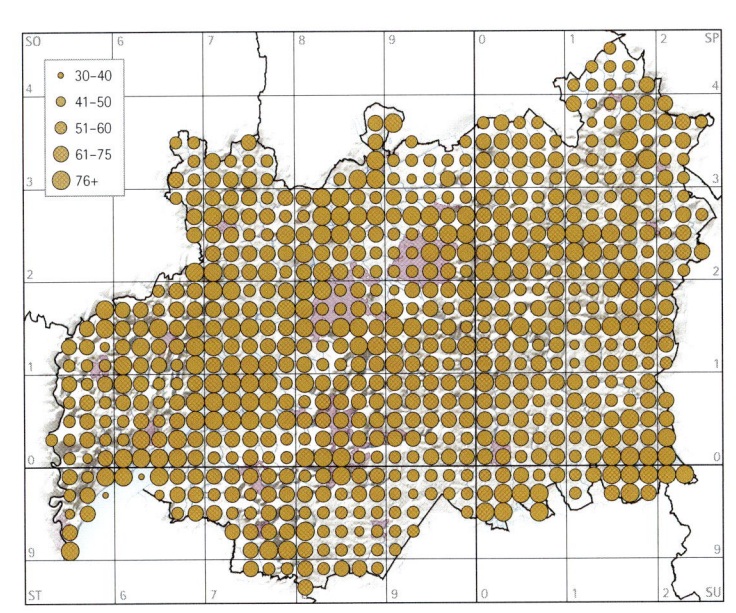

Figure 6. The number of species recorded in each tetrad in the breeding season.

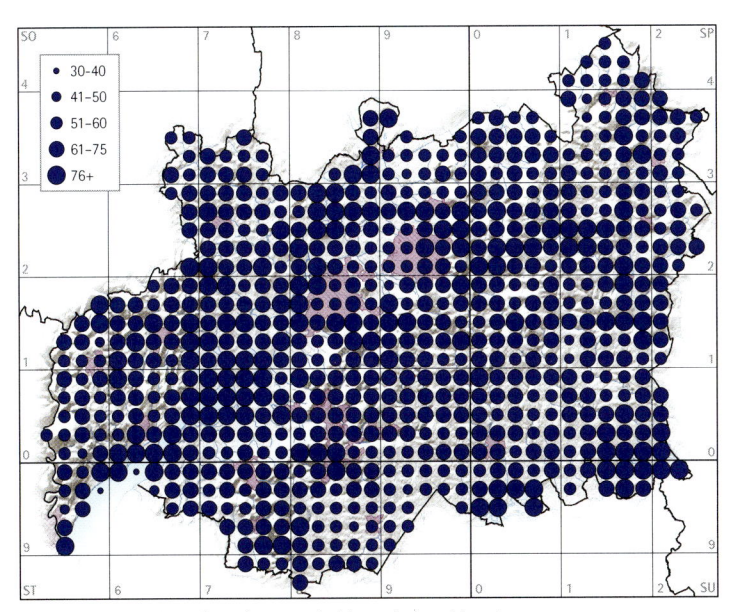

Figure 7. The number of species recorded in each tetrad in winter.

	Breeding season		Winter	Both seasons combined
	Total species	Species with breeding codes	Total species	Total species
SO050*	94	85	83	107
SO051*	93	77	84	105
SO060	131	99	141	175
SO061*	125	98	104	142
SO070	194	109	174	225
SO071	126	93	113	148
SO072	106	89	90	120
SO080	105	84	95	121
SO081	124	88	118	147
SO082	142	93	119	162
SO090	101	83	89	113
SO091	123	93	100	134
SO092	124	92	106	140
SP00	103	78	90	115
SP01	91	82	93	111
SP02	108	89	94	118
SP03*	94	81	84	109
SP10	124	96	113	146
SP11	116	96	102	135
SP12	115	90	104	131
SP13*	103	84	87	115
SP22*	89	76	81	99
ST69*	122	78	117	153
ST79*	103	85	96	121
ST89	105	83	90	123
ST99*	73	67	74	91
Average	113	87	102	131

Table 4. The numbers of species recorded in each of the 26 'core' 10 km squares.

degree. Based on this method, the 20 most abundantly recorded species in each season, with the sum total of higher TTV counts, are shown in Table 3. The sum of all the individual species totals was 248,008 in the breeding season, and 568,409 in winter. Hence nearly one bird in ten seen in the breeding season was a Woodpigeon, as was nearly one in seven in winter.

Excluding the two estuary tetrads that have very little land, the number of species recorded per tetrad in the breeding season ranged from 35 (tetrad SO81N, the Coney Hill–Saintbridge area of Gloucester City) to 156 (SO70H, one of the Slimbridge tetrads). In the winter, totals ranged from 33 (tetrads SO50Q and SO51W, both in the Forest of Dean) to 137 (SO70H, Slimbridge again). The mean number of species per tetrad was 56 in the breeding season and 52 in winter. Figures 4 and 5 show how many tetrads had few, many or intermediate numbers of species at each season.

Figures 6 and 7 show the number of species recorded in each tetrad in the breeding season and in winter. Perhaps the most notable feature is that the areas supporting the highest number of species all include water: the Severn Estuary, the 'Hams' in the Severn Vale, the Cotswold Water Park, Bourton pits and other areas with waterbodies all stand out. The least species-rich areas are those with the most uniform habitats, such as some of the more treeless areas of the Cotswolds and the larger areas of dense woodland.

On a broader scale, the numbers of species recorded in each of the 26 'core' Gloucestershire 10 km squares are shown in Table 4. Note that for squares not wholly in the county, marked with an asterisk, the totals shown here refer only to the Gloucestershire tetrads; the totals for the whole 10 km square are likely to be marginally higher.

Bird surveys in Gloucestershire

In addition to the 2007–11 atlas project, a range of bird surveys organised at both national and county level have been taking place in Gloucestershire for many years (see p. 40). Here we present some results from two of the longest-running – one nationally organised and one locally based.

Breeding Bird Survey

The BBS is the main national scheme for monitoring changes in the numbers of the commoner breeding species. Managed by the BTO on behalf of a partnership made up of the BTO, the Joint Nature Conservation Committee (JNCC) and the RSPB, it started in 1994 and was phased in to replace the Common Birds Census which ran from 1962 to 2000. National and regional results, together with longer term trends, are published annually by the BTO on behalf of the partnership, in a report on *Breeding Birds in the Wider*

Yellowhammers are found in about half of the county's BBS squares.

Countryside (most recently, Baillie *et al.* 2012), which is recognised as the authoritative source of such information.

BBS volunteers survey the same kilometre square twice each year between April and June, counting all the birds they find, and also record habitats. The number of squares surveyed in Gloucestershire rose quickly from 20 in 1994 to 41 in 1999 and is now over 50. A sample size of this magnitude means that the county BBS results can be used to obtain a measure of the well-being or otherwise of the

Linnets have declined through the life of the BBS, but less so locally than nationally.

Bird surveys in Gloucestershire

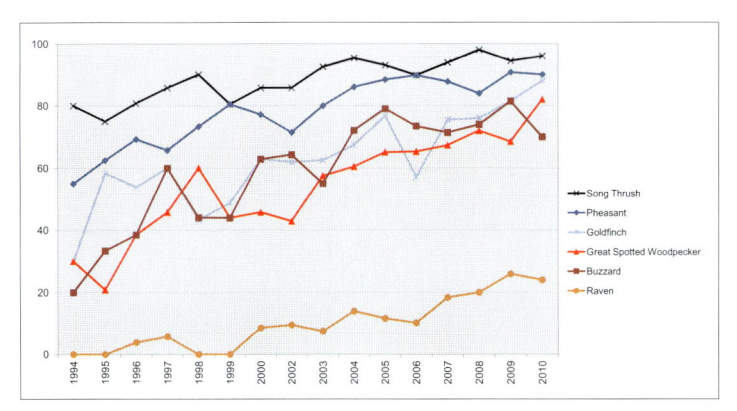

Figure 1. Six increasing residents: percentage of BBS squares in which recorded in Gloucestershire, 1994–2010.

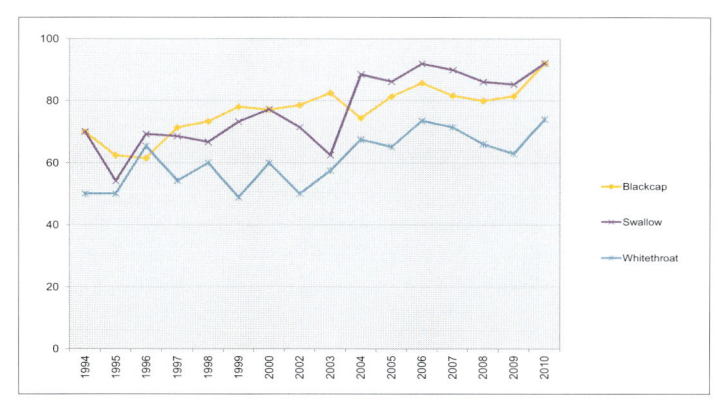

Figure 2. Three increasing summer visitors: percentage of BBS squares in which recorded in Gloucestershire, 1994–2010.

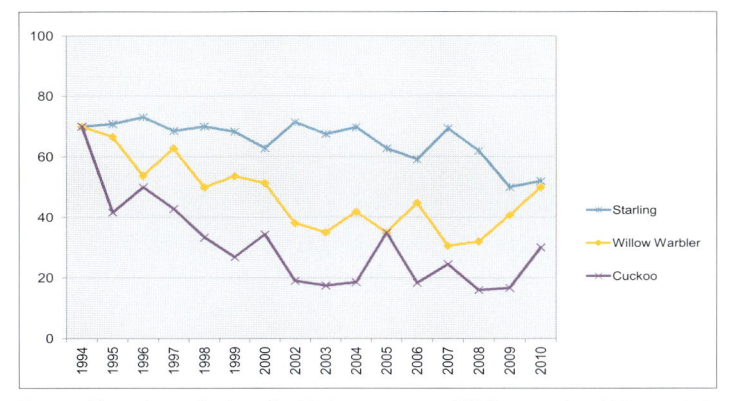

Figure 3. Three decreasing breeding birds: percentage of BBS squares in which recorded in Gloucestershire, 1994–2010.

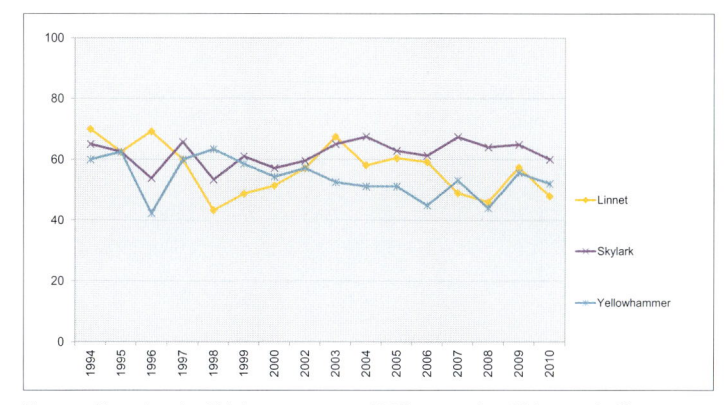

Figure 4. Three farmland birds: percentage of BBS squares in which recorded in Gloucestershire, 1994–2010.

commoner species, simply by calculating the percentage of surveyed squares in which they were recorded. Although such figures measure distribution rather than abundance, they can nevertheless be used to provide an indicator of trends that is reasonably reliable.

Figures 1–3 show the results for 12 species for which the trend in the county seems to be unmistakeable, although it should be noted that the data have not been tested for statistical significance. In every case the time period is 1994 to 2010 but includes no figures for 2001, the year when BBS fieldwork was suspended because of the outbreak of foot-and-mouth disease.

Skylark, Linnet and Yellowhammer (Figure 4) are among those farmland species that are red listed (see p. 57) because of long-term population declines. The county BBS data suggest that, since 1994 at least, they may be holding their own better in Gloucestershire than in some other areas.

Skylark: a species for which county BBS figures have been fairly constant for the last two decades.

A satellite photograph of part of Gloucester shows the amount of 'green' space provided by gardens.

The Gloucestershire Garden Bird Survey

In 1993 GOCC launched a county-wide survey, in which observers counted birds using the feeding stations in their gardens for a nine-week period, starting in early January. A total of 76 forms were returned for the Feeding Station Survey of 1993 and the results were reported in that year's GBR. Gardens were classified as small, medium or large, the sites as urban, suburban or rural, and 55 species were recorded in total. The report concentrated on the percentage of gardens used by the different species, and also included a table of the 'top 10' recorded species. The survey continued unchanged until 1999 when the methodology was changed so that birds landing anywhere in the garden were recorded, not just those using feeders, and so the name was accordingly changed to 'Garden Bird Survey'. (Note that this project is specific to Gloucestershire and is not part of other similarly named surveys organised by both RSPB and BTO; neither should it be confused with the DBPS Garden Bird Feeding Survey described on p. 39). Also from 1999 onwards, the table of most widely reported species was expanded from 'top 10' to 'top 20'. The survey has attracted increasing numbers of observers, with around 300 currently participating, and the latest summary (Sutcliffe 2010) shows that the number of species seen that year was 63, with 84 in total having been recorded over the last decade. The larger sample size in recent years has enabled more robust analyses to be undertaken, and as time goes on there is obviously more opportunity to study trends. In 1993 the top three birds were Robin, Blue Tit and Blackbird, in that order; the data for 2011 show that these same three species still hold the leading positions, but Blackbird is now number one, followed by Blue Tit and then Robin.

Here we set out some of the results from the Gloucestershire Garden Bird Survey, based on an analysis by Vic Polley of the data for the 13 years from 1999 to 2011, and paying particular attention to those species that show statistically significant trends.

Figure 5 shows that most of the common species show a very stable pattern of occurrence. Further analysis does reveal however that the declines in Blue Tit and House Sparrow, though slight, are significant.

Bird surveys in Gloucestershire

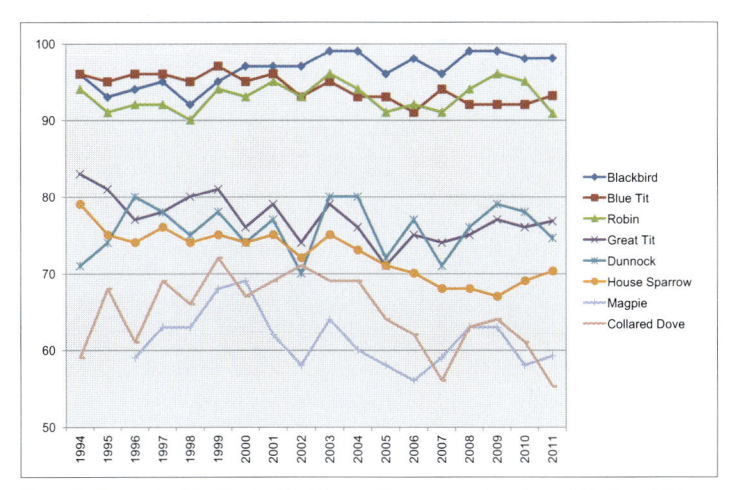

Figure 5. Gloucestershire Garden Bird Survey: Percentage of gardens visited by eight very common species, 1994–2010.

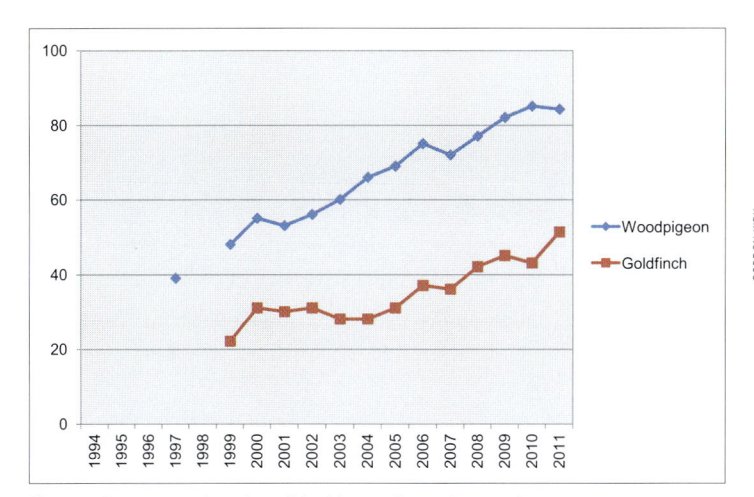

Figure 6. Percentage of gardens visited by two increasing species, 1994–2010.

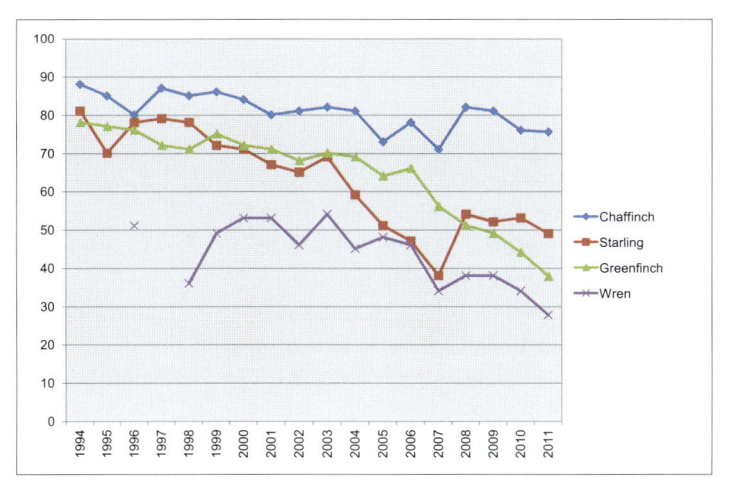

Figure 7. Percentage of gardens visited by four decreasing species, 1994–2010.

Figure 6 shows the rising stars of the survey, Goldfinch and Woodpigeon. The former was recorded in over half of all gardens for the first time in 2011, and the latter muscled its way into the top ten for the first time in 2004 and currently occupies fourth place.

Figure 7 shows the four species that have declined significantly over the period. The decline is less severe for Chaffinch, which fell from fourth place in 1994 to sixth in 2010. Chaffinches have been affected by the Trichomonosis parasite, but not to the same extent as Greenfinches which, as the graph shows, have slumped disastrously. The decreases revealed by this survey are noticeably greater than those among the Greenfinch population as a whole (see the species account for Greenfinch, p. 404) and moreover the survey also shows that Greenfinches declined more in urban gardens than in rural or suburban ones. This is likely to be because a higher proportion of urban-dwelling birds make use of garden feeding stations, where the disease is known to be more readily spread from bird to bird than it is in the wild.

The fall in the number of Starlings visiting gardens reflects the wider decline of that species, but the figures for Wren are less easy to understand, although it is a species that is well known to be susceptible to wide fluctuations in numbers due to the effects of harsh winters, irrespective of any long-term trends.

Great Spotted Woodpecker is a popular visitor to garden feeders.

Introduction to the species accounts

Sources of information

In addition to the data gathered as part of the national 2007–11 Bird Atlas survey, the primary sources of information for the species accounts in this book are the annual GBRs dating back to 1963, and the county bird recorder's database. The latter comprises all the 2007–11 atlas records, all other records submitted from any source since 2002, and many earlier records for less common species.

In general, we have used the previous county avifauna (Swaine 1982) as a basis for describing changes and developments. Accordingly, statements about 'recent' patterns of occurrence or distribution normally refer to the decades since 1980. Swaine in turn relied mostly on Witchell & Strugnell (1892) and Mellersh (1902 and unpublished manuscripts) for historical information relating to birds in the county. When referring to these three books in the accounts we have cited the names of the authors only. We have corrected a small number of errors that we have found in Swaine and have omitted a few records that he included but which are no longer considered acceptable.

We have also made use of national, regional and county information from projects organised by the BTO, such as the BBS, WeBS, Garden BirdWatch and various single-species surveys including the long-running Heronries Census. It should be noted that some of these surveys, including BBS, did not take place in 2001 because of an outbreak of foot-and-mouth disease that restricted fieldwork, so there is often no data for that year.

For additional background information relating to the county, the British Isles, Europe and beyond, we have made great use of the following additional sources. Rather than cite these publications by their conventional author-date references, we have chosen to refer to them in the species accounts by their titles or abbreviated titles as indicated in the bulleted lists below. This is because we feel that it is more convenient for the reader to be reminded of the subject matter of these frequently cited publications. The full titles and other details may be found in the References (p. 442).

For Gloucestershire:

- 1983–87 (or 'first') Cotswolds Atlas: *An Atlas of Cotswold Breeding Birds* (Wright et al. 1990)
- 2003–07 (or 'second') Cotswolds Atlas: *Birds of the Cotswolds: a new breeding atlas* (Main et al. 2009)

Information about breeding waders and other birds in the Severn Vale comes from regular reports by Mike Smart and others, notably in the pages of GBR and *GNS News*.

We have referred a number of times to the Random Square Surveys carried out in winter and summer by members of NCOS: each observer counts birds in a single kilometre square of the Ordnance Survey national grid, using a consistent methodology designed to allow trends over time to be identified.

Data from the Gloucestershire Garden Bird Survey have also been used and results from this study are described in more detail on p. 50.

For status and changes in distribution and abundance in the British Isles and Europe:

- 1875–1900 Atlas: *The Historical Atlas of Breeding Birds in Britain and Ireland* (Holloway 1996)
- 1968–72 Breeding Atlas: *The Atlas of Breeding Birds in Britain and Ireland* (Sharrock 1976)
- 1981–84 Wintering Atlas: *The Atlas of Wintering Birds in Britain and Ireland* (Lack 1986)
- 1988–91 Breeding Atlas: *The New Atlas of Breeding Birds in Britain and Ireland* (Gibbons et al. 1993)
- BWP: *Birds of the Western Palearctic* (Cramp et al. 1977–94; Snow & Perrins 1998)

We have also drawn on material from the BirdFacts and BirdTrends pages on the website of the BTO (www.bto.org/about-birds/birdfacts; www.bto.org/about-birds/birdtrends), which in turn are based on Baillie et al. (2012) and its predecessors, Baker et al. (2006), Burfield

Introduction to the species accounts

and van Bommel (2004), Eaton *et al.* (2011), Hagemeijer & Blair (1997) and occasionally other sources.

In addition, the BTO provided us with summaries of data from the previous atlases for the British Isles.

For information about migration routes and seasonal distribution:
- BWP (as above)
- Migration Atlas: *The Migration Atlas: movements of the birds of Britain and Ireland* (Wernham *et al.* 2002)

For ringing recovery data:

The BTO online ringing report (www.bto.org/volunteer-surveys/ringing/publications/online-ringing-reports) provided information on ringing recoveries involving Gloucestershire up to 2010.

For information about migrants and rarities:
- RBBP: the Rare Breeding Birds Panel website (www.rbbp.org.uk) and reports, notably Holling & RBBP (2009), for information about the numbers and status of rare breeding birds in the UK.
- BirdGuides: the birders' website, for general information about rarities (www.birdguides.com).

We also referred to the British Birds Rarities Committee (BBRC) website (www.bbrc.org.uk) and reports for information about current and former national rarities, and to BirdFacts (see above) for statistics such as average numbers of records per year of scarce migrants.

Finally, we have been provided with much useful information through personal contacts, and this has been acknowledged by citing the individuals' names in parentheses.

Species included

All bird species included in categories A, B and C of the British List, as defined by the British Ornithologists' Union (BOU), that were on the Gloucestershire list on June 30th 2012 are treated in full in individual accounts. This essentially means wild and naturalised or feral species – 330 species in total. In addition, Gloucestershire records of species in categories D and E (essentially escapes or deliberate releases of birds which are not found 'wild' in the country) are summarised. No attempt has been made to gather additional evidence to check the authenticity of old records; in almost all cases we have accepted the judgement of Swaine and Mellersh with any exceptions mentioned in the species accounts. However, we have taken account of recent guidelines from the BBRC concerning historical records (Harrop 2011). Application of the recommended BBRC criteria to the single Gloucestershire record of Alpine Accentor *Prunella collaris* (dated 1860) has rendered it 'no longer accepted', and as a consequence it has been removed from the county list. Although this is the only Gloucestershire record of a national rarity to be affected in this way, the 1930 record of Crested Tit (European Crested Tit) *Lophophanes cristatus* included by Swaine similarly fails to meet modern standards for acceptance and has also been deleted from the county list.

Species order

The sequence in which the species accounts appear in this book generally follows the official BOU taxonomic order in force in 2010. However, in places we have grouped together the rarer species within a given taxonomic group, such as birds of prey or gulls. This is partly to make best use of the space available and in some cases it has also allowed us to make some general remarks about a group of rarities as a whole, for example American waders. We trust readers will find that the arrangement is helpful.

Species names

Throughout this book we have used the current vernacular English names of birds, as used by birdwatchers and the general public in Britain on a day-to-day basis. The headings of the individual species accounts also include the current 'official' English names of birds, as defined by the International Ornithological Committee (IOC) in 2012 (Gill & Donsker 2012), for the benefit of any readers who may be unfamiliar with the more traditional names.

Localities

We have endeavoured to refer to locations that appear on the 1:50,000 British Ordnance Survey maps wherever possible, and to retain the same spellings for place-names that are used on these maps. In the case of more obscure sites such as tiny hamlets or woods, we have tried to provide the name of a nearby larger settlement or mapped feature ('near Cirencester' for example) to assist those readers who are less familiar with the county.

For many people but most especially those from outside the county, mention of the name 'Slimbridge' immediately evokes the WWT reserve and birding site. However, the actual name for this well-known area by the Severn Estuary near the village of Slimbridge, home to the WWT, is the New Grounds; similarly, the area of salt-marsh and grassland immediately adjacent to the estuary here is called the Dumbles. Although these names are familiar to many local birdwatchers and are often used in the pages of the GBR and other local publications, for clarity we have retained the name 'Slimbridge' to refer to the whole of the foreshore and floodplain extending from about Tites Point near Purton to about Frampton on Severn, bounded inland by the Gloucester and Sharpness Canal. Specific sites within this larger area are distinguished by name only when a more precise location is required. Where 'Slimbridge village' is intended, it is referred to in that form.

There is more than one village in Gloucestershire called 'Frampton', but in this book the name refers to Frampton on Severn, unless stated otherwise.

Birds often move between the lakes at Frampton village, the nearby wetland locally known as '100 Acre', and Slimbridge, and in some respects these collectively form one large, if discontinuous, site of wetland habitat. In this book, the phrase 'the Frampton–Slimbridge area' means the whole of this larger area.

The Cotswold Water Park is a huge area of wetland, divided at the time of writing into two sections, west and east. As previously mentioned, local birdwatchers commonly use the numbers allocated to the former gravel-pits when referring to specific lakes. However, as these numbers are not well known outside the region and, in any case, birds very often move around within the Water Park, we have decided, in general, to distinguish only between the west and east sections rather than between individual lakes.

Ringing information

We have used ringing data to give a general flavour of the movements of some birds to and from Gloucestershire. For many species the recoveries to date have not provided any particularly noteworthy information, and in such cases they have not been mentioned. It should be noted that some ringing and recovery information dates from periods when the British counties were organised and named differently, so there are occasional references to 'Hereford & Worcester', 'Avon' and the like, which no longer exist as administrative entities. In the same way, some older recoveries involving 'Gloucestershire' could relate to what is now South Gloucestershire and therefore outside the scope of this book. It would not be possible to eliminate all such records without a disproportionate amount of effort, especially given that the precise ringing and recovery locations are often not provided in the summaries on the BTO website.

Information about summer visitors and passage migrants

The average, earliest and latest arrival and departure dates for seasonal visitors quoted here are based on records from the mid-1970s to 2010. In line with national trends, most summer visitors have tended to arrive a few days earlier in recent years; this fact is not repeated in all the relevant species accounts but any particularly noticeable changes or apparent exceptions to the general trend are pointed out.

Data relating to the annual and seasonal occurrence of scarcer passage migrants have been extracted directly from the GBR. Where graphs are presented for the pattern of occurrence of these species, only the finding date has been taken into account, so a bird found in April but remaining until June will only be graphed for April. The accounts for many of these scarcer species, especially waders and terns, make reference to 'peak counts'. Birders are familiar with the fact that many migrants regularly 'stop over' for days or weeks at a time, and it is often impossible to know just how many Black Terns or Curlew Sandpipers have moved through a given site over a whole season when numbers fluctuate from day to day. The peak count (the maximum count on any one day, anywhere in the county during a given spring or autumn) is a crude measure of total passage, but we believe it to be adequate for describing general patterns and trends.

For some commoner migrants, we have produced graphs showing the total number of records per month between 2003 and 2010, based on the raw data in the county records database. The figures in these graphs are by no means precise, as a single bird can generate a number of 'records' if it stays longer than one day or is reported by more than one observer, but we feel that they do give a realistic impression of the seasonal patterns of occurrence of these commoner migrants in the county.

It should be noted that not all of these graphs run from January to December. For some species, a clearer picture of the seasonal pattern emerges if the graphs start and end in the middle of the calendar year.

Observer effects

There are fairly frequent references in the species accounts to 'observer effects'. This is shorthand for the general trend, especially over the past 50 years or so, of increasing numbers of birdwatchers, equipped with ever-improving optical equipment and benefiting from huge steps forward in the establishment of identification criteria for species that were formerly considered to be difficult, or even impossible, to distinguish in the field. The main result of this trend is that an increasing proportion of the birds present, particularly migrants and visitors, will have been encountered by birders and identified. In some cases this may even have masked declines in the actual numbers occurring. Another result will be a tendency for the dates of the first sightings of seasonal migrants to become earlier, because with more birdwatchers in the field, the first few arriving birds are more likely to be encountered. This effect may tend to exaggerate the real trend among many summer visitors towards earlier arrivals in recent years. The same effect will also tend to result in later apparent departure dates for these seasonal visitors.

It is impossible to quantify such observer effects, but as an illustration of one aspect in Gloucestershire, the number of contributors to the GBR each year increased from about 100 in 1970 to 200 in 1980 and 250 by 2000. Between 2007 and 2009 there were over 400 contributors each year, rising to a very impressive 750 in 2010, but this was largely due to the extra interest generated by the atlas project.

Great Tit is one of the more common species to be found in Gloucestershire.

Introduction to the species accounts

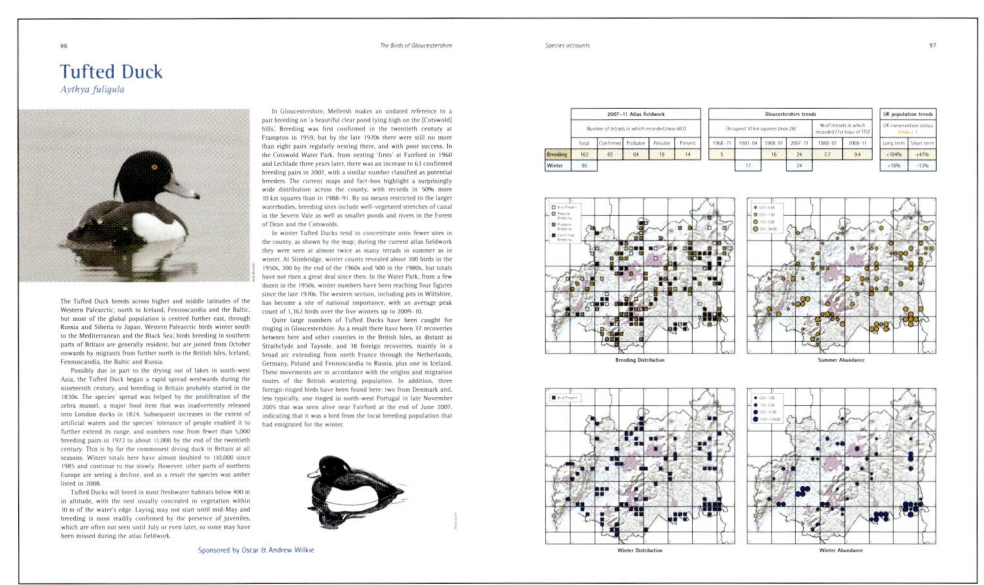

Figure 1. A typical species account for a bird present in both seasons.

Layout of the species accounts

Commoner species: residents and regular summer or winter visitors to the county

The accounts for most of the common species are based on information up to the end of July 2011, when recording for the national 2007–11 Bird Atlas finished, but in a few cases we have included notable records up to 2012. These accounts usually occupy two pages (Figure 1) and include a variable number of maps to illustrate distribution and abundance over the 2007–11 atlas period. Common residents have four maps, showing distribution and abundance for both winter and breeding seasons. Summer and winter visitors generally have two maps, and some scarcer species also have fewer than four because there were insufficient TTV records to produce valid abundance maps.

The *distribution* maps simply show all tetrads in which the species was recorded in each season during the Atlas period, plus categories of breeding evidence for the breeding season, as shown in Figure 2 for Tufted Duck.

The *abundance* maps are based on the average numbers of birds encountered per hour during TTVs. For example, if the first winter visit to a given tetrad produced ten Robins in the first hour and eight in the second, and in the second winter visit the hourly totals were 12 and two, the figure used for that tetrad when producing the winter abundance map for Robin would be [10+8+12+2] divided by four, i.e. 8. The larger the dot on the map, the higher this average figure. As far as possible the TTV data for each species were divided into four roughly equal groups so that most abundance maps contain similar numbers of dots of four sizes; we feel this makes the best use of the data to present a visually informative pattern. For example, the winter abundance map for Robin is shown in Figure 3.

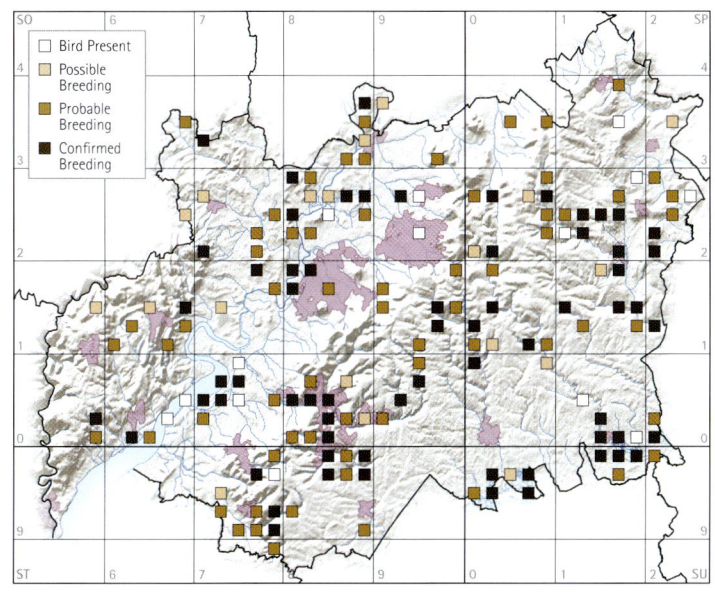

Figure 2. Breeding distribution map for Tufted Duck.

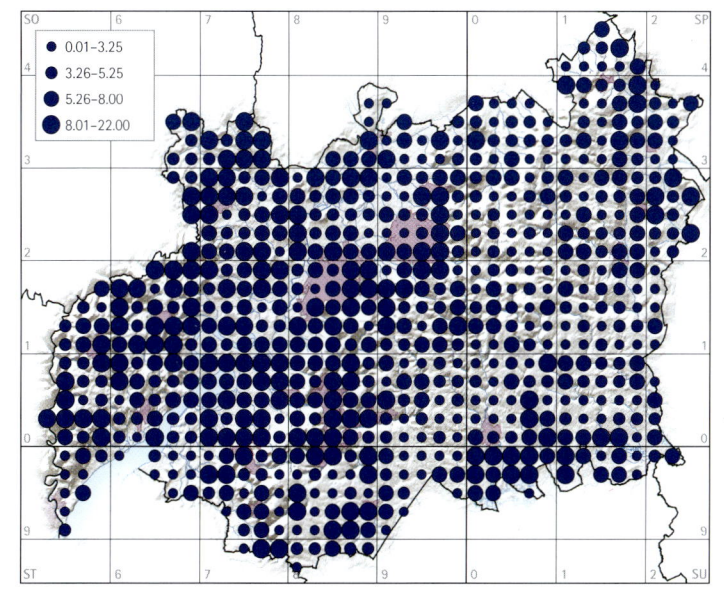

Figure 3. Winter abundance map for Robin.

	2007–11 Atlas fieldwork					Gloucestershire trends					UK population trends	
	Number of tetrads in which recorded (max 683)					Occupied 10 km squares (max 26)				% of tetrads in which recorded (1st hour of TTV)		UK conservation status: Amber 1	
	Total	Confirmed	Probable	Possible	Present	1968–71	1981–84	1988–91	2007–11	1988–91	2008–11	Long term	Short term
Breeding	162	65	64	19	14	5		16	24	7.7	9.4	+104%	+47%
Winter	96						17		24			+16%	–13%

Figure 4. The fact-box from the Tufted Duck species account.

These accounts also contain 'fact-boxes' showing summary data from the atlas period and longer-term trends taken from various sources; for example, Figure 4 shows the fact-box for Tufted Duck.

The first section shows the results of the 2007–11 atlas fieldwork, i.e. for the four winters 2007–08 to 2010–11 and the four breeding seasons from 2008 to 2011. The second section shows the number of occupied 'core' 10 km squares in each of the three breeding atlases and the two winter atlases (including the current national atlas, Balmer *et al.* 2013). For the breeding season, only records with 'possible', 'probable' or 'confirmed' breeding evidence have been used, in order to make the comparisons as valid as possible. In addition, for the 1988–91 and 2008–11 breeding surveys some of the fieldwork methods were identical, so we show the percentage of tetrads in which the species was recorded during the first hour of TTVs.

The third section shows the conservation status and the available UK population trend information for that species. This is taken from various sources, and a dash (–) in this section means that information is not available, usually because the species is not well covered in regular surveys. The 'winter' trends are derived from WeBS, so in general only some wildfowl and waders are included. In this context 'long term' and 'short term' mean 25 (1982–83 to 2007–08) and 10 years (1997–98 to 2007–08) respectively. The breeding season trends are derived mainly from the Breeding Birds Survey and its predecessors, so most of the species involved are the more common land birds; here the timescales are 39 (1970–2009) and 14 years (1995–2009). Finally, for seabirds the breeding season trends are from specific monitoring programmes, with 'long' and 'short' periods of 24 (1986–2010) and 10 years (2000–10) respectively. Full details can be found in Eaton *et al.* (2011).

Dotterel is a scarce migrant in the county.

Less common residents, seasonal visitors and passage migrants

Accounts for these species are normally based on records up to the end of 2010, and occupy one page or less. They generally do not have maps, but many include tables or graphs to illustrate seasonal patterns or long-term trends. A few particularly noteworthy records up to the middle of 2012 are also included.

County rarities

In general the length of the accounts for rare migrants and visitors corresponds with the species' rarity in the county. For species that have been recorded on fewer than ten occasions all records are listed, whilst sightings of rather less rare species are summarised. Some of these shorter accounts also include tables or graphs to illustrate patterns or trends. All records up to the end of 2011 are usually included.

Short-eared Owl is a seasonal visitor to Gloucestershire.

Interpreting the maps

We are confident that the maps in this book give a reliable picture of the general distribution and level of abundance of the county's birds, but the reader should bear the following in mind:

Beware of spurious precision

It is important not to place too much reliance on the fine detail of the maps at the tetrad level. Some features, for example a small gap in distribution or an apparent concentration of a given species in a small area, will be due to chance, not to any real differences in abundance or distribution.

Birds move around

One bird might give rise to more than one dot on a map. For example a single Shelduck moving around Saul Warth, where four tetrads meet in the very centre of the best birding area, could easily generate a cluster of four dots on the map. Similarly, an observer might have seen a Kestrel carrying prey in a particular tetrad during the breeding season, correctly recording 'FF' (signifying confirmed breeding). However the bird might have been taking the prey to its nest in a neighbouring tetrad, where another observer might have (again correctly) recorded 'ON' meaning an occupied nest, also signifying confirmed breeding; the result is two confirmed breeding records mapped for one pair in adjacent tetrads.

The snapshot effect

The distribution maps show the cumulative records for a four-year period and therefore might give the impression that a bird is more widespread than it actually is in any single year. This is especially true for irregularly occurring species such as the Brambling, a visitor that is quite common in some winters but almost absent in others. The first winter in the survey period (2007–08) was a good Brambling year, and the dots on the map mainly refer to this one winter: see the Brambling species account (p. 402) for more details and discussion. Similarly, individual birds can change their nesting site from one breeding season to the next, possibly moving into a new tetrad, so again the maps might indicate more breeding activity than is actually the case in any one year.

Clearly these factors will be balanced, to an unknown extent, by the fact that not all birds present will be detected, in this or any other similar survey.

Breeding status

Observers were encouraged to use the standard breeding codes (see p. 44), based on observations of bird behaviour in the field. These codes are grouped into categories indicating 'possible', 'probable' and 'confirmed' breeding. The resulting breeding distribution maps give a good overall impression of where a given species can be found, but not necessarily such an accurate picture of its breeding status in different parts of the county. The extent to which breeding status was recorded varied from observer to observer (and thus from place to place), and it is much more difficult to confirm breeding for some species than for others. Perhaps the most important thing to remember when looking at the breeding season maps, especially for commoner birds, is that they probably did breed in most of the tetrads where they were found, even if they are not marked as 'confirmed'. In particular, apparent differences in breeding status at the *tetrad* level should not necessarily be interpreted as reflecting real differences, while at the *10 km square* level a preponderance of 'confirmed' dots in one square and only 'possible' in another square is, in general, more likely to reflect a genuine difference.

Red and amber listing

The status of the UK's birds is determined by a panel made up of representatives of the country's leading bird conservation organisations, and from time to time a report on 'Birds of Conservation Concern' is published (see Eaton *et al.* 2009 and its predecessors). Species that are categorised as rare or threatened may be amber or red listed, according to the following criteria:

Red listing

1. Identified by BirdLife International as being globally threatened.
2. Historical decline. Severe decline in the UK between 1800 and 1995, without substantial recent recovery.
3. Severe decline in the UK breeding population, either of more than 50% over 25 years or longer-term if data exist.
4. Severe decline in the UK non-breeding population, either of more than 50% over 25 years or longer-term if data exist.
5. Severe decline in the UK range, as measured by number of 10 km squares occupied by breeding birds, either of more than 50% over 25 years or longer-term if data exist.

Amber listing

1. Categorised as a Species of European Conservation Concern.
2. Red listed for historical decline in a previous review but with substantial recent recovery (more than doubled in the last 25 years).
3. Moderate decline in the UK breeding population. As for red list criterion 3 above, but with a decline of between 25% and 50%.
4. Moderate decline in the UK non-breeding population. As for red list criterion 4 above, but with a decline of between 25% and 50%.
5. Moderate decline in the UK range. As for red list criterion 5 above, but with a decline of between 25% and 50%.
6. Rarity. A UK breeding population of less than 300 pairs or non-breeding population of less than 900 individuals.
7. Localisation. At least 50% of the UK breeding or non-breeding population found in 10 or fewer sites.
8. International importance. At least 20% of the European breeding or non-breeding population is found in the UK.

All regularly occurring species that do not qualify under any of the red or amber criteria are green listed. The green list also includes those species listed as recovering from historical decline in the last review that have continued to recover and do not qualify under any of the other criteria.

Mute Swan
Cygnus olor

The Mute Swan has a fragmented breeding distribution across northern and central Eurasia, where it will use virtually any fresh water below about 300 m altitude that is open enough to allow take-off and landing. Western European populations are largely sedentary, although some birds undertake fairly long movements.

Mute Swans lived wild in Britain from the earliest times, but by the Middle Ages they had been hunted almost to extinction for food. However more recently a pair or two of swans became a desirable fashion accessory among the owners of private waters, and it was the descendants of these tame birds that began to re-establish a wild population in the nineteenth century. Because of these origins many early ornithological writers, including those in Gloucestershire, viewed the species as domesticated and barely mentioned it.

The British population continued to increase until the late 1950s, when breeding was most prevalent in a triangle from south-east England, west to Somerset and north to Cheshire. A series of cold winters then stabilised the national population at about 19,000 birds in summer, including about 4,000 breeding pairs. However from the 1960s many counties, including Gloucestershire, saw a marked decrease in numbers associated with poisoning from the lead weights used by anglers. These were banned in 1987, as was the use of lead gunshot over wetlands in 1999. Since the mid-1980s, numbers of both breeding and wintering birds have risen, though by no means uniformly across Britain, and by 2002 there were around 31,700 birds including 6,150 territorial pairs in summer, and about 74,000 birds in winter.

Being so obvious in stature, colour, nest and cygnets, aggressive in the defence of its nesting territory and showing no fear of people, the Mute Swan is one of the easiest species to survey.

In Gloucestershire, the number of Mute Swans in summer fell from 361 (including 57 breeding pairs) in 1956 to just 185 (39 breeding pairs) in 1983. The Severn Vale suffered the greatest declines and in 1977 there were just five pairs breeding along the 20 km of river between Gloucester and Tewkesbury, although in the same year there were 19 at the Cotswold Water Park. The 1987 ban on lead weights paved the way for a recovery, while the creation of new wetland in the Water Park boosted the population there; in the western section, for example, about 100 summering birds including ten breeding pairs in 1982 increased to over 400 birds and 45 breeding pairs by 2007. Numbers at Slimbridge have also been increasing since the late 1980s, with many of the birds originating from Midland counties further up the Severn.

Whilst there is little seasonal variation in the overall distribution of Mute Swans, as shown by the maps, immatures and non-breeders tend to form summer flocks at a few traditional sites, such as the Water Park, Slimbridge and the Severn Hams. These flocks can give rise to counts well in excess of the number of nesting pairs: for example the maximum breeding season TTV count during the current atlas survey was 127 birds in May 2011 at Slimbridge. Winter numbers here have also increased: from barely double figures during the early 1980s, they reached 100 in the 1990s and exceeded 300 in the early years of the current century, including the first winter of the present survey. The highest count during a winter TTV was 173 in February 2011 at Slimbridge. On the other hand, in the Water Park peak winter totals have shown a much more modest increase, from about 200 in the 1980s to about 250 at present, despite the ever-expanding area of water and more co-ordinated counting.

There have been some fairly intensive, systematic Mute Swan ringing programmes in Britain, generating large numbers of recoveries, and Gloucestershire is no exception: some 700 movements of ringed birds involving the county had been recorded up to 2010. However 40% of these movements were entirely within the county, and another 40% were to and from adjoining counties, reflecting the species' largely sedentary nature. Of the remaining movements, 55 (8% of the total) were to and from the Midlands counties of Shropshire, Staffordshire and West Midlands, whilst the furthest were between Gloucestershire and Lancashire, West Yorkshire and Cornwall.

KEITH SHACKLETON

Sponsored by Peter Ormerod

Species accounts

2007–11 Atlas fieldwork					Gloucestershire trends						UK population trends	
Number of tetrads in which recorded (max 683)					Occupied 10 km squares (max 26)				% of tetrads in which recorded (1st hour of TTV)		UK conservation status: **Green**	
	Total	Confirmed	Probable	Possible	Present	1968–71	1981–84	1988–91	2007–11	1988–91	2008–11	Long term	Short term
Breeding	167	106	32	16	13	19		21	25	10.7	13.8	+179%	+23%
Winter	175						23		26			+126%	+2%

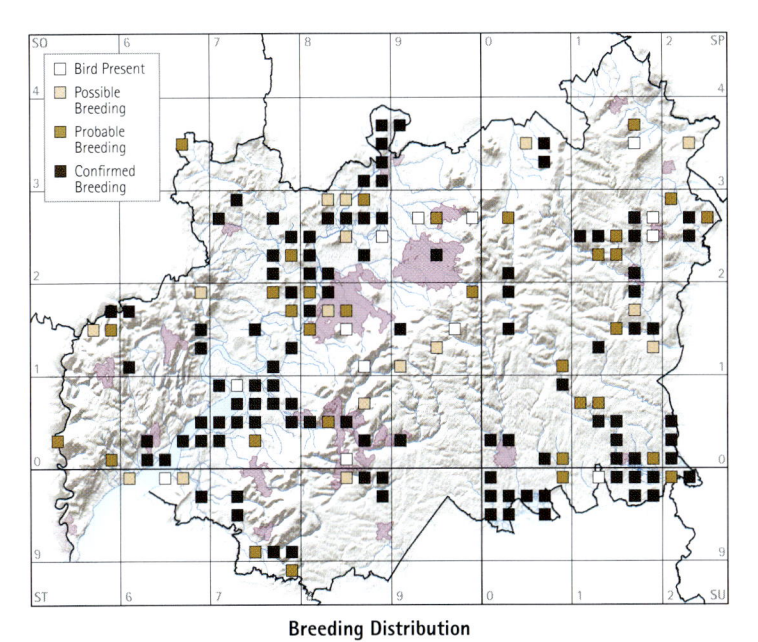

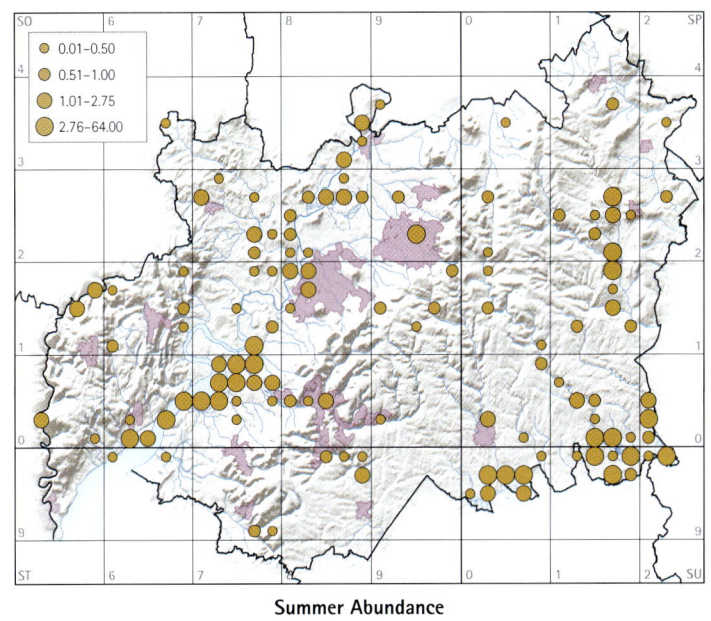

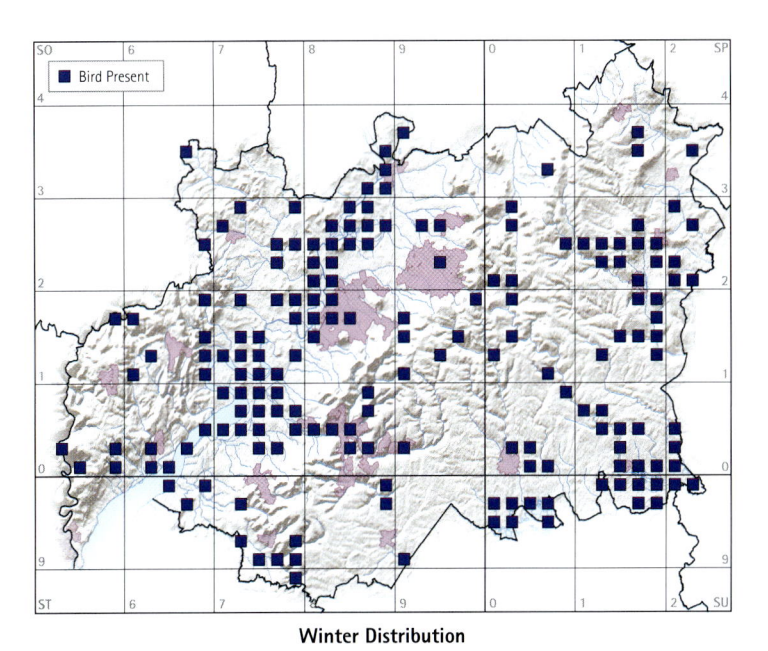

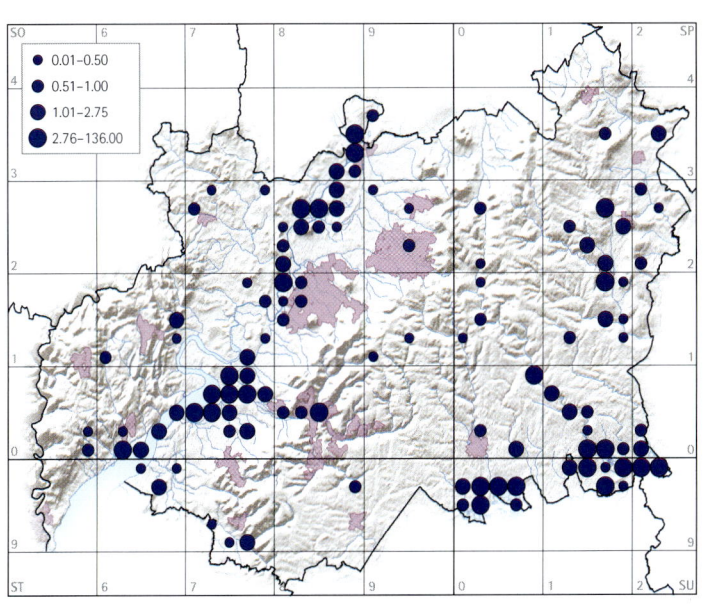

Breeding Distribution

Summer Abundance

Winter Distribution

Winter Abundance

Bewick's Swan (Tundra Swan)
Cygnus columbianus

Bewick's Swans *C. c. bewickii* breed in the tundra zone of north-east Europe and Siberia; in North America there is a different subspecies with an all-black bill, the Whistling Swan *C. c. columbianus*. Bewick's breeding in eastern Eurasia migrate to China and Japan for the winter, whilst western birds winter south to central Europe, mainly in Britain, Ireland and the Netherlands. The British Isles currently host about 40% of these western birds.

The British wintering population grew from a few hundred in 1950 to 1,500 in 1970. Numbers wintering in Ireland decreased over the same period, so a change of wintering area seems likely to have been involved. The British increase continued to a peak of 9,000 by 1991–92, some 30% of the 29,000 in north-west Europe as a whole. Since then, Europe's wintering birds have decreased to 21,500, of which Britain still receives about the same proportion (7,000). Whilst some of this decline may result from an eastward contraction of the wintering range, there has also been an overall reduction in the global population.

Bewick's Swans traditionally feed on aquatic vegetation and flooded pasture, but since the 1970s they have increasingly taken to arable fields. They will readily accept scattered grain, as they do for example at Slimbridge, where Bowler (1996) also discovered the first evidence of feeding on invertebrates on mud at low tide.

Bewick's Swans were no more than a rarity in Gloucestershire until the 1950s. Mellersh referred to the species as a 'very rare straggler to the Severn; no records since 1861', and the next reports were of 12 birds near Tewkesbury in December 1938 and 19 at Slimbridge two months later. From 1955 though they became annual at the Coombe Hill Meadows and on the Dumbles at Slimbridge. In February 1964 a group of 24 appeared in the Rushy Pen in the Wildfowl Trust's enclosures, probably attracted by the presence of seven captive Bewick's there. The regular provision of grain and the lack of disturbance encouraged them to continue to visit, and birds returned to the Rushy Pen the following winter. Thus began the spectacle that is now the hugely popular 'Floodlit Swan Feed'. Numbers at Slimbridge rose quickly through the remainder of the 1960s, reaching 400 for the first time in winter 1969–70, and they have remained broadly at that level since, albeit with a suggestion of a recent fall (see graph), in line with the national trend.

Once the swans began to visit the wildfowl enclosures, allowing views at close range, the Scott family realised that individuals could be identified by their unique bill patterns. So began an ongoing study that has been instrumental in explaining the life histories and social habits of the species. Cygnets remain with their parents during their first and sometimes their second winter, and the birds show high fidelity to certain sites; almost half those at Slimbridge at any time have been there in the past (Bowler & Rees 1998).

These days the swans arrive in the second half of October and leave in March. High counts correlate closely with low temperatures, while flooding on Walmore Common, the Severn Hams and the Avon Meadows draws some birds away from Slimbridge, as indicated by the map. Single-figure groups have been almost annual in the Cotswold Water Park since 1969 and appear to involve different individuals from those visiting the Severn Vale (Bowler & Rees 1998).

There have been many recoveries of ringed birds moving between Slimbridge, the breeding grounds in Russia, and the staging areas en route. More surprisingly, an adult female ringed here in January 1995 was seen in Germany in March the same year before being reported in Iceland in April 1996. Bewick's are very rare visitors to Iceland, and it seems likely that they arrive there after joining up with Whooper Swans. A Slimbridge-ringed bird also holds the current longevity record for the species; ringed in 1968 as an adult male, it was still alive in Germany in 1989, 20 years, three months and nine days later.

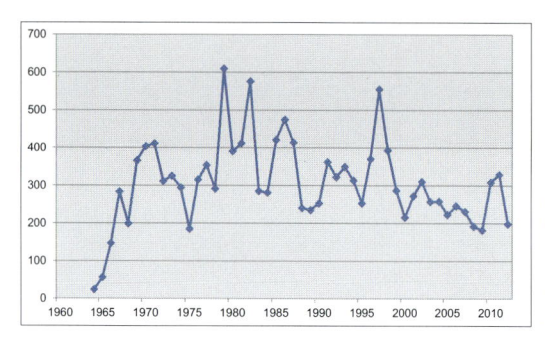

Peak count of Bewick's Swans at Slimbridge, 1964–2012 (note that '1964' means winter 1963–64).

In memory of Jim Cooke

Species accounts 61

	2007–11 Atlas fieldwork				Gloucestershire trends				UK population trends	
	Number of tetrads in which recorded (max 683)				Occupied 10 km squares (max 26)			% of tetrads in which recorded (1st hour of TTV)	UK conservation status: Amber 1,7,8	
	Total	Confirmed	Probable	Possible	Present	1968–71	1981–84	1988–91	2007–11	1988–91	2008–11	Long term	Short term
Breeding	2	0	0	0	2	0		0	0	0	0	–	–
Winter	26							10	7			–24%	–44%

Two Bewick's Swans at Slimbridge: the bird on the left is the famous 'Crinkly'.

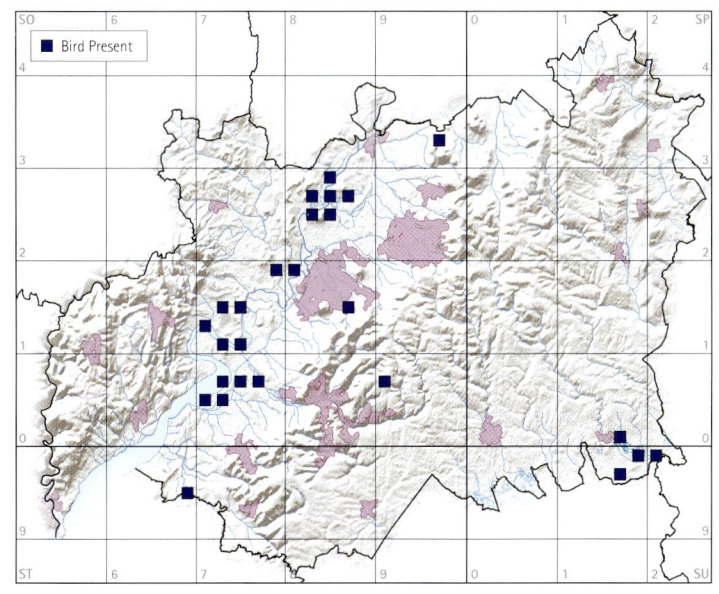

Winter Distribution

Whooper Swan
Cygnus cygnus

Whooper Swans breed in Iceland, parts of arctic Europe and right across northern Asia, with a very few pairs in northern Scotland. Much of the increasing Icelandic population (over 20,000 birds) winters in the British Isles, occurring very widely across Scotland and Ireland, in north-west Wales and in England north of a line joining the estuaries of the Thames and the Dee. The most important site is the Ouse Washes in Cambridgeshire, where almost 6,000 birds can gather nowadays. South of the Thames–Dee line, Whooper Swans are less common, but still occur widely in small numbers. They are perhaps somewhat less tied to natural wetlands than Bewick's Swans and can be found in a wider range of habitats, from high-altitude tarns and lochans to low-lying farmland.

In Gloucestershire this has never been a common bird; Mellersh said that a small flock would appear in 'some winters', not necessarily on the Severn. Swaine referred to approximately one record per decade up to 1950, after which they had become more frequent. He noted that in 1960 five birds appeared on Noxon Pond near Bream in the Forest of Dean, and that up to 14 wintered there almost every year up to 1980; small numbers continued to be recorded there until early 1988. This is typical of these large, noisy swans, which are very faithful to wintering sites, the same family group returning to the same area, year after year.

Whooper Swans have been recorded in the county in all but three of the 30 winters since 1979–80, albeit often in very small numbers. On some occasions their visits have been brief, but a small group can be said to have spent the whole season here in about 20 of those winters. Although occasionally seen in October they often do not arrive until mid-November, and normally leave around the third week of March. There are of course exceptions, and on two occasions birds have stayed until mid-April.

In the 20 years since 1990 the favoured area for wintering groups has been the Severn Hams, with Ashleworth perhaps the most reliable site. Birds in this area tend to be rather mobile, making them difficult to count, but careful observers can identify individuals by their bill markings. They are occasionally seen at other sites such as the Frampton-Slimbridge area, but this is quite unusual. During these two most recent decades the highest estimated winter totals in the county have been 14 in 2000–01 and ten in 2005–06; no other winters have produced double figures.

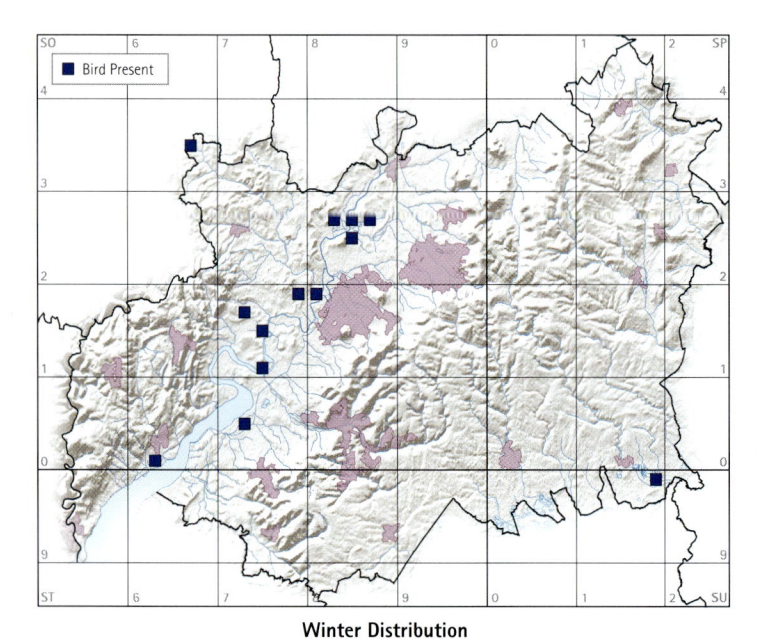

Winter Distribution

Sponsored by Ken & Pam Proud

> **A note about Bean and Pink-footed Geese**
>
> In 1902 Mellersh wrote that up to 2,000–3,000 'Bean Geese' might be present in the Slimbridge area by the end of September. Swaine felt that such references to Bean Geese by early writers should be treated with caution, because of possible confusion between Bean, Pink-footed and other 'grey geese'. Indeed Bean and Pink-footed were formerly considered to be conspecific and were only officially 'split' as recently as 1980. Swaine concluded that Mellersh's statement was 'surely incorrect', and this view is now generally accepted.

Bean Goose
Anser fabalis

Two subspecies of Bean Geese winter in Britain. The more western nominate race breeds in wooded taiga regions including parts of Fennoscandia, while *A. f. rossicus* breeds further east in the Russian tundra. Some authorities treat them as separate species, with English names corresponding to their preferred breeding habitats. Their main wintering grounds are centred around the Netherlands and the southern Baltic Sea.

Swaine reported that between 1940 and 1980 Bean Geese were more or less regular in Gloucestershire, with one to six reported almost every year from Slimbridge. Noting that the races were 'ill-defined', he thought that most were probably *A. f. fabalis*. Assuming he was correct, the balance has changed in recent decades: although a few hundred 'Taiga' Bean Geese regularly winter in central Scotland and Norfolk, this is now a rare visitor to our county, reported just eight times since 1980. Six of these records were of single birds at Slimbridge, and one was of five birds there, but most notable was a flock of 21 which frequented the border between Gloucestershire and Wiltshire in the Cotswold Water Park for a few days in February 1997.

'Tundra' Bean Geese do not winter regularly in the British Isles, occurring merely as wanderers from wintering sites further east, perhaps in response to cold weather. Nevertheless, they are more or less annual in Gloucestershire, having occurred in all but seven winters since 1979–80. The earliest date recorded in this period is November 1st 2009, and the birds normally leave in mid-March. They are normally seen in small groups, with only four records of double-figure flocks and an unusually high maximum count of 28 on December 13th 1987. Almost all records are from the Slimbridge area.

Pink-footed Goose
Anser brachyrhynchus

Pink-footed Geese have a very limited breeding distribution, with one population in Iceland and Greenland and another in Spitsbergen. The former, which increased from c.30,000 birds in the 1950s to c.225,000 in 1999, winters almost exclusively in Scotland and England; the latter, with fewer birds, winters in the Netherlands and Belgium (Migration Atlas).

Swaine cited apparently reliable records of 500 to 1,200 Pinkfeet in the Frampton–Slimbridge area in the 1930s, followed by a steady decline to no more than 50 to 130 birds between the late 1940s and the early 1960s, in line with a 'general retreat northwards' of birds wintering in Britain. He noted that, between 1960 and 1980, small parties arrived very occasionally in September and early October, and assumed that these were Icelandic birds, whereas stragglers found among the White-fronts later in the winter are thought more likely to have moved across from the Netherlands.

Since then little has changed, with the majority of records continuing to come from the Slimbridge area. Although Pink-footed Geese have been seen in the county every winter except one since 1979–80, they are usually very few in number, and have rarely stayed for more than few days. In only 13 winters between 1979–80 and 2009–10 have any Pinkfeet stayed for more than a week or so and many of the larger flocks in particular have only been seen in flight or have stayed very briefly. This is true of the four highest counts since 1980: 55 at Slimbridge on December 28th 1999 and 89 at Twyning two days later; 52 at Slimbridge also on December 28th in 1984; and 33 seen in flight over Minsterworth Ham and briefly settled on the Severn at Sudmeadow, near Gloucester, on January 6th 1997. In addition, 140 'grey geese' circling Frampton Sands and Saul Warth on March 28th 2001 were thought likely to have been this species. The biggest long-staying flocks of what were considered to be wild birds since 1980 were in the winters of 1995–96 (maximum 18), 1997–98 (15), 1998–99 (29) and 1999–2000 (11).

There have been two recoveries of ringed Pink-footed Geese involving Gloucestershire, both dating back to the 1950s and both involving birds ringed in southern Scotland in October and shot in the county in December the same year, showing onward passage from autumn into winter.

White-fronted Goose (Greater White-fronted Goose)
Anser albifrons

White-fronted Geese breed on tundra and swamp discontinuously from western Siberia east to Alaska, and in western Canada and Greenland. Western Eurasian populations of the subspecies *albifrons* winter south to southern Europe, Egypt and the Middle East. A very small percentage of this population winters in South Wales and in southern England, where the major concentration has traditionally been at Slimbridge. Birds from Greenland, of the subspecies *flavirostris*, now winter almost exclusively in north and west Scotland, Ireland and parts of Wales, having ceased to visit north-west England in the 1950s. In the British Isles as a whole, this subspecies outnumbers *albifrons* by 13,000 to 2,400 birds.

It has been estimated that the loss of tundra habitat due to climate change could lead to a 50% reduction in the global population of White-fronted Geese during the present century (Zöckler & Lysenko 2000). However numbers of both subspecies wintering in north-west Europe rose from 50,000–100,000 in the 1960s to 450,000–600,000 in the 1990s and continue to grow (up to one million by 2005) as populations redistribute themselves in response to recent restrictions on hunting, increased food availability and milder winters. At the same time, less severe winters have resulted in more of the European subspecies remaining on the Continent, and numbers reaching England have been in decline since the 1930s. Wintering birds feed mainly on salt-marsh and semi-natural wet grassland, though arable fields are also used. Leaving their breeding grounds by early October, they migrate in stages and generally start to arrive in England in November. Numbers usually peak in January and most birds have departed by early March.

The Severn Estuary near Slimbridge has supported wintering wildfowl for centuries, but it was probably the presence of White-fronted Geese there that encouraged the Lords of Berkeley to preserve these areas of rich grazing pasture and salt-marsh. All geese are loyal to their wintering grounds, but White-fronts are unique in

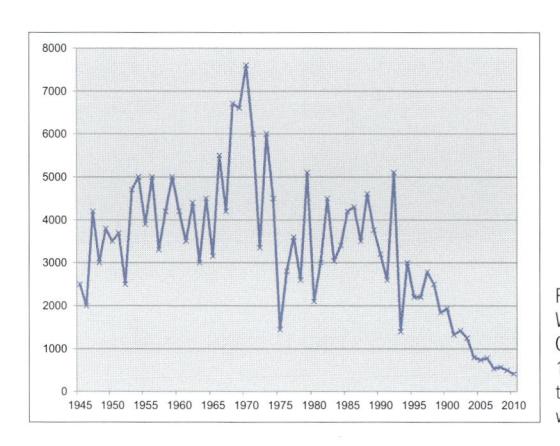

Peak count of White-fronted Geese at Slimbridge, 1945–2010 (note that '1945' means winter 1944–45).

Sponsored by Paul Walkden

| | 2007–11 Atlas fieldwork ||||| Gloucestershire trends |||||| UK population trends ||
| | Number of tetrads in which recorded (max 683) ||||| Occupied 10 km squares (max 26) |||| % of tetrads in which recorded (1st hour of TTV) || UK conservation status: Green ||
	Total	Confirmed	Probable	Possible	Present	1968–71	1981–84	1988–91	2007–11	1988–91	2008–11	Long term	Short term
Breeding	2	0	0	0	2	0		0	0	0	0	–	–
Winter	11						0		4			–	–

using the same sites for both feeding and roosting, making them an ideal quarry for wildfowlers (Walkden 2009).

Probably as a result of the protection provided at Slimbridge following the establishment of the Wildfowl Trust reserve, numbers of White-fronted Geese wintering there increased during the 1950s and 1960s, with the high point being the four consecutive winters from 1967–68, in all of which the peak count was 6,000 or more birds. Far fewer birds visit Britain nowadays, and the Slimbridge flock now numbers mere hundreds (see graph).

Fourteen English sites have regularly held nationally important numbers of White-fronts. Slimbridge has historically attracted 50–65% of *albifrons* visiting Britain and was of international importance for the species until the recent population redistributions, but was displaced as the top British location for the first time in winter 2009–10 by sites in Kent. Other sites in the west have lost their wintering birds altogether and, unthinkable as it was when Peter Scott founded the Wildfowl Trust, it is possible that the White-fronted Goose may one day abandon Slimbridge.

Away from the estuary there are occasional records of small numbers from further up the Severn Vale and at the Cotswold Water Park, while reports of groups in flight, ranging from a handful of birds to dozens, can come from anywhere in the county.

There have been records of Greenland White-fronted Geese at Slimbridge in just over 20 winters since November 1945. The largest flocks were of nine birds in 1945 and 1986 and eight in winter 2001–02. The only double-figure flock of this subspecies in Gloucestershire, and indeed the only record away from the estuary, involved five adults and five juveniles at Coombe Hill Meadows on January 15th 2006.

The majority of recoveries of White-fronts ringed at Slimbridge have been in Russia, the Netherlands, Germany and France, reflecting the origins and migration routes of the British wintering population. Far more unusual were three individuals ringed here during the 1950s that moved to Greece, Italy and Macedonia in subsequent winters. There is also one recovery of a ringed Greenland bird at Slimbridge, also in the 1950s.

Greylag Goose
Anser anser

Greylag Geese were once widely distributed across the boreal and temperate regions of Europe and southern Siberia, but as a result of land drainage, disturbance and persecution the range became fragmented, leaving only isolated populations by the start of the twentieth century. One such pocket remains in the Outer Hebrides and the extreme north of Scotland, while the English population, which used to extend as far south as the Fens, was extirpated by 1831. More recently though reintroductions, mainly during the 1960s and 1970s and coinciding with the development of reservoirs and gravel-pits, have helped the species to become naturalised and widespread in Britain once more. Indeed the 'natural' and 'naturalised' populations have both increased and merged to such an extent that it has recently been proposed that it is no longer practical to continue to treat them as separate (Mitchell *et al.* 2012). The preferred habitat was originally inaccessible swamps, lakes and reed-beds with open grassland for feeding, but naturalised birds are more tolerant of people and will readily breed at ornamental and artificial waters, and feed on farmland.

Icelandic birds winter as far south as northern England, but Greylags in any season south of a line from the Isle of Man to Teesmouth are almost exclusively derived from introduced stock.

The 1968–72 Breeding Atlas recorded a national population of 700–800 breeding pairs, three-quarters of which were derived from introduced birds. By the time of the 1988–91 Breeding Atlas there were 22,000 wild and introduced birds, 75% of them in England. Numbers continued to grow rapidly (12% per year in southern Britain), reaching a total of 37,000 birds by 1999. Current estimates suggest a winter population of 140,000 birds, with strongholds in East Anglia and the East Midlands, Kent, Yorkshire and Cumbria, and fewer towards the south-west.

In Gloucestershire before the twentieth century, the Greylag was known only as a scarce winter visitor to the Severn Vale. Witchell & Strugnell mention one shot in Woodchester Park, with no date, and Mellersh refers to three or four county records but gives no details. There were ten reports from Slimbridge between 1933 and 1956, mainly of single birds. Six escaped from the enclosures there in 1964, and are assumed to have given rise to the breeding flock of semi-domesticated birds at Frampton, which numbered 60 by 1979. Breeding in the Cotswold Water Park was first reported in 1976, and the first record from the Forest of Dean was apparently of two in flight in June 1980 (Swaine). The current map shows an established breeding presence in the Frampton–Slimbridge area, the Severn Hams and the Water Park, with small numbers on scattered waters in the Dean and the Cotswolds.

Naturalised Greylags are widely thought to make only local movements, but an annual moult migration from Gloucestershire to Hogganfield Loch near Glasgow, a distance of about 460 km, has recently been described (Hearn 2005). These failed breeders or non-breeding birds, including some from the Forest of Dean, head north in June and are part of a flock of perhaps 350 birds which gather there. Up to 80% of these birds apparently originate in Gloucestershire and are back by early August, most of them forming part of the wintering flock of 400–500 birds at Slimbridge. Numbers in the Water Park are lower; 380 in September 2010 was double the peak count normally recorded there.

A few Greylags occasionally arrive with the wild geese at Slimbridge but even these may well also be naturalised birds. Usually they are in single figures, but in 2008 there were 18 birds together in late February and early March that appeared to be wild; in addition they showed characteristics of the more eastern Continental populations.

As well as ringing recoveries between Gloucestershire and the Scottish moulting area, there have been a few movements to and from other counties in England and Wales. More unusual was a female ringed as a gosling in June 1994 in Denmark (possibly from wild stock) which was seen at Slimbridge in April 1999 and at Martin Mere, Lancashire several times between autumn 1999 and 2001, before finally being shot 'somewhere in Lancashire' in January 2004.

Species accounts

2007–11 Atlas fieldwork					Gloucestershire trends					UK population trends	
Number of tetrads in which recorded (max 683)					Occupied 10 km squares (max 26)				% of tetrads in which recorded (1st hour of TTV)		UK conservation status: Amber 7,8	
	Total	Confirmed	Probable	Possible	Present	1968–71	1981–84	1988–91	2007–11	1988–91	2008–11	Long term	Short term
Breeding	63	30	8	8	17	0		2	13	0.6	2.9	–	+148%
Winter	51						3		14			+527%	+54%

Breeding Distribution

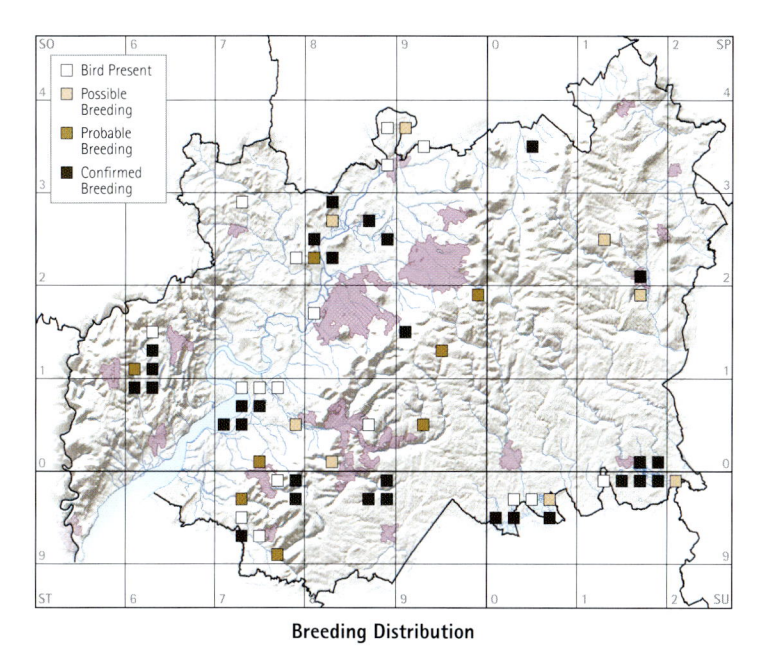

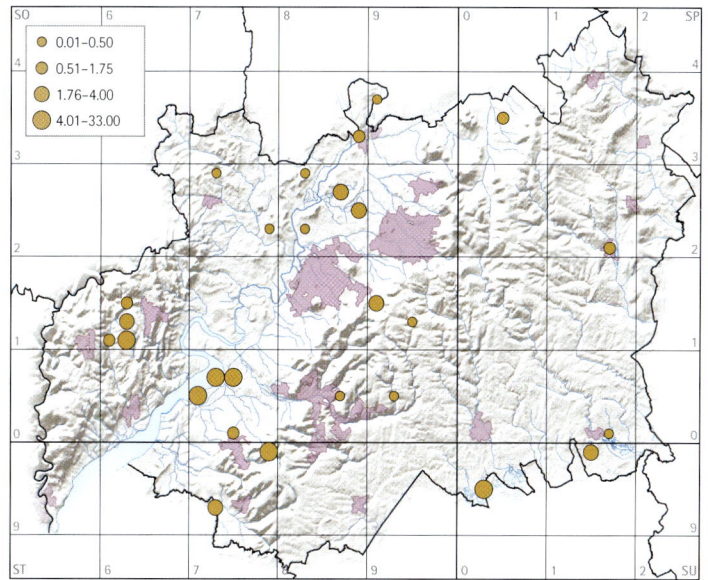

Summer Abundance

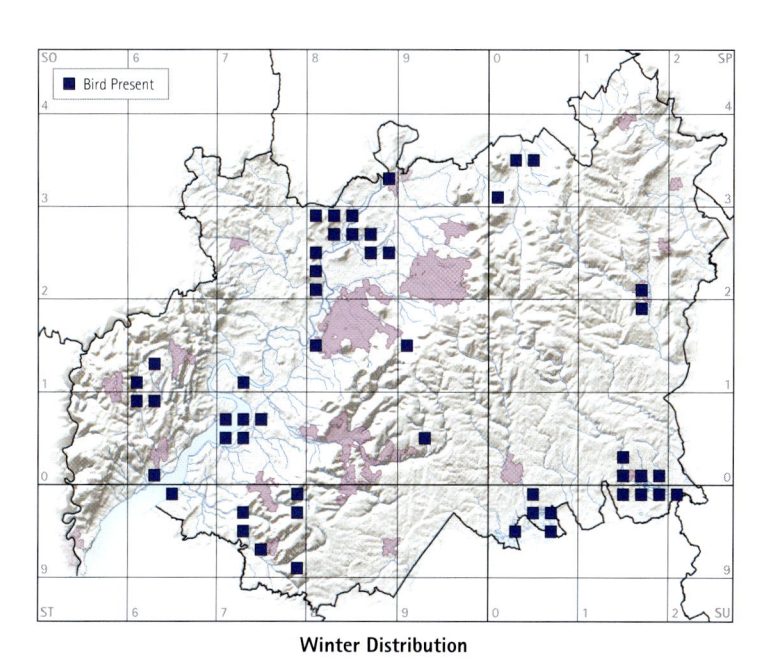

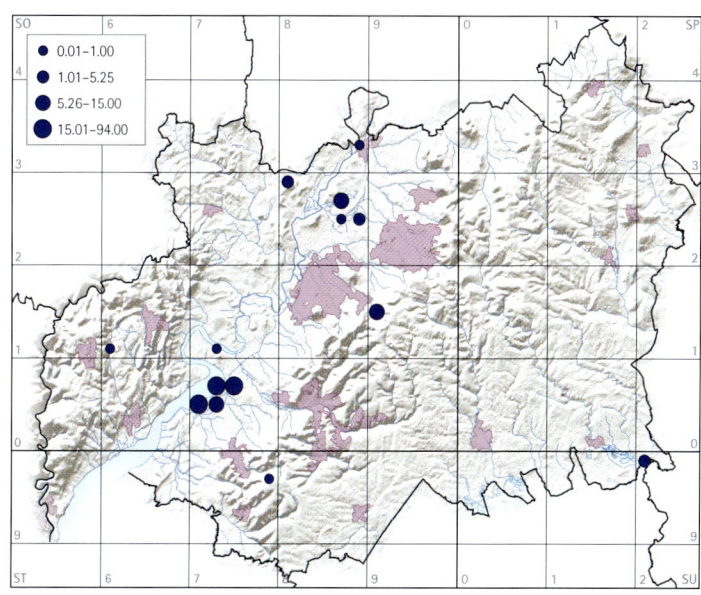

Winter Distribution

Winter Abundance

Canada Goose
Branta canadensis

A native of North America, the Canada Goose has been widely introduced in north-west Europe. The first introduction in Britain was to St James's Park in London in the mid-seventeenth century, and a number of country estates followed suit. Most released birds were of the nominate race, but at least some *B. c. maxima* were probably also involved. The species is now a widespread, naturalised resident, but for 200 years it was regarded as being confined to parks and private estates, with only localised winter movements, and its status as a free-living feral species was accepted only in the late nineteenth century. Consequently, published records from before 1900 are rare and in no way reflect its distribution at that time. *The Handbook* (Witherby *et al.* 1938–41) was the first ornithological publication to treat the species as living wild in Britain.

In Britain, Canada Geese prefer lowland pools and ornamental lakes with open grazing and scattered trees, at the base of which they like to nest. Islands are particularly favoured, and they will nest semi-colonially at sites that are biologically productive enough to support them in numbers. They generally avoid coasts, deep waters and poorly vegetated reservoirs.

As the numbers of geese around introduction sites steadily increased they began to cause damage to crops and, other methods of control having failed, many birds were translocated around Britain in the 1950s and 1960s. However reducing competition by allowing them more space resulted in a population explosion: numbers grew from 3,000 birds in 1953 to 20,000 by 1977 and now stand at 190,000.

Swaine was correct in 1982 to foresee that 'further increase and spread seems inevitable' in Gloucestershire. Records were few here until 1953, when over 40 birds were released at Frampton Pools. Twenty years later there were sometimes more than 100 birds there in winter and, although some were moved away, winter numbers changed little. Slimbridge, which averaged peak counts of 50 in the late 1970s, was soon seeing the flocks of over 400 which are still found there today. Sites elsewhere in the Severn Vale can also attract quite large numbers, and the highest TTV count during the atlas fieldwork was of 375 birds in February 2010 in tetrad SO82I, Hasfield Ham. Both sections of the Cotswold Water Park currently host 100–200 birds each winter.

Away from the Frampton area, Canada Geese bred at Fairford in 1955 and in the recently created Water Park early in the 1960s. The 1968–72 Breeding Atlas showed confirmed breeding in the county only at Slimbridge and the eastern section of the Water Park but 20 years later during the 1988–91 Breeding Atlas survey, breeding was confirmed in 14 10 km squares. Bourton pits were colonised in 1978 and Ashleworth Ham in 1987, and there are now a few pairs in the Forest of Dean. The Cotswolds Atlases reveal a threefold increase from 15 to 47 tetrads with confirmed breeding records between 1987 and 2007. Indeed, the current maps show that most of the county's major waterbodies have now been colonised, with widespread confirmed or probable breeding.

Although indigenous North American Canada Geese are migratory, introduced birds in Britain remained within a few kilometres of their breeding sites until the first translocations of the 1950s, since when moult migrations of usually less than 50 km have become a feature. The longest and best-known such movement in Britain, between northern and central England and the Beauly Firth, involves only a small proportion of the population. There have been about 120 records of ringed Canada Geese moving between Gloucestershire and 20 other British counties. The majority (65) moved to and from nearby 'Avon', Herefordshire and Worcestershire, but one ringed at the Beauly Firth was found here, and others which moved between Gloucestershire and Cumbria, North Yorkshire and Lancashire could also have been en route to and from the moulting site there.

Apparently wild, migrant Canada Geese of various subspecies sometimes reach Scotland and Ireland, but those occasionally seen in Gloucestershire belonging to races other than the nominate are almost certain to be of captive origin.

Species accounts   69

	2007–11 Atlas fieldwork					Gloucestershire trends					UK population trends	
	Number of tetrads in which recorded (max 683)					*Occupied 10 km squares (max 26)*				*% of tetrads in which recorded (1st hour of TTV)*		*UK conservation status:* **Introduced**	
	Total	Confirmed	Probable	Possible	Present	1968–71	1981–84	1988–91	2007–11	1988–91	2008–11	Long term	Short term
Breeding	183	80	41	29	33	4		18	23	5.7	10.1	–	+93%
Winter	133						13		24			+138%	+23%

Breeding Distribution

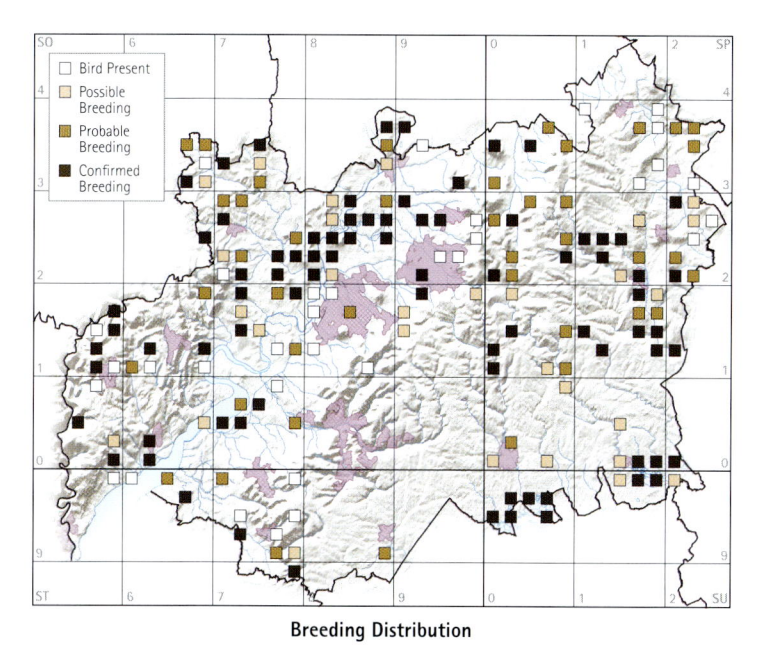

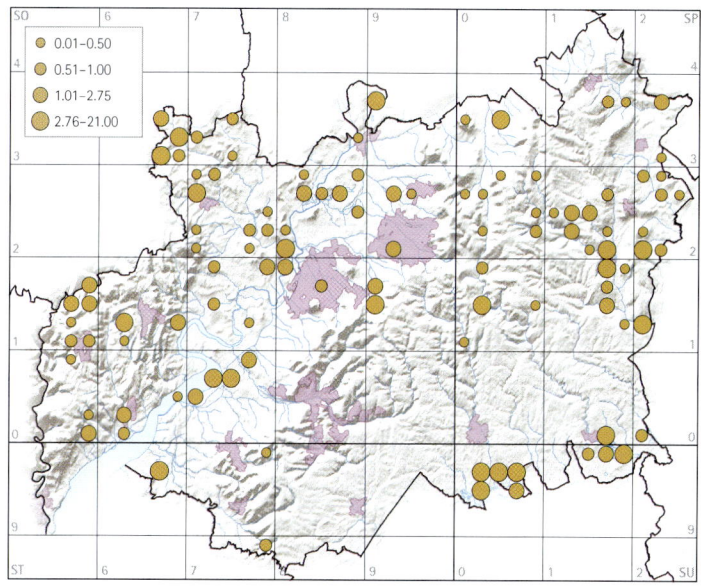

Summer Abundance

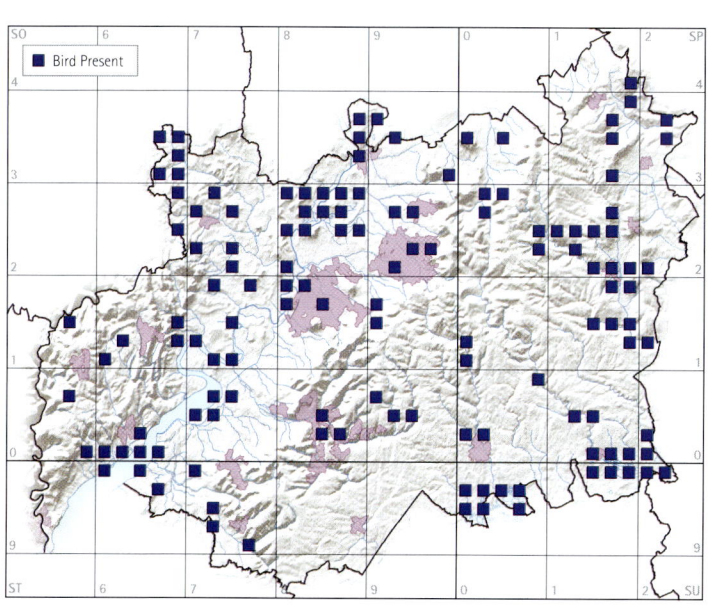

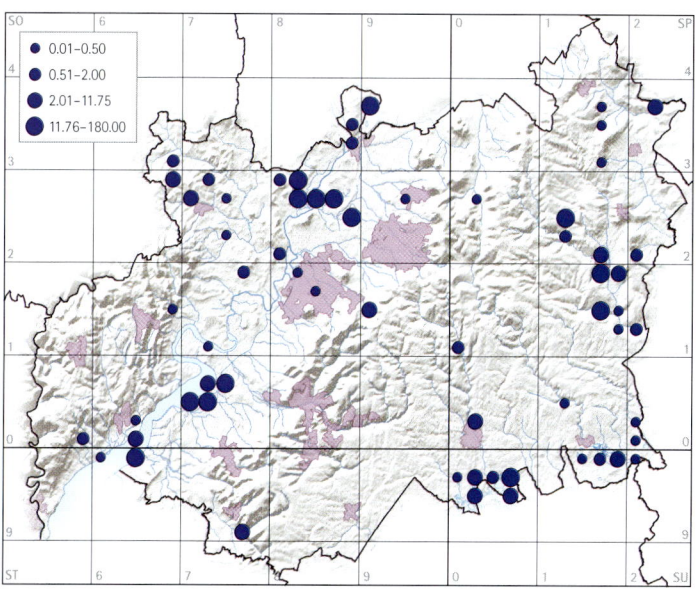

Winter Distribution

Winter Abundance

Barnacle Goose
Branta leucopsis

Barnacle Geese breed in Greenland, Spitsbergen and arctic Russia, wintering in Scotland and Ireland and on North Sea coasts between Denmark and France. There are also breeding populations originating from captive birds in several European countries, including Britain.

In the nineteenth and early twentieth centuries this was a very rare visitor to the county; Mellersh includes just two records. According to Swaine, small numbers started to occur at Slimbridge 'in most winters' from the 1930s, with nine birds present in 1963–64 and ten in 1976. Since then, apparently wild birds have been identified there in four winters in the 1980s, six in the 1990s and just two since 2000. They usually arrive in December with groups of European White-fronted Geese, with peak numbers in January. Normally single figures are involved, the largest flocks being 17 in 1992, 27 in 1994 and 26 in 2007, all in January. Of particular note are two records in 1987: a group of six that arrived on the unusually early date of October 8th included one that had been ringed in western Ireland, indicating that it was from the Greenland breeding population; and five that arrived in December included two colour-ringed birds from the Russian breeding population that had been caught in the Netherlands.

There is also a flock of full-winged Barnacle Geese at Slimbridge, descended from captive birds, and breeding has taken place at nearby Frampton Court Lake since 1979. Numbers here remained fairly low until the mid-1990s, when a steep increase began; in September 2009 there were 152 birds. They are quite mobile and feed in the same areas as the wild geese, so it can be difficult to determine whether there are any truly 'wild' Barnacles in the area.

Feral birds probably account for most if not all other sightings around the county. They occur regularly at the Cotswold Water Park, where they have hybridised with Canada Geese, and they can turn up at any suitable body of water. Breeding was also recorded at Tirley Court in the Severn Vale in 2007 and Lower Swell in the Cotswolds in 2009.

Brent Goose (Brant Goose)
Branta bernicla

The three differently coloured forms of Brent Goose are officially given subspecific status at present, but are considered by some to be separate species. The nominate subspecies is the Dark-bellied Brent, breeding in a single population in arctic Russia and wintering in north-west Europe, with large and increasing numbers on the south and east coasts of England. The Pale-bellied Brent *B. b. hrota* has at least two distinct breeding populations: one in north-eastern Canada, wintering in Ireland; the other mainly in Spitsbergen, wintering around the North Sea, including Northumberland. Black Brants *B. b. nigricans* breed in eastern Siberia, Alaska and north-western Canada, and winter in western North America.

Swaine described this species as 'formerly very scarce, now annual' in Gloucestershire, noting that although there were very few records from the early twentieth century it had been recorded more often since the 1930s and annually since 1964.

Dark-bellied Brents have been seen every year since then, almost always on the Severn Estuary near Slimbridge. Numbers are generally small; more than ten birds have been recorded in about one year in three since 1980. Occasional feral birds can confuse the issue, but the earliest autumn date for wild birds is usually the last week of October, and apart from the occasional straggler they are rarely seen after mid-March. They often move on, rather than staying for the whole winter. The only counts over 50 are of passage birds seen briefly on single days in mid-March: 70 in 1996, 67 in 2000 and 61 in 2009.

There are seven Gloucestershire records of Pale-bellied Brents, all from the Slimbridge part of the estuary.

1941: one from February 23rd to March 2nd.
1946: one from September 30th to November 25th.
1976: two adults on December 27th stayed until January 14th 1977.
1994: one on November 21st.
1997: one on December 27th.
2006: one juvenile on November 4th.
2011: two on March 20th.

There is just one county record of a Black Brant: an adult at the Dumbles, Slimbridge on December 20th 1989.

A bird seen at Slimbridge on November 2nd 2001 showed characteristics of the 'Grey-bellied' form, a small population of which breeds in central Canada. These birds may be hybrids, but some authorities consider that they should be treated as a separate subspecies.

Sponsored by Colin Studholme

Lesser White-fronted Goose
Anser erythropus

Although this neat little goose changed the course of ornithological history in Gloucestershire (see p. 39) it is no more than a very rare visitor nowadays. Lesser Whitefronts breed in a narrow band across Eurasia south of the Arctic Ocean, including parts of Fennoscandia. The population has suffered a dramatic decrease since the mid-twentieth century, to the extent that the species is close to extinction in Fennoscandia and reintroduction schemes are in place there.

Swaine described its status before 1945 as 'unknown' but felt that it was highly probable that birds had been overlooked among the large flocks of White-fronted Geese. Between 1945 and 1980 it was an almost annual visitor to Slimbridge, with about 65 birds recorded in total, although this figure quite possibly includes some individuals returning in successive years. Sightings since then have reflected the large-scale decline, with records in six winters in the 1980s and three in the 1990s, and just one bird this century, in February 2003. In addition a collared captive-bred bird from a reintroduction scheme in Finnish Lapland arrived in 1990–91 and returned for the following two winters. The only record away from Slimbridge involves one in the Cotswold Water Park in the winter of 1996–97 which, as it fed on bread, is assumed to have escaped from a collection.

Sponsored by Paul Walkden

Snow Goose
Anser caerulescens

Snow Geese breed on arctic tundra from north-eastern Siberia eastwards through northern North America to north-west Greenland, with the Greater Snow Goose *A. c. atlanticus* having a more easterly distribution than the Lesser Snow Goose *A. c. caerulescens*. A darker, 'blue' phase occurs in both subspecies. Snow Geese have been kept in wildfowl collections since at least the nineteenth century, and small feral populations have become established in western Europe, including Britain, so it is practically impossible to determine whether Snow Geese seen here are wild or not. The presumption must be that most are not, although birds seen in winter in the company of Greenland White-fronted Geese may be genuine vagrants.

Gloucestershire records, which are all from Slimbridge and Frampton and date from as early as 1890, must be subject to the same doubt, and the species' uncertain status means that some sightings are not even reported by the observers. It might be thought that larger groups would be more likely to be wild, but that this is not necessarily true was proved in 2011 when a party of eight Lesser Snow Geese (three adults and five first-summers) arrived at Slimbridge on June 10th and stayed until June 13th. Their behaviour and general condition suggested that they were not escapes from a wildfowl collection. A few dropped feathers were collected and sent to a Canadian laboratory for isotope analysis. This revealed that the feathers could not have been grown in North America, so these birds probably originated from a feral breeding population in western Europe.

Red-breasted Goose
Branta ruficollis

Red-breasted Geese breed in the arctic tundra of the Taimyr peninsula, often choosing to nest near Peregrines, and their main wintering area is the Bulgarian Black Sea coast. There are nine Gloucestershire records, all of singles and all but one from the Slimbridge area. Most were with flocks of White-fronted Geese, suggesting that they may well have been wild birds, although as with other wildfowl the possibility of escapes cannot be entirely ruled out.

1941: an immature at Slimbridge from February 16th to 26th.
1954: a first-winter bird at Slimbridge from January 8th to 25th and again from February 13th to March 5th; one shot at Hasfield in December.
1959: one at Frampton foreshore from January 24th to March 13th.
1963: an adult, probably a male, at Slimbridge from December 31st to March 8th 1964.
1967: a first-winter bird at Slimbridge from January 5th to 15th, also seen in flight over Frampton sailing lake on January 8th; an adult at Slimbridge from February 4th to 28th, thought probably to have been a different bird.
1969: an adult at Slimbridge from January 19th to 31st.
1984: an adult at Slimbridge from January 17th to March 1st.

Egyptian Goose
Alopochen aegyptiaca

This is an African species, popular in wildfowl collections, with feral populations originating from introduced or escaped birds in several European countries including Britain. Norfolk is the stronghold here, but there are smaller numbers elsewhere.

Egyptian Geese were seen regularly at Frampton Pools in the 1950s and 1960s, and Swaine felt that they 'may be on the point of settling down as feral breeders' in the county. Subsequently one bird was recorded in 1979, three in the 1980s, five in the 1990s and five since 2000. Most were seen in the Slimbridge area, but they have also been recorded on the Severn Hams, Witcombe reservoir and near Lechlade. In the early 1990s four birds were seen sporadically in the Slimbridge area for three consecutive years, and in 2008 a pair nested there, but no young were seen and evidently the anticipated colonisation of the county has not yet taken place.

Shelduck (Common Shelduck)
Tadorna tadorna

The range of the Shelduck extends widely but discontinuously through the middle latitudes of the Palearctic, from Ireland to western China. European birds inhabit shallow muddy shores and estuaries around the Atlantic, Baltic and North Sea coastlines, where they feed on invertebrates sieved from the surface layers of mud. In some areas they have also recently begun to colonise inland waters. Although they are regarded generally as burrow-nesters and readily take to boxes, the nest site may also be in dense ground cover, walls and rock fissures.

Most of the north-west European population undertakes a post-breeding moult migration to the Waddenzee in north-west Germany, although birds from Britain are increasingly likely to moult nearer to home, for example in Bridgwater Bay in Somerset and on the Mersey and Humber estuaries. In winter the British population is augmented by some continental birds.

Until the mid-nineteenth century, breeding populations in Britain were fairly stable, and included some inland sites such as the Brecks in East Anglia. Warreners, whose business it was to raise rabbits for food, then started to become concerned that Shelduck were displacing the rabbits from their burrows, and drastically reduced the birds' numbers in south and east England. However from the 1880s onwards the trend reversed as rabbit farming declined, and the twentieth century saw increasing numbers around Britain. The 1968–72 Breeding Atlas commented on 'an inclination to breed inland ... [though] even now very few nest more than 20 km from tidal water'. By the time of the 1988–91 Breeding Atlas they had colonised almost 100 new 10 km squares and the British population had more than doubled to 10,600 pairs, almost a quarter of the breeding birds in north-west Europe. Numbers have been fairly stable since then. Wintering numbers in Britain grew by over 6% per year from 1960 to reach 78,000 by the mid-1990s, but have since declined and currently stand at 61,000, a figure last seen in the late 1970s.

Mellersh referred to the 'Barrow-duck' or 'Burrow-duck' nesting on the Severn cliffs and mentioned a nest site on the top of Stinchcombe Hill near Dursley. Swaine described them as breeding only on the Severn Estuary and the lower Wye, and formerly on Walmore Common. Nests were first found at Sudmeadow near Gloucester in 1982, Ashleworth Ham three years later and the Cotswold Water Park in 1991. A summer survey of the entire Severn Estuary by the Wildfowl Trust in 1988 found 2,500–2,700 Shelduck, of which 170 pairs attempted to breed; 18 pairs were in Gloucestershire, including 13 at Slimbridge.

The 2007–11 breeding season distribution map shows records in a surprisingly high number of tetrads, with a concentration of confirmed breeding records along the Severn, especially downriver from Slimbridge. Shelduck also probably bred on the Severn Hams, one pair was confirmed right on the county boundary east of Tewkesbury, and a handful of pairs bred in the Cotswold Water Park.

The Severn Estuary is a site of international importance for wintering Shelduck; five-year mean counts across the whole estuary have tripled from 1,500 in the 1970s to 4,480 currently. Of these about 10% use the Gloucestershire section, where numbers before the 1980s did not reach 200 but now total 400–500 birds. Only very small numbers are found in winter further up the Severn Vale and in the Cotswold Water Park.

There have been a total of six interchanges of ringed Shelduck between Gloucestershire and Germany, Norway and the Netherlands, as well as ten recoveries involving movements to and from seven other English counties.

Sponsored by the Dursley Birdwatching and Preservation Society

Species accounts 75

	2007–11 Atlas fieldwork					Gloucestershire trends					UK population trends	
	Number of tetrads in which recorded (max 683)					Occupied 10 km squares (max 26)				% of tetrads in which recorded (1st hour of TTV)		UK conservation status: Amber 7,8	
	Total	Confirmed	Probable	Possible	Present	1968–71	1981–84	1988–91	2007–11	1988–91	2008–11	Long term	Short term
Breeding	70	15	28	5	22	4		7	7	3.6	4.8	+145%	+2%
Winter	52						8		10			–1%	–19%

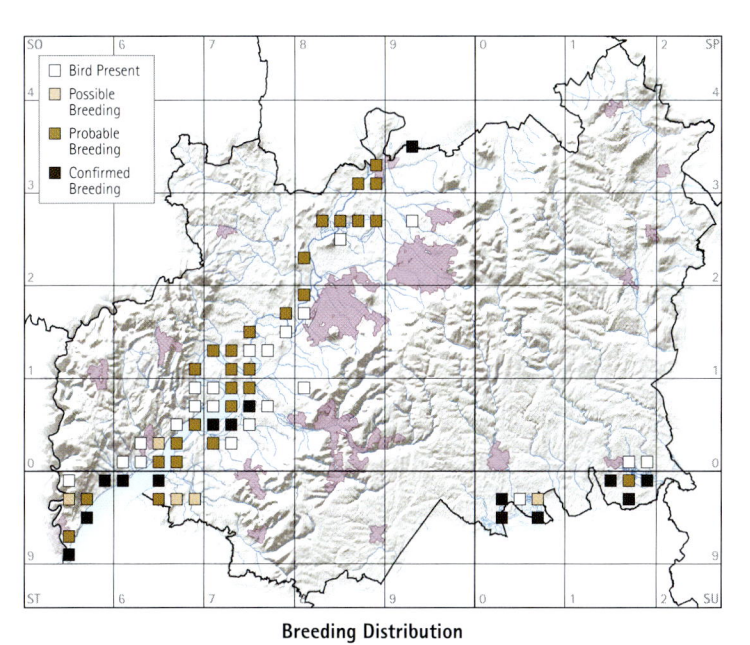

Breeding Distribution

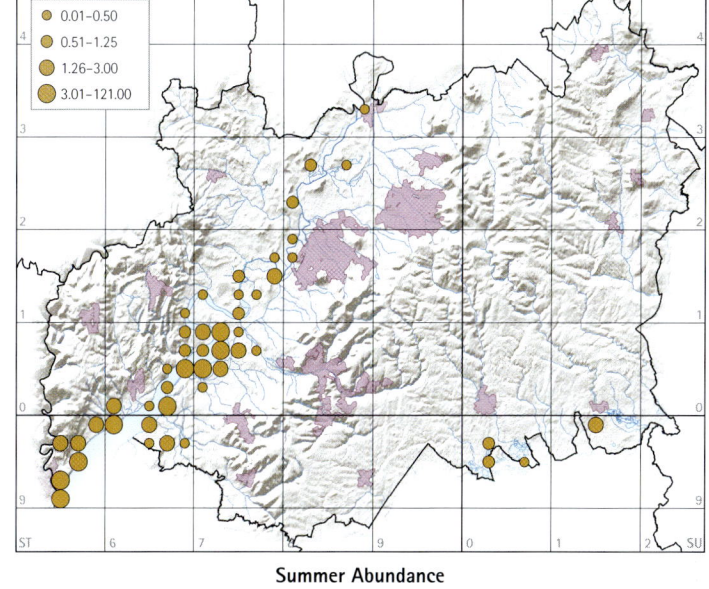

Summer Abundance

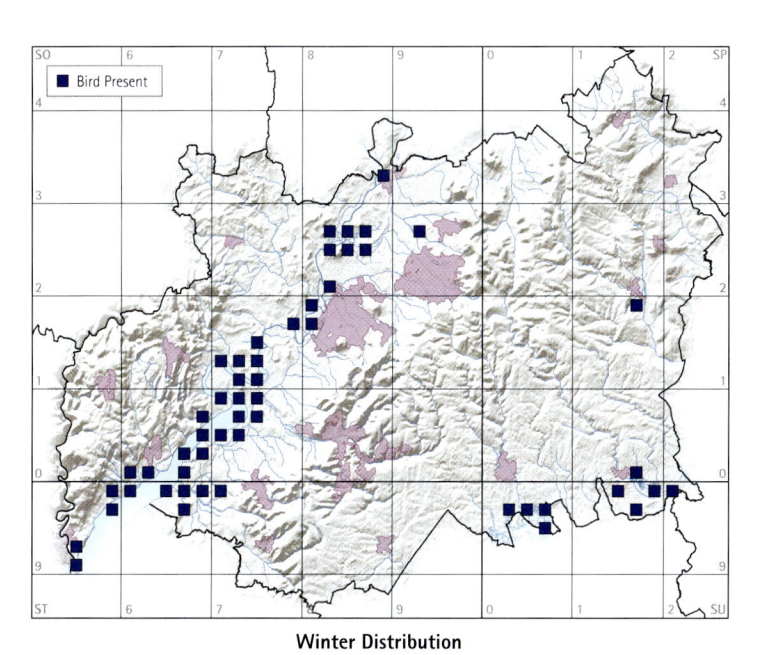

Winter Distribution

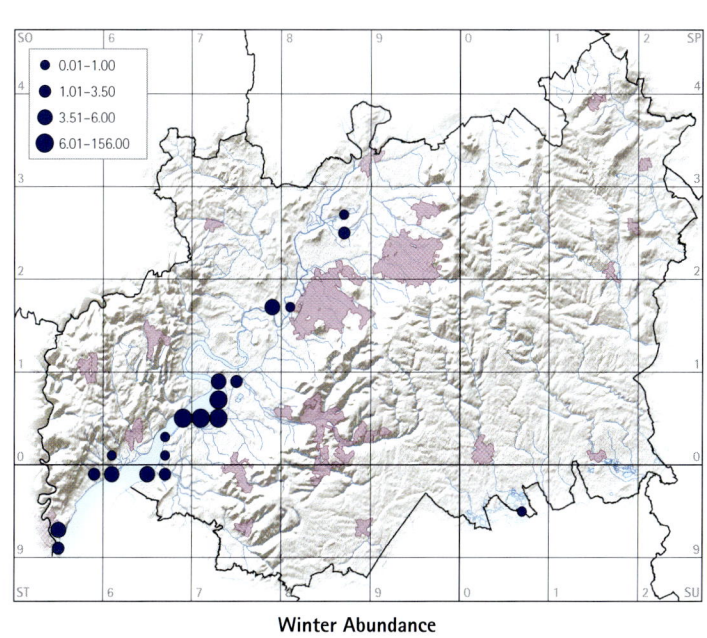

Winter Abundance

Mandarin Duck
Aix galericulata

With the drake's extraordinary plumage evoking its oriental origins, the Mandarin is one of the few non-native species to appeal to birders – perhaps because there is nothing so far to suggest that the population is having any negative effects on native wildlife, unlike most alien species. Originating in eastern Asia, Mandarin were introduced into Britain and became naturalised here during the twentieth century, following the establishment of a nucleus of breeders in Surrey and east Berkshire in the 1930s. The species was not admitted to the official British list until 1971. There are also smaller but increasing populations in a few other European countries, notably Switzerland. Mandarin are very secretive when near the nest site, and partly for this reason numbers in their native range have been greatly underestimated in the past, giving the impression that the feral population in Britain was globally more significant than is the case. In reality, China, Korea and Japan hold a total of at least 70,000 birds (Callaghan & Green 1993), whilst the best recent British population estimate is about 7,000 individuals.

In its natural range the species is migratory and dispersive, but British birds have largely lost this instinct and, although post-breeding flocks will gather on local waters, there has been only a gradual spread into the Midlands, northern England, Scotland and Wales. Numbers are still on the increase however, as the species exploits a previously vacant ecological niche for a hole-nesting perching duck in woodlands surrounding standing or sluggish fresh water. The nest site is typically close to a tree-fringed lake or pond, deep inside a tree hole up to 15 m above the ground, although they will also nest on the ground. They also sometimes use nest-boxes, for example those designed for Tawny Owls.

The first record of Mandarin in Gloucestershire was apparently a single drake at Cannop in the Forest of Dean in January 1965. Breeding was first recorded in the county in 1978 at three sites: Frampton, Uley near Dursley, and Stowell Park near Bourton-on-the-Water. The first two records at least are assumed to have involved birds from the Wildfowl Trust at Slimbridge. Swaine remarked a few years later that the species was showing signs of establishing a feral breeding population in the county. In the Forest of Dean area the first nesting records were at Longhope in 1988 and at further sites in the following two years; it is likely that these birds were escapes from a local wildfowl collection (Ivan Proctor).

Numbers in the county have doubled since the 1988–91 Breeding Atlas (see fact-box). The maps show a distribution unique amongst our wildfowl, with a clear preference for the Forest of Dean and the wooded waters of the Cotswolds, but there is also a lesser presence along the Severn Vale. Indeed the atlas fieldwork has revealed just how widespread breeding Mandarins are, with records from suitable wooded waterbodies throughout the county; for example there is a strong, previously unreported, presence on the river Leadon and its tributaries in the north-west of the county. Mandarin are widespread in the Cotswolds: the 2003–07 Cotswolds Atlas recorded its presence on six river systems, with particularly good numbers in the Batsford–Sezincote area (near Moreton-in-Marsh, SP13).

The winter population has shown a particularly steep rise and WeBS reports state that 'the Forest of Dean ponds are the UK's traditional stronghold for the species'. Totals from co-ordinated autumn counts in the Dean are impressive, with between 220 and 270 recorded in a number of years since 1998. Favoured areas include the Cannop Valley and the Soudley area, but the birds are highly mobile and on occasion almost the whole Dean population can be found at a single site.

An adult female Mandarin ringed at Slimbridge in October 2008 died after hitting wires 120 km away in Northamptonshire in December of the same year: rather a long movement for a bird from a generally sedentary population.

Sponsored by Mr S J Palmer

Species accounts

| | 2007–11 Atlas fieldwork ||||| Gloucestershire trends |||||| UK population trends ||
| | Number of tetrads in which recorded (max 683) ||||| Occupied 10 km squares (max 26) |||| % of tetrads in which recorded (1st hour of TTV) || *UK conservation status:* **Introduced** ||
	Total	Confirmed	Probable	Possible	Present	1968–71	1981–84	1988–91	2007–11	1988–91	2008–11	Long term	Short term
Breeding	135	50	40	29	16	0		8	21	2.2	4.6	–	–
Winter	62						3		21			–	–

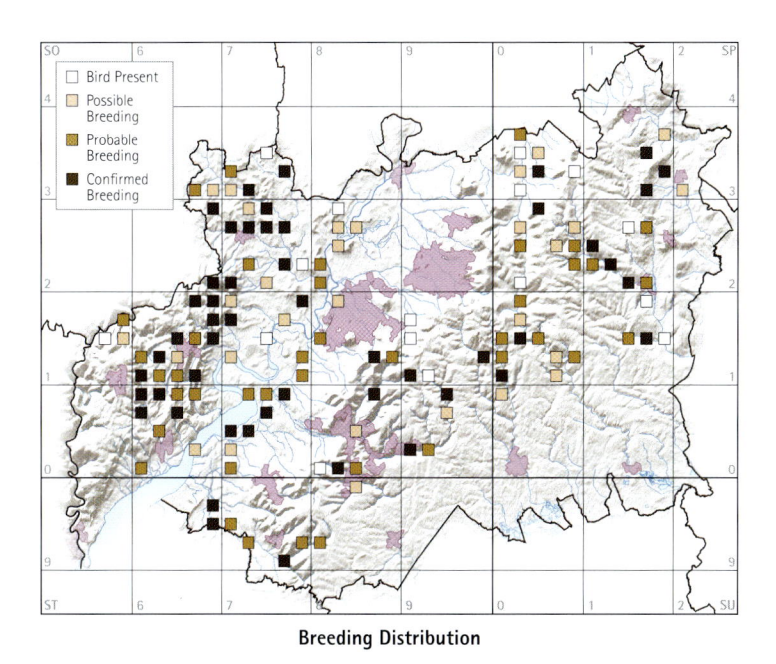

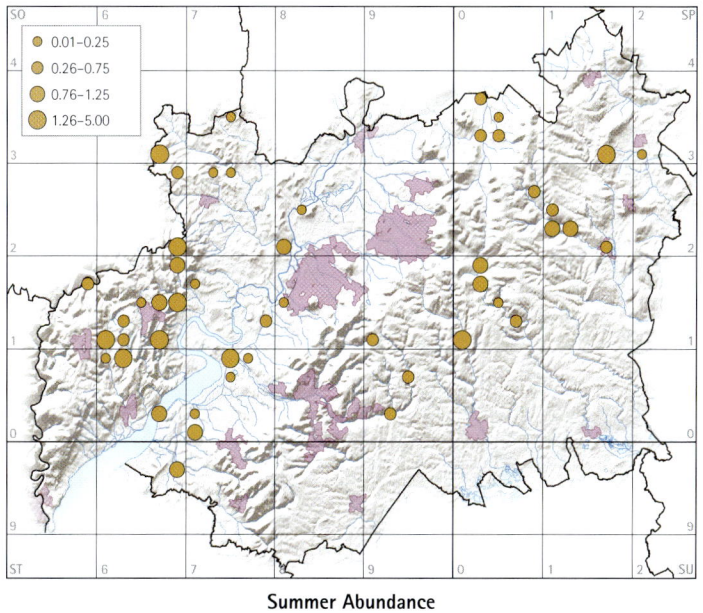

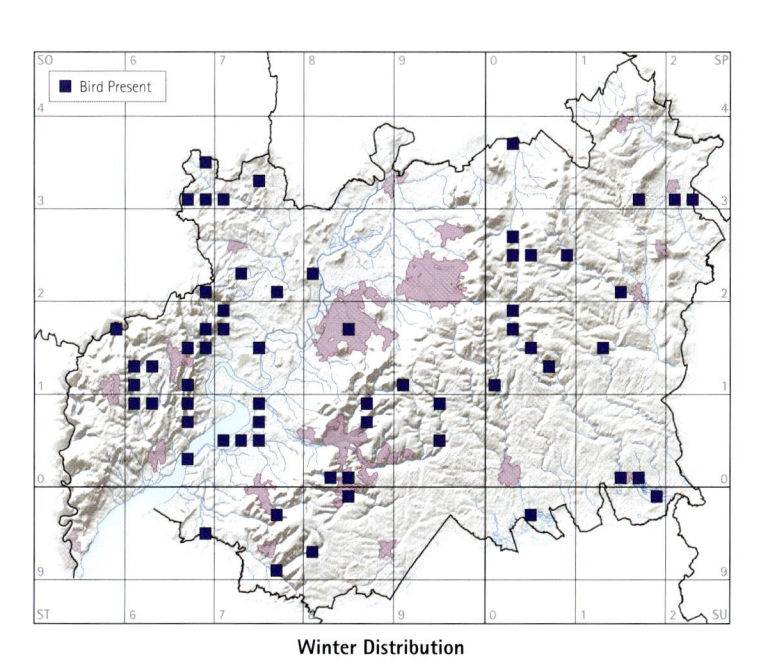

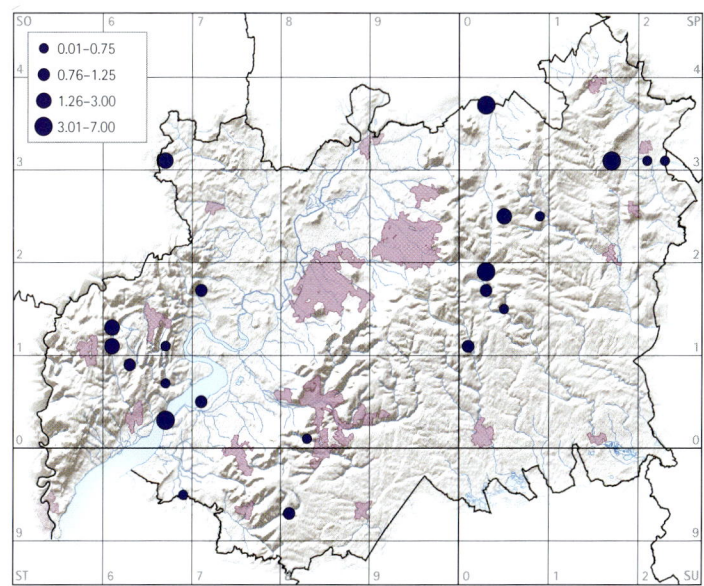

Breeding Distribution

Summer Abundance

Winter Distribution

Winter Abundance

Wigeon (Eurasian Wigeon)
Anas penelope

Wigeon breed across the boreal and subarctic regions of the Palearctic from Iceland to the Pacific Coast, with fewer further south in temperate areas, and winter south to tropical Africa and Indo-China. They require shallow fresh water with submerged or floating vegetation and open banks for breeding.

The first proof of breeding in Britain came from northern Scotland in 1834. Probably helped by increasing numbers of winter visitors during the cold years of the mid-nineteenth century, they spread south to northern England by the 1880s and halted at the north Pennines in the 1930s. Elsewhere in England and Wales breeding has only ever been sporadic, often involving injured or escaped birds. Total numbers nesting in the country have never risen above 500 pairs, and it is estimated that only about 100 pairs breed at present.

This small breeding population is vastly augmented in winter. The few Scottish-nesting birds travel no further than Ireland, whilst Icelandic breeders winter in northern England; migrants arrive in

Sponsored by Elspeth Williams

| | 2007–11 Atlas fieldwork ||||| Gloucestershire trends |||||| UK population trends ||
| | Number of tetrads in which recorded (max 683) ||||| Occupied 10 km squares (max 26) |||| % of tetrads in which recorded (1st hour of TTV) || UK conservation status: Amber 7,8 ||
	Total	Confirmed	Probable	Possible	Present	1968–71	1981–84	1988–91	2007–11	1988–91	2008–11	Long term	Short term
Breeding	14	0	0	0	14	0		0	0	0	0.4	–	–
Winter	83							13	18			+69%	–2%

southern Britain from Fennoscandia and Siberia, and there is often a midwinter influx from the Continent, giving maximum counts in January. Although traditionally a coastal species in winter, relying on the tidal zone and salt-marsh, there has been an increasing tendency over the last century for Wigeon to feed inland, by floodwater and on farmland, though many still return to coastal waters to roost. As herbivores, they need to feed for some 14 hours each day in order to maintain weight, and they therefore often continue to feed through the night. Winter populations in the British Isles were stable from 1930 to 1980 at about 200,000–250,000, representing half of the birds in north-west Europe. Numbers have generally increased since then and approximately 440,000 birds now winter in Britain.

Mellersh's assertion that Wigeon bred around Sharpness 'as late as 1862' has not been substantiated, and in any case it is likely that introduced or escaped birds would have been involved; certainly nowadays they are known in Gloucestershire only as winter visitors. As shown by the maps, the main concentrations are found on the Severn Estuary and Severn Hams, with smaller flocks in the Cotswold Water Park and along the river Windrush around Sherborne. Peak numbers vary greatly with the severity of the winter, but totals have frequently exceeded the threshold for national importance (currently 4,400) at a number of sites. Five-year mean counts at Slimbridge exceeded 6,000 for a few years in the mid-1980s, and although numbers subsequently fell sharply they have regularly reached 4,000 since the turn of the century, with several counts once again in excess of 6,000. On the Severn Hams, flocks of more than 1,000 became routine in the 1980s; over 5,000 briefly visited around the turn of the century, but about 2,000 is now the average winter peak. The Water Park also began to record totals exceeding 1,000 during the 1980s but, despite more thorough counting, figures here have not increased greatly since then.

Rather few Wigeon have been ringed in Gloucestershire compared with some other species of wildfowl and there had only been 48 foreign recoveries up to 2010. The majority (29) were in Russia, with six each in France and Denmark and singles in Iceland, the Netherlands, Germany, Norway, Sweden, Finland and Italy. Birds ringed in the Netherlands (two), Denmark, Finland and Russia have also been recovered in the county.

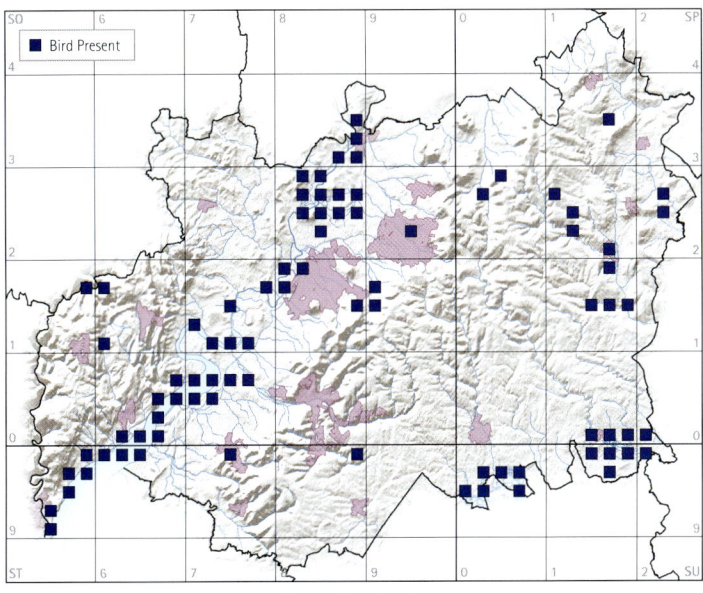

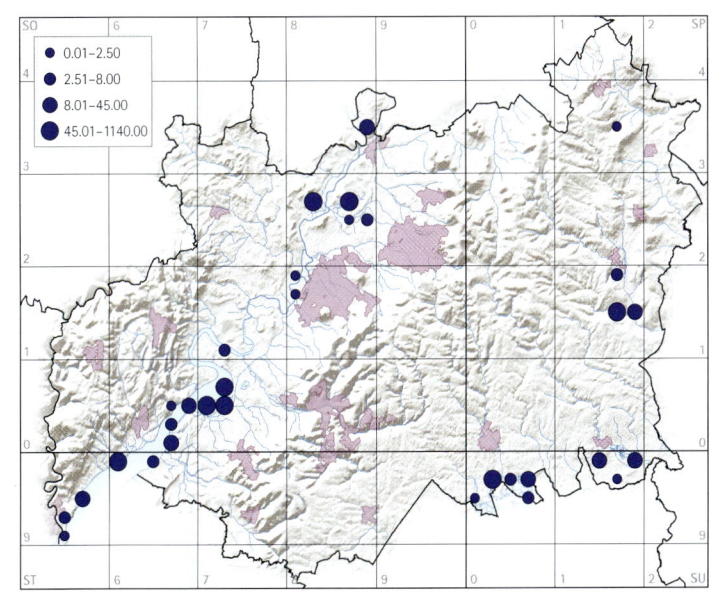

Winter Distribution

Winter Abundance

Gadwall
Anas strepera

The breeding range of the Gadwall lies well to the south of that of most dabbling ducks, across Europe, northern and central Asia and North America, but in Eurasia it has been extending north and west for almost 50 years, quite possibly assisted by global warming. Western Palearctic birds winter mostly south to the Mediterranean and Black Seas, some birds reaching East Africa.

The preferred habitats are lakes, reservoirs, freshwater marshes and slow-flowing streams. Nests are built in dense cover but are rarely more than 20 m from open water, so are relatively easy to locate. Both adults and young feed largely on submerged vegetation and so usually require shallow, nutrient-rich waters, but Gadwall will also steal water weed brought to the surface by Coot, Pochard and Red-crested Pochard. Not only does this tactic reduce energy expenditure, it has also allowed Gadwall to colonise deeper waters than previously. In winter the species extends onto estuaries and sheltered coasts.

Through most of the nineteenth century Gadwall were only very rare winter visitors to Britain. However in England, introductions from 1850 to as recently as 1970 established a number of discrete and localised breeding populations which at first grew very slowly, no doubt augmented by overstaying winter visitors attracted by the feral birds. Since 1960 though, breeding numbers have increased by about 5% per year, to reach 600 pairs by 1983 and almost 2,000 pairs at present. The great majority of these are in England; they represent no more than 1% of the European population.

Numbers wintering in Europe have increased on average by 9% per year since the 1960s, with the most rapid rises in Britain during the 1980s and 1990s. The winter distribution here largely overlaps the breeding range, with 80% of birds on inland lakes and gravel-pits, generally in flocks of fewer than 200. Up to a quarter of our breeding birds emigrate in winter but these are more than compensated for by visitors from Iceland, Fennoscandia, and central and eastern Europe, and the British winter population numbers about 25,000.

According to Mellersh, wintering Gadwall were sometimes caught in the decoys on the Berkeley Estate, but only in very small numbers; fewer by far than Goldeneyes and barely more than Scaup. Generally, Gadwall were rarely encountered in Gloucestershire until the Wildfowl Trust was established in 1946 and became a magnet to wintering wildfowl. Some captive birds escaped, and a nest was discovered at Frampton Pools in 1956. Twenty birds were released around Slimbridge in 1967 and, two years later, 20 feral pairs were breeding in the vicinity and attracting up to 200 more in winter (Swaine). Within 20 years, this breeding population had become naturalised. New waterbodies have played a large part in the increase in numbers and range of Gadwall in Britain since 1930, and it was inevitable that the rapid development of the Cotswold Water Park after 1950 would attract growing numbers, although breeding was not confirmed here until 1984. The county now holds perhaps 40 breeding pairs, heavily concentrated in the Frampton–Slimbridge area and the Water Park, but with outliers on ponds in the Dean and Wye Area and at the Severn Hams.

As the map shows, in winter Gadwall can now be found on most suitable county waters. Totals at Frampton Pools, which sometimes exceed 100, were once of international importance but they have not reflected the rising national trend. However, the Water Park and the Severn Estuary, both of which extend into neighbouring counties, do hold nationally important numbers, with recent peak counts averaging 370 and 243 respectively. The Gloucestershire section of the Water Park averages maximum counts of 300, and Slimbridge 150–200.

There have been almost 120 foreign recoveries of Gadwall ringed in Gloucestershire, mostly at Slimbridge. Nearly 100 of these were in France and the Netherlands, but there have also been movements as far as Latvia, Poland, north Russia, Spain and north-east Algeria. The sole foreign-ringed bird ever to be recovered in the county had been ringed in Germany.

Species accounts

2007–11 Atlas fieldwork						Gloucestershire trends						UK population trends	
Number of tetrads in which recorded (max 683)					*Occupied 10 km squares (max 26)*				*% of tetrads in which recorded (1st hour of TTV)*		*UK conservation status:* **Amber 1,8**	
	Total	Confirmed	Probable	Possible	Present	1968–71	1981–84	1988–91	2007–11	1988–91	2008–11	Long term	Short term
Breeding	31	8	11	5	7	0		3	5	1.2	2.1	–	–
Winter	58						10		17			+310%	+19%

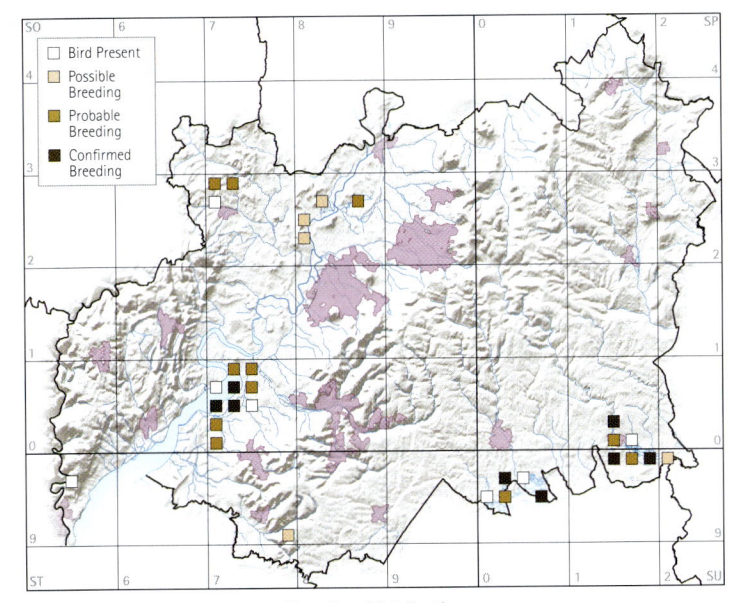

Breeding Distribution

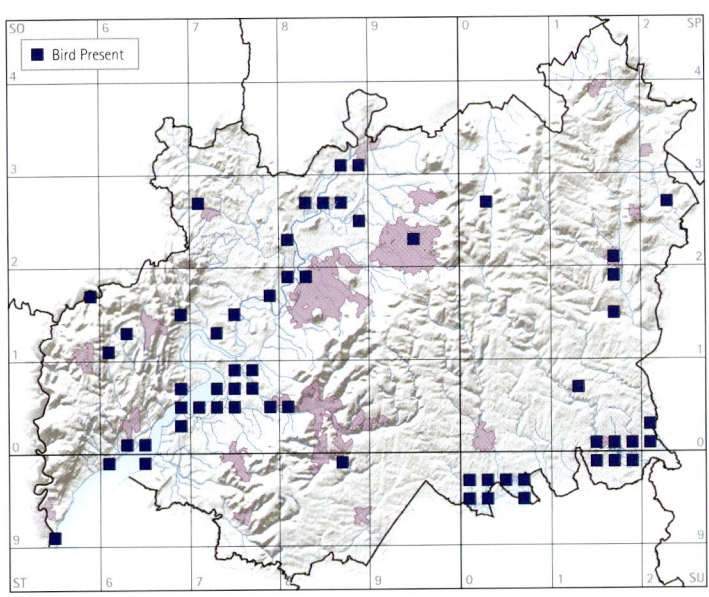

Winter Distribution

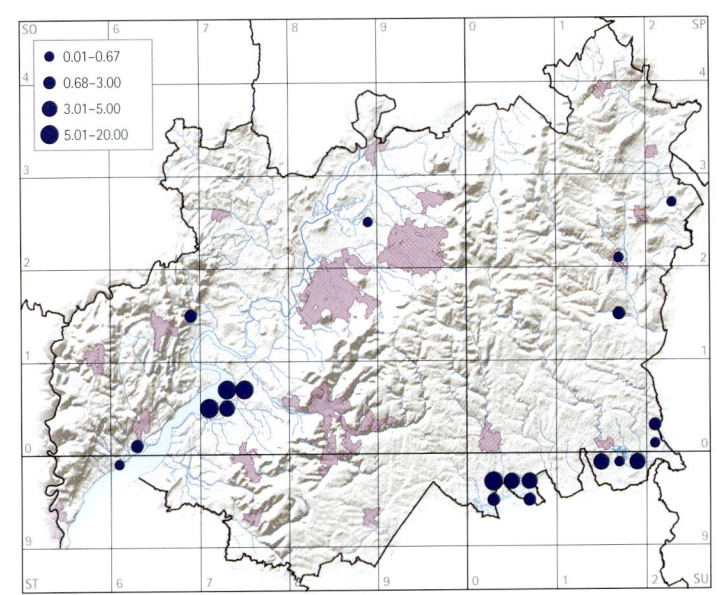

Winter Abundance

Teal (Eurasian Teal)
Anas crecca

Our smallest native duck, the Teal breeds across northern and central Eurasia, from coastal tundra through steppe to desert fringes, and winters south to central Africa and southern Asia. It feeds in shallow water, often at night, and breeds on small pools, wet moorland and bog, and slow-flowing rivers with ample cover. It is unobtrusive in the nesting season and is a notoriously difficult species for which to obtain proof of breeding. Teal will readily resort to shallow coastal waters, estuaries and salt-marsh during winter.

The British breeding population was never numerous and has been declining steadily for at least 70 years due to drainage, agricultural changes and afforestation. The 1988–91 Breeding Atlas recorded a major contraction in range, with almost 20% fewer squares occupied than reported in the 1968–72 Breeding Atlas and a reduction in breeding pairs by at least one-third. The estimate of 1,500–2,600 pairs was considered to be on the optimistic side. There now remain perhaps 1,400 pairs, mainly in the higher, more remote regions of the north and west, with a scattering through more southern counties.

Teal are more familiar in Britain as passage migrants and as winter visitors mainly from the near Continent, Iceland and Fennoscandia. The highest counts are often recorded in September and October, as many migrants pass through on their way further south. Winter counts increased on average by 3% per year between 1960 and 1990 and currently about 210,000 Teal winter in Britain.

It is likely that Teal used to breed occasionally in Gloucestershire before the widespread farming changes that began in the nineteenth century. Mellersh states that 'as late as 1862, Teal ... were supposed to breed occasionally ... about the old Severn Channel near Sharpness' but this, together with other infrequent suggestions of breeding near the Severn, Churn and Windrush up to the 1950s, was never satisfactorily proved. In 1981, however, young Teal were seen on Frampton 100 Acre in July and, if this seems too close for comfort to the WWT collection at Slimbridge, young were reported at Ashleworth Ham in 1999 and 2000, and predated eggs there in 2003. Breeding was not proved in Gloucestershire during the current survey, despite a number of 'probable' breeding records, none of which could be substantiated.

Although Teal can form flocks of several thousand, the 1981–84 Wintering Atlas pointed out that 40% of birds are found in groups of fewer than 200, and the winter distribution map for Gloucestershire confirms their presence here in small numbers on many waters. However the main concentrations are found at the Severn Estuary, on the Severn Hams and, to a lesser extent, in the Cotswold Water Park. The average peak count at Slimbridge in the late 1980s was 733; in the next five years it increased to over 2,000 due to the creation of new wetland habitat by the WWT. Over the the four winters of the current survey, the average peak here was 3,514, boosted by a very high count of 6,643 birds in January 2008. Any

Sponsored by Norman & Wendy Cooke

Species accounts

2007–11 Atlas fieldwork						Gloucestershire trends						UK population trends	
Number of tetrads in which recorded (max 683)					Occupied 10 km squares (max 26)				% of tetrads in which recorded (1st hour of TTV)		UK conservation status: **Amber 8**	
	Total	Confirmed	Probable	Possible	Present	1968–71	1981–84	1988–91	2007–11	1988–91	2008–11	Long term	Short term
Breeding	29	0	12	0	17	0		0	4	0.6	0.7	–	–
Winter	131						20		24			+33%	–4%

site holding over 2,100 birds is currently of national importance, and counts above 5,000 birds are internationally significant.

Mainly as a result of some fairly intensive ringing programmes at Slimbridge, there have been over 250 foreign recoveries of Gloucestershire-ringed Teal. The majority moved to France (71), Finland (58), Russia (32), Denmark (29) and Sweden (20), reflecting known origins and migration routes as well as the presence of ringers, wildfowlers or interested members of the public. There were also ten or fewer recoveries in 15 other countries, including single birds in Greece, Italy, Morocco and Portugal. Three of these four were ringed in autumn, when they were likely to be passing through Gloucestershire on migration, but the bird that went to Greece was ringed in February 1981 and reported shot in April 1982, indicating that it had changed its wintering area.

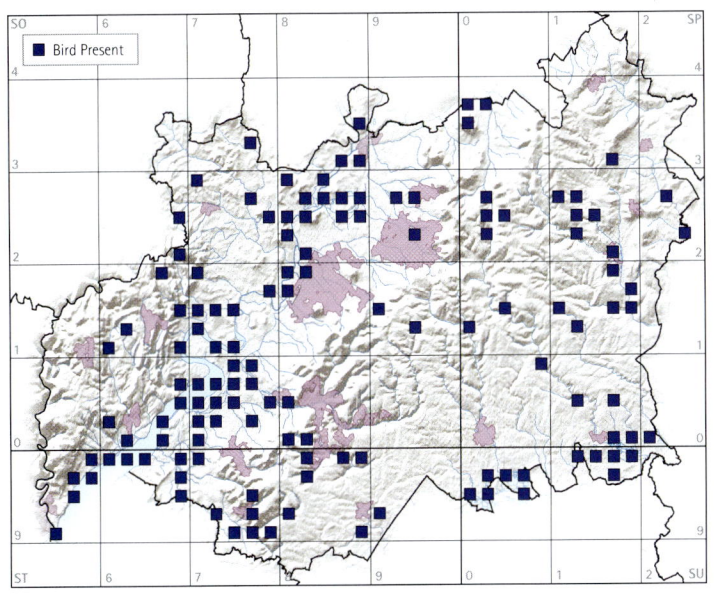

Winter Distribution

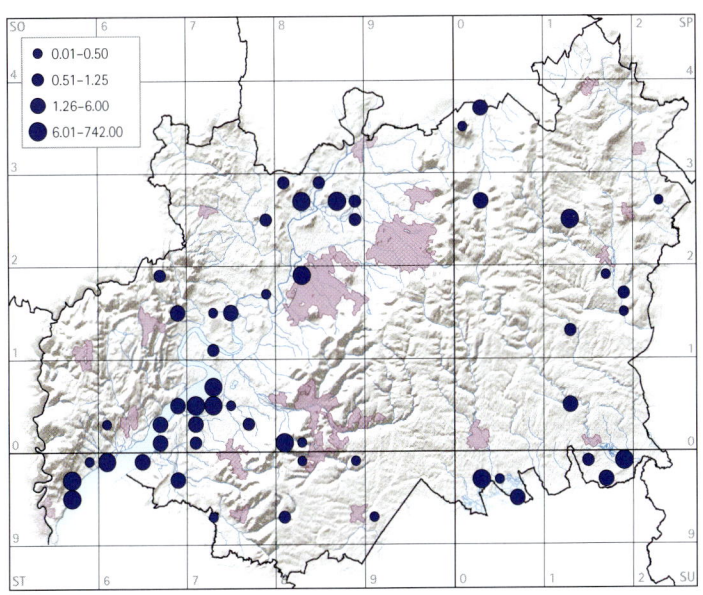

Winter Abundance

Mallard
Anas platyrhynchos

Our most familiar duck, the Mallard is widely distributed throughout Eurasia and North America. The British resident population is augmented from September onwards by almost half a million winter visitors from Iceland, Fennoscandia, the Baltic, Poland and parts of Germany. Mallard will use almost any type of waterbody, from the smallest pond to flowing rivers, but generally prefer the water to be no more than a few metres deep. They will resort to sheltered coasts, especially in winter, and may move well away from water to nest, as indicated by some of the records on the breeding season maps.

The Mallard was domesticated centuries ago and is the progenitor of over 20 recognised breeds of 'farmyard' duck today. Wild birds too were once an important source of food and have long been hunted, originally using traps and decoys (of which there were two in Gloucestershire, at Slimbridge and Purton), and more recently guns. Despite this economic importance, numbers of Mallard fell steeply as a result of agricultural changes from the eighteenth century onwards, leaving the species thinly distributed in southern England. Over the last 50 years, however, the British breeding population has doubled, no doubt partly due to the 400,000 captive-bred birds that are released for shooting every year – although half as many again are shot annually. Populations have also probably been boosted by the spread of domesticated birds, though these have not always been well recorded. The 1988–91 Breeding Atlas still found Mallard to be relatively scarce in south-west England, but subsequently the BBS recorded a 61% regional increase between 1995 and 2008, while the national increase was only 20%. Recent estimates suggest a total British breeding population of around 100,000 pairs.

Conversely, winter numbers have declined substantially since 1980 – by 40% in the decade to 1998, for example – and for this reason the Mallard was amber listed in 2009. Initially, 'short-stopping' in Europe due to milder winters was thought to be the cause, but numbers appear to be declining on the Continent too, suggesting that the birds are staying well to the east. It may also be that milder, more ice-free winters allow Mallard to use smaller waters that are not covered by the WeBS. In 2010, 680,000 were estimated to be wintering in Britain.

Mallard do not winter in vast congregations, but they are relatively easy to survey in the breeding season, with flotillas of ducklings a common sight. Although unpaired birds readily consort together in groups and might have been regarded as 'pairs in suitable habitat', most breeding evidence was of a higher status.

Mellersh stated that Mallard bred in Gloucestershire 'only in small scattered numbers'. More recently, the Cotswolds Atlases and the comparative TTV data (see fact-box) both point to a slight increase, in line with the national trend. The summer maps show Mallard across most of the county, even where standing water is scarce, with gaps in distribution only on some Cotswold tops and parts of the Forest of Dean.

It seems that numbers wintering in Gloucestershire have not declined as much as the national picture would suggest. Swaine's comments in 1982, just as the national decline became noticeable, still hold good for much of the county: of Slimbridge, he stated that 'totals of 1,000 to 2,000 birds are not unusual ... and up to 3,000 have been noted occasionally'. This is still the case, and the Severn Estuary in its entirety is now the only site in Britain that regularly attracts over 3,000 Mallard in winter. Likewise, Swaine's comment that 'totals in excess of 1,000 birds have been noted from time to time since 1975' in the Cotswold Water Park still applies but, despite the increasing water area and better co-ordination of counts, it requires the totals from both sections of the Park to be combined in some winters for Mallard numbers to reach four figures.

Very large numbers of Mallard have been ringed in Gloucestershire and there have been as many as 1,600 recoveries, revealing movements to and from all parts of the British Isles. In addition there have been about 630 recoveries of birds moving to or from 19 foreign countries, ranging from Norway, Finland and Poland to Spain, Italy and Hungary, and with a few birds travelling as far as Belarus, Ukraine and Russia.

'Domestic Mallards' are sometimes treated separately and indeed in the atlas fieldwork observers were asked to record them. However the fact that there were only 120 county records between 1980 and 2010 suggests that in general they go unrecorded.

Sponsored by T & E Butler

Species accounts

2007–11 Atlas fieldwork						Gloucestershire trends						UK population trends	
Number of tetrads in which recorded (max 683)					Occupied 10 km squares (max 26)				% of tetrads in which recorded (1st hour of TTV)		UK conservation status: **Amber 4**	
	Total	Confirmed	Probable	Possible	Present	1968–71	1981–84	1988–91	2007–11	1988–91	2008–11	Long term	Short term
Breeding	514	271	131	71	41	26		26	26	44.8	49.0	+98%	+18%
Winter	458						26		26			−38%	−22%

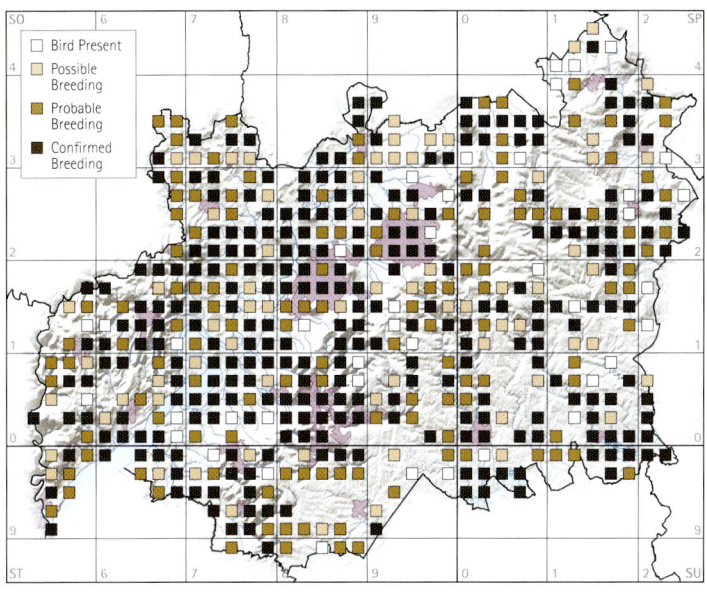

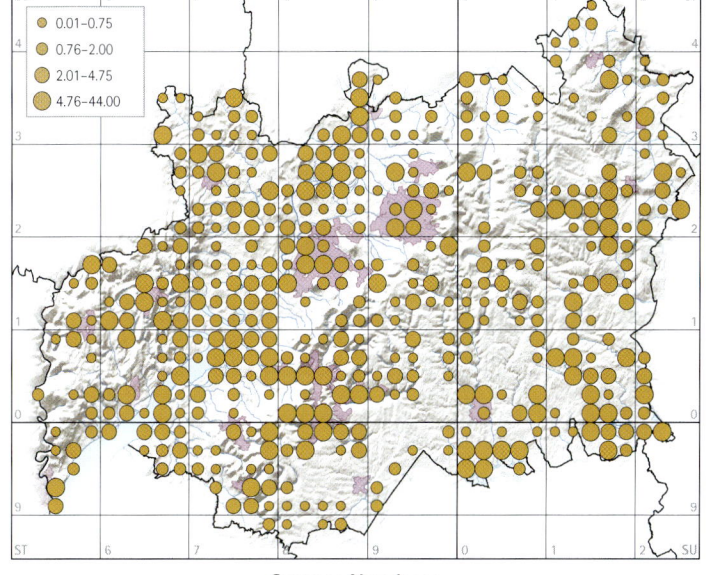

Breeding Distribution

Summer Abundance

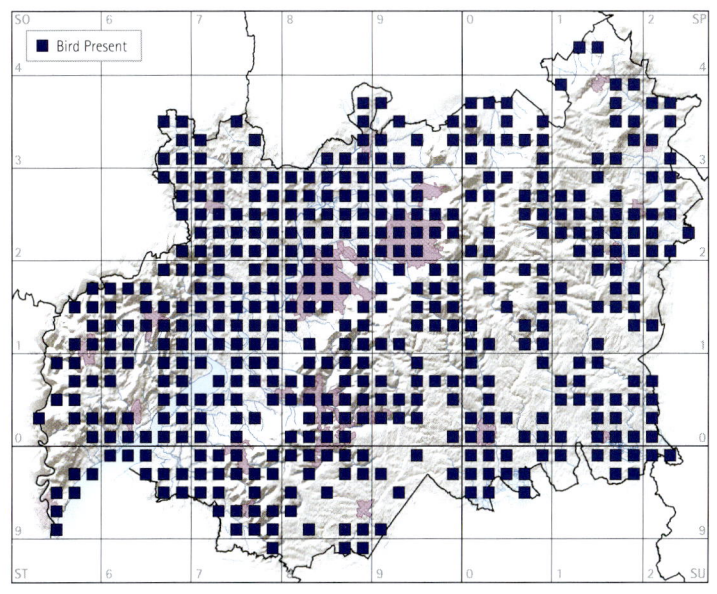

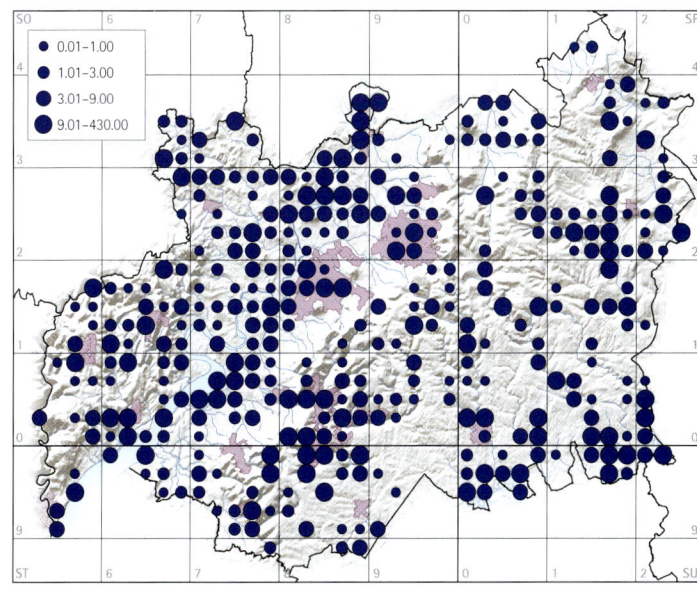

Winter Distribution

Winter Abundance

Pintail (Northern Pintail)
Anas acuta

The elegant Pintail is the most northerly of all dabbling ducks, breeding widely across Eurasia and North America, with the largest populations in the most northern parts of the range. The species generally breeds inland, with a preference for shallow, open, lowland waterbodies. Pintail can be shy and wary and often prefer to feed by night.

The first British breeding records date from 1869 in Scotland and 1910 in England but the species has never established a large or widespread breeding population here. By 1970 there were about 50 pairs but they began to decline soon after to fewer than 35 pairs by the turn of the century.

Birds from northern Europe and western Siberia winter south as far as North and East Africa, using flyways which bring many of them over Britain. They begin to arrive here in late September, many continuing to winter quarters further to the south-west. Numbers remaining in Britain usually peak in December at about 29,000, almost half the wintering population of north-west Europe. This figure has been stable since 1980, having increased from 18,000 over the previous two decades. These wintering birds come from Iceland, Fennoscandia and Russia and favour a few large estuaries, mainly in north-west England, and one notable inland site on the Ouse and Nene Washes in Cambridgeshire and Norfolk. Pintail will also feed on farmland and will readily move around to take advantage of temporary shallow floodwaters.

The Pintail has never bred in Gloucestershire and is known here only as a passage migrant and winter visitor, mainly frequenting the Severn Estuary. Average numbers in the estuary as a whole, extending beyond the Gloucestershire boundary, rose from 250 in the early 1960s to 400 in the 1980s, 630 a decade later and 830 in recent years. These figures are of international significance. During the current survey, however, a slight downward trend seemed to be developing. At Slimbridge, apart from an exceptional figure of 1,104 in January 2007, annual peak counts fell from 437 in 2006 to 250 four years later.

Pintail often use Walmore Common and the Severn Hams during times of flood: nationally important flocks of 520 in February 2004 and 350 in February 2008 were present on receding floodwater on Ashleworth Ham. Double-figure counts are fairly regular at the Cotswold Water Park, but elsewhere they are usually present in single-figure groups. The winter distribution map confirms just how localised Pintail are within the county, with the vast majority of records confined to the Severn Estuary and Hams, the Water Park and Bourton pits.

Ringing at Slimbridge has resulted in many recoveries from abroad, particularly Russia (99 recoveries) and the northern European countries, but also from as far south as Spain and Italy (three recoveries each).

In memory of Peter Jones

Species accounts

| | 2007–11 Atlas fieldwork ||||| Gloucestershire trends |||||| UK population trends ||
| | Number of tetrads in which recorded (max 683) ||||| Occupied 10 km squares (max 26) |||| % of tetrads in which recorded (1st hour of TTV) || UK conservation status: **Amber 1,6,7,8** ||
	Total	Confirmed	Probable	Possible	Present	1968–71	1981–84	1988–91	2007–11	1988–91	2008–11	Long term	Short term
Breeding	6	0	0	0	6	0		0	0	0	0	–	–
Winter	30						7		9			–4%	–5%

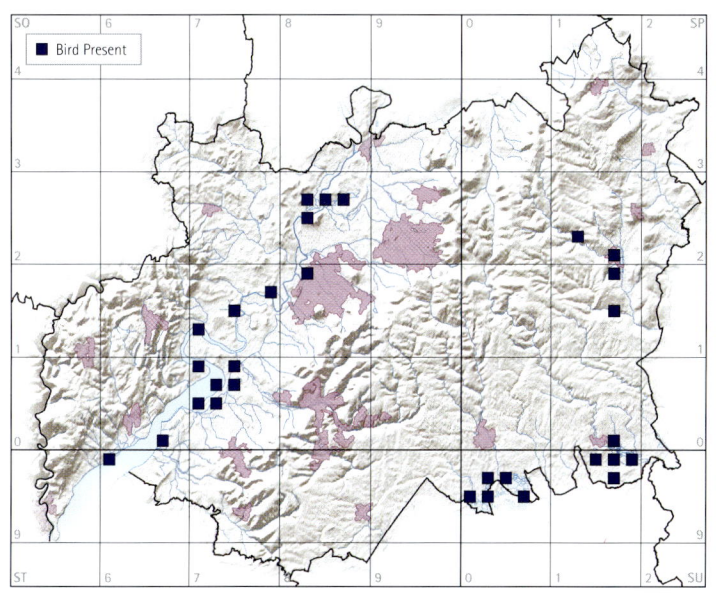

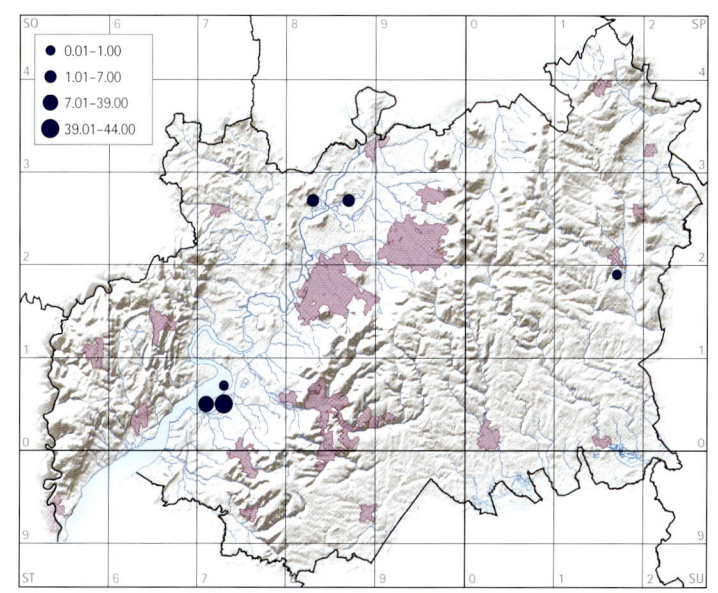

Winter Distribution

Winter Abundance

Shoveler (Northern Shoveler)
Anas clypeata

The Shoveler breeds widely across much of the Northern Palearctic and Nearctic. It is almost exclusively a duck of the lowlands, requiring shallow, permanent and productive fresh water for breeding, usually fringed by reeds or other emergent vegetation and surrounded by fairly open country.

Shovelers can eat up to 10% of their body weight daily, filtering food through their unique sieve-like bills. They feed by repeatedly sweeping the bill left and right, by up-ending or by diving. Small groups of surface-feeding birds are often seen swimming together in circles, head-to-tail, presumably mutually benefiting from the food that is stirred up by the flock. The high demand for food can significantly deplete resources so, outside the breeding season, individuals can be very mobile – more so given the added risks of shallow waters either drying out or freezing. Counts will therefore tend to underestimate the total number of individuals using a site over a complete season.

Breeding and wintering numbers in Britain declined during the nineteenth century, at least in part due to wildfowling, so that by mid-century Shovelers were only breeding for certain in Norfolk, Essex, and the Clyde area of Scotland. Legal protection from 1876 allowed these nuclei to expand in number and range during the first half of the twentieth century into most of England, South Wales and lowland Scotland. The English strongholds now lie from East Anglia across to the West Midlands. British breeding numbers have remained fairly stable at about 1,000 pairs, just a fraction of the European population of 40,000 pairs. Better breeding success at protected sites has masked an overall contraction in numbers and key areas.

European-breeding Shovelers winter south as far as North and East Africa. Most British birds winter in southern Europe, and the British Isles receive wintering birds from the Baltic, Fennoscandia and Russia. Wintering flocks are found mainly at inland waters, but also on estuaries. Autumn migration is earlier than for most Palearctic ducks, with many British breeders already on their wintering grounds by late October. There is a major passage through Britain in November and again in March and April, whilst winter numbers generally peak in December. Individual flocks rarely exceed a few hundred birds but overall totals have gradually risen to about 18,000 birds, 37% of the north-west European wintering population.

In Gloucestershire breeding was first proved in 1937 at Elmore in the Severn Vale downriver of Gloucester, which at that time was a marshy area (Mike Smart). Up to the start of the current atlas fieldwork it had only been recorded eight more times, all in the Frampton–Slimbridge area except for a brood at the Cotswold Water Park in 1972. During the atlas survey breeding was confirmed only at Slimbridge, with possibly two nests in 2010 and certainly four broods in 2011.

In winter, the Severn Estuary in its entirety holds internationally important numbers of about 600 Shovelers, while individual sites in Gloucestershire support nationally important levels (over 180). Peak counts at Slimbridge currently average 200–300 birds, and in the Water Park the western section holds almost 200 whilst the eastern section may support 120–40. The Severn Hams can also host three-figure flocks during times of flood.

Up to 2010 there had been 83 foreign recoveries of Shovelers ringed in Gloucestershire, mainly at Slimbridge. The majority were found in France (32), Russia (22), the Netherlands (13) and Denmark (five), reflecting the main origins and migration routes, with fewer recoveries in Finland and Spain (three each), Italy (two), Estonia, Latvia and Portugal (one each).

Species accounts 89

2007–11 Atlas fieldwork					Gloucestershire trends						UK population trends	
Number of tetrads in which recorded (max 683)					*Occupied 10 km squares (max 26)*				*% of tetrads in which recorded (1st hour of TTV)*		*UK conservation status:* **Amber 1,8**	
	Total	Confirmed	Probable	Possible	Present	1968–71	1981–84	1988–91	2007–11	1988–91	2008–11	Long term	Short term
Breeding	18	2	8	0	8	0		0	2	0.2	0.7	–	–
Winter	45						7		11			+69%	+27%

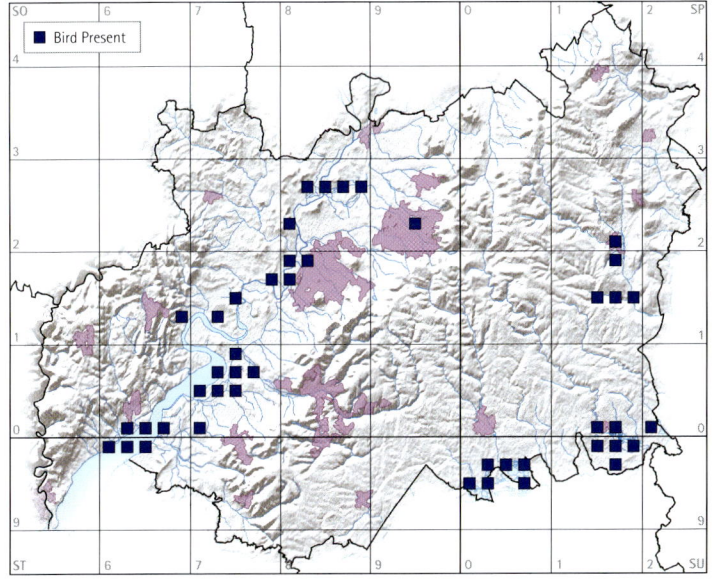

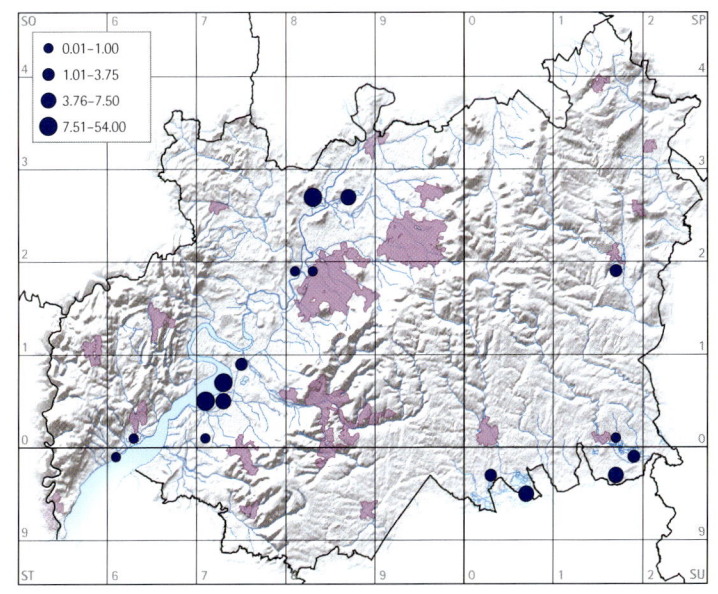

Winter Distribution

Winter Abundance

Garganey
Anas querquedula

This very pretty little duck breeds across much of Eurasia and, unusually among wildfowl, most Western Palearctic breeders are trans-Saharan migrants. Garganey breed in rushy marshlands, wet meadows and rough grasslands intersected with ditches or dykes, and are extremely secretive when breeding. Since 1970 they have suffered a widespread decline over most of their range, probably as a result of habitat loss and possibly exacerbated by hunting.

This is the only duck that is essentially a summer visitor to the British Isles, where it breeds in low and variable numbers, the estimate for 2010 being between 15 and 98 pairs. Nesting records tend to be concentrated in central and south-eastern England, with a stronghold in the Ouse Washes in Cambridgeshire.

Swaine noted that Garganey were much more frequent in 1980 than they had been in Mellersh's day. Indeed Mellersh had received reports of just six birds between 1880 and 1900, whereas Swaine reported about 165 birds in 1958–68 and around 100 in the following decade (an early indication of the decline mentioned above, perhaps). He added that breeding had been confirmed in five years between 1928 and 1937, but not subsequently.

Since 1980 Garganey have been seen in the county every year apart from 1984. In half of these years the total number of birds recorded has been in single figures, and in the other half it has been 10–20, with no discernible trend. Spring records outnumber autumn records (Swaine said the ratio was 3:1, it is now nearer 2:1) but this might simply be because the handsome drakes are so much more noticeable in their spring plumage than in the autumn, when they are more likely to be overlooked among Teal. Many sightings are of single birds, although it is not unusual to see two or three; a record of five pairs together at Frampton on May 23rd 2001 was exceptional.

Garganey have occasionally stayed through the winter in the wildfowl enclosures at Slimbridge, having become accustomed to associating with the tame ducks there. These birds apart, the earliest accepted spring arrival date is March 3rd 2002. The average first date in the decade to 2009 was March 24th, an advance of 11 days compared with the 1980s. Most sightings in the county are in April or May, with a concentration at the well-watched Frampton-Slimbridge area, but they are also regular at the Severn Hams and in the Cotswold Water Park.

In 1997 a pair may have bred in the Slimbridge area and there was thought to have been an unsuccessful breeding attempt at Ashleworth Ham. In 2000, ducklings were seen at Ashleworth, providing the first confirmed breeding record since 1937. Breeding was suspected, but not confirmed, at other sites in 2007 and 2008.

Sponsored by Anser Birding

American Wigeon
Anas americana

Very much the Nearctic counterpart of the Eurasian species, American Wigeon breed in northern North America, especially on the western side of the continent. They winter in southern parts of the USA and in Central America.

There have been nine county records, all except two from the Frampton–Slimbridge area of the Severn Estuary. All were singles and seven of these were males; females are more likely to have been overlooked than the more distinctive-looking drakes.

1946: Frampton 100 Acre, March 9th.
1982: Ashleworth Ham, from April 16th to 30th.
1990: Cotswold Water Park east section, from December 16th until January 24th 1991.
1991: Slimbridge, March 10th.
1992: Slimbridge, a first-winter male on September 15th.
2000: Slimbridge, December 27th.
2008: Frampton 100 Acre, a female or first-winter male from February 27th until March 1st.
2009: Slimbridge, a first-winter male from February 23rd until March 31st.
2010: Slimbridge, a female from October 21st until November 4th.

Green-winged Teal
Anas carolinensis

Breeding widely in North America, and until 2001 regarded as a subspecies of the Teal *A. crecca*, this is one of the more common transatlantic vagrants to Britain.

Swaine mentioned just two county records, in 1964 and 1979, but since then birds have been found in four years in the 1980s, seven years in the 1990s and every year but two between 2000 and 2011, involving about 25 birds (note that the summary in the 2010 GBR is inaccurate). The vast majority of records are from the Slimbridge area and all are of single males, the females being virtually indistinguishable from Eurasian Teal. Birds have been found in all months from October through to May; March and April account for about half the records, but a few birds have arrived in December and overwintered.

Blue-winged Teal
Anas discors

Breeding in the USA and Canada, Blue-winged Teal winter south as far as South America.

There are four county records, all of single males. Remarkably, one spent a whole summer here.

1956: Slimbridge, from December 24th to 28th. This bird was caught and pinioned.
1979: Ashleworth Ham from April 12th until May 1st, and at Slimbridge on May 2nd.
1982: Ashleworth Ham on December 27th.
1993: Slimbridge, from May 29th until October 16th.

Red-crested Pochard
Netta rufina

The Red-crested Pochard is mainly a central Asian species, occurring mostly east of the Caspian and Black Seas where it frequents fairly large, deep reed-fringed lakes with plenty of open water and few flanking trees. There is also a naturally occurring but fragmented population in western Europe. This western population declined during much of the nineteenth century but then its fortunes reversed, and by 1930 growing numbers had spread into many areas, from the Netherlands and Denmark south to Spain and north-west Africa. Spain is now the main centre of a fairly secure continental population, although numbers are falling in eastern Europe. Western birds have traditionally wintered around the Mediterranean and Black Seas, but a shift in distribution over recent decades has seen the core wintering range move north of the Alps, with correspondingly increasing chances of wild birds reaching Britain.

The 50 or so British records in the nineteenth century, all from the area between the Thames and the Humber, very probably related to escaped birds; in addition to the natural spread westward in the early twentieth century captive birds were released in the 1930s and 1940s at Woburn in Bedfordshire and in the London parks, with the first feral breeding noted in Essex in 1958. The only possible British breeding record of truly wild birds came from near the Lincolnshire coast in 1937. A recent estimate suggests that there are about 30 pairs in Britain at present (RSPB website, www.rspb.org.uk).

In Gloucestershire there is one undated nineteenth-century record of a bird shot in Woodchester Park, and another was shot at the Coombe Hill Canal in 1907. Breeding was first reported in 1964 at Frampton Pools, presumably involving birds that had escaped from the collection at Slimbridge. A pair or two have attempted to breed there in many subsequent years, but the young have usually been taken by predators and, as the maps suggest, these attempts may now have ceased. Individuals were occasionally seen around Fairford and nearby Dudgrove in the 1960s, and the first breeding was reported in the Cotswold Water Park in the same area in 1975, and at Bourton pits a year later. The current atlas survey found very small numbers breeding at Bourton and nearby Sherborne, but it is the Cotswold Water Park that has become the main breeding area in the county and, including the Wiltshire section, the main stronghold in Britain. In 2007 a thorough survey there found as many as 191 individuals, and although only six pairs were actually confirmed as breeding that year, there were 20 breeding pairs in 2008. Allowing

Species accounts

	2007–11 Atlas fieldwork					Gloucestershire trends						UK population trends	
	Number of tetrads in which recorded (max 683)					Occupied 10 km squares (max 26)				% of tetrads in which recorded (1st hour of TTV)		UK conservation status: **Introduced**	
	Total	Confirmed	Probable	Possible	Present	1968–71	1981–84	1988–91	2007–11	1988–91	2008–11	Long term	Short term
Breeding	21	11	6	0	4	1		0	3	0	1.3	–	–
Winter	20						0		4			–	–

Breeding Distribution

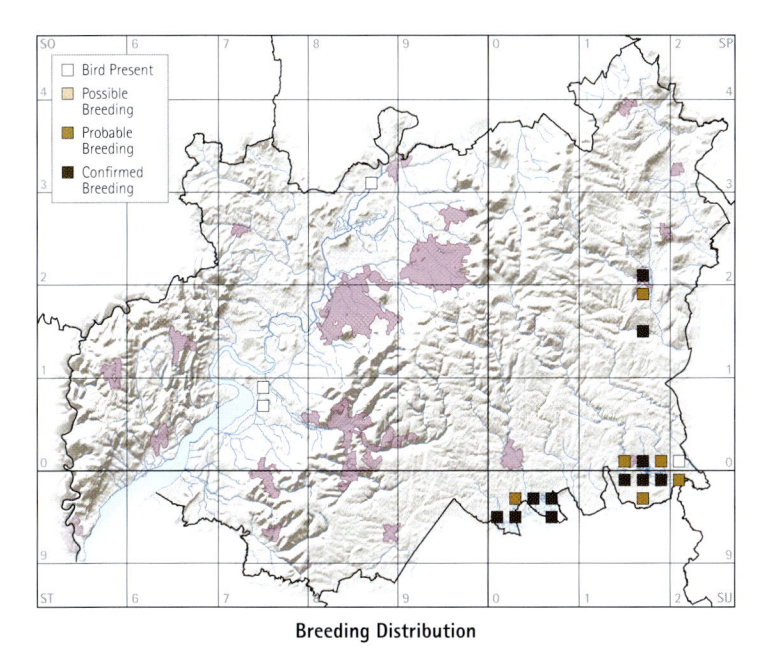

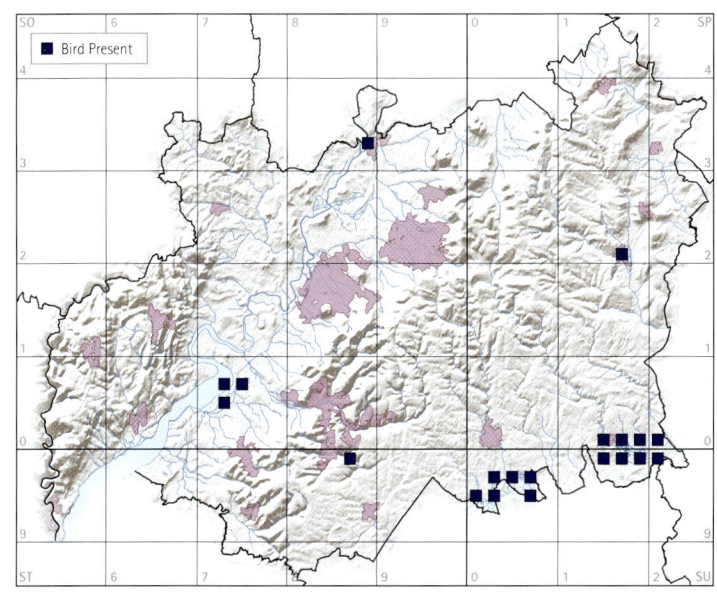

Winter Distribution

for some of these being in Wiltshire but including a few at Bourton and Sherborne, 20 pairs would seem to be a fairly accurate figure for the current breeding population in Gloucestershire. This amounts to over 50% of the national population.

Post-breeding numbers are of course greater, and WeBS reports confirm that the Water Park holds the 'core of the UK population' during winter. This was the only site in the country to average peak counts of more than 48 birds over the five winters to 2009–10, with 89 and 215 in the eastern and western sections respectively. This accounts for just about all the estimated 320 birds wintering in Britain as a whole.

There are occasional winter sightings away from the Water Park, Frampton and Bourton, although there was just one during the current survey.

Pochard (Common Pochard)
Aythya ferina

The Pochard began to spread westwards across Europe in the mid-nineteenth century, possibly because breeding sites in its native Asia were drying up. It currently breeds across northern and central Eurasia, extending further south than most wildfowl, and winters south to central Africa and southern Asia. For breeding, Pochard prefer open water with densely vegetated banks and not too much floating vegetation, but with submerged plant food making up 85% of the diet, the number of suitable freshwater sites is limited. Probably as a result they have become more maritime as they have spread across Europe, with brackish lagoons constituting an important breeding habitat in Britain.

Lingering winter visitors and/or releases may account for the handful of breeding records in nineteenth-century Britain, dating back possibly as far as 1818 in Norfolk. Low breeding success and susceptibility to disturbance ensured that colonisation was slow, with sites often used just once and then abandoned. However by 1930 Pochard were widely but thinly spread throughout England, eastern Wales and southern Scotland. More recently, breeding numbers have increased from 200 pairs in 1970 to about 600 pairs at present, mainly in south-east England.

The species was known in Britain as a winter visitor long before it began to breed here regularly. Pochard from central Europe and western Russia arrive here from late September onwards, with the drakes appearing first and numbers peaking around New Year. In the mid-1970s, the British winter peak of 50,000 birds amounted to 10% of the total in north-west Europe. Since then, populations have been declining across the Western Palearctic. However, numbers

Species accounts

2007–11 Atlas fieldwork					Gloucestershire trends						UK population trends	
Number of tetrads in which recorded (max 683)					Occupied 10 km squares (max 26)				% of tetrads in which recorded (1st hour of TTV)		UK conservation status: Amber 1,4,8	
	Total	Confirmed	Probable	Possible	Present	1968–71	1981–84	1988–91	2007–11	1988–91	2008–11	Long term	Short term
Breeding	12	0	4	4	4	1		5	2	1.2	0.6	–	–
Winter	45							18	15			–43%	–46%

wintering in Britain continued to increase up to the mid-1990s, reaching an all-time peak of 60,000 birds, or 17% of the north-west European population. Numbers then stabilised in some parts of Europe, but there have been severe declines in the British Isles and the Netherlands, and the British winter population now totals just 38,000 birds. Winter 2008–09 saw WeBS counts drop by 20% compared to the five-year average, and numbers remained at this level the following winter.

In Gloucestershire, Mellersh noted that the Pochard was the fifth commonest winter duck in the decoys of the Berkeley Estate during the nineteenth century. More recently, wintering totals in the county have decreased, in line with the national decline. In the eastern section of the Cotswold Water Park, four-figure flocks were regularly present in the 1990s but not since 1998, although both sections still hold nationally important numbers in excess of 380 birds. The Water Park has also become an important area during July and August for moulting drakes, many of which are from continental breeding populations. Similarly, winter counts at Slimbridge, which peaked at 1,431 in January 1997, have not reached four figures since 2001 and now average 650. Frampton Pools, where 750 Pochard were counted in January 1979, now averages just 30 birds each winter. The maps clearly show the concentrations of birds in the Frampton–Slimbridge area and in the Water Park, with scattered records from reservoirs, gravel-pits, lakes and ponds elsewhere in the county.

Breeding was not yet common on artificial waters at the time of the 1968–72 Breeding Atlas, a period which saw Gloucestershire's first breeding record at Frampton Pools in 1971. Since then, breeding has only been confirmed 11 times in the county, at eight different sites, and was not recorded during the current atlas survey.

Up to 2010 about 330 Pochard ringed in Gloucestershire, nearly all at Slimbridge, had been recovered abroad. The majority were found in Russia (112) and France (47), with between ten and 40 reports in each of Belarus, Denmark, Germany, Poland, Netherlands and Ukraine, and fewer in a number of other north European countries. Rather less typical were birds which moved to Switzerland (five), Kazakhstan (four), Italy (three), the Czech Republic and Hungary (two each), and Austria, Moldova, Serbia and Slovakia (one each). The contribution of the Gloucestershire ringing effort is highlighted by the fact that there had been not more than five recoveries of BTO-ringed Pochard in any of these nine countries up to 2010.

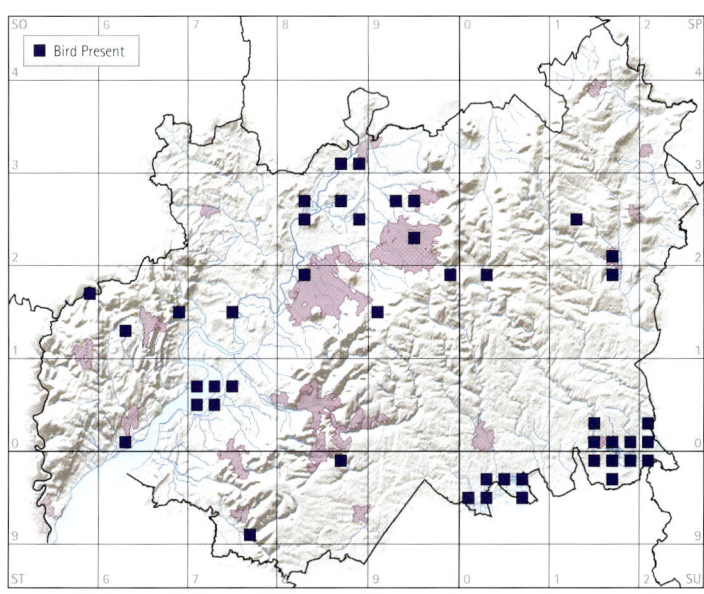

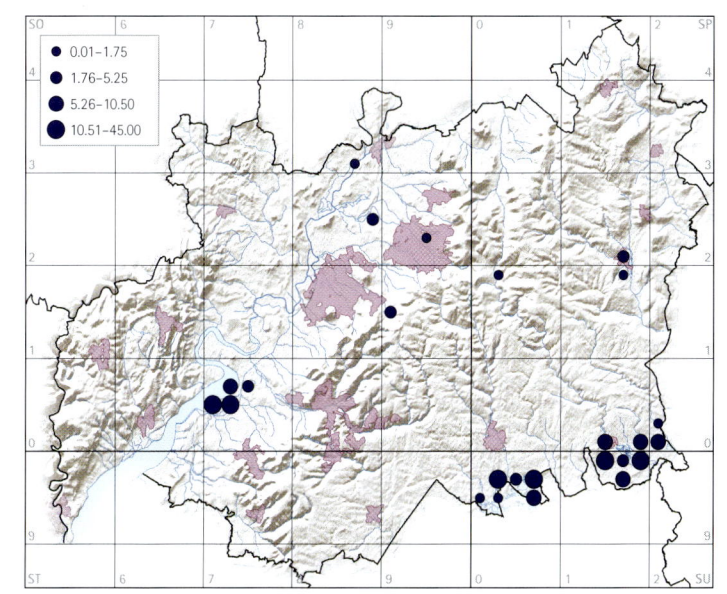

Winter Distribution

Winter Abundance

Tufted Duck
Aythya fuligula

The Tufted Duck breeds across higher and middle latitudes of the Western Palearctic, north to Iceland, Fennoscandia and the Baltic, but most of the global population is centred further east, through Russia and Siberia to Japan. Western Palearctic birds winter south to the Mediterranean and the Black Sea; birds breeding in southern parts of Britain are generally resident, but are joined from October onwards by migrants from further north in the British Isles, Iceland, Fennoscandia, the Baltic and Russia.

Possibly due in part to the drying out of lakes in south-west Asia, the Tufted Duck began a rapid spread westwards during the nineteenth century, and breeding in Britain probably started in the 1830s. The species' spread was helped by the proliferation of the zebra mussel, a major food item that was inadvertently released into London docks in 1824. Subsequent increases in the extent of artificial waters and the species' tolerance of people enabled it to further extend its range, and numbers rose from fewer than 5,000 breeding pairs in 1972 to about 11,000 by the end of the twentieth century. This is by far the commonest diving duck in Britain at all seasons. Winter totals here have almost doubled to 110,000 since 1985 and continue to rise slowly. However, other parts of northern Europe are seeing a decline, and as a result the species was amber listed in 2008.

Tufted Ducks will breed in most freshwater habitats below 400 m in altitude, with the nest usually concealed in vegetation within 10 m of the water's edge. Laying may not start until mid-May and breeding is most readily confirmed by the presence of juveniles, which are often not seen until July or even later, so some may have been missed during the atlas fieldwork.

In Gloucestershire, Mellersh makes an undated reference to a pair breeding on 'a beautiful clear pond lying high on the [Cotswold] hills.' Breeding was first confirmed in the twentieth century at Frampton in 1959, but by the late 1970s there were still no more than eight pairs regularly nesting there, and with poor success. In the Cotswold Water Park, from nesting 'firsts' at Fairford in 1960 and Lechlade three years later, there was an increase to 63 confirmed breeding pairs in 2007, with a similar number classified as potential breeders. The current maps and fact-box highlight a surprisingly wide distribution across the county, with records in 50% more 10 km squares than in 1988–91. By no means restricted to the larger waterbodies, breeding sites include well-vegetated stretches of canal in the Severn Vale as well as smaller ponds and rivers in the Forest of Dean and the Cotswolds.

In winter Tufted Ducks tend to concentrate onto fewer sites in the county, as shown by the map; during the current atlas fieldwork they were seen at almost twice as many tetrads in summer as in winter. At Slimbridge, winter counts revealed about 100 birds in the 1950s, 300 by the end of the 1960s and 500 in the 1980s, but totals have not risen a great deal since then. In the Water Park, from a few dozen in the 1950s, winter numbers have been reaching four figures since the late 1970s. The western section, including pits in Wiltshire, has become a site of national importance, with an average peak count of 1,362 birds over the five winters up to 2009–10.

Quite large numbers of Tufted Ducks have been caught for ringing in Gloucestershire. As a result there have been 37 recoveries between here and other counties in the British Isles, as distant as Strathclyde and Tayside, and 38 foreign recoveries, mainly in a broad arc extending from north France through the Netherlands, Germany, Poland and Fennoscandia to Russia, plus one in Iceland. These movements are in accordance with the origins and migration routes of the British wintering population. In addition, three foreign-ringed birds have been found here: two from Denmark and, less typically, one ringed in north-west Portugal in late November 2005 that was seen alive near Fairford at the end of June 2007, indicating that it was a bird from the local breeding population that had emigrated for the winter.

Sponsored by Oscar & Andrew Wilkie

Species accounts

2007–11 Atlas fieldwork					Gloucestershire trends						UK population trends		
Number of tetrads in which recorded (max 683)					Occupied 10 km squares (max 26)				% of tetrads in which recorded (1st hour of TTV)		UK conservation status: Amber 1	
	Total	Confirmed	Probable	Possible	Present	1968–71	1981–84	1988–91	2007–11	1988–91	2008–11	Long term	Short term
Breeding	162	65	64	19	14	5		16	24	7.7	9.4	+104%	+47%
Winter	96						17		24			+16%	−13%

Breeding Distribution

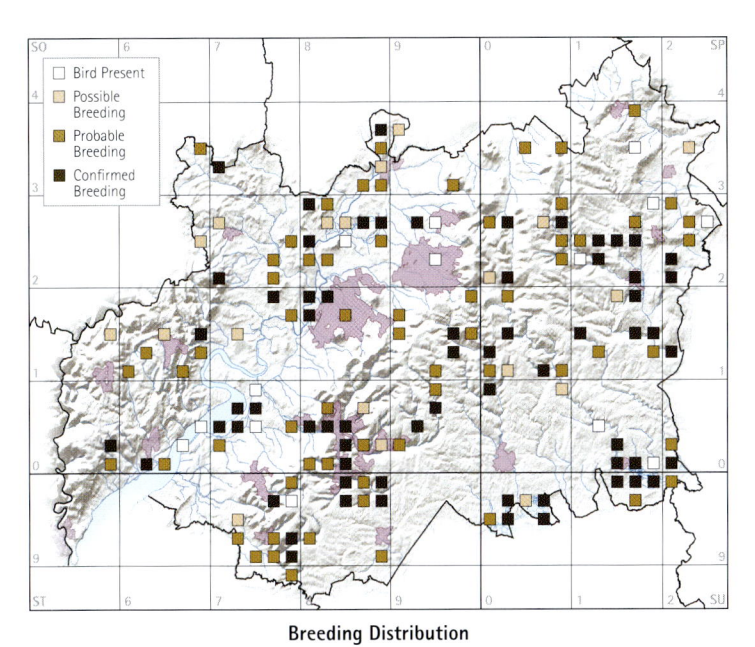

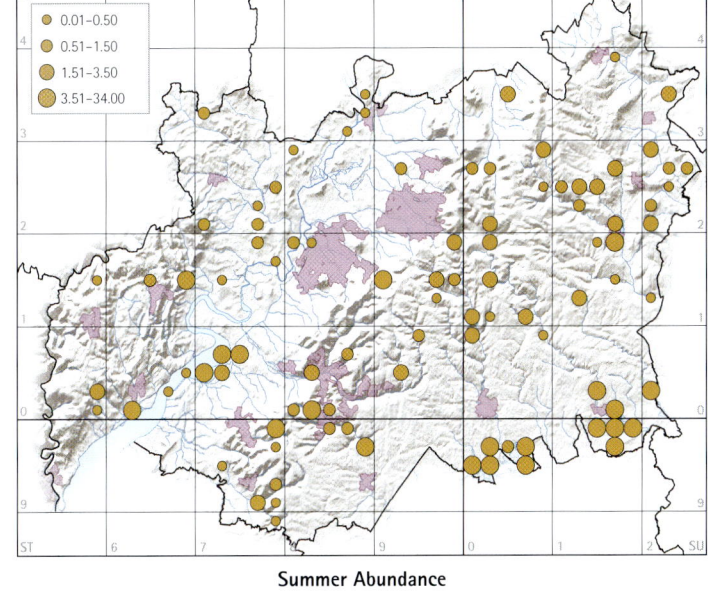

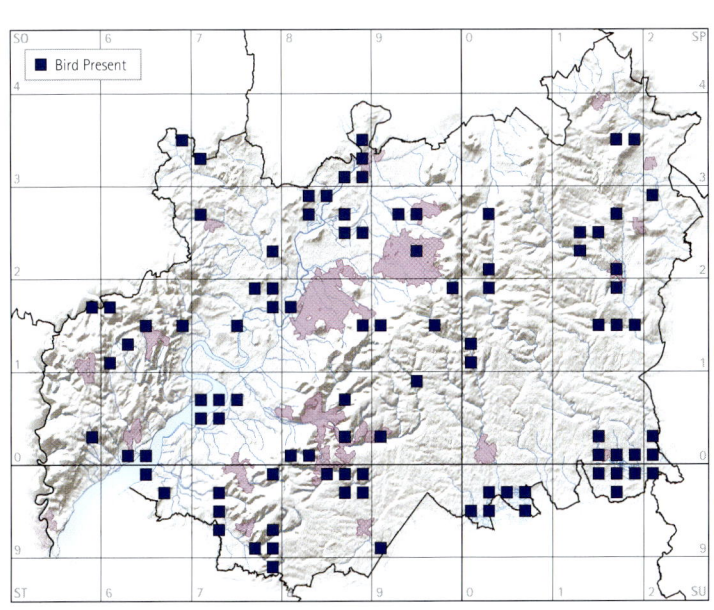

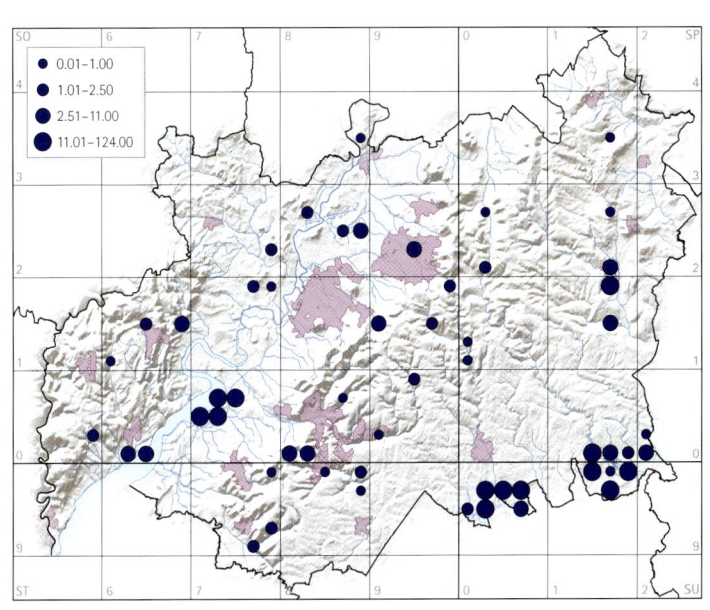

Summer Abundance

Winter Distribution

Winter Abundance

Scaup (Greater Scaup)
Aythya marila

Scaup have a circumpolar breeding distribution in Europe, Asia and North America, chiefly occupying lower arctic latitudes; in Europe they breed in Iceland, northern Fennoscandia and Russia. This is Britain's rarest breeding duck, nesting less than annually and with no regular sites. Scaup are largely coastal in winter, feeding on mussel beds, and European breeders winter mainly in the western Baltic and the Netherlands but also in other areas including the British Isles. Here they occur mainly in the north, especially in estuaries on the east coast of Scotland, and south-west England is one of their least favoured areas (1981–84 Wintering Atlas). When it was still common practice in Scotland to discharge waste grain from breweries and distilleries though sewage outfalls, Scaup were attracted to such areas, which provided a ready food supply.

In Gloucestershire, Swaine described the Scaup as 'a winter visitor occurring almost annually in small numbers', and that still holds true today. They have been seen in the county in all but three years since 1980, but usually in low numbers, with an average of around five birds per year (see top graph). Most records are from November to March (see bottom graph), but with a scattering of sightings in all other months except August.

Scaup have been found at a surprisingly wide range of waterbodies in the county. Many reports are from the Frampton–Slimbridge area and other sites along the estuary, but they have been seen at the Cotswold Water Park and other 'inland' lakes and also, unexpectedly, on quite small ponds at the landfill sites at Gloucester and Stoke Orchard; it seems that most waterbodies are potential sites for this species. Some have been quite long-staying: for example a first-winter male commuted between Huntsman's Quarry (near Stow-on-the-Wold) and Bourton pits from December 3rd 2000 until April 28th 2001.

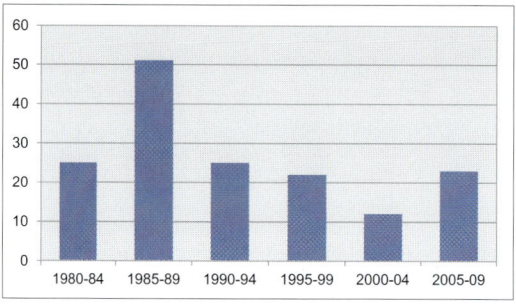

Scaup numbers, 1980–2009.

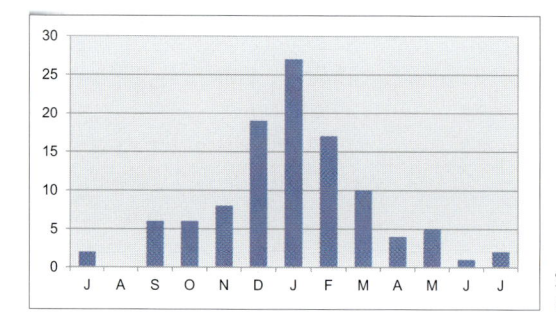

Scaup records by month, 1980–2010.

Ring-necked Duck
Aythya collaris

The New World equivalent of the Tufted Duck breeds across southern Canada and the northern USA, wintering in the southern USA, Central America and the Caribbean.

The 15 county records are all of single birds and almost all males, with 11 in spring (March to May). The first was at Slimbridge from March 12th to 14th 1955, and was the first accepted record for Europe. The second was also at Slimbridge, on March 1st 1977. This bird was caught and ringed and subsequently recovered in south-east Greenland on May 23rd of the same year, evidently attempting to return across the Atlantic. There were three records in 1978 and 1979 from the Cotswold Water Park, and four in the 1980s from four different locations: Flaxley Pool (1984), Witcombe reservoir (1985), Frampton sailing lake (1988), and Bourton pits (1988). The Frampton bird was the first female recorded in the county. There was then a gap until 2000, since when there have been six records, all in the Slimbridge area: in 2000, 2001, 2002, 2006, 2007 and 2010. The 2006 bird was also seen at Mythe Pools near Tewkesbury two days after being recorded at Slimbridge.

Ferruginous Duck
Aythya nyroca

Classified as 'Near-threatened' by the International Union for Conservation of Nature, Ferruginous Ducks have a fragmented breeding distribution from eastern Europe to western Mongolia, and also in a few restricted outlying areas in western Mediterranean countries. Numbers have decreased significantly across their range, probably mainly due to the drainage of wetlands. Ferruginous Ducks are commonly kept in wildfowl collections, and many British records are undoubtedly escapes; this may well also be true of some of the 11 Gloucestershire records. The first sighting in the county was on December 21st 1955 at South Cerney Pit (Cotswold Water Park), and another was recorded in the Water Park in 1957. The next record was not until December 23rd 1978, when an immature male was at Frampton Court Lake. This was followed by a different bird at Dowdeswell reservoir from January 6th to 14th 1979. A bird seen in both 1980 and 1981 in the Water Park was thought likely to be an escape. Subsequent sightings came in 1987, 1993, 1994, 1999 and 2002; three were from the Water Park, the 1993 record (a pair) was from Bourton pits, and the last one was at Slimbridge, where it was established that it was not from the WWT collection. In total, ten of the 11 county records have been during the period from December to March, and all except one have been of single birds.

Lesser Scaup
Aythya affinis

The Lesser Scaup breeds in Canada and in western parts of the USA, wintering in the southern USA and parts of northern South America. Formerly considered to be an extremely rare vagrant to Europe, it has been recorded more frequently here in recent years. It is impossible to know to what extent this is due to a real increase in occurrences on this side of the Atlantic or to improvements in identification skills and optical equipment. There are five county records:

1994: a male in the eastern section of the Cotswold Water Park from November 10th until December 28th.
2007: a male in the western section of the Water Park from February 18th to 20th.
2008: an immature male at Lydney Lakes from October 31st until November 15th and at Frampton Court Lake from November 22nd until December 5th.
2010: a first-winter female at Slimbridge from December 27th until May 12th 2011.
2011: a female at Slimbridge from December 13th to April 6th 2012, quite probably the same 2010 bird.

Common Scoter
Melanitta nigra

Common Scoters breed across northern Eurasia, mainly in the tundra zone and usually nesting well inland. Very small numbers also breed in northern Scotland. All populations are migratory and in winter this is a predominantly marine species, with a liking for sandy bays. British waters receive wintering birds from breeding areas such as Iceland and Fennoscandia, and also hold fairly large numbers of non-breeders throughout the year. These non-breeding birds are joined by moulting birds from midsummer onwards, when they form large flocks. The largest winter concentrations are off the coasts of Wales, north-west England, north Norfolk and eastern Scotland. Carmarthen Bay is of international importance for the species, regularly holding 20,000 birds (Kershaw & Cranswick 2003).

Mellersh mentioned very few records of this species, but Swaine noted that although it had been very irregular in the past, it had become an almost annual visitor to Gloucestershire by 1980. Since then, there have been records in every year except 1999. The seasonal pattern (see graph) is perhaps surprising for a bird often thought of as a winter visitor; the most likely months to see a Common Scoter in the county are July and August. In all probability these birds are involved in the moult-related movements mentioned above, perhaps associated with the Welsh sites. There is a noticeable preponderance of males in these summer records; it is known that males form flocks earlier in the year than females (BWP). The peaks later in autumn and in spring probably involve migrants en route between their breeding and wintering grounds.

The vast majority of county sightings involve small numbers, often just one bird, and only on seven occasions since 1980 have more than ten birds been seen together. Six of these were between June and August, involving groups of between 13 and 26 birds. The seventh was an exceptionally large flock: 98 birds settled on the Severn near Slimbridge 'during bad weather' on April 2nd 2002.

Not surprisingly for a sea-duck almost all sightings are from the estuary, and quite a few involve birds drifting upriver on the flooding tide. Two notable exceptions to this are a lone bird dabbling in shallow water with Wigeon at Walmore Common on November 16th 1998, and a group of 15 at Dowdeswell reservoir on June 14th 2000.

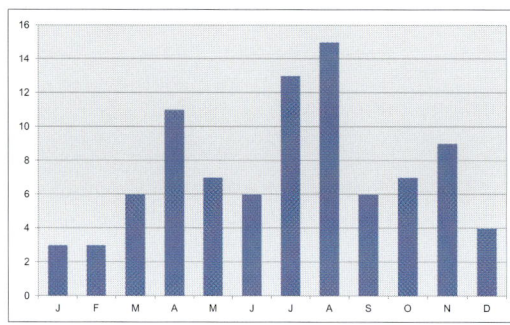

Common Scoter records by month, 1980–2010.

Velvet Scoter
Melanitta fusca

Western Palearctic Velvet Scoters breed on the coasts of the Baltic Sea and the Arctic Ocean, and inland across northern latitudes. Most of these birds winter in the southern and eastern Baltic, in general not moving as far south as Common Scoters, but about 3,000 winter at a small number of traditional sites on the east coast of Britain; they are much rarer in the west. There are four county records from modern times; several older records have never been corroborated.

1986: three flew over floodwater at Walmore Common on January 1st.
1987: a juvenile male was found grounded in a car park in Gloucester city centre on January 24th. It was cared for by WWT staff at Slimbridge and later released.
1989: a female at Frampton sailing lake from January 22nd until February 26th.
1993: a female was with nine Common Scoters in the Cotswold Water Park on November 17th.

Eider (Common Eider)
Somateria mollissima

Eiders are almost entirely coastal throughout the year, and apart from leaving the high Arctic do not make regular migratory movements; they are partial or dispersive migrants. They enjoy an almost circumpolar range, and have increased in the UK, with their range expanding southwards.

There have been 16 Gloucestershire records involving 88 birds, mostly from the Severn Estuary and particularly the Slimbridge area. Twelve of the 16 were between August and December and three in April and May, suggesting passage rather than wintering, and most sightings have been brief. The first record was of two males shot at Witcombe reservoir on an unknown date. The first modern record was on November 28th 1965, when a bird described as a female or immature male was at Bourton pits for seven days, and the second was in 1969. There were no records in the 1970s, but the 1980s produced four, including the longest-staying bird, a juvenile male at Dowdeswell reservoir from December 28th 1985 until January 18th 1986. In the 1990s there were three records, including counts of 18 and 19 at Slimbridge in 1993 and 1997 respectively. Since then, 2001 brought three sightings and there were single birds in 2004, 2008 (a moribund bird near Slimbridge) and 2010.

Long-tailed Duck
Clangula hyemalis

Long-tailed Ducks have a circumpolar distribution and breed in huge numbers, with a range including Iceland, Fennoscandia and the northernmost parts of Eurasia, and from Alaska to Labrador and Greenland. Most European breeders migrate to the Baltic but about 10,000 winter off the British Isles, mainly in the north-east. Surveys of the wintering population in the Baltic Sea indicate that the species has undergone a precipitous decline there, from over four million individuals in 1992–93 to less than 1.5 million in 2007–09 (Skov *et al.* 2011).

Gloucestershire records reflect the fact that this is a rare duck inland. Swaine referred to a few early records, and noted about 20 between 1950 and 1980. Since then, there have been sightings in six years in the 1980s, eight in the 1990s and just four since 2000, the most recent being on April 1st and 2nd 2011. In the first winter period of 1989 during a widespread influx into the country, six different birds were seen, including three together in early February in the eastern section of the Cotswold Water Park. Otherwise nearly all county records are of singles.

About half of all birds were first seen in November, although perhaps surprisingly there are records from all months except June, August and September. About half of the sightings have come from the Water Park and about half from the Severn Estuary and Vale, where they have been seen on Frampton Pools and the Gloucester and Sharpness Canal as well as around Slimbridge. Although some birds have stayed for one day only, it is not unusual for individuals to remain for several weeks.

Goldeneye (Common Goldeneye)
Bucephala clangula

Goldeneye breed widely across northern Eurasia and North America, mainly in the boreal coniferous forest zone. Natural nests are nearly always in holes in trees with easy access to a lake, pond or river, and if there is a shortage of holes this can lead to competition for sites. However Goldeneye will readily move into nest-boxes, and in some countries boxes have been in use for more than three centuries. North-west European breeding populations winter mainly in western Europe, south to Mediterranean France.

The first British breeding record was in Scotland in 1970. With the provision of nest-boxes, numbers increased to about 200 pairs by 2009, and breeding was confirmed south of the border for the first time in 2008, when a pair nested in Avon. The species is amber listed in the UK for its small breeding population and, in England and Wales at least, Goldeneye are far better known as winter visitors, mostly from Fennoscandia. Females tend to winter further south and west than the males, and over 70% of those wintering in Britain are 'morillons', an ancient wildfowling term for female and immature Goldeneye, which were widely thought at the time to be a different species from the male (Bannerman 1958). Our winter population mostly arrives in November and leaves in February and March. The Goldeneye was long considered to be a coastal species and many of England's largest counts come from sheltered bays and estuaries, but inland freshwater sites are also readily used. Such broad tastes in habitats meant that during the 1981–84 Wintering Atlas survey it was the fourth most widespread duck after Mallard, Teal and Tufted Duck. However, winter numbers in Britain are much lower than for many other wildfowl. Numbers rose from 10,000–12,000 in 1970 to 32,000 in the late 1990s (of a total in western Europe of 300,000) but have since decreased to 20,000, as birds have stayed further north in the milder winters.

Historically, Goldeneye in Gloucestershire were concentrated in the Severn Vale. In the decoys of the Berkeley Estate in the late nineteenth century it was the fourth commonest winter duck after Mallard, Teal and Wigeon. The centre of attraction then moved to Frampton Pools, which were greatly extended early in the twentieth century, but the Cotswold Water Park has been the prime site in the county since the mid-1970s, when counts of 40–50 birds became regular there. With an ever-increasing area of water, total numbers now regularly reach nationally important peaks of over 200 birds across the Water Park as a whole. Wintering Goldeneye tend not to form large flocks, and this is reflected in the fact that that highest count in a TTV during the current atlas fieldwork was only ten, in SU19Z in the eastern section of the Water Park, in January 2009.

As implied by the map, away from the Frampton area and the Water Park there are records from only a handful of other places each year, mainly the Cotswold reservoirs and along the river Severn.

Sponsored by the Cheltenham Bird Club

Species accounts

2007–11 Atlas fieldwork						Gloucestershire trends						UK population trends	
Number of tetrads in which recorded (max 683)					Occupied 10 km squares (max 26)				% of tetrads in which recorded (1st hour of TTV)		UK conservation status: Amber 6	
	Total	Confirmed	Probable	Possible	Present	1968–71	1981–84	1988–91	2007–11	1988–91	2008–11	Long term	Short term
Breeding	4	0	0	0	4	0		0	0	0	0	–	–
Winter	24							8		9		–17%	–41%

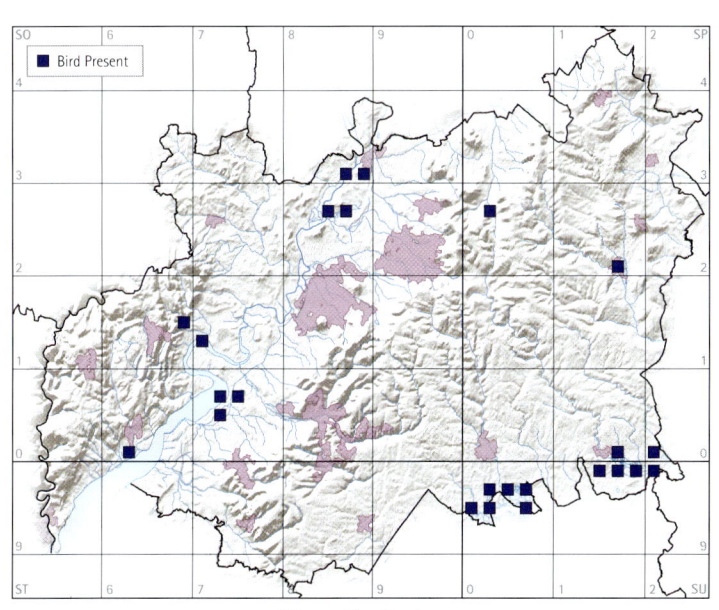

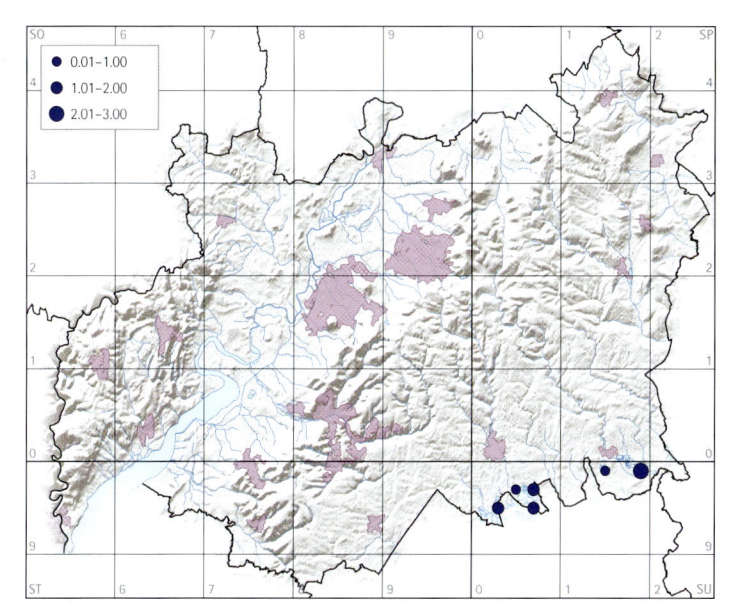

Winter Distribution

Winter Abundance

Smew
Mergellus albellus

Nesting in tree-holes in the boreal zone, mainly south of the Arctic Circle, Smew breed from northern Fennoscandia east to Kamchatka, with a European population of just a few thousand pairs. Western breeders winter mainly in the west Baltic and the Netherlands, and in Britain Smew are mostly restricted to south-east England. With only about 300 occurring here in an average winter (although many more can appear if Dutch waters freeze), this is a sought-after species, especially the adult males with their very striking 'cracked-ice' appearance.

In 1902 Mellersh simply reported '10 recorded killed since 1880, Severn', suggesting that Smew were at least reasonably regular then, but Swaine wrote that 'since 1954 ... reports have been much more frequent'. Since the 1980s there has been a rapid increase in numbers, though with a recent tendency to decline. These more recent decreases have also taken place elsewhere in England, and are presumably linked to the increasing numbers wintering in Sweden and the Czech Republic (WeBS).

Most Gloucestershire records come from the Cotswold Water Park, and the graph shows the highest WeBS counts each year for those Water Park lakes which are wholly in Gloucestershire. Smew are very mobile, making them difficult to count where there are many lakes, but these simultaneous counts provide an absolute minimum figure for the total number of birds present each winter. They evidently prefer the western section of the Water Park, which extends into Wiltshire; this has become the second most important site in the country for the species (WeBS).

Away from the Water Park small numbers, often single birds, are seen in the Frampton–Slimbridge area in most years, and one female is thought to have returned there for five winters in succession, feeding in the same outlet ditch. She was last seen in 1999 on the very late date of April 28th, but did not return in the following winter. It is extremely unusual for Smew to be recorded outside the December to March period in Gloucestershire, and peak numbers usually occur in January.

They also occasionally turn up on other waterbodies, even on rivers if lakes are frozen, and an exceptional 14 birds were on the river Avon at Twyning in January 1985.

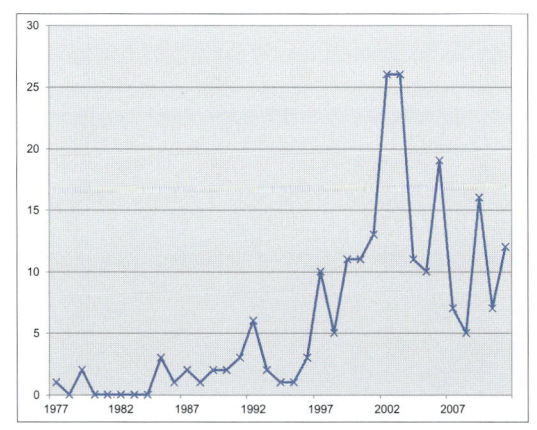

Smew: highest WeBS counts in the Cotswold Water Park (Gloucestershire lakes), 1977–2011 (note that '1977' means winter 1976–77).

Red-breasted Merganser
Mergus serrator

Red-breasted Mergansers breed across northern parts of Eurasia and North America, and in Iceland and Greenland. They nest widely in Scotland and spread south in the twentieth century, reaching England in 1950 and Wales in 1953. In winter they are almost exclusively coastal, unlike Goosanders, and in Britain they are a fairly common sight offshore during that season. These birds are likely to be a mixture of British breeders, which are thought to be partial migrants, and visitors from central Europe, Iceland and Greenland, where they are wholly migratory.

Swaine noted that 'since 1960, birds have occurred in most years' in Gloucestershire, and this is still the case, with only three blank years since 1980. Almost all sightings involve just one or two birds; since 1980 there have only been five reports of more than two birds together, the most being a group of five on the Severn at Tewkesbury during cold weather in January 1997.

The majority of sightings are along the estuary (the closest approximation to 'coast' in Gloucestershire), particularly the well-watched Frampton–Slimbridge area, but there have also been a number at the Cotswold Water Park. Red-breasted Mergansers are less likely than many other wildfowl to appear elsewhere in the county; the only other locations reported since 1980 are the river Severn near Wainlode (in January 1985, January 1987 and February 1993), Bourton pits (October 1993) and Abbey Grounds Lake, Cirencester (December 1999).

As the graph shows, Red-breasted Mergansers have been recorded in nine months of the year, with a noticeable peak in January. The next highest totals are in October and April, suggesting that many of the birds seen in Gloucestershire are on passage to and from southern coasts rather than winter visitors; this is supported by the fact that very few Red-breasted Mergansers stay long in the county.

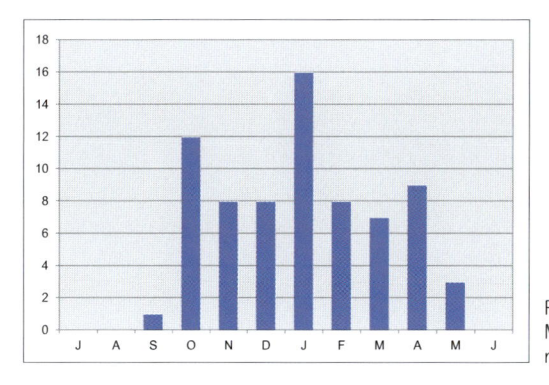

Red-breasted Merganser records by month, 1980–2010.

Goosander (Common Merganser)
Mergus merganser

Goosanders breed throughout the temperate and boreal zones of north and central Eurasia and northern North America, and Western Palearctic birds winter south to the Mediterranean, Caspian and Black Seas. They nest in tree-holes, crevices, hollows and artificial boxes and will use a range of different waterbodies from lakes to fast-flowing rivers, provided there is not so much vegetation that catching fish becomes difficult.

Goosanders were first proved to breed in Britain in 1871, in Perthshire. They subsequently spread steadily, northward at first and then, in the 1940s, southward into southern Scotland and northern England. There were still fewer than 1,000 pairs in 1970, but between the 1968–72 and 1988–91 Breeding Atlases the population not only consolidated in northern England but also colonised Wales (in force) and south-west England (sparsely), bringing the total number of breeding pairs to 2,700. Since then they have continued to increase, to between 3,000 and 3,500 pairs by the end of the twentieth century, compared with a European population of approaching 75,000 pairs.

While some drakes moult in the Beauly Firth in Scotland, it has recently become clear that most fly to northern Norway to do so, leaving the females to incubate the eggs and moult in Britain. However, the males return here for the winter, along with visitors from northern Scandinavia, the Baltic and parts of Russia. These birds arrive in November and leave again in March. Winter numbers in Britain increased from about 5,000 in 1980 to 9,000 in 1995 (while numbers in Europe tripled to almost 300,000 birds), but more recently there has been a decline, from 16,000 at the start of the twenty-first century to 12,000 in 2010.

Since the 1980s they have bred regularly in the Wye catchment in Herefordshire and occasionally in Somerset and Devon, but in Gloucestershire at present the Goosander is known only as a non-breeding visitor, mainly between December and February. Mellersh stated that one or two were to be found in most winters in the Severn Vale and, whilst Swaine implies that they were less frequent in the early twentieth century, they became annual again after 1956, often on the river north of Gloucester. One to five birds is the usual total here, so 14 in 1963 and 16 in 1979, during cold snaps, were noteworthy counts. Single-figure flocks also visit Witcombe and Dowdeswell reservoirs, so again 18 seen on Dowdeswell in the bumper year of 1979 was exceptional. There were few records from the Cotswold Water Park until 1970, when 16 birds were at Horcott and 20 at Dudgrove, and the species has been just about annual there since then, with double-figure counts on many of the lakes. In the Forest of Dean, Swaine mentions single reports from the Wye in 1963 and Cannop in 1973, but the Wye and the Forest ponds are now regular haunts, often hosting double-figure flocks. Indeed the maximum number recorded in the county during a TTV during the present atlas fieldwork was at Woorgreens Lake in the Dean, tetrad SO61G, where 22 were counted in December 2008. There are also frequent sightings of low numbers elsewhere in the county.

2007–11 Atlas fieldwork					Gloucestershire trends						UK population trends	
Number of tetrads in which recorded (max 683)					Occupied 10 km squares (max 26)				% of tetrads in which recorded (1st hour of TTV)		UK conservation status: Green	
Total	Confirmed	Probable	Possible	Present	1968–71	1981–84	1988–91	2007–11	1988–91	2008–11	Long term	Short term
Breeding												
7	0	1	0	6	0		0	1	0	0	–	–
Winter												
51						5		16			–21%	–42%

Sponsored by the Cheltenham Bird Club

Ruddy Duck
Oxyura jamaicensis

The Ruddy Duck is a localised breeding bird of North America and the West Indies. A number were brought to Slimbridge in the early days of the Wildfowl Trust and, although adults were pinioned, about 70 young birds flew free between 1956 and 1963. The first report of feral breeding in Britain came from Somerset in 1960, and the first for Gloucestershire in 1962. However, it was the West Midlands reservoirs and the Cheshire and Shropshire meres that quickly became their stronghold. The species was added to the official British list in 1971.

Ruddy Ducks commonly raise two broods per season, and also frequently practise brood parasitism or 'egg-dumping', laying their eggs in the nests of Tufted Ducks and Pochard. As a result, the feral population multiplied rapidly, with numbers increasing by 25% per year between 1965 and 1975 to a total of almost 60 pairs. During the 1988–91 Breeding Atlas fieldwork period alone, the number of breeding pairs increased from under 400 to 570, with the species now common throughout the Midlands and northern England.

Whilst Ruddy Ducks are migratory in their natural range, British birds move only short distances. Winter flocks, which are often found on larger waters than those used for breeding, build up from September to December and disperse in March and April. Winter numbers in Britain grew rapidly from 1960, in line with the increasing breeding population, to reach over 3,400 by 1991. Unfortunately by then the species had also been found in a dozen or more other European countries, including Spain, where in 1991 a hybrid with the indigenous and already endangered White-headed Duck *Oxyura leucocephala* was seen. This raised the level of concern for the future of the native species, so the WWT and others reviewed potential control measures and an eradication programme was begun. The breeding population of Ruddy Ducks in Britain probably peaked in 1994 at 660 pairs, but subsequently thousands have been shot and recent estimates suggest that as few as 100 birds may remain.

In Gloucestershire, breeding presumably by recently escaped birds took place occasionally at Frampton and Slimbridge from 1962 onwards, but success rates were low. Swaine commented in 1980 that 'a feral population is showing some signs of becoming established in the county', but even by 1986 the GBR could state that breeding was rarely confirmed here. Two years later came the first suspected breeding in the Cotswold Water Park, where it apparently became regular but was rarely reported, so numbers involved are hard to assess. Breeding was also confirmed occasionally at Bourton pits from 1991 onwards.

The western section of the Water Park became the county's prime site for wintering birds, with a mean maximum count of 111 birds for the five winters up to 2004–05. The following five years saw the average peak reduced to just 32 and, with a maximum of just eight individuals in winter 2009–10, the species looks set to disappear from the county, albeit by design.

Red-legged Partridge
Alectoris chukar

The natural range of the Red-legged Partridge is restricted to south-west Europe, where it is currently contracting towards the south-west. Its habitat requirements are similar to those of the Grey Partridge but it tends to prefer areas with drier and lighter soils, for example chalk downland and even coastal bare ground. In Britain, birds of the nominate race from France and north-west Italy have been repeatedly introduced for shooting since the eighteenth century. The first successful introduction, in Suffolk in 1770, resulted in a self-supporting population which spread as far as Somerset, Shropshire and North Yorkshire by about 1930. This was probably the widest distribution attained by the species in Britain. The range then contracted until about 1959, after which numbers again began to grow substantially, especially in Norfolk. However, the vast majority of Red-legs, especially outside East Anglia and certainly in west and south-west England, are captive-bred birds, and many attempted introductions in the west and north have failed, quite probably because the climate is simply too wet.

Red-legged Partridges are considered to be a second-rate quarry compared to the indigenous Greys: they tend to run rather than fly, and present a poor target when they do take wing; they also apparently have an inferior flavour. It is, therefore, rather surprising that as many as 6.5 million Red-legs are released here annually, compared with a mere 100,000 Greys. This is a huge increase on the 800,000 of 30 years ago, and equates to the entire wild population across the species' limited global range. However, even with the ability of pairs to incubate two clutches of eggs simultaneously, one by the cock and one by the hen (BWP), the British feral population, excluding the widely fluctuating stock of released birds, is evidently unable to increase beyond the current baseline estimate of about 136,000 summer territories. In fact, whilst it is very difficult to assess feral numbers when so many birds are released every summer only to be shot by the end of the next winter, estimates suggest that the self-supporting population has probably declined since 1985. On the other hand, one factor that will have acted to boost this population is the 1991 ban on introductions of the closely related Chukar *Alectoris graeca* and Red-leg x Chukar hybrids. It had been realised that the breeding output of hybrid pairs was only one-seventh of that of pairs of pure Red-legs, and that the effect of shooting on a mixed population would eventually be to drive the pure Red-legs to local extinction (Potts 1989). What is certain is that since about 1966 the Red-legged Partridge has outnumbered the rapidly declining Grey Partridge in Britain.

The species was local and rare in Gloucestershire until about 1865 when, as Mellersh stated, 'twenty brace' were released in the north of the county near Stow-on-the-Wold. They established a population which was still increasing in some parts of the Cotswolds at the end of the nineteenth century and was 'even extending its range almost down to the Severn' where it had been unknown five years previously. The 2003–07 Cotswolds Atlas reported an increase in occupancy to 28% of tetrads, compared with 14% two decades earlier. This was no doubt due partly to increased surveying effort, but mainly to the growing numbers of released birds. The current maps confirm that the densest concentrations are still to be found on the higher Cotswolds, with breeding widespread on the dip-slope across to the eastern county boundary. Swaine remarked that Red-legs were scarce south of a line from Cirencester to Slimbridge and this still holds true, presumably because releases here are more limited, but they do now occur in places on the high, flat arable farmland between Wotton-under-Edge and Tetbury. West of the Severn they are much more thinly distributed, with a few birds around the fringes of the Forest of Dean and a concentration along the western shore of the Severn Estuary near Lydney, where large numbers are released for shooting. Breeding further up the Severn Vale too is occasional and irregular.

As in other parts of the country, the feral population in Gloucestershire is almost certainly not self-sustaining and the species' continuing presence here is probably dependent on releases for shooting.

Species accounts

2007–11 Atlas fieldwork					Gloucestershire trends						UK population trends	
Number of tetrads in which recorded (max 683)					*Occupied 10 km squares (max 26)*				*% of tetrads in which recorded (1st hour of TTV)*		*UK conservation status:* **Introduced**	
	Total	Confirmed	Probable	Possible	Present	1968–71	1981–84	1988–91	2007–11	1988–91	2008–11	Long term	Short term
Breeding	397	27	244	86	40	17		22	26	13.8	27.6	−14%	+27%
Winter	305						18		26			–	–

Breeding Distribution

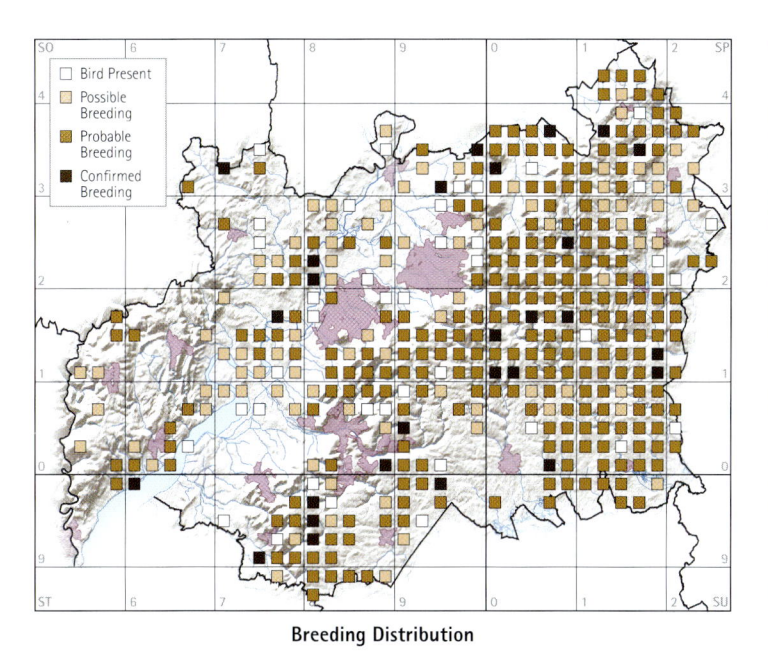

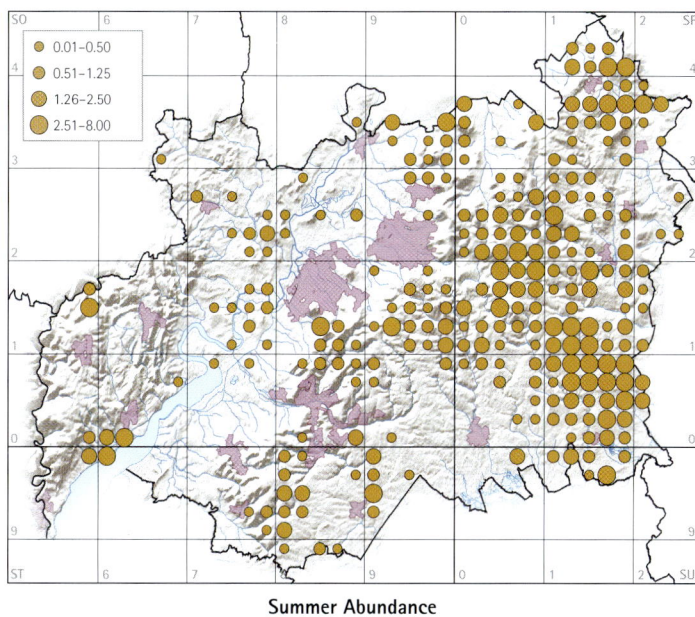

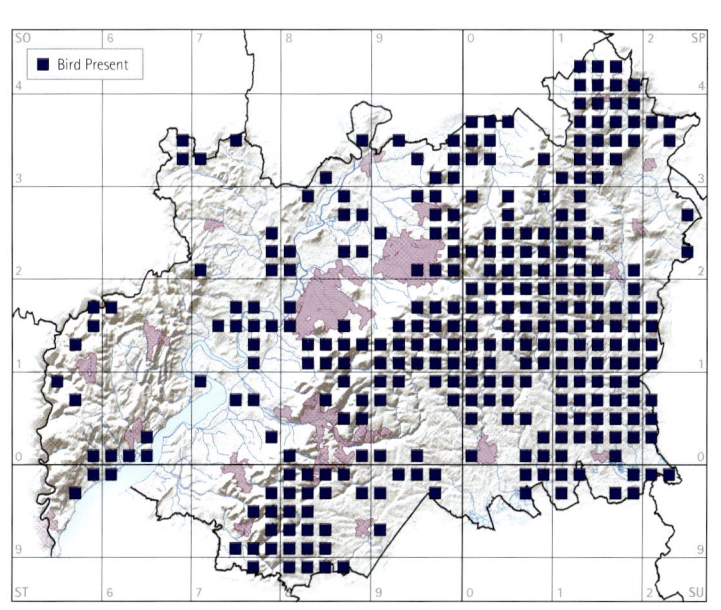

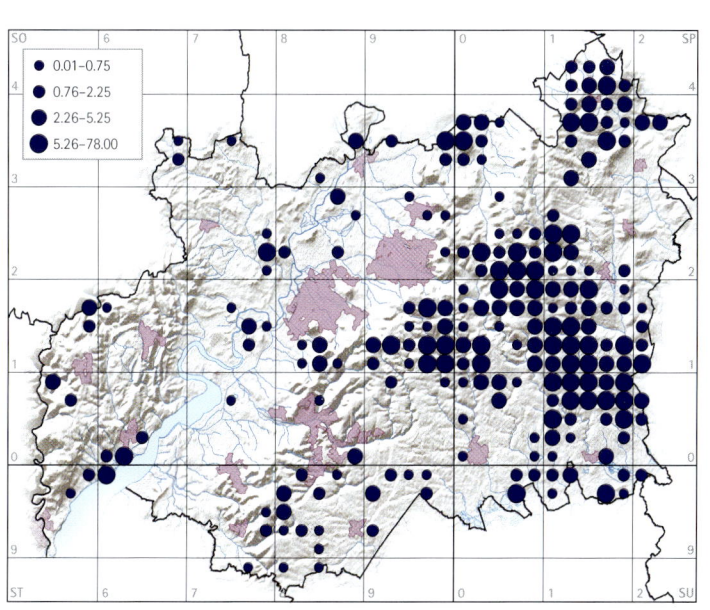

Summer Abundance

Winter Distribution

Winter Abundance

Grey Partridge
Perdix perdix

Grey Partridges are resident from northern Spain and Ireland across Europe to central Asia, and have also been introduced into North America. They were formerly widely known as 'English' Partridges, to distinguish them from the introduced Red-legged or 'French' Partridge, and the name is still sometimes heard today.

For feeding, Grey Partridges require bare ground within fairly low crops or grassland, but they also need taller, denser vegetation nearby for cover and nesting. In Britain today this effectively means agricultural land, but the Grey Partridge was formerly found on low moorland, heath, dunes and brecks. This is possibly the most sedentary of all our birds.

Across Europe, the Grey Partridge probably increased fourfold in the 100 years up to 1880, due to the spread of agriculture to formerly marginal areas; numbers in its natural range were at an all-time high between 1880 and 1914. It was found throughout Britain, except for the north and west of Scotland, and was the most numerous bird species on much farmland, especially in the east. Starting in the 1930s there was a noticeable decline, again largely due to changes in agricultural practices and also perhaps hastened by a run of mild, wet spring seasons. By 1962, the use of agricultural chemicals and the associated reduction in insect food meant that chick survival rates in the first six weeks of life had fallen below 30%, the critical level to maintain the population. So while the 1968–72 Breeding Atlas could state that, despite the long decline, the species 'still has a widespread and almost continuous distribution' through its former range, the 1988–91 Breeding Atlas recorded a retreat eastward of some 50 km over the country as a whole and a reduction in numbers of about 75%. This still left a population of 132,000 pairs, 88% of them in England, but the decline has continued unabated since then. In all, the twentieth century saw the loss of 5.5 million birds or 95% of the British and Irish population, leaving perhaps 75,000 pairs by 1999, with more recent estimates being no higher. The annual release of some 100,000 hand-reared birds in Britain provides no sustained boost to the natural population at all, whilst a new threat in the form of a parasitic infection passed on by Pheasants has recently been identified.

Grey Partridges were evidently so common in Gloucestershire at the turn of the twentieth century that Mellersh did not consider the species to be even worthy of a mention. Just 30 years ago, Swaine described it as 'a common resident and distributed over most of the county' despite a 'gradual decline in numbers'. The 1983–87 Cotswolds Atlas, covering the county's prime Partridge habitat, commented that the species was thought to be holding its own. This optimism was unfounded: 20 years later, the second Cotswolds Atlas reported a 60% decrease in tetrad records, which in reality, allowing for greater observer effort, probably closely reflected the 75% national decline. 'The medium-term future of the species as a regular Cotswolds breeding bird is under serious threat,' was the conclusion.

The current maps and figures serve only to reinforce this very pessimistic assessment and some observers believe that even the remnant population on the Cotswolds now derives from captive-bred birds, or at least depends upon them for its continuation. Only on the high wold and dip-slope can small and declining numbers be found and even here breeding was confirmed at few sites, towards the south of the area. Maximum TTV counts were of a mere ten birds in tetrad SP11Q near Aldsworth, north-east of Bibury in December 2009 (close to a known release site), and in SP00K to the east of Cirencester in July 2010. Away from the Cotswolds, the species has now effectively disappeared from Gloucestershire with the few isolated records undoubtedly relating to the short-lived presence of birds released for shooting.

Sponsored by Dr J W Bennett and Andrew Cleaver, and in memory of Mike Freeman

Species accounts

2007–11 Atlas fieldwork					Gloucestershire trends						UK population trends	
Number of tetrads in which recorded (max 683)					Occupied 10 km squares (max 26)				% of tetrads in which recorded (1st hour of TTV)		UK conservation status: **Red 3**	
	Total	Confirmed	Probable	Possible	Present	1968–71	1981–84	1988–91	2007–11	1988–91	2008–11	Long term	Short term
Breeding	69	8	24	15	22	26		22	13	10.3	1.9	–91%	–54%
Winter	60						20		15			–	–

Breeding Distribution

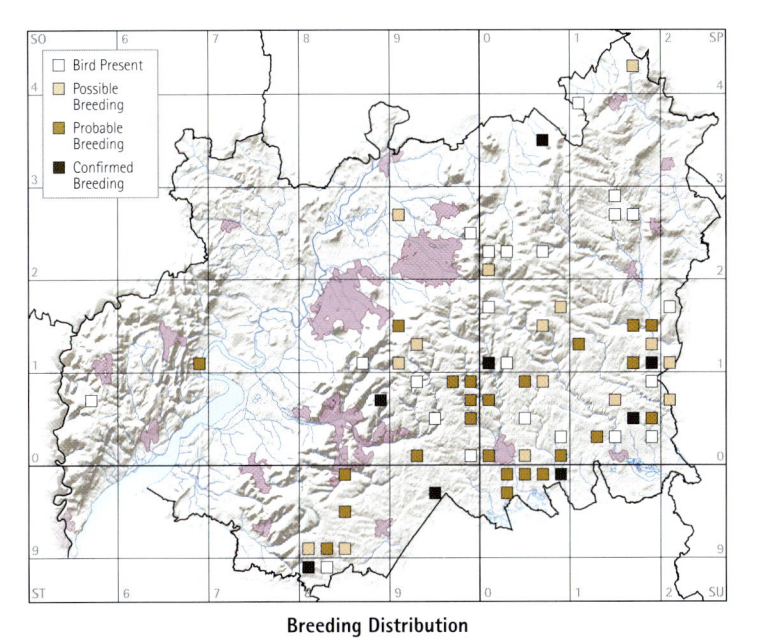

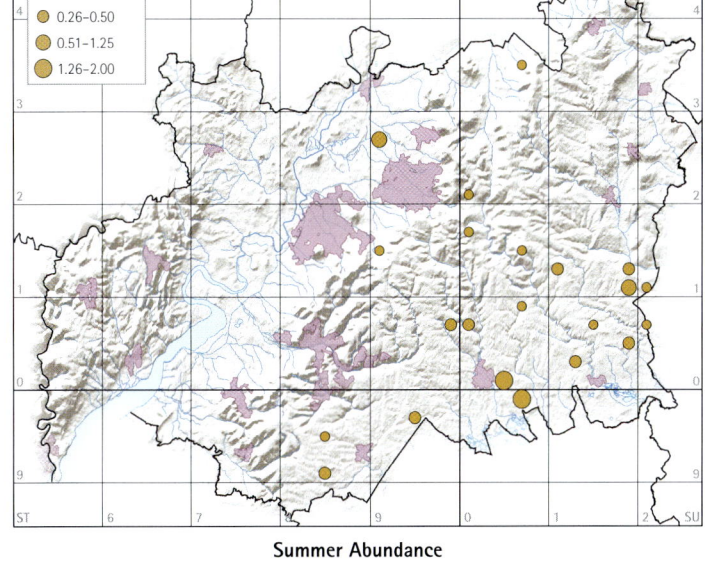

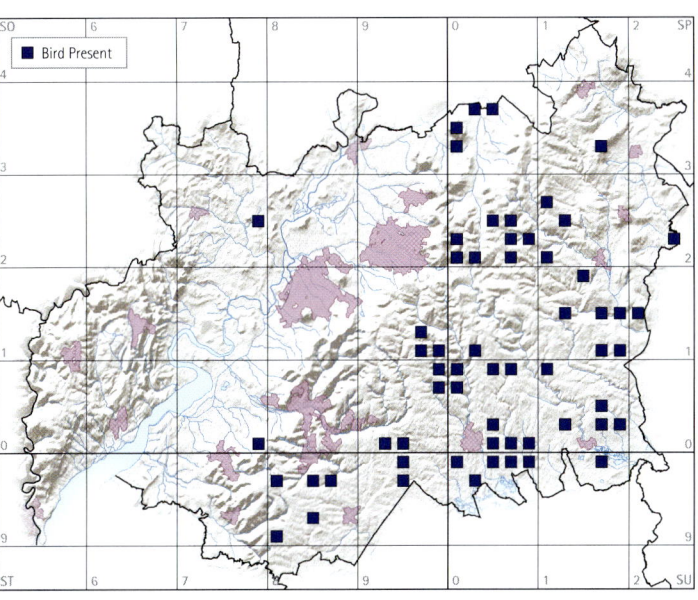

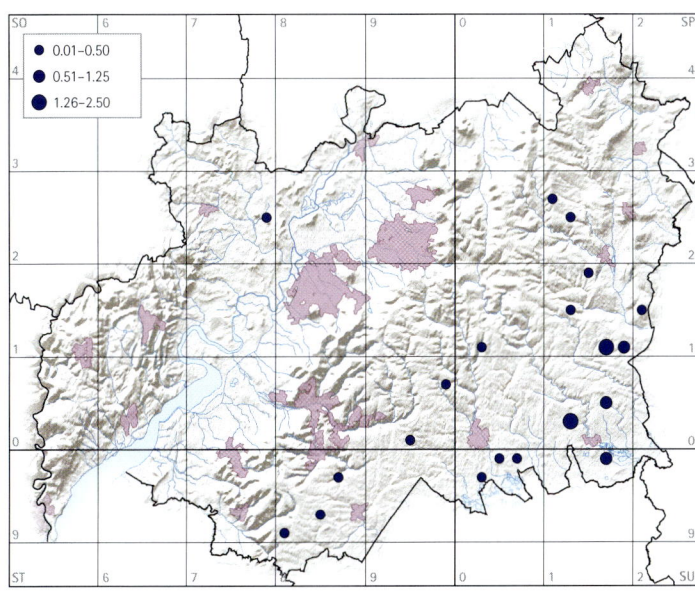

Summer Abundance

Winter Distribution

Winter Abundance

Pheasant (Common Pheasant)
Phasianus colchicus

The nominate race of the Pheasant was originally a bird of the south-central Palearctic, occurring naturally in Europe only in the northern Caucasus between the Caspian and Black Seas. It was introduced widely across Europe from Roman times and was certainly in Britain by the middle of the eleventh century. From the mid-eighteenth century other races were imported, most notably the 'Ring-necked' Pheasant *P. c. torquatus* of eastern Asia. Interbreeding quickly confused the mix and most Pheasants in Britain soon showed the white neck of *torquatus*, though Mellersh stated that individuals of the original and darker 'Common' (or 'Old English') Pheasant were to be found in Gloucestershire until about 1880.

In Britain, Pheasants avoid only high mountains and open moorland. They feed widely on cultivated land and in damp or waterside habitats, but need trees or scrub for shelter. They are susceptible to cold and wet weather, and being very sedentary will succumb rather than move far to escape severe conditions.

From the 1860s onwards game shooting became fashionable and had two immediate and long-lasting effects on the British countryside: the creation and assiduous management of artificial coverts often composed of alien plant species, which still account for much of the Pheasant's breeding habitat, and the captive rearing and release of stock to create a greater density than the birds could otherwise maintain. Anecdotally, the large numbers released 'eat everything in sight' and the full effect of this not inconsiderable alien biomass in the countryside has never been fully researched. Numbers of feral birds fell during the two world wars as active gamekeeping was interrupted and have fallen further due to agricultural intensification, although there has been little recent change in the national distribution apart from a slow expansion into parts of Scotland and Ireland. On the other hand, a staggering 35 million birds are released in Britain every year, of which perhaps 22 million fall to the gun, so it is no surprise that past population estimates have varied markedly between seasons. The 1988–91 Breeding Atlas estimated 3.1 million birds, and numbers have probably been stable or slightly higher since then. As the proportion of captive-reared birds in the wild increases, their poorer productivity means that the breeding output per female decreases in the population as a whole.

Swaine remarked that Pheasants were probably not common in Gloucestershire until well into the nineteenth century, but they have been gradually increasing since then and BBS results show that this trend continues (see graph on p. 49). The 2003–07 Cotswolds Atlas suggested that breeding success may have decreased over the preceding 20 years, although it is difficult to be certain because proof of 'wild' breeding can be hard to obtain and also because recorders have often been indifferent towards a species which is largely artificially maintained – although the two atlas fieldworkers who had to reschedule their survey visits because they found themselves in the middle of Pheasant shoots were probably not indifferent! Nevertheless, it is clear from the current maps that high numbers of Pheasants breed throughout Gloucestershire; they are completely absent only from towns and the most densely wooded parts of the Forest of Dean, and there is certainly a feral breeding population very much at large. Across the Cotswolds the effect of large-scale releases is clear, with a huge maximum TTV count of 700 birds in November 2008 in tetrad SP01C on the high wold, 10 km south-east of Cheltenham.

Sponsored by John & Sue Bolton

Species accounts

	2007–11 Atlas fieldwork					Gloucestershire trends						UK population trends	
	Number of tetrads in which recorded (max 683)					Occupied 10 km squares (max 26)				% of tetrads in which recorded (1st hour of TTV)		UK conservation status: **Introduced**	
	Total	Confirmed	Probable	Possible	Present	1968–71	1981–84	1988–91	2007–11	1988–91	2008–11	Long term	Short term
Breeding	643	85	335	192	31	26		26	26	71.0	78.9	+76%	+34%
Winter	639							26	26			–	–

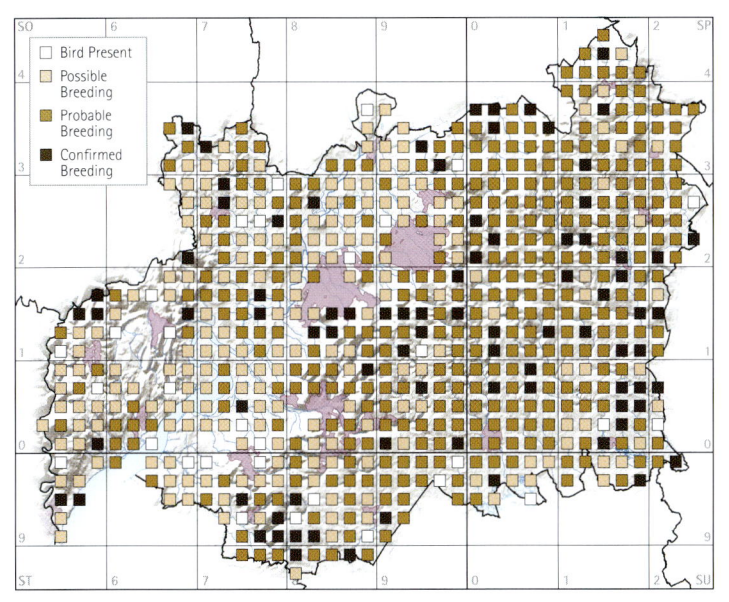

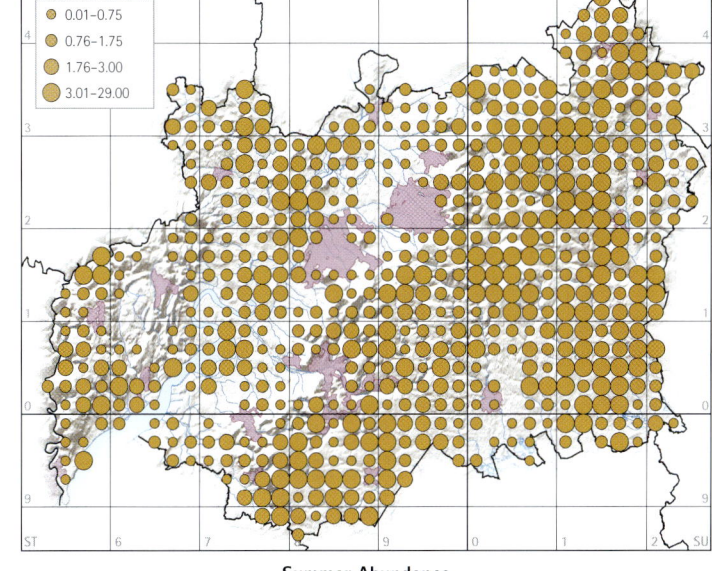

Breeding Distribution

Summer Abundance

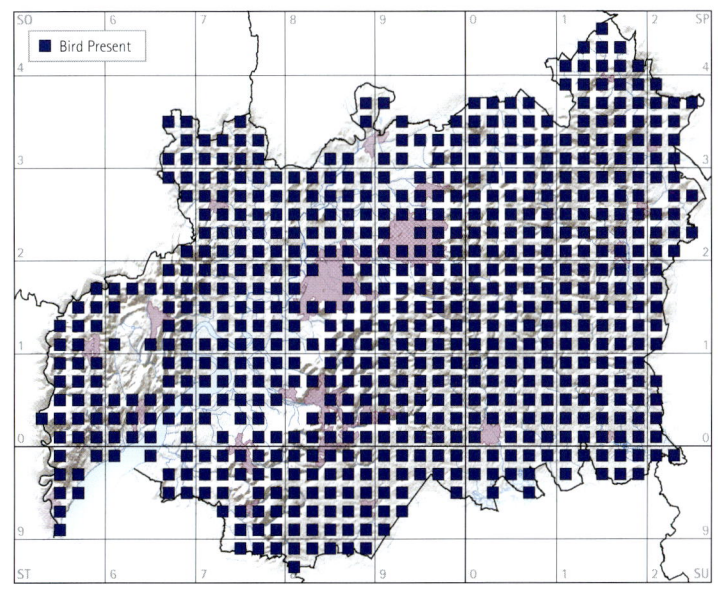

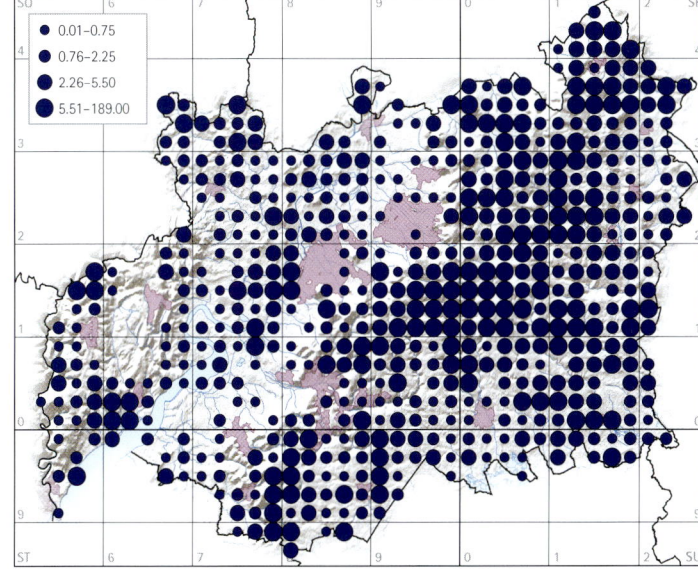

Winter Distribution

Winter Abundance

Quail (Common Quail)
Coturnix coturnix

The breeding range of the enigmatic and secretive Quail, Europe's only migratory gamebird, extends widely over Eurasia and parts of Africa. Quail used to breed further north in Europe but nowadays they only reach the southern shores of the North and Baltic Seas, so Britain is on the northern edge of the range. Western Palearctic birds winter mostly in Africa as far south as the equator but, since the 1960s, growing numbers have remained around the Mediterranean. With the decline in hunting in recent decades, the most serious current threat to the future of the Quail in Europe is possibly the release of captive-bred Japanese Quail *C. japonica* for shooting. This very closely related species threatens the genetic integrity of the indigenous species through interbreeding.

In Britain, Quail breed mainly in arable crops, although they also use hay fields and tussocky pastures, and unlike the Corncrake they may have benefited from the increased acreage under crops in recent decades. They are unique among European birds in that some young that fledge early in the year migrate further north and breed before the season ends (in the same way as some insects, for example painted lady butterflies). Arrivals in Britain from late April to early June are assumed to be part of this second migration, and it is fascinating to realise that many of the Quail we hear calling in the Gloucestershire fields were themselves hatched only a matter of weeks previously. The earliest reported arrival in the county was on April 20th, in 1987.

Wide annual variations in numbers are only part of the problem of assessing breeding populations. As the Migration Atlas pointed out, their status can only be estimated by the number of calling males, with nests and young being near-impossible to locate. They stop calling once they have found a mate, so reports of persistent calling imply that the males are remaining unpaired. Conversely, sporadic calling could suggest rapid pair-formation and widespread breeding. Between 1988 and 1998 the average number of calling males nationally was 532 (ranging from 107 to 1,655) but confirmed breeding records averaged just nine per year.

Given all these provisos, Quail numbers in Britain are thought to have declined to their lowest ebb by about 1865. From 1942, five years after restrictions were placed on the hunting of Quail in the Mediterranean region, numbers here began a slow increase which has continued, though with large fluctuations. Nowadays they breed in small numbers in many English counties, and the RBBP report for 2010 states that Wiltshire and Gloucestershire respectively held the second and third highest numbers of reported singing males in that year (after Yorkshire).

Swaine refers to an 1865 survey which confirmed that Quail were breeding regularly in Gloucestershire and were quite common, at least on the Cotswolds. Mellersh refers to '16 couple' killed at Ablington on one September day in 1862 and 50 eggs taken from a single field four years later. If this coincided with the lowest ebb of British populations, it says a great deal about numbers in Gloucestershire up to that point. Since then numbers in the county have evidently fluctuated just as much as they have nationally. Swaine wrote that between 1950 and 1980 'numbers have varied considerably', with some years entirely lacking in records (1955–60 and 1973–74). Almost all reports were from the Cotswolds which, as the map shows, is still true today. The most frequent habitat in the county is large cereal fields, but legumes, weedy set-aside and uncut meadows are also used, the latter especially in the Severn Vale. During the atlas period, 2008 and 2009 were both good 'Quail years' nationally, but they were overshadowed by an exceptional summer in 2011, when numbers were thought to be at least twice the average level, and this was reflected in Gloucestershire. Quail were recorded at 20–25 locations in the county in each of 2008 and 2009 but at about 50 in 2011, including a remarkable 11 birds near Windrush on August 5th. Hence the map shows the records from a Quail-rich four-year period that may not be typical; we should not overestimate the very patchy and variable distribution of the Quail in Gloucestershire.

Sponsored by the North Cotswold Ornithological Society

Species accounts

	2007–11 Atlas fieldwork					Gloucestershire trends						UK population trends	
	Number of tetrads in which recorded (max 683)					Occupied 10 km squares (max 26)				% of tetrads in which recorded (1st hour of TTV)		UK conservation status: Amber 1,2	
	Total	Confirmed	Probable	Possible	Present	1968–71	1981–84	1988–91	2007–11	1988–91	2008–11	Long term	Short term
Breeding	81	0	29	51	1	8		6	18	0.8	1.0	–	–
Winter	0							0		0		–	–

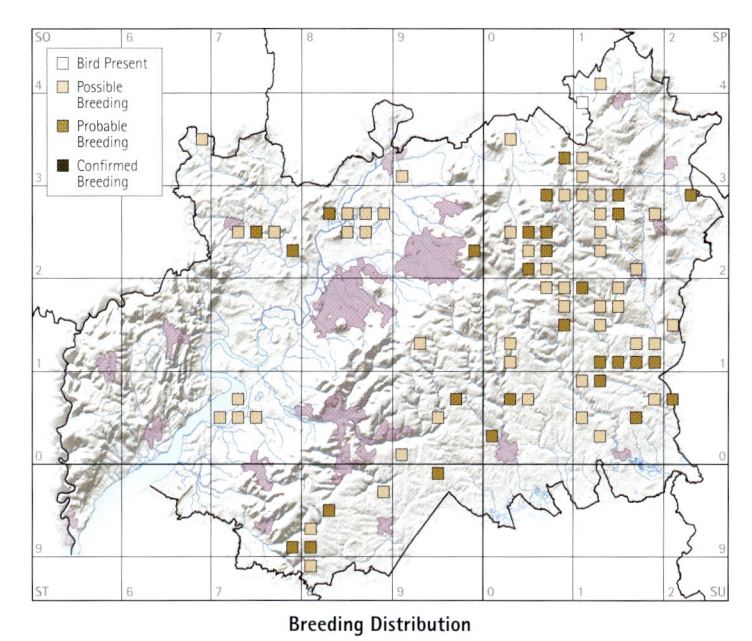

Breeding Distribution

PHIL AND CHRIS ANDREWS

Black Grouse
Tetrao tetrix

Perhaps the most surprising species to feature in this book, Black Grouse breed from Britain east across Eurasia, although the distribution is very patchy in western Europe. They appear to have been fairly widespread in Britain before about 1800, although the situation is complicated by releases, but over the next 50 or so years they disappeared from many English counties (1875–1900 Atlas).

Swaine felt that Black Grouse were 'probably not uncommon in the Forest of Dean during the first 60 years of the nineteenth century', and cites an apparently reliable account of four or five leks in 1859. There have been no satisfactory reports in the county since that time.

Pallas's Sandgrouse
Syrrhaptes paradoxus

Pallas's Sandgrouse sometimes undertake large-scale emigrations both eastward and westward from their normal breeding areas on the steppes of central Asia, and very occasionally there are major irruptions into Europe, possibly when heavy snowfall makes food difficult to find. Such events took place in 1863, 1888 and 1908, and in the first two instances birds arrived in Gloucestershire. As was the norm in Victorian times they were often welcomed with guns, and there are several old records of these birds being seen or shot in the county. Swaine mentioned 15 near Wotton-under-Edge in June 1863, eight or ten 'down the Gloucester Canal' on June 3rd 1888, and one shot at Naunton in October 1888. After the 1888 influx in particular there were instances of birds breeding in Britain, but not in Gloucestershire.

Red-throated Diver (Red-throated Loon)
Gavia stellata

With a circumpolar breeding range mostly in the subarctic and boreal zones, Red-throated Divers nest in small numbers on Scottish lochs and many more winter around the coasts of the British Isles.

There is a record of a bird being shot in 1859 on the Thames and Severn Canal at Cirencester, and there are four Gloucestershire records from later in the nineteenth century. Since then there have been 22 sightings, all between 1934 and 2008: roughly three records per decade, with no indication of any long-term change in frequency. Dates range from October to May, but more than half have been in January and February. Ten of the 22 were found on reservoirs and other lakes (including five records from the Cotswold Water Park), four on the lower Severn, four on floodwater and three on canals. The remaining record was of a bird found alive in Newent in March 1988 and released at Swansea the next day. All these records involve single birds, except for three recorded at Hewletts reservoir, Cheltenham on November 1st and 2nd 1954.

Black-throated Diver (Black-throated Loon)
Gavia arctica

Always the scarcest of the three regular British divers, Black-throats breed from northern Europe, including Scotland, east to Alaska. They are more migratory than their Red-throated cousins, Western Palearctic birds wintering as far south as the Bay of Biscay and the Adriatic Sea.

Although Swaine mentions 'two old and inconclusive records' from the nineteenth century, the earliest satisfactory record for the county dates from January 27th 1947, when one was killed on the river Windrush at Bourton-on-the-Water. The only other records concern a remarkable influx in 1979, when on February 17th and 18th the arrival was noted of four birds (three adults and one immature): two at Frampton sailing lake and two at separate pits in the western section of the Cotswold Water Park. Two more appeared in the Water Park in the following two weeks, whilst an immature seen at Witcombe reservoir from February 24th to March 27th may well have been one of the early arrivals. One adult stayed at the Water Park until April 30th, attaining summer plumage, and an immature remained on the river Churn at North Cerney from about April 6th until June 30th.

Pacific Diver (Pacific Loon)
Gavia pacifica

This close relative of the Black-throated Diver breeds in eastern Russia, Alaska and northern Canada and winters in the countries bordering the Pacific, both on the coast and further inland. Although the first British record came as recently as 2007 there had been another four sightings by 2010, probably including returning individuals.

Quite remarkably, given the rare status of all divers in Gloucestershire, an adult in winter plumage arrived on the estuary off Slimbridge during south-westerly gales on November 18th 2009 and was seen again off nearby Sharpness the next day (Lees 2009).

Great Northern Diver (Great Northern Loon)
Gavia immer

Great Northern Divers breed mainly in northern North America but also in Greenland and Iceland, the latter holding about 300 pairs. They winter further north than the smaller divers, but the waters around the British Isles nevertheless hold internationally important numbers, estimated at around 3,500 to 4,500 birds.

Great Northerns tend to be seen inland more frequently than the other divers, and Gloucestershire records reflect this. Swaine reports that about a dozen were 'killed' in Severn Vale localities between 1870 and 1912, and another near Fairford in 1906. More recently there have been 26 records since 1954. Although recorded dates range from the end of October until early April, almost 90% are in November, December and January. About half are from the Cotswold Water Park, with most of the rest from the Severn Estuary area and others from the reservoirs at Dowdeswell (1954) and Witcombe (1993). In

November 1968 an adult was found alive on a road in Dumbleton near Tewkesbury and released onto Dowdeswell reservoir.

Most county records are of singles but, following storm-force south-westerly winds in early December 2006, two birds were seen several times from Sharpness and Purton (a single was also recorded at the Water Park during the same period). The only other record involving more than one bird was in 2009, when a first-winter that arrived at the Water Park on November 28th was joined by a second individual on December 12th. These well-watched birds stayed in the area until January 3rd 2010, and were often seen feeding on American signal crayfish.

Fulmar (Northern Fulmar)
Fulmarus glacialis

Fulmars breed in huge numbers around the Arctic, North Atlantic and North Pacific Oceans and winter both inshore and further out to sea. Swaine mentioned just three Gloucestershire records prior to 1950 and four between 1950 and 1980, but since then there have been sightings in five years in the 1980s, seven in the 1990s and eight since 2000, with one or two per year being the recent norm. The apparent increase in frequency may simply be due to observer effects, although Fulmars increased strongly in the north-east Atlantic through most of the twentieth century. Most sightings are after strong winds and birds are sometimes found grounded, in poor condition or dead. The majority are seen at the Severn Estuary, but 'inland' records are not unknown. There have been records in all months except February and December, with 80% between April and September. On only two occasions between 1980 and 2010 was more than one bird seen at any one time: three off Beachley Point on August 15th 1990 and two at Sharpness on July 11th 2001.

There is one ringing recovery involving the county: an adult ringed on the Welsh coast near Aberystwyth on June 2nd 1992 was found freshly dead at Aylburton Warth on May 21st 2007. Fifteen years between ringing and recovery would be a long time for most birds, but Fulmars are long-lived: the maximum recorded age is over 40.

Manx Shearwater
Puffinus puffinus

Manx Shearwaters breed on small islands in the northern and eastern Atlantic from the subarctic to the Canaries, with the British Isles holding some three-quarters of the world population, and they winter as far away as the seas off eastern South America.

Swaine mentioned a few early county records and about 16 between 1950 and 1980. Since then they have been seen here in seven years in the 1980s, six in the 1990s and seven since 2000. Sightings are invariably associated with strong westerly or south-westerly gales, and 95% have been in late August and September. Most are seen along the Severn Estuary, but of all the storm-blown species this is the most likely to be found grounded inland, with more than 20 birds suffering this fate since 1980. The most noteworthy recent case was in 1988, when six individuals were found between August 26th and September 6th in various places including Newent, Cheltenham and Gloucester. Some of the birds at the estuary fare no better, as in their weakened state they easily fall prey to Peregrines and gulls.

It is a credit to seabird ringers on the Welsh islands that as many as five of the birds found stranded in Gloucestershire were carrying rings, revealing rather tragic histories: four were found in early September within a week of having been ringed as nestlings in Pembrokeshire in 1948, 1967 (two) and 1974. The fifth was an adult which was recovered on June 8th 1952 having been ringed in Manchester six days previously. This bird had presumably been 'rehabilitated'; it is unclear whether it was released in Manchester or taken to the coast.

Storm Petrel (European Storm Petrel)
Hydrobates pelagicus

'Stormy' Petrels breed in the north-east Atlantic, especially in north and west Britain and Ireland, and also in the Mediterranean. They winter off the coasts of southern and western Africa. In Gloucestershire they occur only as storm-driven strays, and Swaine mentioned just seven pre-1980 records. Since then they have occurred roughly one year in three, with one record in May (29th, in 2011), four in July, two in August, three in September, two in October, three in November and one in December. The November and especially December records are surprising, as this is a summer visitor to the British Isles and winter records are very unusual here. All records are from the Severn Estuary, apart from one that was found exhausted at Rodborough near Stroud on October 18th 1983 and subsequently died. All have been singles, except for two seen from Guscar Rocks on September 4th 1983. In November 1993 one was brought to Slimbridge having been found on a ship moored at Sharpness; it had apparently embarked off the coast of Portugal.

Leach's Petrel (Leach's Storm Petrel)
Oceanodroma leucorhoa

Possibly the most oceanic of all the birds occurring in Britain, Leach's Petrels have a wide breeding distribution, with the largest concentrations in the north-west Atlantic and northern Pacific but with smaller numbers in the north-east Atlantic, including some Scottish islands. They winter at sea as far south as the South Atlantic.

In Gloucestershire this is the quintessential storm-driven species, and a sustained autumn south-westerly will find birders braving the gales at watch points along the Severn Estuary in the hope of glimpsing a Leach's wheeling past. They are by no means annual here; Swaine mentioned a dozen or so pre-1950 records and six between 1950 and 1980, and since then they have been recorded in four years in the 1980s, two in the 1990s and eight since 2000. They are seen mostly between September and December, and unlike many storm-driven species they often occur in groups, especially later in the year. Recent maxima include nine near Slimbridge on December 24th 1989, 36 at Sharpness on December 4th 2006 (many of which were seen further north along the estuary on subsequent days), and at least six at Sharpness on November 23rd 2009. However none of these matches the extraordinary events of 1952, when a severe 'wreck' of this species along the western seaboard in late October produced 'many' both alive and dead at Sharpness on 26th and 27th, at least 260 seen in flight in the Slimbridge area at the same time, and individuals reported grounded and dead from widespread inland localities across the county.

Gannet (Northern Gannet)
Morus bassanus

The Gannet is endemic to the North Atlantic, with largely separate populations in Europe and Canada. Britain and Ireland hold about two-thirds of the eastern population, and numbers here have increased substantially since the 1960s. Some winter in the North Atlantic and the western Mediterranean, while others, especially first-year birds, go as far south as the seas off West Africa.

Gannets arrive in Gloucestershire only as storm-blown or lost individuals. Swaine cited 12 or more pre-1900 records, but there were few until the late 1950s except in 1935, when about 30 were seen in September after gales. From 1957 until 1980 however they were almost annual, with records apparently increasing. In the last 30 years numbers have continued to rise: there have been only four years with no sightings, and whereas in the 1980s an average year produced one or two records, nowadays it tends to be three or four. Gannets have been seen in all months except March, with over two-thirds of reports between May and September, and when the observer mentioned the age of the bird, some 70% were adults. Most sightings are from the lower Severn Estuary but, as with all storm-driven species, they can be found grounded or dead in all manner of places. One of the more unusual of these records was a bird found in a weakened state on the Gloucester northern by-pass on June 21st 1997. It was taken into care and soon recovered (after eating over £100 worth of fish), and was later released from the Gower peninsula in South Wales. Another (pictured below) was found exhausted in a field of kale at Longborough near Stow-on-the-Wold on October 14th 2007.

Almost all recent sightings have involved single birds, a notable exception being in 1983 when after gales in early September up to 18 were seen off Sharpness and Frampton. Four were seen from Saul Warth on May 20th 2006, and three from Sharpness on two dates in November 2009.

Three birds found sick or dead in the county were carrying rings. One ringed as a nestling in June 1974 on the island of Great Saltee (Co. Wexford, Ireland) was found freshly dead on December 12th 2007 near Sharpness, having reached the grand age of 32 (the current record is 37). The other two fared less well, having been found sick and injured in Gloucestershire just a few weeks after being ringed as nestlings on the Bass Rock off south-east Scotland in 1974 and in Shetland in 1987.

Cormorant (Great Cormorant)
Phalacrocorax carbo

Of the four subspecies of Cormorant found in the Western Palearctic, two occur in Britain: *P. c. carbo* breeds on North Atlantic coasts from eastern Canada to Norway and south via the British Isles to north-west France, and is only partially dispersive outside the breeding season, whilst the 'white-headed' *P. c. sinensis* occurs in central and southern Europe and through Asia and, being migratory, may account for up to 10% of the Cormorants wintering in Britain, as well as breeding here in small numbers. Both of these races are amber listed for the importance of British breeding colonies.

A lack of waterproofing in their plumage ensures that Cormorants do not wander far at sea. In the British Isles they used to breed mainly in small colonies on coastal cliffs, especially along the western seaboard. Increasing numbers took to wintering inland, and since the early 1980s they have been regularly wintering and breeding at inland waters in southern and central England. A good proportion of these birds are of the race *sinensis*, presumably originating from the inland nesting colonies in Holland and Denmark.

Cormorant numbers in Britain declined in the nineteenth century because of persecution by fishermen and egg collectors. The decrease slowed through much of the twentieth century but did not cease until its final quarter, during which time breeding numbers recovered from about 6,000 to 9,000 pairs, 1,400 of which were at the new inland colonies. The first decade of the present century saw a renewed reduction of 7%, with an increasing inland population, now estimated to be over 2,000 pairs, masking a steeper decline on the coast. Wintering numbers are currently stable at about 35,000 birds.

In Gloucestershire trends have closely mirrored the national pattern. Mellersh reported only that one or two Cormorants visited the Severn Vale each autumn or winter, and there were no documented county records at all between 1900 and 1945 (Sellers 1979), although some birds were almost certainly present because regular reports began as soon as the Wildfowl Trust was established at Slimbridge in 1946. In the early years of the Trust there were winter counts of up to 20 birds there, but these declined to no more than four by 1972. Swaine reported a steady increase after about 1970, with regular winter counts of about ten and up to three birds staying during the summer. At the same time, winter reports in single figures were coming from the Severn Hams, the Cotswold reservoirs and the Cotswold Water Park. In the last 30 years the highest counts at Slimbridge have averaged 30 birds, with 40 sometimes at nearby Frampton, where Cormorants began to roost in 1971. The western section of the Water Park has occasionally held numbers in three figures since the year 2000, with a maximum count of 199 in January 2006; in the eastern section, double figures were first recorded when a roost was established in 1988 and now as many as 50 birds can be found there.

Since the 1981–84 Wintering Atlas, the winter range in Gloucestershire has increased threefold to take in all but one of the 26 core 10 km squares, emphasising how familiar this once-uncommon visitor has become. The maps clearly show the species' preference for the Severn Vale, the Water Park and other major waterbodies, although records away from these favoured spots show that Cormorants do wander, especially in winter.

To complete the picture of Gloucestershire mirroring the national trend, the first breeding record in the county was confirmed in 2010, with three nests at a confidential site. Recently, a handful of birds showing characters of the subspecies *sinensis* have been reported here each year, but identification is not always straightforward and some may have been overlooked.

TERENCE LAMBERT

	2007–11 Atlas fieldwork					Gloucestershire trends						UK population trends	
	Number of tetrads in which recorded (max 683)					*Occupied 10 km squares (max 26)*				*% of tetrads in which recorded (1st hour of TTV)*		*UK conservation status:* **Green**	
	Total	Confirmed	Probable	Possible	Present	1968–71	1981–84	1988–91	2007–11	1988–91	2008–11	Long term	Short term
Breeding	92	1	0	11	80	0		0	3	1.0	4.6	+10%	−7%
Winter	133						8		25			–	+10%

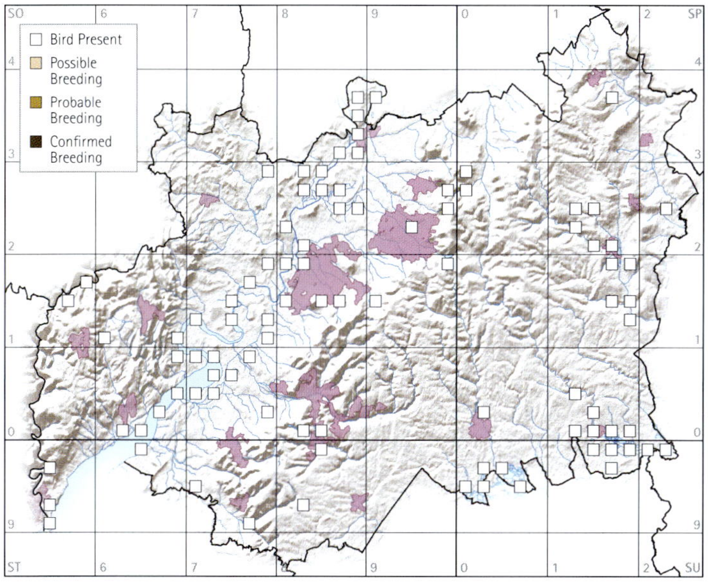

Breeding Distribution
(to preserve confidentiality, breeding status is not shown)

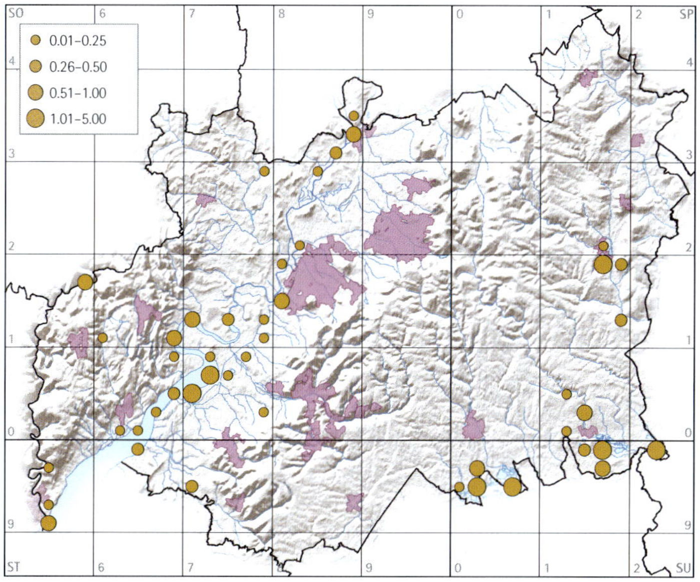

Summer Abundance

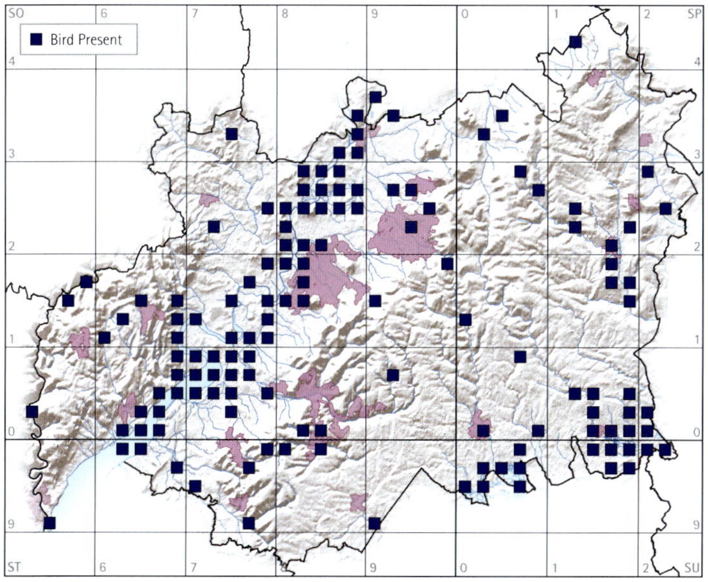

Winter Distribution

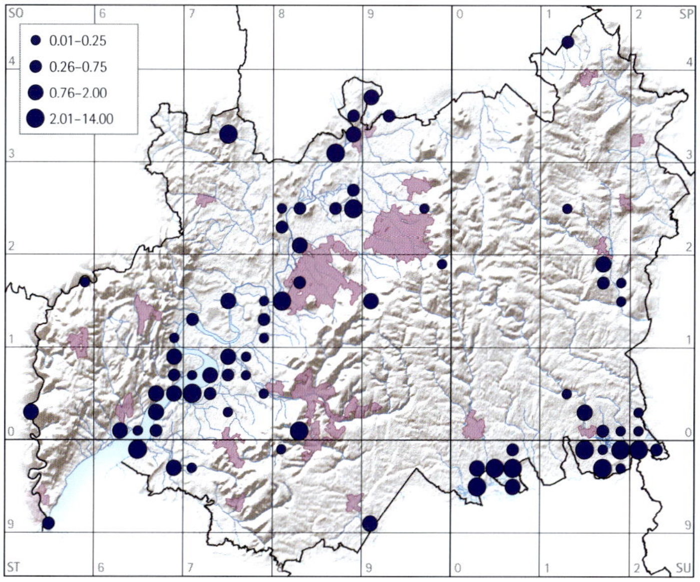

Winter Abundance

Shag (European Shag)
Phalacrocorax aristotelis

Found only in the Western Palearctic, Shags breed on rocky coasts in the north-east Atlantic, the Mediterranean and the Black Sea. Their range extends around the northern coast of Fennoscandia and as far south as the Atlantic coast of Morocco. They are maritime birds and do not normally occur inland, unlike Cormorants. In general they are not migratory, but some dispersal takes place after breeding, especially in the far north.

In Gloucestershire Shags are mainly associated with Atlantic gales. Swaine cited a few early records, followed by just four in the first half of the twentieth century and a further nine up to 1980, and he noted that all were from the Severn Vale. Since then sightings have been more frequent, perhaps because of observer effects, with records from eight years in the 1980s, six in the 1990s and eight since 2000, and with a typical year now bringing two or three sightings. Spring and summer records are rare, but Shags have been found in all months except July (see graph). Most involve single birds, and immatures predominate. The majority are from the Severn Vale, where this species seems to have a particular affinity for the Gloucester and Sharpness Canal, although they do turn up elsewhere and, like other storm-driven birds, some are found dead or dying in unlikely places. One at the Cotswold Water Park on December 10th 1989 was the first for that area (there have been others since), and one which was found dead at Soudley Ponds on March 13th 1986 was the first for the Dean. Occasional influxes occur: in February 1993 as many as a dozen immatures arrived in the county as part of a more widespread movement and a few stayed in the Purton area until mid-June; and on August 22nd 2008 12 birds were seen at Sharpness.

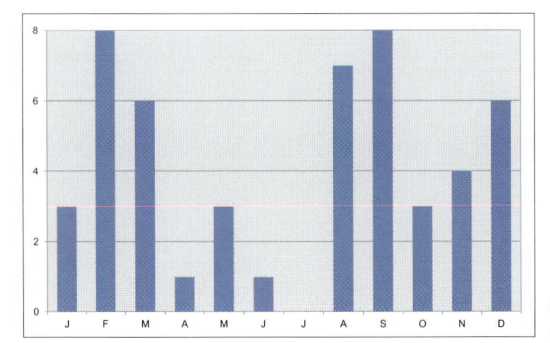

Shag records by month, 1980–2010.

There have been five ringing recoveries in the county, all of birds ringed as nestlings. Two originated in Ireland and one in each of Wales, Scotland and the Scilly Isles.

Species accounts

Bittern (Eurasian Bittern)
Botaurus stellaris

Restricted to lowland swamps and particularly reed-beds, Bitterns breed across the middle latitudes of Eurasia and also in parts of southern Africa. The more northern and eastern European populations are migratory, moving south and south-west, and winter brings visitors to Britain to join our resident birds.

Early sources suggest that Bitterns were formerly plentiful in Britain. However they were commonly hunted, and after years of heavy persecution and the loss of many wetlands they became extinct as a breeding species by the 1880s. After recolonisation numbers rose to a peak in the 1950s, but soon slumped again so that by 1997 the number of 'booming' males was in single figures. Since then though, thanks largely to the creation and management of reed-beds by conservation organisations, numbers have increased steadily, and 104 males were recorded in 2011 (Brown *et al.* 2012). Meanwhile Bitterns have always continued to occur as winter visitors, with numbers dependent on weather conditions on the Continent.

It is quite likely that Bitterns would once have bred in Gloucestershire. Swaine cited several nineteenth-century sources that referred to them being shot here, and a later report that mentioned 'at least thirty Bitterns being shot in various parts of the Severn Vale' in the winter of 1925–26. There were about 25 county records between then and 1980, and subsequently they were seen in eight years in the 1980s, in 1993, and then every year since 1995. The average number of records per year has risen from around one in the 1980s to about five since 2000. This noticeable increase is no doubt influenced by the development of reed-beds at Slimbridge and the Cotswold Water Park as well as the recovery of the British breeding population. An indication of the way in which numbers seem to be building up is that in January 2010 there were sightings of two birds both at Frampton and at a site in the eastern section of the Water Park. Single birds were also seen at a few other places in the county at the same time, and probably at least six were present in total.

About 90% of reports are between November and March, and the most reliable sites are Slimbridge (where in recent years Bitterns have obligingly used a small reed-bed in front of a hide), Frampton and both sections of the Water Park, where a fleeting glimpse is the norm. They are also sometimes seen elsewhere, especially in very cold weather. Many remain for quite long periods, although they will often move short distances between sites, a habit which, together with their extraordinary camouflage and famously skulking habits, makes it very difficult to estimate the total number of birds present.

A particularly remarkable county record came on December 29th 1999, when a Bittern spent the day roosting in a first-floor window-box in Newnham-on-Severn; it flew away when an attempt was made to 'rescue' it.

The only ringing recovery affecting Gloucestershire dates from a time when populations were very low, but it does show the origin of some wintering birds: a nestling ringed in Belgium in May 1960 was found dead at Norton near Gloucester on January 12th 1961.

Little Egret
Egretta garzetta

At the beginning of the last century the Little Egret was hunted to the verge of extinction in southern Europe for its white nuptial plumes, which were used as 'aigrettes' to adorn ladies' headwear. Revulsion at this practice played a large part in the beginnings of the European bird conservation movement.

The Little Egret is widely distributed in three subspecies through temperate and tropical latitudes in the Palearctic, African and Oriental regions. The nominate subspecies occurs in Europe, where in recent years it has expanded its range rapidly northwards from the Mediterranean region. This is often cited as a prime European example of the effects of climate change. The rate of colonisation in the British Isles has been so fast that many birders now barely give Little Egrets a second glance, even though as recently as the 1988–91 Breeding Atlas the species was only found in three tetrads in the whole of Britain and Ireland and was discussed just briefly in an appendix.

Over much of the world range the preferred habitat is shallow lowland lakes and pools and gently flowing streams, but in the British Isles and western Europe Little Egrets are particularly associated with estuaries and coastal waters; they are also partial to floodlands and temporary or fluctuating waterbodies. For nesting they choose large trees, scrub such as willows, or sometimes reed-beds.

Following the first British breeding record in Dorset in 1996 the species' status in Britain is clearly still very dynamic, and it is too soon to say when and at what level the population might stabilise. In 2009, WeBS logged a record national count of 4,709 individuals in September, and the peak count had actually exceeded that for Grey Heron in three of the four most recent years, although this was largely due to Little Egrets' preference for coastal habitats, which are better covered by WeBS. An average of 739 pairs of Little Egrets were estimated to be breeding annually in Britain between 2006 and 2010; the species is amber listed because of its localised breeding population, but this could well change if expansion continues.

The remarkable increase and spread affecting the British Isles has certainly been reflected in Gloucestershire. Whereas Swaine could list a total of only four records for the county, and the 1990 GBR proudly noted the eighth sighting, 20 years later no less than 460 reports were submitted in 2010 alone. The first Gloucestershire breeding record was in 2001 in a Grey Heron colony, since when a dozen pairs have continued to breed in the county each year. It seems likely that Little Egrets will continue to spread as a breeding bird here, and indeed the current atlas fieldwork revealed a regular summer presence along some Cotswold rivers and in the Cotswold Water Park. More generally, as might be expected, summer distribution was concentrated around the Severn Estuary, in the upper Vale, at the Water Park and along the Cotswold rivers; there were almost no records from the Forest of Dean, the Cotswold scarp or dip-slope, nor (surprisingly perhaps) along the river Leadon.

Winter atlas records were more widespread than in summer, with not only the estuary, but Cotswold rivers and the Water Park particularly well represented. The GBR for the last two or three years has recorded several counts of 20 or more birds on the estuary and in the Water Park outside the breeding season. At this time they can also be found on quite small streams and ponds as long as they are fairly undisturbed. After the Severn floods in June and July 2007, Little Egrets (together with Grey Herons and Cormorants) gathered round floodwaters in the Severn Hams to exploit dead fish, and a short-lived roost of 21 egrets was found there in July. The maximum count during an atlas TTV was 11, in tetrad SU29E on the Wiltshire border near Lechlade, in December 2008.

Little Egrets tend to disperse quite widely after fledging, and a nestling colour-ringed in Norfolk in July 2007 was seen in February the following year near Cirencester (and in July near Oxford). Similarly a chick colour-ringed in Gloucestershire in June 2003 was seen alive on the Hampshire coast two months later.

Sponsored by the Dursley Birdwatching and Preservation Society

Species accounts 125

2007–11 Atlas fieldwork					Gloucestershire trends						UK population trends		
Number of tetrads in which recorded (max 683)					Occupied 10 km squares (max 26)				% of tetrads in which recorded (1st hour of TTV)		*UK conservation status:* **Amber 7**	
	Total	Confirmed	Probable	Possible	Present	1968–71	1981–84	1988–91	2007–11	1988–91	2008–11	Long term	Short term
Breeding	69	2	0	9	58	0		0	5	0	2.3	–	–
Winter	115						0		20			–	–

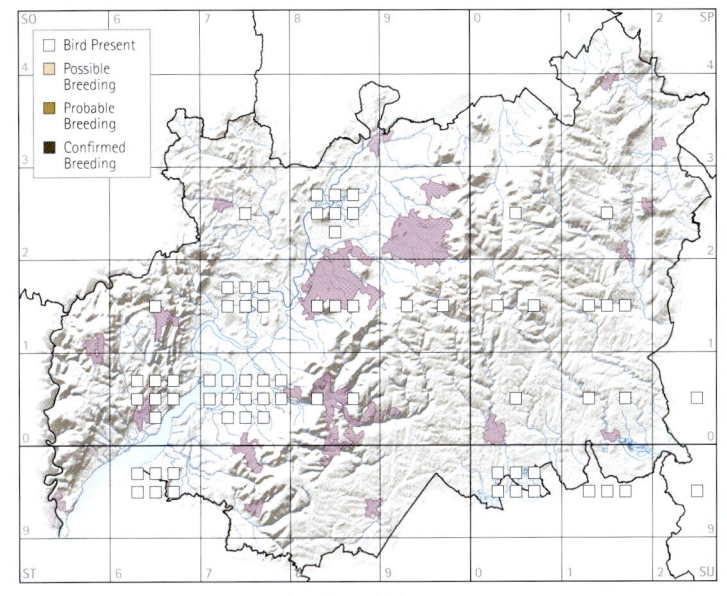

Breeding Distribution
(to preserve confidentiality, breeding status is not shown, and the dots for each 10 km square are grouped together)

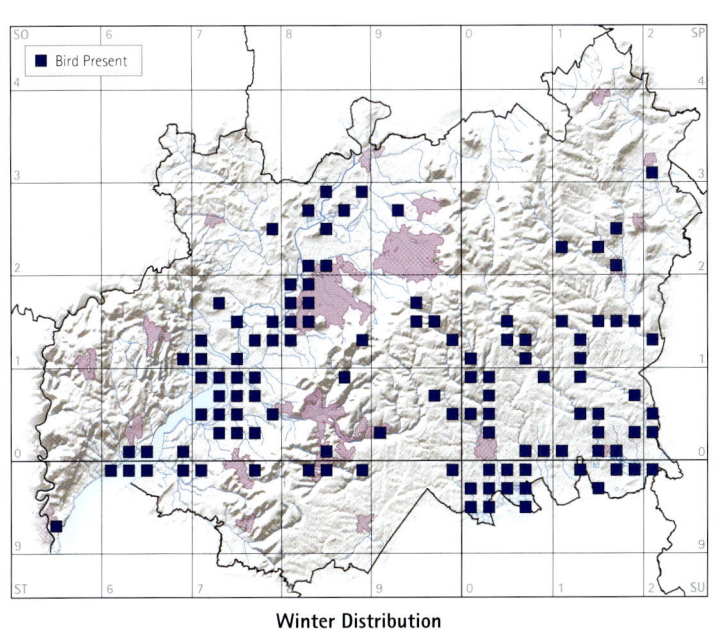

Winter Distribution

JAMES S. LEES

Grey Heron
Ardea cinerea

The Grey Heron is the largest and most northerly distributed of the European herons. The nominate subspecies breeds from Iberia, Ireland and coastal Norway right across the Palearctic to Japan, with a few pairs in North Africa. Other races occupy eastern and south-east Asia and sub-Saharan Africa. Grey Herons are commoner in lowland areas, where there are suitable wetlands for feeding and trees for nesting, this being one of the more arboreal nesters among the herons. In Britain they feed in a fairly wide range of habitats: various types of fresh water (including garden ponds), estuaries and shallow rocky seashores. For nesting they often show a preference for conifers, particularly Scots pines if they are available, but they also use a number of other tree species and may nest in low bushes and on the ground in reed-beds.

Few British-breeding Grey Herons migrate, but many that breed further to the north and east come here to winter, mostly from Fennoscandia and the Netherlands.

This is one of the best-monitored birds in Britain. Systematic counts of the breeding population began in 1928, when there were an estimated 9,000 pairs. Grey Herons are well known to be badly affected by severe winters, and there were corresponding sharp drops in breeding numbers here in 1948, 1964, 1979 and 1986. Since then numbers have increased gradually to just over 13,000 pairs, though the cold winters in the current atlas period have resulted in a recent fall (BTO Heronries Census data). National WeBS indices show little annual variation in the numbers wintering in Britain since 1995–96, though this is a species that is not very well monitored by WeBS.

Grey Herons breed early: in some years the first clutches of eggs may appear in late January, and incubation is normally well under way by March. Most young have fledged by the end of May, and some summer atlas records will undoubtedly have included recently fledged juveniles.

Swaine described the Grey Heron as a 'resident, breeding in small numbers, and a winter visitor' in Gloucestershire. Counts for the national Heronries Census show that the number of breeding pairs in the county has been fairly steady over the last ten years, generally in the same 14 heronries, which were all surveyed during the current atlas fieldwork. The presence of a large colony on the Gwent bank of the river Wye above Chepstow probably explains the lack of heronries in the Gloucestershire part of the Forest of Dean, although a probable nest site was found in the county west of the Severn in 2011. Annual total numbers breeding in the county increased (along with improving coverage) from 91 pairs in 2002 to a peak of 130–32 in 2007, dropping to 96–113 in 2011 following the two colder winters. However, at some sites there were considerable fluctuations in numbers over this period.

The distribution of Grey Herons in the county is equally wide-ranging in summer and winter. At both seasons the favoured areas are, perhaps not surprisingly, the Severn Vale and Estuary, the Frome valley, the Cotswold rivers and the Cotswold Water Park. All the county's heronries are situated close to the reliable food sources provided by these areas, and there are fewer records at all seasons from the Forest of Dean and the drier parts of the Cotswolds. At the most favoured sites, aggregations of up to about 15 birds may be seen at times, particularly in late summer after the young have fledged and become independent.

Considerable numbers of Grey Herons have been ringed in the county and some have also been given individually identifiable wing tags. As a result there have been over 130 interchanges of marked birds between Gloucestershire and 20 other English and Welsh counties. Most moved from here to nearby 'Hereford & Worcester' (41) and Powys (29); the longest movements within Britain were from Gloucestershire to Kent and West Yorkshire. In addition a Gloucestershire-ringed chick was killed by a car on the French Atlantic coast in its first winter, and birds ringed as nestlings in Germany, Sweden (two) and the Netherlands (two) have been found here.

In memory of Hilary Channon

Species accounts 127

2007-11 Atlas fieldwork					Gloucestershire trends						UK population trends	
Number of tetrads in which recorded (max 683)					Occupied 10 km squares (max 26)				% of tetrads in which recorded (1st hour of TTV)		UK conservation status: **Green**	
	Total	Confirmed	Probable	Possible	Present	1968-71	1981-84	1988-91	2007-11	1988-91	2008-11	Long term	Short term
Breeding	302	18	4	25	255	21		25	16	13.8	19.1	+21%	+2%
Winter	359						25		26			–	–

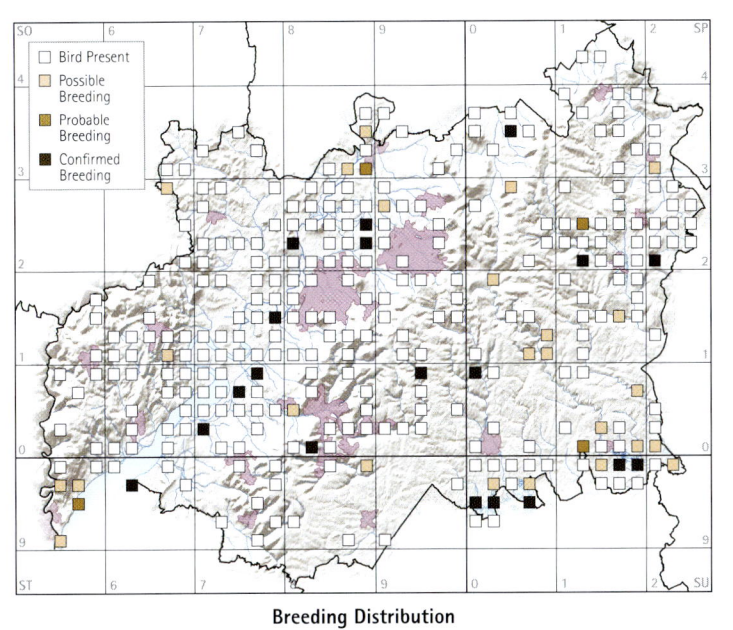

Breeding Distribution

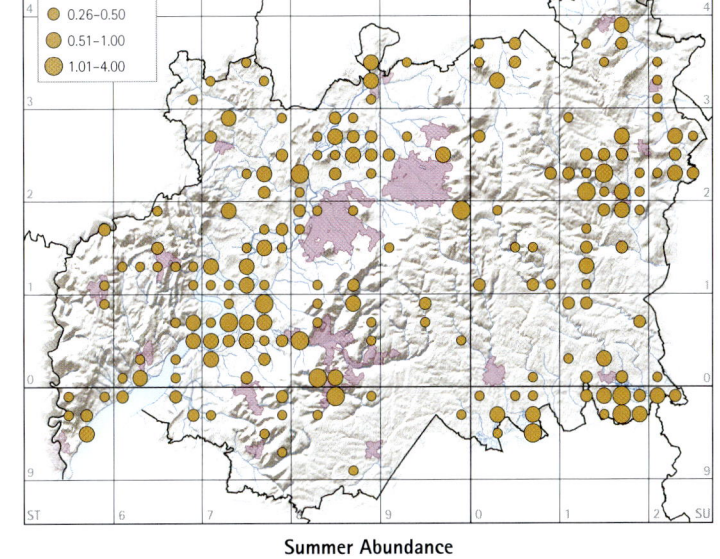

Summer Abundance

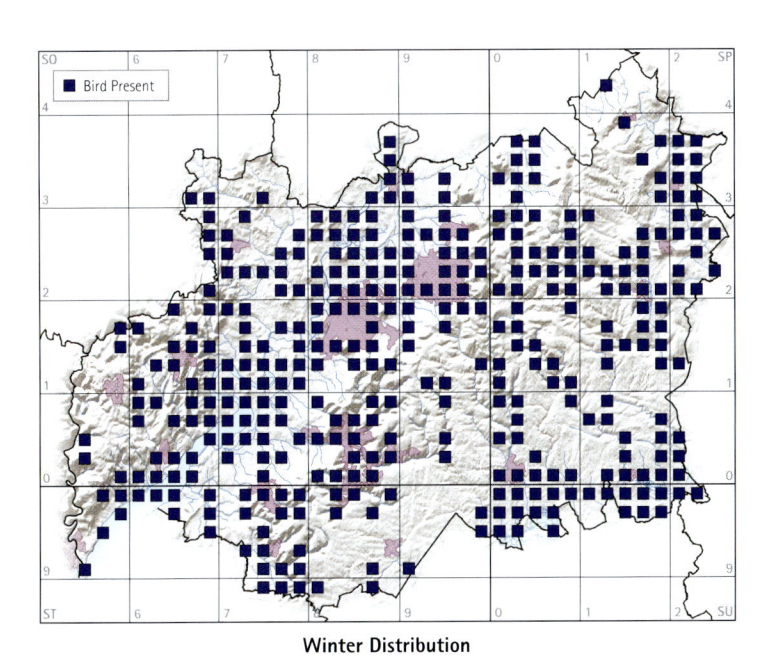

Winter Distribution

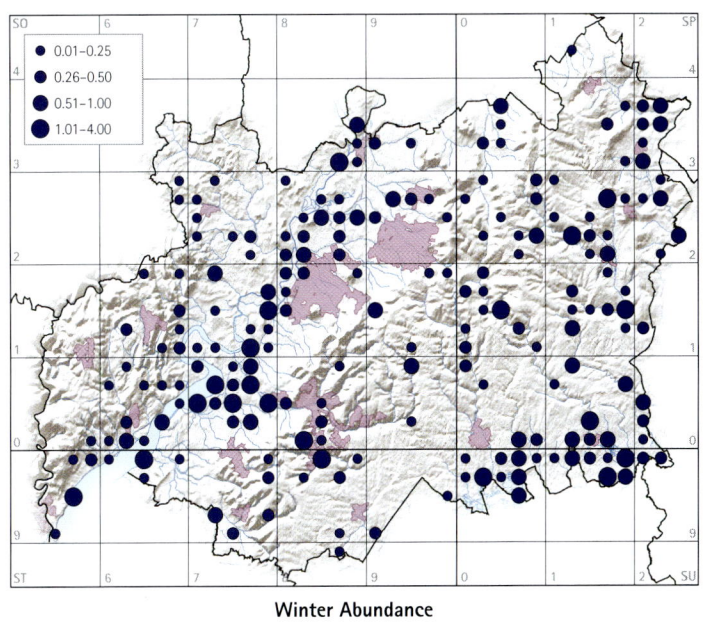

Winter Abundance

Rare herons and allied species

Only a few species of 'long-legged marsh birds' breed in the British Isles, but there are many more in other parts of Europe. All are migratory to some degree, with most moving to Africa for the winter, and often these migrations are rather leisurely, with birds wandering for considerable distances. In addition, juveniles disperse widely after fledging, often in all directions from the breeding site. Several species (Squacco Heron, Cattle Egret, Black Stork, White Stork and Glossy Ibis) have expanded their breeding ranges northwards in recent times. These features, taken together, have resulted in increased vagrancy to Britain.

The graph shows that, although there are more county records for this group in May than any other month, they can turn up at any time of year.

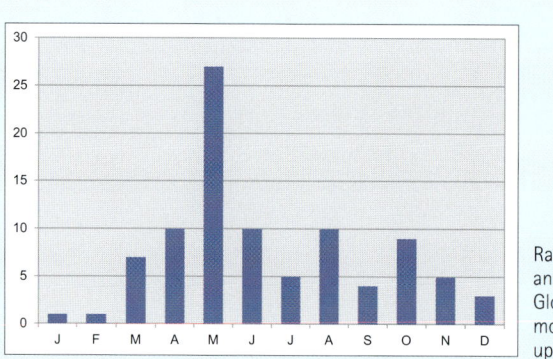

Rare herons and allies in Gloucestershire by month of finding, up to 2011.

Little Bittern
Ixobrychus minutus

Breeding widely across the Old World, Little Bitterns are summer visitors to a wide range of freshwater habitats across much of southern and central Europe, though somewhat more patchily in the west. The European population is declining, probably because of drought on their wintering grounds, which are primarily in East Africa. Little Bitterns occur in small numbers in Britain in most years, usually in southern and eastern England. There are two confirmed British breeding records, in Yorkshire in 1984 and Somerset in 2010.

Mellersh mentioned two Gloucestershire records from 1872 and 1883, but Swaine noted that corroborative evidence was lacking. The only other county record is of a male, seen three times at close range at Frampton Court Lake on May 31st 1964.

Night-heron (Black-crowned Night Heron)
Nycticorax nycticorax

In Europe Night-herons occur as summer visitors, breeding patchily mainly south of latitude 50°N. The world range is very extensive and they use a wide variety of habitats, sometimes foraging away from water.

Swaine mentioned that one was reputed to have been shot near Colesbourne between 1867 and 1875, but the first verifiable county record was not until 1950, when an adult was seen at Slimbridge on September 4th. There were then two records in the 1970s, two in the 1980s and three in the 1990s. Single records in 2000 and 2002 were followed by a fascinating series of sightings at Frampton sailing lake, assumed to involve the same returning individual. It was first seen on August 27th 2003 and it returned, usually on a very similar date, every year until 2008. Its average stay was 38 days. In addition one was recorded at the same site on March 29th and 30th 2007 and one appeared at Slimbridge on May 19th 2011.

Squacco Heron
Ardeola ralloides

Preferring still fresh waters flanked by dense vegetation, Squacco Herons breed from southern Spain across to south-west Asia, although rather thinly in southern Europe, and winter in sub-Saharan Africa. As a result of hunting (for their plumes) and habitat loss, they suffered steep declines in the early twentieth century. More recently there has been evidence of population increases in the western part of the range (Spain, France and Italy). It is likely that most British records concern birds from these populations; in recent years Squaccos have occurred more or less annually in small numbers in southern England. There are just two Gloucestershire records:

1867: an adult shot at Slimbridge in August was presented to City Museum, Gloucester in 1911.
1997: an adult on a garden pond in Cerney Wick near Cirencester from June 25th until July 1st.

Cattle Egret
Bubulcus ibis

Cattle Egrets are less dependent on aquatic habitats than other Western Palearctic herons, using pastures, steppes and arable fields as well as wetter areas. Following recent widespread population expansions they are now virtually cosmopolitan, and look set to follow Little Egrets in colonising parts of Europe where they have previously occurred only as vagrants. The first confirmed British breeding record was in 2008 on the Somerset levels.

The occurrence of Cattle Egrets in Gloucestershire reflects this expansion. The first record was of an adult at the Slimbridge reserve on August 20th 1974, with possibly the same bird at Slimbridge village on March 2nd 1975. The next was not until 20 years later: what was assumed to be a single individual was seen intermittently at Twyning, Walham, Sudmeadow and Sandhurst, in the Severn Vale, between December 26th 1993 and September 2nd 1994. On April 4th 2005 one was found at Frampton sailing lake and stayed around the Slimbridge area until April 9th. December 2007 saw a large influx of Cattle Egrets into the south-west of England, and one found its way to Frampton, where it associated with Little Egrets. It stayed in the area until June 22nd 2008 and was joined by a second bird from April 17th onwards. In 2009 a single bird was seen in March in the same area, and then between August and November there were regular sightings there, with a maximum of four together in the first week of October. In 2010 singles were seen at Slimbridge on June 9th and flying over Clapton-on-the-Hill, near Bourton-on-the-Water, on December 1st. Finally, in 2011 one was at Slimbridge from March 19th to 21st, one was in the Frampton–Slimbridge area from October 28th to November 2nd, and what was presumably the same individual was seen intermittently in the Lydney Harbour area from November 11th into 2012.

Great White Egret (Great Egret)
Ardea alba

Restricted mainly to extensive wetlands in lowland regions, Great White Egrets were formerly extremely rare in Europe, having been hunted for their plumage in the past, but they have increased dramatically in recent times in both range and numbers.

The pattern of Gloucestershire records mirrors this increase. Following the first county record on June 18th 1989 the next was not until 2000, but between then and 2010 there were no fewer than 17 records, including 12 since 2006. All these involved single birds but in 2011, following three more singletons in March and April, four or possibly five birds were seen together several times in late October, flying in to a roost.

There are records from most months of the year but over half have been in May and June. Although the majority have been in the Severn Vale, there are six records from various sites on the Cotswolds.

A female seen in 2010 at Ashleworth Ham from March 17th and then in the Slimbridge area until 30th had been colour-ringed as a nestling in north-western France the previous year. After touring north-west England, south-east Wales and Gloucestershire, she settled in Somerset from April 2010 into 2012, when she achieved fame by becoming one half of the first pair to have bred in Britain (Pitches 2012).

Purple Heron
Ardea purpurea

Purple Herons are summer visitors across Europe south of 50°N, and are also widespread residents in Africa and southern Asia. They are strongly associated with extensive reed-beds. Numbers have decreased across much of their European range, though there have been signs of a recovery in some countries in more recent years and they bred in Britain for the first time in 2010, at Dungeness, Kent. Most British records are of spring migrants.

There have been 16 Gloucestershire records, all involving single birds. The first, at Frampton Court Lake from April 28th until May 4th 1968, was followed by six during the 1980s, one in 1997 and eight between 2000 and 2010. Most were seen in the Slimbridge and Frampton area, the exceptions being singles at the Cotswold Water Park, Moreton-in-Marsh and Lydney Lakes. The dates of these 16 sightings range between April 23rd and August 7th, but only four were later than May 25th.

Black Stork
Ciconia nigra

Black Storks inhabit undisturbed forest areas, usually well away from human interference. They breed across much of Eurasia, European birds wintering in tropical Africa. After a prolonged decline in numbers, European populations started to recover in the middle of the twentieth century and several countries including France, Italy and Denmark have been colonised or recolonised since about 1980. Black Storks have occurred in small numbers in Britain in most recent years.

There is just one Gloucestershire record, of a single bird in the Perrott's Brook area of the Churn valley in the Cotswolds from July 14th to 16th 1995.

White Stork
Ciconia ciconia

Often closely associated with humans, White Storks use cultivated areas for feeding and make considerable use of man-made structures for nesting. Breeding mainly in Europe, the Middle East and North Africa, they winter mostly south of the Sahara. There has been a general population decline in most parts of the European range, although more recently numbers have grown in some areas, notably France, probably accounting for an increase in British records in recent years.

The first for Gloucestershire was on September 20th 1972, when one of two birds that had been near Ashton Keynes in Wiltshire crossed the border and was seen at Cerney Wick. This bird, originally ringed in Denmark, had been captured in Somerset in 1971 and released in August 1972.

Subsequent records in 1986 and 1998 were followed by a spate of six between 2004 and 2008, and another in 2011. County records follow the national seasonal pattern, with most in spring but two in September.

Glossy Ibis
Plegadis falcinellus

Although they enjoy an almost cosmopolitan (if very patchy) range, Glossy Ibises suffered huge population declines in the last century, due mainly to habitat loss and also locally to hunting (BWP). However as with White Stork, there have been recent colonisations in the Camargue (France), and elsewhere in western Europe, which probably accounts for an increase in sightings in Britain. They have rather specialised wetland habitat requirements and are usually considered to be intolerant of human disturbance. There are five accepted county records:

1943: one at Barn Farm, Elmstone Hardwicke near Cheltenham from October 5th to 19th.
2004: one seen briefly at the western section of the Cotswold Water Park on May 2nd (first reported in the 2007 GBR).
2007: a remarkable 17 birds arrived at Frampton on April 20th. The whole group stayed until May 7th, also spending time at nearby Saul Warth, and three remained until May 14th.

2009: one at Lydney Marsh on October 15th moved to Frampton the following day.
2010: one, which spent most of its time in the Wiltshire part of the western section of the Water Park, crossed the border into Gloucestershire a few times between August 30th and November 1st.

In addition one was reported shot at Arlingham about 1909, but Swaine rejected this record as 'not supported by further data'.

Spoonbill (Eurasian Spoonbill)
Platalea leucorodia

Spoonbills breed in rather few scattered localities in Europe, and across central Asia. Most are summer visitors, wintering further south, although not necessarily travelling far. There are also resident populations in a band extending from north-east Africa to India. For feeding they need extensive shallow waters of even depth, and they nest in scattered shrubs or trees in dense reed-beds. The Eurasian population has been in long-term decline because of the loss of wetlands, although there have been recent substantial increases in the Netherlands and Spain and recolonisation of several other western European countries, albeit in very small numbers. Spoonbills bred in Britain until the seventeenth century but there were then none until the late 1980s, when a pair bred in England. In subsequent years there were only records of occasional pairs here and there, but in 2010 a small colony was established in Norfolk, with six successful nests.

Swaine noted just seven Gloucestershire records from 1838 until 1953, and then eight between 1960 and 1980. Since then Spoonbills have become more frequent (see top graph) and have been recorded every year since 1991. Most are seen in the spring, but there are records in all months except for January (see bottom graph). The majority of sightings are at Slimbridge, but they were also seen at Coombe Hill in 2006, 2007 and 2009. At the Cotswold Water Park there were records in 1987, 1991 and 1992 but, perhaps surprisingly, none since. If the British population follows the upward trend of others in western Europe we can surely expect to see more of these fine, statuesque birds in the county.

A nestling colour-ringed in the Netherlands in 2006, and sighted in Devon in October that same year, passed through Slimbridge on April 16th 2007 en route to Norfolk.

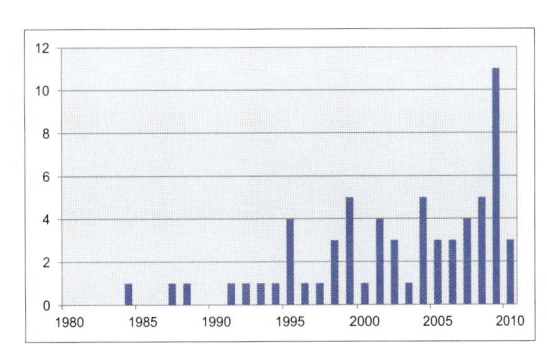

Number of Spoonbills recorded per year, 1980–2010.

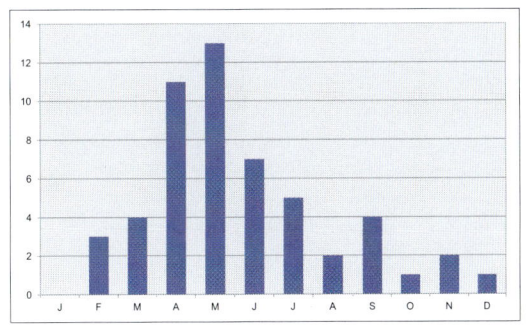

Spoonbill records by month, 1980–2010.

Little Grebe
Tachybaptus ruficollis

Little Grebes are very widely distributed across the Old World; the nominate subspecies is found in Europe, north-west Africa, Turkey and Israel. They breed on shallow, open and often quite small fresh waters with submerged vegetation and muddy bottoms, with fringing reeds or other dense growth for nest sites. Canals and reservoirs are used as well as rivers, lakes and ponds. Obtaining proof of breeding is a good deal more difficult than for Great Crested Grebes; Little Grebes are secretive and unobtrusive when nesting, and it is the loud trilling call that often betrays the presence of a breeding pair.

Northern and eastern populations are migratory, but further west and south the degree of dispersal depends on the severity of the winter. In Britain, many move to more open waters or sheltered coastlines in winter, especially in hard weather.

At the end of the nineteenth century the Little Grebe was widely distributed as a breeding bird across the British Isles, except for Shetland and Scilly, and was generally quite common in lowland areas. This is apparently still the case but the species is notoriously difficult to census and assessments of breeding numbers have been spectacularly vague and variable; an estimate in the year 2000 suggested between 4,000 and 13,000 pairs. An overall shortage of data resulted in the species being given amber listing in the UK in 2009. Some recent assessments of trends have been rather contradictory: the Waterways Breeding Bird Survey suggests some decline along linear waterways since 1990, while the BBS indicates a slight increase on other waterbodies. Estimates of wintering birds have likewise varied enormously, possibly due in part to fluctuating numbers of migrants from the Continent. Over the longer term however the WeBS has recorded a slow, steady increase since 1985. The most recent winter estimate, in 2010, was of 16,000 birds.

At the end of the nineteenth century Mellersh listed the species as a resident breeder in Gloucestershire, while remarking that 'It is not known that ... the Little Grebe ... is resident anywhere along the Severn'. Correspondents to Witchell & Strugnell referred to it variously as plentiful, often met with, frequently met with, and 'breeds at Rendcombe'. Swaine described it as being widely distributed but not abundant. More recently, the two Cotswolds Atlases recorded a 31% increase in the number of tetrads where the species was recorded (from 49 to 64) between 1987 and 2007, though much of this was thought to have resulted from greater observer effort. During the current survey, Little Grebes were found on many waters across all parts of the county in summer, and it seems likely that they have increased in numbers and range here since the 1988-91 Breeding Atlas. The surprisingly high percentage of confirmed or probable breeding records is perhaps because a single pair can raise up to three broods per year, giving observers several chances of finding the young. Although there are noticeable concentrations around Slimbridge and the eastern section of the Cotswold Water Park, the widespread distribution reflects the fact that Little Grebes will use the smallest and apparently most unlikely looking ponds for nesting. Similarly in winter, as the map shows, they can be found on a very wide range of waters throughout the county, from ponds in the Forest of Dean to the rivers of the Cotswold dip-slope. At this season even quite small waterbodies can sometimes hold numbers in double figures; the maximum count during an atlas TTV was 13 in SO70T on the river Frome near Frampton in November 2007, but there were as many as 36 on Gatcombe Water near Stroud in October 2009.

Sponsored by Julia Evans

Species accounts

2007–11 Atlas fieldwork						Gloucestershire trends					UK population trends	
Number of tetrads in which recorded (max 683)						Occupied 10 km squares (max 26)				% of tetrads in which recorded (1st hour of TTV)		UK conservation status: **Amber 3**	
	Total	Confirmed	Probable	Possible	Present	1968–71	1981–84	1988–91	2007–11	1988–91	2008–11	Long term	Short term
Breeding	117	54	21	32	10	18		15	24	5.5	5.9	−40%	+15%
Winter	129						21		26			−	+23%

Breeding Distribution

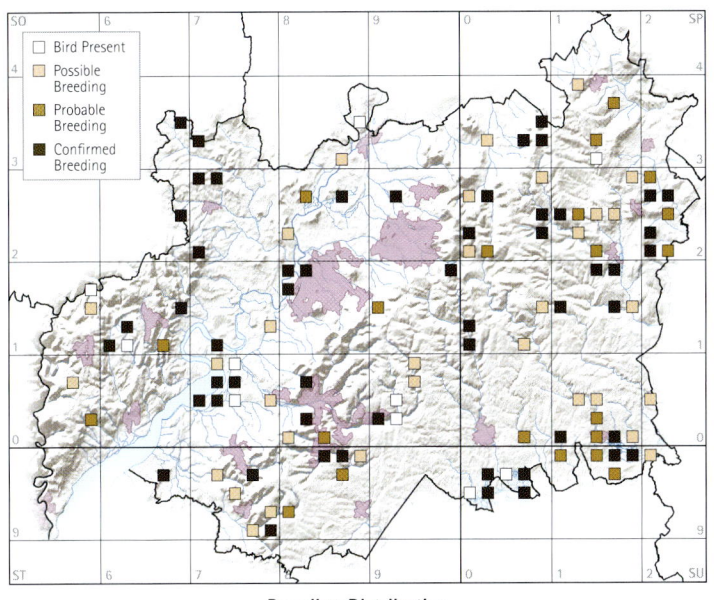

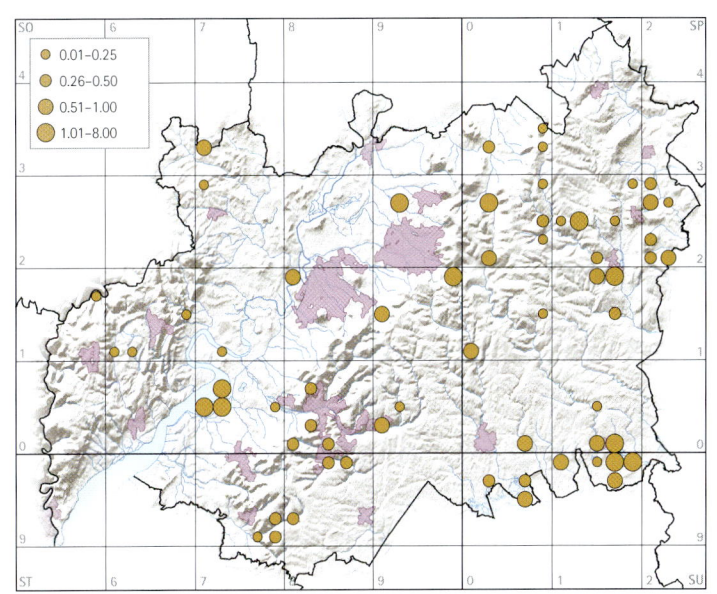

Summer Abundance

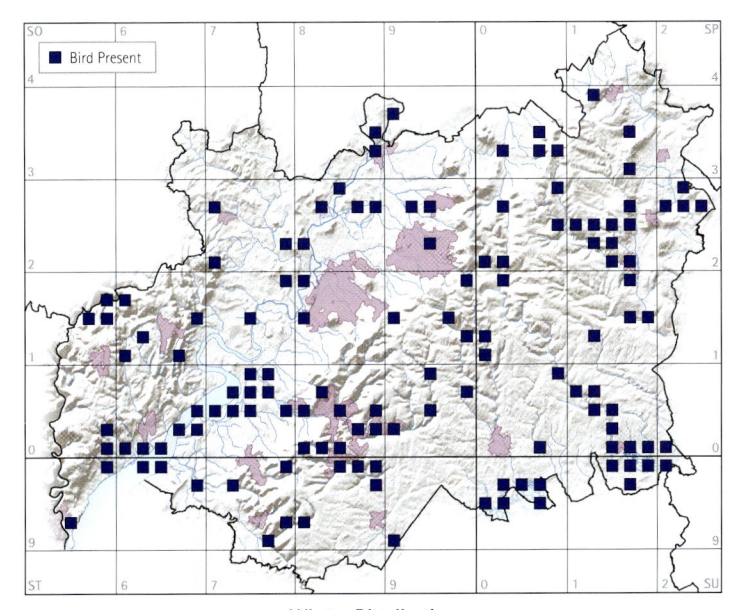

Winter Distribution

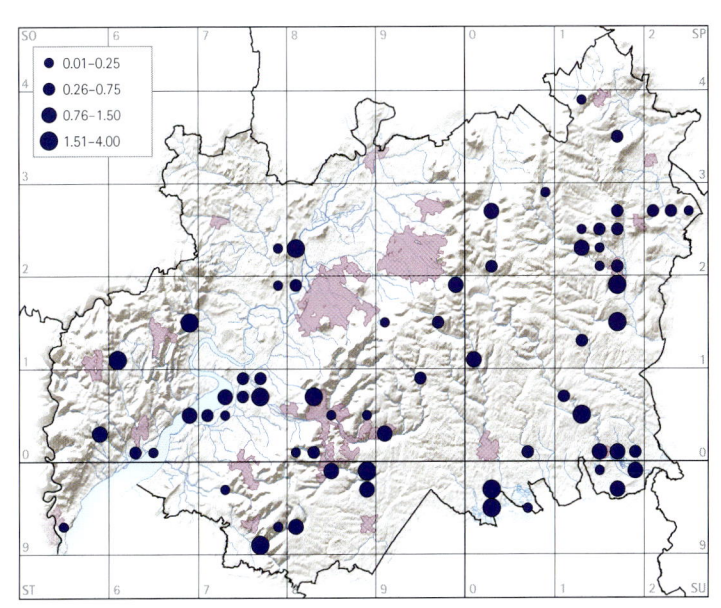

Winter Abundance

Great Crested Grebe
Podiceps cristatus

The Great Crested Grebe is widely distributed from Fennoscandia south through Europe to the coastal fringes of North Africa and east to Korea and Japan, with two different subspecies in Africa and Australasia. Many populations are at least partly migratory, including north European birds which move to the Mediterranean region after breeding; others are more dispersive, such as the British birds which winter on the coast or at reservoirs.

Breeding occurs generally in lowland regions on large, shallow, eutrophic lakes, canals or slow-moving rivers, with fringing vegetation for cover. Nests are fairly visible, the young remain dependent for up to nine weeks (sometimes engagingly riding on a parent's back), and their striped heads make them identifiable as juveniles for much longer, so breeding is relatively easy to prove.

In the early nineteenth century Great Crested Grebes were distributed widely but sparsely across England and Wales. In some areas they were controlled to preserve fish stocks, and in addition their eggs were a popular delicacy. When their plumes became fashionable for ornamenting hats in the mid-nineteenth century, the persecution became unsustainable and numbers declined to fewer than 50 pairs in England by 1860. They started to recover some 20 years later, probably before the first of the Bird Protection Acts in 1876 began to have any significant effect, and by 1931 there were about 2,800 adult birds in Britain. The steady increase has continued, thanks largely to the development of gravel-pits and reservoirs and the species' growing willingness to use rivers. Birds in breeding condition numbered 4,500 in Britain in 1965; in the UK as a whole there were some 8,000 birds in 1991, increasing to just over 6,000 pairs in 2000.

After the moult during August to October, birds gravitate towards their winter quarters. Hard weather in Britain can force many to leave the country, whilst cold conditions on the Continent can double the numbers here, so winter totals vary considerably. However there has been an overall increasing trend in recent decades, with average winter counts in Britain practically doubling from fewer than 10,000 in 1984 to 19,000 by 2010.

In Gloucestershire, Mellersh described the Great Crested Grebe as a winter visitor to the Severn Vale and Cotswolds, scarce in spring. Early records came from Siddington in 1854 and Chaxhill, Purton, Gloucester and Withington during the 1880s. In the twentieth century, regular breeding was reported from Frampton Pools, the Cotswold reservoirs and Cirencester Park between 1914 and 1960. In the Cotswold Water Park nesting was first recorded in 1955 and numbers here increased rapidly to 148 adults, including 30 confirmed breeding pairs, in 1975. By 2007 there were 106 pairs definitely breeding there, with at least the same number possibly breeding. Swaine reported that there had never been a record from the Forest of Dean, but by 1994 a pair was breeding near Cinderford. During the current atlas survey period Great Crested Grebes bred at all these locations and also at Bourton pits and sites along the Severn Vale from the Hams towards Tewkesbury.

The map shows that birds are also present at all the main county waters during winter. The Water Park, including the pits beyond the county boundary, holds wintering numbers of national importance, and in the western section alone the average peak was 326 birds over the five winters up to 2009–10.

Sponsored by Julie Harper and by the Cotswold Water Park Trust

Species accounts

2007-11 Atlas fieldwork					Gloucestershire trends						UK population trends	
Number of tetrads in which recorded (max 683)					Occupied 10 km squares (max 26)				% of tetrads in which recorded (1st hour of TTV)		UK conservation status: **Green**	
	Total	Confirmed	Probable	Possible	Present	1968-71	1981-84	1988-91	2007-11	1988-91	2008-11	Long term	Short term
Breeding	47	31	7	1	8	8		6	10	1.6	3.8	–	+16%
Winter	46						8		12			–	–3%

Breeding Distribution

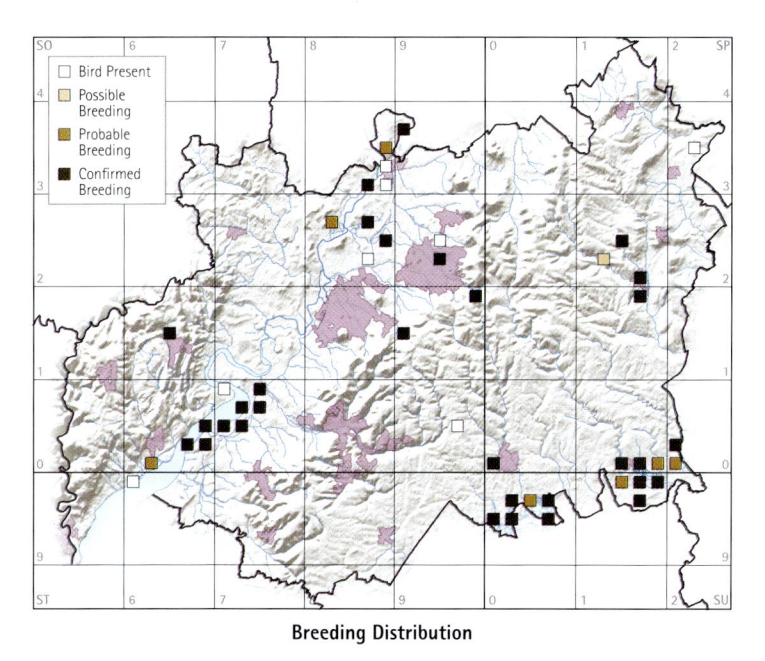

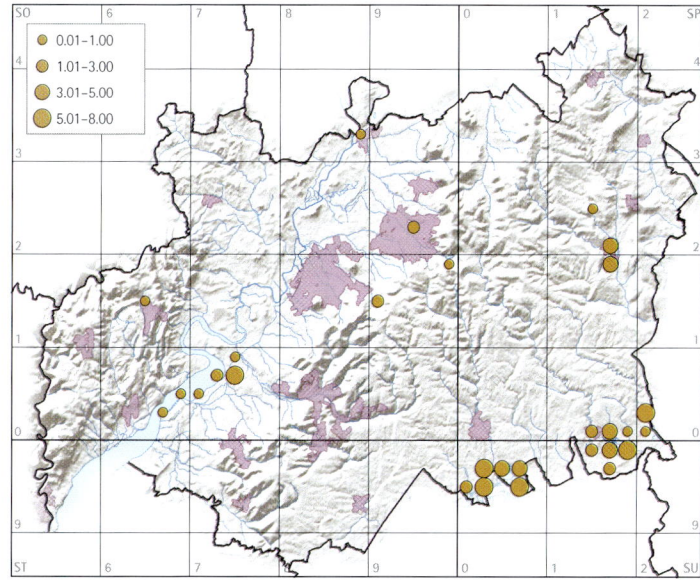

Summer Abundance

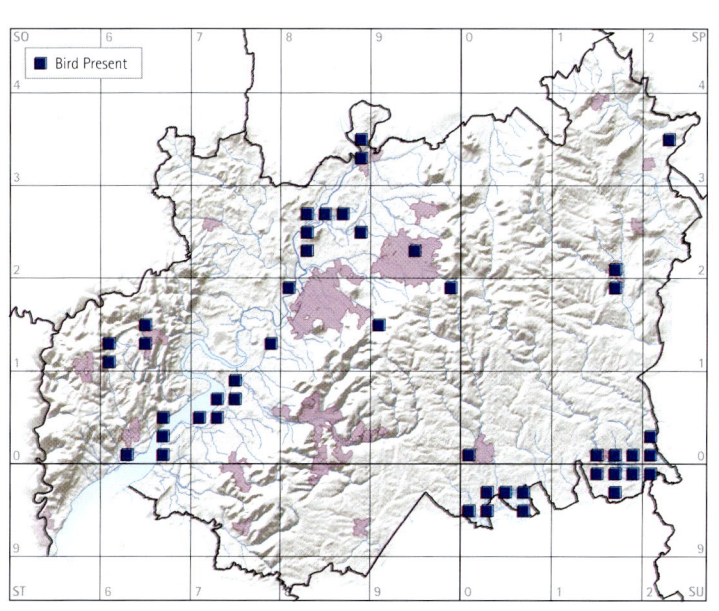

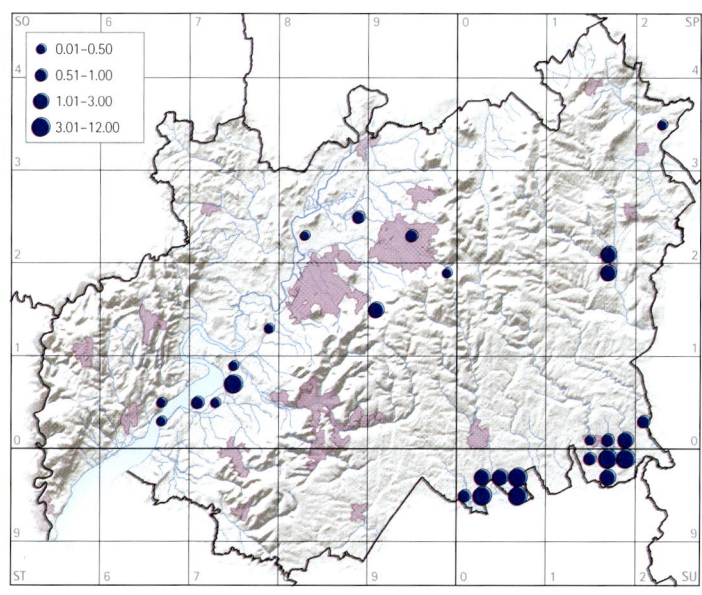

Winter Distribution

Winter Abundance

Red-necked Grebe
Podiceps grisegena

Red-necked Grebes breed in two distinct populations: one from the Baltic region eastwards across central Europe into western Asia, and another in eastern Asia and North America. Nesting on small reeded waters, most move to coastal areas for the winter, and the coasts of the North Sea, including the east coast of Britain, hold wintering European birds. Occurrences inland tend to coincide with periods of very cold weather when birds move from frozen waters further east, and this holds true in Gloucestershire, where this is the least frequently seen of all the grebes. Swaine referred to a few early records, noting just four between 1966 and 1978. He also described an 'unprecedented influx' in early 1979, when as many as ten different birds were seen across the county in very cold conditions, with most in the Cotswold Water Park, including three together at a pit near Lechlade in February. There has been no repetition of such events since, with sightings in just 11 years since 1980; perhaps 13–15 birds in 30 years. All but two were seen at the Water Park, the others being on the Severn by Wainlode Hill and at Frampton. Half were in December or January, although birds have been seen in all months from October through to April. Red-necked Grebes can be long-stayers; at least three of these birds have lingered for more than a month.

Slavonian Grebe (Horned Grebe)
Podiceps auritus

Breeding in the northern temperate zone across Eurasia and North America, this migratory grebe winters mainly in coastal waters. Overall the European breeding population is classified as declining. It first bred in Scotland in 1908 but it is very rare there; numbers have decreased recently to just 22 pairs in 2010. A few hundred winter around British coasts, especially in the north.

Swaine described this species as scarce in Gloucestershire and referred to several early records as well as a dozen or so between 1960 and 1980. Records since then seem to have reflected the European decline, with six in the 1980s and eight in the 1990s but only one since 2000, in winter 2008–09; in all, around 16 birds in 30 years. They have been seen in all months from October through to May, but the vast majority are from December to February. About 60% of sightings since 1980 have been from the Cotswold Water Park and 25% from the Frampton and Slimbridge area; the others were at Witcombe reservoir, on the river Severn near Tewkesbury and on a millpond near Winchcombe. All records except one have involved single birds, the exception being two at the Water Park on April 18th 1990.

Black-necked Grebe
Podiceps nigricollis

Black-necked Grebes have an unusual world distribution, perhaps reflecting their preference for unstable or temporary habitats. They breed in most north European countries, although very patchily in the west, and also in the Middle East, southern Africa and western North America. They require small, shallow, plentifully vegetated and highly productive waters. Such habitat may only appear in wet years, which means that their presence at any particular site may be more or less temporary, as they move from place to place in search of suitable conditions. However, sizeable colonies can quickly establish themselves if conditions are suitable (BWP). Northern birds are migratory, wintering on lakes, reservoirs and coastal waters; they are much less tied to salt water than Slavonian Grebes.

Very small numbers nest in Britain, with a current (2006-10) average of 51 breeding pairs per year, but in this country this species is mainly a passage migrant and, to a lesser extent, a rare winter visitor.

In Gloucestershire this is a scarce bird and, as shown by the graph, most occur during the spring and autumn passage periods. Swaine mentioned just four records between 1861 and 1940 (the latter involving suspected breeding), and a further five up to 1979. Since then there are indications of an increase, possibly linked to the availability of suitable habitat in the Cotswold Water Park, with records from three years in the 1980s, five in the 1990s and nine in the 2000s; a total of 33 birds in the 30 years. In all cases except one (see below) single birds have been involved, and they have all been seen on fresh water. The Water Park has provided more than half of the sightings, although since 2000 birds have also been seen at Frampton Pools, Dowdeswell reservoir, Harbour Road Lakes near Lydney, Ashleworth Ham and Woorgreens.

The notable exception to single-bird records was in 2004, when a pair nested at the Harbour Road Lakes: an adult and a chick were seen on August 4th, providing the only confirmed breeding record for the county.

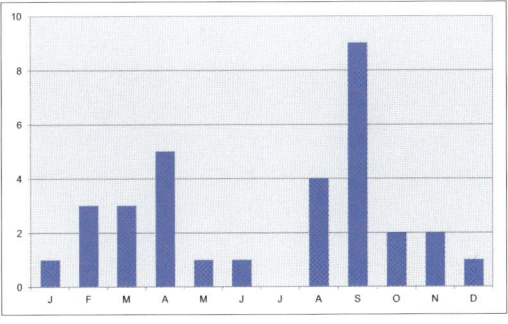

Black-necked Grebe records by month, 1980–2010.

Red Kite
Milvus milvus

Red Kites are almost entirely confined to the Western Palearctic, breeding from Morocco through Iberia, France and Germany to the Baltic, and also in the British Isles, the islands of the western Mediterranean, Italy and mid-eastern Europe. The world population numbers about 20,000 pairs.

The history of the Red Kite in Britain has been well documented. In brief, following centuries of persecution this formerly abundant bird was reduced to a handful of pairs in mid-Wales by about 1900. This tiny population only just survived into the 1960s, but in more recent decades improved adult survival and nesting success, linked to the reduction in persecution, have resulted in an increasingly strong recovery and spread. In 1989 the well-publicised reintroduction programme began in the Chilterns and Scotland; breeding by reintroduced stock was first recorded in both areas in 1992, and from these and other re-established nuclei there has been a steady spread into new areas. In 2011 the British population was estimated at about 1,800 breeding pairs, of which half were in Wales (RSPB website, www.rspb.org.uk) and around 600 in the Chilterns (Chilterns AONB website, www.chilternsaonb.org).

Eastern European Red Kite populations are migratory, wintering mainly in the northern Mediterranean basin, while western birds are resident or undertake short-range or dispersive movements. Welsh adults are largely sedentary but some juveniles move further, and some juveniles from reintroduction schemes have undertaken movements as far as Iberia.

In Gloucestershire, Red Kites had disappeared from the Cotswolds by about 1860 and from the Forest of Dean by about 1875. Up to 1980 there had only been seven twentieth-century records: one in 1955, two in the 1960s and four in the 1970s. This slight increase was probably due partly to observer effects and partly to the gradual recovery of the Welsh population. Between 1980 and 1994 there were usually fewer than three records per year, and the species was still on the county rarities list until well into the 1990s, but from 1995 to 2000 the reporting rate rose to about 20 sightings per year. This level was maintained until 2004, since when there has been very steep increase: 42 in 2005, 130 in 2008, 176 in 2010. In 2007 it was suggested in the GBR for the first time that observers were no longer submitting all their sightings. The majority of records are in the Cotswolds, implying that most of our birds come from the Chilterns rather than Wales, and at the time of writing (2012) Red Kites are a fairly common sight along much of the Oxfordshire border.

Records since 1980, including the current atlas survey period, show a distinct peak between March and June. While this could be exaggerated by multiple reports of lingering individuals, sizeable accumulations have been a feature in south-west England in recent springs. In 2009, Red Kites were reported from eight Gloucestershire localities on a single day, May 10th, including eight birds heading south-west together over New Fancy in the Dean, and in 2010 eight flew north over Slimbridge on May 25th.

In 2003 a pair of Red Kites summered in the east of the county but did not breed. In 2004 and 2005 a pair was displaying in the same area, but breeding was not confirmed; a report of confirmed breeding in 2005 (Holling & RBBP 2009) is incorrect. In 2006 near Withington on the Cotswolds one was observed flying off a nest, calling, and in mid-April 2007 in the same area a male was seen bringing food to a female. Mating was observed and a nest located, but the pair apparently deserted soon afterwards. In spring 2011 a farmer in the Blockley area reported a nest and filmed the birds collecting wool for nest-lining, and later in that year a family group was seen elsewhere. Finally in 2012 an active nest was found at this latter location, presumed also to have been occupied in 2011 (Terry Fenton). It is reasonable to assume that the Red Kite will become a regular breeding bird in our county.

There have been a few sightings here of wing-tagged Red Kites from reintroduction schemes in England and Scotland. More intriguingly perhaps, a chick ringed in June 1975 in mid-Wales was found dead in the county later that summer. If seen alive, this bird would have been an exciting find at the time.

In memory of Peter Jones

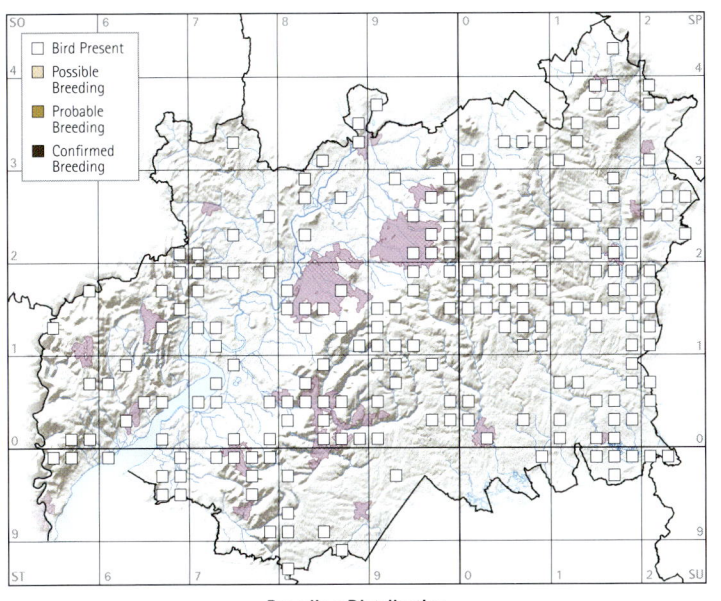

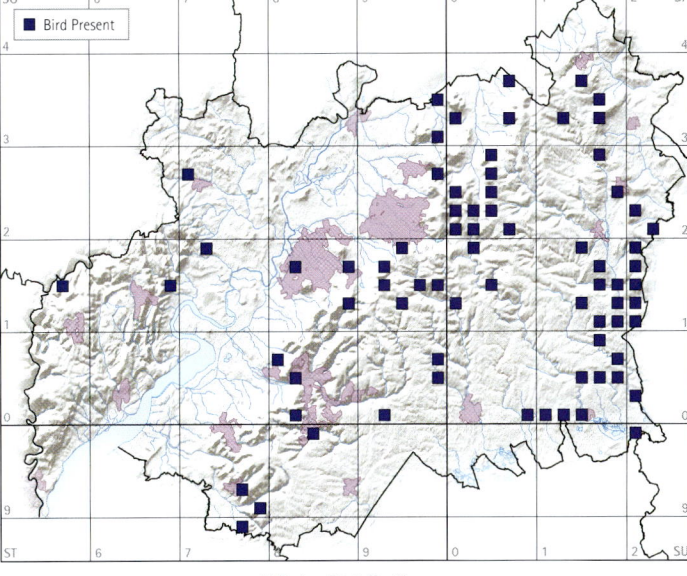

Breeding Distribution
(to preserve confidentiality, breeding status is not shown)

Winter Distribution

Honey-buzzard (European Honey Buzzard)
Pernis apivorus

Although it nests in Britain only in very small numbers, the Honey-buzzard is one of the world's most abundant raptors, breeding in wooded habitats from Spain to Sweden and eastwards in a broad band across Europe and western Asia. It is migratory, wintering in equatorial Africa, and the autumn passage of thousands of birds at sites such as the Straits of Gibraltar is one of the most impressive bird migration spectacles.

At no time in written ornithological history has the Honey-buzzard been anything but a rare summer visitor to Britain. In the last quarter of the nineteenth century one of the few counties where it was definitely recorded was Herefordshire, and some of the records came from areas very near the Gloucestershire border (1875–1900 Atlas). Mellersh suggested that Honey-buzzards bred in the Forest of Dean area in the late 1870s, but added that 'it has been ... difficult to obtain dates'. Swaine noted that 'several early books and manuscripts mention specimens obtained, birds seen and some breeding reports', chiefly from the Forest of Dean but also from several other localities, but similarly remarks that 'details are lacking'. Despite the anecdotal and unsubstantiated nature of these early reports it is probably safe to conclude that there were small numbers of Honey-buzzards in the county in past centuries, although it is impossible to be more precise about the species' true historical status.

Since the Second World War most records in Gloucestershire have been of birds on passage. Their frequency has increased since the turn of the twenty-first century: of the total of about 18 post-1970 county records, nine have been since 2000. This might be partly due to observer effects, but there has probably also been a real increase in the numbers of birds summering, if not breeding, fairly close by in the southern Welsh Marches and South Wales valleys; for example, breeding probably occurred in Gwent in 2000 and 2002 (Venables *et al.* 2008). There is some uncertainty about the total number of birds due to the possibility of multiple observations of the same individuals, but since 1980 there have been 13 sightings of passing migrants in Gloucestershire, of which ten were in autumn (between August 2nd and October 7th) and three in spring (April 16th to June 1st).

In addition to these migrants, birds were seen in 1976, 1979, 1980 and 1981 in the Forest of Dean on dates and in circumstances which suggested that breeding may have been taking place, especially in 1980 and 1981. Only the 1976 record was mentioned by Swaine and the GBR; presumably the others were omitted in order to protect the birds. Since then there has been only one sighting in the county during the breeding season: in July 1989, probably a male.

During the night of August 30th 2008 a female Honey-buzzard that had been satellite-tagged in North Wales was tracked flying over Cleeve Cloud on the Cotswold scarp – the only example to date of a bird on the Gloucestershire rarities list being recorded in the county without actually having been seen!

Marsh Harrier (Western Marsh Harrier)
Circus aeruginosus

Marsh Harriers breed across Eurasia from Iberia to the Pacific, in areas with temperate and Mediterranean climates. In early times Marsh Harriers bred in Britain but they became extinct here around 1900. The Norfolk Broads were recolonised in the 1920s, but after a limited spread into other parts of East Anglia, numbers again fell until by 1971 just one British pair remained at Minsmere in Suffolk (Taylor & Marchant 2011). Since then a remarkable recovery has occurred, with the current UK population estimated at around 450 pairs, mainly but by no means exclusively in the south and east of England. The species has enjoyed similar fortunes in most of Europe, with quite steep increases in the 1980s in particular. The Marsh Harrier is well named; it needs extensive wetlands with reed-beds for breeding, although it will also hunt over nearby grassland or crops.

Many Marsh Harriers move south for the winter and there is widespread dispersal from breeding areas. In Gloucestershire they occur only as migrants; our nearest breeding birds are probably in Somerset. Swaine referred to some old reports, but felt they lacked 'adequate detail'; he knew of about 24 sightings between 1910 and 1980. Since then there has been a remarkable increase, with about 20 in the 1980s, 40 in the 1990s and almost 100 since 2000 (numbers are approximate, as the same bird may be recorded more than once). Marsh Harriers have been seen in all months except December, but as the graph shows, the great majority occur in April, May and August. Almost all sightings are of single birds and about 60% have been in the estuary area, especially around Slimbridge and Frampton. The remainder are equally divided between the Severn Hams, the Cotswold Water Park and elsewhere.

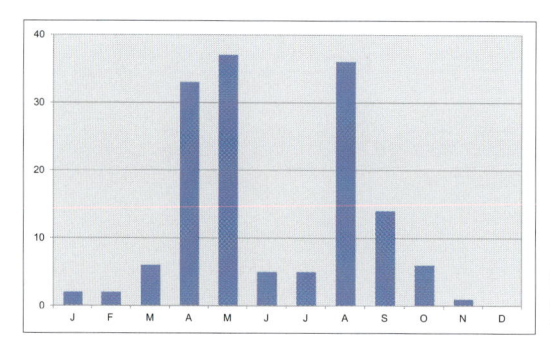

Marsh Harrier records by month, 1980–2010.

The county probably does not currently hold a wetland with a large enough reed-bed for Marsh Harriers to breed, although this may change in future. In the meantime it is heartening to know that there is an ever-increasing chance of seeing one of these magnificent raptors drifting over the marshes.

The only ringing recovery of a Marsh Harrier in Gloucestershire dates from the days when the species was very rare in Britain: a nestling male ringed near Leipzig in Germany on June 30th 1963 was found 'long dead' at Snowshill near Winchcombe in May 1964, a movement of 1,024 km.

Hen Harrier
Circus cyaneus

Ranging further north than other harriers, Hen Harriers breed in open country in the temperate climate zones of northern Eurasia. Although in Britain breeding birds are more or less restricted to upland moors, elsewhere they occupy a range of grassland habitats and even cultivated areas. They are migratory in northern and north-eastern Europe, but only partially so elsewhere. In winter the British population is boosted by arrivals from further north, though the numbers of immigrants appear to be fewer than previously thought (Dobson *et al.* 2012).

The breeding habitat and prey of British birds has put them into conflict with shooting interests, especially on grouse moors, and they have suffered long-term intense persecution. This has been so severe that at times in the early twentieth century the British population was restricted to Orkney and the Outer Hebrides. There has been some recolonisation and a partial recovery since then; in 2010 there were estimated to be around 660 pairs, about 80% of them in Scotland. However, this implied a decrease of almost 20% since 2004 and illegal persecution continues to be a serious problem; indeed in 2012 none may have bred in England.

Hen Harriers appear to have bred in Gloucestershire until the middle of the nineteenth century; Mellersh cites reports of breeding on open ground in the Forest of Dean around 1800. He described the bird as 'once a resident on the wolds but no longer so', adding 'it really is a serious question, whether it is worth while banishing every species of hawk from so many areas in England, for the sake of a little game'. The last breeding record appears to have been around 1860.

It was therefore all the more remarkable that in 2009 one of the very few English pairs bred in Gloucestershire. A hunting male was first seen by an observer during an atlas TTV, and the nest was located when another observer saw a food-pass. With the landowner's co-operation the nest was diligently guarded and monitored by a small team of local birders supported by the RSPB and Natural England, and the pair successfully raised one male chick. The nest was in a cereal field, suggesting that the pair may have originated from France, where this habitat is frequently used, rather than from British moorland. Breeding has not been recorded in the county since.

Setting aside this extraordinary event, it is as passage migrants and winter visitors that Hen Harriers are normally encountered in Gloucestershire. Swaine reported 15 to 20 birds between 1950 and 1980, with most records coming from the Cotswolds. Since then they have been recorded in every year except two, almost always as single birds and with a pattern of sightings suggesting that rather more pass through on migration than spend the winter here (see graph). The number of sightings in the last decade (on average about five birds each year) is rather higher than in the previous two, but this may well be due to observer effects. Nowadays most records of passage birds are from the Severn Vale, but this too may reflect the distribution of birdwatchers. The late spring peak (in May) is somewhat surprising and may include Fennoscandian birds making their way back north. Around a third of all sightings, and the majority of winter records, are from the Cotswolds, where set-aside and rough grassland can provide an abundance of prey for these graceful, charismatic hunters.

Occasionally observers report 'ring-tail' harriers: females or immatures that could not be specifically identified. These records are not included here.

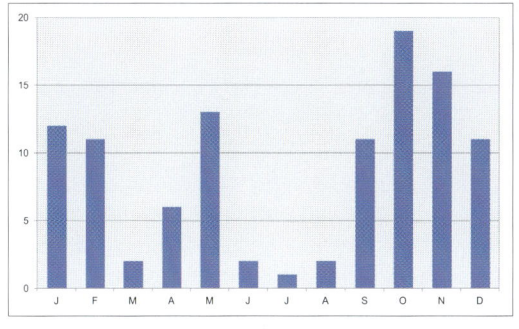

Hen Harrier records by month, 1980–2010.

Sponsored by David Evans and Vic Polley

Goshawk (Northern Goshawk)
Accipiter gentilis

Goshawks are seen less often than might be expected for such a large raptor, but the New Fancy viewpoint in the Forest of Dean has become one of the prime sites in Britain for watching their spring display flights. They have a Holarctic distribution: in Europe they are found from Spain to the Urals, and from Crete to northern Finland. They inhabit extensive woodlands and are largely sedentary, although juveniles can disperse away from their natal sites.

They had ceased to breed in most of Britain by the mid-nineteenth century, and their history here is not well documented. It was only during the fieldwork for the 1968–72 Breeding Atlas that regular nesting was proved to have resumed, but by the time of the 1988–91 Breeding Atlas they had become established in several areas, including the Dean and the Wye Valley. The present British population of about 450 pairs is considered to consist entirely of lost or escaped falconers' birds and their descendants.

Early records both national and local are difficult to assess, and Swaine was evidently unable to confirm some of those reported by Mellersh. The first definite modern Gloucestershire breeding record did not come until 1980, when a pair that had bred in Gwent crossed the border and nested in the county. The early years of the colonisation of the Dean and Wye were well documented (Anon 1989, 1990), but since Goshawks in other parts of Britain were suffering from thefts of eggs and chicks, the decision was taken not to divulge the breeding area. This undoubtedly benefited the birds, which spread rapidly both in the Gloucestershire Dean and in Gwent. Measurements of moulted feathers have confirmed that these early colonists were of the large, pale northern European type formerly favoured by falconers, though more recent measurements suggest a mixing with smaller birds. Some individuals have been seen to be wearing the remains of falconers' jesses, sure proof of their captive origin.

Sponsored by Terry Fenton

2007–11 Atlas fieldwork						Gloucestershire trends						UK population trends	
Number of tetrads in which recorded (max 683)					Occupied 10 km squares (max 26)				% of tetrads in which recorded (1st hour of TTV)		UK conservation status: Green	
	Total	Confirmed	Probable	Possible	Present	1968–71	1981–84	1988–91	2007–11	1988–91	2008–11	Long term	Short term
Breeding	76	14	29	15	18	0		8	16	1.2	1.2	–	–
Winter	70						2		19			–	–

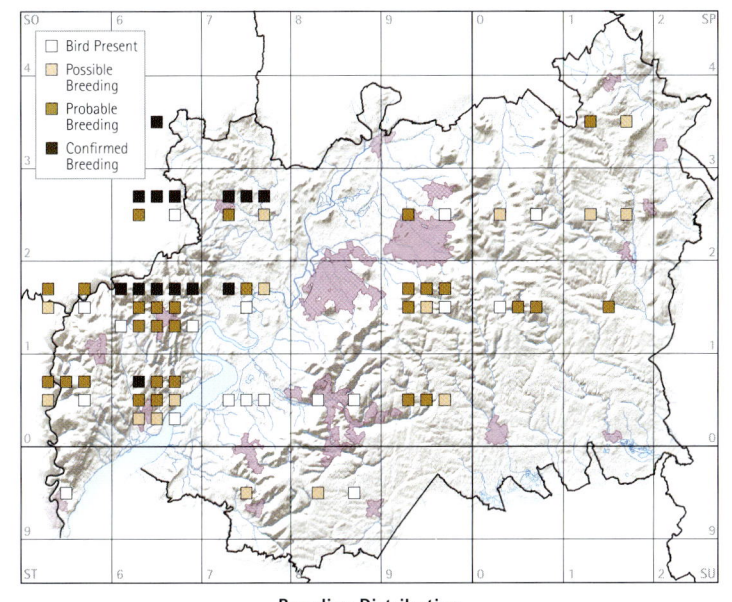

Breeding Distribution
(to preserve confidentiality, the dots for each 10 km square are grouped together)

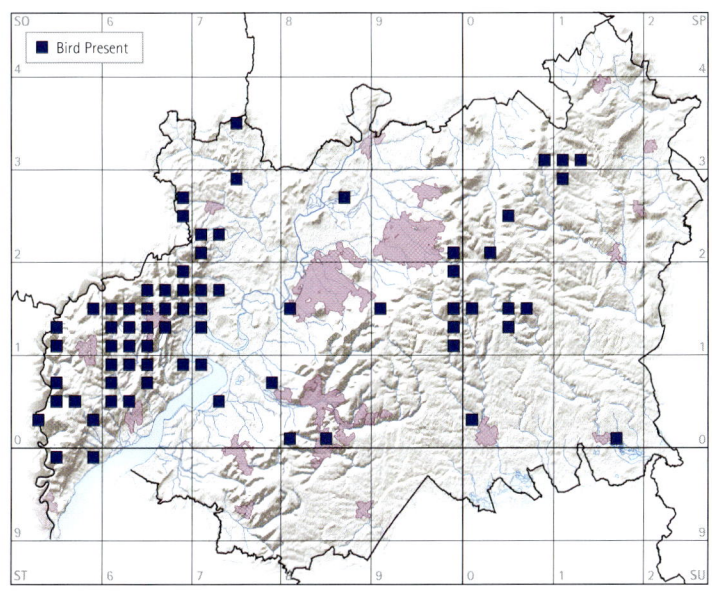

Winter Distribution

By 1984 there were five known pairs in Gloucestershire, increasing to 21 nesting sites by 1995, and the population in the Dean is now likely to have reached saturation level, with 62 known sites in 2011. Some 25 to 30 nests are monitored annually, along with a similar number in Gwent. As the population has increased so clutch and brood sizes have decreased, possibly due to intraspecific competition (Jerry Lewis), but the greatest negative effect on breeding success has been nest failure. Ten clutches of eggs are known to have been stolen between 1990 and 1994, but overall the main cause of failure has been the disturbance resulting from forestry operations. Although Petty (1996) considered that conflicts between Goshawks and tree harvesting had largely been overcome, this disturbance can still be a significant cause of reduced productivity at the high nesting densities found in the Dean and Wye (1.5–2 km spacing, and as close as 700 m when the topography allows separation on either side of a ridge). The Forestry Commission trains staff to identify nests in advance of operations, and they endeavour to carry out their work in such a way as to minimise disruption, noting breeding activity and waiting until the young have fledged, but even so a degree of conflict between large-scale forestry activities and wildlife conservation is inevitable. In any case, the greatest overall threat to Goshawks at present is probably from illegal killing during the autumn, when dispersing juveniles are attracted to young Pheasants being kept in pens prior to release for shooting.

As the main Dean and Wye Valley woodlands are surrounded by a mostly farmed landscape, with little suitable nesting habitat, it is not surprising that it was not until 2000 that Goshawks began to be recorded at all frequently elsewhere in Gloucestershire, with breeding first confirmed outside the Dean as recently as 2007 (Terry Fenton).

Most movements of Gloucestershire-ringed Goshawks involve short distances of up to about 20 km. However one flew 150 km to the Welsh coast near Cardigan, where it was found 'oiled' and rehabilitated before release. Another Gloucestershire bird holds the record for the longest-lived British Goshawk: 18 years, eight months and 27 days.

Sparrowhawk (Eurasian Sparrowhawk)
Accipiter nisus

Sparrowhawks are widespread in most of Europe, north-west Africa and Asia Minor and eastwards across Asia to the Pacific. They nest in almost any kind of woodland apart from the very smallest, and will hunt in a wide range of habitats where there is sufficient cover to enable them to take their prey by surprise. Southern and western birds, including those in Britain, are mostly resident, but from Fennoscandia and Russia eastwards many are migratory, some wintering as far south as the northern tropics.

The marked decline of the Sparrowhawk in Britain due to toxic seed dressings during the late 1950s and early 1960s has been well documented, and the population has long since recovered from that setback. The European population currently numbers about a quarter of a million pairs, with some 40,000 pairs in Britain.

Nesting Sparrowhawks are quite secretive, but their presence can often be detected by their aerial display flights during the spring. Later in the season the nestlings soon become noisy to the extent that they may give away the presence of a nest, although during the current atlas fieldwork in Gloucestershire breeding was confirmed in only about 15% of the tetrads in which birds were recorded.

Swaine noted that Sparrowhawks were 'probably most numerous in the Forest of Dean and in the wooded parts of the Cotswold river valleys', but today a great many records also come from suburban garden feeding stations, which provide good hunting opportunities for this small, agile hawk. The 2003–07 Cotswolds Atlas registered a 54% increase in occupied tetrads and a 150% increase in confirmed breeding since the 1983–87 survey, although this could well have been influenced by more intensive surveying. County BBS figures have fluctuated quite widely, but have tended to be rather higher since 2003 (records in 16% of survey squares per year on average) than from 1994 to 2002 (12% of squares on average).

The current maps, both summer and winter, reveal a widespread distribution across the county, but also indicate that Sparrowhawks may be less numerous in the more open areas of the Cotswolds and the Severn Vale. Contrary to Swaine's assessment, there are also apparently gaps in the distribution in some parts of the Forest of Dean. It could be that the habitat here makes Sparrowhawks less easily detectable, and nowadays there is also the possibility that some may be preyed upon by Goshawks.

Sparrowhawks are usually solitary outside the breeding season, and the maximum TTV count of six in tetrad SP14V in the far north-east of the county, at Ebrington on New Year's Eve 2010, though noteworthy, is unlikely to have referred to a 'flock'. On the other hand, up to six were seen hunting together at the huge Starling roost at Slimbridge during the winter of 1997. Sparrowhawks will take a wide range of prey, and more unusual victims in the county have included Little Stint, Jack Snipe, Red-necked Phalarope and Green Woodpecker.

Gloucestershire Sparrowhawks evidently do not travel far: of 29 ringing recoveries involving the county up to 2010, 24 related to movements within the county and another three to or from neighbouring counties. The only two longer-distance movements were by a male nestling ringed near Barnsley, South Yorkshire in June 1992 and killed by road traffic later that year near Broadway, and another male chick ringed in central Finland in July 1983 and found dead from injuries at Miserden, near Stroud, on November 29th that year.

Sponsored by Colin Studholme

Species accounts   145

2007-11 Atlas fieldwork					Gloucestershire trends					UK population trends	
Number of tetrads in which recorded (max 683)					Occupied 10 km squares (max 26)				% of tetrads in which recorded (1st hour of TTV)		UK conservation status: **Green**	
	Total	Confirmed	Probable	Possible	Present	1968-71	1981-84	1988-91	2007-11	1988-91	2008-11	Long term	Short term
Breeding	436	66	62	230	78	24		25	26	22.7	16.3	+81%	-8%
Winter	492						25		26			–	–

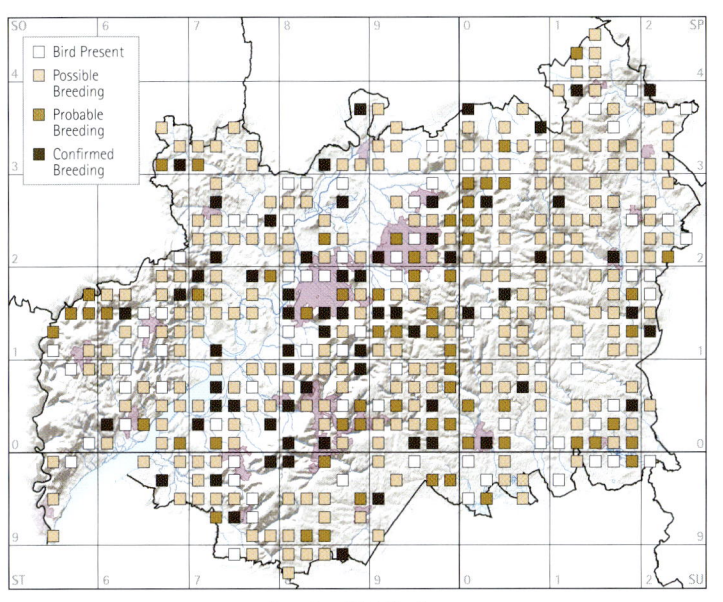

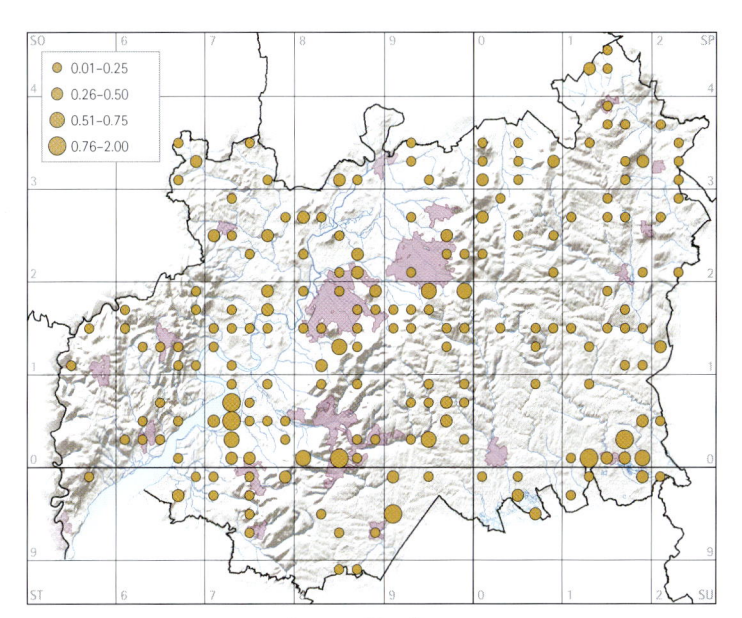

Breeding Distribution

Summer Abundance

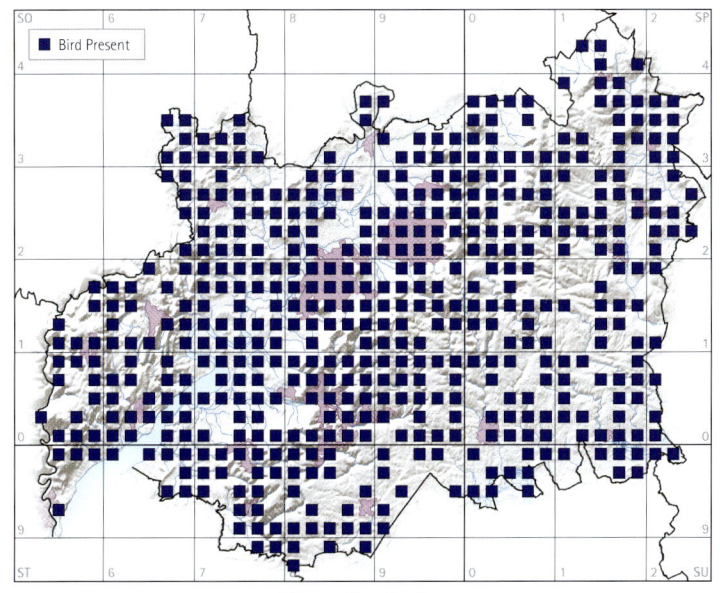

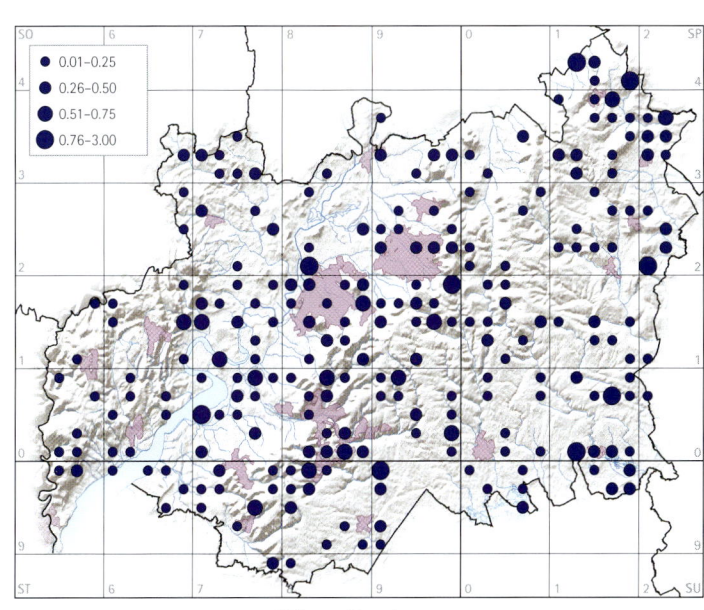

Winter Distribution

Winter Abundance

Buzzard (Common Buzzard)
Buteo buteo

The recolonisation of lowland England by the Buzzard has been one of the most dramatic events in the birdlife of the British Isles over the last few decades.

Buzzards range over all but the most northern parts of Europe, and eastwards across middle latitudes of Asia. Those in the east of the range are long-distance migrants, but in southern and western Europe, including the British Isles, they are mainly short-distance migrants or residents. They were formerly widespread throughout Britain, but persecution by gamekeepers and others from the eighteenth century onward meant that by 1900 they were largely confined to strongholds in Wales, Scotland and the west of England. There was a partial recovery after about 1920, but the myxomatosis epidemic starting in the early 1950s and the ill-effects of toxic agricultural chemicals in the 1950s and 1960s caused further setbacks. By the time of the 1968–72 Breeding Atlas they were still mainly restricted to the South-west Peninsula, Wales, the Lake District and much of Scotland, with a few in the north of Ireland. There was rather little change up to the 1988–91 Breeding Atlas, with a slight expansion eastwards in England and a more noticeable consolidation in Ireland. Since then however there has been a truly remarkable push eastwards across England, and today they are to be found almost throughout the country.

The fortunes of the Buzzard in Gloucestershire have closely followed national developments. It was quite common here until about 1850, but there was then a sharp decline and it became extinct as breeding bird by about 1890. It remained a scarce visitor until the 1940s, when breeding recommenced. The setback due to myxomatosis in the 1950s was fairly temporary, but the Buzzard remained decidedly uncommon for several decades: by 1980 it was still a 'scarce and local breeding species', in the Dean, Wye Valley and parts of the Cotswolds (Swaine). The next two decades were the main period of increase and spread. By about 1990 some 400 records were being submitted to the county recorder each year, with increasing numbers relating to breeding. By the year 2000 well over 500 records were being received each year, pairs had become established in the Severn Vale, and it was estimated that the number of pairs in the Cotswolds had doubled, from about 60 to 120, in the four years since 1996. The 2001 GBR stated that 'the breeding population must be in the low hundreds ... groups of up to five birds are no longer unusual'. In 2007 the second Cotswolds Atlas revealed an astonishing increase from 78 to 289 occupied tetrads since 1987, and estimated that the number of breeding pairs there could have increased by a factor of 20 over the same period. County BBS figures also show a steady increase since the mid-1990s, although numbers have recently levelled off (see graph on p. 49).

The maps confirm that Buzzards are widespread at both seasons, the only noticeable gaps being in the larger built-up areas. The breeding season abundance map hints at higher densities along the Cotswold scarp and in the north-west around Newent, while they are apparently less common in some parts of the Vale. Breeding densities also appear to be relatively low in the Forest of Dean; this might seem surprising, but feeding opportunities may be better in farmed landscapes than in areas dominated by trees. In any case this relative scarcity of birds in the Forest is less obvious in winter.

The highest number seen during atlas TTVs was 27, at both seasons: in December 2007 in SO50W on the edge of the Dean plateau near Lydney, and in April 2008 in SP10Y near the Oxfordshire border. In recent years some large groups of birds have been recorded, especially in autumn when they feed on earthworms in ploughed fields; the largest count to date is 56 in October 2009 near Birdwood, between Gloucester and Mitcheldean. These numbers would have been unimaginable when Swaine was writing at the beginning of the 1980s.

Of the 12 Buzzard ringing recoveries involving Gloucestershire up to 2010, one revealed a flight of more than 100 km: a 2005 chick from the New Forest, Hampshire was found dead in August that year near Winchcombe.

Sponsored by Norman Hockley, and in memory of R J B Christian

Species accounts 147

	2007-11 Atlas fieldwork					Gloucestershire trends						UK population trends		
	Number of tetrads in which recorded (max 683)					Occupied 10 km squares (max 26)				% of tetrads in which recorded (1st hour of TTV)		UK conservation status: Green		
	Total	Confirmed	Probable	Possible	Present	1968-71	1981-84	1988-91	2007-11	1988-91	2008-11	Long term	Short term
Breeding	675	279	236	137	23	17		23	26	19.9	76.9	+435%	+72%
Winter	676						21		26			–	–

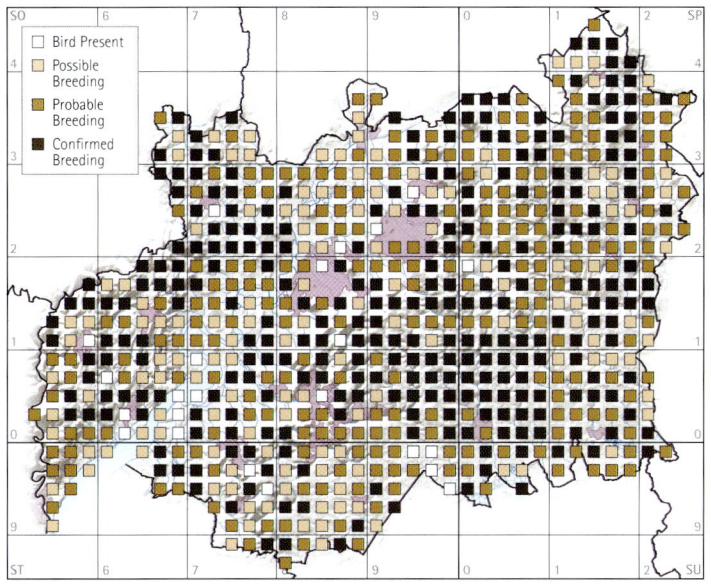

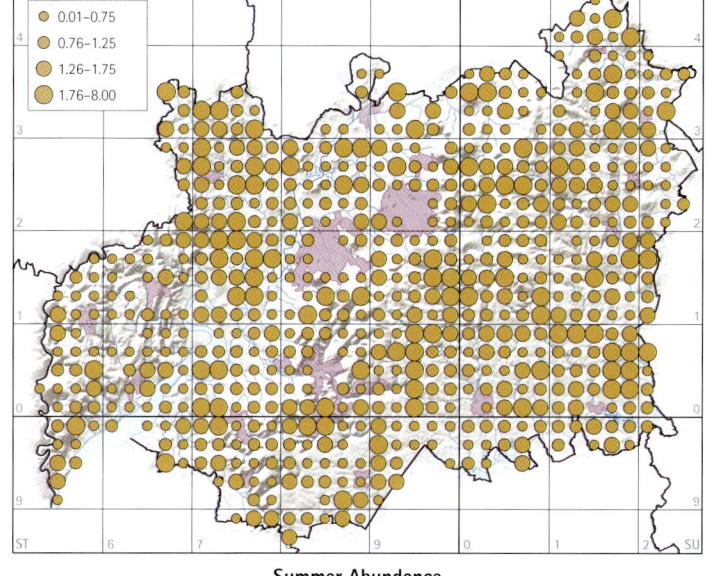

Breeding Distribution

Summer Abundance

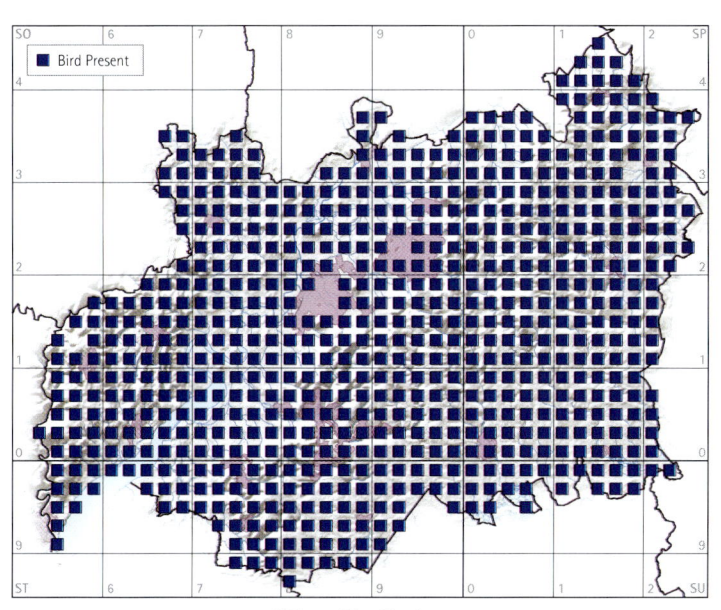

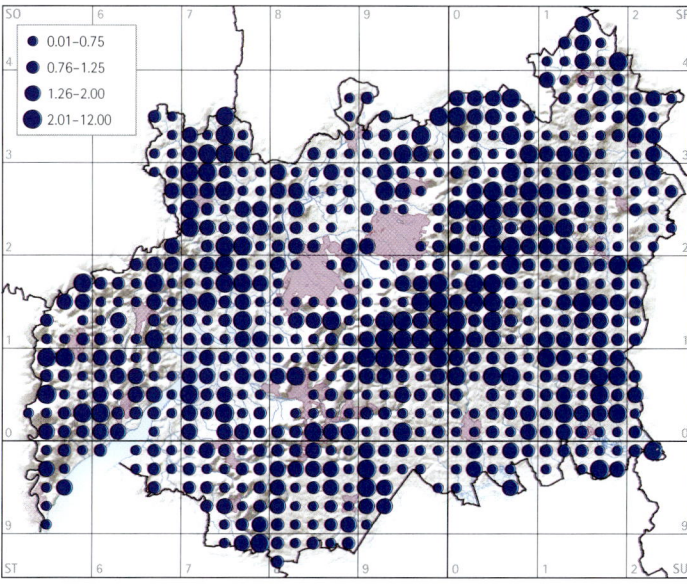

Winter Distribution

Winter Abundance

Osprey
Pandion haliaetus

Ospreys occur on every continent except Antarctica, breeding right across the northern hemisphere and wintering further south, and with a breeding population in Australia as well. By the nineteenth and early twentieth centuries they were absent from many parts of their former European range, because of persecution by egg collectors and hunters and through conflict with sport-fishing interests. Since then there has been some recovery, including the well-publicised recolonisation of Scotland in the mid-1950s following their extinction there in 1916, and the subsequent spread south into England and Wales. There are currently thought to be between 250 and 300 breeding pairs in the UK (RSPB website, www.rspb.org.uk), but they are still threatened by persecution and disturbance.

Most west European birds migrate to sub-Saharan Africa for the winter, and British birds migrate through Spain to winter in West Africa; it is as migrants that they occur in Gloucestershire. Mellersh referred to just three records, all involving birds that were shot. However by 1980 Swaine was able to report that half of the 30 county records since 1850 had been post-1960, reflecting the general recovery. This upward trend has continued since, with records in every year. The average number of sightings per year has risen from two in the 1980s to four in the 1990s and ten since 2000; numbers unimaginable a generation ago. Almost all records are of single birds and most are in spring (see graph), hinting at different migration routes or behaviour in spring and autumn.

Satellite tracking is starting to reveal more information about Osprey migration, but there is still much to learn.

The earliest and latest dates in Gloucestershire are March 13th 1993 and November 6th 1998. About a third of records are from the well-watched parts of the Severn Estuary, but Ospreys have been recorded county-wide and if they find suitable water for fishing they will stay for a day or two. A notable sequence of sightings from Symonds Yat (two in 2002, two in 2007, one in 2008 and two in 2009) may reflect the presence of sharp-eyed birders at the Peregrine viewpoint there, but it is tempting to speculate that they follow the generally north–south running Wye valley on migration.

If the breeding range of this iconic species continues to expand, the Cotswold Water Park must surely be a candidate for colonisation.

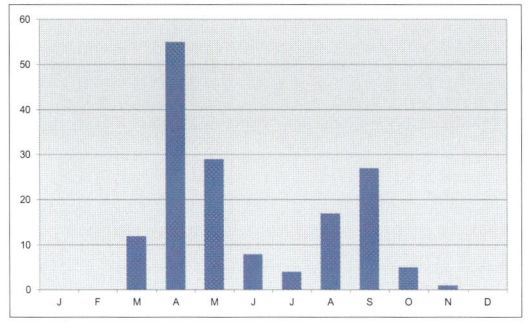

Osprey records by month, 1980–2010.

Sponsored by Ken Garrington

Black Kite
Milvus migrans

Occurring across most of the Old World, Black Kites are probably the most numerous of all raptors. They are summer visitors to Europe, breeding as far north as the Arctic Circle. There is just one county record, a single bird seen over Symonds Yat on May 15th 1985.

Montagu's Harrier
Circus pygargus

Breeding across Europe and Asia, with Western Palearctic breeders wintering south of the Sahara, Montagu's Harrier is one of Britain's rarest breeding birds. The tiny English population includes (in good years) a few pairs in our neighbouring county of Wiltshire. They prefer low or sparse vegetation for hunting, but need rather taller, undisturbed cover for breeding.

Swaine mentioned 'about six' reports from the nineteenth century, but considered none of them convincing. He also cited 'apparently reliable' reports of a 'late bird' in Gloucester on November 17th 1922, and one at Colesbourne on April 1st 1963, but these dates are so far outside the normal range that some doubt must be attached to them. If they are excluded, there are 11 Gloucestershire records, with dates between April 27th and August 15th. The first was a juvenile shot at Northleach on August 15th 1923 which was given to the Cheltenham Museum. The rest have all been since 1958, with seven from 1995 onwards, but the increase in frequency is probably due to observer effects. All have been near the Severn Estuary or in the Cotswolds, apart from one at Coombe Hill in May 2010.

Rough-legged Buzzard
Buteo lagopus

Breeding on the tundra at high latitudes in Eurasia and North America, Rough-legged Buzzards move south for the winter, preferring open and largely treeless terrain. They are regular winter visitors to eastern England, albeit in small numbers, but rarely come very far west. Swaine described several old records as being without convincing evidence. Thus there are just four accepted county records, all of single birds:

1907: one trapped at Guiting Wood in the Cotswolds on March 30th was preserved and presented to Gloucester Museum.
1920: one was killed on Dumbleton Hill, November 17th.
1969: Aylburton Warth, April 9th.
1989: Guiting Power, June 1st.

Golden Eagle
Aquila chrysaetos

Golden Eagles breed discontinuously across Eurasia, including Scotland, and in North America, mainly preferring mountainous terrain. Although the American population is migratory, most European birds, including those in Scotland, are sedentary, so sightings of birds away from their core areas are very unusual.

Mellersh cited a single record at Whiteshill near Painswick from before 1870, which is not considered reliable, and one at Bibury in 1954 was considered to be an escape (the species does not appear in Swaine). The only confirmed record is of one at Symonds Yat on July 9th 1989. This individual, an immature at least two years old, was also seen in Herefordshire and Wales.

Red-footed Falcon
Falco vespertinus

Red-footed Falcons breed from eastern Europe eastwards, wintering in southern Africa. Their migration route lies significantly further west in spring than in autumn and, in the spring of some years, many wander well to the west of the European breeding range.

Mellersh referred to two records of birds being killed, one near Colesbourne in 1870 and another at nearby Duntisbourne 'possibly in the same year'. More recently there were ten county records between 1973 and 2008, nine of which fell between May 15th and June 2nd (the exception being an adult male on September 16th 1974). Eight of the ten were at or near the Cotswold Water Park, with several crossing the Gloucestershire–Wiltshire border. All were of singles except for two instances when two females were recorded together.

Gyr Falcon (Gyrfalcon)
Falco rusticolus

Gyr Falcons are mainly sedentary in their circumpolar Arctic range; most records from further south relate to dispersing immature birds. A few are recorded in the British Isles in most years, the majority in the north and west of Scotland and Ireland.

There is an extraordinary, detailed account in Witchell & Strugnell of a bird near Cheltenham which was seen to dash itself on the ground while chasing small birds, whereupon Mr Strugnell 'seized it in his soft felt hat'. A local taxidermist identified it as a young Gyr Falcon, and this appears to have been confirmed when it was independently identified (from a drawing) as an immature white morph, probably from Greenland. The only other county record is of one at Slimbridge on January 26th, February 15th and March 11th 1964.

Kestrel (Common Kestrel)
Falco tinnunculus

Kestrels breed over practically the whole of Europe, and widely in Asia and Africa. Birds from western and southern Europe, including those nesting in Britain, are only partially migratory, but those from further north and east mostly undertake longer migrations, some wintering as far south as sub-Saharan Africa. Kestrels use a very wide range of habitats but avoid extensive dense woodlands, and in Britain they breed mainly in relatively low-lying areas. Optimal habitats contain some rough grassland, where they can find food (mainly voles, although Kestrels will take a wide range of prey), and tree-holes for nesting (though they also use holes or ledges on cliffs or buildings, disused nests of other birds, and nest-boxes).

The whole of the western and northern European population suffered severe declines between the 1950s and the late 1960s, due to the effects of toxic farm chemicals. Numbers recovered subsequently, but more recently there have been further declines in the British Isles, as shown in the fact-box, and elsewhere in Europe. There are currently about 55,000 pairs in Britain. The 1968–72 Breeding Atlas described the Kestrel as 'the most widespread and numerous raptor' here, but in recent years, in most parts of the country at least, it is a Buzzard that is more likely to be spotted in flight over the motorway. Kestrels are conspicuous when hunting, but when nesting they can be surprisingly unobtrusive until the young are at the point of fledging. Of the county records during the current atlas survey for which a 'confirmed' breeding code was provided, nearly half related to fledged young.

Swaine described the Kestrel as quite a common breeding species throughout Gloucestershire and present at all seasons: 'the decline in Eastern England ... attributed to toxic chemicals, was not noticeable in this county.' Kestrels are still fairly common and well distributed here, and there appears to be little evidence of any significant local decline. Indeed, although county BBS figures have fluctuated, the long-term situation has been remarkably stable, with records in 25% of survey squares per year on average both between 1994 and 2002 and between 2003 and 2010. In the area covered by the Cotswolds Atlases there was actually a 70% increase in the number of tetrads with sightings of Kestrels between 1987 and 2007, and although this rise was thought possibly to be due to greater survey effort, such a substantial change seems likely to reflect a real increase in numbers. The current breeding distribution map shows a similarly wide range in the Cotswolds area, and indeed the only major gaps in the whole county are, as might be expected, in the densely wooded Forest of Dean and around the larger conurbations. The breeding season abundance map confirms that the most favoured areas are in the eastern half of the county, mainly on the Cotswold dip-slope. This is presumably associated with good feeding habitat, although Kestrels are noticeably less abundant in what seem to be equally suitable areas in some parts of the Severn Vale.

The winter maps reveal a very similar picture, with records from slightly more tetrads, and again a concentration on the Cotswold dip-slope. In conclusion it would seem once again that recent significant declines in Kestrel numbers in some parts of the country have apparently not taken place to any noticeable degree in our county.

Up to 2010 there had been 50 recoveries of ringed Kestrels involving Gloucestershire, about half of which revealed movements within the county or to and from neighbouring counties. Most of the rest involved interchanges with other English and Welsh counties, the notable exceptions being a bird ringed as a chick in Dumfries & Galloway in June 1983 and found dead in Gloucestershire in October that year, and three ringed as nestlings in the Netherlands (two) and Sweden which were found dead here during their first winters. These recoveries suggest that the slightly wider distribution of Kestrels in Gloucestershire in winter compared with summer could be partly due to an influx of winter visitors from elsewhere, as well as to post-breeding dispersal within the county.

Sponsored by the Cheltenham Bird Club

Species accounts   151

2007–11 Atlas fieldwork					Gloucestershire trends						UK population trends		
Number of tetrads in which recorded (max 683)					Occupied 10 km squares (max 26)				% of tetrads in which recorded (1st hour of TTV)		UK conservation status: Amber 1		
	Total	Confirmed	Probable	Possible	Present	1968–71	1981–84	1988–91	2007–11	1988–91	2008–11	Long term	Short term
Breeding	546	103	119	260	64	26		26	26	37.3	32.7	–39%	–28%
Winter	588						26		26			–	–

Breeding Distribution

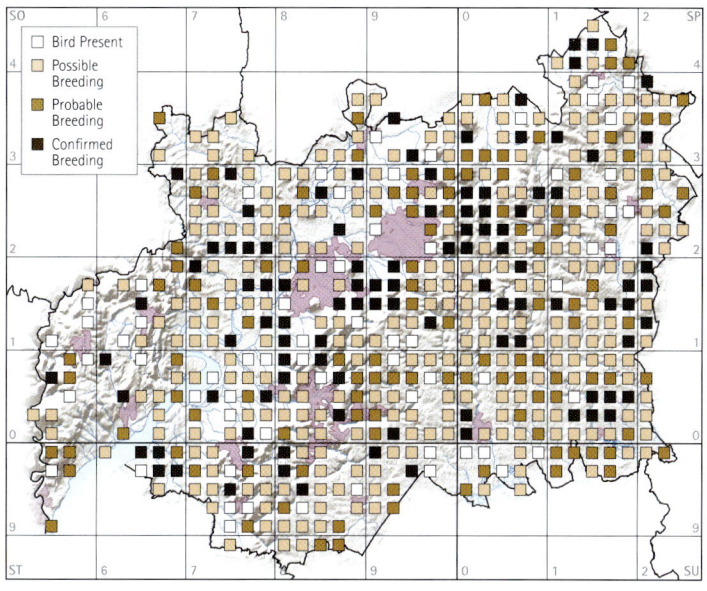

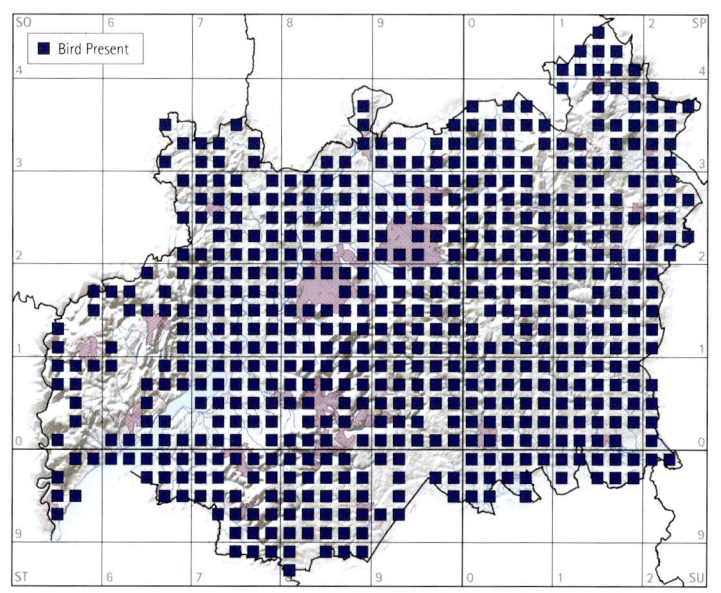

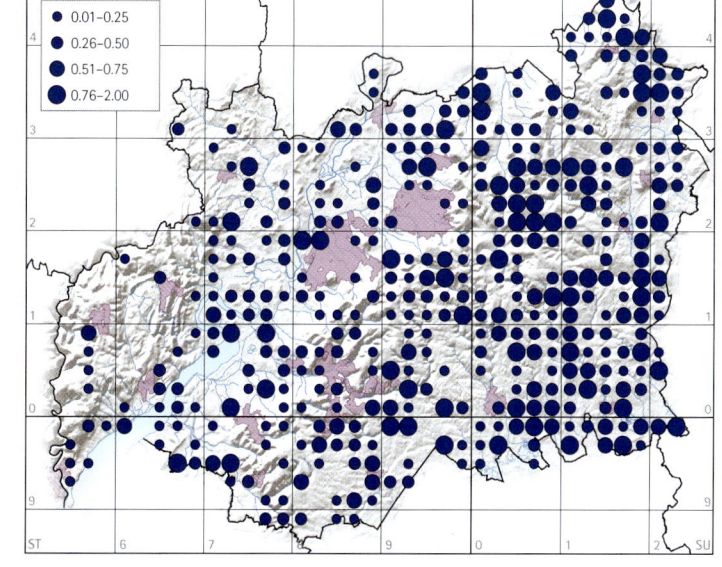

Summer Abundance

Winter Distribution

Winter Abundance

Merlin
Falco columbarius

This small, fierce falcon breeds in Iceland and across wide areas of northern Eurasia and North America, with most birds wintering well south of their breeding range. The European population numbers between 11,000 and 19,000 pairs. An increase in numbers in the British Isles since the 1980s has been attributed to the use of forest margins for breeding; a survey of the British breeding population in 2008 produced an estimate of about 1,100 pairs. However, most British Merlins nest on moorland in Scotland, northern England and Wales, and this is now a very rare breeder in south-west England with just the odd pair present on Exmoor, though a pair did breed in Wiltshire in 2005. Most of the British population remains in the country all year round, but many move to lowland areas, particularly coastal marshes, during the winter months. Winter also sees the arrival in the British Isles of migrants from Iceland.

Swaine referred to breeding records from the Forest of Dean 'a hundred years ago or more', but there is no firm evidence to confirm this. Otherwise he described Merlins as scarce but regular visitors from autumn to spring, mostly from October to April and generally with just one to four reports per year.

Even allowing for increasing numbers of observers and better recording, it is clear that Merlins are now occurring in Gloucestershire more frequently, as revealed in the comparative winter data in the fact-box. There were over 70 sightings in the county in 2008 alone, for example. The vast majority of records concern single birds, though occasionally two are seen together. The Severn Estuary and its margins produce most records, but fairly regular sightings come from other open areas of the Severn Vale and Hams. The Cotswolds are also well represented; a typical sighting here is of a hunting bird

ROB BROOKES

| | 2007–11 Atlas fieldwork ||||| Gloucestershire trends |||||| UK population trends ||
| | Number of tetrads in which recorded (max 683) ||||| Occupied 10 km squares (max 26) |||| % of tetrads in which recorded (1st hour of TTV) || UK conservation status: **Amber 2** ||
	Total	Confirmed	Probable	Possible	Present	1968–71	1981–84	1988–91	2007–11	1988–91	2008–11	Long term	Short term
Breeding	12	0	0	0	12	0		0	0	0	0	–	–
Winter	58							5	20			–	–

speeding across a stubble field, sending finches, buntings or Skylarks into a panic. On the other hand, despite the increase, records from the Forest of Dean and the Over Severn area are still fairly unusual.

The first autumn birds typically appear in late September or early October and most have departed by April, though there are a few records in late August and in May. Sightings in midsummer are very unusual; since 2000 there has only been one June record (two birds at Slimbridge on June 15th 2008), with three in July and one in the first half of August.

Some fairly intensive Merlin ringing programmes in the British Isles in recent years have resulted in three recoveries in the county. All were ringed as nestlings, in North Yorkshire, Co. Durham and Dumfries & Galloway, 230–360 km from their Gloucestershire recovery sites. One was found dead and one injured, and the third was unlucky enough to be killed by a cat. All three were ringed between 1987 and 1992 and at least two died in their first winter.

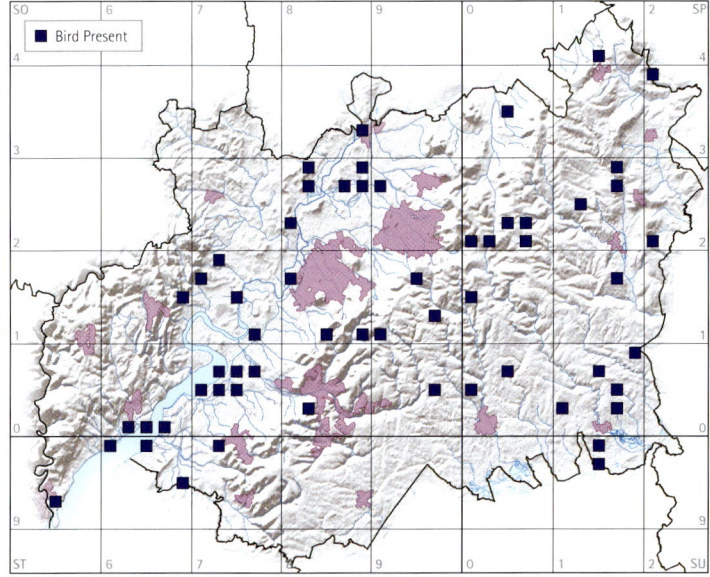

Winter Distribution

PETER SCOTT

Hobby (Eurasian Hobby)
Falco subbuteo

The fast-flying, graceful Hobby breeds across all but the most northern parts of Europe, and in parts of North Africa and much of northern and central Asia. It is a migrant, wintering in southern Africa and the north of the Indian subcontinent. The European population is in the region of 41,000–60,000 pairs.

Formerly much less common and restricted to southern England, the British population has expanded in recent times, though this is still rather a scarce bird in much of Wales and a rare breeder in Scotland. The latest estimates suggest that there are up to 2,200 pairs in Britain. Hobbies breed in a variety of habitats as long as their usual prey (hirundines, insects and even occasionally bats) is available. They tend to avoid uplands and also large areas of dense woodland, although a very recent study in south-east England concluded that not only have their numbers been significantly underestimated in the past, but that most nests were on the edges of woods or just inside (Clements & Everett 2012). They almost always nest in old Carrion Crows' nests, often making use of nests that have already been occupied by Crows earlier in the season. However the nests are not easy to find, and Hobbies are very late breeders, typically laying in June and having young in the nest well into August, so some pairs may well have been overlooked even during the intensive atlas surveying. The most likely way to obtain proof of breeding is to hear noisy young calling near the nest late in the season.

Numbers in Gloucestershire have certainly increased since 1980. The 2003–07 Cotswolds Atlas reported confirmed breeding in nine tetrads in that area compared to just one tetrad 20 years previously, and in 2009 it was estimated that there were at least 21 breeding pairs in the county as a whole. These figures are likely to be minima and clearly demonstrate that the species is doing well,

Sponsored by Rob Husbands and by the Cotswold Water Park Trust

Species accounts

	2007–11 Atlas fieldwork					Gloucestershire trends					UK population trends		
	Number of tetrads in which recorded (max 683)					Occupied 10 km squares (max 26)				% of tetrads in which recorded (1st hour of TTV)		UK conservation status: Green	
	Total	Confirmed	Probable	Possible	Present	1968–71	1981–84	1988–91	2007–11	1988–91	2008–11	Long term	Short term
Breeding	204	26	17	96	65	11		12	24	1.2	2.1	–	+20%
Winter	0							0		0		–	–

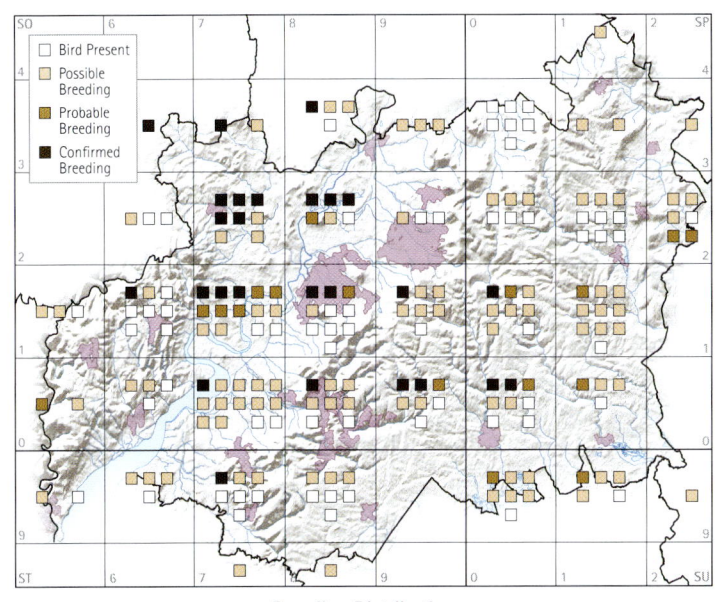

Breeding Distribution
(to preserve confidentiality, the dots for each 10 km square are grouped together)

although it should be borne in mind that the map reflects four years of fieldwork, during which time some pairs may well have moved from one tetrad to another. Indeed, one observer recorded what was probably the same pair nesting in two or possibly three different tetrads during the survey, even though they had moved only a few hundred metres between years.

The map shows that Hobbies occur across much of the county but that they evidently avoid not only treeless areas but also heavily wooded regions; although they have bred in the Forest of Dean, sightings there are generally few and usually of single birds. The high concentration of confirmed breeding records in the north-west (in and around 10 km square SO72) may be due to the nest-finding skills of two observers who are licensed to ring legally protected raptors, rather than a higher density of Hobbies. Specific breeding sites cannot be disclosed, as sadly Hobbies are still illegally persecuted for their beautiful red-brown eggs.

The earliest spring sighting on record for the county is one at Edgeworth near Stroud on April 4th 1986, but the third week of April is the more usual time for the first migrants to appear. Since the late 1980s most years have produced double-figure counts at the Cotswold Water Park, particularly during May in the western section, for example 25 in May 2003 and 24 in May 2006. However this area is not a breeding stronghold and some of the birds seen there are likely to be passage migrants, or breeding birds from the wider area gathering around a good food source. Another favoured site is the Frampton area, though single figures are more usual here.

By early October most have departed south and later records are unusual, but they do include an unusually late bird in the eastern section of the Water Park on October 30th 1988.

A fully grown Hobby ringed in Belgium on August 11th 2004 was found dead near Lydbrook in the Dean in July 2010. The dates suggest that it may have been a British breeding bird that was ringed on passage.

Peregrine (Peregrine Falcon)
Falco peregrinus

This powerful falcon is often regarded as the fastest creature on earth, reaching speeds of up to 300 km per hour during an attacking 'stoop'. It breeds on every continent except Antarctica. In Britain its strongholds have traditionally been in the upland and coastal regions of the west and north. The population here had already been reduced by around 50% by the end of the Second World War, when many were killed because of the threat they posed to the carrier pigeons which were vital for wartime communications. During the 1950s and early 1960s numbers declined even more as a result of toxic farm chemicals, and Peregrines disappeared from most parts of southern England. Although still subject to illegal persecution in some areas, numbers have gradually recovered since then and there are now about 1,500 pairs in Britain.

Swaine described Peregrines as chiefly autumn and winter visitors to Gloucestershire, with up to four birds noted annually in the Severn Vale, especially in the Slimbridge area; elsewhere in the county sightings seem to have been rather rare at that time. Swaine also referred to a record of a pair nesting on the old Severn railway bridge near Sharpness before construction was finished in 1879, and there were breeding attempts in the Wye Valley in 1929 and in 'several years' between 1937 and 1960. After a long absence Peregrines again bred in the county in 1982, when a pair raised young near Symonds Yat in the Wye Valley. They returned the following year but the nest was robbed on two occasions, prompting the RSPB to introduce wardening at the site. Since then Peregrines have bred there every year, with consistently high breeding success although, deplorably, one of the young was shot in 1987. This site has become a very popular visitor attraction.

During the 1980s records from elsewhere in the county increased steadily and the Ashleworth and Hasfield Ham area joined Slimbridge as a regular wintering site for Peregrines. It was not until 1991 that a second breeding site was located, in the Forest of Dean, but by 1999 five pairs were breeding in the west of the county. In 2002 a pair was found nesting in the Cotswolds, and subsequent years have seen a further increase and a spread into the Vale. In 2007 a pair nested successfully for the first time on Gloucester Royal Hospital, and in 2010 a pair raised young in a nest-box on Christ Church in the heart of Cheltenham. Urban nesting by Peregrines has become increasingly common in Britain in recent years. Elsewhere, pairs have also bred in old Ravens' nests on tall electricity pylons, but most nests are still in more natural sites in the Dean and Wye area. Ten pairs definitely bred in the county in 2009, with possible breeding at four more sites. The prospects for the Peregrine look good, though it still faces persecution from certain quarters, as demonstrated by an adult female found shot close to a nest site in the Dean in June 2009.

Outside the breeding season records are much more widespread and Peregrines may now be encountered anywhere in the county. During the current atlas survey nearly a quarter of tetrads produced at least one winter record. Most sightings come from the Severn Vale, particularly near the estuary and at the Severn Hams, where potential prey is plentiful. There are also frequent reports from the Cotswold Water Park and in the northern part of the Cotswolds, though there are still relatively few sightings further south.

Peregrines will take a wide variety of prey, and in Gloucestershire they sometimes take advantage of stormy conditions when exhausted seabirds such as petrels, Manx Shearwaters and auks are blown into the Severn Estuary and present an easy target. Elsewhere, prey remains found at the Christ Church nest site have included Teal, Snipe, Great Spotted Woodpecker and Great Grey Shrike!

Up to 2010 there had been eight recoveries of ringed Peregrines revealing movements between Gloucestershire and mainly western areas of England and Wales. In addition, two ringed as chicks in Sweden and Finland were recovered here during their first winters, showing that some birds seen in the county have come from far afield.

Sponsored by Brian Channon

Species accounts 157

2007–11 Atlas fieldwork					
Number of tetrads in which recorded (max 683)					
	Total	Confirmed	Probable	Possible	Present
Breeding	84	15	2	7	60
Winter	156				

Gloucestershire trends					
Occupied 10 km squares (max 26)				% of tetrads in which recorded (1st hour of TTV)	
1968–71	1981–84	1988–91	2007–11	1988–91	2008–11
0		2	13	1.2	1.5
	5		24		

UK population trends	
UK conservation status: Green	
Long term	Short term
–	–
–	–

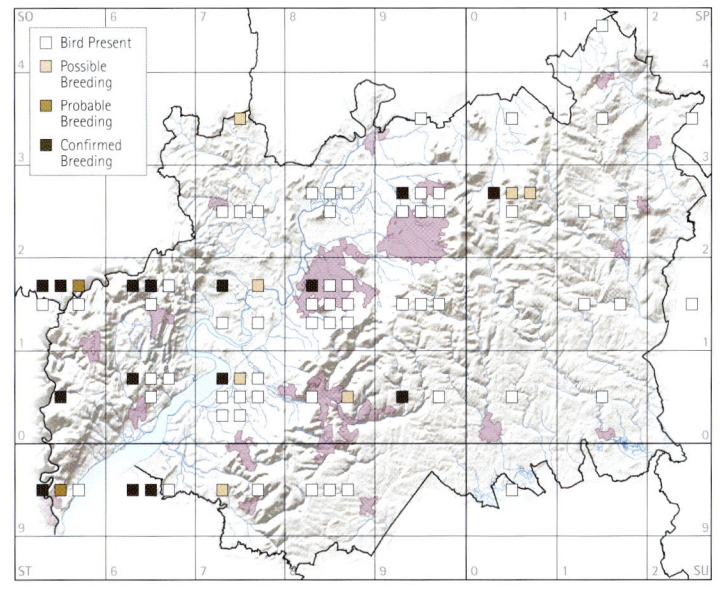

Breeding Distribution
(to preserve confidentiality, the dots for each 10 km square are grouped together)

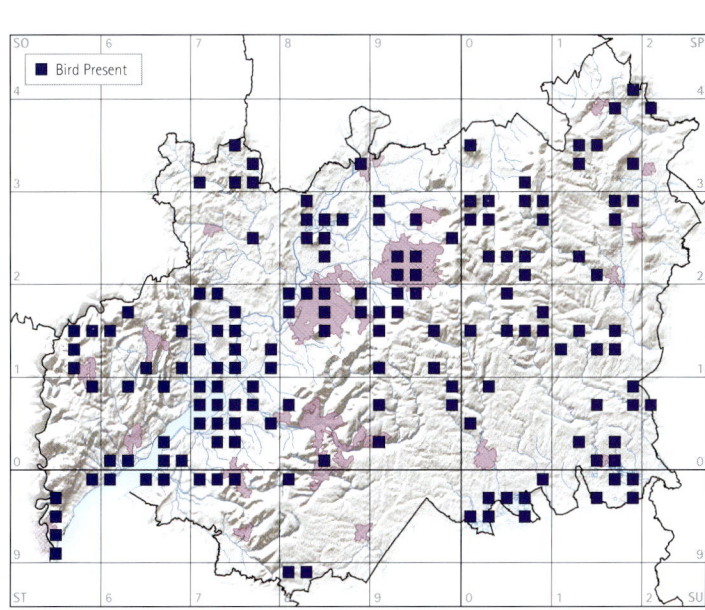

Winter Distribution

DAVE PEARCE

Water Rail
Rallus aquaticus

The Water Rail breeds throughout most of Europe, including Iceland, and discontinuously across southern and central latitudes of the Palearctic. It is mainly resident in the west and south of its range, but despite its weak-looking flight it is capable of long-distance movements, and birds breeding in eastern Europe winter as far south and west as the Mediterranean basin. In winter the resident British breeding population is joined by immigrants from as far away as Sweden, Poland and the Czech Republic.

The European summer population numbers between 125,000 and 310,000 pairs. Since 2006, when the RBBP first began monitoring this species, there have been around 1,100 territories in Britain, though the Panel notes that 'most county totals are probably underestimates' because of the birds' very unobtrusive, skulking habits.

Water Rails favour reed-beds and other dense and fairly tall aquatic vegetation, but may be found in all kinds of freshwater habitat, even small ditches and drains, particularly in winter and on migration. They are one of the most elusive birds, though they are often vocal, and many records come into the 'heard only' category.

The status of the Water Rail in Gloucestershire does not appear to have changed a great deal since Swaine described it as mainly an autumn to spring visitor in small numbers, but with records for all months and with occasional reports of breeding. Since then breeding records have continued to be sporadic. In 1983 broken eggshells were found at Slimbridge, and in 1989 a juvenile was seen in the western section of the Cotswold Water Park on June 23rd, too early a date for a migrant. Two heard at Estcourt Park near Tetbury during July of the same year could also have been breeding, as could birds heard at Slimbridge in June and July 1996. Breeding was again suspected at Slimbridge in 1998 with a juvenile seen on August 14th, still rather early for a migrant. A wet spring in 1999 produced ideal conditions at Ashleworth Ham and three birds were heard calling during June, with one still present in August. In the area

Sponsored by M J & J Bridge

2007-11 Atlas fieldwork						Gloucestershire trends						UK population trends		
Number of tetrads in which recorded (max 683)						Occupied 10 km squares (max 26)				% of tetrads in which recorded (1st hour of TTV)		UK conservation status: Green		
	Total	Confirmed	Probable	Possible	Present	1968-71	1981-84	1988-91	2007-11	1988-91	2008-11	Long term	Short term
Breeding	18	3	4	6	5	6		1	6	0.2	0.1	-	-
Winter	66							0	20			-	-

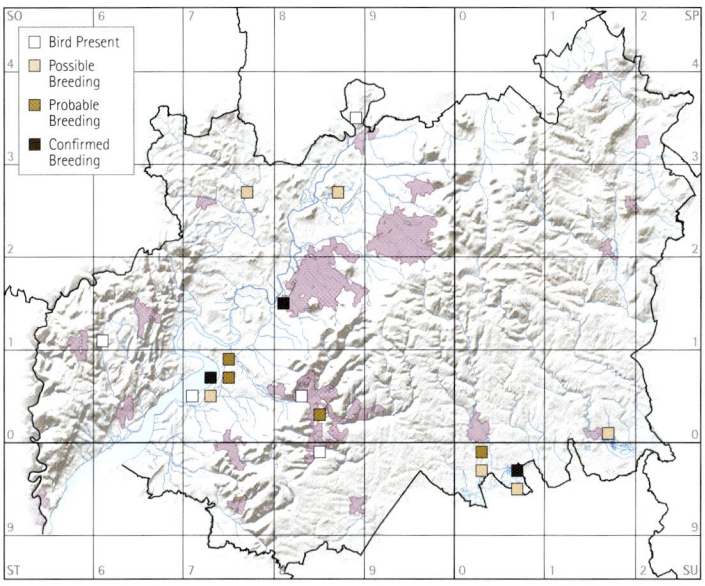

Breeding Distribution

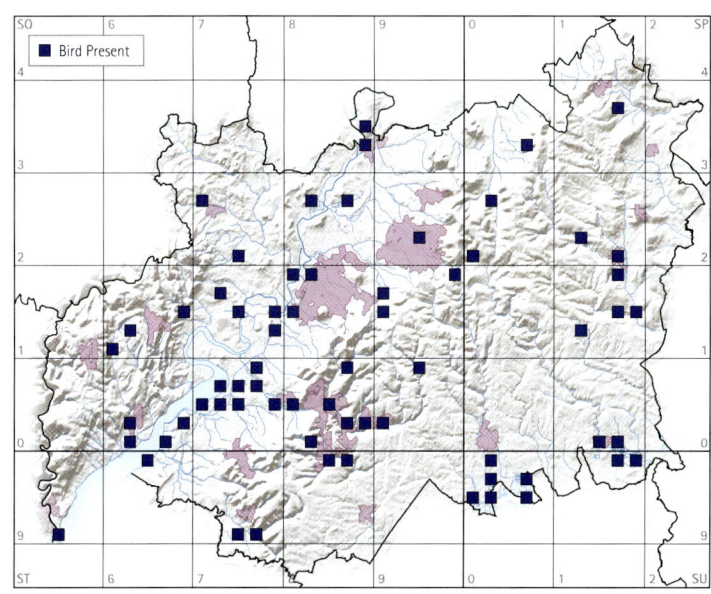

Winter Distribution

covered by the Cotswolds Atlases there was no evidence of breeding in 1983-87, but 2003-07 produced summer records in the north of the region near Chipping Campden. A survey of nesting waterbirds in the Water Park in 2007 located eight possible breeding pairs in the western section, including the Wiltshire part. In the same year an adult was seen feeding two juveniles at Quedgeley in the Severn Vale and, during the atlas fieldwork, breeding was confirmed there, and also at Frampton and the Water Park. In addition, probable breeding was recorded in four other tetrads.

As autumn migrants begin to arrive from the end of September, Water Rails are seen and heard increasingly widely in the county, with numbers tending to peak in December and January. During the current atlas fieldwork most winter records came from the Vale, the Stroud valleys and the Water Park, though reports were characteristically scattered throughout the county at waterbodies including Dowdeswell and Witcombe reservoirs, the lakes at Miserden and Woodchester Park in the Cotswolds, and a few sites in the Forest of Dean. The vast majority of records relate to single birds; the only area in the county where there are regular counts in double figures is the Slimbridge reserve, where there have been estimates of up to 35 birds during winter. Here and in the Water Park, Water Rails can be seen feeding on the ground at bird-feeding stations in the winter. Records tail off rapidly everywhere in the county during April, as wintering birds depart.

There is one Gloucestershire recovery of a foreign-ringed Water Rail: ringed at Bellum, Belgium on March 15th 2009, it was killed by a car exactly a year later at Poole Keynes in the Water Park. Whether its breeding origins were in Belgium or more distant, it was perhaps forced to migrate further than usual by the cold weather of winter 2009-10.

Corncrake (Corn Crake)
Crex crex

Making their presence known by their unmistakable and endlessly repeated 'crex-crex' song, Corncrakes breed from Ireland to southern Siberia and winter in eastern parts of sub-Saharan Africa.

When traditional hay and water meadows predominated in British river valley landscapes Corncrakes were well known and widely distributed throughout almost the whole of Wales, Scotland and Ireland, and in most of England. However there has been a well-documented, severe decline across much of western Europe since the late nineteenth century, resulting in the complete disappearance of Corncrakes from many areas. The decline has been caused mainly by agricultural intensification, notably the replacement of traditional haymaking by silage production, which involves cutting grass much earlier in the season and often repeatedly.

According to the available evidence the Corncrake was familiar and locally common in Gloucestershire in the nineteenth and early twentieth centuries, particularly in the Severn Vale and along the lower valleys of the Cotswold rivers. Witchell & Strugnell simply considered it 'common' and made little further comment, and Mellersh appears to have regarded it as sufficiently common to warrant a mention only in the context of a lack of birds in some specific areas. They were certainly common enough in the Vale to have been caught for the table as part of the traditional foraging activities of the local people there. Dr Oliver H. Wild, a curator at the Gloucester City Museum in the 1930s, assembled a collection of various devices – some comb-like, others more like football rattles – from several places along the river between Tewkesbury and Longney. These 'callers' produced sounds that mimicked the Corncrakes' calls and apparently so stimulated the birds that they would approach close enough to be killed with a short stick, whereupon they were skinned and stewed (Christian 1999a). Gloucester Folk Museum now hosts this collection of callers.

Drawing on the work of his Gloucestershire predecessors and on national surveys (Alexander 1914; Norris 1945), Swaine summarised the bird's history in the county as follows: 'The long decline of the Corncrake in Britain began to affect Gloucestershire late in the nineteenth century. By 1914 the bird was becoming scarce but some still bred, chiefly in the river flats. The decrease was very marked by 1930. Nesting ceased in the southern areas first and on the Cotswolds earlier than in the Severn Vale, where breeding continued into the 1950s.'

He continued that 'no more than one or two are reported in most years' and he may well have written this somewhat earlier than 1982, as there are only a handful of reports between the late 1960s and the late 1970s. The last confirmed breeding record reported by Swaine was 'a nest of broken eggs' at Tidenham Chase on the Dean plateau in 1964, and a pair was reported from the same place in 1968. However Christian (1999a) cast some doubt on both of these records, writing that the eggs were not found in a nest and apparently did not reach the county recorder until September, by which time they would have faded and dried out. In neither case was any calling reported, and Christian noted that the 1968 record involved two birds 'seen together', which would be highly unusual for this species.

The remaining county records all probably relate to passage rather than breeding birds. One was flushed from cover at Coombe Hill in 1966, and 1969 brought three sightings: one at Guiting Wood on May 4th, one found dead at Winchcombe soon afterwards, and one at Epney on May 27th. In 1974 birds were calling in May at Ashleworth, Slimbridge and Witcombe. One was found dead near Eastleach in 1975 and one was calling there in 1976, one stayed around Cowley for a week in June 1978, and there were then records in 1980, 1984, 1987, 1991 and 1992. In 1994 a first-winter bird was picked up alive at a Pheasant shoot near Avening one day in January, a most unusual date. It subsequently died and its identity was confirmed by the county recorder. The next record was not until 15 years later, when one was flushed by a grass mower at Slimbridge on September 22nd 2009, and most recently one was heard calling in a hay meadow at Coombe Hill on May 30th 2011.

Spotted Crake
Porzana porzana

Spotted Crakes breed very patchily in western Europe, but are more widespread further east, as far as western China; for breeding they favour sedge bogs and wet meadows. Western birds winter mainly in sub-Saharan Africa, but also in smaller numbers in the Mediterranean region and apparently very occasionally in Britain (Migration Atlas). In fact their numbers and distribution are not well understood: they are extremely secretive, call at night, sing on passage, and in any case breed very sporadically depending on habitat conditions. In the British Isles they were certainly more widespread in the past, declining rapidly in the first half of the nineteenth century as a result of large-scale drainage and reclamation of wetlands (1875–1900 Atlas), and nowadays this is a very rare breeding bird. In the five years up to 2010 the average number of singing males in the UK was just 33 (RBBP).

Swaine quoted notes from Mellersh's manuscripts which described various records from the turn of the twentieth century, including '30 or 40 at Coombe Canal' and also eggs being taken in that area, but they seem to have declined quickly in the county after about 1915. There were just 13 records between 1900 and 1980, mostly in the autumn but with one or two in winter. Since 1980 there have been sightings of passage migrants in nine years, including annually from 2007 to 2010, mostly at Slimbridge and mostly in autumn. In addition, in the three years from 1999 to 2001 calling birds were present in spring at Ashleworth Ham; in 1999 song was sustained over two months, and in 2000 up to three birds were present. Calling was also heard there in May 2003, and at Severn Ham, Tewkesbury in June 2005. It is notoriously difficult to confirm breeding for this species, which is rarely *seen* on its breeding grounds, and it is impossible to say whether breeding took place at any of these sites.

Little Crake
Porzana parva

Breeding in reed-beds in eastern Europe and into Asia, and very patchily further west, Little Crakes are so skulking and difficult to survey that little is known about them. There are just two county records:

1951: one was at Slimbridge from April 22nd to 29th, finally being found dead in one of the pipes in the duck decoy. The specimen is at the Natural History Museum.
2005: one at Slimbridge from September 14th until October 2nd.

Swaine, quoting Mellersh, referred to one 'said to have been obtained near Deerhurst about 1876', but this record is not considered to be acceptable.

Baillon's Crake
Porzana pusilla

The breeding range of this species is broadly similar to that of Little Crake, although it is said to prefer sedge bogs with somewhat shallower water. Its habits are equally skulking and elusive. The only county record is of one killed at Over, near Gloucester, in 1882.

Moorhen (Common Moorhen)
Gallinula chloropus

The Moorhen has a widespread distribution across much of Europe, but it is absent from Iceland and northern Fennoscandia and in the east it is only a summer visitor. It also breeds widely in Africa, Asia and North and South America. Up to 1.6 million pairs breed in Europe, with Britain estimated to hold 240,000 territories. In winter the British population is augmented by visitors from the near Continent.

Moorhens are found in a wide variety of freshwater habitats but are probably most familiar as inhabitants of small ponds with sufficient surrounding vegetation to provide cover. Being mainly sedentary and territorial they are rarely seen together in any great numbers. The Moorhen is unusual in that immature birds often help their parents to raise chicks from second or occasionally third broods.

Swaine described it as a common breeding bird, present at all seasons, and noted a population increase in the Thames Area as a result of the proliferation of new gravel-pits in what is now the Cotswold Water Park. His account also includes an example of this species' susceptibility to severe winter weather, citing a record of between 60 and 70 found dead at Stowell Park near Chedworth in the Cotswolds in early 1963.

There has probably been little change in status in the county since 1980 apart from continuing expansion into newly created habitat in the Water Park. In the Cotswolds there was little change between the 1983–87 and 2003–07 Atlases; the latter noted that 'it was unusual to find a suitable piece of water without a pair of Moorhens in residence', and this comment holds true for the whole county, even the urban areas. Both of the current distribution maps tend to mirror the locations of waterbodies, and the only obvious larger gaps are in the higher and drier parts of the Cotswolds and the Forest of Dean. The winter and summer abundance maps have a very similar pattern, indicating that our Moorhens are largely sedentary under normal weather conditions. The maximum breeding season TTV count was of 15 in SU09I at the Water Park in May 2008, whilst the maximum winter count of 200 came from SO70C in November 2010. Not surprisingly this tetrad includes part of the Slimbridge reserve, where Moorhens are among the many species that have taken full advantage of the daily feeding of the captive wildfowl and wintering Bewick's Swans. Counts there are regularly the highest in Britain and often amount to several hundred birds, with maxima since 1980 ranging from 292 in 1982 to 879 in 1990.

An indication of the origin of some of the Moorhens wintering in the county is provided by the recovery of a nestling ringed near Antwerp in Belgium in May 1937 and found at Quedgeley near Gloucester, in unknown circumstances, on March 10th 1938.

Sponsored by Peter Ormerod

Species accounts 163

2007–11 Atlas fieldwork					Gloucestershire trends						UK population trends		
Number of tetrads in which recorded (max 683)					Occupied 10 km squares (max 26)				% of tetrads in which recorded (1st hour of TTV)		UK conservation status: Green		
	Total	Confirmed	Probable	Possible	Present	1968–71	1981–84	1988–91	2007–11	1988–91	2008–11	Long term	Short term
Breeding	442	274	52	85	31	26		26	26	36.5	34.9	−5%	+14%
Winter	393						26		26			–	–

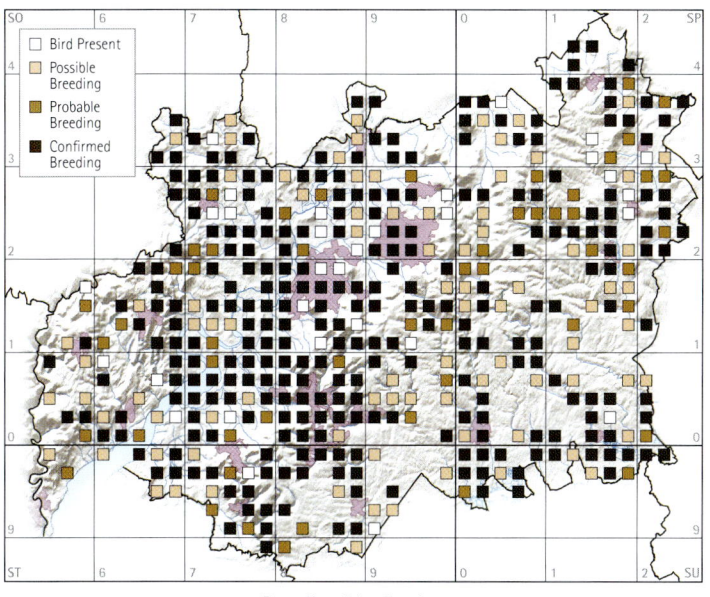

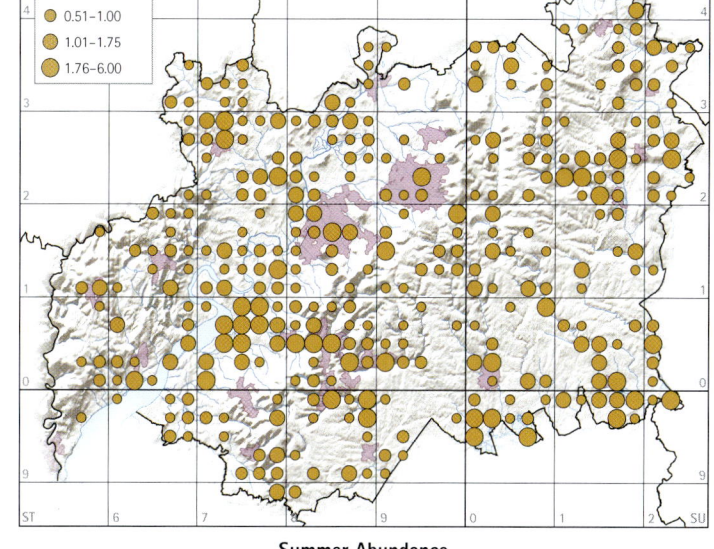

Breeding Distribution

Summer Abundance

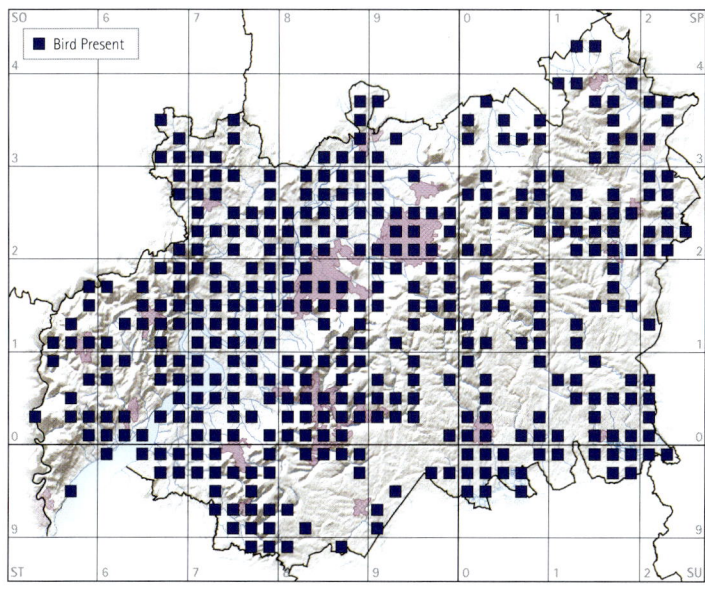

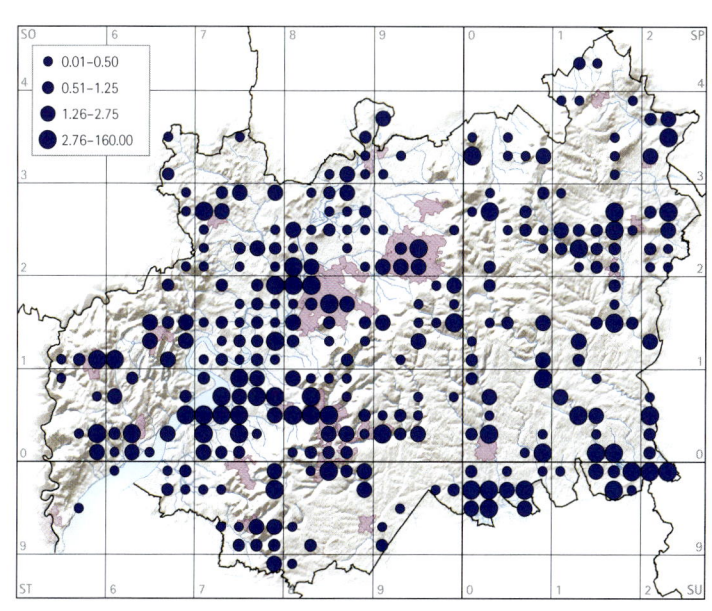

Winter Distribution

Winter Abundance

Coot (Common Coot)
Fulica atra

The Coot now breeds widely across Europe, following an increase and northward spread into Fennoscandia during the late nineteenth and early twentieth centuries. It also breeds across much of Russia, where it is a summer visitor, and in the Indian subcontinent, Australasia and North Africa. The mostly resident British population numbers around 25,000 pairs, but visitors from the Continent swell the winter population to 180,000 birds. Compared with the Moorhen, the Coot prefers larger waterbodies and generally avoids small ponds and streams.

This is one of the easiest species to confirm breeding, as the nests and young are so conspicuous. Of all atlas breeding season records of Coots from Gloucestershire that were allocated a breeding code, 68% were 'confirmed'. Only for Rook was an equally high figure achieved.

According to Mellersh, Coots were apparently rather scarce in the county during the nineteenth century, but Swaine described a significant increase during the twentieth, especially in the Thames Area where the proliferation of gravel-pits in the Cotswold Water Park provided perfect habitat. Here the breeding population probably already exceeded 100 pairs by 1978, and since then numbers have continued to increase; a survey of breeding waterbirds in the Water Park as a whole in 2007 recorded a total of 782 pairs, 565 of which were confirmed to be breeding.

Outside the breeding season, peak numbers at the main sites occur between October and January, though casual observations suggest that Coot are more widespread through the county in the late winter and early spring, presumably as immigrants from elsewhere in Britain and the Continent start their return migration. In 1978 what were then record winter numbers were counted during December, with nearly 6,000 in the Water Park and 700 at Frampton Pools. The continued expansion of the Water Park has seen numbers continue to rise, and in November 1995 the combined WeBS count for the two sections produced a new peak of about 7,100 birds. Although totals in subsequent years were somewhat lower, current numbers there are once again close to that figure. Frampton Pools has also remained an important wintering site, often holding several hundred birds, and Bourton pits also regularly produce high counts, notably about 660 in December 1981. In recent years habitat improvements have resulted in increasing numbers at Slimbridge, with over 500 recorded in October 2008. Winter counts of over 100 are also not unusual at Witcombe and Dowdeswell reservoirs and are occasional at Ashleworth Ham

The maps highlight the fact that in view of its general preference for larger bodies of water, the Coot is surprisingly widespread in the county, with confirmed breeding records from over 140 tetrads. Coots will evidently colonise almost any sufficiently large waterbody, whether it be a disused or active canal, a slow-moving Cotswold river, one of the larger ponds in the Forest of Dean or a park lake in one of the urban areas. In the area covered by the Cotswolds Atlases, where there was 'little change' between 1987 and 2007, the distribution was still broadly the same during the current survey, with breeding pairs concentrated along the main river valleys.

The widely travelled nature of some Coots is demonstrated by the ringing recoveries involving Gloucestershire. Up to 2010, in addition to 18 recoveries showing movements within England as far afield as Cambridgeshire, Cheshire and Devon, four birds ringed here in autumn or winter in the 1960s and 1970s had been recovered, all shot, in Denmark (three) and the Moscow area of Russia.

Species accounts 165

2007-11 Atlas fieldwork					Gloucestershire trends					UK population trends	
Number of tetrads in which recorded (max 683)					Occupied 10 km squares (max 26)				% of tetrads in which recorded (1st hour of TTV)		UK conservation status: **Green**	
	Total	Confirmed	Probable	Possible	Present	1968-71	1981-84	1988-91	2007-11	1988-91	2008-11	Long term	Short term
Breeding	199	144	20	24	11	23		22	26	12.8	14.8	+81%	+37%
Winter	158							25	26			–	-8%

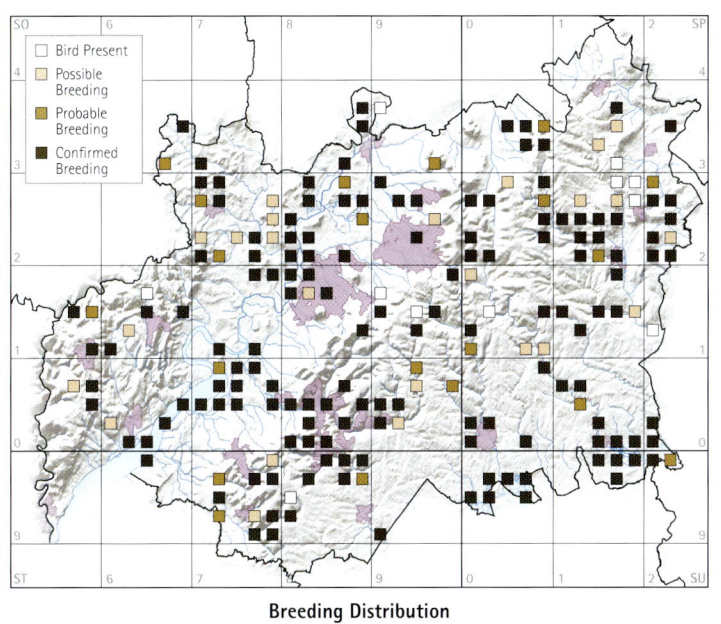

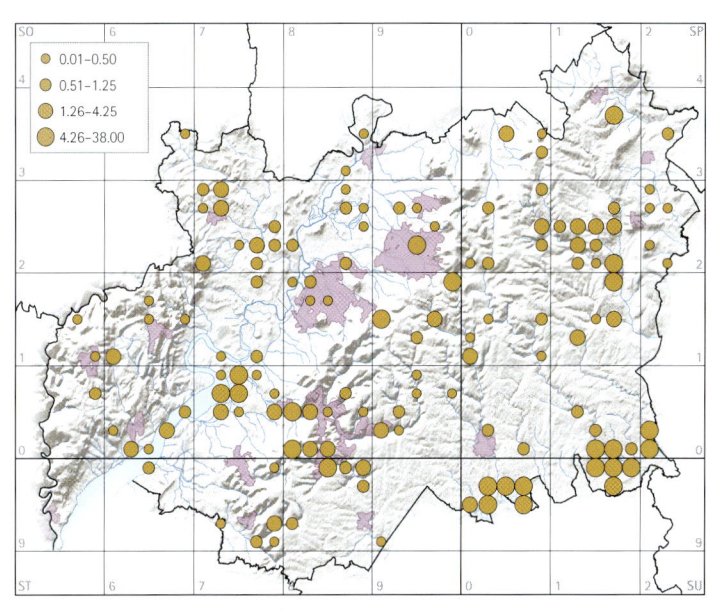

Breeding Distribution

Summer Abundance

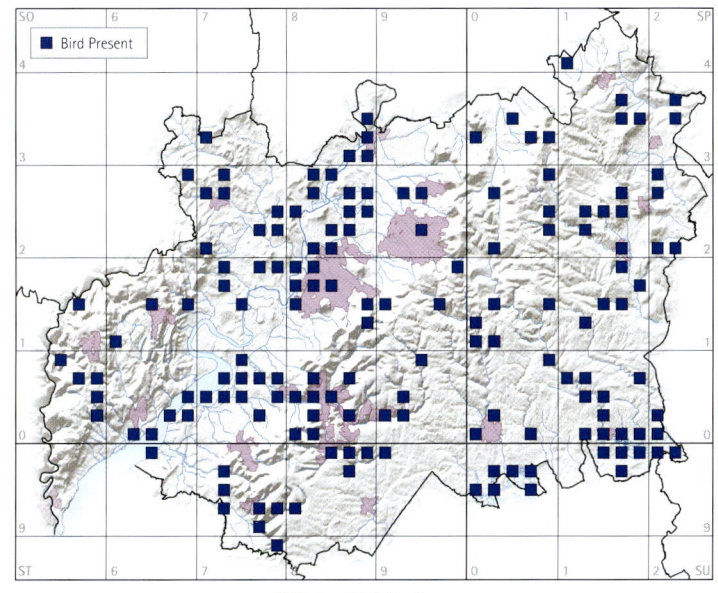

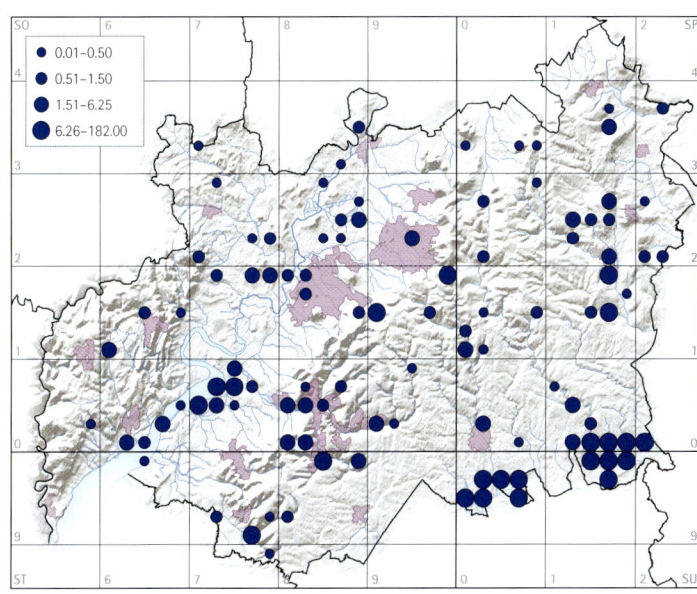

Winter Distribution

Winter Abundance

Crane (Common Crane)
Grus grus

Cranes breed from Fennoscandia and northern Germany eastwards to central Siberia, but their breeding range has decreased everywhere in Europe since the Middle Ages. In Britain they were familiar birds up to the sixteenth century and were hunted for food. They were then absent for several centuries, but they have bred every year since 1981 in the Norfolk Broads and have spread to Humberside and the East Anglian Fens since 2000. By 2011 there were 17 nesting pairs in Britain (Stanbury & Sills 2012). European populations are mainly migratory and have two different wintering areas; some fly south-west to North Africa, Iberia and parts of Italy and France, while others move south-east to Asia Minor and the Middle East. However the new British colonists are largely resident (Stanbury 2011).

Swaine noted one record of a Crane, shot near Tewkesbury in 1869, but there were no more in Gloucestershire until one in April 1976. This was followed by sightings in every year from 1979 to 1983, in 1990, and in 1999. Since 2000 there has been a noticeable increase, with reports in six years up to the end of 2011. Many records are of singles, but three were seen in flight over Shurdington on December 15th 1981, a group of two adults and three immatures at Woorgreens Lake in the Dean on February 23rd 2003 moved to Slimbridge later that day and remained until March 2nd, and three flew over Eastington near Stonehouse on April 22nd 2008. In total there have been 17 records since 1970, involving 25 birds, with sightings in most months of the year but none in May, June or July.

Currently Cranes are being bred at Slimbridge for release on the Somerset Levels, as part of a reintroduction scheme (the 'Great Crane Project'). If this is successful, this most elegant of birds may become a regular sight in Gloucestershire.

Little Bustard
Tetrax tetrax

Formerly breeding in open terrain across much of mainland Europe, Little Bustards became extinct in many countries by the first half of the twentieth century. There are still populations in Iberia and France. The only Gloucestershire record is of an adult female first seen at Castle Farm, Turkdean near Northleach on May 20th 1946. It remained in the area until it was shot on July 30th.

Great Bustard
Otis tarda

Great Bustards became extinct in Britain by the 1830s. Salisbury Plain is considered to have been one of their strongholds (Wiltshire Ornithological Society 2007) and they may well have bred in Gloucestershire, although there are no specific records. Globally their numbers have declined massively, and although they range as far east as Mongolia, many populations are isolated and threatened.

During the 1970s and 1980s attempts were made to establish a breeding population from captive pinioned birds at Porton Down in Wiltshire, but without success. A more recent reintroduction scheme in Wiltshire produced the first 'wild' chicks in 2009 and it is hoped that this stately bird will regain a foothold in Britain.

In Gloucestershire the only known nineteenth-century record refers to a female shot near Cheltenham in early February 1891 (BirdGuides). More recently, one was seen in flight at Leckhampton Hill on May 24th 1977. On November 23rd 2007 two wing-tagged birds from the Wiltshire reintroduction scheme were found in a field near Sharpness, staying for several days. One of them was subsequently seen at several other places in the county before it took up residence in a crop field at Calmsden in the Cotswolds (see photograph) from February 2nd to March 17th 2008.

Avocet (Pied Avocet)
Recurvirostra avosetta

The Avocet has become familiar to birdwatchers and the British public alike since 1970, when the RSPB adopted it as its logo. Avocets have specialised breeding requirements (shallow lagoons or marshes with sparse vegetation) and the world distribution is correspondingly patchy, but they range quite widely across Eurasia and parts of Africa.

Up to the early eighteenth century Avocets bred regularly along the east coast of England, but egg collecting and loss of habitat led to their disappearance by the mid-nineteenth century. They recolonised East Anglia in 1947 and, thanks largely to the efforts of the RSPB and other conservation bodies, the British population has increased to about 1,500 pairs. British-breeding Avocets are partly migratory, some wintering in Britain but others ranging as far south as Senegal.

There were no definite Gloucestershire records prior to the early 1900s and the first substantiated sighting in the county was of four 'at Stonehouse on the Severn' in March 1913 (Robinson 1914). Stonehouse is about 7 km from the Severn and although Swaine assumed that the report related to the Frampton–Slimbridge area, it is possible that it should have referred to Stonebench, near Gloucester. There were no more records until 1954, when five were on the estuary in August. Since then there has been a steady increase (see top graph) and by the start of the twenty-first century Avocets had become near-annual visitors to the county. Nearly all records have been from the Frampton–Slimbridge area, with fewer elsewhere on the estuary, at the Cotswold Water Park, and more rarely at other sites in the Severn Vale. About half of all sightings have involved single birds; the largest flock recorded so far was 23, at Saul Warth near Frampton on April 22nd and 23rd 2005. There have been records in all months, with a noticeable peak between March and May (see bottom graph).

The first hint that breeding might take place in the county came in April 2010, when a pair displayed and began nest-building at Slimbridge. They did not stay to breed that year, but in 2012 a pair raised three young in full view of the public Holden Tower hide.

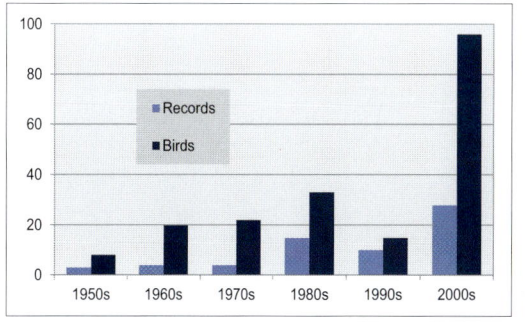

Avocet records, 1950–2010.

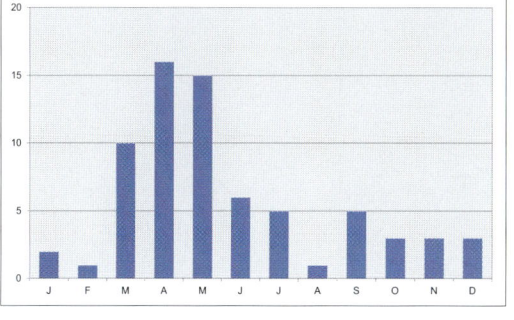

Avocet records by month, 1980–2010.

In memory of Peter Jones

Oystercatcher (Eurasian Oystercatcher)
Haematopus ostralegus

The noisy and conspicuous Oystercatcher breeds in north-west Europe including Iceland, locally in parts of southern Europe, and in west-central and eastern Asia. Northern populations are migratory, many wintering around the North and Irish Seas but some moving as far south as West Africa. Oystercatchers favour coastal areas, but also commonly breed inland in some regions.

The 1968–72 and 1988–91 Breeding Atlases revealed a considerable increase in the British population between about 1970 and 1990, accompanied by an increasing tendency to nest inland. Recent estimates suggest a total of around 113,000 pairs in Britain in summer, while in winter the population rises to around 320,000 birds.

Swaine described the Oystercatcher as an annual visitor to the Severn Estuary and occasionally elsewhere in the county, mostly from March to October and usually in just ones and twos but sometimes in parties of up to 16 birds. This picture remained much the same until 1987, when a record flock of 30 was seen on the Severn shore at Frampton during May and two birds lingered in the area throughout the summer. Presumably the same pair returned for the next two years, but the first confirmed breeding in the county came from further down the estuary at Guscar Rocks, where a pair raised at least one young in 1990. In the following years breeding attempts became almost annual at Guscar and also at Slimbridge, where there were up to three pairs. In 1999 breeding was suspected at the western section of the Cotswold Water Park, and in 2000 at least six pairs attempted to breed around the estuary, though again with no success. However in 2001 a pair raised two young at Slimbridge, and since then successful breeding has occurred every year, with a gradual increase to nine pairs at Slimbridge and up to three pairs at the Water Park. Breeding has also continued to take place or to be suspected elsewhere by the estuary, for example at Beachley Point, Berkeley Shore and Sharpness. In 2010 the first breeding on the Severn Hams was recorded when a pair hatched

Species accounts

2007–11 Atlas fieldwork					Gloucestershire trends						UK population trends		
Number of tetrads in which recorded (max 683)					Occupied 10 km squares (max 26)				% of tetrads in which recorded (1st hour of TTV)		UK conservation status: Amber 7,8	
	Total	Confirmed	Probable	Possible	Present	1968–71	1981–84	1988–91	2007–11	1988–91	2008–11	Long term	Short term
Breeding	45	12	7	6	20	0		1	6	0.4	2.1	–	–8%
Winter	23						3		7			0	–14%

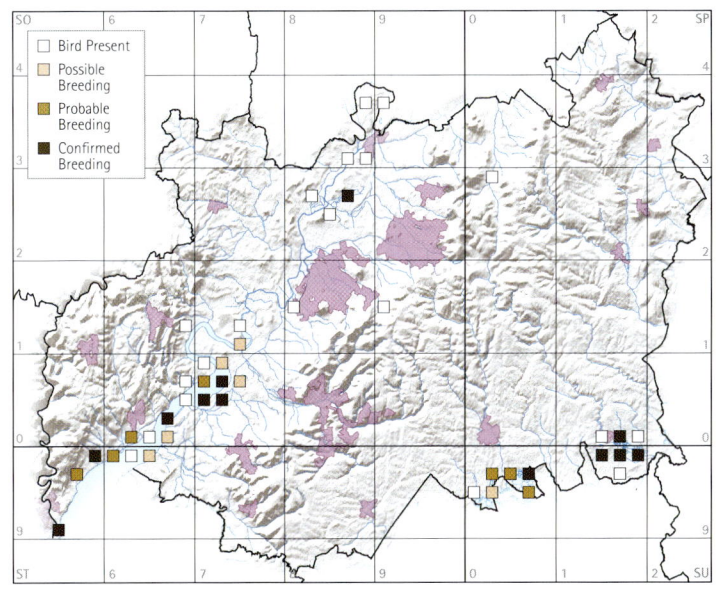

Breeding Distribution

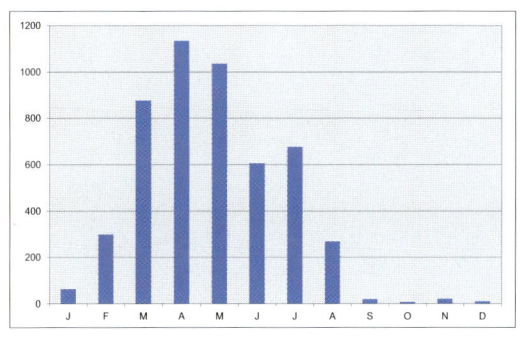

Oystercatcher numbers reported 2003–10, by month.

Winter Distribution

two chicks at Coombe Hill Meadows. This reflects a national trend towards increased use of lowland damp grassland by nesting Oystercatchers.

Since breeding began, peak counts in the county have also increased; these have included 25 at Beachley Point in February 1995, and at Slimbridge 30 in March 2004, 38 in late July 2005 and 37 in June 2006. During the current atlas fieldwork the maximum TTV count was 11 in ST69K at Beachley Point in June 2009.

By September most birds have deserted the county, and there are very few records from then until February, as shown in the graph. The first breeding pairs return and start to establish territories in late February, and although the two seasonal distribution maps are very similar, with birds along the estuary and in the Water Park, all the 'winter' Water Park records relate to February birds returning to their breeding grounds; the very few truly wintering birds all occur along the estuary.

The origins of Oystercatchers wintering in the county are illustrated by two ringing recoveries: an adult ringed at Slimbridge in February 1957 and found freshly dead in Iceland in August 1961, and a nestling ringed in the Netherlands in June 1997 that was found dead, killed by a raptor, at Sharpness Docks in March 2001.

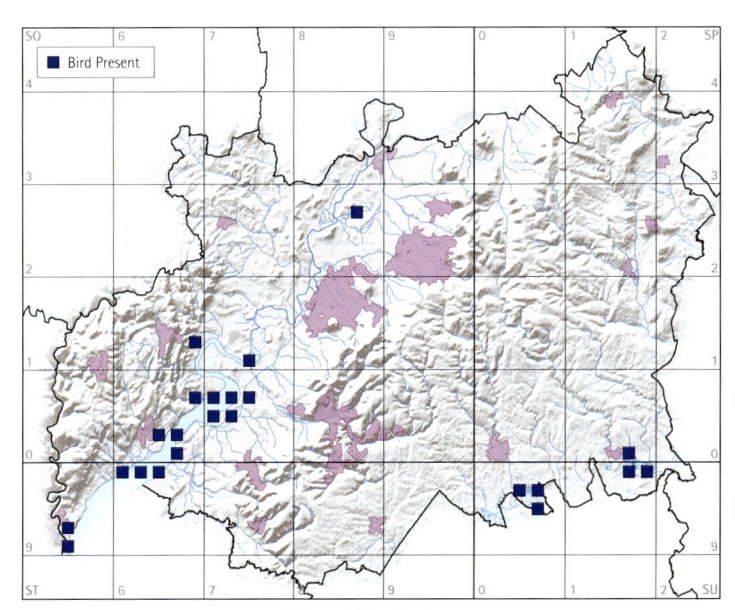

Little Ringed Plover
Charadrius dubius

The very extensive summer range of the Little Ringed Plover includes parts of North Africa and much of Eurasia. The European population numbers between 70,000 and 115,000 pairs and most of these birds winter in the northern Afrotropics. Following a range expansion, and aided by new reservoirs and gravel-pits, the species first began colonising Britain in 1938, when a pair bred in Hertfordshire. After several decades of steady spread a national survey in 2007 located 891 pairs, though it is estimated that the total may be up to 1,100 pairs.

Swaine described the Little Ringed Plover as a very local summer visitor to Gloucestershire and documented the colonisation of the county, with the first three breeding pairs near South Cerney in 1953 increasing to 25 pairs in the Cotswold Water Park by the late 1970s. Breeding also occurred at new gravel workings near Frampton in 1966, and at a Cotswold quarry west of Stow-in-the-Wold in 1974. Around 15 pairs were still present at the Water Park in the early 1980s, but reduced gravel extraction meant that numbers declined to just a few pairs during the 1990s and breeding was not always proved in some years. Perhaps as a result of more sympathetic management by the mineral companies, numbers seem to have recovered somewhat over the past decade and a survey in 2005 located 15 pairs in the Gloucestershire section; the sight of one of these tiny waders sitting tight on its nest while huge machines manoeuvre around it is almost surreal. However some areas of apparently suitable nesting habitat in the Water Park are unoccupied, so factors other than the availability of suitable sites may be limiting the numbers here (Gareth Harris, Cotswold Water Park Trust). As a ground-nesting species,

Sponsored by the Cotswold Water Park Trust

2007–11 Atlas fieldwork					Gloucestershire trends						UK population trends	
Number of tetrads in which recorded (max 683)					Occupied 10 km squares (max 26)				% of tetrads in which recorded (1st hour of TTV)		UK conservation status: Green	
	Total	Confirmed	Probable	Possible	Present	1968–71	1981–84	1988–91	2007–11	1988–91	2008–11	Long term	Short term
Breeding	21	5	9	1	6	2		3	5	0.6	0.6	–	–
Winter	0						0		0		–	–

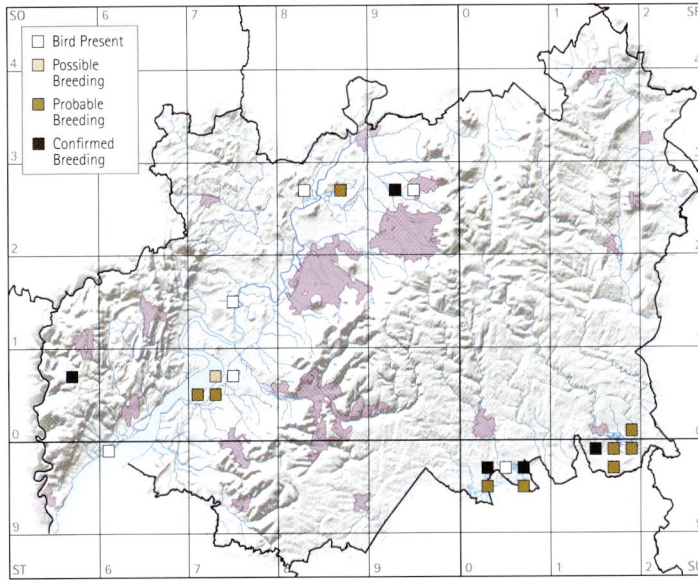

Breeding Distribution

Little Ringed Plovers are especially vulnerable to predation and the increasing number of summering gulls almost certainly presents a threat.

There have been occasional breeding attempts elsewhere in the county, though with limited success. The Slimbridge reserve, particularly the South Lake, has been the most regular site, but nest failures have been frequent due to predation by Moorhens, Grey Herons and others, and also to flooding. Breeding has succeeded at Coombe Hill Meadows and at the landfill site at Stoke Orchard near Cheltenham, and has been attempted at Ashleworth Ham. During the atlas fieldwork, nesting was confirmed at a quarry site in the Forest of Dean. The latest available figures from the RBBP give a total of 16 confirmed or probable breeding pairs in Gloucestershire in 2009.

In spring and autumn migrating Little Ringed Plovers can be found at places in the county where they do not breed, particularly in the Severn Vale, though records of more than four or five together are unusual. The last week of March normally sees the first spring arrivals but sightings have become earlier in recent years, with one at Slimbridge on March 9th 2010 the earliest on record. Autumn migrants appear from July onwards, most have departed by mid-September, and by far the latest report concerns two still in the western section of the Water Park on October 10th 2005.

There is one ringing recovery of a Gloucestershire Little Ringed Plover: a colour-ringed 2008 chick from Shorncote Quarry in the Water Park was seen alive 84 km away at a gravel-pit near Little Marlow, Buckinghamshire, on March 28th 2010. It seems likely that it had moved away from its natal site to breed.

Ringed Plover (Common Ringed Plover)
Charadrius hiaticula

The nominate subspecies of the Ringed Plover breeds in eastern Canada, Iceland and Spitsbergen, and from southern Fennoscandia south to Brittany, including the British Isles. Some of the declining British and Irish population are resident, while others winter south to northern Spain. There is also a marked passage through the British Isles of north-western birds en route to and from their wintering sites in West Africa, and in winter local birds are joined by migrants from northern and western continental Europe. The species is amber listed, due to a longer-term decline in the breeding population and because the UK holds a significant proportion of the European wintering population. The preferred habitat at all seasons is wide sandy or shingly tidal beaches, but in Britain and elsewhere they have also taken to various wetland sites inland.

There have been a few Gloucestershire breeding records, mostly at the flooded gravel-pits of the Cotswold Water Park. An unsuccessful attempt here in 1978 was followed by successful nesting in 1982, and further attempts (some successful) by up to five pairs in at least ten years up to 1996. More recently, a nest with eggs was found in the western section in May 2010. In addition, a pair held territory at Slimbridge in 1992.

It is as passage migrants that Ringed Plovers are commonest in the county, with numbers peaking in May and late August (see graph). The date of the spring peak indicates that northern birds are involved, as British breeders are on territory as early as February whereas Arctic birds may not arrive until June. Indeed, one ringed in Gloucestershire in August 1975 was recovered in Iceland in June 1977.

Swaine mentioned occasional records of well over 1,000 birds on passage during the 1960s, and an autumn peak of 800 was recorded in 1976. Since then peaks have averaged around 150 birds in spring (maximum 350, May 15th 2002) and about 150–200 in autumn, with 'exceptional' counts of 600 around August 20th 2004 and 830 on August 25th 2010. All of these large totals have been at the Severn Estuary.

Ringed Plovers are scarce in Gloucestershire in winter, and they have apparently decreased since the mid-1980s, when there were a few counts of around 30 birds; no more than ten at a time have been reported since 2000, and in some winters none are seen at all.

There are just occasional single-figure records from waterbodies away from the estuary and the Water Park.

A few birds showing characteristics of the slightly smaller, darker subspecies *C. h. tundrae*, which breeds from northern Scandinavia eastwards and migrates mainly to eastern and southern Africa, are seen on passage in the county from time to time.

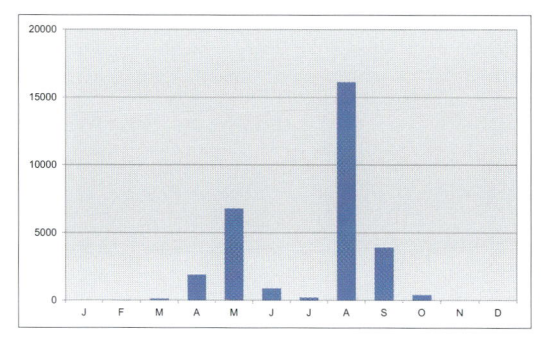

Ringed Plover numbers reported 2003–10, by month.

Sponsored by David & Roni Cramp

Kentish Plover
Charadrius alexandrinus

Kentish Plovers have a wide-ranging world distribution but have declined throughout Europe, probably due to a combination of habitat destruction, disturbance and nest predation. The last British breeding record in was in Lincolnshire in 1979 (BWP). These days this is a scarce annual migrant in Britain, with usually between 20 and 40 records per year.

The first for Gloucestershire was at Slimbridge on April 4th 1960, and there have now been 22 county records. There were only three sightings in the 1960s, but during the 1970s there were records in six years, involving 12 birds and with maxima of three in 1975 and 1977. The 1980s only produced two; there were four records (eight birds) in the 1990s, and one in 2008. Four records have come from the Cotswold Water Park, one from Frampton sailing lake, and the rest from the Frampton–Slimbridge area of the Severn Estuary. All have involved singles, apart from two on June 1st 1991 and a remarkable four birds from September 23rd to 25th 1999; all of these six were at Middle Point, Slimbridge.

In line with the national pattern the majority have been in spring, with 18 records between March 27th and June 11th, and something of a peak (eight records) in the first half of May. The remaining four sightings were in the first half of July (one), late August (two), and the four birds of late September 1999.

Dotterel (Eurasian Dotterel)
Charadrius morinellus

Dotterel have a widespread but patchy breeding distribution from Scotland (occasionally northern England and Wales) and northern Fennoscandia east across Siberia. The British population declined markedly during the nineteenth century, due largely to shooting and egg collecting. They winter mainly in North Africa and the Middle East (BWP) and occur regularly on passage in England, with higher totals in spring than in autumn.

They evidently used to be seen more often in Gloucestershire than they are now. Few of the records cited by Mellersh are dated, but they include 'small parties' near Sherborne Park on the Cotswold dip-slope around 1850, 17 killed on Cleeve Hill in about 1870, and a flock of 14 also on Cleeve Hill in May 1909. Since then there have only been 13 sightings, involving a total of 25 birds: five records (ten birds) between 1934 and 1980, one record of six birds in 1984, two records (three birds) in the 1990s, and five (six birds) since 2000. Nine of these sightings, involving 21 birds, have been in spring, between April 8th and May 11th but mostly in May. Spring has also produced the only sizeable flocks in recent decades: five by the river near Slimbridge on April 26th 1975, and the six in 1984, at Cleeve Hill on May 5th. All other spring records have involved singles and twos, and all four of the autumn sightings have been of single birds, between September 1st and 16th.

It is notable that over half of these 13 records have been at Cleeve Hill, the highest point in the county. Slimbridge has had three records, and the others have been at Aylburton Warth (two), Shab Hill on the Cotswold scarp above Gloucester, and Hewletts reservoir, Cheltenham.

Golden Plover (European Golden Plover)
Pluvialis apricaria

Golden Plovers breed in northern Europe from Iceland east to north-west Russia. They prefer tundra and arctic-alpine habitats, including mountains and moorland in the British Isles. European numbers have declined and the breeding range has contracted northwards since the mid-nineteenth century. They winter on lower-lying farmland and grasslands, in more southern parts of Europe and in North Africa and the Middle East. In summer Britain holds up to 23,000 pairs out of a total European population of around half a million pairs, while about 400,000 birds are estimated to winter here. Once a flock takes wing Golden Plovers are very distinctive, with their direct, rapid flight and plaintive calls, but they are easily overlooked if feeding quietly or roosting on ploughed land.

In Gloucestershire, although three-figure flocks of passage migrants are not unusual and there are occasional reports of midsummer birds in their full breeding finery, this is primarily a winter visitor, with maximum numbers occurring from December to February. As the maps show, it is one of the more widespread waders in the county, with concentrations on the open farmland of the Cotswolds and in some areas of the Severn Vale.

Golden Plovers have always tended to move to the low-lying ground adjacent to the Severn Estuary during severe weather, but in recent years numbers remaining in this area for the whole winter have risen considerably. This is particularly true of Slimbridge, where formerly fewer than 100 birds were usually counted; recent annual maxima there have been around a couple of thousand, with a remarkable peak of 4,700 in January 2005. The highest TTV count during the atlas fieldwork, 3,300 in December 2007, also came from Slimbridge. At the same time numbers at the Cotswold Water Park, which formerly exceeded 1,000 quite regularly and peaked at 3,000 during January and February 1989, have fallen to generally just a few hundred birds. Similarly, numbers in the Tewkesbury area of the Vale, another former stronghold, have decreased considerably. This evident shift towards Slimbridge is no doubt due to improvements in the habitats there since the grassland and the flooding regimes have been managed with conservation in mind.

Some of these Vale-dwelling birds have also used the nearby Framilode and Rodley areas in recent years and counts of several hundred are now not unusual there. Lower down the estuary the Lydney New Grounds area has long been regarded as an important site, but apart from one high count of 1,000 in January 2009, most recent records there refer to much lower numbers. Despite the general shift, the Cotswolds have by no means been completely deserted and often hold sizeable flocks, for example a respectable 1,300 at Hawling in November 2006.

Overall, it seems that the number of Golden Plovers wintering in Gloucestershire has increased in recent decades. For Mellersh this species was mainly a passage migrant in the Vale, and Swaine mentioned no flocks of more than 1,000 birds. Again, this may well be a result of the increasingly high quality of the habitat at Slimbridge, as well as a tendency to remain further north in winter than would formerly be the case due to generally milder weather.

There have been two recoveries of foreign-ringed Golden Plovers in the county: a 1932 Icelandic nestling was found injured after hitting overhead wires at Lydney in its first autumn, and an adult ringed in the Netherlands in April 1991 was killed by a bird of prey at Wotton-under-Edge in December that same year.

Species accounts

2007–11 Atlas fieldwork						Gloucestershire trends						UK population trends	
Number of tetrads in which recorded (max 683)						*Occupied 10 km squares (max 26)*				*% of tetrads in which recorded (1st hour of TTV)*		*UK conservation status:* **Amber 8**	
	Total	Confirmed	Probable	Possible	Present	1968–71	1981–84	1988–91	2007–11	1988–91	2008–11	Long term	Short term
Breeding	36	0	0	0	36	0		0	0	0	0	–	–4%
Winter	154						14		24			+403%	+9%

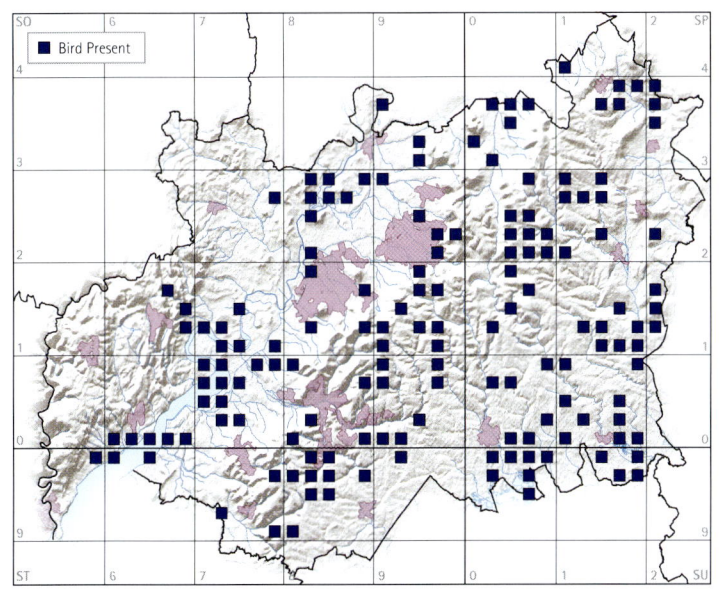

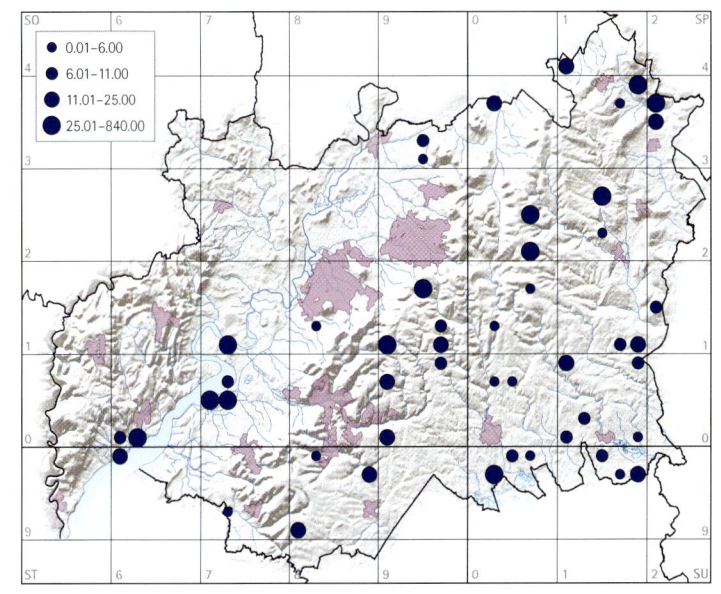

Winter Distribution

Winter Abundance

Grey Plover
Pluvialis squatarola

Grey Plovers breed in the Russian and North American Arctic and winter 'throughout much of the world' (Migration Atlas), extending from western Europe to the southern hemisphere. Following a marked increase after about 1970, some 43,000 birds from the Russian population were wintering on British coasts and estuaries by 1990, mainly between the Wash and the Solent. Many more pass through on migration.

At the end of the nineteenth century Mellersh described the Grey Plover as a 'mere straggler' in Gloucestershire. By the late 1970s numbers in the county had increased significantly, in line with the national pattern: Swaine described it as mainly a passage migrant, with counts of up to 20 in April and May, up to 40 in autumn, and a few in winter.

Since 1980 the pattern has remained much the same, with no obvious changes in average numbers on migration or in winter. In spring the peak passage usually occurs in May and in most years the highest count is between ten and 20 birds (median 15); there have only been six counts of 40 or more, with notable maxima of 110 in May 1990 and 87 in May 1992. Autumn passage extends over a longer period, as also noted by Swaine, with peak numbers usually in October. The highest count is usually between ten and 40 birds (median 25), but there have been nine autumns with peaks of 50 or more, including unusually high counts of 176 in October 1988 and 186 on September 19th 1993.

Nearly every year produces a few winter records, but numbers at this time are usually in single figures. Notable exceptions were 28 in December 1985 and 15 in January 1996.

The majority of records are from the Severn Estuary but there are a few elsewhere, especially in the Cotswold Water Park but also occasionally at wet grassland sites in the Vale.

Black-winged Stilt
Himantopus himantopus

Black-winged Stilts have a wide-ranging world distribution, although the European range is very fragmented and populations are generally small. Western Palearctic breeders migrate mainly to Africa, north of the equator. They have occasionally nested in Britain, with breeding attempts tending to be more frequent in recent years, partly due to improved protection.

There has only been one record in Gloucestershire: a pair at Saul Warth and Slimbridge from May 12th to 15th 2005. Mating was observed, but although the marshy habitat appeared to be suitable for breeding, it was evidently not quite to their liking.

Stone-curlew (Eurasian Stone-curlew)
Burhinus oedicnemus

Stone-curlews breed across a wide area of the Palearctic from the Canary Islands to Vietnam, preferring more or less flat open country. Historically they adapted well to low-intensity farming, but the European range in particular has become increasingly fragmented and numbers have fallen rapidly over the last 150 years or so, due to changes in agricultural practices. However in England the decline has been reversed in recent years as a result of targeted conservation efforts; the population here increased from about 160 pairs in the 1980s to about 370 in 2010 (RSPB website, www.rspb.org.uk).

According to Mellersh, Stone Curlews were not uncommon as breeding birds on the higher parts of the Gloucestershire Cotswolds up to about 1860, after which a rapid decline set in. The last record in his manuscripts was of one shot near Shipton Oliffe in 1923. Swaine mentioned subsequent breeding attempts in June 1953 near Aldsworth, and in 1954 possibly at the same location and also near Turkdean. Since then there have been the following six records:

1980: one at the Cotswold Water Park from July 27th to August 3rd.
1981: one walking across a road at Coombe Hill near Wotton-under-Edge on September 12th.
1982: one on the foreshore at Frampton on March 27th.
1995: one on the shore at Fretherne (near Frampton) on June 27th.
2007: one at the Washpool on Cleeve Hill on April 21st.
2008: one photographed in sheep pasture near Sheepscombe on May 7th.

Collared Pratincole
Glareola pratincola

Collared Pratincoles have declined markedly in Europe over the past 100 years or so, mainly because of loss and degradation of their wetland habitats, disturbance, and the increasing use of pesticides that destroy their insect prey. The European breeding range is now mostly restricted to the Mediterranean countries. They winter in Africa, and vagrants occur annually or near-annually in very small numbers in Britain. Locally there have been two records, both involving birds that were seen to cross briefly into Gloucestershire from neighbouring counties:

1968: one flew into the county from North Meadow, near Cricklade in Wiltshire, on May 30th.
1994: a juvenile flew across from Bredon's Hardwicke (in Worcestershire, near Tewkesbury), on May 4th.

In addition, Mellersh listed an old, unconfirmed record of one killed near Painswick. There is some doubt about the date of this report: either May 1876 or July 1882.

Lapwing (Northern Lapwing)
Vanellus vanellus

The Lapwing's tumbling display flight and exuberant 'pee-wit' calls are familiar over pastures and arable farmland, but it has undergone a severe decline in recent decades.

Lapwings breed from Ireland and France across to eastern Siberia and south to Spain, Greece and Turkey. European breeders winter in south-western parts of the breeding range, including the British Isles, and south as far as North Africa. Those breeding in Britain winter in the British Isles and along the Atlantic coasts of France and Spain. They will nest on a wide range of grasslands and other open habitats where they can obtain access to their invertebrate food; in the British Isles they are essentially birds of farmland, grassy wetlands and moorland edge.

This is one of the most strongly declining bird species in Europe, having decreased in all regions since 1980. In Britain it was moved from the amber to the red list in 2009, because of its strong decline between 1982 and 2007. Changes in farming practices have been responsible for this fall in numbers, notably the reduction in mixed farming together with general agricultural intensification.

A post-breeding influx of continental birds into Britain can begin as early as May, but the majority arrive between September and November. Wintering flocks occur on arable and pastoral farmland and at coastal wetlands; in icy conditions they move to the estuaries of southern and western Britain and Ireland, or to France and Spain. Their widespread distribution and the wide variety of habitats used makes it difficult to estimate numbers wintering in Britain, but there has evidently been a decline; a 1996 estimate of 1.5 million wintering birds was revised down to 620,000 in 2006–07 (Musgrove *et al.* 2011).

As with other breeding waders in Gloucestershire, the atlas fieldwork period was particularly unsuitable for Lapwings in the Severn Vale, because of the negative effects of the floods of June 2007 and September 2008 on food resources in subsequent years and, conversely, because of dry conditions in 2010 and 2011.

Swaine noted that the Lapwing bred 'sparingly in open country around the Forest of Dean; more plentifully in the Severn Vale and towards Newent and Redmarley; widely but somewhat thinly over the Cotswolds and throughout the Thames Area'. Regular surveys over the last ten years have found, as with Redshank, that larger numbers now breed in salt-marshes and flooded fields along the Severn Estuary in the Slimbridge and Aylburton Warth areas, than on meadows in the Vale. Atlas fieldwork during the nesting season found fewer Lapwings around Newent than there were in Swaine's day, except along the Leadon, and there were very few indeed in the Forest of Dean area. The main concentrations were around the estuary, in the upper part of the Vale and on the Cotswolds dip-slope, with a noticeable absence along the scarp. Although the overall distribution of breeding birds remained the same between the 1983–87 and 2003–07 Cotswolds Atlases, population density here decreased.

Swaine remarked on concentrations of several thousand Lapwings in the county as early as June or July; such flocks were still being observed at Slimbridge in the 1980s, but not since 1990 either on the estuary or in the Cotswold Water Park. The 2000 GBR noted that wintering numbers had declined in some previously favoured areas and that the species had virtually disappeared from the high Cotswolds during winter, because of a movement to Slimbridge where feeding opportunities had improved (see also Golden Plover, p. 174). This tendency has continued, with a 40% decrease in numbers wintering on the Cotswolds between the mid-1980s and the 2000s (Peter Dymott) and up to 9,000 at Slimbridge in winter since the turn of the century. Flocks venture up the Severn Vale only when flooding becomes extensive, while winter numbers average about 1,000 in both the eastern and western sections of the Water Park (Gareth Harris).

There have been recoveries in Gloucestershire of Lapwings ringed as chicks in Germany (four), Finland and the Netherlands, and movements from the county to France (four), Portugal (two), Spain (two), Germany, Hungary and the Netherlands. Of these, the only definitely Gloucestershire-bred birds (i.e. ringed as chicks) which moved abroad were one to Spain in 1930 and one to France in 1931.

Sponsored by Andrew Cleaver, E Golding, Pauhla Whitaker, Patrick Wise, and the North Cotswold Ornithological Society

Species accounts

	2007–11 Atlas fieldwork					Gloucestershire trends					UK population trends	
	Number of tetrads in which recorded (max 683)					Occupied 10 km squares (max 26)				% of tetrads in which recorded (1st hour of TTV)		UK conservation status: Red 3	
	Total	Confirmed	Probable	Possible	Present	1968–71	1981–84	1988–91	2007–11	1988–91	2008–11	Long term	Short term
Breeding	226	64	99	25	38	26		25	25	19.9	10.3	−48%	−20%
Winter	310						26		26		26	+137%	−23%

Breeding Distribution

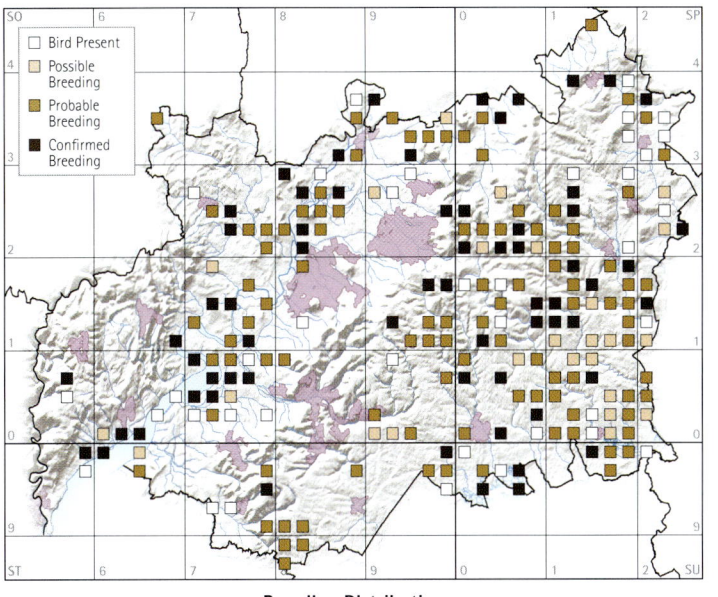

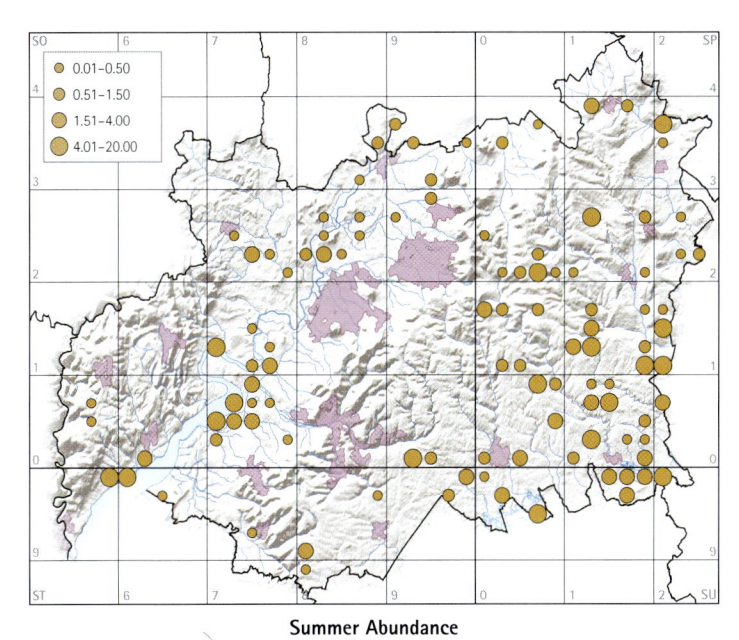

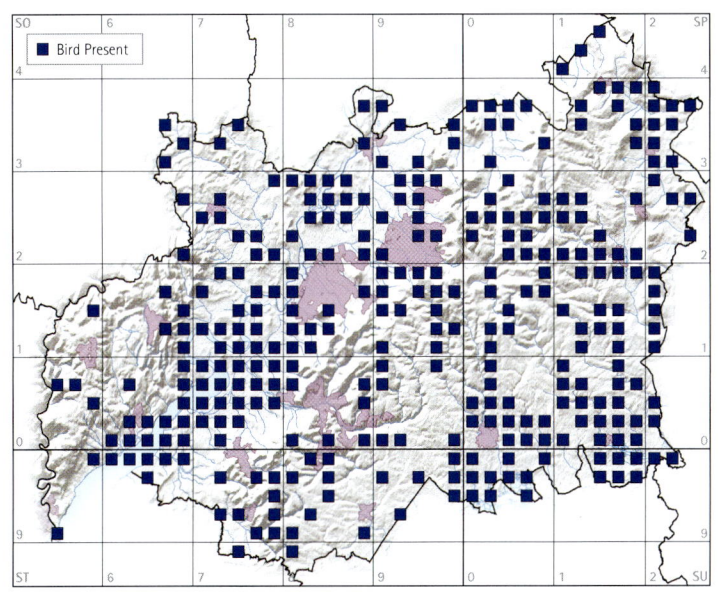

Summer Abundance

Winter Distribution

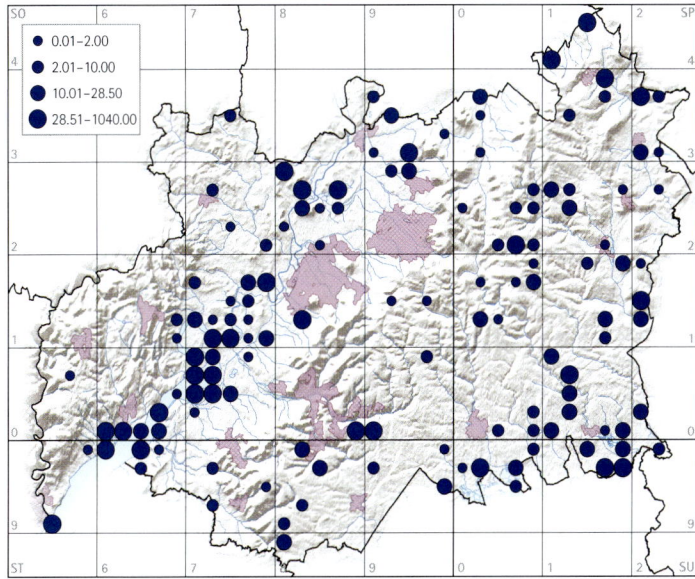

Winter Abundance

Knot (Red Knot)
Calidris canutus

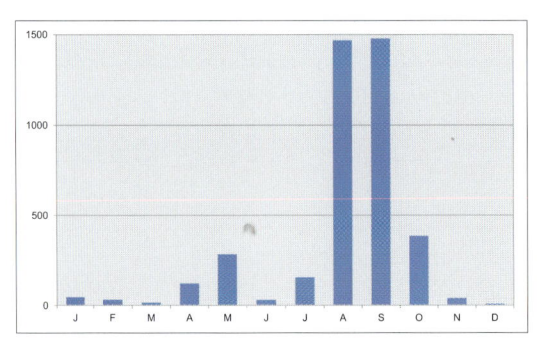

Knot numbers reported 2003–10, by month.

Knot breed in the high Arctic and winter in western Europe, West Africa, south-east Asia and widely in the southern hemisphere. Almost all those wintering in Britain breed in the Canadian Arctic and Greenland, while a few Siberian birds sometimes pass through in autumn.

Swaine described the Knot as 'chiefly a passage migrant, most numerous in autumn' in Gloucestershire, and this is still true today. He referred to occasional totals of 60 to 90 birds, mainly in autumn, with an 'exceptional' flock of 400 on the estuary at Slimbridge in August 1946.

Since 1980, numbers on passage have been very variable at both seasons. In spring the largest flocks at any one site have usually been of no more than 15 birds (median 9), so maxima of 170 at Slimbridge on May 11th 1993 and 73 there in May 2000 were unusual. The highest spring numbers can be at any time between early April and late June, but are usually in May (see graph)

Numbers in autumn have generally been higher, with maximum counts usually ranging between 15 and 60 birds (median 42). There have been four three-figure peaks (maximum 280 at Slimbridge on August 20th 1983), and a very exceptional flock of about 1,000 birds which flew across from Monmouthshire to Beachley Point on September 30th 1985. Autumn peaks are usually in September, but can be any time from mid-August to October (see graph).

Winter records in the county are generally few and far between, with sightings in December, January and/or February in 14 of the 30 years from 1981 to 2009. Swaine mentioned a flock of 60 at Slimbridge in February 1968, but this was unusual; normally fewer than a dozen birds are seen at this season, with a maximum count in recent years of 37 at Slimbridge on January 2nd 2007. There has been a tendency towards more winter sightings since about 1990, but this may be due to observer effects.

Knot are unusual away from the estuary, but there have been a few sightings elsewhere, mainly at the Cotswold Water Park and the Severn Hams. Very unexpected was a single bird in flight over the Cotswolds at Leighterton, near Tetbury, on July 27th 2009.

Sanderling
Calidris alba

Sanderlings breed in the far north of the circumpolar tundra and their only nesting area in the Western Palearctic is Spitsbergen, where there are thought to be no more than 100 pairs. In autumn they undertake very long migrations, some reaching Tierra del Fuego, southern Africa and Australasia. In Britain they are passage migrants and winter visitors. Outside the breeding season they prefer sandy seaside beaches, but migrants can be seen in other wetland habitats, including inland sites.

In Gloucestershire the Sanderling is, as described by Swaine, 'a passage migrant in spring and autumn, chiefly in the Severn Estuary'. He reported that spring flocks of 40 to 60 were 'not infrequent' between March and June, while in autumn 'small numbers' were present in July and August, with a lesser peak between late August and early October. A report of 120 birds on the estuary at Slimbridge on October 26th 1959 was 'surprising at this season'. Swaine knew of only two midwinter records, both in January: three at South Cerney in 1954 and one at Slimbridge in 1972.

Since 1980 Sanderlings may perhaps have become slightly more numerous in the county, at least in spring, when the peak count has usually been between 30 and 70 birds (median 45). There have been three-figure peaks in four springs, with a maximum of 211 on May 30th 2008. Numbers in autumn remain lower, with a peak count usually between ten and 30 birds (median 17), but there have been four years with maxima of between 40 and 55 birds and an unusually large flock of 120 on August 4th 1991. The spring peak passage is usually in the second half of May or the first week in June, while autumn numbers have tended to peak in August or the first half of September. Midwinter records are still very unusual, with singles in January in 1990 and 2003.

Virtually all county records come from the estuary, with a handful of sightings at the Cotswold Water Park and one at Tirley Knowle, near Hasfield Ham, on August 14th 2010.

Sponsored by Geoff Clutterbuck

Little Stint
Calidris minuta

Breeding from arctic Norway and Finland eastwards across northernmost Siberia, Little Stints winter mostly in Africa and southern Asia, though some move only as far as southern Europe. In the British Isles they are mostly passage migrants, but a few overwinter. As with Curlew Sandpipers, some autumns bring unusually high numbers to Britain.

Swaine stated that in Gloucestershire Little Stints were considerably more numerous in autumn than in spring, and that there were very few midwinter records. The main change since then has been a tendency for more to be seen during winter, with records at that season in all but four years since 1981, and annually since 1994. There were always five or fewer in winter each year up to 1995, but an average of eight per year subsequently. There seemed to be something of a peak around the turn of the millennium, with 12 at Slimbridge in winters 1998-99 and 1999-2000, 20 there in 2000-01 and 15 in 2001-02, but there have been no double-figure counts since then.

The general pattern of passage migration in the county has changed little since 1980. Estimated annual total numbers passing through in spring (April to June) have very rarely been greater than five birds, with a notable maximum of ten in 2006. The highest single count (flock) in spring is six, in 1991 and 2007. Autumn passage nearly always peaks in September, with a maximum count of usually between five and 20, though numbers vary widely from year to year. There have been six years with peaks of 40 or more, and a maximum count of 200 on September 27th 1996, a year when many Little Stints were brought to Britain by easterly winds. These autumn figures are comparable with the maxima of 100 in October 1966 and 80 in September 1967 quoted by Swaine.

Little Stints will use a fairly wide range of habitats outside the breeding season and although most county records are from the Severn Estuary, there are occasional sightings at other wetland sites.

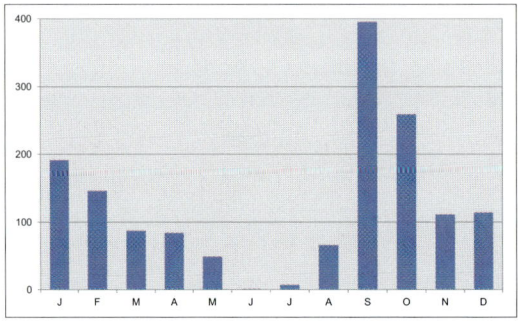

Little Stint numbers reported 2003-10, by month.

In memory of Robert & Lilian Boon

Curlew Sandpiper
Calidris ferruginea

Curlew Sandpipers nest in the coastal zone of the Asiatic high Arctic, and winter over much of sub-Saharan Africa, south Asia and Australasia. In the British Isles they are passage migrants, mainly in autumn when there are sometimes very large influxes, due to high population levels after a successful breeding season combined with easterly winds.

Swaine described the species as 'a passage migrant, usually in small numbers, and more frequent in autumn' in Gloucestershire. In spring only singles were usually seen, in May and June, and not in every year. The highest autumn numbers up to 1980 had been 'somewhat exceptional' counts of 100 in late August 1969 and 140 on August 5th 1975.

This general pattern has changed little since 1980. In spring there have been records in 75% of years, but only two counts of over four birds: six on June 2nd 1991 and 15 on April 30th 2004. The total number seen in spring has very rarely exceeded half a dozen in any year. Apart from a very early record of two on March 30th 2000, spring passage is nearly always between late April and the end of May. In autumn peak numbers have usually been between 5 and 20 birds, with maximum counts of 40 in September 1988 and 51 in September 1998. The total number passing through in autumn in most years probably ranges between 20 and 100 birds. There seems to have been a slight tendency for more to be seen in autumn in recent years, but this may be due at least partly to observer effects. The timing of the autumn peak passage is usually between mid-August and the end of September, with one very late record of a single on November 10th 1991.

There are comparatively few records away from the Severn Estuary and these have nearly all been at the Cotswold Water Park.

Dunlin
Calidris alpina

The Dunlin has a circumpolar breeding range, extending south in Europe to the Baltic region and the British Isles. There are three subspecies in the Western Palearctic. The nominate race breeds in northern Fennoscandia and western Siberia and many winter in western Europe, including the British Isles. *C. a. shinzii* breeds in Britain, parts of north-west continental Europe and south-east Greenland, and *C. a. arctica* nests in north-east Greenland and visits the British Isles on passage; these two subspecies winter mainly in West Africa.

The British breeding population numbers around 9,500 pairs, the vast majority in north-west Scotland. A handful of pairs still nest on Dartmoor, the most southerly breeding area in the world. In autumn around 350,000 Dunlin arrive in the British Isles to spend the winter on coasts and estuaries. Since the mid-1990s there has been a steady decline in wintering numbers here, but this is still one of our most numerous and familiar small waders. Indeed, Dunlin often receive no more than a brief glance from birders in search of rarer species, although a good knowledge of their structure, plumages and behaviour is a very useful starting point for identifying some of these rarities.

The status of the Dunlin in Gloucestershire remains much the same as when Swaine described it as a winter visitor and passage migrant and the most abundant wader on the Severn Estuary. The map shows that during the atlas period wintering Dunlin were largely confined to the estuary, particularly the Frampton–Slimbridge area which regularly holds several thousand birds and, further downriver, the Aylburton Warth–Guscar Rocks area where there are usually a few hundred. In the Slimbridge area the highest count ever recorded was 7,500 in December 2000, though peaks of 2,000 to 3,000 have been more usual here in recent winters, while the maximum at Aylburton Warth was 1,200 in December 1981. Up to 1,000 have also occasionally been reported much further up the estuary in the Rodley and Longney area; these may well be birds that have been temporarily displaced from further down.

Away from the estuary several sites have attracted good numbers in winter, though only rarely in recent years, possibly due to an overall decline in numbers but also perhaps because feeding and roosting conditions at Slimbridge have improved and have tended

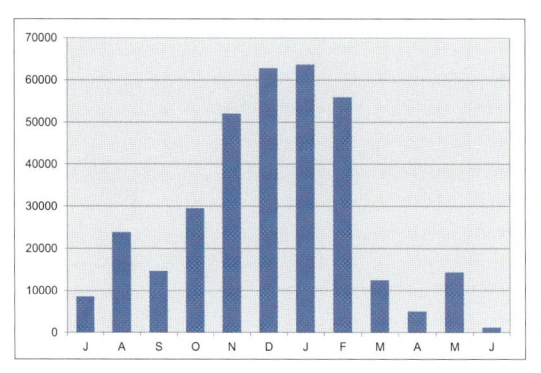

Dunlin numbers reported 2003–10, by month.

Sponsored by Terry Fenton

Species accounts

| | 2007–11 Atlas fieldwork ||||| Gloucestershire trends |||||| UK population trends ||
| | Number of tetrads in which recorded (max 683) ||||| Occupied 10 km squares (max 26) |||| % of tetrads in which recorded (1st hour of TTV) || UK conservation status: Red 4 ||
	Total	Confirmed	Probable	Possible	Present	1968–71	1981–84	1988–91	2007–11	1988–91	2008–11	Long term	Short term
Breeding	19	0	0	0	19	0		0	0	0	0	–	–
Winter	33							6	7			–28%	–39%

to draw birds away. Walmore Common held 1,600 in December 1982 and 1,200 in February 1986, and up to 700 have been seen on the Avon Meadows at Twyning in the past. The Severn Hams also provide suitable habitat following flooding, with both Ashleworth Ham and Coombe Hill Meadows holding up to 250 birds.

During passage periods records are much more widespread and small numbers may appear almost anywhere where there is open water with suitable margins for feeding. Spring passage on the estuary usually peaks during May, though substantial numbers may appear in late April or early June. Maximum counts from the Slimbridge area at this season usually number several hundred birds, though up to 1,000 were present in May 1986. Away from the estuary just single-figure counts are the norm, but larger numbers are occasionally noted, such as 55 at the Cotswold Water Park in April 2008 and 120 at Coombe Hill Meadows in late May of the same year. Return migration begins in earnest during July as adult birds, perhaps failed breeders, head south. Up to 450 have been noted during this month, but the peak, up to 750 birds, typically occurs during August when numbers are swollen by an influx of juveniles. There is then something of a lull in September before the arrival of much larger numbers of wintering birds in October and November (see graph).

There have been about a dozen ringing recoveries showing interchanges of Dunlin between Gloucestershire and the principal English estuaries, especially the Wash. There have also been 15 movements of ringed birds between the county and Iceland, Fennoscandia, Denmark, Germany, the Netherlands and Morocco.

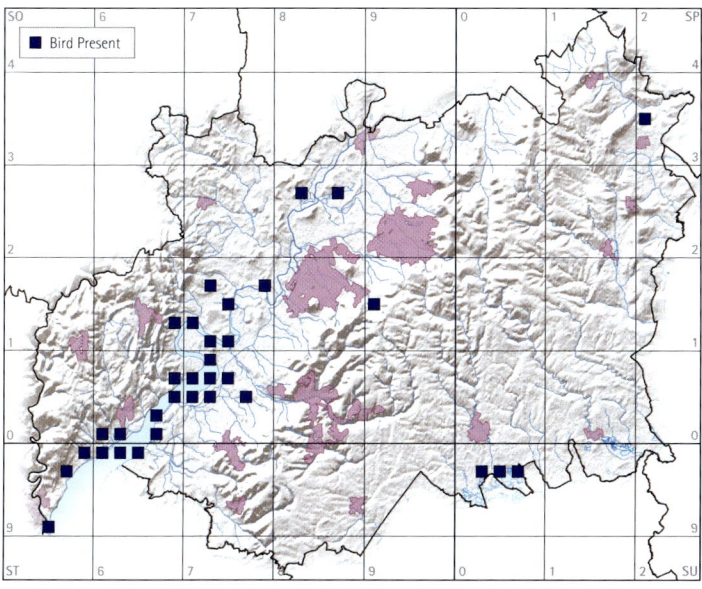

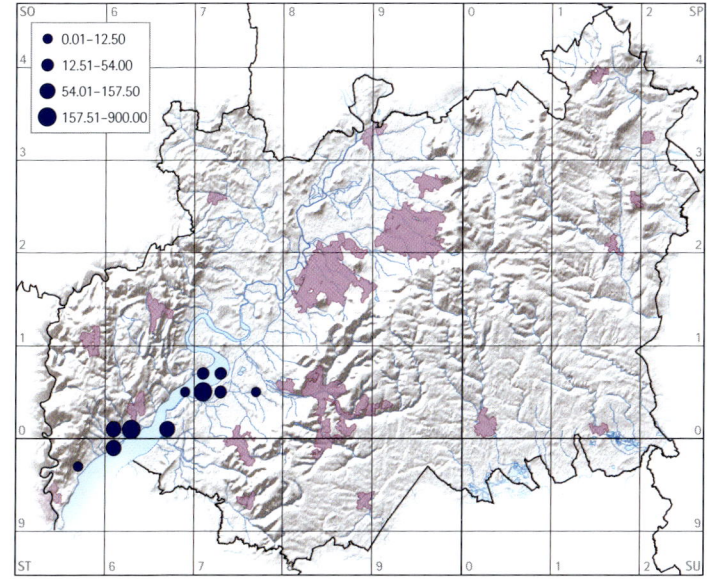

Winter Distribution

Winter Abundance

Ruff

Philomachus pugnax

Ruff breed in marshy grasslands, from Fennoscandia to the Bering Strait and very discontinuously from England and France across west and central Europe to Kazakhstan. Nearly all winter in Africa and outside the breeding season they use a wide range of habitats, including dry grasslands. The English breeding population numbers only a few dozen, and Ruff occur in Britain essentially as passage migrants and, nowadays, winter visitors, although there were no wintering records here prior to 1934.

In Gloucestershire, Swaine noted that Ruff had formerly been regarded only as occasional visitors, but by 1980 they had become much more numerous and regular, mainly as passage migrants from March to May and, somewhat more plentifully, from July to October. The largest group ever recorded was 67, at Slimbridge in March 1976. Occurrence in winter was irregular and mostly in low numbers.

Since then the main change in the county has been an increase in wintering numbers. Ruff now winter here every year, with often up to 15 birds at favoured sites. Indeed, in some years the highest count for the whole year has been in winter, for example 32 in early 2010 at Slimbridge.

Numbers on passage have apparently changed rather little since 1980. Peak counts in spring (usually in April) are normally between five and 15 birds; four years have produced maxima of 20 or more, and the largest spring flock was 64 at Slimbridge on April 16th 1987, a year when numbers were at their highest since 1976. Numbers on autumn passage tend to be higher, with annual peak counts, usually in September, ranging between five and 20 birds; seven years have produced peaks of over 25, the maximum being 45 in September 1998.

While most records come from the Frampton–Slimbridge area, there are also regular sightings away from the Severn Estuary, in particular at the Cotswold Water Park and, when conditions are suitable, at Severn Vale grasslands (notably 55 at Walmore Common in April 1987). There are also quite frequent reports from other localities, including landfill sites and Cotswold farmland.

Jack Snipe
Lymnocryptes minimus

The main breeding range of the Jack Snipe extends from northern Fennoscandia eastwards across Siberia, though there is a small, isolated population in southern Sweden. Within Europe it winters mostly in western and southern areas, including the British Isles. The British wintering population has been estimated at around 100,000 birds.

Many Jack Snipe must go undetected. They inhabit marshy and boggy areas, often preferring wetter areas than Snipe, and such habitats are often inaccessible to observers. They are also usually silent, often solitary and probably partly nocturnal. However, what makes them particularly difficult to find is their superbly camouflaged plumage and their habit of sitting tight until the observer is very close.

Their status in Gloucestershire remains the same as described by Swaine: a winter visitor in small numbers, with the majority of records coming from the Severn Vale. Over half of the 38 tetrads where Jack Snipe were recorded during the four winters of atlas fieldwork were in the Vale. The Cotswold Water Park also produced a loose cluster of records, with just a few sightings elsewhere, on the Cotswolds and in the Forest of Dean.

Swaine mentioned two August reports, but the first birds typically arrive in the county at the end of September and singles at Slimbridge on September 8th 1991 and September 18th 1997 are unusually early by modern standards. Peak counts at any one site are often no more than three or four individuals, but much higher numbers have occasionally been recorded. Up to 18 were seen in the western section of the Water Park during March 1984, and 13 were found there in January 1994, but nowadays such numbers are unlikely to be recorded due to a reduction in suitable habitat and also to restrictions on access. In January 1986 15 were counted at Plusterwine by the Severn, near Lydney, and at Slimbridge 13 were seen on December 2nd 2004 and 19 during January and February 2006. Elsewhere in the Vale, Ashleworth Ham, Coombe Hill Meadows and Walmore Common are regular sites and have all held seven or more birds on occasion. Only two Forest of Dean sites, Woorgreens and Tidenham Chase, have attracted Jack Snipe with any regularity; both have held up to four birds. Occasional reports also come from the higher ground of the Cotswolds.

By the end of March many Jack Snipe have departed for their breeding grounds, but records to mid-April are not unusual and a few stragglers may be still be encountered at the end of the month. The latest spring sighting in recent times was of one near Fairford on May 4th 2009. Summer records are very rare anywhere in Britain, and singles at Bourton pits on June 6th 2002 and Walmore Common on June 19th 2010 are exceptional.

Rather few Jack Snipe are ringed or recovered, so the record of one ringed in the county on October 8th 1969 and shot in Co. Cork, Ireland on January 26th 1970 is of some interest. This bird was evidently on passage when it was ringed.

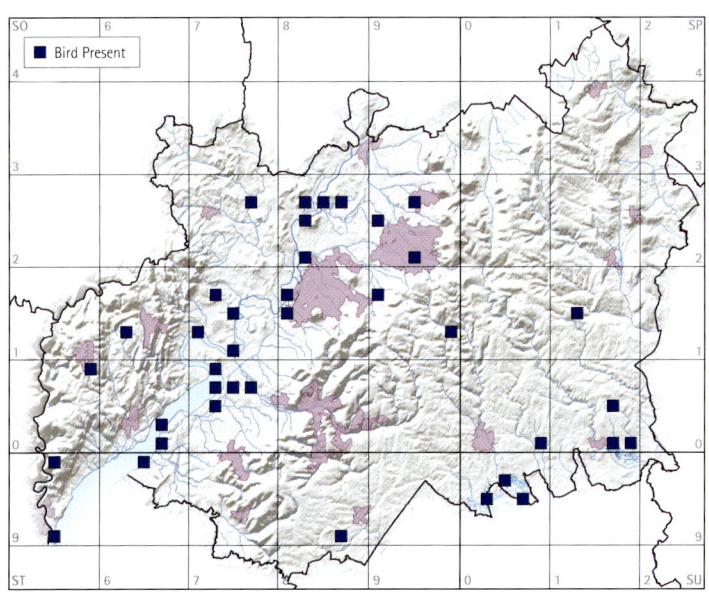

Winter Distribution

Snipe (Common Snipe)
Gallinago gallinago

The Snipe's 'drumming' display ranks as one of nature's most magical sounds, and the disappearance of the species as a breeding bird is one of the most tragic events for Gloucestershire's wildlife in the last 20 years.

Snipe breed across the Northern Palearctic from Iceland to eastern China, and are replaced in North America by the closely related Wilson's Snipe *G. delicata*. European birds are partly migratory, wintering south to the Mediterranean basin. The basic requirement for nesting is soft organic soil, rich in invertebrate food, with clumps of herbage or shrub cover. They breed throughout Britain but drainage and general degradation of wetlands has caused a decline in numbers and a concentration in the few remaining suitable habitats. This was already noticeable by the time of the 1988–91 Breeding Atlas. Approximately 53,000 pairs were thought to be breeding in Britain around 2000, while about a million individuals winter here.

In Gloucestershire, Mellersh mentioned a number of breeding records. Swaine commented that 'a few probably breed every year' but 'records of proven breeding are rather few'; likely nesting areas were the New Grounds at Slimbridge, Walmore Common and 'other places along the Severn', St Briavels in the Forest of Dean, and the Windrush Valley in the Cotswolds. GBRs from the 1980s to 1992 recorded several birds drumming by daylight, a strong indication of breeding, at Walmore, Ashleworth Ham, Coombe Hill, and Upham Meadow along the Avon north of Tewkesbury. However in 1995 a thorough survey of breeding waders in the Severn and Avon Vales (Quinn 1995) found not a single drumming Snipe in Gloucestershire. In April and May 2001 and 2002 one bird drummed consistently for several weeks at Ashleworth Ham, though only after dusk, and quite probably bred. The 2003–07 Cotswolds Atlas concluded that 'it seems unlikely that Snipe breed in the survey area, although historically they probably have done so'.

During the current atlas fieldwork, a Snipe drummed for one day only in each of 2008 and 2009 at Slimbridge; there was no proof of breeding anywhere in the county. Attempts have been made to manage habitat for Snipe at Slimbridge and the Severn Hams, but so far with no success in attracting breeding birds back to Gloucestershire.

Outside the breeding season, Snipe were considered to be widespread and numerous by Mellersh and Swaine. This has always been a popular quarry species: Mellersh mentioned large shooting bags from damp arable land in the Severn Vale, though he considered it much less common on the Cotswolds. Swaine quoted 'numerous records of from 100 to 200 birds, sometimes more' in the Vale and at the Thames Area gravel-pits, and added that in the Cotswolds the species was recorded principally in the main river valleys, with relatively few records in the Forest of Dean. Recent GBRs indicate that three-figure counts do still occur in winter, but are unusual. The largest numbers are often seen during northward spring passage from March to May, when birds sometimes become active at dusk, raising vain hopes that they might stay to breed. Return passage may begin as early as mid-June or July, which explains 'summer' records during the atlas fieldwork; indeed in the unusual 2007 summer floods 270 were noted at Walmore Common on 24 August, suggesting that migrants which would normally have passed

In memory of Keith Garner

Species accounts

	2007–11 Atlas fieldwork					Gloucestershire trends						UK population trends	
	Number of tetrads in which recorded (max 683)					Occupied 10 km squares (max 26)				% of tetrads in which recorded (1st hour of TTV)		UK conservation status: **Amber 1**	
	Total	Confirmed	Probable	Possible	Present	1968–71	1981–84	1988–91	2007–11	1988–91	2008–11	Long term	Short term
Breeding	38	0	1	3	34	12		8	3	1.4	0.6	–	+50%
Winter	184						21		24			–	–

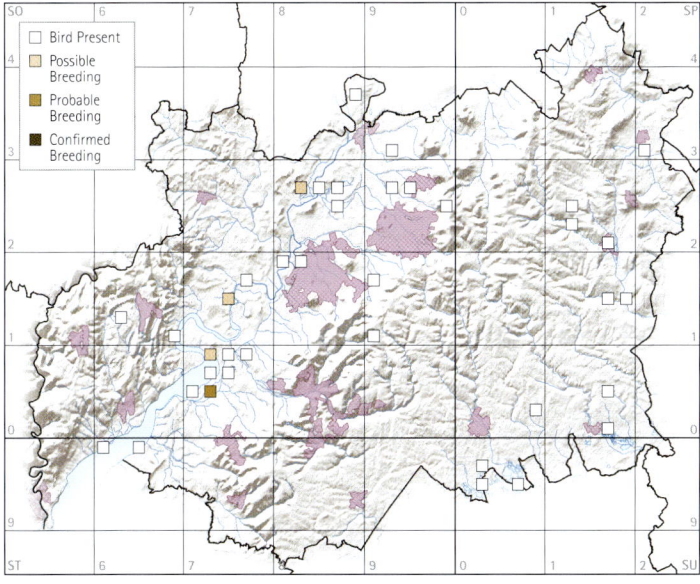

Breeding Distribution

straight over were alighting to take advantage of the unusually wet conditions. Winter records during the atlas fieldwork mirrored the findings of Mellersh and Swaine, with the largest concentrations throughout the Vale, rather few in the Dean, scattered records on the Cotswolds (mostly along the main rivers) and good numbers in the Water Park. The maximum recorded in a winter TTV was 50, in January 2008 in tetrad SO70E on the Awre peninsula between Newnham and Blakeney.

In addition to half a dozen movements of ringed Snipe between Gloucestershire and other English counties, there have been three longer-distance recoveries: a nestling ringed in Finland in 1962 was shot near Cirencester in January 1963, one ringed in Germany in July 1969 was caught by ringers at Coombe Hill in October that year, and one ringed at Frampton in September 2007 was shot two days later in Atlantic France.

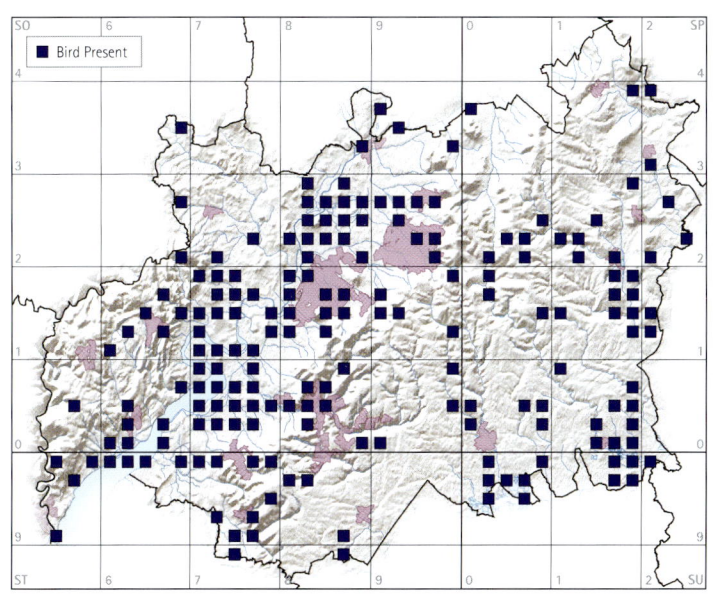

Winter Distribution

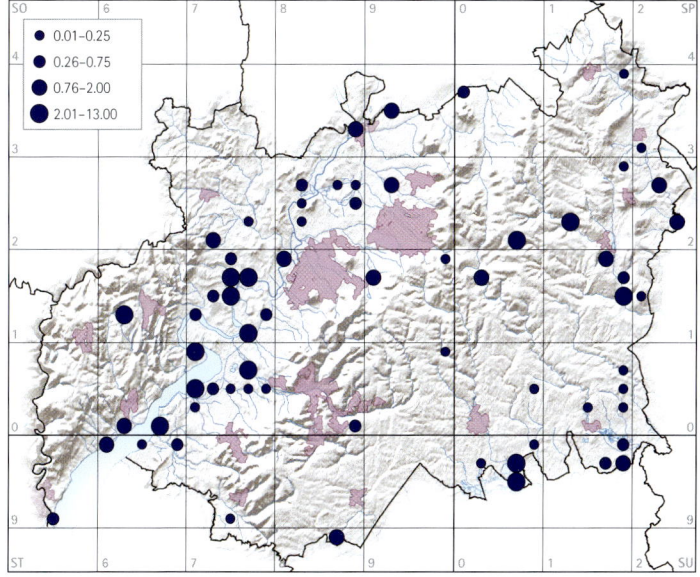

Winter Abundance

Woodcock (Eurasian Woodcock)
Scolopax rusticola

The Woodcock is a fairly common but declining breeder across much of northern Europe including the British Isles, though it is absent from Iceland. Its summer range also extends across central Russia and Asia. It is mostly resident in the west, but in eastern Europe and Fennoscandia it is a summer visitor, wintering in western and southern Europe and also parts of North Africa. Woodcock are thought to be usually promiscuous or polygynous, a single male pairing with more than one female per breeding season. The European population numbers between 600,000 and 1.6 million 'pairs', and a national survey organised by the Game Conservancy Trust and the BTO in 2003 estimated a breeding population of over 78,000 males in Britain. Winter numbers here vary from year to year, but are thought to be around 1.4 million birds.

Woodcock require woodland for breeding, but mostly avoid high altitudes and very dense woods with little shrub layer. Their secretive and mainly nocturnal habits, combined with often overlapping territories, make them a difficult species to census accurately. Most breeding season sightings are of males engaged in their crepuscular territorial 'roding' flights. During the winter they are more widespread and may be flushed from a broader range of habitats.

Swaine described the Woodcock as a regular winter visitor to Gloucestershire in modest numbers and a local breeding species

Sponsored by Acorn Tree and Woodland Services

Species accounts

2007–11 Atlas fieldwork						Gloucestershire trends						UK population trends	
Number of tetrads in which recorded (max 683)					Occupied 10 km squares (max 26)				% of tetrads in which recorded (1st hour of TTV)		UK conservation status: Amber 1	
	Total	Confirmed	Probable	Possible	Present	1968–71	1981–84	1988–91	2007–11	1988–91	2008–11	Long term	Short term
Breeding	31	0	21	4	6	12		8	7	1.6	0.4	–83%	–
Winter	139						20		25			–	–

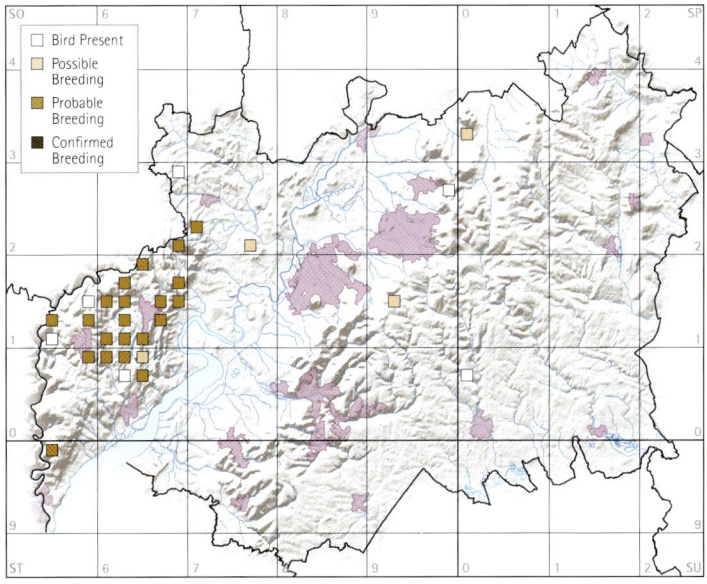

Breeding Distribution

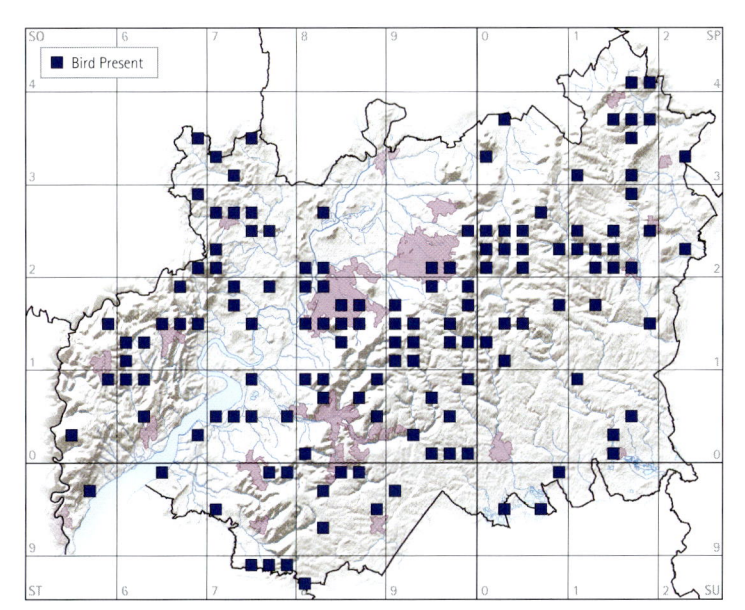

Winter Distribution

with its stronghold in the Forest of Dean, becoming more established on the Cotswolds from 1960 onwards. During the 1983–87 Cotswolds Atlas fieldwork roding Woodcocks were present at several locations, including Bourton Woods near Blockley, Wolford Wood near Moreton-in-Marsh, Foxholes nature reserve near Kingham, and Cirencester Park. In March 1992 three or four birds were reported roding north of Longborough near Stow-on-the-Wold. However, the Cotswold population does not appear to have persisted: during the 2003–07 Atlas surveys the only indication of possible breeding was an 'agitated' bird in the Coln valley between Fairford and Coln St Aldwyns in June 2005. A larger-scale, regional decline was also revealed during the national 2003 survey, when Woodcocks were found in just 11% of woods in the south Midlands, the lowest occupancy rate in Britain, compared with 69% in northern Scotland. During the current atlas there were just two reports from Cotswold localities and no evidence of breeding.

However the Forest of Dean remains an important area, as shown by the map, although the total number of breeding birds is unclear as no detailed survey has been undertaken. The 2003 GBR indicated a minimum of 35 roding birds here, but this was based on a limited survey and a more recent estimate suggests up to 100 nesting females (Ivan Proctor).

The winter map shows a fairly wide spread of records, although open woodland still produces most sightings at this season unless the weather is particularly harsh. Most were from the Dean, the Cotswold scarp and the middle part of the Severn Vale in the Gloucester area. The Thames Area also produced a few records, but the Cotswold dip-slope and the upper Vale were certainly less favoured, due no doubt to a lack of woodland. The vast majority of winter records are of single birds, but occasionally some numbers are reported together, often by shooting parties. The Pegglesworth Estate near Seven Springs held 15 to 20 in the early months of 1981, 11 were flushed at Elmore on February 1st 2002, and the Whittington Lodge Estate near Andoversford reported 20 on a Pheasant shoot on January 3rd 2009.

Shoots also provide the majority of Woodcock ringing recoveries. Birds ringed in autumn in the Netherlands and in winter in northern France were shot in Gloucestershire in winter, while one ringed at Parkend as a chick in June 1986 was shot in Brittany in February 1987.

Black-tailed Godwit
Limosa limosa

The nominate subspecies of Black-tailed Godwit has a patchy breeding distribution from west and central Europe (including a small population in England) eastwards to central Siberia. This race winters mainly in sub-Saharan Africa, but also in Iberia, and is declining in Europe.

The subspecies *L. l. islandica* breeds predominantly in Iceland, with very small numbers in northern Norway and Scotland. Numbers have increased steadily in recent decades, including the Scottish population which however only numbered about ten pairs by 2008. This subspecies winters in western Europe, including Britain where numbers have increased markedly in recent decades, and is the commoner of the two races in Gloucestershire.

Black-tailed Godwits prefer lowland wet grassland and marshes for breeding; wintering *islandica* use similar habitats plus estuarine mudflats and lagoons.

This was clearly a rare bird in Gloucestershire at the end of the nineteenth century. The species was not included by Witchell & Strugnell, Mellersh scarcely mentioned it, and there were few reports prior to the 1930s (Swaine). Subsequently there was a gradual increase on passage, and by about 1980 some 20 to 30 birds were being seen fairly frequently in autumn. Spring numbers were lower, with a maximum of 24 in April 1977. In addition there were a few reports of one or two in winter between about 1960 and 1980; ten in February 1980 were thought worthy of special mention.

Since 1980 there has been a marked and sustained increase, especially after 2000 (see top graph). Winter records were still 'exceptional' in 1988 (GBR) but have been annual since about 2000, and Black-tailed Godwits are now seen in the county in all months (see bottom graph). The bulk of records are from Slimbridge, where habitat improvements may have played a part in the increase, but they are also regular elsewhere, especially the wet grasslands of the Severn Vale. The highest counts are still usually in autumn, but winter flocks sometimes exceed 60 birds. The highest recorded count at Slimbridge is 254 on July 27th 2006.

Breeding was suspected in the Severn Vale in 1969 (1968–72 Breeding Atlas; Swaine) but there are no details.

A number of colour-ringed Black-tailed Godwits from the Icelandic breeding population have been seen in the county, some at least en route to wintering haunts on the English south coast.

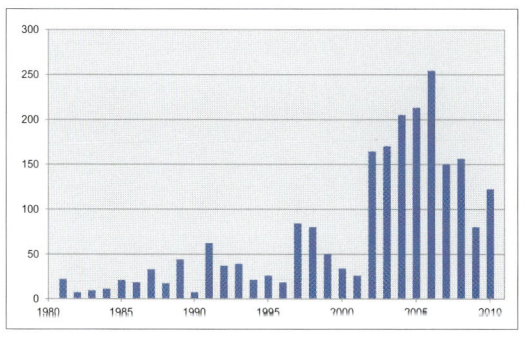

Peak counts of Black-tailed Godwits, 1981–2010.

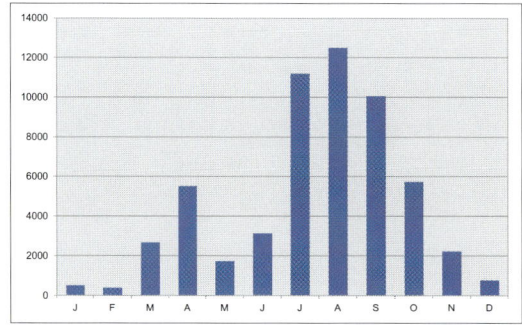

Black-tailed Godwit numbers reported 2003–10, by month.

Sponsored by Beryl Smith

Bar-tailed Godwit
Limosa lapponica

Breeding in the far north of the Palearctic and western Alaska, and wintering south to southern Africa and Australasia, Bar-tailed Godwits are passage migrants and winter visitors to the British Isles. They favour the larger estuaries, but are comparatively uncommon on the Severn (see p. 19). Nevertheless the vast majority of Gloucestershire records are from the estuary, nowadays mainly the Frampton–Slimbridge area.

Swaine described this species as 'chiefly a spring and autumn migrant', with peaks of usually up to 50 birds in April to early May, and normally under 40 in September. The largest flock on record at that time was 300, at Slimbridge in late April 1976, and winter records, of 'single birds or small groups', were unusual.

Since 1980, numbers on passage have been very variable. Peak spring numbers are usually in late April and early May, while autumn peaks can be at any time in August or September (see graph). The spring maximum has usually been between 25 and 80 birds (median 50); there have been six years with three-figure peaks, including a remarkable count of at least 700 on April 27th 1984. In autumn numbers are usually considerably lower, with the highest count normally between five and 25 birds (median 12). There have only been five autumns with peaks of 50 or more birds, and only one three-figure count, an 'exceptional' 120 in late August 1986. At both seasons, peak counts have tended to be slightly lower since 1995 than between 1981 and 1994.

Bar-tails remain scarce in Gloucestershire in winter, with no records at all in January, February or December in about one-third of years since 1980. Usually only one or two birds are found at this time, with ten in February in both 1987 and 1998 being the highest counts.

There are occasional sightings away from the estuary, mostly at the Severn Hams and the Cotswold Water Park. One on May 5th 2000 in an arable field at Longborough, in the Cotswolds near Stow-on-the-Wold, was very unusual.

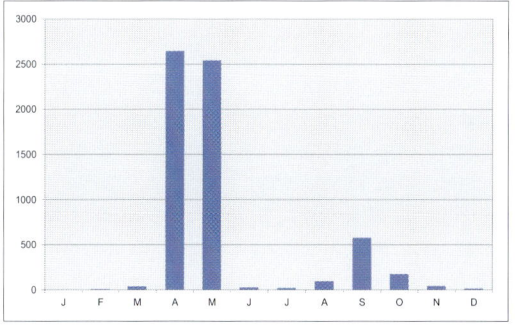

Bar-tailed Godwit numbers reported 2003–10, by month.

Curlew (Eurasian Curlew)
Numenius arquata

The Curlew's long, sickle-shaped bill and haunting 'cour-lee' calls are familiar on the Severn Estuary, while the bubbling display flight is a much-loved feature of early summer, especially in hay meadows by the Severn and Avon. This is the largest wader, and very long-lived: the current longevity record is nearly 32 years.

Curlews breed from Ireland to central Siberia, generally choosing damp or wet terrain and open landscapes with wide visibility. In Britain they breed mainly in upland areas; some agricultural lowlands were colonised in the early twentieth century, but they are still largely absent from south-east England. British breeders winter mainly in western Britain and Ireland, while those from further north and east migrate to southern Africa. The British Isles receive a large influx of wintering birds from Fennoscandia and the Low Countries. British breeding numbers have recently been estimated at 105,000 pairs, a very substantial upward revision since the 1988-91 Breeding Atlas, but numbers have declined again in the last few years, perhaps because of chick predation. Similarly, the British winter population increased from the mid-1970s until the early 2000s but then declined, perhaps because of an eastward shift in distribution associated with milder winters. It is currently estimated at about 140,000 individuals.

In Gloucestershire, Curlews do not lay until late April when the grass is well grown, and their long incubation and fledging periods limit opportunities for replacement clutches. Many nests and eggs are lost to foxes, mink, crows and (a new predator in recent years) gulls. However, Curlews seem to have recovered more rapidly than other breeding waders from the summer floods along the Severn in 2007 and 2008. Nests and eggs are difficult to find, even when the adults' alarm calls suggest they are nearby.

Swaine noted that 'a few pairs breed' in the county, and this remains the case today. Thirty-four pairs nested in the Severn and Avon Vales in Gloucestershire and Worcestershire combined in 2002, and in the Gloucestershire part of the Vale 17-21 pairs attempted to nest in 2009 and 20-22 pairs at 13 sites in 2011. Curlews in this part of the county, where density is greatest and the birds are closely monitored, attempt to breed each year in the same meadows, which often benefit from government agri-environmental schemes that support late hay cuts and restricted use of herbicides. On the Cotswolds the few breeding areas are elevated, uncultivated and largely ungrazed grassland, reminiscent of the moorland habitat used elsewhere. As shown by the map, during the current atlas survey breeding was only confirmed in four tetrads in the Vale; in the Cotswolds it was recorded in two tetrads, the same low figure as during the 2003-07 Cotswolds Atlas. However, breeding was strongly suspected at a number of other sites in the Cotswolds and the Vale, and also in the Cotswold Water Park and in traditional hay meadows in the Forest of Dean.

By late June or July the nesting areas are deserted and flocks of adults gather on the Severn Estuary to moult. The sightings by the estuary shown on the breeding season map will include these birds, in addition to non-breeders and passage migrants. Recent colour-ringing studies on the estuary have revealed remarkable site fidelity among these birds, with at least 90% of birds ringed in September returning the following August.

Swaine noted that 'the two main feeding areas are at the New Grounds and from Aylburton to Guscar Rocks. Counts from these, taken together, have given maximum totals of from 1,200 to 1,800 birds'. These remain the main wintering sites today, with similar numbers. Recent WeBS counts show that September peaks on the whole estuary reach more than 3,000 birds. Until the New Year, flocks concentrate on the estuary and inland records are scarce, but the return to local and continental breeding grounds begins as early as January or February, which explains the 'winter' records in the Vale and the Water Park, where small flocks of migrants also occur in March and April.

Ringing recoveries reveal movements to Gloucestershire of birds ringed on breeding grounds in Finland (four) and the Netherlands (two), and birds ringed in Gloucestershire have been recovered in Finland (four), Sweden, France and the Netherlands.

Sponsored by Mike Smart, and in memory of John Bentley-Taylor and Richard Wilkinson

Species accounts

	2007–11 Atlas fieldwork					Gloucestershire trends						UK population trends	
	Number of tetrads in which recorded (max 683)					Occupied 10 km squares (max 26)				% of tetrads in which recorded (1st hour of TTV)		UK conservation status: **Amber 1,3,8**	
	Total	Confirmed	Probable	Possible	Present	1968–71	1981–84	1988–91	2007–11	1988–91	2008–11	Long term	Short term
Breeding	94	6	23	26	39	14		6	12	3.9	4.4	–60%	–41%
Winter	60						7		10			+27%	–16%

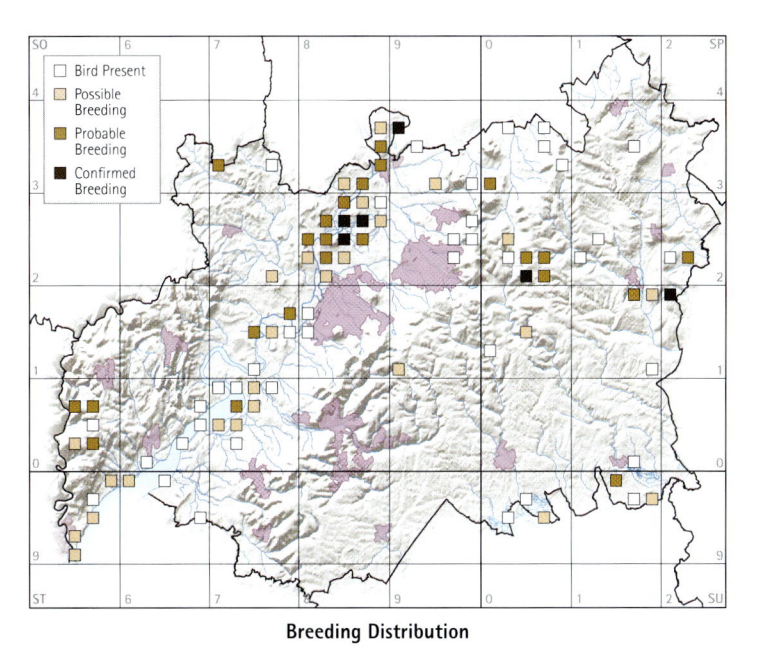

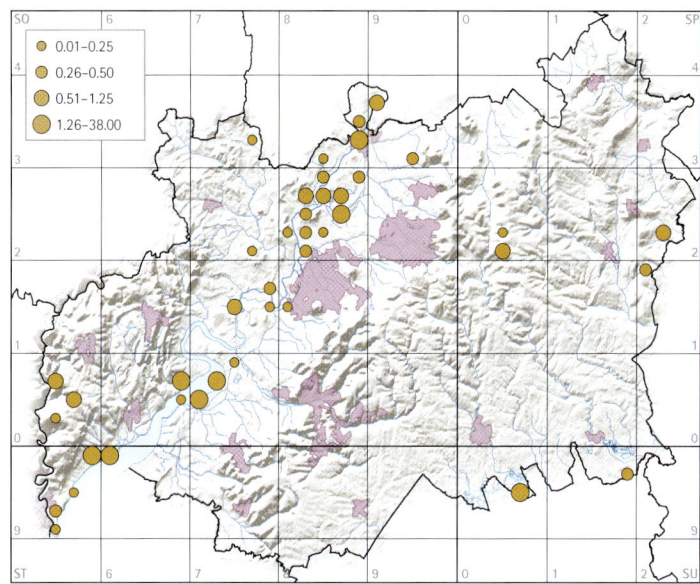

Breeding Distribution

Summer Abundance

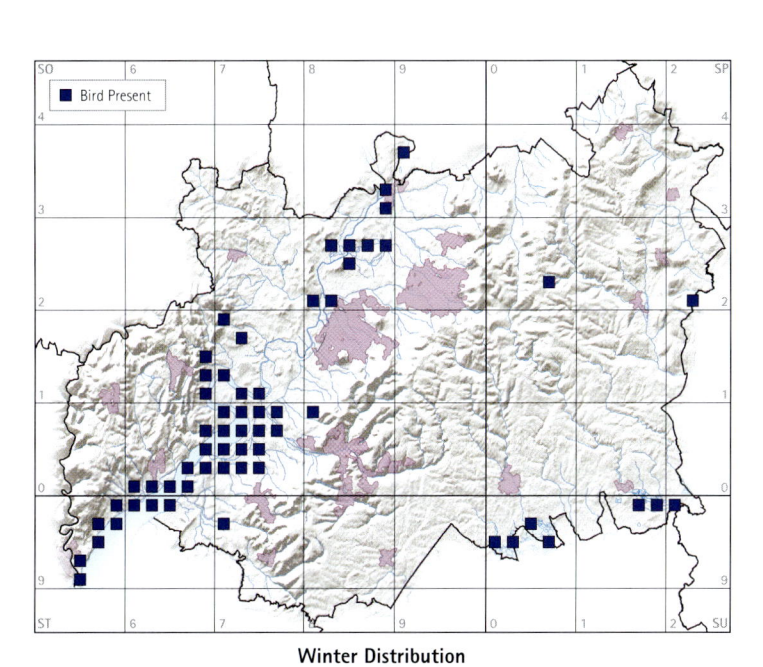

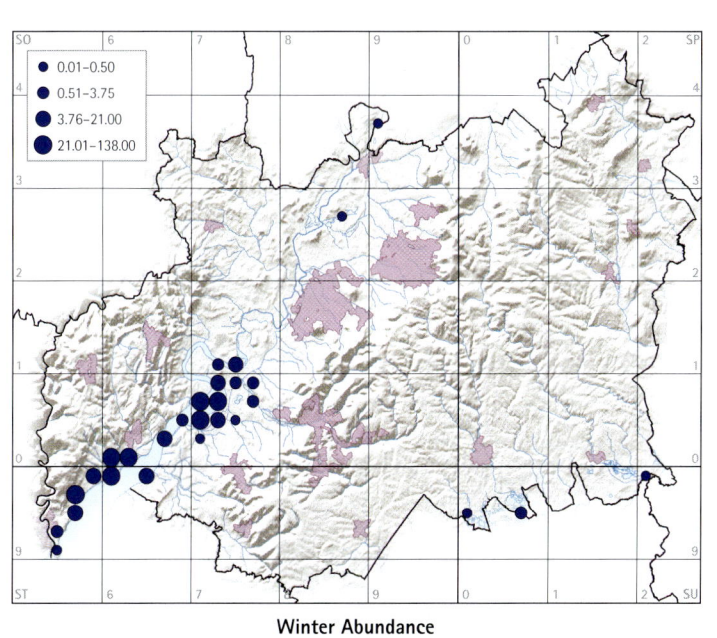

Winter Distribution

Winter Abundance

Whimbrel
Numenius phaeopus

Whimbrel nest mostly on open moorland and tundra in Iceland, Fennoscandia, northern Russia and patchily across Siberia, with a different subspecies, *N. p. hudsonicus*, in North America. There is a tiny population in Shetland, and they sometimes breed elsewhere in north and west Scotland. There are occasional winter records in Britain, but the vast majority of European birds migrate to the Afrotropics.

Most of the autumn passage through Britain is via the North Sea coastline and southern England, whilst in spring the bulk of the movement is further to the west: 'between 1972 and 1975 74% of passage Whimbrel counted in Britain in May occurred at sites around the Severn Estuary, compared with 8% during autumn passage' (Ferns *et al.* 1979).

In Gloucestershire, Swaine described the Whimbrel as 'not uncommon as a passage migrant ... regular in both spring and late summer'. Spring passage peaked in late April and May, with usually up to 40 birds and a maximum count of 150 in May 1968. Up to 30 were seen together in autumn but usually far fewer, with the bulk of the passage in July and August.

Since 1980 there has been very little change. The earliest spring record is of nine on the very early date of March 8th 2003, but the first migrants usually appear between April 5th and 15th, with a slight tendency towards earlier arrivals in recent years. Peak numbers in spring still occur in late April or early May. The largest flocks at this season have usually been between 50 and 75 birds, with four three-figure maximum counts, the highest being 200 on May 2nd 1987. The autumn peak is usually in late July or early August. Since 1980 the largest flock per year at this season has varied between one and 30 birds; the total number recorded in the whole autumn has often been no more than 20.

One at Beachley Point on February 17th 1986 and one at Slimbridge on the same date in 1996 are the only winter records.

While most occur on or by the estuary, there are frequent reports from widely scattered localities throughout the county, particularly the Cotswold Water Park and the wet grasslands of the Severn Vale, but also elsewhere, especially migrating birds in flight.

Common Sandpiper
Actitis hypoleucos

Breeding very widely across the Palearctic, Common Sandpipers prefer to nest by fast-flowing rivers and streams; however they will use a wide range of wetland habitats at all seasons. The British breeding population is mostly confined to more northern and upland areas, and has been declining recently. The winter range is also very extensive, including much of southern Africa and southern Asia. A few winter in western Europe, including the British Isles.

Mellersh cited about five instances of supposed breeding in Gloucestershire, but presented little evidence, and Swaine mentioned a few more unproved records up to 1980. The first well-documented breeding attempt was in 1993, when a pair raised at least one chick by the Severn Estuary near Berkeley. They may have bred in the same place in the following year. In 1999 single pairs were present at two sites and one bred successfully; a single pair was suspected of breeding in 2000, and one pair bred in 2001, but there have been no subsequent attempts.

Swaine stated that Common Sandpipers were 'occasionally reported in winter', and mentioned about 15 records. Winter sightings remained unusual from 1981 to 1999, but ones or twos have been recorded every winter since 2000.

The vast majority of Common Sandpipers seen in Gloucestershire are passage migrants (see graph). They occur at a very wide range of sites throughout the county, though the largest numbers are nearly always at the Severn Estuary (especially in the Slimbridge area and near Berkeley) and at the Cotswold Water Park. In spring the highest counts at any site are usually under ten, with an all-time maximum of 25 at Dowdeswell reservoir on April 20th 1995. Spring passage seems to have become earlier: between 1981 and 1990 the date of the first sighting of the year averaged April 9th, whilst since then it has nearly always been before April 5th, although the picture is complicated by increasing numbers of winter records. Also, between 1981 and 1994 the highest spring count was in April in seven years and in May in six, while between 1995 and 2010 all dated peaks were in April.

In autumn, peak numbers at any one site are usually in the range of 15 to 30 birds, with an average annual maximum of 22 between 1981 and 2010. The highest recent counts were an 'exceptional' 52 at the Berkeley shore on August 14th 1997 and 42 at the Guscar Rocks area in July 1986. The timing of autumn passage has perhaps been slightly later in recent years: from 1981 to 1994 there were nine years with July peaks and five with August peaks, while from 1995 to 2010 the peak came in July in seven years and in August in eight.

Rather few Common Sandpipers have been ringed in Gloucestershire, but there have been three recoveries showing the timing of passage and destinations of migrants: an adult ringed in the county on August 7th 1966 was found dead in western Norway in July 1969, a first-year ringed at Stroud on April 27th 1980 was caught by a ringer in Kintyre, Scotland in May 1981, and a juvenile ringed at Frampton on August 18th 1984 was caught by a ringer in Denmark on July 17th 1985.

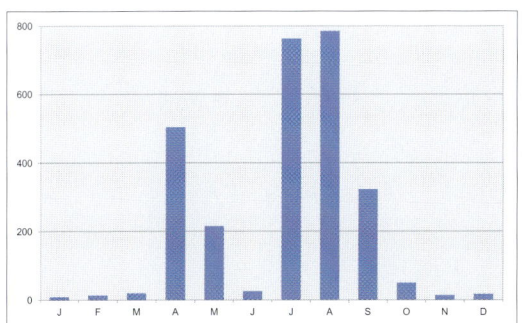

Common Sandpiper numbers reported 2003–10, by month.

Green Sandpiper
Tringa ochropus

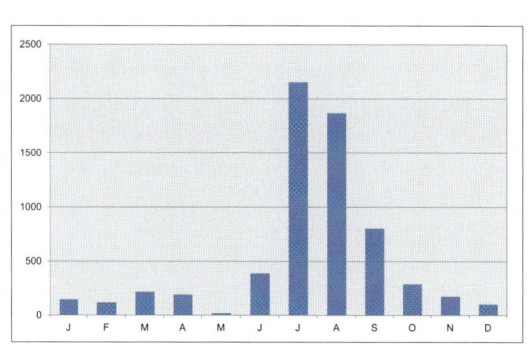

Green Sandpiper numbers reported 2003–10, by month.

Green Sandpipers breed from Fennoscandia and north-east continental Europe across central latitudes of the Palearctic. European breeders winter mostly in the Mediterranean countries and Africa, but some remain in more northern areas including the British Isles, where they also pass through on migration. They use swampy habitats for nesting, often near trees, but outside the breeding season can be found at a wide variety of freshwater sites, including small farm ponds and drainage ditches. Their presence at such places can be unexpected, and the observer is often just as startled as the bird as it is suddenly flushed at close range, calling sharply and showing its contrasting blackish wings and white rump and tail.

Swaine described the Green Sandpiper as a passage migrant and rather scarce winter visitor in Gloucestershire, commonest in autumn; 20 or more could be seen together in August. He noted that wintering seemed to be on the increase, with one or more records almost every year since 1950.

Since 1980 there has been a further increase in winter records, though this could be partly due to observer effects, and as the map shows, sightings were well scattered in winter during the atlas survey. There seems to have been something of a peak in winter records from about the mid-1980s to 2000, when groups of five or more were fairly regular, particularly at the Cotswold Water Park (maximum there of 12, in January 1989). Since 2000 though, no more than four have been seen together in any winter.

Records increase very slightly in March and April as migrants move through the county (see graph). The maximum count at any one site in spring since 1980 is ten, at the Water Park on April 12th 2002; more usually peaks of three to five are recorded.

The autumn passage is far more pronounced. The first returning birds appear in June, and numbers peak around late July to early August. The highest counts per year at any one site are usually between 12 and 25, with three peaks of 30 and a maximum of 31 at Slimbridge in early August 1999. Green Sandpipers seem to have increased on autumn passage over the last decade or two: the average peak count per year between 1981 and 1995 was 15, while between 1996 and 2010 it was 23. This could well be a result of recent habitat management at sites such as Slimbridge and Coombe Hill Meadows.

Spotted Redshank
Tringa erythropus

Elegant and dashing, Spotted Redshanks are always a pleasure to see. They breed on the northern Eurasian wooded tundra; Western Palearctic breeders winter in western Europe, the Mediterranean basin and especially the Afrotropics. In Britain they are passage migrants and uncommon winter visitors and are found in a fairly wide range of wetland habitats.

It seems that Spotted Redshanks may have been overlooked in Gloucestershire up to the mid-twentieth century. Mellersh mentioned only one, shot near Tewkesbury in 1872, and there seem to have been just two or three more records up to about 1940. Swaine described the species as a 'passage migrant in small or moderate numbers', with 'between 20 and 30 birds ... noted fairly frequently' in autumn, and rare sightings in winter.

The main changes in more recent decades have been an increase in the number of winter records and a decrease in numbers on passage. There have been sightings every winter since 1995, usually of one or two birds at any site but with eight on the Severn Estuary shore near Berkeley on January 16th 2009. On spring passage, mainly during the second half of April and May, it is now unusual to see more than three together; the largest group since 1980 was six at Hasfield Ham on May 6th 2000, and the total number of birds passing through the county at this season probably seldom exceeds ten in any year. In autumn groups of three to five birds are not unusual, and the largest flock recorded in the county since 1980 was 16 at Slimbridge in late August 1986. Maximum numbers in autumn can be at any time in August or September, sometimes later; November has produced two larger than average flocks of seven at Walmore Common in 1997 and 14 at the Berkeley shore on November 15th 2008. However, such high counts notwithstanding, the total number moving through Gloucestershire in an average autumn may only be ten or a dozen.

Sponsored by P F Pope

Greenshank (Common Greenshank)
Tringa nebularia

Greenshanks breed from Scotland and Fennoscandia eastward across Siberia, mainly in the taiga and forest zones. The Scottish population has numbered very approximately 1,000 pairs in recent years. They prefer marshy or boggy areas with lakes and ponds for nesting, but will use a wide range of wetlands on passage and in winter. The majority of Western Palearctic birds winter in sub-Saharan Africa, though some remain in southern and western Europe, including several hundred in the British Isles.

In Gloucestershire, Greenshanks are passage migrants and scarce winter visitors. Swaine referred to 10–20 birds being seen quite often between July and September, with fewer in April and May and usually none in midwinter. This pattern is still broadly the same (see graph). Winter sightings remain erratic: there were no records between 1981 and 1989, usually one bird every year from 1990 to 2001 (with two or three in 1998), and singles in only two years since then (2003 and 2008).

The first spring migrants usually arrive in April, with peak numbers normally in the first half of May. Scottish breeders return from late March, so our passage birds are probably from elsewhere. It is unusual to see more than half a dozen together in spring; notable maximum counts since 1981 have been 30 at Slimbridge on May 6th 1990 and another 30 at Ashleworth Ham also on May 6th in 2000. Peak autumn numbers occur in August or September, and a few birds often linger into late October or November. Since 1981, maximum counts in autumn have usually been between eight and 20 birds, but there have been peaks of over 20 in six years, notably 35 at Slimbridge in August 1985 and 45 there on August 12th 1984, the highest ever county total.

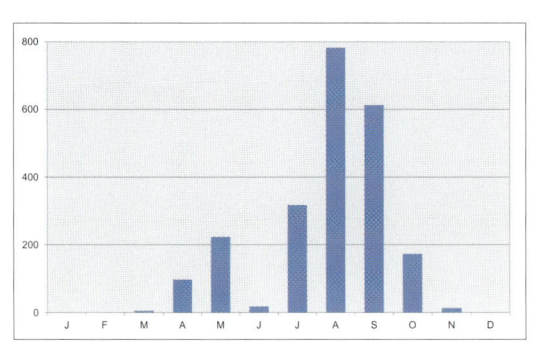

Greenshank numbers reported 2003–10, by month.

On the basis of peak counts, there is no evidence of any change in the volume of passage through the county since 1981.

While many records come from the Severn Estuary, the wide range of habitats used by Greenshanks means that sightings elsewhere are less unusual than for some other shorebirds. The Cotswold Water Park and the Severn Vale wet grasslands regularly attract a few birds, and they are also sometimes seen at sites such as the Cotswold reservoirs and lakes in the Forest of Dean.

Wood Sandpiper
Tringa glareola

Wood Sandpipers breed from Scotland and Fennoscandia eastwards across the whole of northern Eurasia, mainly in and immediately to the north of the coniferous forest zone. They winter mostly in the tropics and subtropics south of the breeding range. They pass through the British Isles in relatively small numbers on migration, mainly in south and east England and more commonly in autumn.

The status of the Wood Sandpiper in Gloucestershire has not changed since Swaine described it as an 'uncommon passage migrant'. The first documented county record was one at Shipton Oliffe, near Cheltenham, in September 1874. Sightings remained very sparse until the early 1950s, when there was a noticeable increase, no doubt influenced by rising numbers of observers. Swaine cites about 60 records between then and 1980, i.e. about two per year. More recently there has been a further increase to usually around five to ten birds per year, again probably mainly due to observer effects but also perhaps influenced by habitat creation and improvements at Slimbridge, the Severn Hams and the Cotswold Water Park.

The timing of the passage through the county mirrors the national pattern, with peaks in May and August (see graph). There are usually only one or two birds in total each spring, and sometimes none at all; notable recent exceptions have been ten in 1987 and nine in 1992. The autumn total is usually about three or four birds, with ten in 1983 and 1987, and about 20 in 2008 (noted in the GBR as 'quite remarkable numbers'). Few are seen after the end of September; one at Slimbridge on November 15th 1995 was very late. Normally only one or two are seen together at either season, but small flocks sometimes build up as lingering birds are joined by new arrivals; six at Slimbridge on May 18th 1992, and seven at the Water Park on August 22nd 1983, were unusually large groups.

Most are seen on the estuary in the Frampton–Slimbridge area, at the Water Park and (increasingly) at the Severn Hams. Individuals have also sometimes turned up at more unexpected sites, including the landfills at Gloucester and Stoke Orchard.

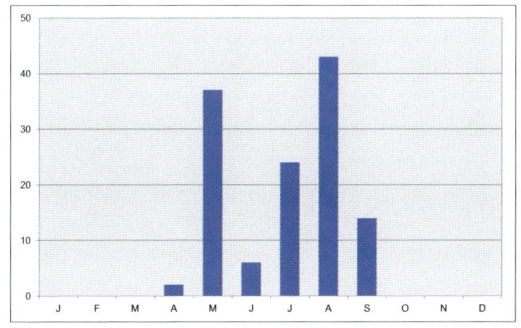

Wood Sandpiper numbers reported 2003–10, by month.

Redshank (Common Redshank)
Tringa totanus

The Redshank earns its nickname of 'warden of the marshes', both on the Severn Estuary in winter and on the wet meadows where it nests, through its agitated movements and constant repetition of its 'too-too-too' alarm call.

Redshank breed across the Palearctic from Iceland to eastern China in the temperate and steppe zones, tolerating a wide range of climatic conditions but seeking openness, look-out facilities and access to wetland food resources. Three different subspecies occur in the British Isles: *T. t. britannica* which breeds here, *T. t. robusta* which breeds in Iceland and comes here to winter, and *T. t. totanus* which breeds in Fennoscandia and western central Europe and winters along Atlantic coasts (Delany *et al.* 2009). An estimate for 1985–98 put the British breeding population at about 39,000 pairs, following a significant decline. Many of these birds winter locally and are joined by large numbers of Icelandic breeders and a few from the Continent. WeBS counts indicate that wintering numbers in UK, totalling 122,000 individuals, have also followed a downward trend over the last decade, and are again approaching the all-time low levels of the early 1980s. The Redshank, known to be site-faithful in winter, is one of the few waders wintering in Britain that have *not* undergone an eastward shift in distribution in recent years under the influence of climatic change, perhaps because of the presence of many birds of westerly, Icelandic origin (Austin & Rehfisch 2005).

Swaine noted that 'small numbers breed annually' in Gloucestershire, citing the Severn Estuary and Vale, the Windrush valley and the Cotswold Water Park. More recent censuses of breeding waders have found the major concentrations of Redshank to be by the estuary: at Aylburton Warth, and in the Frampton–Slimbridge area where specific habitat management for nesting Redshank and Lapwing now takes place. These areas usually hold 10–20 pairs each, but breeding success is low because of predation. In comparison, the number of pairs breeding 'inland' at small wetlands in the Vale (such as Walmore Common, Ashleworth Ham, Coombe Hill, Leigh and Upham Meadow) is very low and has decreased sharply of late. In the current atlas period, breeding numbers in the Vale may have been especially low due first to the abnormal summer flooding in 2007 and 2008, which killed earthworms and other invertebrates and adversely affected food resources in the following years, and secondly to the near-drought conditions in the summers of 2010 and 2011. Even allowing for this and for the difficulty of finding nests and young, the breeding season map confirms the localised distribution in the county. Redshank still breed in the Water Park, but have evidently disappeared from the Windrush valley since Swaine's day: not one breeding pair was found there during the fieldwork for the 2003–07 Cotswolds Atlas or the current survey.

Outside the breeding season, Swaine indicated that Redshank were 'present in all months along the Severn Estuary with numbers between 50 and 100 frequently reported'; he also referred to smaller numbers in the Vale and at the Water Park. The map confirms that Redshank winter almost exclusively on the estuary, with just a few records from the Severn Hams. The single 'winter' Water Park

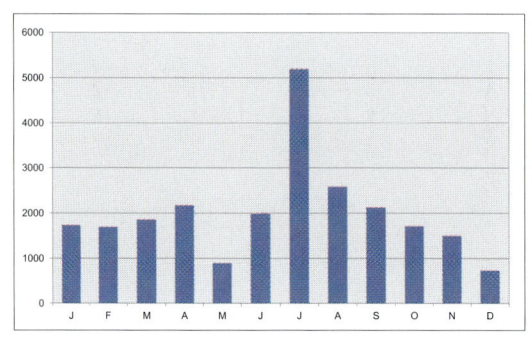

Redshank numbers reported 2003–10, by month.

Sponsored by the Dursley Birdwatching and Preservation Society

Species accounts

2007–11 Atlas fieldwork					Gloucestershire trends						UK population trends	
Number of tetrads in which recorded (max 683)					Occupied 10 km squares (max 26)				% of tetrads in which recorded (1st hour of TTV)		UK conservation status: Amber 1,3,8	
	Total	Confirmed	Probable	Possible	Present	1968–71	1981–84	1988–91	2007–11	1988–91	2008–11	Long term	Short term
Breeding	33	6	12	6	9	8		8	6	2.8	1.5	–	–35%
Winter	27							6	4			+23%	–13%

record was on February 28th, no doubt an early returning breeder or passage migrant. The five-year winter mean for the whole of the Severn Estuary, extending to Bridgwater Bay and Cardiff, is just below the threshold of 2,500 for international importance; however the Gloucestershire proportion of this total is rather meagre. The maximum winter TTV count was 52 at Slimbridge in November 2010.

Recent GBRs record few three-figure counts anywhere in the county, with peak numbers on the estuary of usually between 70 and 80 during autumn passage in July and August. Spring passage appears to be practically indiscernible (see graph).

There have been 14 interchanges of ringed Redshank between Gloucestershire and other counties in England and Wales, the longest movements revealing generally southward displacements from spring and summer to autumn and winter. The three furthest movements were of birds ringed here in autumn and winter and found over 300 km away, in Northumberland, Co. Durham and North Yorkshire, in spring.

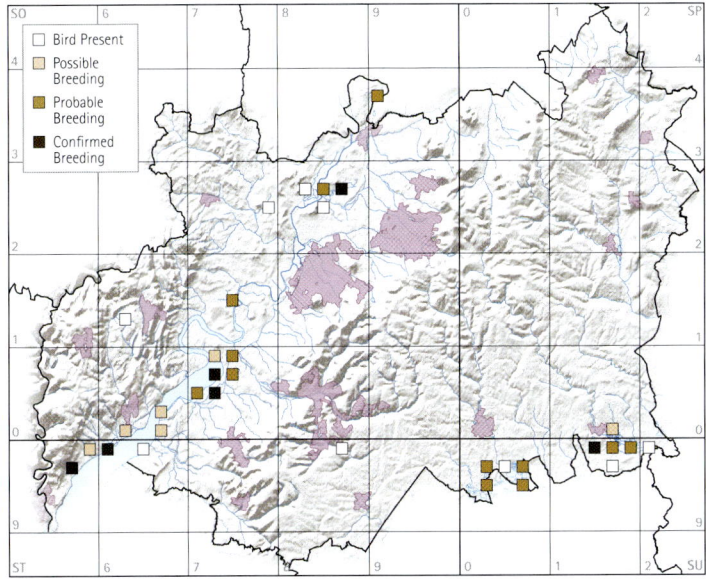

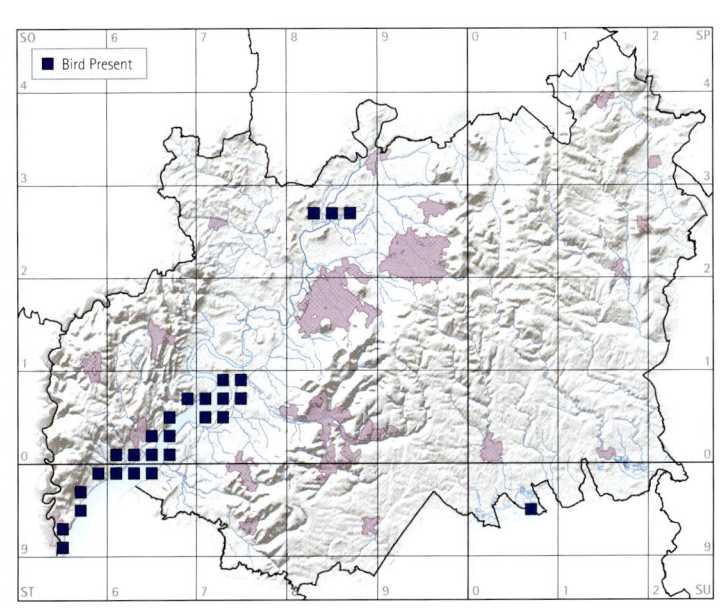

Breeding Distribution

Winter Distribution

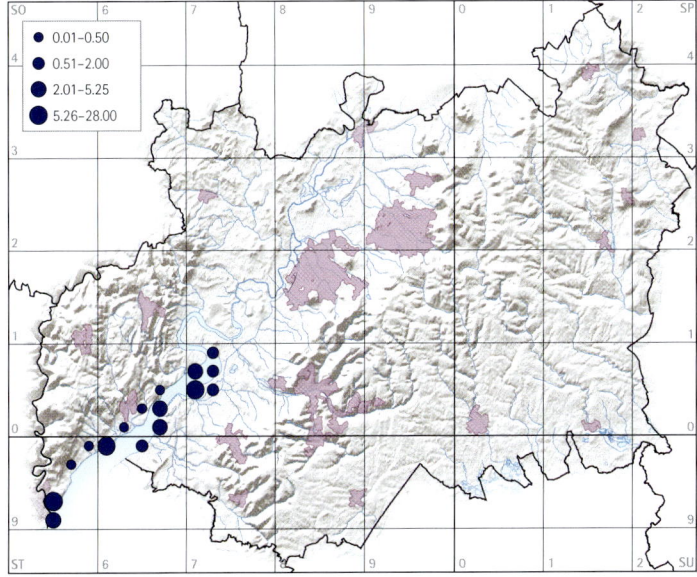

Winter Abundance

Turnstone (Ruddy Turnstone)
Arenaria interpres

Turnstones breed on open shorelines all around the Arctic, and in winter can be found almost anywhere worldwide, south even to the sub-Antarctic. In the British Isles they are mostly passage migrants and winter visitors, mainly from Canada, Greenland and Iceland with fewer from Norway and the Baltic. A few non-breeders remain here through the summer. Although they are largely maritime at all seasons they regularly migrate across continents, and they occur fairly frequently inland on passage in Britain.

Swaine described the Turnstone as 'a passage migrant and winter visitor, but noted in all months' in Gloucestershire, and this is still broadly true today. Most records are, not surprisingly, from the Severn Estuary. When Swaine was writing, the largest numbers ('50 to 100 birds, and sometimes more') had traditionally been recorded at the Guscar Rocks–Aylburton Warth area, in April and September–October. In more recent decades the highest counts of the year have tended to come from the opposite shore at Berkeley, and there appears to have been an increase in the proportion of records in March and November, blurring the distinction between the passage and winter periods. Indeed, since about 1995 the highest counts of the year have been as likely to be in winter as on passage. This may be partly due to observer effects, but there is some indication that numbers on migration, particularly in spring, have tended to decrease slightly. Between 1981 and 2010 the average annual peak in spring was about 55 birds, in autumn about 35; the overall maximum count in spring was 130 (on April 14th 1986) and in autumn 71 (in October 1982). The spring peak still nearly always falls in April, but the highest autumn figures nowadays are more often in October than September. Maximum counts in winter (November to February) have ranged between about 15 and 100.

Away from the favoured parts of the estuary, numbers are much lower and overall this is a fairly scarce species in Gloucestershire. There are occasional records from the Cotswold Water Park, but very few elsewhere. One flying over open farmland near Coln St Aldwyns in the Cotswolds on February 4th 1996 was very much out of the ordinary.

Red-necked Phalarope
Phalaropus lobatus

Red-necked Phalaropes breed all around the sub-Arctic and low Arctic zones in Eurasia and North America, including a tiny population in the Shetlands. They winter at sea, mostly in the Pacific and the northern Indian Ocean, but unlike Grey Phalaropes they are more often seen inland on migration than offshore. In most of Britain they are scarce passage migrants, and there have only been nine modern records in Gloucestershire, all involving single birds:

1950: Hewletts reservoir, Cheltenham, from September 23rd to 26th.
1963: Slimbridge on August 2nd.
1988: Slimbridge from June 8th to 10th.
1998: Slimbridge from September 28th to October 3rd; seen to be killed by a Sparrowhawk.
2005: Slimbridge from October 3rd to 22nd; Walmore Common on October 29th, thought to be a different bird.
2008: moulting adult at Saul Warth near Frampton, August 14th to 22nd.
2010: Slimbridge, from August 31st to September 12th.
2011: female at Slimbridge, June 22nd to 25th.

All the autumn records have been of immatures with the exception of the 2008 bird. In addition, one was reported by Mellersh as having been shot in autumn at Bibury 'prior to 1870' but with no other details.

Grey Phalarope (Red Phalarope)
Phalaropus fulicarius

In the British Isles, Grey Phalaropes are most commonly seen when they are blown close inshore by gales while en route from their Arctic nesting grounds to their wintering areas off West Africa and western South America. This is the most strictly oceanic of the three phalaropes, even on passage, and inland records are correspondingly scarce.

The earliest Gloucestershire record was of one at Tewkesbury in 1832. There were about ten reports during the second half of the nineteenth century, not all of which were substantiated (Mellersh). Swaine listed three records between 1900 and 1950, two in the 1950s and singles in 1968, 1974 and 1978. Since then, despite the increasing numbers of observers, there have only been 16 more records up to 2010: five birds in the 1980s, six in the 1990s and five since 2000.

Nearly all sightings in recent years have been on or near the Severn Estuary, particularly between Berkeley and Frampton. The exceptions are singles at Coombe Hill Meadows in November 2005 and Witcombe reservoir on August 28th 2009. There are records in all months from July (one on the Gloucester and Sharpness Canal at Saul on July 29th 1986) to December, but 11 of the 16 post-1980 birds were in September and October, reflecting the period of peak passage through British waters.

White-tailed Plover (White-tailed Lapwing)
Vanellus leucurus

Breeding in the Middle East and central Asia, with birds from the western part of the range wintering in north-east Africa, White-tailed Plovers are very rare visitors to Britain with just five records up to 2007. In 2010 the much-travelled sixth appeared in Lancashire in May, moved to the Netherlands in June and returned to the London–Essex border on July 7th. It then added itself to the Gloucestershire list by spending July 9th and 10th at Slimbridge, before moving to Kent for the last ten days of its stay in Britain.

Temminck's Stint
Calidris temminckii

Temminck's Stints breed in Scotland (rarely), Fennoscandia and across the far north of Siberia, and winter from the Mediterranean basin and sub-Saharan Africa across southern Asia to Japan. In Britain they are uncommon but annual passage migrants and a few are also recorded in winter.

Swaine cited a report by Mellersh of one 'said to have been shot ... near Stroud, 1878', but no details were given, and the first authenticated record for Gloucestershire was not until 1965: one at Frampton sailing lake on August 31st. Since then there have been just over 30 records, with a sustained eight records per decade since 1980. As with many scarce migrant waders, most sightings have been from the Frampton-Slimbridge area (25 records) and the Cotswold Water Park (seven). Most have involved single birds, but there were 'twos' at Frampton in August 1966 and May 2004, and a remarkable four at the western section of the Water Park in May 2003.

There have been a few winter records from Slimbridge: one stayed for most of November 1980, and singles remained through the first winter period in both 2007 and 2008. There was also one at the western section of the Water Park from December 3rd to 12th 2011. Apart from that, ten records (11 birds) have been in autumn, spread fairly evenly between July 9th and September 29th, and 19 records (23 birds) in spring, between April 25th and May 25th, with a marked peak of nine records in the middle ten days of May. The Migration Atlas gives national peak passage periods as August–September and mid to late May.

Purple Sandpiper
Calidris maritima

Purple Sandpipers have a patchy circumpolar Arctic and sub-Arctic breeding range and migrate just sufficiently far south to winter on ice-free coasts, including quite commonly in the British Isles. In winter this is very much a bird of rocky shores, and inland records are rare.

Mellersh's manuscripts (quoted by Swaine) refer to one 'about 1877 in the autumn from Tewkesbury', but this record does not appear in his book. The first modern Gloucestershire record came in 1971, on April 10th and 18th at Guscar Rocks. The next was at the same site in 1981, and since then there have been about ten records; the exact total is uncertain as it seems likely that some reports refer to the same individuals. Predictably enough, nearly all sightings have been from the Severn Estuary; the two exceptions were in the Vale, at Leigh Meadows for 11 days in November 1984 and at nearby Coombe Hill Meadows on December 7th 1986. All records have been of singles between November and February, apart from two at Longney Crib south-west of Gloucester on October 7th 1990, and a remarkable flock of seven roosting with Dunlin at Sharpness shore on October 17th 1999.

Broad-billed Sandpiper
Limicola falcinellus

Broad-billed Sandpipers breed in Fennoscandia and Siberia. Unlike most Western Palearctic shorebirds they migrate south-east in autumn, and this no doubt explains why they are barely annual visitors to the British Isles. There have been four records in Gloucestershire, all in spring:

1976: one at Slimbridge from May 6th to 9th, presumed to be the same individual there on June 2nd.
1980: one at Aylburton Warth on May 15th.
1987: one at Slimbridge on June 14th.
1991: one by the Severn at Frampton from June 8th to 10th.

As with some American waders, the proportion of spring records in Gloucestershire is higher than for the country as a whole: approximately half the national records are in spring (BWP).

Great Snipe
Gallinago media

There are only two acceptable Gloucestershire records of this vagrant from Fennoscandia, north-east Europe and Siberia: one shot near Cheltenham on September 7th 1897 (BirdGuides) and one seen at Slimbridge on January 28th 1958. Mellersh mentions a number of additional nineteenth-century records, but although the species was commoner in Europe and was seen rather more often in Britain at that time, none of these records is satisfactorily documented.

Nearctic waders

Many North American (Nearctic) shorebirds breed in the Arctic or sub-Arctic and migrate in autumn to Central or South America. Each year, a few find their way to the western European seaboard, through directed flights in non-standard directions and/or having been 'drifted' by strong westerly winds. Over the past half-century or so, some species have proved to be regular in small numbers in Europe, particularly the British Isles. Indeed, records of a few (including White-rumped, Pectoral and Buff-breasted Sandpipers, and American Golden Plover) are now so regular that they are no longer subject to scrutiny by the national Rarities Committee.

They are most often seen on the coast, in common with many rarer migrant waders, and may be found all around the British Isles, though rather more frequently in the west. However, inland records are not exceptional, and Gloucestershire has had its fair share (see graph, top right). In fact, of the 21 species that have been recorded in the British Isles, 11 have been seen in Gloucestershire; many of the remaining ten are extremely rare visitors to Europe.

Also in common with most rare shorebirds, and indeed rare migrants in general, the majority occur in autumn, though spring records are by no means exceptional (see graph, bottom left).

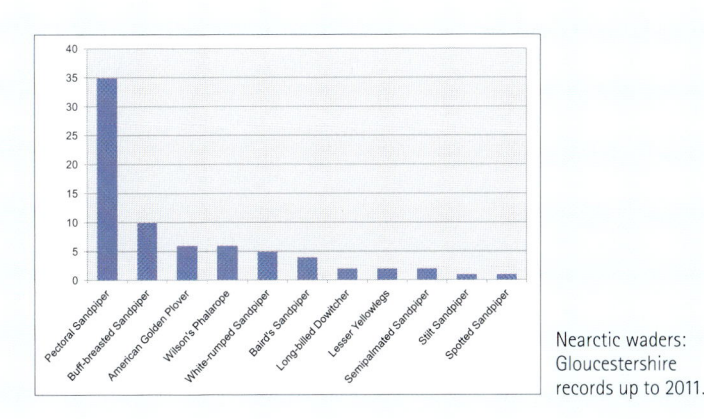

Nearctic waders: Gloucestershire records up to 2011.

In line with the national picture, sightings in Gloucestershire have tended to increase since the middle of the twentieth century (see graph, bottom right). This change is likely to be almost entirely due to observer effects; in fact the breeding populations of some of these species have undergone declines, tending to counteract the general trend.

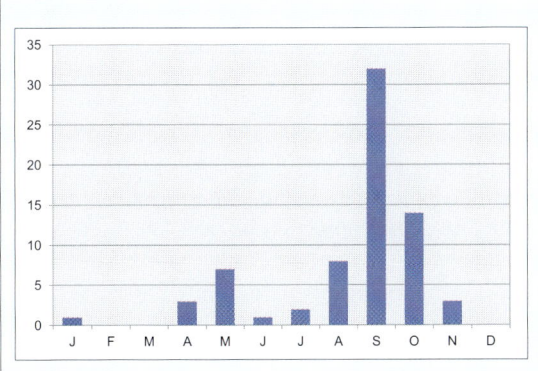

Nearctic waders in Gloucestershire by month of finding, up to 2011.

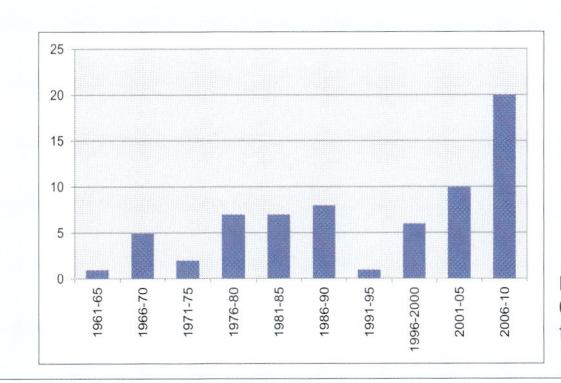

Nearctic waders in Gloucestershire by five-year period, 1961–2010.

American Golden Plover
Pluvialis dominica

The Nearctic counterpart of the familiar European Golden Plover is an annual visitor in low numbers to the British Isles, usually in autumn and winter. In Gloucestershire there have been six records, all in the Frampton–Slimbridge area of the Severn Estuary:

1967: one on October 4th.
1985: a juvenile in October from 7th to at least 12th, perhaps 19th.
1990: one in winter plumage from April 9th to 20th.
1999: one in first-summer plumage on May 20th.
2005: an adult on January 20th.
2007: an immature intermittently from November 1st to December 5th.

Semipalmated Sandpiper
Calidris pusilla

There have been just two county records of this national rarity, both of which were juveniles seen at the Dumbles, Slimbridge: one from September 24th to 26th 2006 (Lees 2006), and one from September 18th to 29th 2011.

White-rumped Sandpiper
Calidris fuscicollis

There have been five Gloucestershire records, all in the Frampton–Slimbridge area of the Severn Estuary:

1976: one on November 14th.
1986: an adult on August 21st and 22nd, during an exceptional passage of shorebirds.
1988: an adult on 2nd October, thought to have been the same individual that had been in the Wiltshire section of the Cotswold Water Park for a few days previously.
2004: a moulting adult at the high-tide roost on August 15th, and a juvenile there on October 4th.

Baird's Sandpiper
Calidris bairdii

There have been four county records, all on the estuary in the Frampton–Slimbridge area:

1966: one on August 30th and 31st.
1967: one on October 18th.
2005: an adult on August 11th and presumably the same individual on 21st; a juvenile from October 6th to 9th.

Pectoral Sandpiper
Calidris melanotos

Pectoral Sandpipers are scarce annual visitors to the British Isles, mostly in autumn; spring records probably involve birds which have crossed the Atlantic in preceding autumns. As the commonest North American wader in Europe, their relatively frequent occurrence here has been linked to their south-eastward migration across Canada, which tends to take them into the paths of eastward-tracking Atlantic depressions.

The first one to be seen in Gloucestershire stayed at Slimbridge from August 6th to 14th 1975. There were then between 31 and 34 more up to 2011 (a few may be duplicate records of the same individuals). Usually no more than one has been seen per year, but there were two in 1987, 2004 and 2011, three in 1977 and 2010, at least six in 2006 and a similar number in 2008. Both these high totals coincided with greater numbers than usual in the British Isles.

Of the approximately 33 individuals recorded in the county, about 29 have arrived in autumn, between July 24th and October 20th, and four in spring, between May 7th and 18th. The proportion of spring records in Gloucestershire is perhaps slightly higher than for Britain and Ireland as a whole.

Slimbridge has hosted the majority of birds, with four at nearby Frampton and seven in the Cotswold Water Park.

Stilt Sandpiper
Calidris himantopus

Stilt Sandpipers are the nearest Nearctic equivalent to Curlew Sandpipers. They breed in the North American tundra and most winter in central South America. This is a rare visitor to the British Isles with only 28 records between 1950 and 2010, so the moulting adult which spent from August 15th to 21st 2008 at Coombe Hill Meadows was a rather unexpected addition to the Gloucestershire list.

Buff-breasted Sandpiper
Tryngites subruficollis

Despite their restricted breeding range and mainly inland migration routes, Buff-breasted Sandpipers appear annually in low numbers in the British Isles, mostly in autumn and sometimes in small flocks. There have been nine records (ten birds) in Gloucestershire. Unless stated otherwise, they were all single birds in the Frampton–Slimbridge area:

1961: September 17th.
1970: Aylburton Warth from September 20th to 22nd.
1975: Cotswold Water Park (western section) on September 11th.
1977: May 9th and 10th.
2000: September 18th to 30th, and another at Cleeve Hill on September 21st and 22nd.
2006: two from September 22nd until October 1st (and possibly a third on September 23rd).
2008: May 3rd and 4th.
2011: September 11th to 28th.

As with Pectoral Sandpiper, the proportion of spring records here is perhaps rather higher than for Britain and Ireland as a whole.

Long-billed Dowitcher
Limnodromus scolopaceus

Most Long-billed Dowitchers migrate through western and mid-eastern North America in autumn, but some make long south-eastward movements towards the American Atlantic coast, which is thought to be a factor influencing their relatively frequent occurrence in the British Isles, where they are annual in very low numbers in autumn.

There have been two records in Gloucestershire: one remained on the estuary at Frampton from October 12th to December 14th 1984, and in 1985 a juvenile spent from September 26th to October 19th at the Dumbles, Slimbridge.

Spotted Sandpiper
Actitis macularius

This is very much the Nearctic counterpart of our Common Sandpiper and the two have been treated as conspecific in the past. It breeds across much of North America and migrates south in a broad front to winter in Central and South America. It is an annual visitor to the British Isles in very small numbers, with 167 records between 1950 and 2010.

The long-awaited first record for Gloucestershire came in 2011, when a juvenile remained by the Severn Estuary just downriver of Lydney Harbour from September 15th to 26th (Phillips & Phillips 2011).

Lesser Yellowlegs
Tringa flavipes

In many ways the North American equivalent of our Redshank, Lesser Yellowlegs are one of the more frequently seen Nearctic waders in the British Isles, with records in small numbers every year, mainly in autumn.

In Gloucestershire there have been two records, both at Frampton: one from April 2nd to 26th 1970 and one from April 26th to May 1st 1998. It is notable that both records have been in spring (see Pectoral and Buff-breasted Sandpipers).

Wilson's Phalarope
Phalaropus tricolor

Wilson's Phalaropes occur annually in very low numbers in the British Isles. In Gloucestershire there have been five records:

1976: one at Frampton sailing lake on September 2nd.
1985: one at Slimbridge on September 14th.
1990: an adult female in full breeding plumage at Slimbridge from June 7th to 10th.
2009: one by the shore at Slimbridge from November 7th to 12th.
2010: a first-winter at Dowdeswell reservoir near Cheltenham on September 29th and 30th.

Arctic Skua (Parasitic Jaeger)
Stercorarius parasiticus

Arctic Skuas breed mainly in the far north of Eurasia and North America, but extend south to the Faeroes, southern Scandinavia and northern Scotland. They winter in the open southern oceans, with very few remaining north of the equator. The Scottish breeding population has suffered a substantial decline in recent decades, and in most parts of the British Isles they are spring and autumn migrants, seen mainly offshore but also fairly frequently inland.

Swaine noted that in Gloucestershire this was 'formerly regarded as an occasional visitor, usually in ... rough weather', but by 1980 was being recorded almost annually, and the tendency for records to increase has continued (see top graph). The vast majority of sightings are during the passage periods (see bottom graph) and most are at the Severn Estuary, where migrants are seen flying upriver in spring and usually downriver in autumn, often in fair weather. It would seem that small numbers of Arctic Skuas regularly take an overland route between the Severn and the east coast between the Wash and the Humber, as postulated by Swaine. In addition, there are often records during strong westerly winds, presumably involving migrants entering the mouth of the Bristol Channel and being blown into the estuary. There are also two midwinter records: one in the western section of the Cotswold Water Park on January 27th 1974, and one off Slimbridge on December 7th 2006, during severe gales which caused a 'wreck' of Leach's Petrels.

Most county sightings are of one or two birds, rarely three to five, and with one record of six off Slimbridge on September 9th 1989. Away from the estuary there have been three records from the Water Park (including a notable five on August 13th 2006) and a handful of sightings of overflying singles elsewhere.

As the top graph shows, there have been considerable fluctuations within the overall increasing trend, notably a paucity of spring records between 1980 and 2000, a period when autumn sightings were at something of a peak. These variations probably result from a number of factors: observer effects (especially between 1960 and 1980), medium-term variations in the incidence of strong winds in autumn, and possibly fluctuations in the size of the breeding populations from which Gloucestershire birds originate.

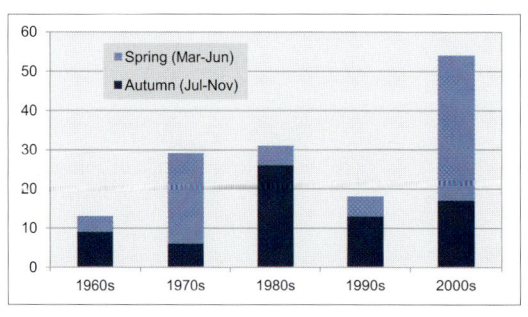

Arctic Skuas on passage: records by season and decade, 1960–2009.

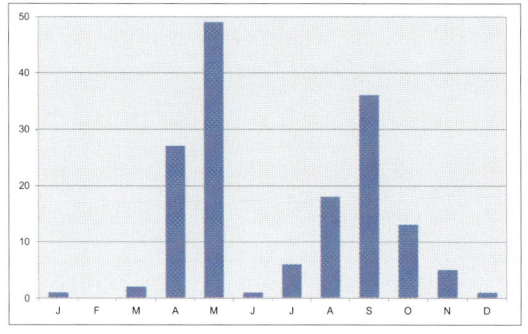

Arctic Skua records by month, 1960–2010.

Great Skua
Stercorarius skua

Great Skuas, often known by their Shetland name 'Bonxie', breed only in the Western Palearctic. During the second half of the twentieth century they spread from strongholds in Iceland, the Faeroes and Shetland to other parts of northern Scotland, Spitsbergen, Bear Island, Jan Mayen, Norway and Russia. Populations have continued to increase in most areas, although in Britain there have been fairly wide fluctuations. Bonxies winter at sea, but many remain in the North Atlantic. They are far less regular inland than Arctic Skuas.

In Gloucestershire, virtually all records of Great Skuas are on the Severn Estuary, during westerly gales. Mellersh listed two records from the nineteenth century, and Swaine described the species as a scarce visitor, with just three sightings between 1900 and 1976 including one record of three birds together in August 1976. Since then there have been sightings in the county in 21 of the 30 years between 1981 and 2010. They have been in all months except March and June (see graph), with peaks in autumn and winter and a suggestion of a smaller one in spring.

Usually single birds are seen, but there have been a few sightings of up to three and one of five, on April 13th (an unusual date) in 1985. Not infrequently, individuals remain around the estuary for days or even weeks, notably one which stayed from early January to mid-May 2007. During their stay they are often seen attacking and sometimes killing other birds, including storm-driven Leach's Petrels, gulls, Shelduck, and once even a White-fronted Goose. On November 28th 2009 one was seen to attack and apparently kill a Little Egret.

The only record away from the estuary was of one found dead in the Cotswold Water Park on September 23rd 2009.

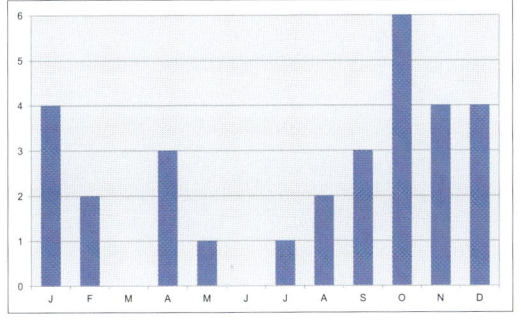

Great Skua records by month, 1981–2010.

Pomarine Skua
Stercorarius pomarinus

Pomarine Skuas breed in the tundra zone and winter mostly in tropical oceans. They are regular migrants in the British Isles, with the biggest flocks appearing offshore in spring. Inland records are fairly frequent, especially during gales in late autumn.

The first Gloucestershire record came as recently as 1970, when three were seen off Slimbridge on May 12th. Since then there have been nine more records, all at the Severn Estuary. All have been singles, apart from another group of three off Beachley on May 6th 1985. There is no indication of any consistent long-term change in frequency, with two records in the 1970s, four in the 1980s, one in 1996 and three since 2000. There have been five records totalling nine birds in spring, between mid-April and mid-June, and five singles in autumn (one on September 3rd 1988, otherwise in October and November). In 2009 a near-adult that arrived at Beachley Point on November 25th remained there until December 9th, feeding on a sheep carcass (see photograph); all others have passed straight through.

Long-tailed Skua (Long-tailed Jaeger)
Stercorarius longicaudus

Breeding around most of the Arctic and sub-Arctic zones and migrating to the southern oceans, Long-tailed Skuas are scarce but regular passage migrants in the British Isles. This is the most oceanic of the skuas and inland records are unusual. There have been three authenticated records in Gloucestershire, all at the Severn Estuary:

1967: an adult off Frampton on May 27th.
1993: a juvenile at very close range off Slimbridge on August 23rd.
2008: on September 6th a juvenile flying downriver with an Arctic Skua was seen from both Slimbridge and Sharpness.

In addition, Mellersh referred to one having been shot near Badgeworth, Cheltenham, in about 1867, but gave no further details.

Kittiwake (Black-legged Kittiwake)
Rissa tridactyla

Kittiwakes nest mainly on cliffs, around the coasts of North Sea countries and elsewhere in the North Atlantic, North Pacific and Arctic Oceans. They are pelagic outside the breeding season, Western Palearctic birds ranging widely over the North Atlantic. Numbers increased markedly during the twentieth century but there have been significant decreases more recently, linked with food shortages. In the UK a sharp decline set in after 1986 and there was a 40% fall in breeding numbers between 1999 and 2009.

In Gloucestershire, Kittiwakes occur as gale-driven strays and passage migrants. As noted by Swaine, they are most frequently seen in spring, often in fairly large flocks flying up the Severn Estuary.

Since 1980 the numbers seen per year have been extremely variable (see graph), albeit within the context of an overall decline. The 1986 GBR noted that there had been a 'marked increase since 1979' and high numbers continued to be recorded up to the early 1990s. However this may well have been largely due to observer effects, as many reports between 1985 and 1995 were from the Beachley Point area, where 'seawatching' has been less popular in more recent years.

The total number of birds per year in spring (usually mid-February to mid-April) has ranged from just one to about 1,500; the largest day count was 600, on March 22nd 1983. The biggest flocks tend to appear during fair weather and fresh to strong south-westerly breezes, lending support to the suggestion by Swaine and others that an overland migration route across the English Midlands might be used in spring if conditions are suitable. Numbers in autumn (September to November) are usually lower than in spring, and are more dependent on the incidence of gales; there were no autumn sightings at all in seven post-1980 years and the maximum day count was 220 on November 12th 1987. In winter (December and January), numbers are similarly variable and dependent on gales; there were some large counts between 1985 and 1995 from the Beachley Point area (notably a total of 630 during December 1990), and the usually far lower numbers in recent winters may be due to weather and observer effects as well as, perhaps, generally smaller breeding populations.

Away from the estuary there are sometimes sightings of wind-blown individuals at sites such as landfills and the Cotswold Water Park, and occasional reports of probable passage flocks. Five in flight at Moreton-in-Marsh on July 3rd 1993 was a very unusual record in terms of date and location.

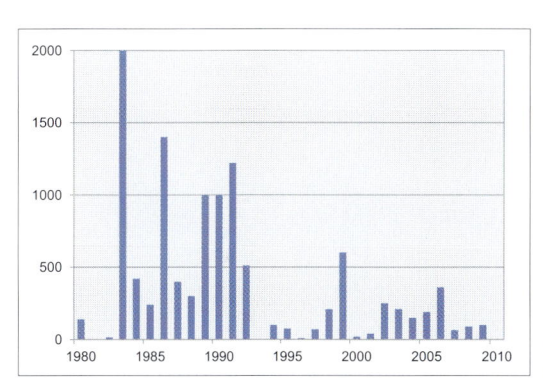

Kittiwakes per year since 1980 (some figures are estimates; no data for 1993).

Black-headed Gull (Common Black-headed Gull)
Chroicocephalus ridibundus

Following an expansion of their breeding range over the last 200 years, Black-headed Gulls now nest over much of Europe and the central latitudes of Asia, as well as in coastal areas of eastern Canada. In Britain, decreasing numbers in the late nineteenth century led to fears of extinction, but subsequently the population grew dramatically and breeding colonies are now widespread, although the national 2007–11 atlas results indicate that there has been a decline in some parts of the country during the past 20 years. Nesting sites include inland freshwater habitats such as lakes, marshes, gravel-pits and moorland, as well as coastal salt-marsh and sand dunes.

Northern and eastern European birds are migratory, and winter south to the Mediterranean countries and beyond. At this season the British population is greatly augmented by an influx of continental birds, and in general it is as a winter visitor that this small gull is most familiar in Gloucestershire, where it exploits a wide range of habitats including landfill sites, playing fields, parks and even gardens, as well as the more traditional grassland and farmland.

Swaine refers to reports of breeding by the Severn at Framilode in 1938 and 1939, but details are lacking and the first confirmed breeding record in the county was in the Cotswold Water Park in 1970. Nesting attempts there have become increasingly frequent (though not always successful) up to the present, with a maximum of 85 pairs and 65 young at a single lake in 2007. Breeding has also been attempted at Ashleworth Ham (1979 and 1986, unsuccessful), and more frequently at Slimbridge (20 pairs in 2009) and Frampton 100 Acre (17 pairs in 2009).

'Autumn' passage in the county, including birds from the Low Countries, can begin as early as mid-June. At this stage many pass straight through, and it is not until October that really large numbers of continental birds begin to build up. Return passage starts in late February, and most of the winter visitors have departed by mid-April.

Results from the atlas fieldwork reflect these seasonal variations, with records from many more tetrads in winter than in the breeding season, although non-breeders are apparently much more widespread in summer now than in the past. Winter counts of up to 5,000 are not unusual at the landfill sites, increasing to as many as 10,000 in freezing conditions. They readily move onto floodwaters in the Vale when the Severn spills its banks, and flocks of up to 3,000 can be seen feeding on waterlogged fields as the floods recede. The only area of the county where they are rarely seen is the heavily wooded Forest of Dean, though in contrast with Common Gulls they are also comparatively scarce on the high Cotswolds. This is one of only ten species for which over 1,000 were recorded during a single TTV: 1,100 were counted in one of the Slimbridge tetrads on February 9th 2011.

Very large numbers of Black-headed Gulls roost at the Noose area of the Severn Estuary. Obtaining accurate counts here is very difficult, but the best estimates suggest that during the early 1990s as many as 100,000 may have been present in winter (Durham 1990; Stewart 1997), with rather fewer in more recent years. Some of these birds may fly a considerable distance from their feeding areas to the roost. There is also a large roost in the Water Park, where over 20,000 were counted in January 2004.

Studies by the SEGG and others over the last 25 years have resulted in well over 400 interchanges of ringed or colour-ringed Black-headed Gulls between Gloucestershire and 16 European countries outside the British Isles, as far away as the Baltic States, Finland, Russia, Poland, the Czech Republic and Spain. Ringing has also revealed that individuals show a high degree of site fidelity, returning to the same area winter after winter.

Sponsored by J A Bailey

Species accounts 215

	2007–11 Atlas fieldwork					Gloucestershire trends						UK population trends	
	Number of tetrads in which recorded (max 683)					Occupied 10 km squares (max 26)				% of tetrads in which recorded (1st hour of TTV)		UK conservation status: **Amber 4,8**	
	Total	Confirmed	Probable	Possible	Present	1968–71	1981–84	1988–91	2007–11	1988–91	2008–11	Long term	Short term
Breeding	155	10	2	6	137	0		1	5	0.4	9.5	+34%	+29%
Winter	457							26	26			–	–

Breeding Distribution

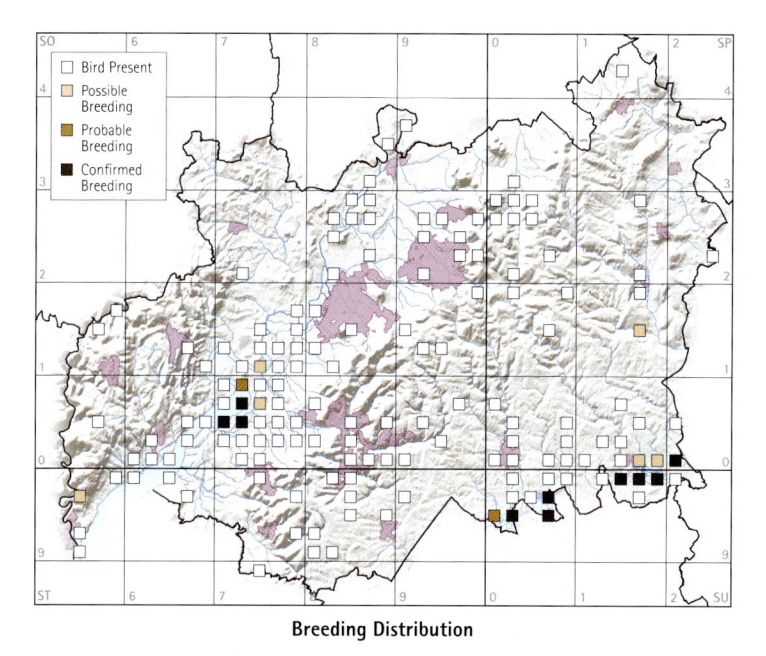

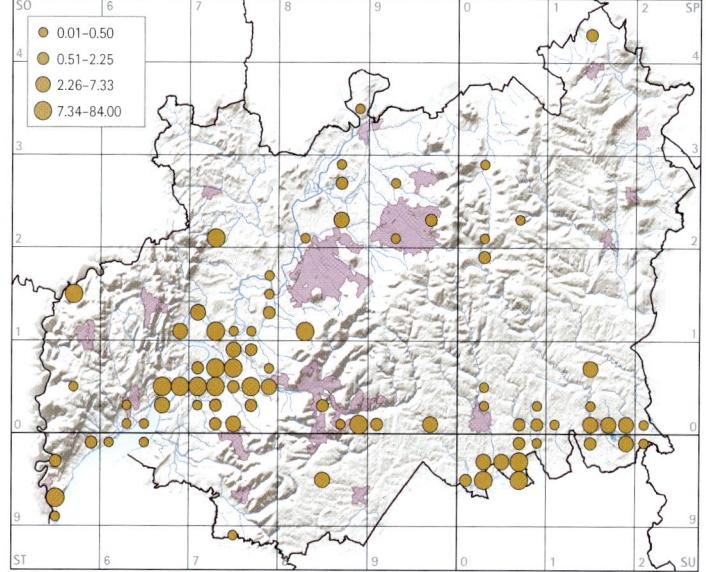

Summer Abundance

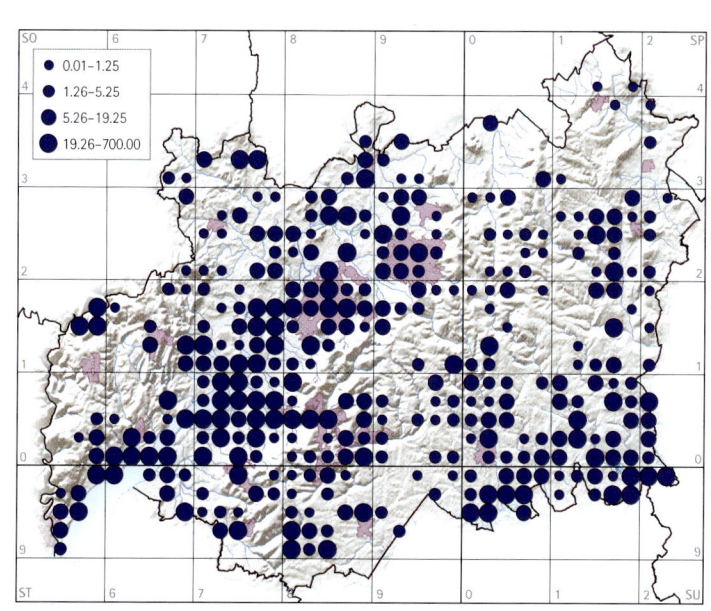

Winter Distribution

Winter Abundance

Little Gull
Hydrocoloeus minutus

the Cotswold Water Park and occasional sightings in the Severn Vale. On average about 15 birds are seen per year, though with wide variations, from just three (in 1982 and 1985) to about 55 or 60 (in 1984, including a record count of 34 flying up the estuary off Slimbridge on April 30th). Most appear in spring, with records at this season every year; about 90% of all records in recent years have been in the three months from March to May. The first migrants usually arrive around the first week in April and in most years the peak count falls between mid-April and mid-May, slightly earlier than the May to June peak indicated by Swaine.

Autumn numbers are generally lower, with rarely more than five birds in any year since 1980 and no records at all in six years. Three were seen together on September 1st 1997 and September 7th 1983, and seven paused briefly in the eastern section of the Water Park on September 10th 2010, but all other autumn records have been of one or two birds.

Sightings in winter (December to February) remain fairly unusual and depend strongly on the incidence of westerly gales; there have been records in 15 years since 1980. Normally only one or two birds are seen in total in winter in any year, so five together on the estuary near Slimbridge on December 29th 2006 was a remarkably large flock for this season.

Little Gulls breed from eastern Europe patchily across northern Asia and in a few places in North America. European birds winter from the Irish and North Seas to the Mediterranean and West Africa, mainly along the coast or just offshore. They have occasionally bred in Britain, but here they are mostly migrants, with a 'remarkable increase in numbers on passage since the mid-1950s' (1981-84 Wintering Atlas).

They have also clearly become more common in Gloucestershire. Witchell & Strugnell mentioned just one record, in 1863, and Mellersh cited only three reports. Swaine described them as 'now regular in small numbers' following 'a remarkable increase ... since about 1960', with 5-10 birds per year on average during the 20 years to 1980, including a few in winter. The largest flock on record at that time was 14 at Slimbridge in June 1971.

Over the 30 years or so since then the increasing trend has continued. Most records come from the Severn Estuary, where birds often fly upriver in spring and stop off for variable periods in the Frampton-Slimbridge area. There are also a number of records from

Mediterranean Gull
Larus melanocephalus

At one time considered to be a 'relict species' heading for extinction (Voous 1960), Mediterranean Gulls made a remarkable recovery in the second half of the twentieth century, spreading west from the eastern Mediterranean and Black Sea region to establish colonies widely across Europe. The first British breeding record came in 1968, and by 2010 there were nearly 1,000 pairs in the country, mainly in south and east England (RBBP). Some birds remain in parts of the breeding range through the winter, but many migrate to Mediterranean and Atlantic coasts, including widely around the British Isles.

There has been a huge rise in the number of records of this beautiful gull in Gloucestershire in recent decades. It seems hardly credible now that Swaine knew of only two county records, at 'a gravel-pit near South Cerney' on April 9th 1962 and in flight near Stroud on April 17th 1968. There were then no more until 1981, and although they became increasingly frequent thereafter the species was still on the county rarities list in 1994. By 1995 the cumulative total had reached about 75 individuals, and the increase has continued, with over 100 records involving more than 150 'bird-days' in 2009 alone.

Estimating total numbers is difficult because individuals remain in the county for variable lengths of time, but the graph is representative of the seasonal pattern, with a noticeable spring passage especially in March, a lesser peak in autumn (July to September), and comparatively few, mainly adults, in midwinter. During passage periods it is now not unusual to see four or five Mediterranean Gulls together; the largest 'flock' so far was of nine birds at the Severn Estuary roost on September 17th 2000.

Although most records are of birds feeding at landfill sites and roosting on the estuary, there are a few sightings from the Cotswold Water Park and increasing numbers of records elsewhere, for example on flooded fields in the Severn Vale or feeding on ploughed land or pasture with other gulls in the Cotswolds.

There have been a number of sightings of colour-ringed birds, especially at landfill sites, from France, Belgium, Holland, Germany and Poland. Some foreign-ringed birds have returned to the county in successive years.

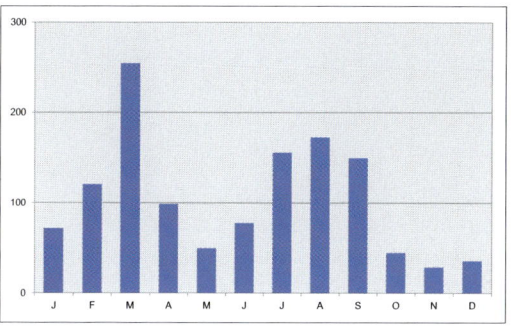

Mediterranean Gull numbers reported 2003–10, by month.

Sponsored by John Phillips

Common Gull (Mew Gull)
Larus canus

Common Gulls breed from Iceland and the British Isles very patchily eastwards across Eurasia to the Pacific, and in north-west North America. They breed and winter inland as well as on the coast; the English name seems likely to be derived from their choice of 'commons' (moors or grassland) as nesting and/or feeding sites, rather than from their perceived status as they are not particularly 'common' here compared with other gulls.

There was a widespread and marked increase in range and numbers during the twentieth century, although more recently there has been a decrease in some European countries (BWP). The British breeding population had declined up to the time of the 1988-91 Breeding Atlas but has tended to increase slowly since then.

In winter, European breeding birds move to the western seaboard, mainly south to Brittany but some reaching the Mediterranean. The British Isles receive a large influx of immigrants at this time, mainly from the Nordic countries, the Baltic states and west Russia. Migration into Britain starts in August or September and continues into early winter; return passage is mostly during March and April.

In Britain, wintering Common Gulls prefer to feed on well-grazed pasture on freely draining soils, where earthworms are readily available. They are also often seen following the plough and will flock onto flooded grassland. In the 1981-84 Wintering Atlas, their liking for pasture was suggested as the reason for a noticeable concentration in the Severn Vale and west Cotswolds compared with areas immediately to the east and north.

Swaine described the Common Gull as a visitor to Gloucestershire in large numbers from late July to April, and noted that it had probably been less plentiful here in the nineteenth century. The large gull roost at the Severn Estuary had been estimated to contain over 30,000 Common Gulls in some years, though there were also some far higher and lower estimates.

There has been little noticeable change since then, except that the maximum estimate from the Severn roost has been no more than 7,500 (in January 2004), though it is very difficult to obtain accurate counts here. There has also been a roost of up to about 5,000 in the Cotswold Water Park.

A few immature birds usually remain in the county all summer but the first autumn migrants appear in August, sometimes July, and numbers tend to stabilise from about November until January or February. The distribution map confirms that Common Gulls are widespread in the county in winter, with records absent only from the Forest of Dean plateau, the 'orchard country' of the north-west, and parts of the extreme east of the county. However the abundance map shows that they are clearly most common in a few parts of the Vale and particularly in the higher areas of the Cotswolds, where pasture or other grassland is regularly available; they are far less abundant in areas of more arable farmland to the east. This confirms the pattern revealed in the 1981-84 Wintering Atlas and contrasts with the picture for Black-headed Gull, which is not so reliant on grassland. Compared with other gulls they are scarce on landfill sites except during freezing conditions (John Sanders). The largest winter flocks away from roosts are usually of no more than a few hundred birds and the most seen during a TTV in the current atlas fieldwork was 700, on February 9th 2011 at Slimbridge.

Passage is far more noticeable in spring than autumn; this may well be because although similar numbers of birds are moving through, they are concentrated into a shorter period of time, mainly March and early April. In recent years the highest counts of the year have almost always been in March. Four-figure flocks are not unusual at this time, for example 2,500 on ploughed land near Syreford on March 19th 2008 and 2,300 in manured pasture near Elkstone on March 26th 2007.

There have been 50 or so ringing recoveries of Common Gulls involving Gloucestershire, the majority moving to the county from Norway but with a few from Germany, Denmark and Estonia. One bird ringed at Gloucester was recovered in north-west Russia.

Sponsored by Philip Boobyer

Species accounts

| | 2007–11 Atlas fieldwork ||||| Gloucestershire trends |||||| UK population trends ||
| | Number of tetrads in which recorded (max 683) ||||| Occupied 10 km squares (max 26) |||| % of tetrads in which recorded (1st hour of TTV) || *UK conservation status:* **Amber 1,8** ||
	Total	Confirmed	Probable	Possible	Present	1968–71	1981–84	1988–91	2007–11	1988–91	2008–11	Long term	Short term
Breeding	88	0	0	0	88	0		0	0	0	3.4	–	–
Winter	456						25		26			–	–

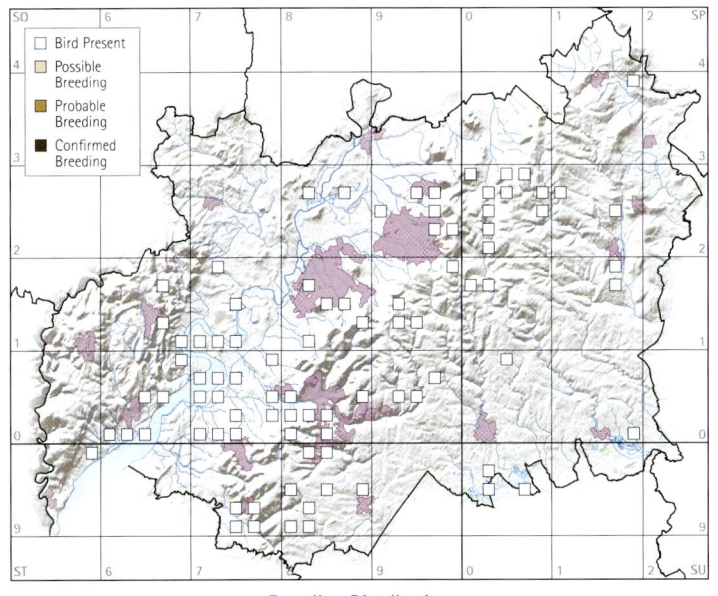

Breeding Distribution

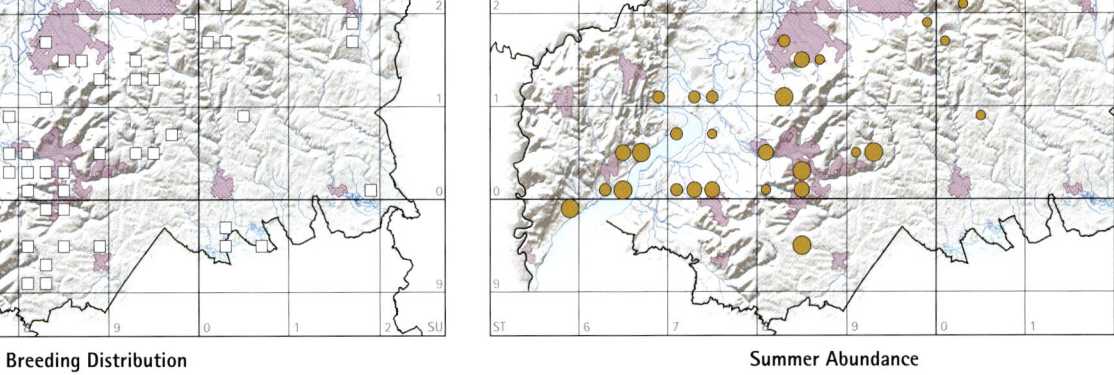

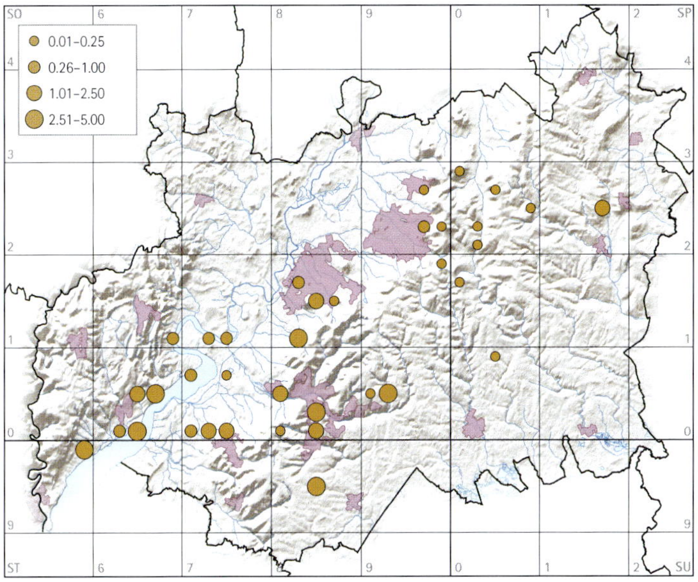

Summer Abundance

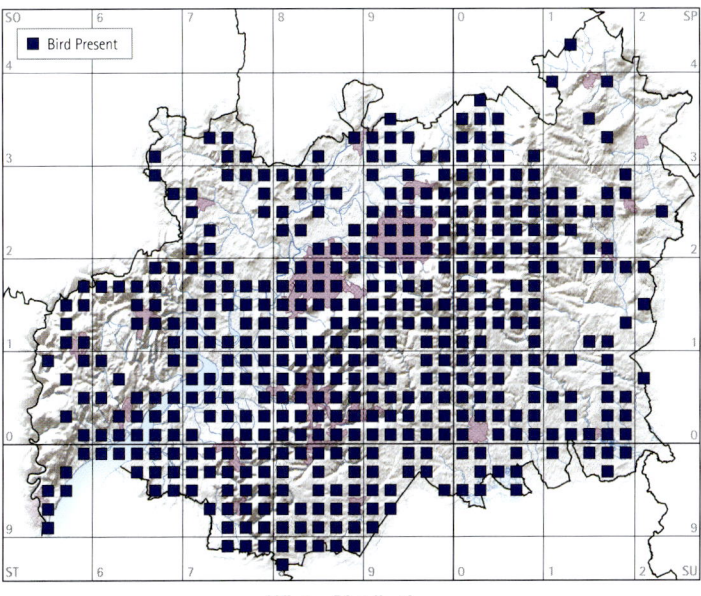

Winter Distribution

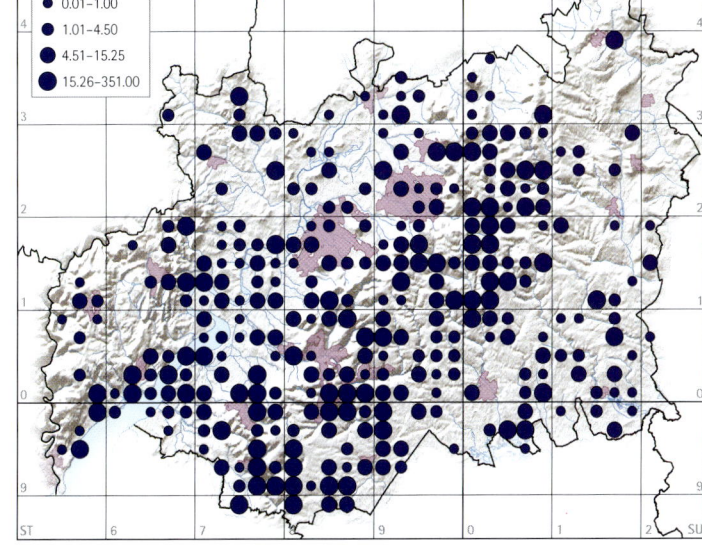

Winter Abundance

Lesser Black-backed Gull
Larus fuscus

Following range expansions during the twentieth century, the paler-backed subspecies of Lesser Black-backed Gull, *L. f. graellsii*, now nests most commonly in Iceland, the Faeroes and the British Isles, with lower numbers in France, Iberia, Greenland and eastern North America. Natural colonies at coastal sites have declined, but there have been major increases in the numbers nesting on roofs, sometimes far inland (see p. 224). Many are migratory, wintering in the Iberian peninsula and coastal regions of north-west Africa.

The well-documented move to inland areas of Britain that started in the second half of the twentieth century initiated a population explosion. For example, breeding numbers in the inner Bristol Channel area increased by 9.1% per year up to 1975 (Mudge & Ferns 1980). Overall, numbers increased during the 1980s and then stabilised, but have decreased since about 2000. The inland breeding population has risen more or less steadily throughout the whole period, whereas the number of coastal nesters has fallen since the early 1990s.

In Gloucestershire, breeding was first noted in Gloucester city in 1967 when there were two pairs. Although there were some temporary setbacks, numbers increased dramatically, especially from the mid-1980s, and new sites on the edge of the city were colonised. A survey of the wider Gloucester area in 2009 to 2011 revealed about 2,500 pairs (Peter Rock) with at least 4,100 pairs for the whole county (see p. 224 for details).

A survey during the winter of 1950–51 only found about 20 birds in the whole of Gloucestershire (Barnes 1952), but colour-ringing has demonstrated that these days about 35% of the county's adults remain during the winter, although some will move to France and the Iberian peninsula if the weather is harsh. Young birds are still very migratory and by October most locally bred juveniles have moved south, to Iberia and beyond. Most of the birds present in the county in winter are from colonies in the north of Britain, with some from Iceland, the Faeroes and the Low Countries.

Lesser Black-backs began to be recorded at the county's many active landfill sites in the 1950s. At the Gloucester site, numbers rose steadily from about 200 in 1959 to at least 5,500 by the winter of 1985–86. Numbers have stabilised since then, apart from a peak of 8,000 during very cold weather in January 1997. At the landfills near Cheltenham, winter numbers have risen steadily from 800 in 1971 to 5,000–6,000 since 2007.

Huge numbers of Lesser Black-backs roost with other gulls on the Severn Estuary, especially downriver of Slimbridge. There could well be considerably more than 10,000 here at times, although the practicalities of counting the roosting birds mean that accurate figures are difficult to obtain. Recent peaks at the smaller but currently rapidly increasing roost in the Cotswold Water Park have been estimated at 6,500 in January 2007 and January 2008 in the western section, and 3,000 in October 2009 in the eastern section.

PETER PARTINGTON

The maps show that Lesser Black-backs have a wider winter distribution in the county than Herring Gulls, extending up onto the Cotswolds. This could reflect the greater overall abundance of Lesser Black-backs, as well as any differences in the two species' feeding ecology. Systematic counts by NCOS suggest that there have been increases in the east of the county since 2002.

Over the last 25 years the SEGG has collected a huge amount of data on the movements of this species (GBR and SEGG bulletins therein). The most northerly recoveries were of two birds ringed at the Gloucester landfill site and shot at Ammassalik in Greenland in 1997 and 1998, while the most southerly was a nestling colour-ringed on the Gloucestershire Royal Hospital, Gloucester on June 27th 2005 and sighted at Bijol Island, Gambia on December 23rd 2006.

The subspecies of the Lesser Black-backed Gull that breeds from Norway south to the Netherlands, *L. f. intermedius*, is a regular visitor to Britain, mainly on passage. There have been sightings in Gloucestershire of over 270 birds colour-ringed in Norway, revealing that the Severn Vale is on a regular migration route for this subspecies.

The breeding range of the nominate race of the Lesser Black-back, known as the Baltic Gull, is contracting, and its numbers are in decline. Its core breeding population is now in Finland and coastal areas of Sweden. There is one confirmed county record: an adult at the Gloucester landfill from April 18th to 20th 2007 (Sanders 2007b). It had been colour-ringed as a chick in Finland in July 2004, and was seen there again in July 2007, just 6 km from where it was originally ringed. This was only the second accepted record for Britain.

Sponsored by John Sanders

Species accounts

2007–11 Atlas fieldwork					Gloucestershire trends						UK population trends	
Number of tetrads in which recorded (max 683)					*Occupied 10 km squares (max 26)*				*% of tetrads in which recorded (1st hour of TTV)*		*UK conservation status:* **Amber 7,8**	
	Total	Confirmed	Probable	Possible	Present	1968–71	1981–84	1988–91	2007–11	1988–91	2008–11	Long term	Short term
Breeding	313	23	6	5	279	2		1	7	0.6	20.9	–2%	–36%
Winter	344						21		26			–	–

Breeding Distribution

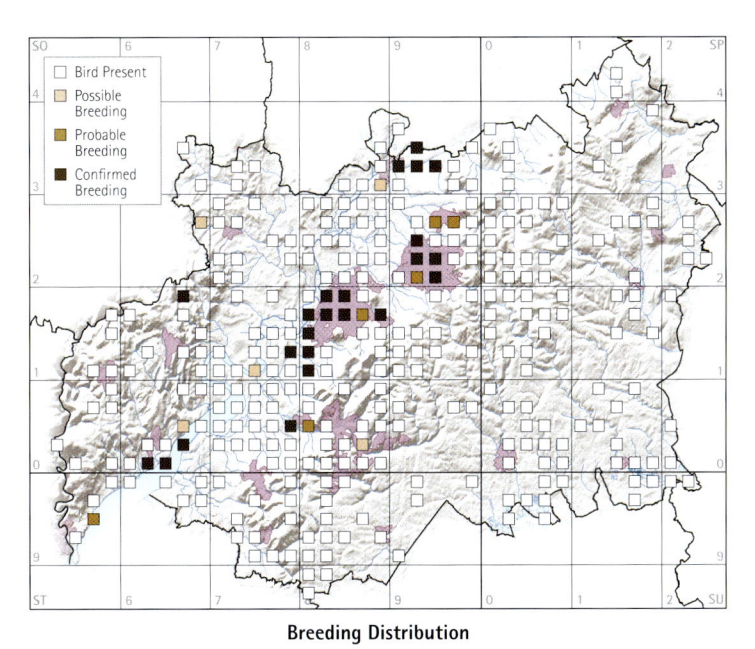

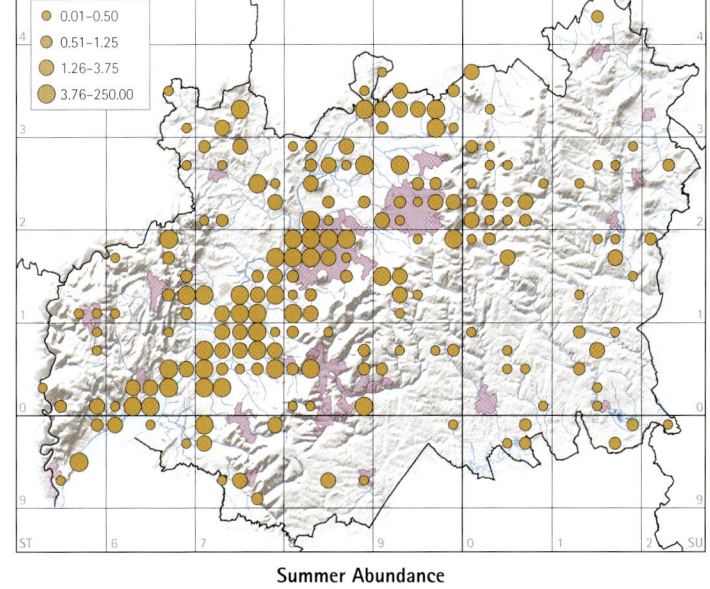

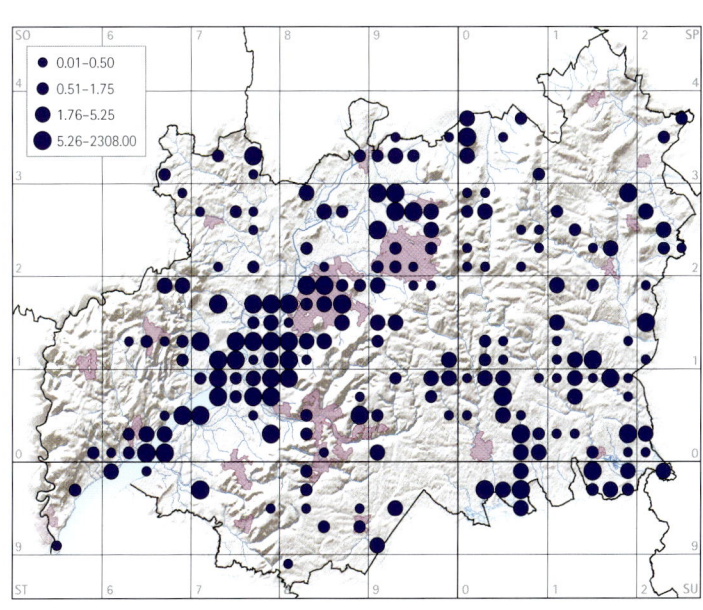

Summer Abundance

Winter Distribution

Winter Abundance

Herring Gull (European Herring Gull)
Larus argentatus

Familiar and seemingly fearless, Herring Gulls provoke mixed reactions: some admire them for their boldness, while others dislike them for their noisy, 'messy' habits. They breed widely across northern areas of Eurasia.

British and Irish breeding birds are of the subspecies *L. a. argenteus*, which also nests in Iceland, the Faeroes, western France and the North Sea coast to Germany. The preferred nesting habitat is rocky cliffs and small islands, and they will also use coastal dunes and shingle beaches as long as they are free from disturbance. They nest around all our coasts, although there are fewer in eastern England where suitable habitat is scarcer. The relatively recent move inland to urban areas is well documented (see p. 224), but urban-nesting gulls are a small proportion of the total population and their success has not compensated for sharp decreases in coastal colonies, which are believed to be related to the decline in the fishing industry.

Swaine noted that breeding was said to have occurred in the Wye valley 'many years ago', but details are lacking, and Mellersh and other earlier writers made no mention of breeding in the county. The present colony by the Wye near Chepstow was first noted in 1947, when one pair bred, and at that time this was the only known breeding site in the county. Following a rapid increase there were about 90 pairs by 1976, but after outbreaks of botulism in the late 1970s and early 1980s numbers declined, and only about ten pairs now nest at this site.

Herring Gulls started to nest on rooftops in Gloucester city in 1971 (Swaine), and they were using old RAF buildings on the outskirts at Quedgeley by 1975. Numbers rose rapidly to 126 pairs by 1980 (Mudge & Ferns 1980). There was then probably a slight fall in the early 1980s, again due to botulism, followed by another period of increase and spread. During the atlas period there were about 1,000 pairs in the county, almost three-quarters of which were in Gloucester (see p. 224 for details).

The first recorded sighting of Herring Gulls at a county landfill site was of 100 at Stroud in 1966. These days it is not unusual to see 5,000 at the Gloucester landfill during winter, and even more during spells of very cold weather. Rather smaller numbers are usually present at the Bishop's Cleeve and Stoke Orchard landfills near Cheltenham, where they are outnumbered by Lesser Black-backs. Ringing data from the SEGG show that numbers of Herring Gulls on landfills have increased since the mid-1980s, despite the fact that populations as a whole have declined over that period. The reason for this is not clear but it is possible that control measures at landfill sites further north, using falconers and noise deterrents, have driven the birds south to Gloucestershire sites where, until very recently, there has been no disturbance.

Outside the breeding season thousands of Herring Gulls join other gulls in the huge roost on the estuary near Slimbridge. A few hundred also roost at the Cotswold Water Park, where numbers have increased considerably in recent years. It is likely that many of these Water Park birds feed in Wiltshire during the day, since the atlas results indicate that there are very few birds across the Cotswolds and in eastern regions of Gloucestershire.

Movements of birds ringed by the SEGG have been mainly short distance and dispersive, with a majority of recoveries coming from the main Bristol landfill site and the shores of the Bristol Channel. Most of the remainder have come from the southern half of England and Wales, with very few from the north of England and Scotland and just three from the Republic of Ireland. However, since the introduction of colour-ringing more interchanges of this subspecies to and from the Continent have been recorded than had previously been suspected. There have been over a dozen movements to and from France and the Channel Islands, and a few between the county and the Low Countries and northern Spain.

The nominate race of the Herring Gull breeds from Denmark and Scandinavia east to north-west Russia. It is a regular winter visitor to Gloucestershire in small numbers, and there have been ten observations of colour-ringed birds from Russia, Denmark, Finland and Norway.

Sponsored by John Sanders

Species accounts

2007–11 Atlas fieldwork						Gloucestershire trends						UK population trends	
Number of tetrads in which recorded (max 683)					Occupied 10 km squares (max 26)				% of tetrads in which recorded (1st hour of TTV)		UK conservation status: **Red 3,4**	
	Total	Confirmed	Probable	Possible	Present	1968–71	1981–84	1988–91	2007–11	1988–91	2008–11	Long term	Short term
Breeding	162	26	5	3	128	1		1	7	0	10.6	−29%	−38%
Winter	230						18		23			–	–

Breeding Distribution

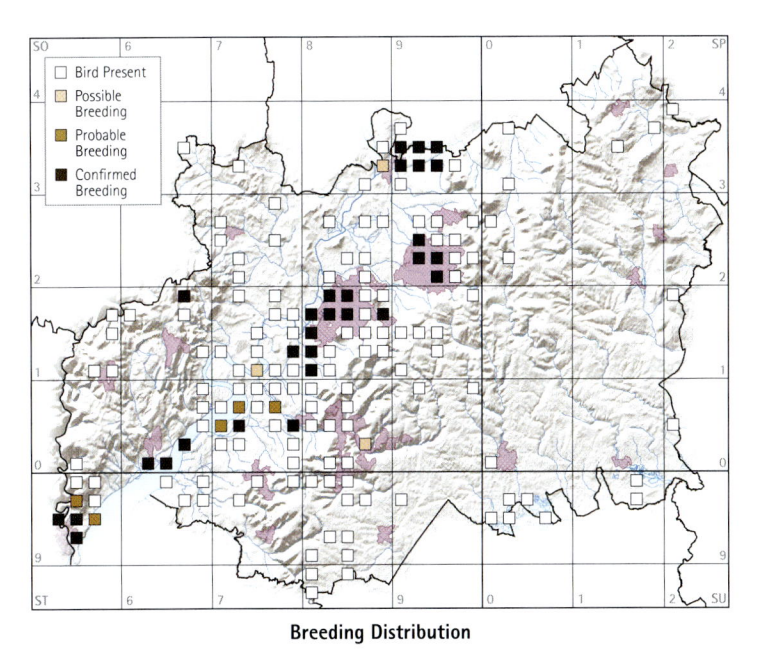

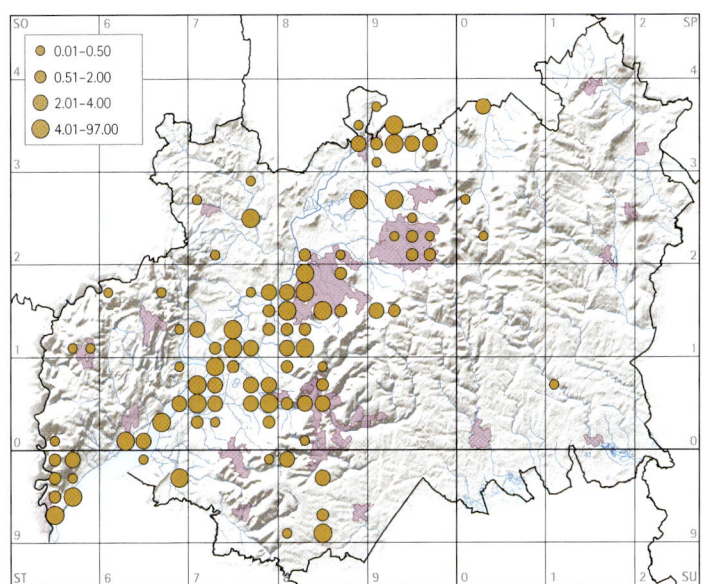

Summer Abundance

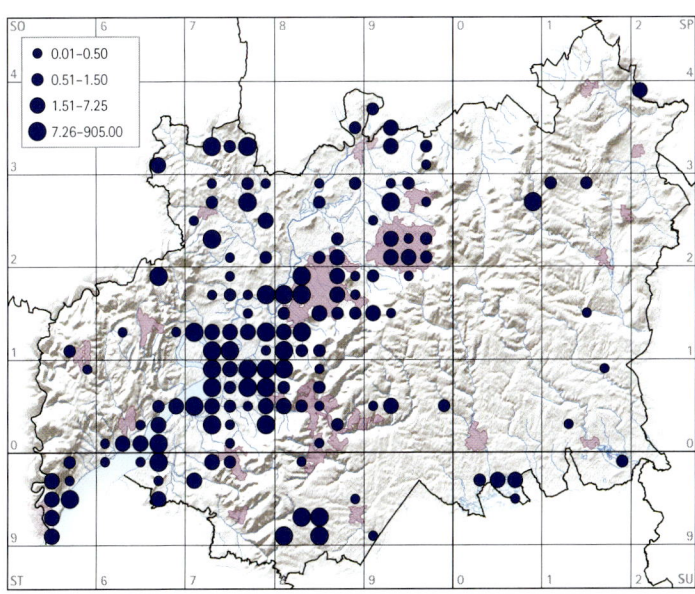

Winter Distribution

Winter Abundance

ARMED AND DANGEROUS

EXCLUSIVE By Sarah Webb
sarah.webb@glosmedia.co.uk

Those pesky gulls are back with a vengeance ..pelting stones at city's new shopping complex

THE city's winged menaces are back and this time they're even more lethal – attacking Gloucester's newest shopping centre!

Seagulls are bombarding the Quays Designer Outlet Centre with stones and wrecking its state-of-the-art roof in the pro-

Urban gulls breeding in Gloucestershire

Those compiling GBRs 50 or more years ago would no doubt have been surprised to be told that by the early twenty-first century the maximum winter counts for Herring Gulls and Lesser-Black-backed Gulls in the county would come not from the Severn Estuary but from two inland localities: the landfill sites near Bishop's Cleeve and Gloucester. Their surprise would surely have turned to disbelief if it was revealed that the species with the highest county *breeding season* TTV count during the 2007–11 atlas survey would be the Lesser Black-backed Gull, with 800 birds on June 4th 2009 at the Bishop's Cleeve landfill.

The fact is that these 'seagulls' are now a familiar sight in many urban parts of the county. Perceived by many as being noisy, dirty and aggressive, they attract a good deal of attention from the local press and are a serious concern for local authorities, who are expected to 'do something about them'. They have been relatively well monitored in Gloucestershire in recent years, and this brief account charts their fortunes.

Following the introduction of the Clean Air Act in 1956, household waste, which had previously been burned, was now dumped, untreated, on open landfill sites. Though tip faces were covered at the end of the day, many birds, including gulls, were able to take advantage of this constant and reliable food source, and numbers of Herring and Lesser Black-backed Gulls quickly increased in non-urban colonies. In essence, these colonies were outgrown and the breeding birds spread into new areas, with rooftops being widely used, and this increase has continued apace to the present day. As soon as they started to nest in urban centres the rate of increase in breeding numbers was phenomenal, with both species estimated to have risen by about 10% per year up to the mid-1970s (Mudge & Ferns 1980). There was a reverse in the late 1970s and early 1980s, caused by outbreaks of botulism which affected Herring Gulls more than Lesser Black-backs and non-urban gulls more than urban gulls (Rock 2005), but numbers recovered very strongly thereafter, with even faster rates of increase. Interchange between urban and non-urban populations is nowadays very rare: a gull hatched on a rooftop is highly unlikely to recruit into a non-urban colony once it is old enough to breed, and vice versa (Rock 2005). In short we now have two populations,

	Lesser Black-backed Gull	Herring Gull
Gloucester area	2,423	746
Ashchurch/Northway	807	134
Cheltenham area	273	47
Mitcheldean	232	17
Stonehouse	179	45
Lydney area	104	45
Sharpness	63	31

Numbers of nests at urban sites in Gloucestershire, 2009–11.

the non-urban and the urban. More recently, Lesser Black-backs, previously summer visitors to Britain, began to overwinter here in increasing numbers instead of migrating to traditional wintering grounds in Iberia and beyond, with urban gulls dispensing with migration at almost twice the rate of non-urban birds (Rock 2006).

Both species will nest on a wide range of structures, but sometimes the places they choose reflect their traditional, 'natural' preferences, with Herring Gulls choosing sites that resemble cliff ledges and crannies, and Lesser Black-backs preferring more open flat roofs. Most nests can be found on the shallow-sloping roofs of large factories and similar buildings on industrial estates, and increasingly in retail parks. Nests are built wherever there is any kind of structure that will serve to retain nesting material, however meagre; this might be a small ledge or merely a protruding bolt. The highest densities, with nests just a few metres apart, occur on older buildings such as military warehouses, where typically there is a series of parallel roofs with gullies between them, providing excellent nest sites. In residential areas of Gloucester and Cheltenham houses are also used, and here a typical nest might be found in the angle between a chimney and a roof.

The table shows estimates of the number of nests in each of the occupied areas of the county during the second half of the 2007–11 atlas period. It should be noted that the colonies were not all visited in the same breeding season. In addition, counting is not straightforward because of the difficulties in accessing the colonies, or indeed in simply being able to see on to the rooftops, so these numbers are therefore likely to be conservative. In particular the sites in and around Cheltenham town centre are on particularly high roofs, so actual numbers there are probably considerably greater than those shown. However it is certain that in 2011 more than 5,000 pairs bred in the county, with Lesser Black-backed Gulls outnumbering Herring Gulls by about four to one overall, although this ratio varies considerably depending on the area.

In addition to these sites, in 2012 both species were found to have colonised factory buildings on the edges of Coleford and Cinderford. Initial estimates suggested that in total, five to ten pairs of Lesser Black-backs and up to five pairs of Herring Gulls were present (Peter Rock).

In the area administered by Gloucester City Council, accurate counts are undertaken annually. From 2002 to 2009 these surveys were done by the same observer, using the same counting and

Nests of Lesser Black-backed Gulls and Herring Gulls in Gloucester, 2002–09.

estimating techniques each year. The graph charts a dramatic rise of 117% in the city in just seven years, and the city of Gloucester is now home to one of the largest urban gull colonies in Britain (Rock 2009). The rate of increase has slowed down, but it is a matter of opinion whether this apparent levelling off is due to recently introduced control measures or to other factors.

Various attempts are made to control gull numbers. Owners of properties with nests have used an imaginative range of measures including the erection of netting, covering buildings with wires and spikes, installing large plastic owls, and playing audio tapes featuring birds of prey and distress calls of gulls. However it seems that at best the gulls are persuaded to move temporarily to a nearby building, whilst at worst they completely ignore these measures (see photo, top left).

For some years now, local authorities have been arranging for eggs to be oiled, a process that renders them incapable of hatching while ensuring that replacement clutches are not laid. This may be partially effective but as the vast majority of nests are inaccessible it has limited impact. As these large gulls are long-lived, it would also take a long time for any effects on breeding populations to be seen.

A large-scale campaign to scare gulls away from the county's landfill sites started in the summer of 2011, when falconers were employed to fly Peregrines and other raptors across the sites five days per week – a technique that had already been used in other parts of the country. The effect has been dramatic, with no gulls present during working hours, although some do visit at other times, when their behaviour is quite different from before; now they feed quickly and there is no loafing at these sites (Sanders 2011). Whether the falconers will have the same impact during periods of extremely cold weather, and whether they will reduce the numbers of gulls nesting in urban areas, as intended, remains to be seen. It has been suggested that some Lesser Black-backs may have resumed their migrations to traditional Iberian wintering grounds in response to the repeated scaring, but as many immature birds spend two years abroad before returning here to breed it will be some time before any conclusions can be drawn.

The large gulls are able to take advantage of a wide range of feeding opportunities and there can be no doubt that they know exactly where to find food throughout their home ranges which, for urban gulls, may extend over thousands of square kilometres (Rock 2004). Certainly, it seems safe to assume that as long as there are plentiful feeding opportunities, there will be large numbers of urban gulls and that, whether welcome or not, they will make their presence felt.

Yellow-legged Gull
Larus michahellis

This Mediterranean counterpart of the Herring Gull has only fairly recently been classified as a species in its own right (Sangster *et al.* 2005). The nominate race breeds from western France and Iberia to the Black Sea, and in recent times has begun to spread into central Europe. The French range now extends to Normandy (Malling Olsen & Larsson 2004). A few have attempted to breed in southern England since about 1995, mainly in mixed pairs with Lesser Black-backed Gulls.

The first record of a Yellow-legged Gull in Gloucestershire was in 1984, and they began to become noticeably more numerous after 1993. In recent years adults have started to arrive in the county in late June, and juveniles two or three weeks later. At the Gloucester landfill site, peaks of up to 50 birds are normal during July and August, with up to ten at the other county landfills. Up to 35 may often be seen on the Severn Estuary off Lydney Harbour at this time of the year, whilst the highest recent count at Slimbridge was 70 in July (Martin McGill). The species is scarce elsewhere in the county; only single-figure reports have been received from the Cotswold Water Park and the floodwaters in the Severn Vale.

Numbers begin to decline from September onwards (see graph). Only about ten are seen daily during the winter months, and usually only a handful of immatures are present during the spring and early summer. However, the sighting of an adult collecting nesting material at the Gloucester landfill on May 7th 2008 has given rise to speculation that breeding might be attempted in future.

Ringing, and particularly colour-ringing, has demonstrated that many of the Yellow-legged Gulls seen in Gloucestershire come from breeding colonies in northern coastal areas of the western Mediterranean, particularly France, and has also proved that a small number of individuals return year after year. Northward migration in late summer is evidently a regular, annual event for part of this Mediterranean population. More unusually, a chick colour-ringed in 1995 on the Berlenga Islands, Portugal, was at the Gloucester landfill on 28 May 1996, and another nestling ringed in Switzerland in June 1997 was trapped there in November 1999, the first Swiss-ringed Yellow-legged Gull to be controlled in Britain.

A third-winter bird showing characteristics of the darker subspecies *L. m. atlantis* ('Azorean Gull'), which breeds on the Atlantic islands and also on the Atlantic coasts of Morocco and Iberia, was seen and photographed at all three county landfill sites on many dates between September 7th and October 18th 2010.

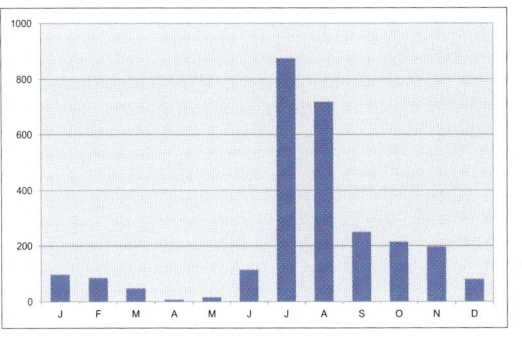

Yellow-legged Gull numbers reported 2003–10, by month.

Caspian Gull
Larus cachinnans

The Caspian Gull was officially 'split' from the closely related Yellow-legged Gull and elevated to species level as recently as 2007. It breeds around the Black and Caspian Seas and eastwards into Asia, and in recent years has spread from Ukraine into Poland and Germany. Hybrids with Yellow-legged and Herring Gulls are fairly frequent (Faber *et al.* 2001), and care needs to be taken in identifying this species.

The first Caspian Gulls were identified in Britain in 1995, and the first for the county was an adult at the Gloucester landfill site on December 7th 1998. There were further records of adults at the Gloucester and Bishop's Cleeve landfills in 1999 and 2001, and the species has been seen regularly from 2003 onwards, averaging just under seven per year. Most have been at the landfills, and following the recent deployment of falconers there to scare gulls away, records of this species seem likely to decline in future years.

Four birds identified as Caspian Gulls when colour-ringed as nestlings in Poland have been seen in the county; two of these proved to be hybrids.

Sponsored by Gordon & Margaret Avery

Iceland Gull
Larus glaucoides

Iceland Gulls are endemic to Greenland, where they breed on cliffs and rocky shores. They are heavily hunted for food, and it is estimated that up to a fifth of the population is taken each year. Many birds, particularly from the east coast, move to Iceland during the winter, and relatively small numbers, mainly first-winters, continue south to the British Isles. Up to 300 are seen here each winter, but numbers vary considerably depending on the harshness of the weather in Greenland.

There was some uncertainty regarding the identification of Iceland Gulls among early county observers, and Swaine referred to birds in 1947 and 1973 that were either this species or Glaucous Gulls. A report of an adult Iceland Gull at Awre on September 16th 1973 was later found to be unacceptable after a review by the County Records Committee, and the first reliable records came in 1984, when five or six were seen. There were then very few until the 1994–95 winter, when more intensive coverage of the county's landfill sites began. In common with other gulls they move between the landfills and the roost on the estuary, and there are many duplicate sightings of the same individuals along the Severn between Gloucester and Slimbridge. In this area up to five Iceland Gulls have been recorded each year since 1994, with the exception of early 2009 when an estimated 14 were present. Determining what caused this unprecedented influx is impossible, but severe weather in Greenland and bird-scaring by falconers on landfills outside Gloucestershire may have been contributory factors.

Very occasionally one or two birds have been recorded at the roost in the Cotswold Water Park, and the only record elsewhere was of an exhausted first-winter at Kingscote, Dursley on January 8th 2005, which was taken into care and later released. About two-thirds of all sightings are of first-winter birds.

The very similar Kumlien's Gull '*L. g. kumlieni*' is currently generally regarded as being a hybrid between Iceland Gull and Thayer's Gull *L. thayeri*. It breeds on Baffin Island and in north-western Quebec, and winters along the east coast of North America. Small numbers are seen in the British Isles each winter, particularly on the west coast of Ireland. There have been about eight records in Gloucestershire, all since 2003 and all at landfill sites or roosting in the Water Park. Most have been found in January or February, the exceptions being one at the Gloucester landfill from December 20th 2004, and one at the Stoke Orchard landfill near Cheltenham on March 18th 2011. Most records have been of adults, and there is the possibility that single individual(s) could have returned in successive years.

Sponsored by John Sanders

Glaucous Gull
Larus hyperboreus

The breeding distribution of the Glaucous Gull lies between latitudes 60°N and 83°N, in the sub-Arctic and Arctic zones. It nests in Greenland, Iceland, Bear Island, Spitsbergen and coastal areas of European Russia. Hybridisation with Herring Gulls is not infrequent where the two species' ranges overlap; the hybrids can be identified in their first-winter plumage by characteristic markings in their primaries. Glaucous Gulls are mainly sedentary or short-distance migrants, but up to about 500 birds winter in the British Isles each year, mainly in northern areas. Numbers vary considerably from year to year depending on the severity of the winter. The majority of sightings are between December and April and most are of immature birds.

The earliest county record quoted by Swaine was of an adult shot near Fretherne in 1906. Between 1950 and 1975 there were a further six records involving seven birds, all from the Severn Estuary. One of these, an adult, was reported on September 24th 1968, extremely early in the season. There were then no sightings until 1983, and between then and 1995 there were only records every other year on average and no more than two birds were reported in any year. Since 1996 though they have been seen in every year except one. Numbers have increased too, with at least five in winter 2007–08 and at least seven the following winter. This increase may be partly due to the fact that falconers are being deployed to deter gulls at many landfill sites in the Midlands and northern England, which is tending to force them to move to less disturbed tips. In addition of course, the figures are likely to reflect the increasing numbers of observers in the county, and in particular the more intensive watching at the landfill sites that began in the mid-1990s.

Of the birds that were aged, 39 were first-winters, four second-winters, one third-winter and two adults. Earliest and latest dates since 1980 were an adult at Hardwicke on November 22nd 1987 and a first-winter at Slimbridge on May 27th 2005.

The vast majority of recent records have come from the three county landfill sites, loafing areas on sandbanks in the Severn, and the gull roost on the estuary. There are very few records from elsewhere: singles at the Cotswold Water Park in 1984, 1985 and 1992, one over the river Wye at Beachley Point on January 17th 1987, one near Tewkesbury from February 1st to 15th 1998, and a first-winter over Windsoredge, Nailsworth on January 26th 2009.

The first county record of a Herring Gull x Glaucous Gull hybrid came in 1991; there have been a few more records subsequently, with annual sightings since 2007.

Sponsored by John Sanders

Great Black-backed Gull
Larus marinus

As its scientific name implies, this is a much more maritime species than Herring or Lesser Black-backed Gulls. It breeds discontinuously along the coasts of northern and western Europe, including the Baltic Sea and the Arctic Ocean, as well as in Greenland and North America. Northern breeding populations are completely migratory, with many frequenting the North Sea in winter, while some range as far south as the Canary Islands. In contrast, southern birds only undertake dispersive movements. There has been an increase in numbers and range in Europe during the twentieth century, and this trend is clearly continuing as in 2010 the species was unexpectedly found nesting in Morocco (Jönsson 2011).

In the British Isles, Great Black-backs nest only rarely in the south-east and east of England, but they are widely distributed in the remaining coastal areas, particularly in Scotland. Numbers have increased over the last 100 years or so, but have tended to stabilise since about 1999.

In Gloucestershire, breeding was unsuccessfully attempted on St Twrog's Island (Chapel Rock), off Beachley Point, in 1955 and 1957, and was thought to have been successful there in 1962 and 1963 (Niles & Cooper 1969), although details are lacking for the 1960s records. A further attempt was made at this site in 1997, and in 2012 a nest with three eggs was found but they disappeared under circumstances suggesting that the nest was robbed (John Sanders). Given the normally very maritime breeding sites, it came as a surprise to learn that three pairs nested among the other gulls on rooftops in Gloucester in 2009, and four in 2010 (Peter Rock), although similar sites have been reported in other parts of the country over the last 15 years.

Great Black-backs are far more common in Gloucestershire outside the breeding season. Swaine noted that there appeared to have been a big increase in the county over the 30 years up to 1980, and this trend has continued. The species was not so adversely affected by botulism as Herring and Lesser Black-backed Gulls (Mudge & Ferns 1980). Numbers are highest in midwinter, and the daytime loafing flock on the Dumbles at Slimbridge has provided the largest counts, with a maximum of 242 on January 9th 2008. Up to 30 are frequently seen feeding at the Gloucester landfill site, with a maximum of 100, also in early January 2008. Single figures are more usual at the Bishop's Cleeve and Stoke Orchard landfills. Only a few, mainly immature birds, remain during the summer months.

Great Black-backs can be seen anywhere on the Severn Estuary, especially downriver from Lydney Harbour. There are also occasional records from the Severn Vale as far upriver as Tewkesbury, and along the Wye between Beachley Point and Symonds Yat, but there have been very few sightings in the Cotswolds. Seven flying over Nailsworth on January 9th 2000 was an unusually large group for this part of the county, and during the current atlas fieldwork there was another unusual Cotswolds record of three feeding on a sheep carcass on high open agricultural land above Nailsworth on June 24th 2010. In the Thames Area, between one and four are usual at the roost in the Cotswold Water Park. (A few records of higher counts at some of these sites have appeared in past issues of the GBR, but they are now considered unreliable).

A fairly high proportion of the Great Black-backs on the Gloucester landfill site carry metal rings. Those few whose rings have been read have all originated from Denny Island, in the Bristol Channel off Avonmouth, which is the nearest colony to Gloucestershire. All movements of birds ringed at the Gloucester landfill have been similarly short-distance, to the Bristol area and landfill sites in the Midlands. One ringed as a nestling in Guernsey in 1989 was shot during a cull at Quedgeley in March 2003, and there have been sightings of three birds colour-ringed as nestlings in France and four from Norway. Norwegian Great Black-backs occur in relatively large numbers on the east coast of England during the winter, but it seems that few continue as far as Gloucestershire.

Sponsored by John Sanders

Species accounts   231

2007–11 Atlas fieldwork					Gloucestershire trends					UK population trends	
Number of tetrads in which recorded (max 683)					Occupied 10 km squares (max 26)				% of tetrads in which recorded (1st hour of TTV)		UK conservation status: Amber 4	
	Total	Confirmed	Probable	Possible	Present	1968–71	1981–84	1988–91	2007–11	1988–91	2008–11	Long term	Short term
Breeding	33	2	0	0	31	0		0	1	0	1.3	−20%	−30%
Winter	39						12		10			–	–

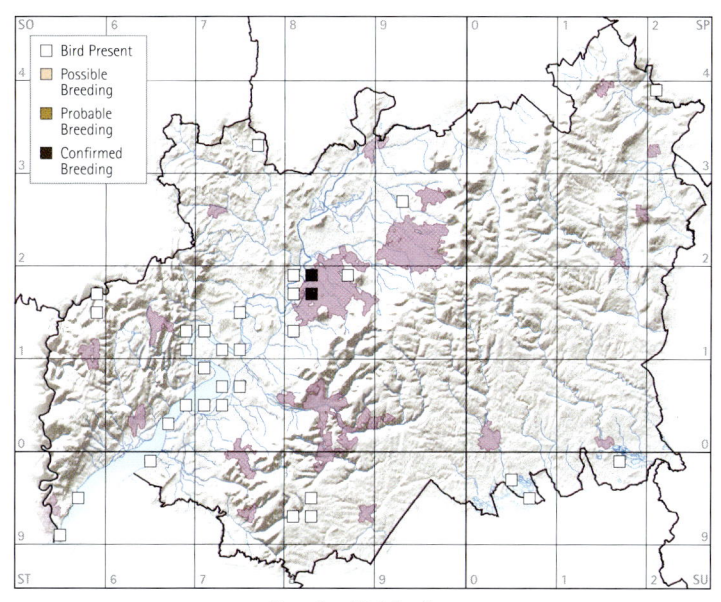

Breeding Distribution

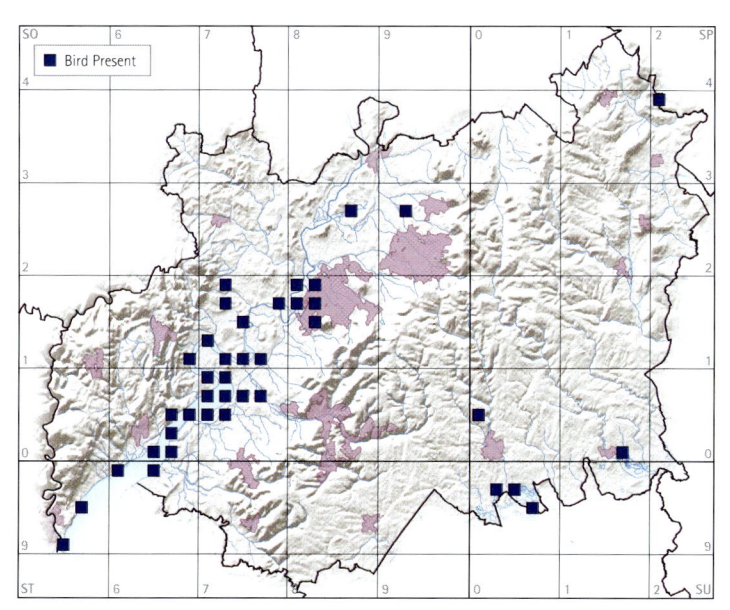

Winter Distribution

Ivory Gull
Pagophila eburnea

A high Arctic species rarely extending beyond the southern edge of the drift-ice, Ivory Gulls are barely annual wanderers to Britain and Ireland, with 53 records between 1950 and 2010. There have been two records in Gloucestershire:

1921: one was shot on the Severn at Longney Sands a few miles downriver of Gloucester in late January.

1990: a first-winter on the foreshore at Frampton on December 30th remained until January 1st 1991.

Sabine's Gull
Xema sabini

Sabine's Gulls breed from north-east Siberia across northern North America, in Greenland and (rarely) Spitsbergen. They winter in the southern Pacific and Atlantic Oceans. In the British Isles, where they are most often seen flying past seawatching points in autumn, they were formerly considered to be rare visitors, but they are now known to be annual, albeit in variable numbers.

The first record for Gloucestershire was of an adult at the Severn Estuary off Tites Point near Slimbridge from August 27th to 29th 1981. This was followed by a number of sightings on several dates between September 4th and 14th 1983, when Atlantic depressions brought unusually high numbers to Britain: at least three different birds (two adults and a juvenile), and quite possibly five, were seen between Tites Point and Frampton. There were then single juveniles, all in the same area of the estuary, on August 30th 1988, November 2nd 2003, and November 14th 2009. Finally, in westerly gales in September 2011, at least one juvenile was seen on several dates between 6th and 11th between Guscar Rocks and Slimbridge, and an adult was off Slimbridge on 10th.

Bonaparte's Gull
Chroicocephalus philadelphia

Breeding in Alaska and Canada and wintering on the coasts of North and Central America, Bonaparte's Gulls have proved in recent decades to be annual visitors in very low numbers to the British Isles, with 170 records between 1950 and 2010. There have been a number of inland records, and it is perhaps surprising that only one has so far been found in Gloucestershire: an adult on the estuary at Slimbridge on September 10th 2006 (Lees 2006).

Ross's Gull
Rhodostethia rosea

Ross's Gulls nest on the north-east Siberian tundra and winter mainly to the south and south-east of the breeding range, in the northern Bering Sea and the Sea of Okhotsk. They are barely annual visitors to Britain and Ireland, with 91 records between 1950 and 2010. The only record for Gloucestershire was on April 16th 2002, when an immature spent the day at Frampton sailing lake in company with Little Gulls.

Laughing Gull
Larus atricilla

Laughing Gulls breed along the western Atlantic coast, from the USA–Canada border to northernmost South America. In winter they extend along both American coastlines. They are annual or near-annual visitors to Britain and Ireland, with 190 records between 1950 and 2010; a fairly high proportion of these were in late 2005 and early 2006 (see below). There have been three records in Gloucestershire:

1981: a first-winter at Slimbridge from December 30th until January 5th 1982.

1997: an adult at the Gloucester landfill site on November 10th.

2006: an adult at Witcombe reservoir on January 29th. This sighting followed an unprecedented arrival of over 50 Laughing Gulls in the British Isles in late 2005 in the wake of North Atlantic storms, the remnants of Hurricane Wilma.

Franklin's Gull
Larus pipixcan

Franklin's Gulls breed in west-central North America and winter mostly on the Pacific coast of South America. They are now known to be annual or near-annual visitors to the British Isles, though the first record was not until 1970; there were 66 records up to 2010. There are three records for Gloucestershire:

1996: an adult remained at the Gloucester landfill site from January 4th to 7th (Sanders 1996).
2005: one on the Severn at Newnham on March 22nd.
2008: one again at Newnham on April 7th.

It is possible that the 2005 and 2008 records refer to the same individual.

Ring-billed Gull
Larus delawarensis

The first British record of a Ring-billed Gull came in 1973 in Glamorgan, following a period of rapid expansion of the North American breeding population. Since then they have been seen annually in variable numbers, with a tendency to decrease slightly in recent years.

The first Gloucestershire record was of an adult at Slimbridge from January 16th to 30th 1982. The next sighting was not until 1989, but subsequently there have been records in most years, usually involving up to three wandering individuals per year and with some birds quite possibly returning over a number of years. The majority of records have been of adults, and they have been found in all months except September (see table). Most have been seen at the well-watched Severn Estuary and the Gloucester landfill site, but there are also records from Ashleworth Ham, in and around the towns of Cheltenham, Gloucester, Stroud and Tewkesbury (particularly on playing fields), and at the M5 motorway service station at Michaelwood. Rather surprisingly there are only two sightings so far from the Cotswold Water Park, in February and December 1992.

Jan	Feb	Mar	Apr	May	Jun	Jul	Aug	Sep	Oct	Nov	Dec
10	5	6	7	1	1	2	1	0	4	4	5

Ring-billed Gull: all county records up to 2010, showing month of first finding.

American Herring Gull
Larus smithsonianus

As the name implies, this is the Nearctic counterpart to our Herring Gull, and it is very similar in appearance. Indeed the BOU has only treated it as a separate species since 2008, although recent genetic studies suggest that the two may not be as closely related as had been assumed (Sangster *et al.* 2007). The first record for the British Isles was in 1994, and there had been 25 more up to 2010. There has been one record in Gloucestershire: a first-winter at the Frampton landfill site on December 15th 1997 (not 1998, as implied in the 1998 GBR).

Glaucous-winged Gull
Larus glaucescens

As an inhabitant of the Pacific Ocean, breeding from Oregon, USA around to Kamchatka and wintering south to Japan and Mexico, this was a very unexpected addition to the Gloucestershire and British lists. An individual in third-winter plumage was found at the Gloucester landfill site on December 15th 2006 and was cannon-netted with other gulls the next day and colour-ringed. It was seen in spring 2007 in Carmarthenshire in early March, at the Gloucester landfill again on March 16th and 17th, and finally in Surrey on April 18th (Sanders 2006, 2007a, 2010). This was only the third record for the Western Palearctic.

Little Tern
Sternula albifrons

Little Terns breed patchily along coasts and major river valleys in the Western Palearctic and parts of Asia; there are also populations in Africa, Australasia and the Americas. West European birds winter in western and probably southern Africa. European populations decreased during the second half of the twentieth century, though they are tending to stabilise more recently; in Britain there have been substantial declines since the 1980s. The nearest breeding colonies to Gloucestershire are in Dorset and Hampshire.

There are few old county records of Little Terns. Mellersh listed the species as an occasional visitor to the Severn in October and November, which is late in the year by modern standards. Swaine described it as an 'uncommon visitor on passage', mostly in May, with singles or small parties of up to 15 in most years. Only since about 1950 had records become more or less regular, although this may well have been due to observer effects.

Since 1980 the county status has remained broadly unchanged. The vast majority of sightings come from the Severn Estuary, where many records are of birds flying straight through, especially in spring. Unusual peaks apart (see graph), there seems to have been a generally decreasing trend from the 1980s until 2000, with a tendency to increase again subsequently.

The earliest date on record is April 14th 2009; the peak spring count can be at any time between mid-April and mid-May. Little Terns were seen at this season in 24 of the 30 years since 1980, with a grand total of spring birds over this period of about 130. In each of the four years when unusually large peaks were recorded (see graph) a single flock accounted for 40% to 60% of the season's total.

In autumn there were records in 18 of the 30 years since 1980, the grand total for autumn over that period being about 50 birds, and the high figure of 12 in 1991 included a single flock of 11 on September 12th. The timing of autumn records is as variable as in spring, but in recent years there have been few sightings after the end of September.

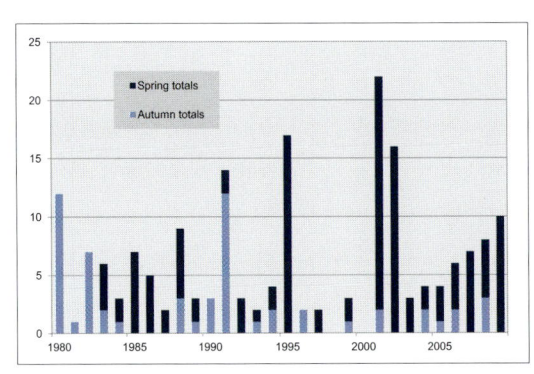

Little Tern numbers, spring and autumn, since 1980.

Gull-billed Tern
Gelochelidon nilotica

Gull-billed Terns have a very widespread world range, breeding on all continents except Antarctica. However their rather specialised habitat and food requirements mean that their distribution is very patchy. Western Palearctic populations declined strongly in the twentieth century, mainly because of agricultural intensification. European breeders winter in sub-Saharan Africa, and in the British Isles they are annual visitors in low and decreasing numbers, with 284 records between 1950 and 2010. There are three records for Gloucestershire:

1967: one over the Severn foreshore at Frampton on October 1st.
1995: an adult in breeding plumage in the high-tide gull roost at Slimbridge on July 28th.
1999: one that was originally found in Wiltshire moved across to the Gloucestershire part of the western section of the Cotswold Water Park from June 27th to July 4th.

Caspian Tern
Hydroprogne caspia

Caspian Terns are globally very widespread, breeding on all continents except Antarctica and South America. However the nesting colonies are very scattered; in the Western Palearctic they are restricted to a very few sites around the Baltic and Black Seas, and in inland Turkey and southern Russia. Numbers fluctuate, but have tended to decrease over most of the European range over the last 50 to 100 years. In the British Isles this is a rare but annual visitor, with 265 records between 1950 and 2010. A high proportion of sightings here are in midsummer. There have been four records in Gloucestershire, all from the Frampton–Slimbridge area:

1971: an adult in summer plumage on the estuary from August 8th to 11th was also seen at nearby Frampton sailing lake.
1976: one at the sailing lake on July 9th.
1979: a first-summer on the estuary on May 21st.
1991: an adult flying upriver on July 27th.

Roseate Tern
Sterna dougallii

This is a very scarce breeding bird in the Western Palearctic, where most colonies are in the Azores and the British Isles. There are also populations in the Pacific and Indian Oceans, and on the Atlantic coast of the Americas. British and Irish populations declined severely during the latter part of the twentieth century, but since 2000 there has been a noticeable recovery. Roseate Terns are highly oceanic at all seasons and inland records are very rare. There have been four records in Gloucestershire:

1968: one at the Severn Estuary near Slimbridge on September 28th.
1971: one at Frampton pools on May 30th.
1989: one at the western section of the Cotswold Water Park on May 11th was also seen in Wiltshire.
2002: one settled by the river near Westbury-on-Severn on May 13th flew off downriver and was watched flying past the Awre peninsula, Slimbridge and Sharpness.

Sandwich Tern
Sterna sandvicensis

Western Palearctic Sandwich Terns have a very scattered distribution on the coasts of Atlantic, North Sea and Baltic countries and further east near the shores of the Mediterranean and Black Seas. The species also extends to the Caspian region, and there are populations in the Americas. In the British Isles they are similarly scattered, with colonies of various sizes dotted around all coasts, and numbers here have fluctuated considerably, with a tendency to increase in recent years. Western European populations winter mainly in West Africa.

Mellersh mentioned only two Gloucestershire records from the nineteenth century and there were apparently none between 1900 and 1950, but Swaine reported that it was 'now noted almost annually'. This change may well have been influenced by observer effects in addition to any population increases. Between 1950 and 1980 there were regular sightings of up to six birds per year between April and September, with 'a slight preponderance in April'.

Since 1980 there have been records in every year except 1998. Total annual numbers have varied widely, with an average (median) of seven birds per year, and a maximum of about 40 in 1983. Spring birds (mostly late March until May, with a marked peak in April) have been seen in 22 years, and autumn birds (late July to early October) in 25; the seasonal grand totals are very similar, with 130 birds in autumn and 140 in spring. The largest day count in spring was nine, on April 28th 2010; autumn flocks are also usually of up to half a dozen or so, with notable exceptions of 19 off Slimbridge on October 1st 1983 and 17 off Pill House Rocks, further down the Severn Estuary, on October 4th 2009.

Most county records of this essentially maritime tern have come from the estuary, with occasional reports from the Cotswold Water Park and more rarely at the Cotswold reservoirs. There have also been a few unexpected sightings elsewhere: one flying over with roosting gulls near Littledean on March 8th 2001, two over Longborough near Stow-on-the-Wold on September 23rd 2003, and one flying over New Fancy viewpoint in the middle of the Forest of Dean on March 14th 2004.

Species accounts

Arctic Tern
Sterna paradisaea

Arctic Terns are famed for their remarkable long-distance migrations; they probably spend a higher proportion of their lifespan in daylight than any other species on Earth. They breed all around the northern hemisphere, mainly in the arctic and subarctic zones, and winter in the Southern Ocean up to the edge of the Antarctic ice. Most of the relatively small British population breeds in north and west Scotland and Ireland. There have been severe declines in recent decades, due to breeding failures linked with overfishing.

The field identification criteria for Common and Arctic Terns were only worked out relatively recently, and up to about 1990 many birds in Gloucestershire, as elsewhere, were identified only as 'commic' terns. Accordingly, in describing Arctic Terns as spring and autumn passage migrants through the county, Swaine could only say that they were 'apparently much scarcer' than Common Terns; the majority of records up to 1980 still referred to 'commics'.

More recently Arctic Terns have proved to be annual on passage, though in very variable numbers. They are much more numerous in spring, when flocks are often seen flying rapidly up the Severn Estuary and gaining height upriver of Slimbridge. The Cotswold Water Park also regularly attracts passing birds, and there are fairly frequent sightings elsewhere.

The first spring birds usually appear in the last ten days of April. Because numbers are so variable and because of the past confusion with Common Terns, a 'normal' spring passage is difficult to quantify; in springs when no large numbers of 'commics' were reported, totals of Arctics have ranged from zero (in 1995) to about 1,000 (in 2004). High totals of definite Arctics also came in 1998 (690) and 1999 (290). In many years most of the spring movement takes place over just a few days, with the maximum day total accounting for the bulk of the passage. For example in 1998, 96% of spring birds were on May 2nd, and in 1999, 86% were on April 28th. The spring passage is usually almost over by mid-May, although there are occasional records up to the middle of June.

Autumn passage by contrast is a much more leisurely process, with small groups often lingering at Frampton or the Water Park for several days. In some years none are seen at all at this season; the maximum autumn total during the post-'commic' era was 34 in 2009, and the largest flock was 21 on September 6th 2008. Usually the first autumn birds appear around early September and the passage is over by early October.

Sponsored by the Dursley Birdwatching and Preservation Society

Common Tern
Sterna hirundo

Common Terns have a widespread distribution in the northern hemisphere, breeding across much of Eurasia and North America. They winter well to the south, with much of the British and European population migrating to the inshore waters of sub-Saharan Africa. Common Terns are more wide-ranging than other terns in terms of breeding sites, and commonly nest inland. The European population is estimated to be between 220,000 and 320,000 pairs, with about 10,000 pairs in Britain.

Criteria for distinguishing Common and Arctic Terns in the field were not fully worked out until about 1980, and many older records combine the two species under 'commic' terns.

Writing in 1982, Swaine described the Common Tern as purely a passage migrant in Gloucestershire, but this was to change very shortly afterwards. In the Cotswold Water Park nesting had already begun in the Wiltshire section in 1979, and the first breeding record in our county came in 1981 when a pair raised two young just inside the border at South Cerney. Over the next few years up to three pairs attempted to breed there on a fairly regular basis, though not always successfully. During the 1990s up to seven pairs were recorded there, and the first nests were also seen in the eastern section of the Water Park. The increase then accelerated, aided by the provision of floating nesting platforms. Both numbers and monitoring effort have varied considerably from year to year, but from 2004 onwards the Water Park as a whole has supported up to 40 pairs, most of them in Gloucestershire (Gareth Harris, Cotswold Water Park Trust).

Elsewhere, a pair laid eggs at Slimbridge WWT in 1999; they failed to hatch, but a pair returned the following year and successfully raised two young. Since then regular breeding has continued here and nearby, again encouraged by the provision of nesting platforms, with up to about eight pairs in the Frampton–Slimbridge area as a whole. In 2007 a pair attempted to breed at Coombe Hill Meadows, but the nest was flooded out. There was another breeding attempt there the following year, though at least one egg was taken by a Raven. During the same season a pair with young was reported at Netheridge Nature Reserve near Hempsted, Gloucester.

Despite the establishment of this breeding population, Common Terns are still most familiar in the county as passage migrants. The majority of records of migrating birds come from the

Species accounts

2007–11 Atlas fieldwork						Gloucestershire trends						UK population trends	
Number of tetrads in which recorded (max 683)						Occupied 10 km squares (max 26)				% of tetrads in which recorded (1st hour of TTV)		UK conservation status: Amber 7	
	Total	Confirmed	Probable	Possible	Present	1968–71	1981–84	1988–91	2007–11	1988–91	2008–11	Long term	Short term
Breeding	40	14	1	9	16	0		1	5	0.2	2.2	+17%	+3%
Winter	0						0		0			–	–

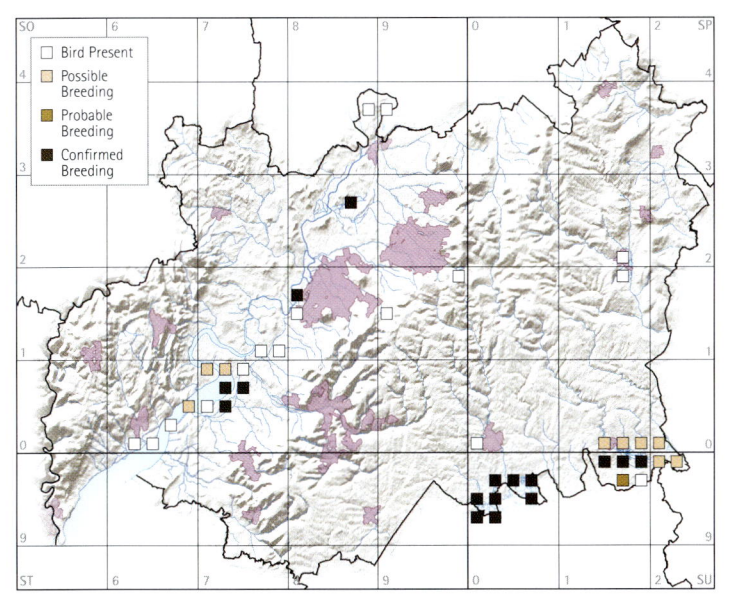

Breeding Distribution

Frampton–Slimbridge area, although they are also regular in some numbers at the Water Park. Mid-April is the usual time for the first arrivals, though there is considerable variation from year to year: one at Frampton Pools on March 22nd 1981 is the earliest ever spring record, whilst in 1985 the first reports did not come until May 4th. Most big counts are during May; the highest recent figures are 114 on May 2nd 1990, 174 on April 26th 1995 and 200 on May 13th 2001. The maximum recorded count from the Water Park is 63 in the western section on May 6th 2007.

Autumn migration is usually much less obvious, often only involving single-figure flocks; a notable exception was a movement of about 300 downriver past Slimbridge on September 11th 1992. Common Terns seem to be leaving the county earlier: in the 1980s the date of the last sighting was often in mid-October, but in recent years it has moved closer to mid-September.

There are four ringing recoveries of Common Terns affecting Gloucestershire, all involving the Water Park. Two suggest spring passage via Zeebrugge, Belgium, while a nestling ringed here in June 1984 and caught by ringers at Farmoor reservoir, Oxford on June 15th 1993 had probably dispersed away from its birthplace to breed. More unexpectedly, a 2006 nestling was found recently killed by a 'bird of prey', presumably a Peregrine, at St Paul's Cathedral, London, on August 2nd 2008.

Black Tern
Chlidonias niger

The main Palearctic breeding range of the Black Tern extends from eastern Europe to eastern central Asia. Further west the distribution is much more patchy, following declines since the nineteenth century caused by land drainage; Black Terns formerly bred regularly in Britain, where today they are passage migrants. European birds winter mainly in the coastal zone of tropical West Africa. Passage through Britain tends to be concentrated in the south and east, and is usually more pronounced in spring, although at both seasons numbers are influenced by the weather, particularly the incidence of easterly winds, and there is much year-to-year variation.

Swaine described Black Terns as irregular spring and autumn passage migrants through Gloucestershire, from April to June and from July to October (and rarely in November). There had been some large flocks on occasion, including groups of 100 or more in May 1958, August 1969 and May 1978. Since 1980 they have continue to be 'irregular', with annual totals ranging from nine in 2009 to about 330 in 1992, a year when high numbers were seen throughout the Midlands in September. Although the numbers seen in an average year have changed rather little, there has been a noticeable trend towards fewer 'big years' more recently: totals of over 100 birds were recorded in four years between 1981 and 1995, but only once between 1996 and 2010 (in 2008).

Many spring sightings are of small groups flying rapidly up the estuary whilst at both seasons, but especially in autumn, flocks stop off for varying periods at Frampton and the Cotswold Water Park. There are also occasional sightings elsewhere.

The date of the first spring sighting is rather variable but normally in the last ten days of April, and peak counts tend to be at the end of April or in the first few days of May. Total spring numbers have ranged between none (in 1982) and 150 (in 1990), and the largest flock recorded at this season was 100 on May 2nd 1990; usually no more than a dozen are seen together. In autumn the peak may fall at any time in August or September; the largest flock at this season was 220 on September 11th 1992. There were similarly high numbers in 1989 (total about 200, with 130 on August 19th); more normally the autumn total has been between 15 and 40. One at Beachley power station from November 5th to 15th 1984 was the latest ever recorded in the county.

Sponsored by Gareth Harris, Cotswold Water Park Trust

White-winged Black Tern (White-winged Tern)
Chlidonias leucopterus

White-winged Black Terns breed at shallow inland waterbodies from eastern Europe to northern China. European populations winter inland in the Afrotropics. They are annual visitors to the British Isles in spring and autumn, and are now seen so regularly that the species was removed from the national rarities list in 2006. There have been nine records in Gloucestershire, involving ten birds:

1960: a moulting adult with Black Terns off Slimbridge on August 27th.
1964: one in the Cotswold Water Park on July 23rd.
1979: an adult in almost complete breeding plumage at Slimbridge on May 18th and 19th.
1980: a juvenile at Frampton sailing lake from September 26th to 28th.
1992: two in a flock of Black Terns off Slimbridge on August 9th.
1994: a juvenile at Frampton on October 31st.
1998: a juvenile in the Water Park from August 22nd to 30th.
1999: a juvenile at Frampton sailing lake from September 15th to 25th.
2005: an adult in breeding plumage adult in the Water Park on May 14th.

Nationally, there have been records in all months from March to November, but with marked peaks in mid to late May and in late August to early September; the county records in July and late October are rather unusual.

Whiskered Tern
Chlidonias hybrida

Whiskered Terns nest on floating vegetation at inland waters in warm climates in parts of Eurasia, Australia and Africa. Western Palearctic birds migrate to tropical Africa and southern Asia, and they are annual in small numbers on passage at both seasons in the British Isles, with 177 records between 1950 and 2010. All four Gloucestershire records have been since 2000, and all have involved spring adults in breeding plumage:

2002: one which spent most of its time in the Wiltshire part of the Cotswold Water Park drifted across into Gloucestershire on April 15th.
2005: another in the Water Park from May 24th to 26th.
2008: one at Frampton from May 10th to 13th.
2009: one at Frampton sailing lake on April 25th, part of a notable influx into the country.

Auks (Alcidae)

The four auk species that have been seen in Gloucestershire all breed in colonies, often containing vast numbers, in the arctic, subarctic and temperate regions of the North Atlantic. Numbers of Puffins, Guillemots and Razorbills breeding in the British Isles have fluctuated quite widely in the past but have tended to increase, or at least to stabilise, in more recent years.

All four species are strictly marine, with broadly similar feeding behaviour, and they all disperse out to sea for the winter and only return to land to breed. As such, inland records in Britain and elsewhere involve gale-driven or otherwise disorientated birds. Most that arrive in Gloucestershire probably do not survive for long without human intervention.

Gloucestershire records are summarised in the tables. They include corpses as well as birds that were alive when found; whilst some may have washed up already dead on the shore, the majority were probably alive when they arrived in the county.

Mellersh noted that there had been 'several' records of each of the four species in the nineteenth century, but gave few figures, and Swaine gave no precise figures for Guillemot and Razorbill for the first part of the twentieth century.

The number of Guillemot records in 1980–2010 was three times the number in 1950–79. Much of the increase may well be due to observer effects, but Razorbills increased by less than twofold over the same period and Puffins and Little Auks increased only slightly. These differences perhaps reflect the differing fortunes of the breeding populations, and/or the varying incidence of severe winter gales; Puffins spend the winter further out to sea than the other two British breeding species, whilst Little Auks are only winter visitors to British waters from the Arctic.

The table of monthly totals, using all available dated records, also shows the difference between the three British breeders and Little Auk: all 18 Little Auks were between October and February with a peak in November, whilst the other species were more likely to be recorded in other months. The overall January peak is due mainly to the number of Guillemots; the other two British species do not show any marked seasonality. It seems surprising that of these dated records, only Little Auks have been found in the county in November, a month when severe gales are fairly frequent.

	1950–79	1980s	1990s	2000s	Total
Guillemot	8	9	13	3	33
Razorbill	5	2	2	4	13
Puffin	3	3	1	0	7
Little Auk	7	5	3	1	16
Total	23	19	19	8	69

	J	F	M	A	M	J	J	A	S	O	N	D	Total
Guillemot post-1950	9	2	1	3	3	1	0	3	4	3	0	4	33
Razorbill post-1950	1	0	2	1	2	0	0	0	2	4	0	1	13
Puffin post-1900	1	1	1	0	1	0	0	1	1	2	0	2	10
Little Auk post-1900	3	4	0	0	0	0	0	0	0	2	7	2	18
Total	14	7	4	4	6	1	0	4	7	11	7	9	74

Guillemot (Common Murre)
Uria aalge

Of the 33 birds since 1950, 11 were dead when found, two were seen to be killed by Peregrines, one was later found dead, and several were reported as oiled, weak or sick-looking. Though most have been on the Severn Estuary, wind-blown birds have been found at Gloucester (May 1970) and Redmarley D'Abitot near Newent (June 1969).

A Guillemot ringed as an adult at Sule Skerry in Orkney in June 1989 was found dead at Lydney Harbour on March 5th 1990.

Razorbill
Alca torda

Swaine knew of only four dated records of live birds in the county, including two found inland, in Stroud on October 21st 1957 (erroneously recorded as 1959 by Swaine), and at Prestbury, Cheltenham in September 1962. All other twentieth-century records have been either at the Severn Estuary, or close by. Two were found dead, and live birds were variously reported as sick, weak, taken into care or 'immediately drowned by gulls'.

Little Auk
Alle alle

Little Auks are regular in winter in the North Sea, but less common off the western coasts of the British Isles. Mellersh noted about ten Gloucestershire records between 1850 and 1900, while Swaine cited reports of 'several' in the Severn Vale after a violent storm in October 1841, and singles in 1912 and 1943.

At least three twentieth-century birds were found dead, one was seen to be killed by a Peregrine, at least another two died shortly after being found, and most of the remainder were in poor condition. All have been singles apart from the 1841 records, although three were reported from different localities in a bad 'wreck' in February 1950. Most records have been at or near the Severn Estuary, but some have been found 'inland' as far as Little Rissington near the Oxfordshire border and Bourton-on-the-Water. One found in a field of sprouts near Chipping Campden on November 21st 1995 was taken to Humberside and released.

Puffin (Atlantic Puffin)
Fratercula arctica

Swaine cited three records between 1900 and 1949. Only three of the total of ten records since 1900 were by the Severn (two near Frampton and one at nearby Epney); the others were at various Cotswold localities. None was found dead, but most were moribund or clearly in poor condition; two notable exceptions were the Epney bird, which flew upriver with the Severn Bore on October 9th 1987, and one seen flying along the Gloucester and Sharpness Canal near Frampton on May 12th in the same year. One found on Minchinhampton Common near Stroud in February 1996 was taken into care and was later flown to the Channel Islands by the BBC to be released.

Feral Pigeon (Rock Dove)
Columba livia

The Feral Pigeon, in common with all domestic pigeons, derives from the wild Rock Doves of the Western Palearctic and now has a near-global distribution, exploiting almost all types of human settlements and becoming so familiar that it is often taken for granted and ignored. Pigeons were widely kept for food from pre-Roman times and more recently the selective breeding associated with the sports of homing and racing has produced a plethora of plumage types. With individuals escaping from dovecotes or becoming lost after release, feral populations formed around human habitation and were certainly known in London by the fourteenth century. As numbers grew some infiltrated the remaining wild Rock Dove populations, while some wild birds forsook the cliffs to join feral flocks in the comfort of the towns, making it impossible to separate 'wild' and 'feral' birds in any meaningful way; indeed some ornithologists argue that any such distinction is erroneous. Further difficulties arise because wild Rock Doves were not widely recognised as being different from Stock Doves until the late eighteenth century (1875–1900 Atlas), and because even today Feral Pigeons go unrecorded by many birders. In Britain, Rock Doves were originally confined to coastal cliffs, and some outcrops and quarries in inland Wales. Until the nineteenth century they were regular on the south coast and even common in the south-west, but they withdrew to increasingly remote areas of north-west Scotland by the mid-twentieth century, and even there completely 'pure' wild birds arguably no longer existed by then. Despite its familiarity then, the Feral Pigeon joined our wild avifauna almost furtively.

Its nesting crevices are now on buildings and under bridges, and it supplements its natural diet of seeds with the scraps and leavings of its human companions. This ready supply of food means that energy can be expended on breeding rather than foraging, and up to five clutches of eggs are laid per year, all year round, and the young can breed from the age of six months. The only limiting factor is the availability of nest sites, so there is always a surplus population ready to replace breeding birds killed by humans or cats, or preyed on by the growing urban Peregrine population.

Between the 1968–72 and 1988–91 Breeding Atlases, numbers in the British Isles possibly doubled to perhaps 200,000 pairs as birds expanded into more rural areas; there was an overall increase of 39% in occupied 10 km squares, but in England the increase was 69%. The national BBS hints at a slight decline in numbers since 2004.

Given its preferred habitat, it is unlikely that the wild Rock Dove ever bred in Gloucestershire. Witchell & Strugnell referred to it as being 'more abundant on the Cotteswolds, where it nests, than in the vale', but this was corrected by Mellersh, who wrote, 'there are no Rock Doves in the county … only tame pigeons … which have returned to a wild state, or Stock Doves.' Mellersh also discounted a report of nesting Rock Doves on the Wye cliffs in the 1870s.

Swaine did not treat the species at all, and nor did the 1983–87 Cotswolds Atlas. The second Cotswolds Atlas made the attempt and found it 'breeding in most towns and many farms, although their occurrence in villages is best described as patchy' in 2003–07, but it then warned that the results reflected birdwatchers' differing attitudes to the species more than its real distribution. County bird reports did not include Feral Pigeon before 1995 and since then there have been only intermittent counts of up to 200 birds in Gloucester and Cheltenham and up to 400 at Sharpness Docks. In the current survey the species was found in about a third of tetrads in both seasons. The highest TTV counts, of 190 birds in winter and 94 in summer, were both from the Gloucester Docks area. The maps clearly show a general avoidance of the Forest of Dean and the high Cotswolds; the greatest numbers and highest levels of confirmed breeding are found in the urban areas and lower-lying villages.

Improved reporting of this species in the county in future would enable better population monitoring than has been the case to date.

Sponsored by P A Tyers

Species accounts

	2007–11 Atlas fieldwork					Gloucestershire trends						UK population trends	
	Number of tetrads in which recorded (max 683)					Occupied 10 km squares (max 26)				% of tetrads in which recorded (1st hour of TTV)		UK conservation status: **Green**	
	Total	Confirmed	Probable	Possible	Present	1968–71	1981–84	1988–91	2007–11	1988–91	2008–11	Long term	Short term
Breeding	227	39	58	81	49	7		24	24	23.9	12.8	–	–8%
Winter	241						22		25			–	–

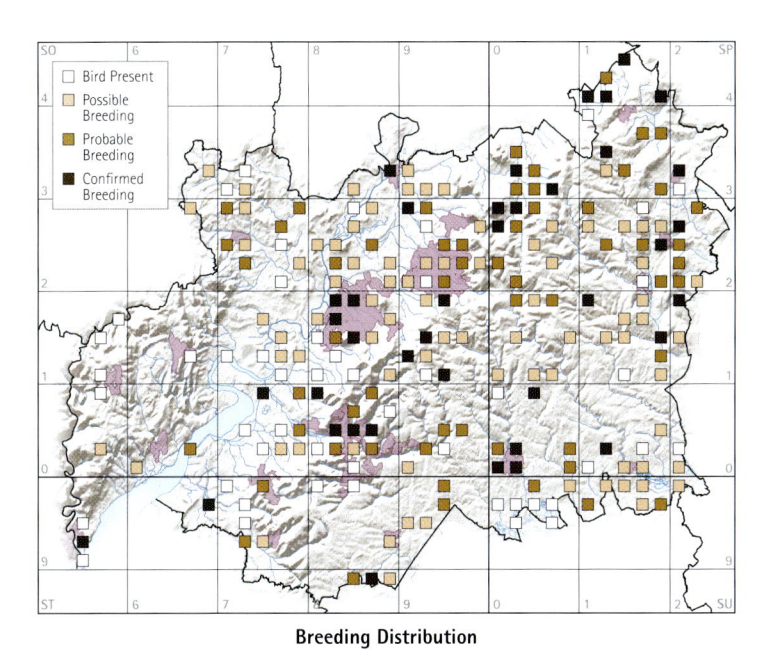

Breeding Distribution

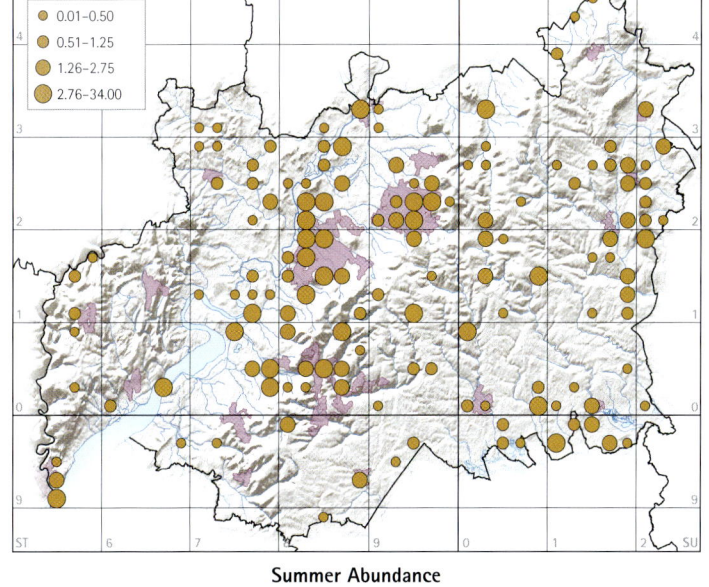

Summer Abundance

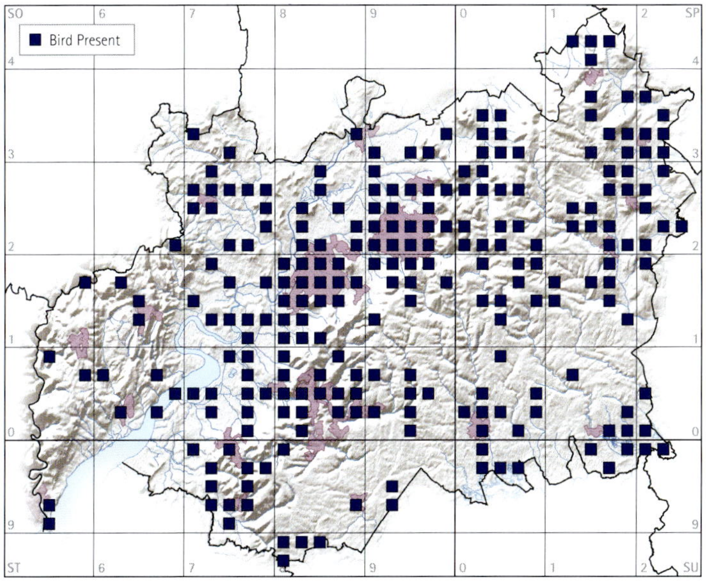

Winter Distribution

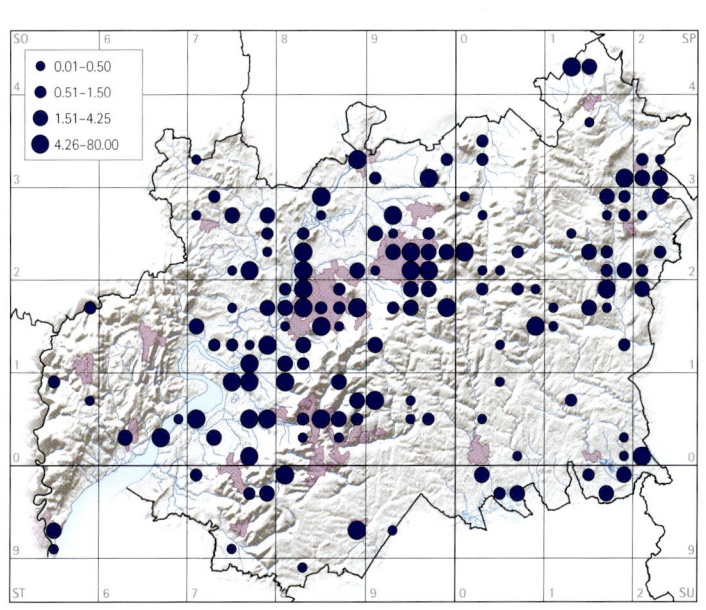

Winter Abundance

Stock Dove
Columba oenas

The Stock Dove breeds throughout most of Europe except in Iceland and northern Fennoscandia. It also occurs in north-west Africa and western Asia. Birds in the west and south of the range are resident, but those breeding further north and east migrate to the Mediterranean region for the winter. Britain is estimated to hold about 309,000 breeding pairs, which is a high proportion of the estimated 600,000 pairs in Europe. The population here increased steadily up to the 1930s but there was a severe decline from 1950 associated with toxic seed dressings, followed by a fairly strong recovery in more recent decades.

Stock Dove nest sites are mostly in tree-holes, but they will also use rock crevices, derelict buildings, barns or even rabbit holes in areas where few other options are available and, like Jackdaws, they also take readily to nest-boxes, such as those designed for owls or Kestrels. As seed-eaters, they prefer nesting sites that are within foraging range of arable land.

Stock Doves are often noticeable by their calls and display flights, but confirming breeding is not always easy as the plumage of juveniles, unless seen closely, is not unlike that of the adults. Most 'confirmed' breeding records during the atlas survey related to adults seen entering nest sites.

Swaine described the Stock Dove as a common resident in Gloucestershire around 1980, probably more plentiful at that time than formerly, and breeding in all parts of the county. He also suggested that birds from further north and east might winter in the county, and mentions a huge flock of up to 1,500 at Didbrook near Winchcombe during the severe weather of February 1979.

Since then, counts of well over 100 birds have been recorded in most years, with the majority of these coming from the lower Severn Vale or the Cotswolds, and mostly during the early spring period from February to April. The highest counts have been 300 at Ebworth in February 1987, 350 at Epney in March 1995 and 700 at Hasfield Ham in February 2000. Other sites in the Vale that regularly attract good numbers include Minsterworth Ham, the Rodley area and Lydney New Grounds (though 'observer effects' may be involved here, as these sites are more popular with birdwatchers than some other, similar areas of farmland in the county). During the current atlas fieldwork the maximum winter TTV count was 122 in December 2008 in tetrad SO91S at Cowley on the Cotswolds, south of Cheltenham.

The maps show that Stock Doves are very widespread in the county at both seasons. The winter abundance map is distinctly patchy, possibly reflecting localised concentrations on temporary or isolated sources of food, particularly stubble fields, unharvested crops or ploughed land. The breeding season abundance map reveals lower densities in the Forest of Dean and in built-up areas, probably due to the lack of arable farmland, and also in parts of the Cotswolds, possibly reflecting a local scarcity of nesting sites. In optimal conditions Stock Doves can reach quite high breeding densities: for example in 1990 as many as 53 pairs bred at Boxbush Farm, Longhope, where nest-boxes were provided.

Although the second Cotswolds Atlas suggested that there had 'probably been a real decrease in breeding density' in that part of the county between 1987 and 2007, BBS figures for the whole of Gloucestershire reveal a trend of increasing numbers, with the average annual occupancy of survey squares rising from about 40% between 1994 and 2002 to about 55% from 2003 to 2010.

British Stock Doves are almost all sedentary, and rather few ringed here have been recovered abroad. Similarly, most ringing recoveries involving Gloucestershire relate to movements within the county. A notable exception concerns a nestling ringed at Longhope on August 25th 2005 and shot at Monsegur in south-west France on November 7th that year, a movement of 932 km south.

Sponsored by the Dursley Birdwatching and Preservation Society

Species accounts 247

	2007-11 Atlas fieldwork					Gloucestershire trends					UK population trends	
	Number of tetrads in which recorded (max 683)					Occupied 10 km squares (max 26)				% of tetrads in which recorded (1st hour of TTV)		UK conservation status: **Amber 8**	
	Total	Confirmed	Probable	Possible	Present	1968-71	1981-84	1988-91	2007-11	1988-91	2008-11	Long term	Short term
Breeding	634	109	354	144	27	25		26	26	60.4	54.9	+83%	+4%
Winter	556						26		26			–	–

Breeding Distribution

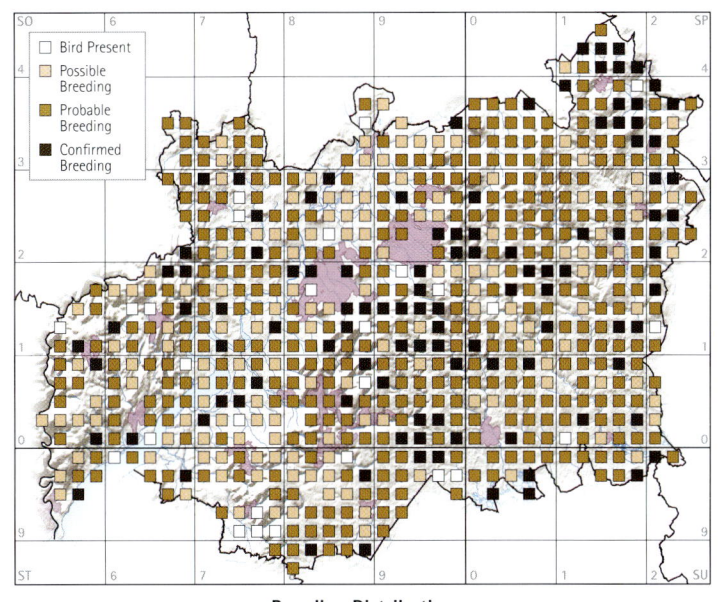

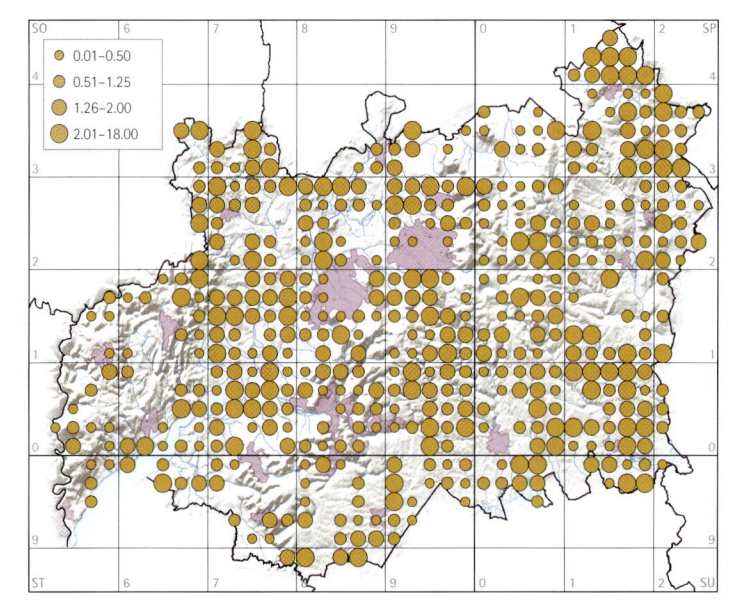

Summer Abundance

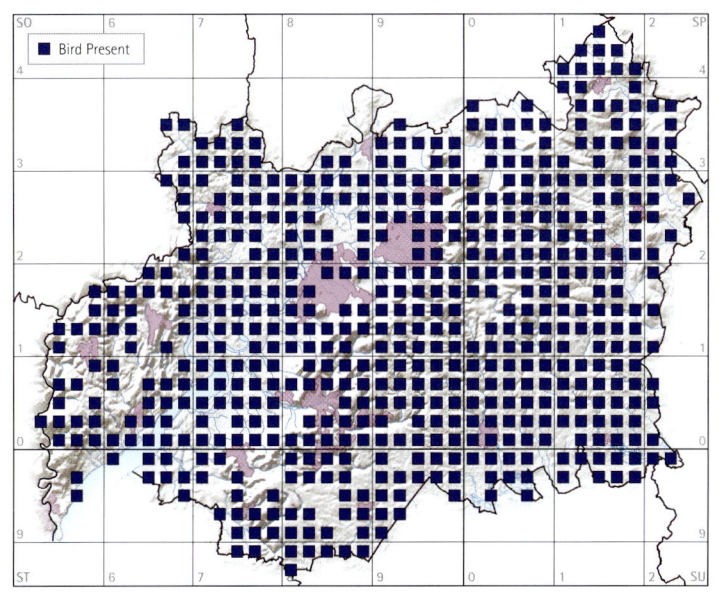

Winter Distribution

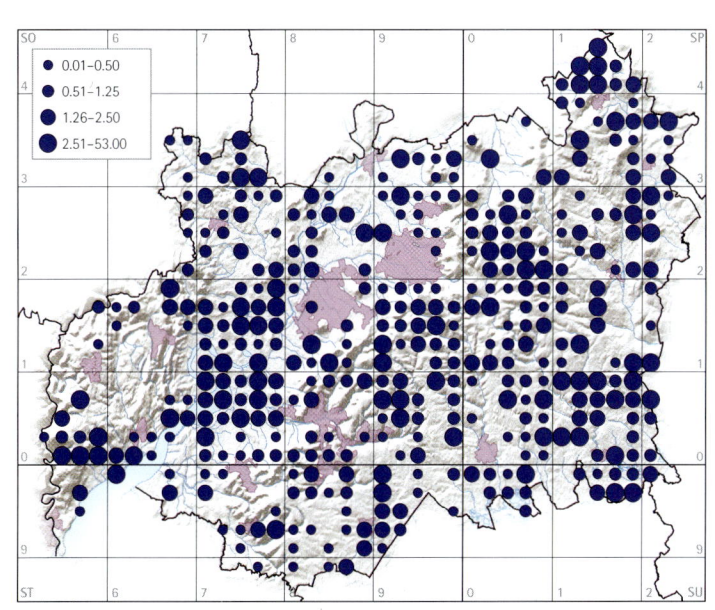

Winter Abundance

Woodpigeon (Common Wood Pigeon)
Columba palumbus

The Woodpigeon is one of the most successful and familiar of British birds and it also breeds across most of Europe, though only occasionally in Iceland. Further afield, its range extends to western Siberia, the Middle East and north-west Africa. Most eastern and northern populations are migratory, retreating south and west for the winter. The European summer population numbers between 8 and 13 million pairs, with 2.5 to 3 million pairs in Britain.

A steady increase has been evident across Europe as a whole since 1980, while numbers in the British Isles have risen considerably since the mid-1970s. The national BBS has registered a continued increase since 1994, except in Scotland where numbers have stabilised. The increase has been attributed to the spread of intensive agriculture and particularly of oil-seed rape, a food source which has helped to improve winter survival rates (Inglis *et al.* 1990). Woodpigeons have also colonised urban habitats, where they will take advantage of garden feeding stations. Readily available food sources allow them to breed at all times of the year, though the vast majority do so between May and September.

Swaine described the Woodpigeon as an abundant resident nesting in all parts of Gloucestershire and mentioned several flocks of 3,000 or more, and recent surveys confirm how ubiquitous it has become. It was recorded in very close to 100% of tetrads during the fieldwork for the 1983–87 and 2003–07 Cotswolds Atlases, and also in the county as a whole during the current atlas survey, when it proved to be the most abundantly recorded species at both seasons (see p. 46). It has been seen in 100% of Gloucestershire BBS squares every year since 1994.

The summer map shows comparatively few tetrads without confirmed or probable breeding and many of these are in areas with fewer observers, such as parts of the Forest of Dean. It is noticeable that there were many confirmed breeding records in the main urban areas. It also seems probable that out-of-season breeding is more likely in the urban areas where there are more reliable food supplies and slightly higher temperatures. A bird was sitting tight on a nest at Prestbury, Cheltenham on December 11th 2007.

Wintering Woodpigeons also occur in all parts of the county, but numbers are clearly lower in the Forest of Dean where food supplies are perhaps more limited, particularly in conifer plantations. Wintering flocks of 1,000 or more have been recorded annually in recent years, usually in the Cotswolds or the Thames Area but also in the Severn Vale. The largest Cotswold concentrations have included 3,000 at Sheepscombe near Stroud in early January 2005 and 2,500 at Compton Abdale near Northleach in February 2009. In the Thames Area, a flock of 3,500 was at Fairford in late December 2010. The highest atlas TTV count was of about 1,270 birds in SO91V near the Cotswold village of Colesbourne in December 2009.

However the largest numbers are often reported during the autumn, and monthly totals show a huge peak in November (see graph), as migrants pass through the county in a generally south-westerly direction. For example, flocks amounting to about 10,000 birds passed over North Nibley on the Cotswolds scarp near Dursley on October 23rd 2005, whilst at Pope's Hill on the east edge of the Forest of Dean, 5,000 moved south-west in just 30 minutes on November 19th 2008 and two days' movements here in early November of the following year totalled around 10,000 birds. These movements suggest that at least some of our winter birds are migrants from elsewhere. Most probably originate from more northerly parts of Britain, though some birds from the near Continent, particularly the Low Countries, are known to winter in Britain, and at the same time a number of our birds move south into France.

There had only been 15 ringing recoveries of Woodpigeons involving Gloucestershire up to 2010, and 11 of those related to movements within the county. However the remaining four do help to shed some light on their migrations: three birds ringed in Oxfordshire, Warwickshire and Shropshire were found here, and a nestling ringed at Hasfield Ham in June 2005 was found dead on the Normandy coast of France in November that year.

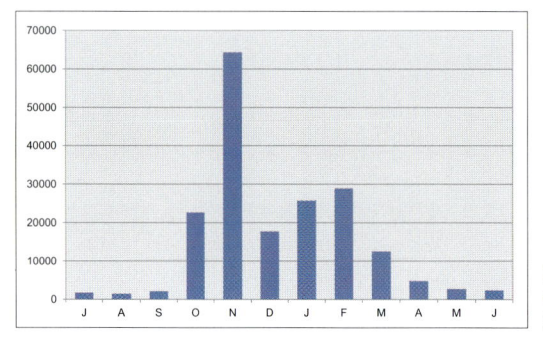

Woodpigeon numbers reported 2003–10, by month.

Sponsored by Chris Britton

Species accounts

2007–11 Atlas fieldwork					Gloucestershire trends						UK population trends		
Number of tetrads in which recorded (max 683)					Occupied 10 km squares (max 26)				% of tetrads in which recorded (1st hour of TTV)		UK conservation status: Green		
	Total	Confirmed	Probable	Possible	Present	1968–71	1981–84	1988–91	2007–11	1988–91	2008–11	Long term	Short term
Breeding	682	429	202	45	6	0		26	26	100.0	99.9	+130%	+38%
Winter	682						26	26				–	–

Breeding Distribution

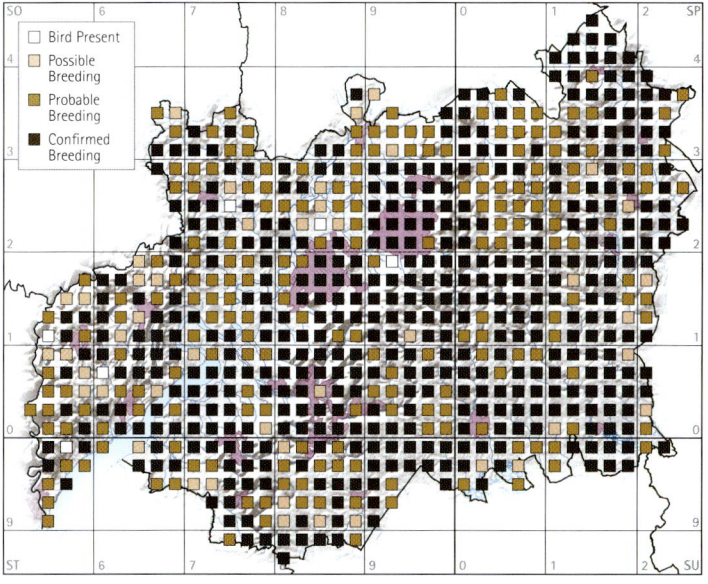

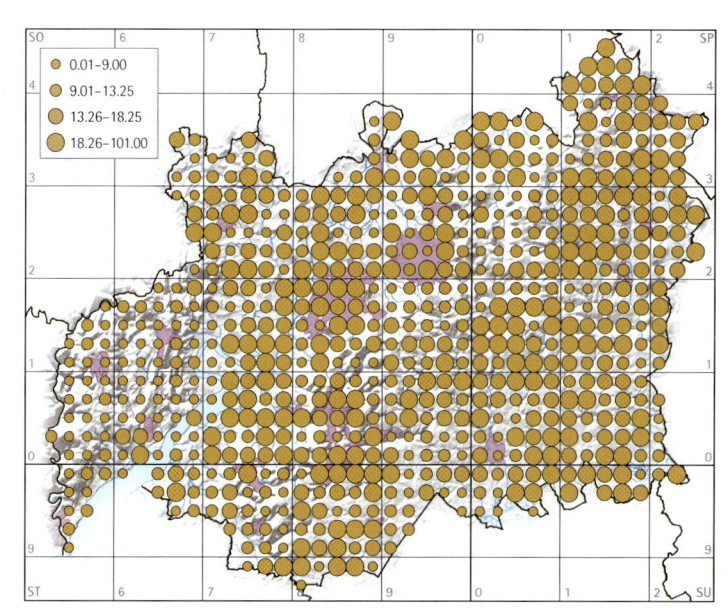

Summer Abundance

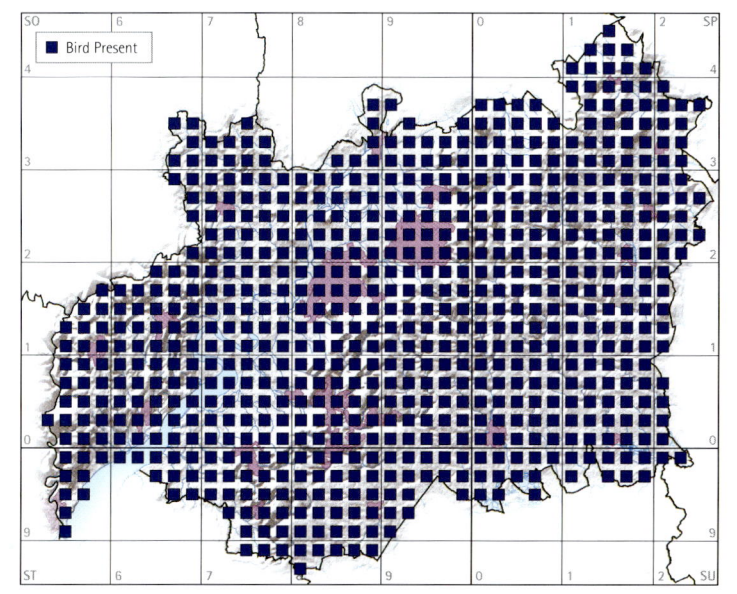

Winter Distribution

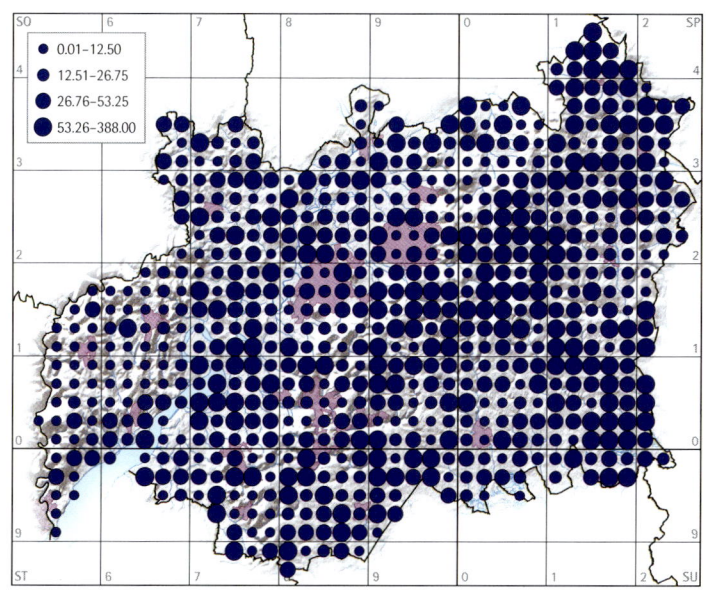

Winter Abundance

Collared Dove (Eurasian Collared Dove)
Streptopelia decaocto

Eighty years ago the Collared Dove was essentially a bird of the Middle East and northern India, but during the 1930s it began an astonishing north-westward expansion, initially at an average rate of over 40 km per year. By 1970 it had colonised 2.5 million square kilometres of Europe.

In the British Isles the first Collared Dove was recorded in 1952 in Lincolnshire and the first breeding record came three years later in Norfolk. Between 1955 and 1965 numbers in Britain doubled every year to 3,000 pairs, and by 1966 it had bred in every English county and was regarded as common in many areas. By the time of the 1988-91 Breeding Atlas there were about 200,000 pairs and the range had consolidated over the whole country. The population growth has since been slowing and has possibly stalled since 2005, but there are now about 300,000 pairs in Britain.

In Europe more than in its original range, the species associates closely with human habitation, especially where grain is left to lie, and it is commonest around docks, farmsteads, villages and suburbs. Its repetitive calling makes it an easy species to locate. In Britain the breeding season extends from February to October and up to five broods may be raised each year, with the female often still feeding young while already incubating the next clutch of eggs. Nevertheless, of over 1,000 county atlas records for which a breeding code was provided, only 10% were 'confirmed', mostly involving fledged young. This low percentage perhaps reflects the fact that these young look very similar to their parents.

The first records for Gloucestershire came in 1961 with six birds at Gloucester Docks, where numbers had risen to over 50 two years later. Breeding was first confirmed in 1963 at the docks, Slimbridge, Sherborne and Coln St Aldwyns, and by 1968 Collared Doves had colonised the whole county, though they were still scarce in the Forest of Dean. Maximum counts at Slimbridge rose from 200 in 1966 to 900 in 1974. In some subsequent years so few records were received that the GBR did not even mention the species, but the local population continued to consolidate: the 1983-87 Cotswolds Atlas recorded it in 75% of tetrads and that of 2003-07 in over 83%, very similar to the figure for the whole county during the current atlas survey. Since 1994, Gloucestershire BBS figures have fluctuated quite widely but with no discernible overall trends: Collared Doves were found in an average of 52% of study squares both between 1994 and 2002 and between 2003 and 2010.

The maps show that the species' distribution is effectively the same throughout the year, extending over most of the county but with noticeably lower densities in areas with the sparsest human habitation, on the higher ground of the Cotswolds and in the Forest of Dean.

Flocks have become very much smaller in recent years as the flour and grain storage facilities at the county's docks have become tidier or ceased to operate and the amount of spilt grain on farms has declined. Fewer than five flocks of more than 40 birds have been recorded in the last decade, the maximum being 74 at Berkeley in November 2006. During the current atlas fieldwork the highest TTV count was 50, in tetrad ST69P near Berkeley power station in November 2007. In some recent years running up to this survey only one or two breeding records were submitted to the GBR, which says less about the Collared Dove than it does about observers' loss of enthusiasm for a species which was completely unknown here until 50 years ago.

Of about 30 ringing recoveries involving Gloucestershire up to 2010 nearly half relate to movements within the county. The four longest documented movements, to southern and central Scotland (three) and western Ireland, all took place between 1967 and 1974, during the period of rapid colonisation of the British Isles. In addition, one ringed on the Channel Islands in February 1977 was found dead at Slimbridge in June that year.

Sponsored by J S Burrows

Species accounts 251

	2007–11 Atlas fieldwork					Gloucestershire trends					UK population trends		
	Number of tetrads in which recorded (max 683)					Occupied 10 km squares (max 26)				% of tetrads in which recorded (1st hour of TTV)		*UK conservation status:* **Green**	
	Total	Confirmed	Probable	Possible	Present	1968–71	1981–84	1988–91	2007–11	1988–91	2008–11	Long term	Short term
Breeding	585	149	284	121	31	26		26	26	59.6	56.2	+400%	+25%
Winter	561						26		26			–	–

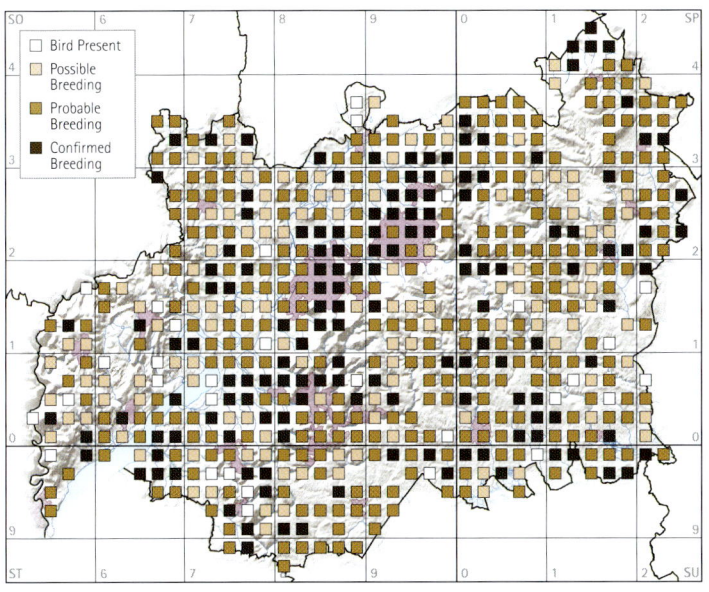

Breeding Distribution

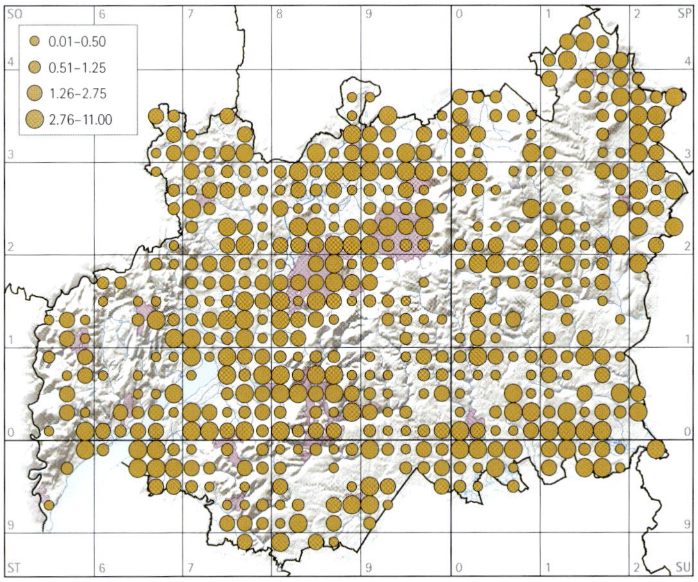

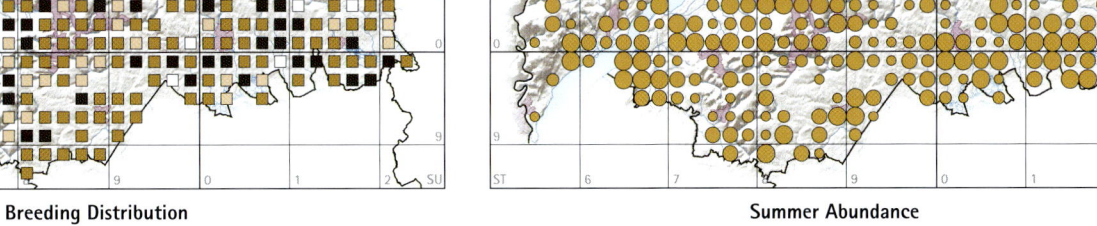

Summer Abundance

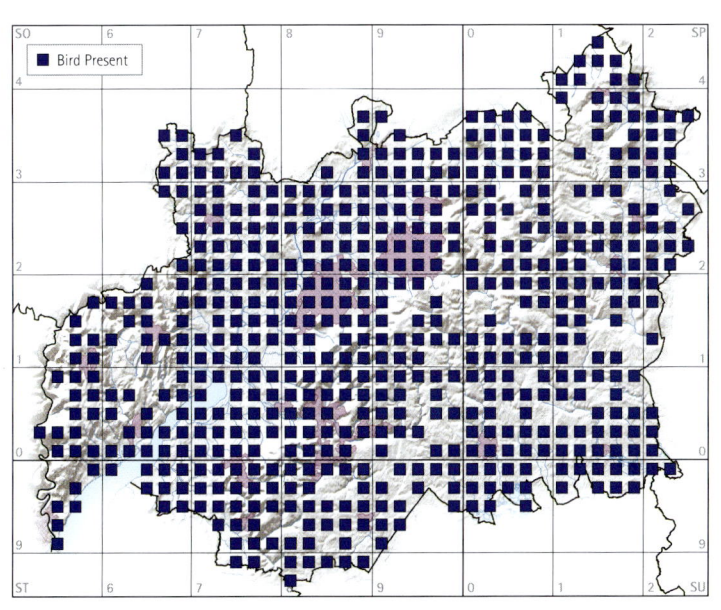

Winter Distribution

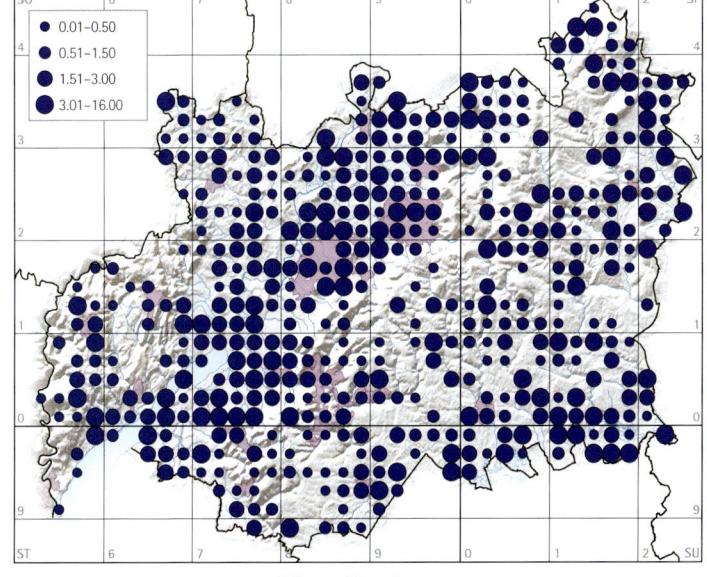

Winter Abundance

Turtle Dove (European Turtle Dove)
Streptopelia turtur

The Turtle Dove is a widespread summer visitor to much of Europe, apart from northern regions such as Iceland and Fennoscandia. Its breeding range also includes parts of North Africa, the Middle East and central Asia. It winters south of the Sahara, where it often forms huge roosts in favoured areas. The European population is upwards of 2.5 million pairs. In the British Isles it has occasionally bred in Scotland and Ireland, but its main range has always been restricted to England and Wales, where its soft, purring song is one of the most evocative sounds of summer.

The Turtle Dove is one of the most rapidly declining species in Europe. This decline, which first became evident during the late 1970s, is attributed to agricultural intensification, climatic changes and hunting (often illegal) during its migration through southern parts of Europe. The British population was estimated at 44,000 pairs in 2000, but has continued to decrease.

Swaine considered Turtle Doves to be 'not uncommon, but rather sparsely distributed' in Gloucestershire. He described them as breeding quite commonly in the Forest of Dean and as locally numerous in parts of the Severn Vale, the Cotswolds and the Thames Area. Flocks of up to 40 had been recorded during the 1960s, but such numbers had not been reported since and there had been some evidence of a decline during the 1970s. Swaine's account therefore

Sponsored by Fraser Hart and Jennifer Rogers

Species accounts

	2007–11 Atlas fieldwork					Gloucestershire trends						UK population trends	
	Number of tetrads in which recorded (max 683)					Occupied 10 km squares (max 26)				% of tetrads in which recorded (1st hour of TTV)		UK conservation status: **Red 3**	
	Total	Confirmed	Probable	Possible	Present	1968–71	1981–84	1988–91	2007–11	1988–91	2008–11	Long term	Short term
Breeding	53	3	9	25	16	26		17	10	4.7	1.5	–91%	–74%
Winter	1						0		1			–	–

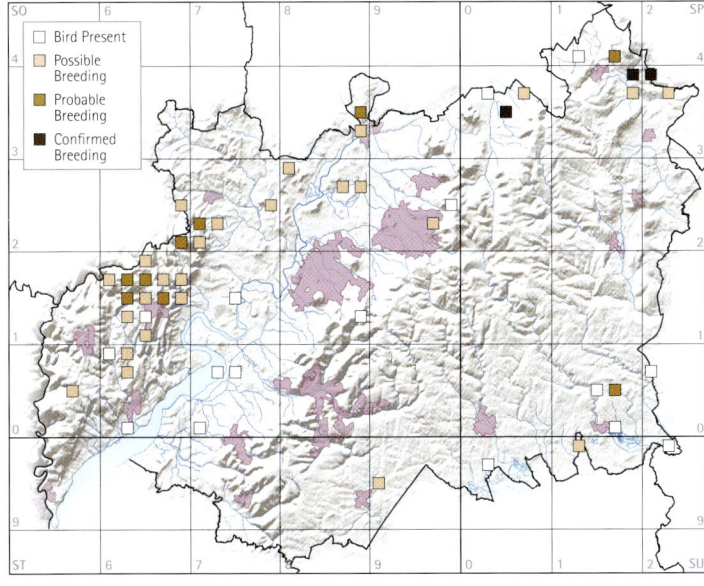

Breeding Distribution

hints at the beginning of the catastrophic population crash that continues to this day. The national decline has been accompanied by a range contraction and Turtle Doves no longer breed in Wales, so Gloucestershire now lies on the edge of its British and European distribution.

During the 1980s this remained a widespread breeding species in the county and it was evidently still familiar enough to be under-reported by some observers. By 1988 however the GBR was acknowledging a severe decline and requested that all records be submitted. Despite some annual fluctuations the demise accelerated during the 1990s: at the Nagshead RSPB reserve 13 pairs were located in 1992, but only 'one or two' by 1995. Frampton Pools, a traditional breeding site, had no records at all in 2000 and the following year the Cotswold Water Park also drew a blank. The most recent flock of any size recorded in the county was one of seven birds near Naunton on the Cotswolds in August 2000. The 2003–07 Cotswolds Atlas recorded Turtle Doves in less than 8% of tetrads, compared to 30% in 1983–87. In the same area of the county during the current atlas survey they were located in only 3% of tetrads, although the only three confirmed breeding records for Gloucestershire were from the northern Cotswolds. Most of the remaining Turtle Doves in the county are confined to the Forest of Dean, where they seem to prefer dense, thicket-stage plantations or regrowth for nesting. There were just a few potential breeding records from the upper Vale and elsewhere during the atlas fieldwork. There may be as few as ten or a dozen nesting pairs in the county at present and it seems very likely that the Turtle Dove will soon be lost as a breeding bird.

The earliest spring arrival date on record in the county during the last few decades was fairly recent, on April 18th 2003 at Rudford near Highnam. More usually the first spring record is during the last few days of the month. In some years there are no autumn records later than August, and sightings after mid-September are unusual. However, the few October records include one notable example of late passage when a total of 42 were counted moving south-west at Frampton Pools during the mid-afternoon of October 8th 1983. One which paused briefly at Ebworth Woods, Sheepscombe on October 11th 1988 is the latest on record.

A few Turtle Doves occasionally winter in Europe, and there are two recent county records at this season: one was seen at The Moors, Slimbridge on January 8th 1985, and one visited a garden at Berkeley with Collared Doves between November 6th 2008 and March 30th 2009.

Cuckoo (Common Cuckoo)
Cuculus canorus

The song of the Cuckoo is arguably the best-known 'wild' sound in Britain, but sadly it no longer heralds the spring as widely as it did in the past; this is a species in headlong decline.

Cuckoos breed widely in all climatic zones in the Western Palearctic except for arctic tundra and desert. They are also widespread in Asia, and they winter in Africa, mainly south of the equator. Their breeding distribution depends on that of their host species, and they are spread thinly across a range of different habitats; in Britain they mainly occupy rough grassland and moorland (where their principal host is the Meadow Pipit), bushy areas and scrub (Dunnock) and reed-beds (Reed Warbler).

Cuckoos have suffered long-term declines across much of their European range, perhaps because of changes in land management practices. Their main food is large caterpillars, and populations of moths and butterflies are known to have declined in recent decades. Pressures from human activities in the wintering quarters may also be detrimental and a BTO radio-tracking study, recently begun, aims to shed more light on the wintering areas and requirements of the species.

At the time of the 1988–91 Breeding Atlas the decline was only moderate, but since then ongoing surveys such as BBS have revealed a dramatic population crash. This appears to be nowhere worse than in south-west England, where there was a fall of 73% between 1995 and 2009. On the other hand, the evidence from the current national atlas and BBS is that although the dramatic declines are continuing in the whole of southern and eastern Britain, Cuckoo populations are faring much better in the north, especially in Scotland (see Spotted Flycatcher, p. 366, for possible explanations).

Swaine described Cuckoos as widespread, being recorded in all parts of Gloucestershire in a variety of habitats, but added that there had been a general decline since about 1955. He also listed 22 host species recorded in the county, including Nightingale, Marsh Warbler and Spotted Flycatcher, and mentioned a juvenile Cuckoo in the Nagshead RSPB reserve, Forest of Dean, that was being fed by both a Wren and a female Pied Flycatcher on the same day in 1978!

In Gloucestershire the first Cuckoos are usually heard in the second week of April (earliest record April 2nd 1989), and by the end of June most adults have left the breeding areas. Juveniles also migrate early and the vast majority have left the county by early September; the latest date on record is October 6th 1985. As they are nest parasites it is not easy to record their breeding behaviour; most atlas records refer to singing birds or sometimes to territorial interactions, and it was rare to confirm breeding during the fieldwork. However there were a few occasions when young birds were seen being fed by their host parents, and one lucky observer saw a female Cuckoo carrying a host's egg in her bill, having just replaced it with one of her own.

The 2003–07 Cotswolds Atlas described the Cuckoo as a species that had suffered one of the biggest declines over the previous 20 years, and the results of the current atlas fieldwork give no grounds for optimism; numbers in the county are evidently still falling in line with the national pattern. In fact the map is likely to give an overoptimistic impression of their distribution, as the far-carrying song and restless, mobile habits mean that the same bird is likely to be recorded independently by different observers. In addition, some migrating birds probably sing as they pass through the county. Moreover, the map shows all records over the four-year atlas survey period and therefore exaggerates the distribution in any single year; there were only 18 tetrads in which Cuckoos were recorded in all four years. The maps show that the Cleeve Hill area still holds breeding Cuckoos, where they probably use Meadow Pipits as their host species, and there are also records in the more rural parts of the Severn Vale, where the main host could well be Reed Warbler. However, in terms of density of records the stronghold appears to be the Forest of Dean and the areas to the north around Newent and the Herefordshire border, where Dunnocks are likely to be the main hosts. In 2011 at Coombe Hill a young Cuckoo was seen being fed by a Reed Bunting, a rather unusual host species.

Sponsored by the Cheltenham Bird Club

Species accounts

2007–11 Atlas fieldwork					Gloucestershire trends						UK population trends		
Number of tetrads in which recorded (max 683)					*Occupied 10 km squares (max 26)*				*% of tetrads in which recorded (1st hour of TTV)*		*UK conservation status:* **Red 3**	
	Total	Confirmed	Probable	Possible	Present	1968–71	1981–84	1988–91	2007–11	1988–91	2008–11	Long term	Short term
Breeding	271	6	40	189	36	26		26	25	43.0	12.2	–61%	–48%
Winter	0						0		0			–	–

Breeding Distribution

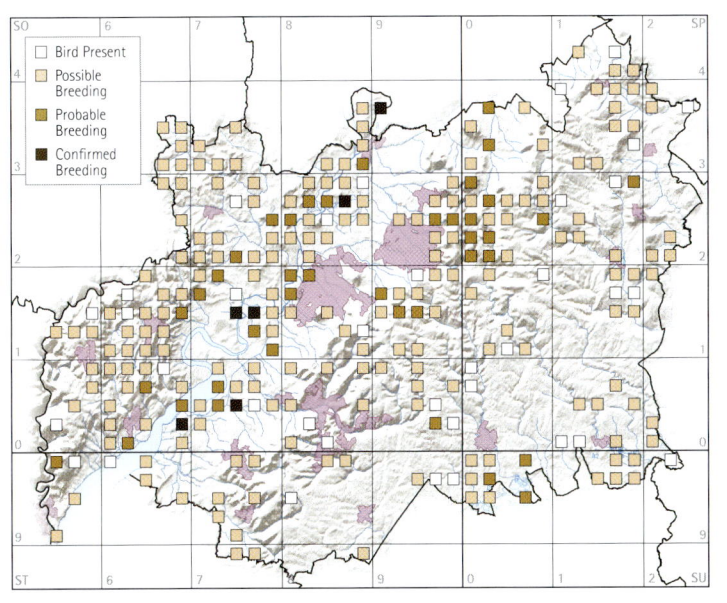

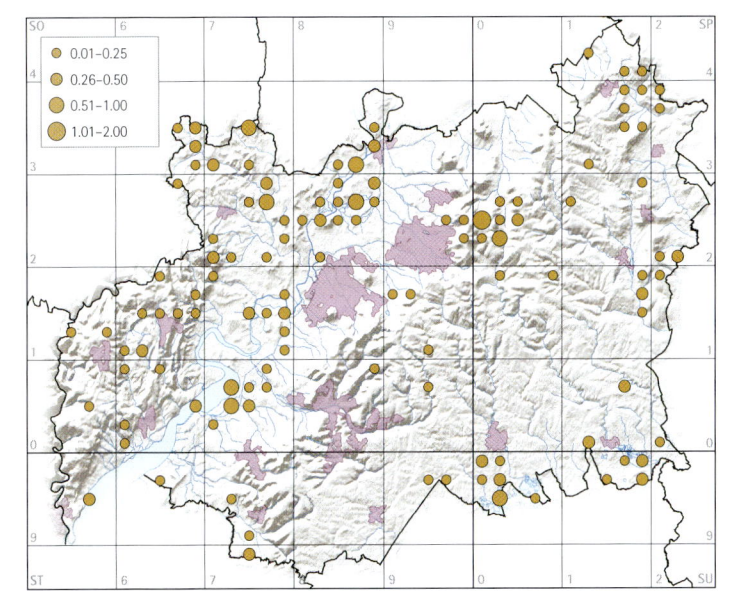

Summer Abundance

Juvenile Cuckoo being fed by a Reed Warbler.

Barn Owl
Tyto alba

Barn Owls have a very wide global distribution but are mostly confined to warmer climatic zones. Their British range has extended northwards in recent decades to include northern Scotland, but the British Isles remain firmly on the northern edge of their distribution and they can suffer very high mortality here during cold winter weather. In 1998 it was estimated that 93% of the British population bred at an altitude of 150 m or below, usually in warm, low-lying river valleys (Shawyer 1998). They nest in tree cavities and on cliff faces as well as in barns and other buildings, and readily use nest-boxes. Their prey consists mainly of small mammals, and they need largely open habitats in which to hunt; this may include arable farmland, riverside or lakeside vegetation and woodland edge, as well as rough grassland.

Barn Owls are not easy to survey. Like most owls they are largely nocturnal, and they are also less vocal than the other species. They are more likely to be recorded in winter, when the days are shorter and they tend to hunt more during daylight. On the other hand, atlas fieldworkers were sometimes told about the presence of Barn Owls by landowners, often resulting in a confirmed breeding record.

British Barn Owl populations declined markedly in the twentieth century as a result of the intensification of farming, in particular losses of habitat and the use of pesticides. The 1988–91 Breeding Atlas highlighted continuing declines, with the population estimated at just 4,400 pairs. Since then numbers have recovered strongly, perhaps as a result of agri-environment schemes (notably wider field margins and set-aside) and the provision of nest-boxes.

The fact-box shows that Gloucestershire has followed this national pattern, but the raw figures may not do justice to the scale of either the decline or the subsequent recovery. For example the 1983–87 Cotswolds Atlas estimated that there were 'almost certainly less than ten pairs' in the North Cotswolds in an average year during the 1980s, whereas 20 years later there were estimated to be 'approaching 50 pairs'. The welcome recovery of this charismatic bird in Gloucestershire may be due in part to efforts in Wiltshire, where the Salisbury Plain area in particular has seen a spectacular rise in numbers since a major nest-box scheme began in the 1980s.

Barn Owls are widely distributed across the county where there is suitable habitat. In particular, over the atlas winter periods they were recorded in almost a quarter of county tetrads. As well as being more visible during winter they sometimes disperse away from breeding areas at this time, and the periods of cold weather during the last two winters of the atlas survey may have forced some into areas where they would not normally occur.

Swaine stated that the Cotswolds 'have always been its stronghold' in Gloucestershire. The current distribution maps suggest strong populations in areas to the west and south of Stow-on-the-Wold, in parts of the Severn Vale, and also in the Cotswold Water Park which, including the Wiltshire section, holds about 25 pairs (Gareth Harris, Cotswold Water Park Trust).

Between January and May 2006 five Barn Owls were found dead at Slimbridge, thought possibly to have been killed by Tawny Owls. If so, this would be a very unusual occurrence; Mikkola (1983) lists 38 cases of Tawny Owls killing other owl species, but the majority

Sponsored by Margaret Headon

Species accounts

	2007–11 Atlas fieldwork					Gloucestershire trends					UK population trends	
	Number of tetrads in which recorded (max 683)					Occupied 10 km squares (max 26)				% of tetrads in which recorded (1st hour of TTV)		UK conservation status: Amber 1	
	Total	Confirmed	Probable	Possible	Present	1968–71	1981–84	1988–91	2007–11	1988–91	2008–11	Long term	Short term
Breeding	124	43	15	33	33	19		4	22	0.6	1.3	–	+501%
Winter	170						13		23			–	–

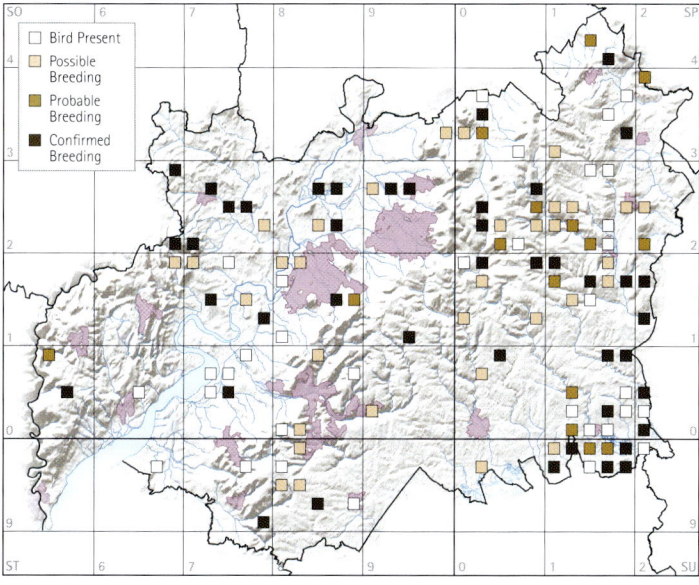

Breeding Distribution

of the victims were Little Owls and (elsewhere in Europe) other small owls, and only one was a Barn Owl.

Barn Owls ringed as nestlings in Devon, Lancashire, Lincolnshire, Merseyside and Oxfordshire have been found dead in Gloucestershire, and a Gloucestershire nestling moved to Bedfordshire. Most of these movements are likely to have involved juveniles dispersing shortly after fledging. At least three were killed by road traffic.

Swaine mentions two sightings in the county in the late 1970s of birds showing characteristics of the dark-breasted continental race *T. a. guttata*, but the records are not now considered to be safely acceptable.

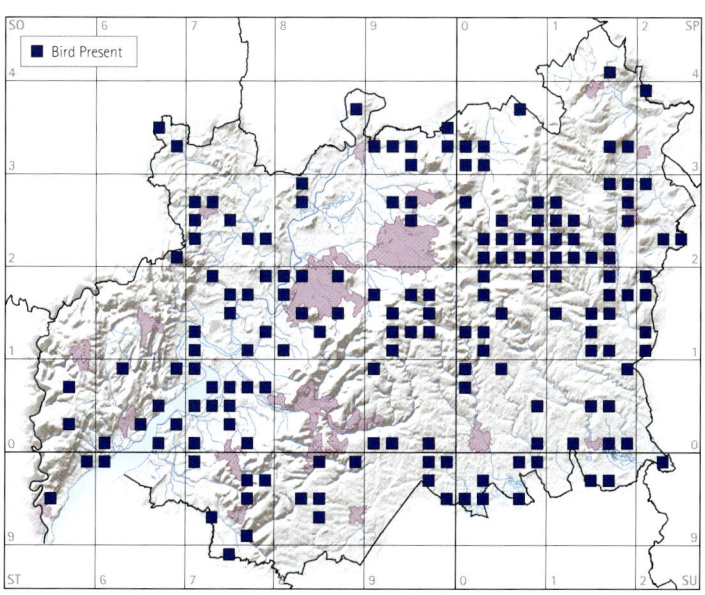

Winter Distribution

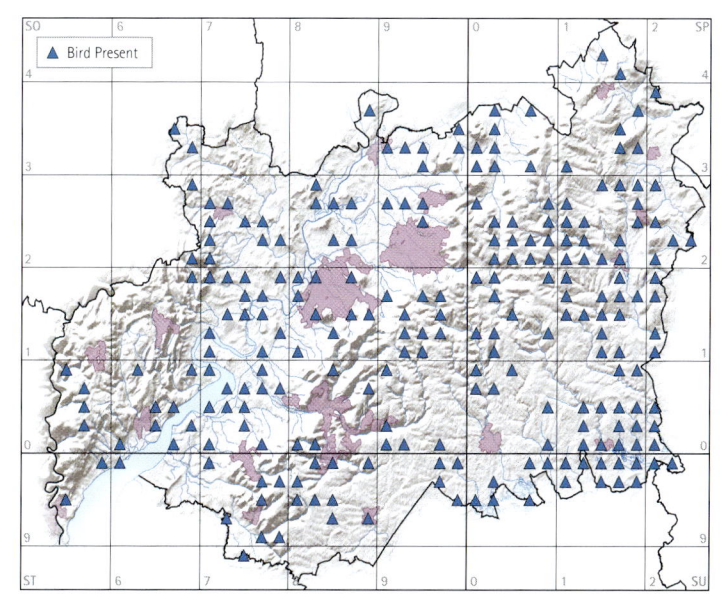

Year-Round Distribution

Little Owl
Athene noctua

Little Owls are found across much of Eurasia and parts of North Africa. They were introduced into Britain in the late nineteenth century and spread rapidly over England, Wales and southern Scotland. They use a wide range of habitats, though not dense woodland, and nest in tree-holes, natural rock-faces, quarries, farm outbuildings and nest-boxes. Like Barn Owls they are very vulnerable to hard winters, and in addition their numbers may vary in parallel with cyclical fluctuations in the populations of voles and other small rodents, which form an important component of their diet at times. This makes it rather difficult to assess long-term trends, but it is clear that the national Little Owl population has decreased in recent decades. The 1988–91 Breeding Atlas suggested that nest sites may have been lost through the felling of hedgerow and streamside trees, the destruction of old orchards and the demolition of older farm buildings.

They are less nocturnal than either Barn or Tawny Owls and are frequently seen perched conspicuously in daylight or at dusk, especially on summer evenings. Nevertheless this is not an easy species to detect, and some will have been overlooked during the atlas survey work.

Although Mellersh stated that one was shot near Cheltenham in 1868, Swaine cited the date of the first reliable Gloucestershire record as 1908, with breeding confirmed in 1916. They use a range of different habitats in the county, particularly farmland in the Cotswolds and old orchards in the Severn Vale and elsewhere, and in all areas they make use of the boles of old pollards and other tree cavities for nesting.

For at least 20 years the GBR has reflected a widespread belief among the county's birdwatchers that Little Owls have been decreasing, in line with national populations, and the 2003–07 Cotswolds Atlas also suggested a reduction in numbers. The results of the current atlas fieldwork confirm this, as is shown by the figures in the fact-box. However, the maps show that Little Owls still occur in most parts of the county, although not surprisingly they are absent from the densely wooded areas of the Forest of Dean, and they are very thinly distributed on the Dean plateau generally. Swaine stated that they were less numerous in the Vale and the Thames Area than in the Cotswolds, but this appears to be no longer true; the maps suggest that the lower-lying Vale may be more favoured nowadays. It may simply be that fewer birds were chanced upon in the less populated areas of the county, and there are certainly far fewer roving records for this species from the Cotswolds than the Vale, but the TTV data also suggest that the species' stronghold in the county is centred around the 10 km square SO71, to the west of Gloucester.

The median distance between ringing and recovery sites for Little Owls ringed in Britain is just 2 km, which is very short given that there is usually some postnatal dispersal away from the nest site. Gloucestershire ringing recoveries reflect this very sedentary character, but one record of interest concerns a bird ringed at Tickmorend, Nailsworth as a first-year female in November 1985 and recovered alive nearby in June 1994. Given that the longevity record for this species is just over 10 years, this must be one of the oldest Little Owls ever recorded.

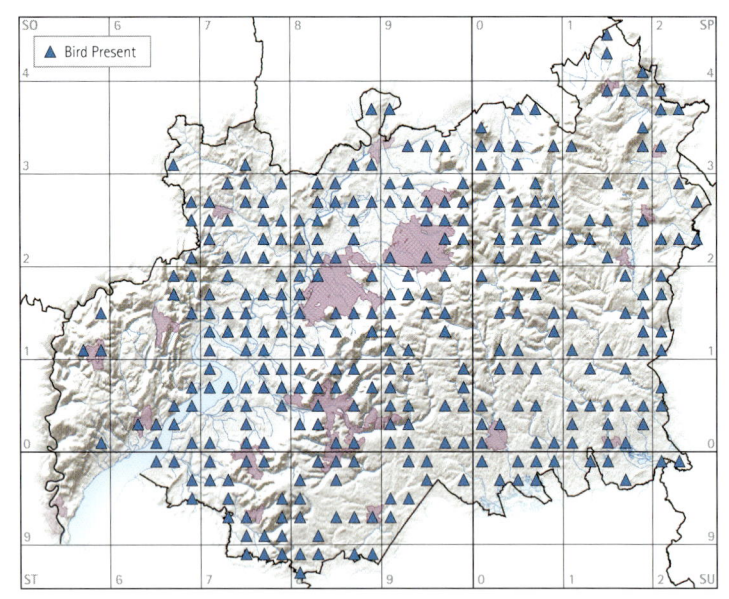

Year-Round Distribution

RICHARD BAATSEN

Sponsored by Mr S J Palmer and Athene Whitaker, and in memory of Andy Stevens

Species accounts

2007–11 Atlas fieldwork					Gloucestershire trends						UK population trends	
Number of tetrads in which recorded (max 683)					*Occupied 10 km squares (max 26)*				*% of tetrads in which recorded (1st hour of TTV)*		*UK conservation status:* **Introduced**	
	Total	Confirmed	Probable	Possible	Present	1968–71	1981–84	1988–91	2007–11	1988–91	2008–11	Long term	Short term
Breeding	235	62	43	89	41	26		25	24	16.2	6.2	–43%	–29%
Winter	179						25		26			–	–

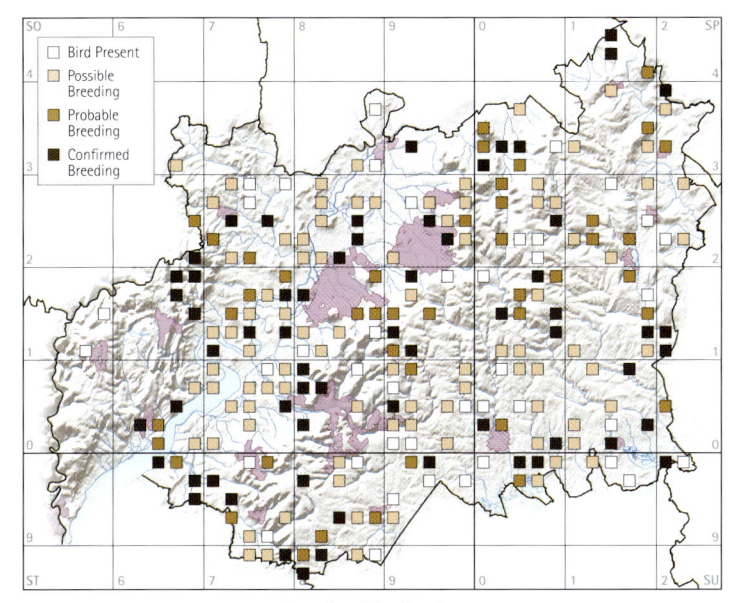

Breeding Distribution

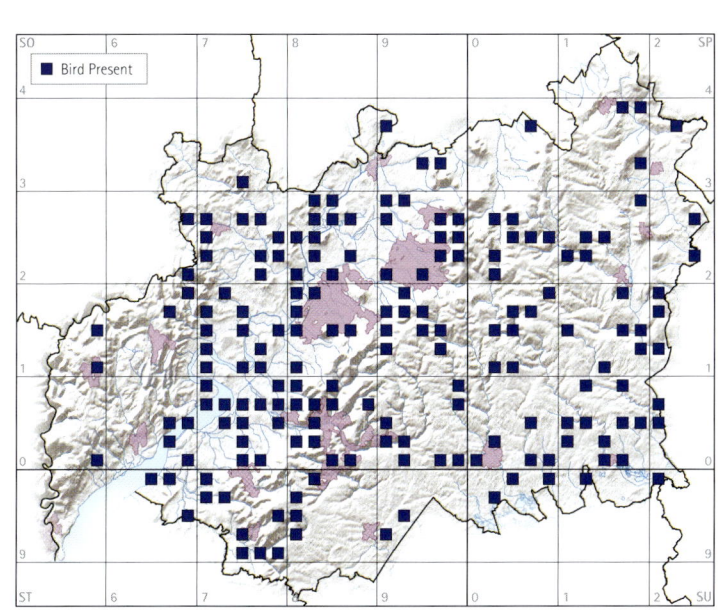

Winter Distribution

GRAHAM WATSON

Tawny Owl
Strix aluco

Tawny Owls are found in most of Europe and discontinuously across Asia. In Britain they are widespread everywhere except in largely treeless areas of the Scottish highlands and islands. They are also absent from Ireland, and on the Isle of Man breeding was confirmed for the first time as recently as 2005 (Sharpe 2007).

This is primarily a woodland owl, and its main habitat requirement is the presence of sufficient mature trees to provide roosting and nesting sites. More open, cultivated landscapes with copses and hedgerow trees are also used, as are built-up areas provided there are parks or large gardens. Tawny Owls are quite tolerant of the presence of humans and will use nest-boxes and occupy buildings if the surrounding habitat is suitable.

The 1988–91 Breeding Atlas referred to increases that 'must have taken place recently in, for example, new areas of forestry plantation', while Swaine suggested that there was likely to have been a considerable increase in Gloucestershire during the twentieth

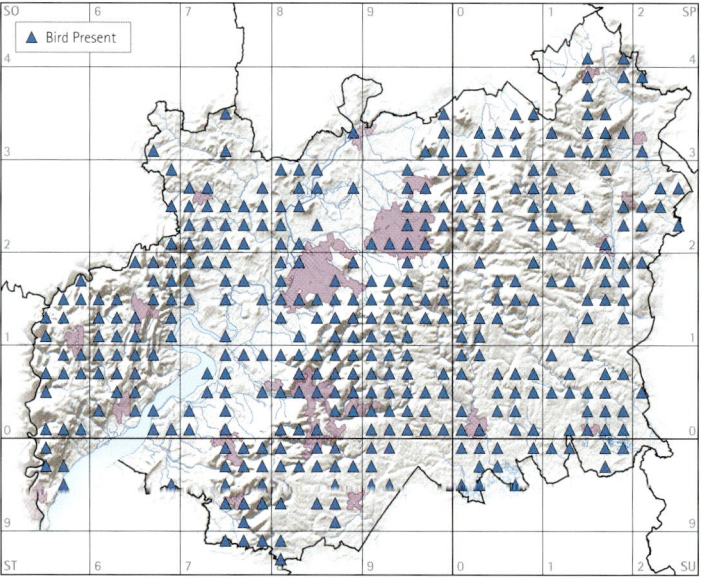

Year-Round Distribution

century due to a relaxation of human persecution. However current national studies indicate a long-term shallow decline in numbers, especially in England, and this also appears to be the case locally, where all the relevant indicators are negative (see fact-box). In the area covered by the Cotswolds Atlases, a 34% increase in occupied tetrads was recorded between 1987 and 2007, but this was thought to be largely due to increased survey effort and by 2007 'the general feeling among observers ... is that Tawny Owl numbers may have declined since the early 1990s.' Nevertheless they can still be present

Sponsored by the Dursley Birdwatching and Preservation Society

2007–11 Atlas fieldwork					Gloucestershire trends						UK population trends	
Number of tetrads in which recorded (max 683)					Occupied 10 km squares (max 26)				% of tetrads in which recorded (1st hour of TTV)		UK conservation status: Green	
	Total	Confirmed	Probable	Possible	Present	1968–71	1981–84	1988–91	2007–11	1988–91	2008–11	Long term	Short term
Breeding	268	81	44	103	40	26		23	26	9.9	4.7	–32%	–18%
Winter	243						25		26			–	–

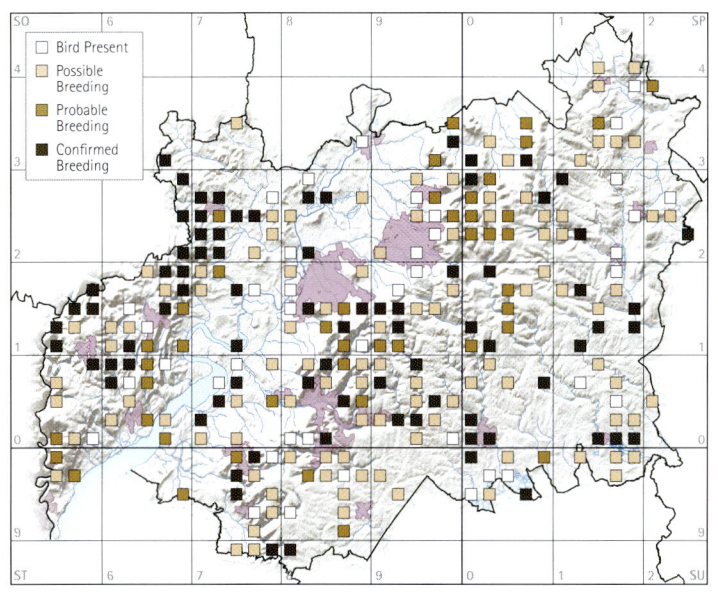

Breeding Distribution

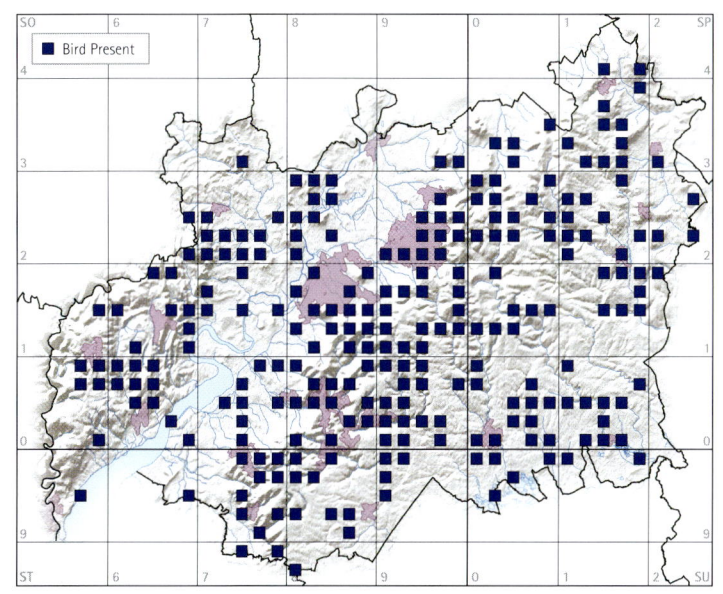

Winter Distribution

at quite high densities in the best habitats: for example one observer found at least five 'singing males' in a small area of Woodchester Park near Stroud during a 'bat-walk'.

As with other nocturnal species, surveying Tawny Owls using standard atlas methodology is rather unsatisfactory. Atlas fieldworkers were encouraged to undertake nocturnal visits, but only a minority did so and hence the maps show the distribution of casual observers as well as of Tawny Owls. A further complication is that pairs establish territories in winter and breed early in the year, typically laying eggs in March. They are very vocal during this period, but this may not have been recorded as breeding evidence by many observers as it will have occurred outside the designated atlas 'breeding season'. Once the eggs are laid, the birds' presence is much more difficult to detect, although later in the year the young can be noisy when begging for food. In any season, the observer may be lucky enough to come across a Tawny Owl being mobbed by a group of small birds.

These factors mean that caution should be exercised when interpreting the maps for this species. First, it will be underrecorded, so the maps almost certainly underrepresent its true distribution. Secondly, the early breeding behaviour means that the 'winter' map imparts more information about breeding distribution than does the 'breeding' map. However, even allowing for these difficulties, it is clear that Tawny Owls are still well-distributed in the Forest of Dean and in the more wooded areas of the Cotswolds, particularly along the scarp.

Most Tawny Owls are very sedentary, staying in or very near to their breeding territories all year round, but some birds occasionally undertake longer movements. Ringing recoveries affecting Gloucestershire reflect this pattern, with 13 movements within the county and five to and from neighbouring counties. Rather more unusual was one ringed in Lancashire and found here; quite a long journey for this species.

Long-eared Owl
Asio otus

Long-eared Owls must rank as one of the most difficult species to study or monitor. Elusive and almost exclusively nocturnal, they are very unlikely to be recorded during routine fieldwork.

They breed across much of North America and Eurasia, although not in the far north, and also in the Canary Islands and locally in parts of Africa. Fennoscandian birds are mainly migratory and some reach the British Isles in the winter, although the numbers migrating and the distances moved vary greatly depending on fluctuations in the populations of their prey, particularly voles. The British breeding population is thought to be decreasing, but the causes are not well understood; competition with the larger Tawny Owl is probably one factor. They can make use of a wide range of habitats, from heathland to dense woodland (though always requiring open areas for hunting), and they often use the old nests of Carrion Crows.

Mellersh noted that in the nineteenth century dense conifer plantations on the Cotswolds held breeding birds, but in the Forest of Dean area, they were (and had been) very scarce, with no breeding recorded. Swaine cited sources stating that Long-eared Owls bred quite commonly in the Bourton-on-the-Water area until the 1930s, when there was a sudden decrease and disappearance. Remarkably, there were then no reliable county records at all until a large autumn influx into Britain in autumn 1975 brought a group to Eastleach, where numbers peaked at 17 in February 1976. Several were recorded in the following few years, and in 1979 an adult was seen taking food to two young in an undisclosed location, the first Gloucestershire breeding record for over 70 years. Since then though there have only been definite nesting records in five years (1981, 1982, 1994, 1996 and 2002) although there have been a few tantalising summer records in other years, suggesting that they might breed more regularly.

In winter there have been records in the county every year since 1980, usually in small numbers (up to four or five) but occasionally more. Long-eared Owls form winter roosts, the locations of which are not widely disclosed in order to avoid disturbance by birdwatchers and photographers. The total number of birds in these roosts varies from year to year, and undoubtedly not all roosts are located; indeed in some years none are found. The highest number of roosting birds recorded was in 1991–92, when a total of 'nearly thirty' were counted at five roosts, and in 1999–2000, when up to 13 were found. There are also occasional winter records of single birds away from roosts, usually in the Vale.

Sponsored by the Rev & Mrs P van de Kasteele

Short-eared Owl
Asio flammeus

Short-eared Owls have an extensive breeding range, occupying high and middle latitudes across Europe, Asia and northern North America, with separate subspecies in the Caribbean, parts of South America, and even on the Falklands, Hawaii and the Galapagos.

Northern breeders are wholly or partially migratory and some Fennoscandian birds winter in Britain. British breeders nest mainly on moorland and in young plantations in Scotland, northern England and Wales. In winter they vacate higher ground and move to lower altitudes, especially by the coast. This is a highly nomadic species, travelling long distances in response to prey availability; northern breeding population levels are closely linked to fluctuations in the numbers of Norway lemmings.

Short-eared Owls are passage migrants and winter visitors in Gloucestershire, where thanks to their more diurnal habits they are more likely to be seen hunting than other large owls. Mellersh said that the species 'almost entirely keeps to the Cotswolds', but Swaine noted that by the 1970s the Severn Vale was the main source of records. This is still true today, with the grassland habitats by the estuary providing sightings almost annually, usually of one or two birds at a time. Currently there are also a few areas on the Cotswolds where Short-eared Owls occur reliably in most winters, on undisturbed, ungrazed, uncultivated grassland or set-aside, and in these locations they can occur in greater numbers than in the Vale, providing a fine spectacle as several birds hunt together on a winter's afternoon. One such site is the Hawling–Brockhampton area east of Cheltenham, which has held up to six birds in recent years. This species' ability to exploit any area where prey is temporarily available was apparent in 1988–89, when eight wintered at a young plantation (essentially rough grassland) at Pamington, near Tewkesbury.

The graph shows the number of sites at which Short-eared Owls have been reported each year, and the estimated total number of birds involved. The increase in numbers might not be simply due to observer effects, as there is every indication that more birds are being seen at each site than previously.

Although most records are from the winter months, birds can arrive early and linger well into spring. Since 1980 the earliest autumn bird was one at Lydney on August 5th 2002, and in the following spring one stayed in the Slimbridge area until May 15th. It is difficult to say whether the single bird seen on June 14th 1996 at Slimbridge was early or late!

A hint at the origin of some of our Short-eared Owls is provided by the recovery of one ringed as a nestling on the west coast of Finland on June 20th 2005 and found dead at Winchcombe on November 11th that year.

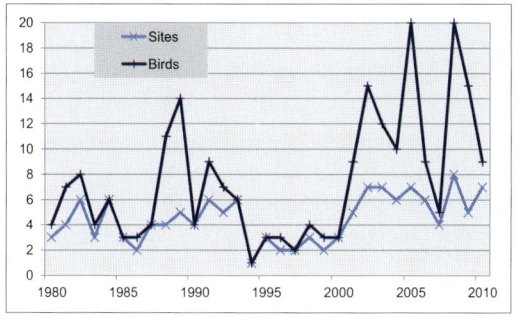

Short-eared Owl sites and estimated minimum number of birds, 1980–2010.

Sponsored by Gordon & Jenny Kirk

Nightjar (European Nightjar)
Caprimulgus europaeus

Nightjars breed from North Africa and the British Isles east to northern China and the north-west Himalayas. Nearly all winter in Africa south of the Sahara. They breed in open, scrubby areas, laying their eggs in a scrape on bare ground. Typical habitats vary from large expanses of heathland to dunes and woodland clearings.

In Britain, Nightjars are most numerous in the east and south of England, from East Anglia to the Dorset heaths, but they also breed in smaller numbers elsewhere in England, Wales and southern Scotland. Only a few pairs remain in Ireland.

The twentieth century saw a steep decline in Britain's Nightjars. Formerly fairly abundant and widespread, they decreased to the extent that it became possible to obtain accurate counts of the whole population in national surveys. The decrease has been linked to changes in the management of heath and a decline in numbers of insect prey, particularly moths. Between the 1968–72 and 1988–91 Breeding Atlases, the range in Britain and Ireland declined from 655 to only 285 10 km squares. Since the 1980s numbers have edged upwards again, probably helped by increasing areas of forestry clear-fell: national surveys by the BTO revealed 3,400 males in 1992 (a rise of 50% since 1981) and 4,600 males in 2004, with most of the increase occurring within the reduced breeding range.

Because of their nocturnal habits Nightjars are rarely recorded other than by targeted searches at dusk on spring and summer evenings. They are the last of the summer visitors to arrive; in Gloucestershire the average first arrival date is May 17th and the earliest on record was on April 26th 1984. The male's distinctive churring song, which makes them easy to locate, continues throughout the summer, becoming more intermittent in late July

Sponsored by Hugh Manistre

Species accounts

2007–11 Atlas fieldwork					Gloucestershire trends						UK population trends	
Number of tetrads in which recorded (max 683)					Occupied 10 km squares (max 26)				% of tetrads in which recorded (1st hour of TTV)		UK conservation status: **Red 5**	
	Total	Confirmed	Probable	Possible	Present	1968–71	1981–84	1988–91	2007–11	1988–91	2008–11	Long term	Short term
Breeding	21	1	11	7	2	5		1	4	0.2	0	–	–
Winter	0						0		0			–	–

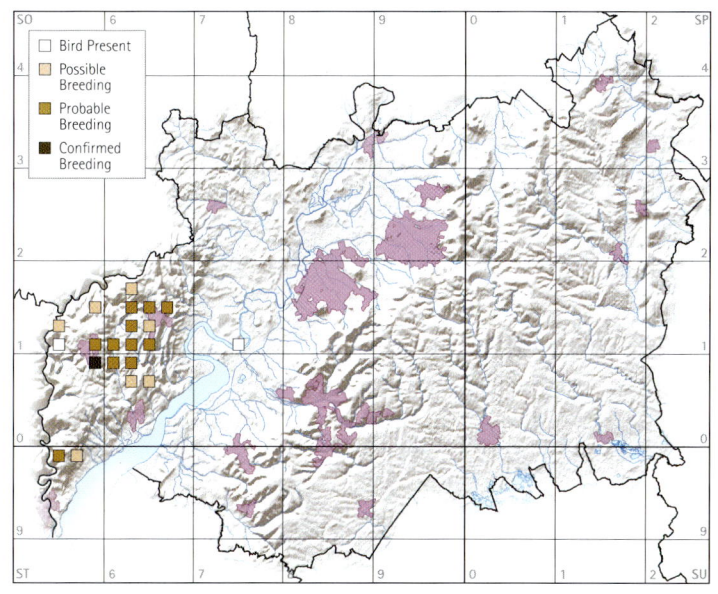

Breeding Distribution

and August. Unsuccessful breeders may desert breeding sites as early as mid-July, and in most years all the county's Nightjars have left by the end of August.

The Gloucestershire Nightjar population has reflected the fluctuations at the national level. In the mid-nineteenth century it was said that 'The fern owls are very numerous' in the Forest of Dean (Nicholls 1858), and in 1902 Mellersh not only described Nightjars as being 'in great profusion' in the Dean but also spoke of them being widespread in the Cotswolds and breeding in the Vale at Highnam and Michaelwood. Christian (1999b) suggested that there had been an increase in numbers in the mid-twentieth century following the extensive felling of oak woodland during and after the Second World War, but Swaine made no mention of any such increase and described the Nightjar as 'very local' with only ten pairs found in a 1979 survey, all in the Forest of Dean. Since then the Gloucestershire population has varied within narrow limits. A low point came in 1989–90, when only three or four sites held single calling males and the county population seemed to be on the brink of extinction. However there has been a gradual recovery in numbers since then and it is likely that the current breeding population for the Forest of Dean is at least 20–25 pairs. Elsewhere, there have been just two sightings of single birds in the Cotswolds since 2000. All the breeding sites in the Dean are in small areas of relict or restored heath, such as the Park at Tidenham and Crabtree Hill near Cinderford, or in areas of clear-fell, which are used by the birds for five to ten years until the regenerating or replanted tree crop develops to the thicket stage.

Although Nightjars in Gloucestershire have now recovered slightly from their lowest point, they enjoy nothing like the abundance and widespread distribution described by Mellersh 100 years ago. No longer is their song familiar to people throughout the county; they have become a 'birdwatchers' bird', found only by those making a special journey to known sites to hear that magical call and to enjoy in the summer dusk their graceful buoyant flight.

JACKIE GARNER

Swift (Common Swift)
Apus apus

Swifts are remarkable birds because they feed, sleep and mate on the wing, landing only to visit their nests. The young fly and feed independently as soon as they fledge and may not land again for up to three years. Swifts breed across nearly all of Europe and eastwards across the middle latitudes of Asia, wintering almost entirely in sub-Saharan Africa.

For such a well-known and apparently widespread bird, it is perhaps surprising that the British population is estimated to be just 80,000 pairs. Although they have not been surveyed very systematically in the past, recent work by the RSPB has concluded that their numbers have almost halved since about the year 2000. One reason may be that the replacement of old building stock is depriving them of nesting opportunities. Older buildings often provide the type of cavities they need, and they have a particular preference for the loose-fitting roof tiles that can be found in many towns and villages, where noisy 'screaming parties' betray their presence. Unlike House Martins, Swifts are unable to exploit most modern buildings unless special provision has been made for them, so they are absent from many housing estates.

Swifts' eggs are very unusual in that they can survive periods of cold for several days at any stage of development. Similarly, the newly hatched young can enter a torpid state, giving them the ability to survive if adults are away from the nest for long periods, as may happen if prolonged wet weather makes it impossible to catch aerial food in the vicinity of the nest. In these conditions the adults will undertake long journeys in search of better conditions, and it is likely that this often involves flying all the way around a low pressure system to avoid rainfall, a non-stop flight of perhaps 1,000–2,000 km (BWP).

Swifts are one of the last migrants to arrive in Britain, and the first Gloucestershire birds normally appear in the last few days of April. The earliest record is of four at Slimbridge on April 6th 2008. They are also among the first to leave, the bulk of the population often departing en masse over just a few days. Sightings after the end of August are uncommon, and there has been an apparent tendency towards earlier departures in recent years. However there is a remarkable record in the 1980 GBR of young still being attended at the nest on September 22nd at Swells Hill, Stroud, and there have been a few extremely late reports, as late as December 1st 1994. Recent experience suggests that swifts in Britain after the end of October may be just as likely to be Pallid Swifts *Apus pallidus*.

Swaine noted older reports of Swifts nesting in natural rock crevices in quarries on Cleeve Hill and near Lancaut in the Wye Valley, but nowadays breeding birds in Gloucestershire are wholly dependent on human sites. They are found in many villages and smaller towns and also penetrate into the larger conurbations, with breeding confirmed in central Gloucester, Cheltenham and Stroud.

The distribution map shows many records of 'possible' breeding across the county. These were mainly based on birds seen in 'suitable habitat', and some may well have related to Swifts feeding over open country rather than near breeding sites. The map may therefore give the impression that breeding is more widespread than it really is. Similarly, some areas of high density shown on the abundance map will be due to aggregations of feeding rather than nesting birds. A few flocks of 100 or more Swifts are reported in the county in most years, often over or near waterbodies, with a maximum of around 300 being the norm. On the other hand, despite their noisy displays it is not always easy to confirm breeding. The distribution map shows a concentration of 'confirmed' records in the three 10 km squares between Stroud and Cirencester (SO80, SO90 and SP00), but this may be influenced by the fact that some observers were more likely than others to record breeding status.

Sponsored by Les Brown, T R Guest and Mary Jennings

Species accounts 267

2007–11 Atlas fieldwork						Gloucestershire trends						UK population trends	
Number of tetrads in which recorded (max 683)						Occupied 10 km squares (max 26)				% of tetrads in which recorded (1st hour of TTV)		UK conservation status: **Amber 3**	
	Total	Confirmed	Probable	Possible	Present	1968–71	1981–84	1988–91	2007–11	1988–91	2008–11	Long term	Short term
Breeding	546	141	99	155	151	26		26	26	66.3	45.1	–	–31%
Winter	1						0		1			–	–

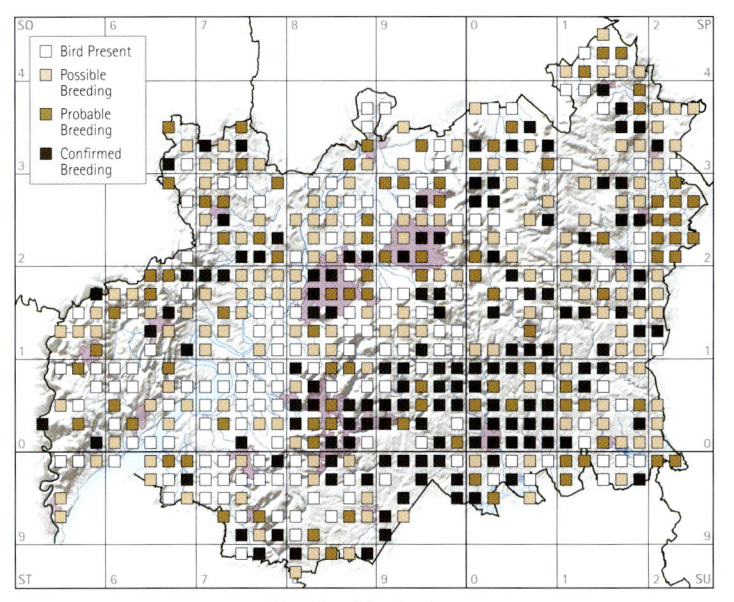

Breeding Distribution 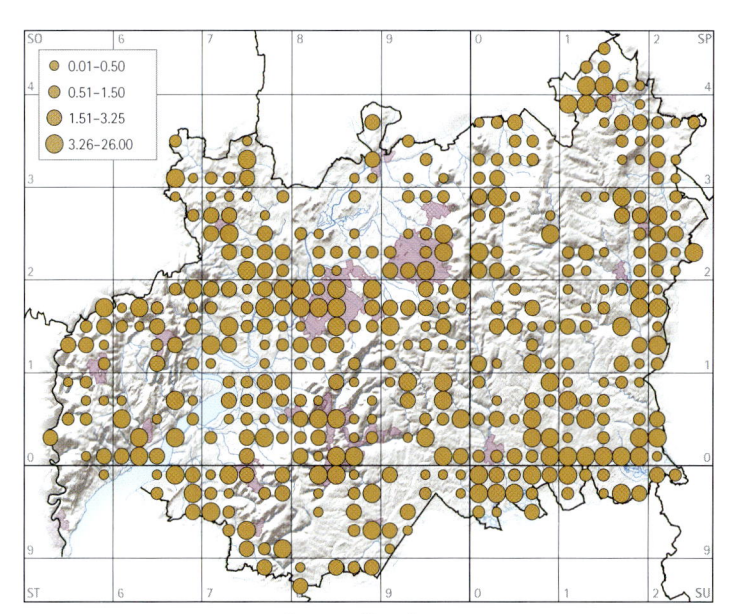   **Summer Abundance**

Kingfisher (Common Kingfisher)
Alcedo atthis

Kingfishers breed across much of Europe apart from the more northerly areas, as well as in central, eastern and southern Asia. Over a large part of their range they migrate south for the winter, but this is not the case in western Europe. However even in our region they do undertake weather-related movements and they are frequently seen at the coast in winter, when freshwater sites may be frozen.

They can be found in most parts of Britain except for the Scottish highlands and islands, and the long-term national population trend appears to be fairly steady although they are subject to shorter-term fluctuations due to hard winters. For breeding they require waters that support fish prey of a suitable size, which can include lakes and garden ponds as well as rivers and streams, and they also need banks in which to excavate the tunnels that lead to their nest chambers. These conditions are satisfied in many parts of Gloucestershire, including the higher ground of the Cotswolds and the Dean Plateau as well as the Severn Vale and the Thames Area although, as Swaine pointed out, suitable nesting banks are scarce on the Cotswold streams and along the Severn itself. He noted that the Vale and the Cotswold Water Park were the most favoured areas, with a noticeable increase in records from the latter area as it was being developed in the 1970s.

Kingfishers are among the most colourful of British birds, but very often all the observer sees is a blur of blue and green hurtling along a watercourse; detection relies on sound as often as sight, as their high-pitched calls can be heard above the sound of the water. They are fairly noisy and conspicuous when feeding young, but their nesting sites are often inaccessible, which might account for the relatively small proportion of confirmed breeding records during the atlas surveying. It is noticeable that there are a number of areas in the Cotswolds (for example along the river Coln north of Fairford) where breeding was confirmed during the 2003-07 Cotswolds Atlas fieldwork but not during 2007-11. However, this could well be due to less intensive effort during the later survey, and the fact that it extended over four years rather than five.

The second Cotswolds Atlas suggested a possible increase between 1987 and 2007, and the current data indicate a further increase since then, but it is unwise to rely on such 'snapshot' data (even when carefully collected over four or five years) as a true indicator of trends for a species that is so susceptible to harsh weather. Mortality can be severe in very cold winters, but recovery can be similarly rapid, thanks to the birds' ability to raise two or three broods in a season with up to six young per brood.

Given their specific habitat requirements, it is perhaps surprising that Kingfishers were recorded in over 20% of county tetrads at both seasons. Even though the four-year recording period tends to exaggerate the extent of their distribution to some degree and they were not recorded in all these tetrads every year, it is clear that they are reasonably widespread in the county. The Vale is the most densely populated region, where the streams flowing into the Severn provide the best habitat. The Cotswold Water Park is also an important area at all seasons, and may well receive additional birds in the winter in the same way that coastal sites do. The winter map suggests some possible dispersion away from the breeding areas.

By far the longest movement by a ringed Kingfisher involving Gloucestershire was by a bird ringed 179 km away in Nottinghamshire and killed by a cat here in its first winter.

Sponsored by Brian & Margaret Channon and by the Cheltenham Bird Club

Species accounts

2007–11 Atlas fieldwork					Gloucestershire trends						UK population trends	
Number of tetrads in which recorded (max 683)					*Occupied 10 km squares (max 26)*				*% of tetrads in which recorded (1st hour of TTV)*		*UK conservation status:* **Amber 1**	
	Total	Confirmed	Probable	Possible	Present	1968–71	1981–84	1988–91	2007–11	1988–91	2008–11	Long term	Short term
Breeding	160	28	19	75	38	21		14	26	3.4	5.1	–11%	–17%
Winter	164						23		24			–	–

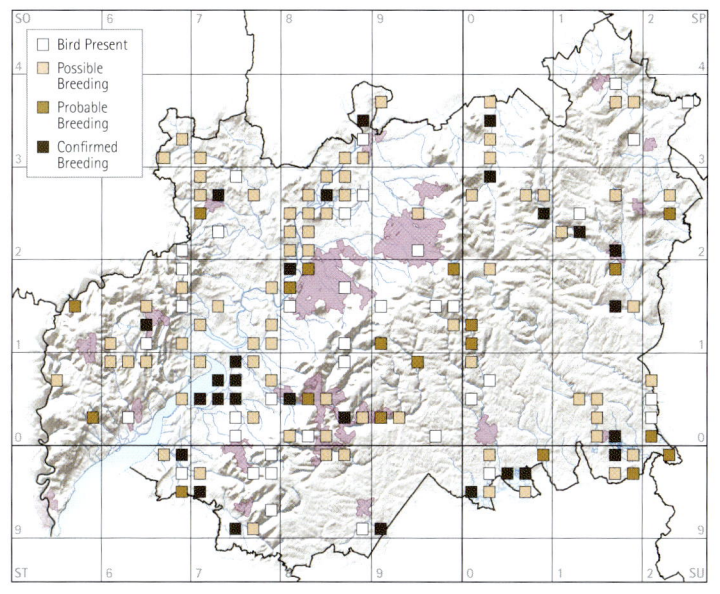

Breeding Distribution

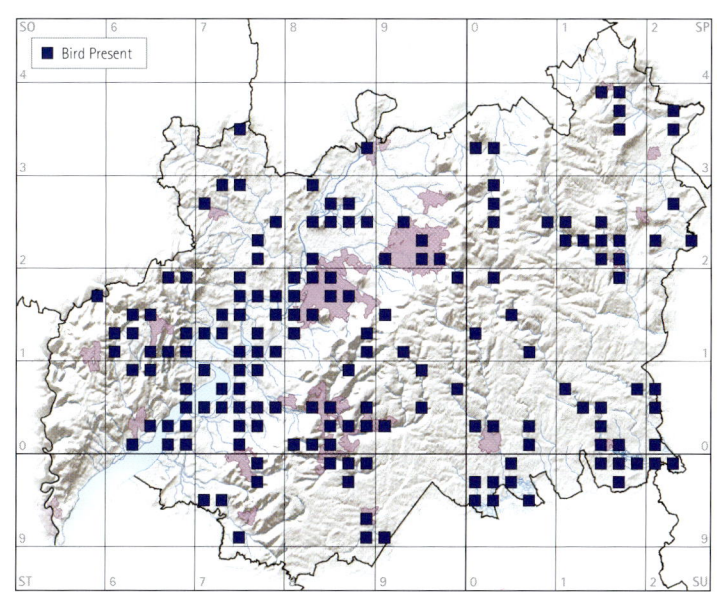

Winter Distribution

Alpine Swift
Apus melba

Alpine Swifts are summer visitors to southern Europe and there are usually up to about a dozen records in Britain every year, mainly in spring and concentrated in the southern counties. The species was removed from the national rarities list in 2006. There have been two records in Gloucestershire:

1970: one at Cainscross, Stroud on April 16th.
1977: one at South Cerney sewage farm (Cotswold Water Park area) on June 1st.

Mellersh referred to two unsubstantiated records: one 'killed' near Cirencester in 1863, and one 'north of Colesborne' in about 1869.

Bee-eater (European Bee-eater)
Merops apiaster

The spectacular and colourful Bee-eater has spread north from its Mediterranean stronghold in recent decades. It is now an annual visitor to Britain, with up to 30 or 40 records per year; there are also a few breeding records. It was removed from the national rarities list in 1991. Despite the recent increase, the only record in Gloucestershire is of one photographed at South Cerney near Cirencester on May 31st 1979. Mellersh also mentioned an unsubstantiated record of one killed at Shurdington near Cheltenham in about 1871.

Hoopoe (Eurasian Hoopoe)
Upupa epops

The startlingly exotic-looking Hoopoe breeds across southern and eastern regions of the Western Palearctic and in central and southern Asia. Those breeding in more northern parts of Europe move south to winter in North Africa and the Mediterranean basin. Hoopoes occupy open country with mature trees and, at least in western Europe, they are often associated with rural human settlements. They are annual visitors to the British Isles, especially in the south and west, and most commonly in spring. There have been 30 or so cases of proved breeding in Britain since the 1830s, apparently with peaks around the turn of the twentieth century and in the 1950s, and an exceptional total of four pairs in 1977.

Swaine felt that Hoopoes had become more frequent in Gloucestershire since the late 1940s. There had been over 40 records between 1955 and 1980, three-quarters of which were in April and May, and by 1980 they had become 'almost annual'. This increase seems unlikely to have been simply due to observer effects because Hoopoes are quite often found by non-birdwatchers as, like Wrynecks, they seem to favour gardens and especially those with large lawns. More recently, as the left-hand graph shows, there seems to have been something of a peak in the frequency of sightings in the county during the 1990s, and at the time of writing we appear to be in rather a lean period. The spread of records through the year is unchanged; half of the sightings since 1980 have occurred in May (see right-hand graph). There is just one confirmed breeding record, at Longhope in 1925. Between 1966 and 1980 there were several occasions when breeding was suspected, such as in 1980 when two birds were seen for a fortnight at Highnam Woods in late May and early June, but in none of these cases was it confirmed.

Since 1980 all records have involved single birds, and they have come from all parts of the county. Perhaps the most noteworthy was in 1995, when an unfortunate Hoopoe was found moribund in a woodshed at Adsett near Westbury-on-Severn during freezing weather on December 27th, having been present in the area for about ten days.

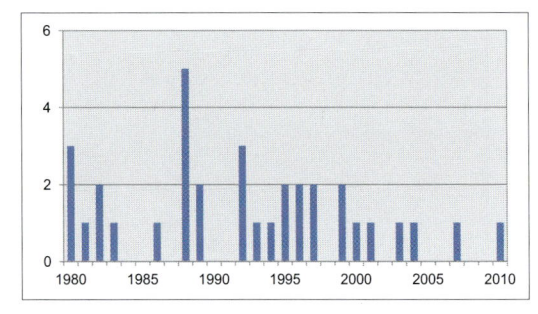

Number of Hoopoes recorded per year, 1980–2010.

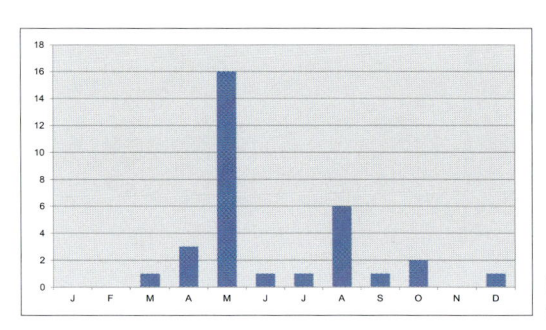

Hoopoe records by month, 1980–2010.

Wryneck (Eurasian Wryneck)
Jynx torquilla

Wrynecks breed across much of Europe except the far north, and their range extends eastwards to Japan. Western populations migrate mostly to sub-Saharan Africa for the winter, passing through Europe on a broad front. Wrynecks have suffered a very long-term and widespread decline in Britain and beyond, which has been attributed to habitat degradation and possibly climate change (BWP). By 1970 the British population was confined to south-east England, where it became extinct by 1980; more recently there have been occasional breeding attempts in Scotland, probably involving birds from Fennoscandia.

A bird of open woodland as well as parks and orchards, up to the beginning of the twentieth century the Wryneck was a not uncommon summer visitor to Gloucestershire. Mellersh described it as being still quite common in the Severn Vale and widely distributed in the Forest of Dean, though scarcer in the Cotswolds. There was evidently a very rapid but poorly documented decrease thereafter, reflecting the national decline.

Swaine noted that 20 migrant Wrynecks had been recorded in the county between 1960 and 1980, of which seven were in 1976, which was evidently an exceptional year. They have been seen rather more frequently since 1980, with records in all but eight years, though the true status has probably changed little given the increasing numbers of observers. Of a total of 51 birds in this period, ten were in August and 32 in September; indeed, over half of all sightings were between August 16th and September 15th. Spring records have occurred in only 1984, 1987 (two), 2007 (two) and 2008. The earliest date was April 19th, in 1987 and 2007, and the latest record was on October 19th 1986. The maximum in any year was four, in 1995, 2000 and 2010, with one or two per year being more usual.

In common with Hoopoes, many of these Wrynecks were seen in gardens, although this strange woodpecker's cryptic plumage and furtive behaviour mean that it is far more likely to be seen in an observant birdwatcher's garden than in one belonging to a member of the non-birding public. Given these attributes it is very likely that more must visit the county than are actually recorded. Wrynecks are not normally seen in large numbers anywhere in Britain, even at the most favoured coastal migration sites, and it seems surprising that they still regularly pass through Gloucestershire, well to the east of their current breeding range.

Sponsored by Mike King of Gloster Birder

Green Woodpecker (European Green Woodpecker)
Picus viridis

Present across most of Europe but thinning out rapidly north of latitude 60°N, Green Woodpeckers require grassland for feeding and mature trees for nesting. Hence in Britain they occupy parkland, well-grazed pasture, orchards, larger gardens and woodland edges, and they often find suitable habitat in and around villages. They prefer warmer climates, and although numbers in Britain as a whole have increased markedly over the last 40 years or so they are still commonest in the south and east and absent from much of Scotland, as well as Ireland. This is a highly sedentary species, with adults very loyal to their breeding areas.

Green Woodpeckers are specialist feeders, using their long tongues to probe ants' nests to find adults, pupae and eggs. This results in high mortality when prolonged periods of frost and ice render the ground too hard to penetrate, and it can take many years for numbers to recover from a very hard winter. They may also be adversely affected by long periods of summer drought.

Although they are rather wary birds, both sexes are very vocal all year round, and their easily recognised far-carrying calls and song made for straightforward recording during atlas visits. However it is much more difficult to find their nests than is the case with Great Spotted Woodpeckers; despite broadly similar total numbers of records in Gloucestershire during the atlas period, observers recorded Green Woodpeckers with an 'occupied nest' or 'nest with young' on just five occasions, whereas for Great Spotted Woodpeckers the figure was 116. Once they leave the nest, though, the loud begging calls of the juveniles make them easy to locate, and many observers were able to confirm breeding in that way.

Swaine interpreted comments by Mellersh as indicating that Green Woodpeckers may have been rather less plentiful in Gloucestershire at the end of the nineteenth century than towards the end of the twentieth. The comparative atlas figures suggest that there may have been a slight overall increase in more recent years, although perhaps not on the same scale as at the national level (see fact-box). The county BBS figures certainly show a clear increase, with records in an average of 53% of squares each year between 2003 and 2010 compared with 41% between 1994 and 2002. Similarly, the 2003–07 Cotswolds Atlas and regular winter surveys from that area of the county also suggest substantial increases in the last 15–20 years.

Despite the long-term national population increases, very recent BBS results and the current atlas fieldwork are pointing to declining numbers in Wales and parts of south-west England. However there is no sign of any decrease as yet in Gloucestershire, and the maps show that Green Woodpeckers are still widespread in our county. In particular the Cotswold scarp appears to hold good numbers, offering as it does plenty of mature trees and areas that are not as intensively cultivated. The Newent area also seems to be favoured, probably because it still has many traditional orchards. Most places where there are relatively few Green Woodpeckers are areas of arable farmland with few hedges, an exception being the extreme south-west of the county, which appears to have suitable habitat, but in which rather few Green Woodpeckers were recorded.

Reports in the GBR reveal that this is a species that can produce surprises; in April 1995 no fewer than seven birds, all calling, were in the same tree at Edgeworth, near Stroud, and in July 2005 one was seen swimming in Dowdeswell reservoir.

Sponsored by Viv Phillips

Species accounts

2007–11 Atlas fieldwork					Gloucestershire trends					UK population trends	
Number of tetrads in which recorded (max 683)					Occupied 10 km squares (max 26)				% of tetrads in which recorded (1st hour of TTV)		UK conservation status: Amber 1	
	Total	Confirmed	Probable	Possible	Present	1968–71	1981–84	1988–91	2007–11	1988–91	2008–11	Long term	Short term
Breeding	595	158	137	267	33	26		26	26	43.4	51.5	+127%	+47%
Winter	566						26		26			–	–

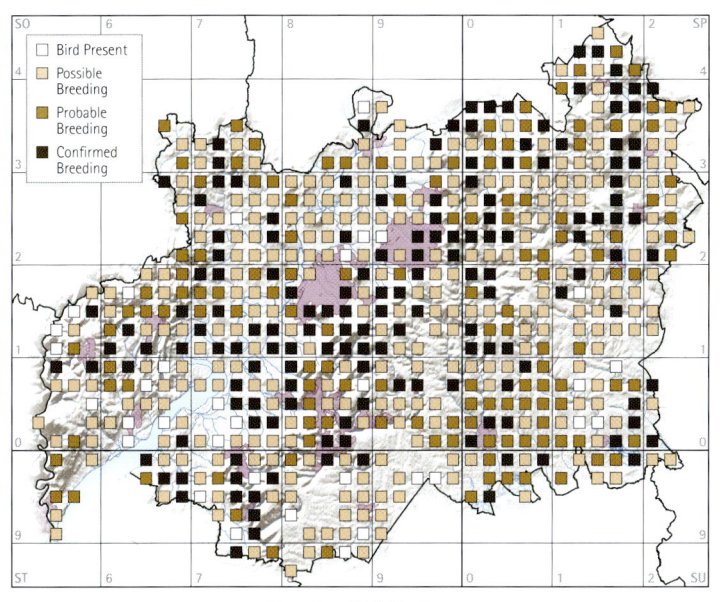

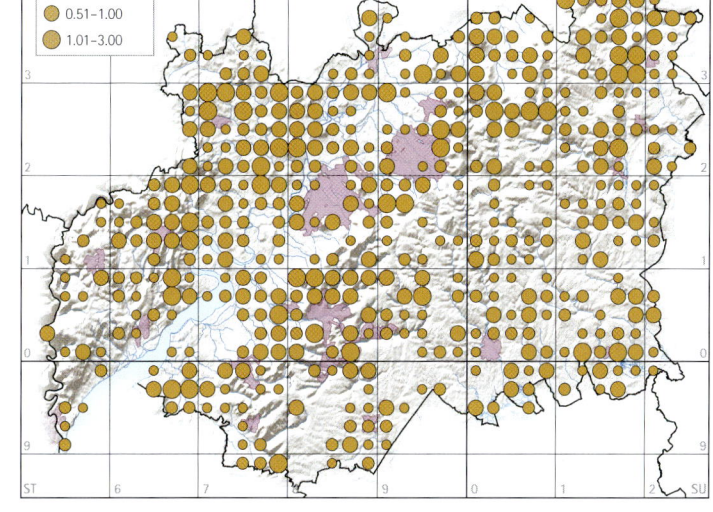

Breeding Distribution

Summer Abundance

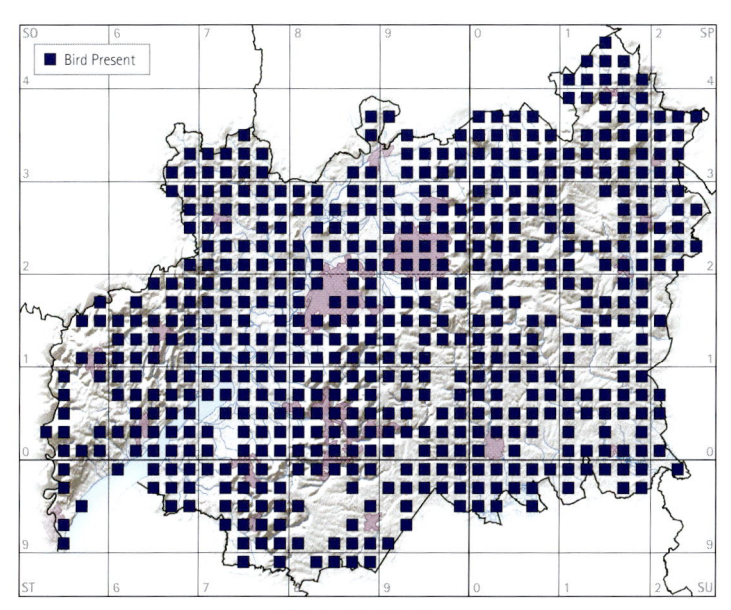

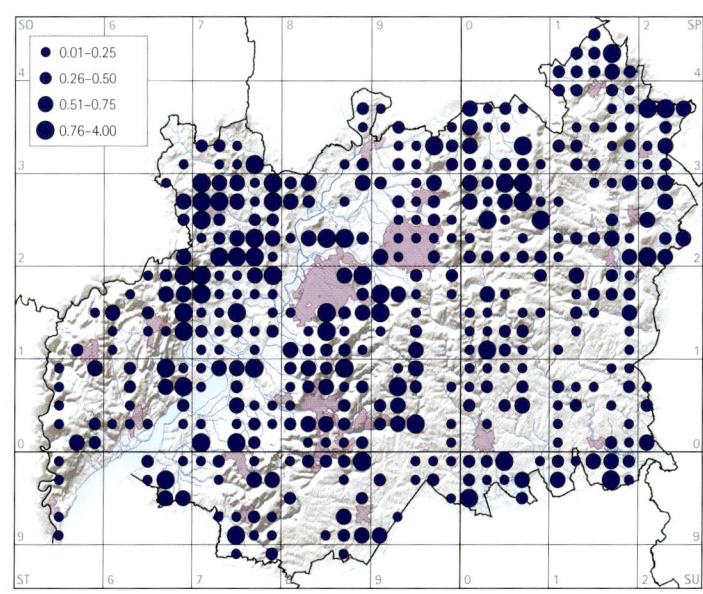

Winter Distribution

Winter Abundance

Great Spotted Woodpecker
Dendrocopos major

Great Spotted Woodpeckers occupy most of Europe, being absent only from treeless areas in Iceland and elsewhere in the extreme north, and their range extends right across Eurasia to Japan and parts of south-east Asia. In recent decades their populations have increased in a number of European countries including Britain, and a significant range expansion was confirmed during the current national atlas fieldwork, when they became the first species of woodpecker to colonise Ireland. Now that they have established a foothold, it seems likely that they will thrive there.

They occur in any habitat with trees big enough to provide holes of the size needed for nesting, and in Britain this precludes very few areas. They feed mainly on invertebrates and their larvae extracted from rotten branches or from beneath the bark of trees, but also on nuts and seeds. They also take the eggs and nestlings of other hole-nesting species by breaking into their nests, including those in nest-boxes, and in some places they are major nest predators of tits, especially Willow Tits (BWP). They are frequent visitors to gardens in all but the most urban areas, using feeders in both winter and summer.

Great Spotted Woodpeckers are often detected by their unmistakable loud 'tchik!' call, which is used all year round. Also, the males 'drum' very frequently from January into May, especially on mild sunny days. Occasionally they make themselves even more obvious by choosing to drum on man-made items such as the metal caps on telegraph poles, thereby advertising their territories over an even wider area. In addition the nestlings can become extremely noisy as fledging time approaches, so all in all this is a species that reveals itself readily to surveyors.

All available sources of data confirm that the recent national increase has been mirrored in Gloucestershire (see fact-box). For example, systematic winter surveys by NCOS indicate that numbers have doubled in the last 15 years, and there was a substantial increase in occupied tetrads between 1987 and 2007 in the area covered by the Cotswolds Atlases. Figures from the countywide Gloucestershire Garden Bird Survey reveal a very significant rise in the number of gardens visited to over 20% since 2000. The distribution maps confirm that this is now the most widespread woodpecker in the county by some margin, with records from about 95% of tetrads in both summer and winter during the atlas fieldwork. This would have surprised Mellersh, who wrote in 1902 that it was scarce in the Severn Vale and 'rarely if ever' entered Cheltenham. It is clear from the abundance maps that Great Spotted Woodpeckers are scarcest in areas where there is high-intensity arable farming with few trees, such as some parts of the high wold and the Vale. These maps also show that the highest densities occur mainly to the west of the river Severn, in and around the Forest of Dean. The maximum number of birds seen during an atlas TTV was 11, in SO62X just west of Newent in June 2009.

Ringing recoveries involving Gloucestershire have confirmed the species' very sedentary nature: up to 2010 there were 12 movements within the county and singles between here and neighbouring 'Avon' and 'Hereford & Worcester'. In addition though, there is a noteworthy record of a bird ringed as an adult in June 1984 at Frampton and seen alive there in August 1993 (the ring having been read in the field!). It must have been at least ten years old when resighted, making it one of the oldest Great Spotted Woodpeckers on record; the maximum age determined by BTO ringing is just short of 11 years.

Sponsored by the GWT Snows Farm Reserve Team

Species accounts   275

2007–11 Atlas fieldwork					Gloucestershire trends						UK population trends	
Number of tetrads in which recorded (max 683)					Occupied 10 km squares (max 26)				% of tetrads in which recorded (1st hour of TTV)		UK conservation status: **Green**	
	Total	Confirmed	Probable	Possible	Present	1968–71	1981–84	1988–91	2007–11	1988–91	2008–11	Long term	Short term
Breeding	646	286	149	186	25	25		25	26	38.1	62.8	+364%	+139%
Winter	651						26		26			–	–

Breeding Distribution

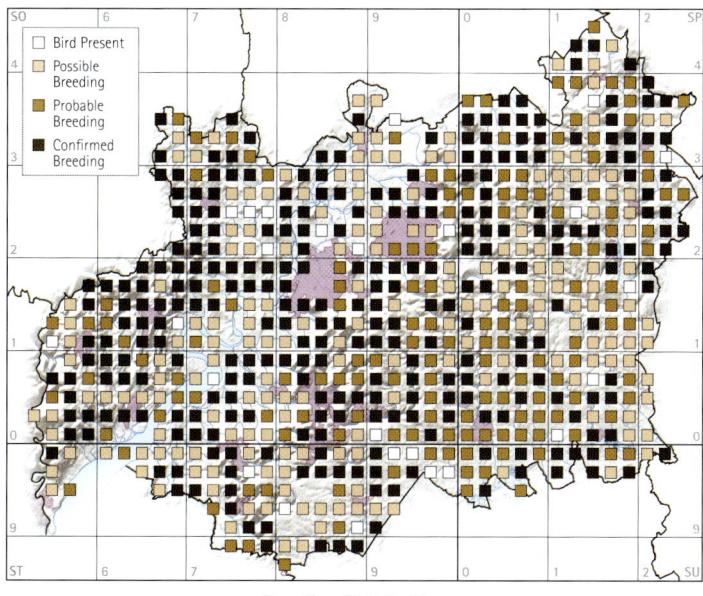

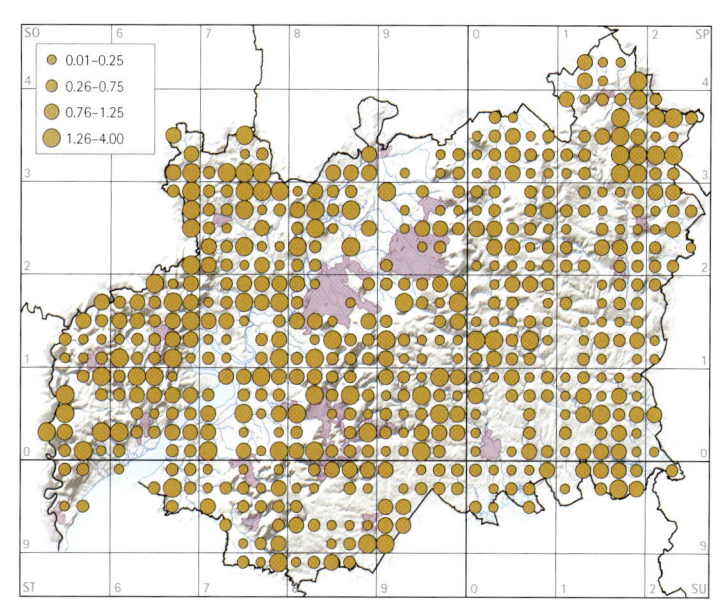

Summer Abundance

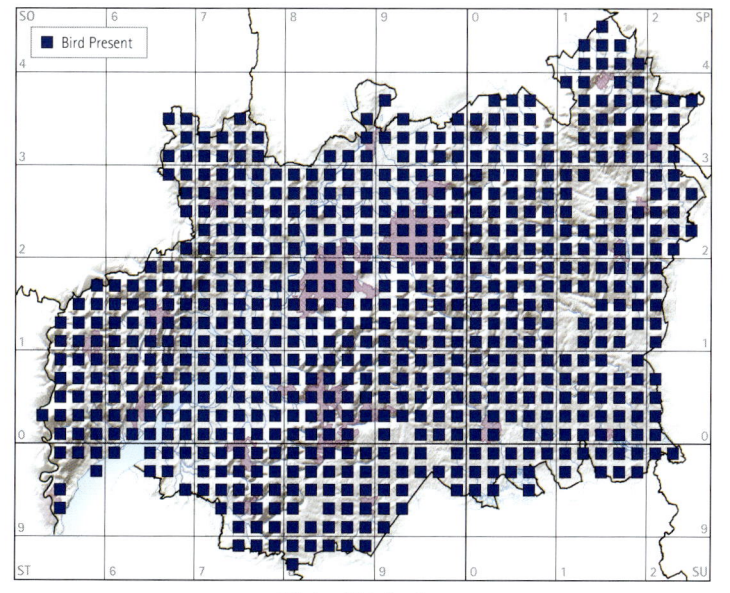

Winter Distribution

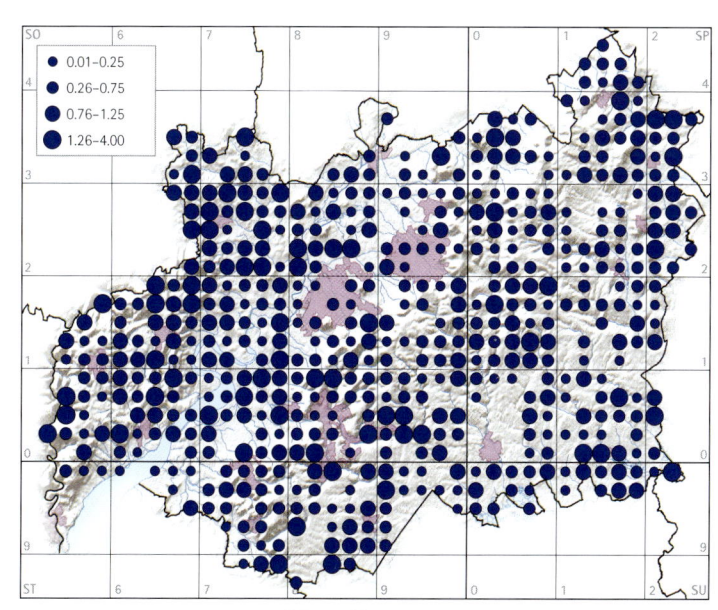

Winter Abundance

Lesser Spotted Woodpecker
Dendrocopos minor

Lesser Spotted Woodpeckers breed in most European countries (although they are very local in Iberia) and across Asia as far as Japan. On the Continent they extend well north of the Arctic Circle, but in Britain they are southern birds, becoming very sparse north of Yorkshire and Lancashire. They inhabit wooded landscapes with plenty of dead standing timber, including mature woodland, parkland, orchards and stands of mature alders along streams.

Surveying Lesser Spotted Woodpeckers is not easy; they are difficult to locate in the canopy and although their calls are readily identifiable, their scarcity means that they can be missed in general surveying. Also many observers find it difficult to distinguish their drumming from that of the much more common Great Spotted Woodpecker.

There is evidence that Lesser Spotted Woodpeckers require larger home ranges than might be assumed from their diminutive size (Wiktander *et al.* 2001) and they appear to be particularly sensitive to changes in habitat. This has implications for conservation because it means that large areas of suitable habitat need to be preserved. In the nineteenth century, the widespread cessation of cider production in south-west England resulted in disused orchards with much dead wood, ideal for Lesser Spotted Woodpeckers. The grubbing up of these ancient orchards in the 1940s led to the species' almost complete disappearance from some areas (1875–1900 Atlas). Conversely, there is evidence that the 1970s saw a temporary population increase because of dead trees left behind by Dutch elm disease (1988–91 Breeding Atlas).

Sadly, since then numbers in Britain and indeed in much of Europe have fallen at a rate which can only be described as catastrophic. In 2011 the national population was estimated to be just 1,000 pairs, and the species was added to the list of birds monitored by the RBBP. Recent research suggests that breeding success is currently low because of chick starvation, but more work is required to understand the causes of this (Smith & Charman 2012). The remaining populations appear to be mainly associated with more open wooded areas such as orchards and parkland, but landscape-scale effects appear to be more important than local effects; woods are more likely to be occupied if they are 'connected' within heavily wooded landscapes (Baillie *et al.* 2010).

According to the GBR, Lesser Spotted Woodpeckers were still 'widely reported from most parts of the county' in 1976, and Swaine described the species as 'a widespread but thinly distributed resident', with no evidence of any marked change since the nineteenth century. Since then though numbers have fallen dramatically; all available data suggest a decline in excess of 80% in 20 years and this is now a rarely encountered species for most Gloucestershire birdwatchers.

It is clear that the county stronghold, if such a word is still appropriate, is the eastern Dean area, but there are still scattered pairs elsewhere; almost all are in lightly wooded or orchard landscapes. This is a largely sedentary species, so the best indication of their true distribution is probably achieved by combining the winter and breeding distribution maps. For example, in the 10 km square SO82

In memory of Peter Jones

Species accounts

2007–11 Atlas fieldwork					Gloucestershire trends					UK population trends	
Number of tetrads in which recorded (max 683)					Occupied 10 km squares (max 26)				% of tetrads in which recorded (1st hour of TTV)		UK conservation status: **Red 3**	
	Total	Confirmed	Probable	Possible	Present	1968–71	1981–84	1988–91	2007–11	1988–91	2008–11	Long term	Short term
Breeding	51	8	9	24	10	21		12	14	3.2	0.6	–70%	–
Winter	49						16		18			–	–

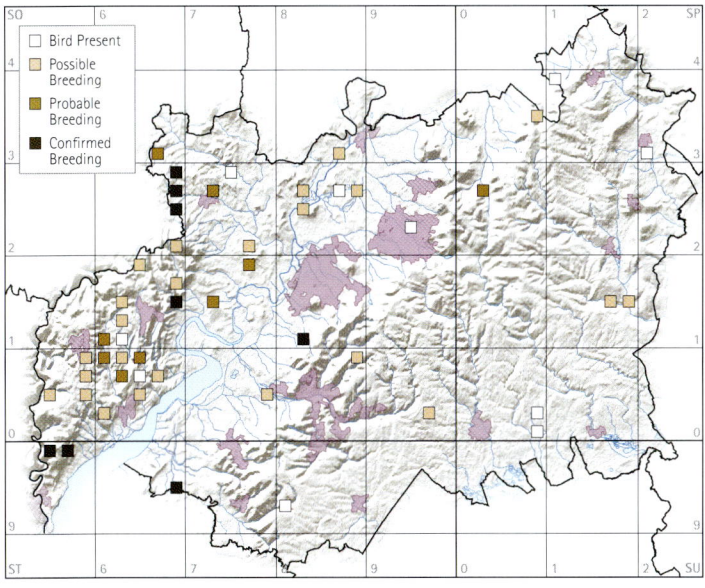

Breeding Distribution

there are several breeding season records, and the absence of any sightings there in winter is quite probably due to the birds being overlooked during that season.

The small group of confirmed breeding records along the border with Herefordshire suggests that the species might be holding on in suitable habitat there, but enquiries suggest that only a few isolated pairs are involved and this is not the eastern fringe of a larger population (Chris Robinson).

Given the scale of the current decline there must be serious doubts about the long-term prospects for Lesser Spotted Woodpeckers in the county. Detailed surveying in 2010 and 2011 suggested that there may be as few as 20 widely scattered pairs left (Ben MacDonald), so the chances of the species clinging on seem rather remote.

Lesser Spotted Woodpeckers are not frequent visitors to garden feeders, so it was especially satisfying for one atlas volunteer in Chargrove, near Cheltenham, to photograph a male (shown opposite) that became a garden regular during very cold weather in December 2009.

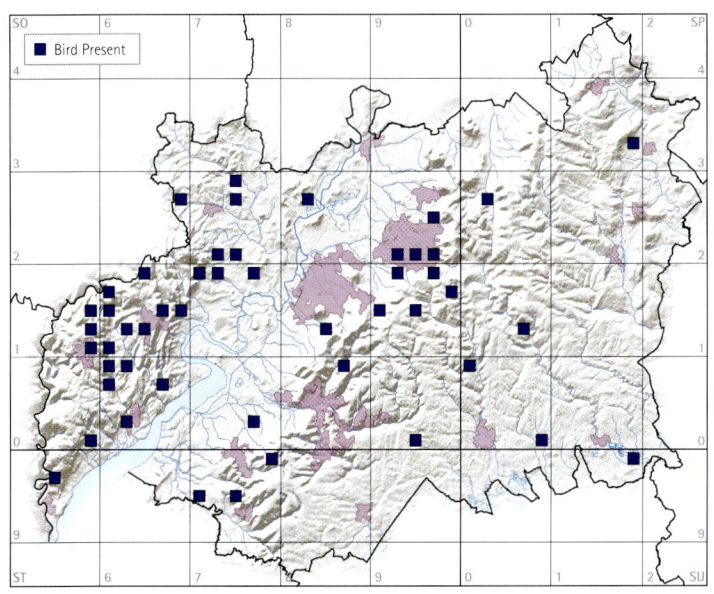

Winter Distribution

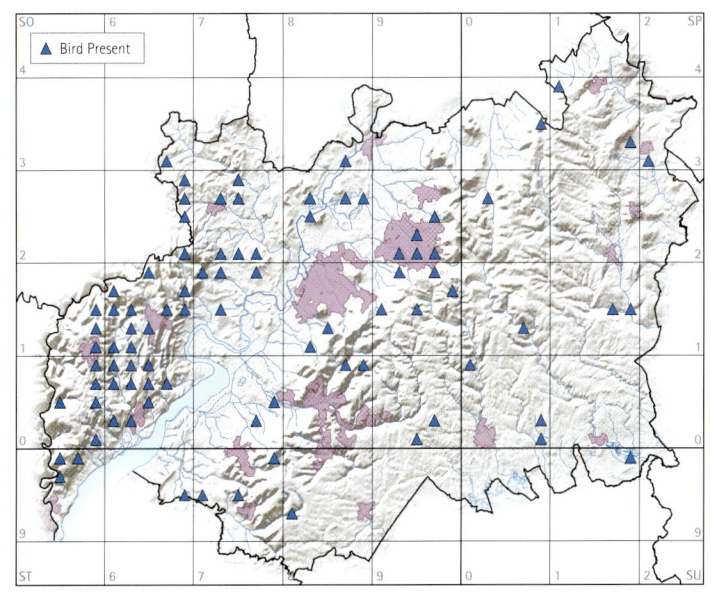

Year-Round Distribution

Red-backed Shrike
Lanius collurio

Red-backed Shrikes are summer visitors to temperate areas in Europe and eastwards to western Siberia. They winter in eastern and southern Africa, and even the westernmost breeders migrate round the eastern end of the Mediterranean (BWP). Their overall range has contracted severely since the nineteenth century, thought to be due at least in part to a decline in the abundance of large insects (1988–91 Breeding Atlas), no doubt resulting in turn from agricultural intensification and other changes in the countryside. In Britain, Red-backed Shrikes have declined from being a familiar and widespread bird over much of England and Wales to near extinction. The rate of loss appears to have accelerated from the 1930s and regular breeding ceased around 1988, since when there have been only scattered infrequent instances, including most recently in Devon.

Mellersh is remarkably brief in dealing with this species, almost to the point of dismissal; he simply states, 'Gloucestershire is visited ... regularly by large numbers of the Red-backed Shrike in the summer'. It appears that they were breeding virtually throughout the county at the end of the nineteenth century, with records and anecdotal notes to indicate pairs across the Cotswolds, all through the Severn Vale and in many open areas of the Forest of Dean. Records tended to decline subsequently but nests were regularly being found in the Dean as recently as the 1960s, and one report even noted that the species had increased there on land cleared of oaks during the Second World War (Andrew Bluett). Sadly, this bucking of the national trend was short-lived, and the last breeding record for the county came in 1966 at Crabtreehill Plantation near Cinderford, although two birds were seen near Fairford in July the following year. The decline has been so rapid and complete that since then there have been only five records of this magnificent little bird:

1971: one at Frocester Hill, on the Cotswold scarp between Stroud and Dursley on May 26th.
1973: an adult male near Daglingworth, Cirencester on May 6th.
1976: an immature at Ozleworth, Wotton-under-Edge on June 27th.
1997: a female at Cannop crossroads, Forest of Dean on May 25th.
2006: an adult male at Tidenham Chase in the Dean on June 16th.

Great Grey Shrike
Lanius excubitor

Great Grey Shrikes breed patchily in France and Germany and northwards into Fennoscandia, and more continuously across parts of eastern Europe, Asia and North America. The Fennoscandian population is migratory and in recent years an average of about 60 have wintered in Britain, though numbers vary in relation to breeding success in the previous nesting season, which in turn depends on the population levels of their rodent prey, in the same way as for some owl species (Migration Atlas). Individual birds will sometimes return to the same wintering area in successive years, but in general their presence is unpredictable and the surprise discovery of a shrike watching for prey from a prominent perch is guaranteed to enliven a winter's day.

Mellersh stated that Gloucestershire held 'one or two in most winters' but this was regarded by Swaine as 'perhaps an exaggeration', noting that there were scarcely any published reports for the nineteenth century and that Mellersh himself had only mentioned about a dozen instances from 1875 to 1902. Swaine knew of only two reports between then and 1960, but there were 14 from 1960 to 1980. Since then they may have become more frequent in the county: in the 1980s they were recorded in only two years, but this rose to six years in the 1990s and every year except one since 2000. Moreover until 2000 it was very unusual for more than one bird to be seen in any year, whereas since then this has happened on seven occasions. It is difficult to be certain about total numbers as individuals are known to range widely, but it seems likely that in both early 2008 and early 2009 three different birds were present in the county. It is possible that the increase of clear-felled plantation in the Forest of Dean accounts for the higher overall numbers, as they were not recorded regularly from that area in the past and this is now a favoured habitat. Almost all other sightings are from higher ground on the Cotswolds, where uncultivated grassland and scrub can harbour sufficient prey.

Wintering birds can arrive in the last week of October, and it is not unusual for individuals to remain until April; in 2009, for example, one was seen at a favoured Forest of Dean site until April 22nd. A remarkable record came in 2010 when the remains of a Great Grey Shrike were found among the birds killed by Peregrines at Christ Church, Cheltenham. This discovery was made on October 10th, when it was estimated that the remains were less than a week old; this is the earliest autumn date for the species in the county.

Isabelline Shrike
Lanius isabellinus

There were 80 records of this Asiatic shrike in the British Isles between 1950 and 2010. There has been one record in Gloucestershire: a first-winter bird was photographed in the western section of the Cotswold Water Park on October 28th 2001.

Woodchat Shrike
Lanius senator

Woodchat Shrikes are summer visitors to southern Europe and are seen in Britain every year in low numbers, most frequently in the month of May. The species was removed from the national rarities list in 1991, although the increase in sightings here since the mid-twentieth century is likely to be due to observer effects. There have been three records in Gloucestershire:

1905: one on the Oxfordshire border at Little Rissington airfield from May 5th to 8th.
1958: one near Dursley on May 27th.
1961: one at Coombe Hill Canal on June 6th.

Mellersh refers to three birds taken near Cheltenham: at Dowdeswell Wood before 1875 and at Shurdington and Badgeworth in 1893. These reports remain unsubstantiated. The absence of any county records in the last 50 years, despite the huge increase in the number of birdwatchers, is entirely in accordance with the severe declines in the northern part of this shrike's European range.

Golden Oriole (Eurasian Golden Oriole)
Oriolus oriolus

Golden Orioles are fairly common summer visitors to much of continental Europe, the Middle East and parts of North Africa, and the breeding range extends to Mongolia and the eastern Himalayas. Western birds winter widely over sub-Saharan Africa. The tiny British breeding population, mainly in East Anglia, has decreased recently.

In Gloucestershire there are some historical records, but with few details. Since 1910 there have been 23 records: singles in 1920, 1949 and 1962, four in the 1970s, eight in the 1980s, three in the 1990s, and five since 2000. The peak in the 1980s coincided with something of a high point in the fortunes of the English breeding population.

Finding dates have ranged between April 16th (1977) and July 14th (1949), with about three-quarters between mid-May and mid-June, which is typical for the species in Britain. Also characteristically, many have involved singing males. About half were in the Severn Vale, the remainder divided between the Thames Area (Cotswold Water Park) and the Cotswolds; surprisingly, none has been recorded in the central part of the Dean. Nearly all stayed for only one day, but in 2004 a pair was seen at the Water Park on April 28th and a male was heard there on a few dates at the end of May, although there were no indications of breeding.

Nutcracker (Spotted Nutcracker)
Nucifraga caryocatactes

European Nutcrackers are largely sedentary, but birds of the subspecies *N. c. macrorhynchos* from Siberia sometimes erupt south-westwards, making the species a rare and erratic visitor to Britain with 375 records since 1950.

The sole accepted Gloucestershire record is of one at Humblebee Wood near Winchcombe on September 28th 1963. Mellersh (quoted by Swaine) refers to one at Shurdington near Cheltenham in 1866, but gives no supporting details, and this record does not satisfy modern criteria for acceptance.

Magpie (Eurasian Magpie)
Pica pica

The Magpie is a very successful, familiar and widespread species, ranging over practically the whole of the Western Palearctic and wide areas of Asia. It is essentially sedentary throughout its range, but it colonised Ireland in the late seventeenth century. Magpies nest in trees or bushes but can be found in a wide range of habitats, avoiding only very densely wooded areas, large wetlands, deserts and high mountains in addition to completely treeless landscapes.

In Britain, Magpies were formerly heavily persecuted, especially by gamekeepers, because they will readily eat the eggs and young of other birds during the breeding season. During the nineteenth century there were widespread declines as a result of this pressure. There was some recovery during the First World War, due to lapses in keeping and to legislation against poison baits, and then a more pronounced increase from the mid-1940s onward. Nowadays they are still subject to control, but on a reduced scale, and as a result of this relaxation of pressure they continued to increase dramatically during the late twentieth century and at the same time spread into suburbs and even town centres, in Britain as well as in a number of other European countries. Since about 1995 population levels here have been more or less stable at about 600,000 territories. There has been concern in some quarters that because of their predation of eggs, nestlings and fledglings, Magpies might be adversely affecting songbird populations, but there is no evidence that they have any significant large-scale effects.

Swaine confirmed that the national increase since the 1940s had affected Gloucestershire, with birds found regularly 'even in town parks and far up onto the higher Cotswolds'. These days, as the maps show, they can be seen anywhere in the county, even including the centres of larger towns. However, TTV results appears to show a decrease in occupancy at the tetrad level since the 1988–91 Breeding Atlas (see fact-box). This is in line with a slight decline in the regional BBS figures for south-west England (a 4% drop between 1995 and 2009), although within the county the BBS data show no noticeable trend either way.

The abundance maps show noticeably lower numbers in the more heavily wooded parts of the Forest of Dean, and especially across the Cotswold dip-slope. As well as perhaps providing less suitable breeding habitat, with more open countryside and fewer hedges, it is in these areas of the Cotswolds where gamebird shooting is most likely to take place, and where Magpies are accordingly more likely to be persecuted. It is notable that densities were relatively high in the 10 km squares including Gloucester, Cheltenham and Stroud, the county's largest built-up areas, reflecting the successful penetration by Magpies into suburbs and the edges of towns. Indeed, the largest count during a TTV, of 44 birds, was on the outskirts of Cheltenham in tetrad SO92A in November 2007.

The Magpie's sedentary nature means that ringing recoveries revealing movements of more than a few kilometres are unusual, and movements of more than 100 km are decidedly rare. There has been one such long-distance recovery involving Gloucestershire: a juvenile ringed at Portland Bill, Dorset in July 2007 was reported dead near Lechlade in April 2008.

Sponsored by Jake King

Species accounts

2007–11 Atlas fieldwork				
Number of tetrads in which recorded (max 683)				
	Total	Confirmed	Probable	Possible	Present
Breeding	636	286	177	142	31
Winter	665				

Gloucestershire trends					
Occupied 10 km squares (max 26)				% of tetrads in which recorded (1st hour of TTV)	
1968–71	1981–84	1988–91	2007–11	1988–91	2008–11
26		26	26	93.3	75.3
	26		26		

UK population trends	
UK conservation status: **Green**	
Long term	Short term
+94%	–3%
–	–

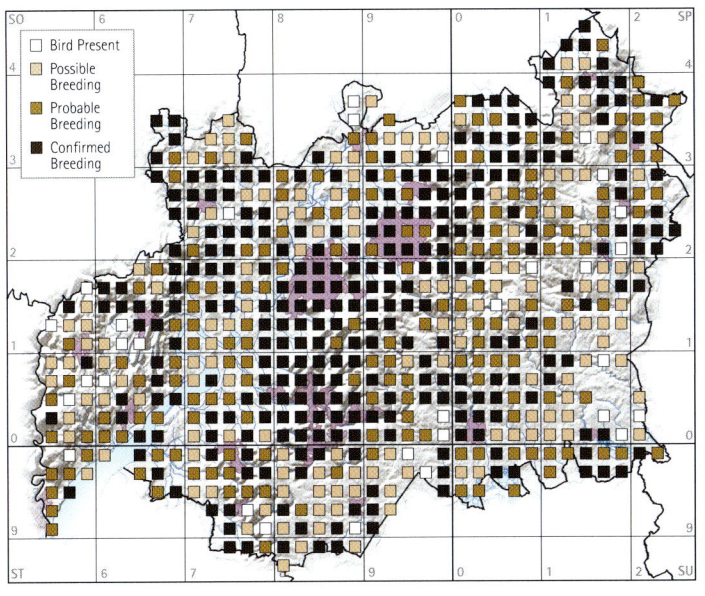

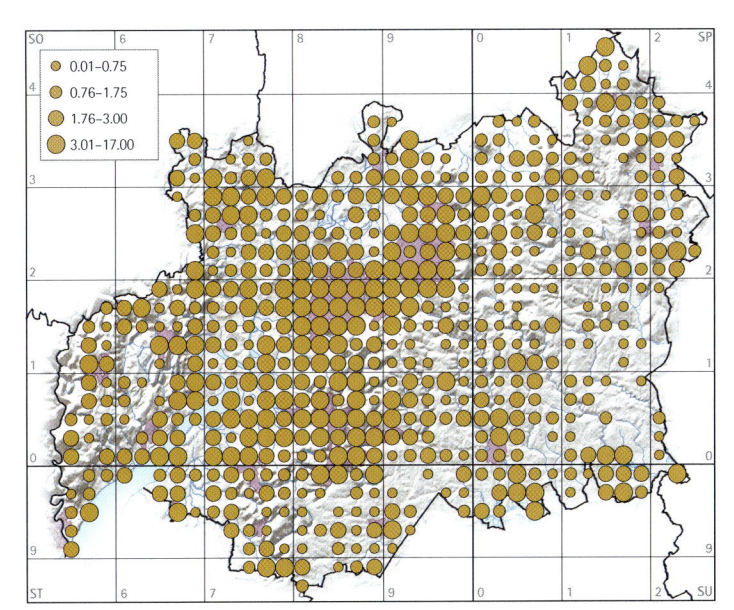

Breeding Distribution

Summer Abundance

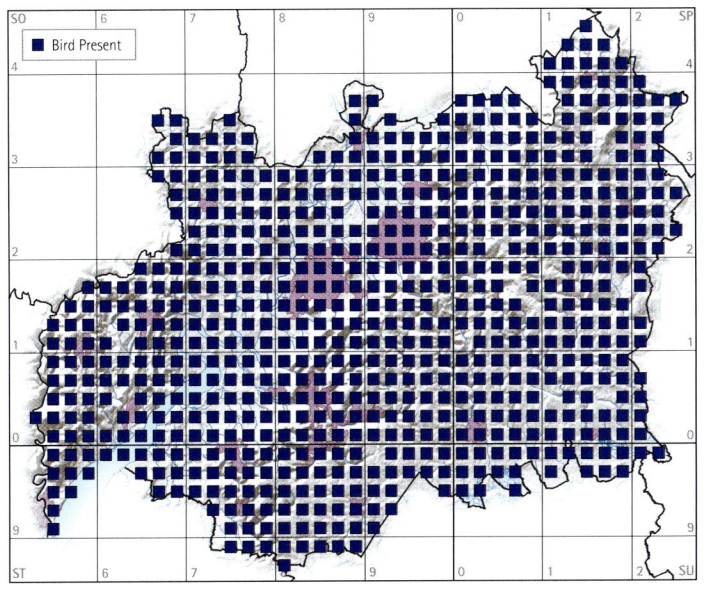

Winter Distribution

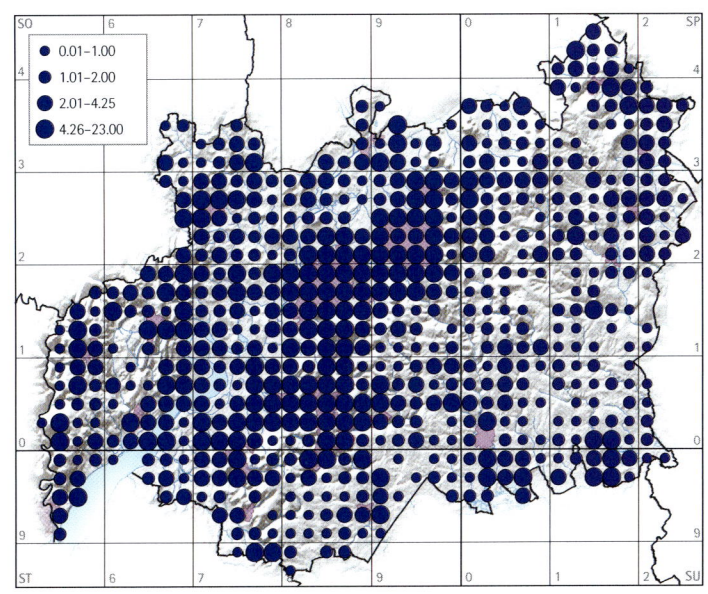

Winter Abundance

Jay (Eurasian Jay)
Garrulus glandarius

Jays breed from North Africa, the British Isles and Fennoscandia across wide areas of Eurasia as far as the Pacific. Their habitat is mainly broad-leaved woodland, especially oak, beech and hornbeam. In Britain they are strongly associated with oak, and in autumn they can be seen busily burying acorns for future consumption, often carrying them for considerable distances. It is probably this caching behaviour that enables oak woodland to spread uphill and across open country, as many buried acorns remain uneaten and eventually germinate. Jays are essentially sedentary, but in some years northern and eastern populations undertake eruptive movements in response to shortages of food, particularly acorns. The most recent major irruption into Britain was in 1983.

Jays often come into gardens and will readily take food provided at bird tables and feeders. They will also take the eggs of other birds during the breeding season, and because of this they have always been heavily persecuted by gamekeepers and others over much of their range. However, some relaxation of this pressure in recent years has resulted in an increase in numbers in parts of Europe, including Britain, and despite their sedentary nature they have spread into areas of northern Scotland and western Ireland.

Swaine stated that the Jay was a common resident in wooded areas of Gloucestershire and was being increasingly found in large gardens and parks. He also quoted a figure of 300 killed by one gamekeeper over an area of about 1,000 acres (400 ha) in a single year (1900) in the Forest of Dean – a measure of the intensity of persecution as well as the density of the Jay population.

The spread from woodland into other habitats has continued over the last three decades, and the distribution maps show that Jays occur throughout the county. The only noticeable gaps are in some comparatively treeless areas of the Severn Vale, Cotswolds and Thames Area. The abundance maps show clear concentrations in heavily wooded regions, as might be expected especially the Forest of Dean (including the Newent area), but also along the Cotswold scarp and in some other parts of the Cotswolds, notably 10 km squares SO90 (Cirencester Park), SP01 (Withington Woods), and SP02 (Guiting Wood and numerous other smaller woodlands).

In the area covered by both Cotswolds Atlases the number of tetrads where Jays were found increased from 154 to 183 between 1987 and 2007. On the other hand, for the county as a whole there seems to have been a decrease in tetrad occupancy between the 1988–91 Breeding Atlas and the current survey (see fact-box). However, county BBS data show no clear trends over the last 16 years and these apparent changes may reflect short-term population fluctuations as well as the vicissitudes of fieldwork.

Jays sometimes gather into small flocks, even when not undertaking long movements. Quite possibly the highest count during a winter TTV, of 15 in SO62X near Newent in November 2008, involved such a gathering. On the other hand, the highest breeding season count, again of 15 birds in SO80S near Stroud in June 2008, probably simply reflected a high breeding density in that area.

The fact that this largely resident bird will nevertheless sometimes undertake fairly long movements is reflected in the recoveries of two Jays ringed in Gloucestershire, in Shropshire and 'Hereford and Worcester' respectively.

Sponsored by the Newent Wildlife Watch Group

Species accounts

2007–11 Atlas fieldwork					Gloucestershire trends						UK population trends	
Number of tetrads in which recorded (max 683)					Occupied 10 km squares (max 26)				% of tetrads in which recorded (1st hour of TTV)		UK conservation status: Green	
	Total	Confirmed	Probable	Possible	Present	1968–71	1981–84	1988–91	2007–11	1988–91	2008–11	Long term	Short term
Breeding	483	63	155	210	55	26		25	26	43.6	34.2	+6%	+16%
Winter	590							26	26			–	–

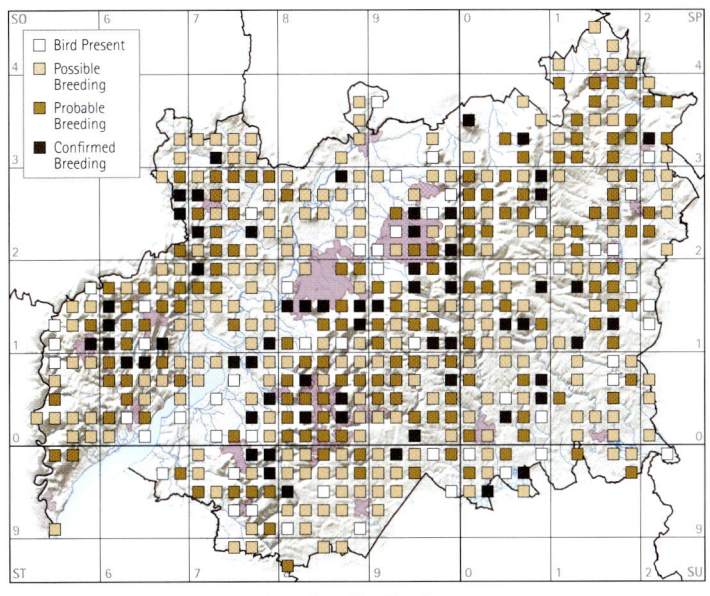

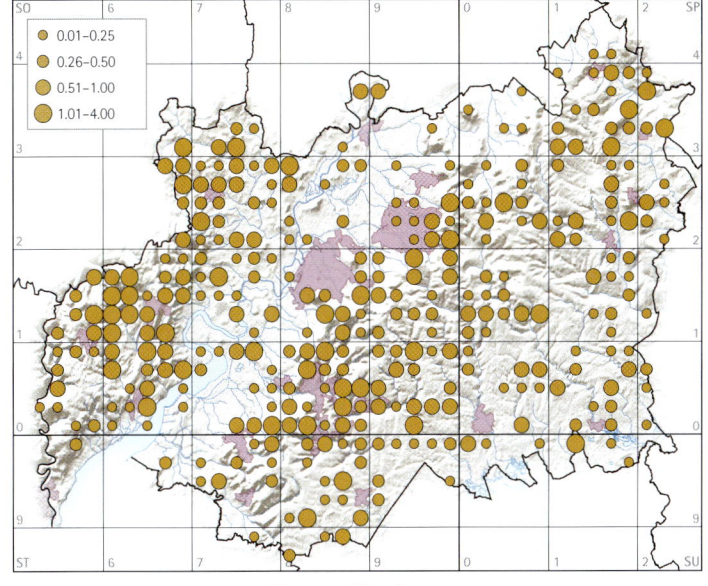

Breeding Distribution

Summer Abundance

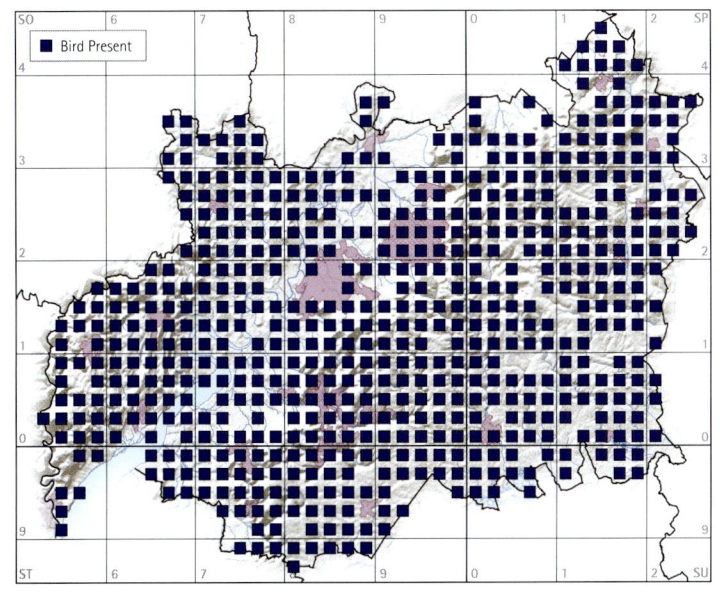

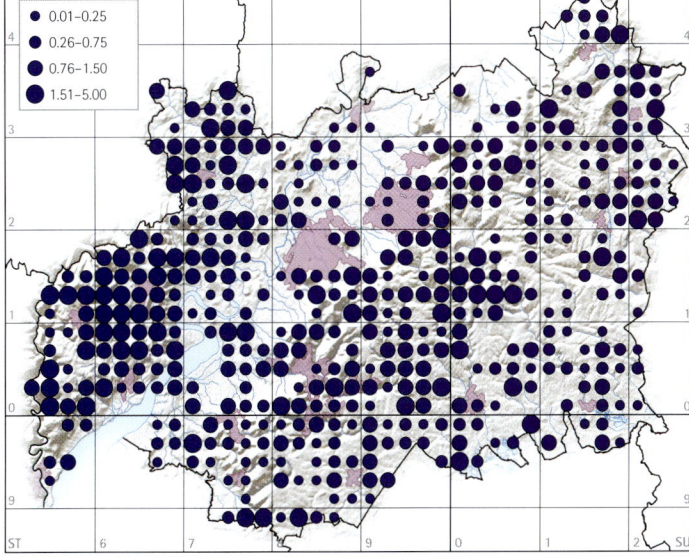

Winter Distribution

Winter Abundance

Jackdaw (Western Jackdaw)
Corvus monedula

Jackdaws breed from North Africa, the European Atlantic seaboard and southern Scandinavia east to central Siberia and the north-west Himalayas. Northern and eastern birds are migratory but in most of Europe they are resident. They are found throughout the British Isles, except in treeless moorland and mountainous areas. However the distribution over the entire range is 'remarkably patchy and fluctuating' (BWP), probably as a result of their requirements for nesting holes (in trees, rock-faces and buildings) in sufficient number and density to enable breeding colonies to exist. Jackdaws have adapted well to artificially modified landscapes including farmland, and in Britain at least they are commonest in areas where there are extensive areas of sheepwalk or cattle pasture, where it is easy for them to find food. The young are fed mainly on invertebrates, while adults also eat carrion, 'scraps' (foraging on landfill sites and in farmyards), seeds and fruits. More rarely they will take birds' eggs, and in late summer they often move into woods, where they feed in flocks on caterpillars in the canopy. These habits and their frequent loud calling mean that Jackdaws are usually easy to find during atlas surveying.

There was little change in distribution at the national level between the 1968–72 and 1988–91 Breeding Atlases but, as the fact-box indicates, there have been considerable increases in numbers within the British range.

In Gloucestershire, Swaine remarked that Jackdaws were abundant and widespread and had increased considerably at least since 1940. The current atlas results show that they are still common here and have certainly not decreased. In the area covered by the Cotswolds Atlases the occupancy rate apparently rose by about 9%, from 274 to 298 tetrads, between 1987 and 2007. This was thought to be possibly a result of improved coverage, but the county BBS data also seem to show an increasing trend between 1994 and 2010.

For a relatively large hole-nesting bird, confirmed breeding records are surprisingly widespread, probably reflecting a fairly high density of old hedgerow trees in most parts of the county as well as the birds' willingness to use artificial nesting sites, including conspicuous ones such as chimneys. The only area where records are noticeably sparser is in the central, densely wooded part of the Forest of Dean, where grassland foraging habitat is scarce and where large old trees with suitable holes may, unexpectedly perhaps, be in shorter supply. There are also areas of low density in Gloucester and especially Cheltenham, and in some of the more treeless parts of the Cotswolds. In winter Jackdaws are even more widespread, though they were still not recorded in some Dean tetrads; the abundance map tends to suggest that they prefer higher land at that season, with fairly noticeable areas of low density in the Severn Vale around Cheltenham and Gloucester and in some lower-lying parts of the Cotswolds and Thames Area. This could reflect the distribution of pasture to some degree.

Flocks of over 500 Jackdaws are by no means exceptional in the county, especially in late summer when numbers are boosted by fledged young, and in winter when they gather to roost. The largest count in recent years was of 2,000 flying to roost by the western section of the Cotswold Water Park on October 30th 2005. The highest counts during atlas TTVs were 550 in December 2007 in tetrad SO91Y, in the Cotswolds near Cheltenham, and 200 in July 2010 in SO73G, on the county border near the southern end of the Malvern Hills.

Sponsored by Peter Ormerod and Alan Richards

Species accounts 285

2007–11 Atlas fieldwork					Gloucestershire trends						UK population trends		
Number of tetrads in which recorded (max 683)					Occupied 10 km squares (max 26)				% of tetrads in which recorded (1st hour of TTV)		UK conservation status: **Green**	
	Total	Confirmed	Probable	Possible	Present	1968–71	1981–84	1988–91	2007–11	1988–91	2008–11	Long term	Short term
Breeding	660	468	116	58	18	26		26	26	85.6	85.5	+124%	+39%
Winter	664						26		26			–	–

Breeding Distribution

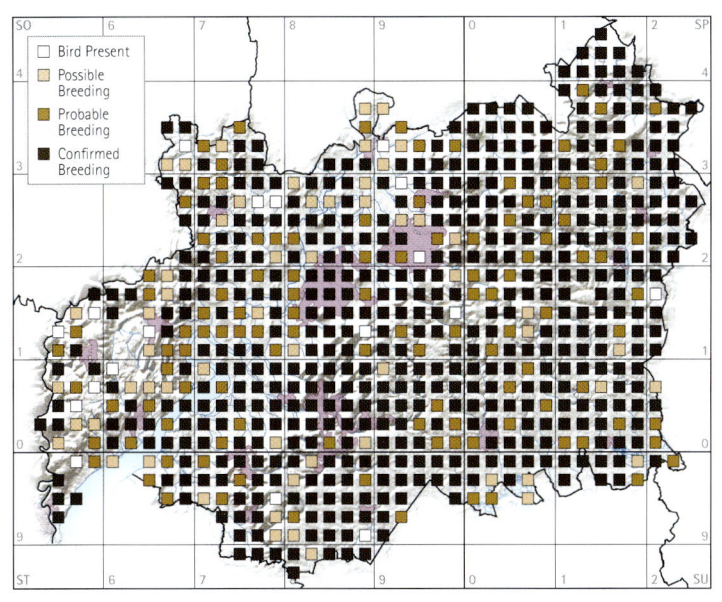

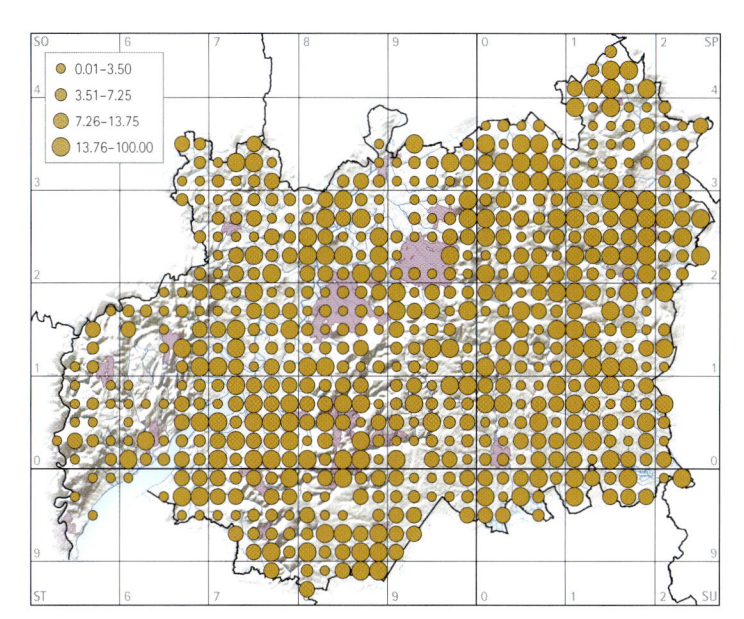

Summer Abundance

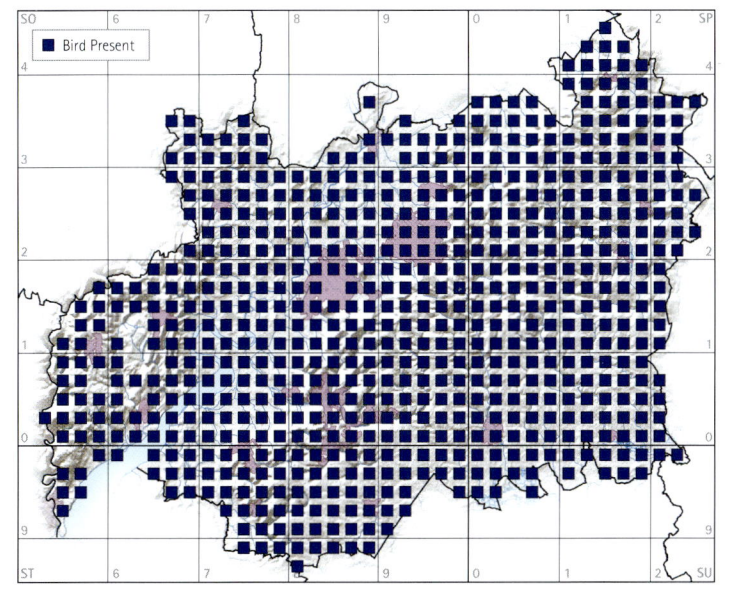

Winter Distribution

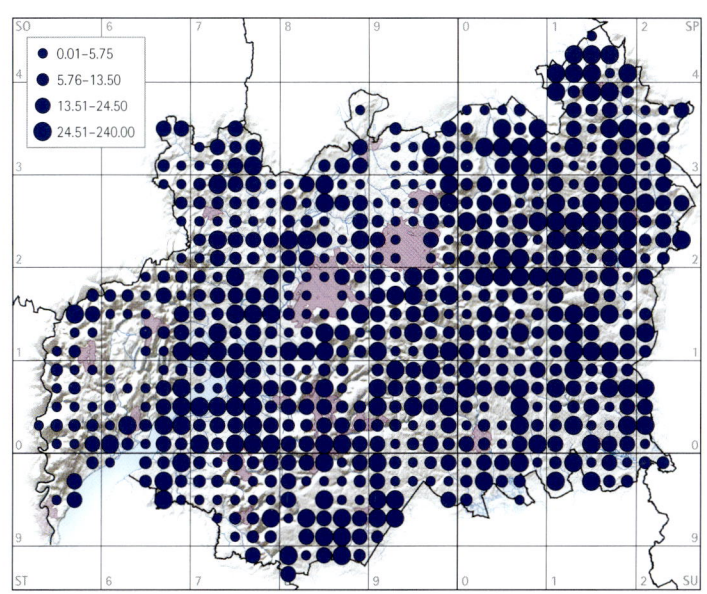

Winter Abundance

Rook
Corvus frugilegus

Their ability to exploit open habitats, particularly grasslands, means that Rooks must have benefited enormously from the conversion of vast areas of woodland to farmland from prehistory up to modern times. These days the breeding range extends from France and the British Isles across Europe and southern Siberia as far as central China. Over much of the range they are at least partially migratory, and many northern European breeders winter south to the Mediterranean countries, but British and Irish birds are essentially resident. One requirement which restricts their distribution is the need for fairly tall trees for nesting, so they are absent in summer from extensive treeless areas such as moors and high mountains.

Despite the overall long-term increase in the amount of suitable habitat, the more recent fortunes of the Rook have been rather mixed in much of Europe. In Britain they increased considerably during the 1920s and the 1940s but then declined quite markedly between about 1950 and 1975, with something of a recovery since.

Swaine referred to reports by Mellersh of a roost of 20,000 to 25,000 birds in Dixton Wood near Winchcombe and similar 'immense flocks' in other parts of Gloucestershire. Such numbers would have been remarkable around 1980 when Swaine was writing, but he still described the Rook as an 'abundant resident' at that time; there had apparently been an increase in the county from about 1930 to 1950 followed by a subsequent decline, approximately paralleling national trends. Both national and local declines are thought to be due to the use of toxic pesticides, agricultural intensification (notably the conversion of grassland to arable farming) and persecution (which is largely misguided: 'on balance the species is beneficial', 1968–72 Breeding Atlas).

The maps show that Rooks are still very widespread in Gloucestershire, although numbers are clearly lower in the Forest of Dean, where there is less farming and more extensive woodland. Although rookeries are noisy and active places they can still be missed during atlas fieldwork, especially those with few nests, but breeding was nevertheless confirmed in more than 50% of tetrads in the county, an unexpectedly high total. In winter Rooks are if anything even more widespread, though there is still a noticeable area of low density or absence in the Dean area, and the abundance map for this season clearly confirms that larger towns tend to be avoided.

The comparable TTV figures shown in the fact-box hint at a slight decline in range over the last 20 years, but on the other hand county BBS figures give no indication of any decrease and in the area covered by the Cotswolds Atlases the number of occupied tetrads was similar between 1987 and 2007.

The largest flocks reported in recent GBRs have contained around 500 birds, while during atlas TTVs the maximum counts were 617 in December 2008 in SP10S (in the Cotswolds near Fairford), and 600 in May 2011 in SO70C (Slimbridge). These numbers pale into insignificance compared with Mellersh's tens of thousands, but it seems likely that the Rook population here is currently fairly stable.

There have been very few ringing recoveries of Rooks involving Gloucestershire, but there is one notable movement of an adult ringed in northern Germany in May 1933 and shot at Deerhurst, near Tewkesbury, in January 1942.

Sponsored by Phil Davis

Species accounts

2007–11 Atlas fieldwork						Gloucestershire trends						UK population trends	
Number of tetrads in which recorded (max 683)					Occupied 10 km squares (max 26)				% of tetrads in which recorded (1st hour of TTV)		UK conservation status: Green	
	Total	Confirmed	Probable	Possible	Present	1968–71	1981–84	1988–91	2007–11	1988–91	2008–11	Long term	Short term
Breeding	573	392	23	79	79	26		26	26	70.2	60.5	–	–12%
Winter	626							26	26			–	–

Breeding Distribution

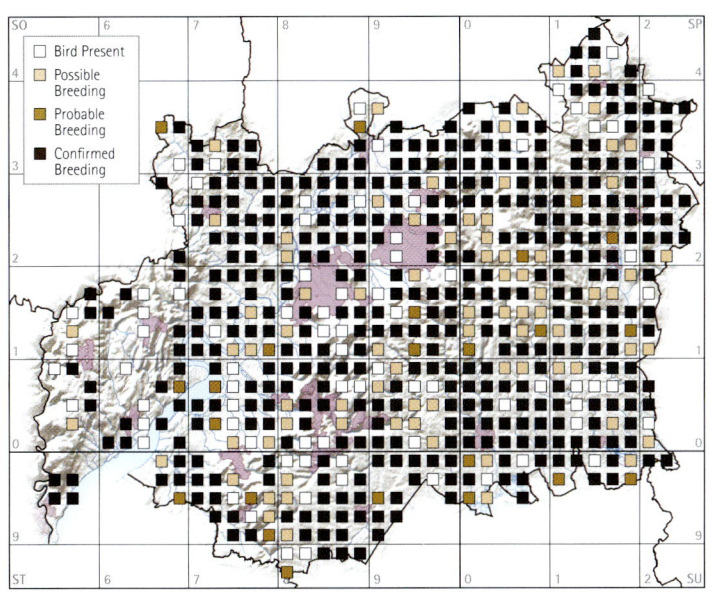

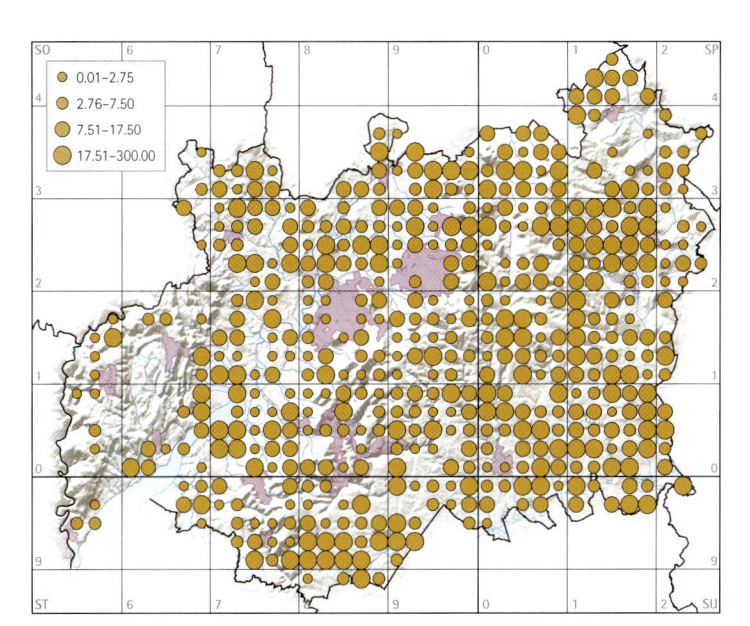

Summer Abundance

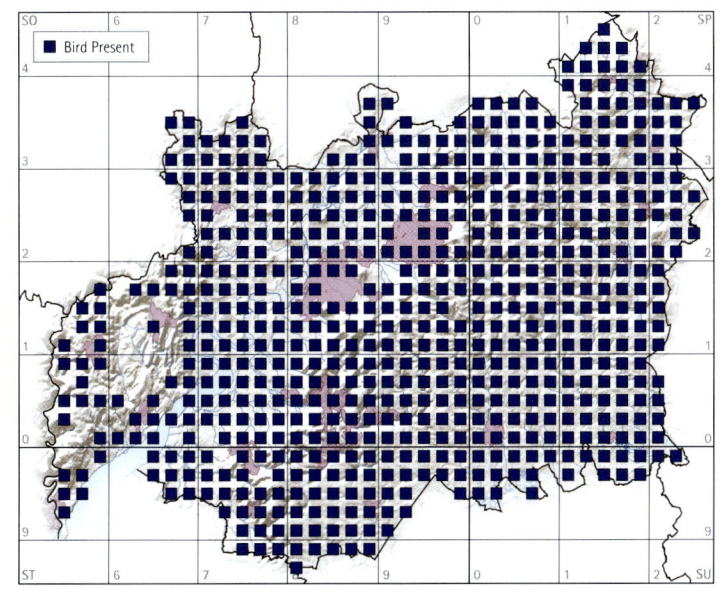

Winter Distribution

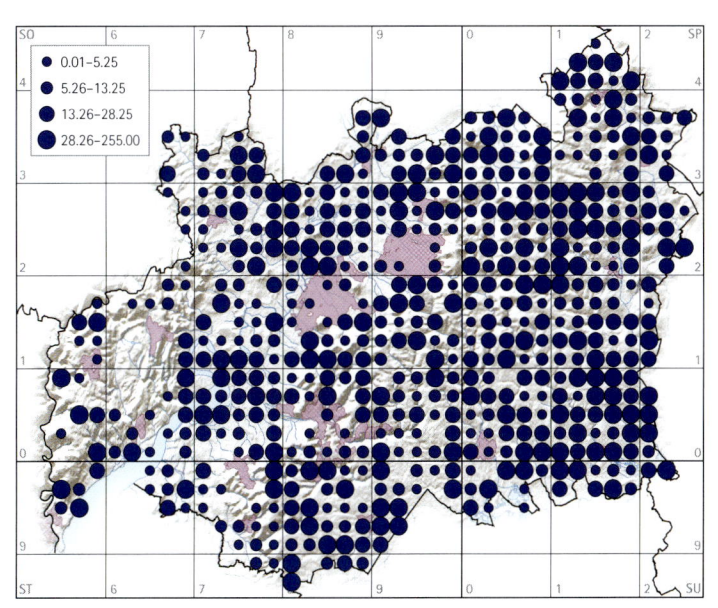

Winter Abundance

Carrion Crow
Corvus corone

One of the most familiar species on the British list, the Carrion Crow breeds in western Europe, including England, Wales and all but the far north and west of Scotland; there is another subspecies in central and eastern Asia. Elsewhere, including in Ireland, Fennoscandia and eastern Europe, it is replaced by the very closely related Hooded Crow, with which it hybridises freely and with which it was formerly considered to be conspecific. Western European Carrion Crows are essentially resident. The habitat is basically 'open country with scattered trees, copses and woodland' (BWP). In Britain this includes very wide areas of countryside, and in addition the adaptable and successful Crow has successfully colonised suburbs and towns.

That Crows are so widespread and common is partly due to the very diverse range of food that they will take and to their adaptability in exploiting new food sources. As the English name implies, dead animal material such as road kills, sheep carrion and refuse from landfill sites does form a high proportion of the diet, but they will also readily eat invertebrates and small mammals, as well as cereal seeds and other vegetable food. They also take eggs and young birds, and will attack helpless or sick livestock. As a result they are unpopular even among some birdwatchers, as well as sheep farmers and gamekeepers, and they have long been heavily persecuted. Nevertheless they have increased in numbers steadily, especially during the twentieth century.

This is an easy species to find during atlas work – the birds are often noisy and make their presence known, and the large tree nests are conspicuous and are built or repaired early in the breeding season, when the trees are not yet in full leaf. In winter, the unwary observer may confuse Carrion Crows with Rooks: contrary to popular myth, large flocks of Crows are not necessarily 'Rooks', and a single Rook is not necessarily a 'Crow'!

In Gloucestershire, Swaine described the Carrion Crow as 'a common resident in all parts of the county' and mentioned the large flocks to be found at landfill sites; there were records of winter roosts of 'up to 40 or more birds in various places'. There has certainly been no decrease since then, and they must breed in practically every kilometre square in the county. The Cotswolds Atlases recorded no significant changes in breeding distribution between 1987 and 2007, and since 2006 Crows have been recorded every year in 100% of county BBS squares. The abundance maps show that, as with Magpies, numbers are lower in some farmland areas, particularly in parts of the Cotswolds and the Thames Area where gamebird shooting is most prevalent and where Crows are likely to be subjected to heavier control by keepers. They are also comparatively scarce in the more densely wooded parts of the Forest of Dean, although they were recorded at fairly high densities in the nearby region of mixed farming and orchards around Newent. They appear to be more concentrated in the Severn Vale in winter than in the breeding season; the highest count during a winter TTV was 347, in SO81D at the Gloucester landfill site in December 2007. Even during the breeding season, when they tend to be less gregarious, 210 were counted during a TTV at SO92I, Bishops Cleeve (also near a landfill site) in April 2009.

Hooded Crow
Corvus cornix

Although in early times the Hooded Crow was considered to be a species in its own right, it was regarded as a subspecies of Carrion Crow for a while, before being 'split' again in 2002. The main breeding range is from Fennoscandia and eastern Europe eastwards across large areas of Asia, but they also occur in Ireland, the Isle of Man, north-west Scotland and the Faeroes. Hence the Hooded Crows of the British Isles are separated from continental birds by land occupied by Carrion Crows, in addition to the North Sea. The British population is sedentary, but Fennoscandian birds move south-west for the winter and in the past Hooded Crows wintered regularly in England, especially on the eastern seaboard. In recent times these birds are wintering further north, probably in response to climatic amelioration, so they are no longer regular here (Migration Atlas).

Against this background it is not surprising that in 1902 Mellersh reported that this species was recorded annually on the Cotswolds, with larger flocks of up to ten occurring every two or three years. Perhaps because of observer effects, or the bird's perceived lowly status as a subspecies, there were no reports between the turn of the twentieth century and 1946, but Swaine described them as irregular visitors between then and 1980, with 'nearly 30' recorded. This may be an error, as only 19 are detailed in the relevant county bird reports. The last record of more than one bird was of three at Leckhampton Hill on September 4th 1971, and since Swaine's time records have dried up almost completely; singles were at Cheltenham on December 12th 1982 and in flight at Slimbridge on May 1st 1991.

Sponsored by Colin & Ingrid Twissell, and in memory of Mr Colin H E Minchin

Species accounts

2007–11 Atlas fieldwork					Gloucestershire trends						UK population trends		
Number of tetrads in which recorded (max 683)					Occupied 10 km squares (max 26)				% of tetrads in which recorded (1st hour of TTV)		UK conservation status: Green		
	Total	Confirmed	Probable	Possible	Present	1968–71	1981–84	1988–91	2007–11	1988–91	2008–11	Long term	Short term
Breeding	681	463	144	62	12	26		26	26	100.0	98.1	+85%	+9%
Winter	683						26		26			–	–

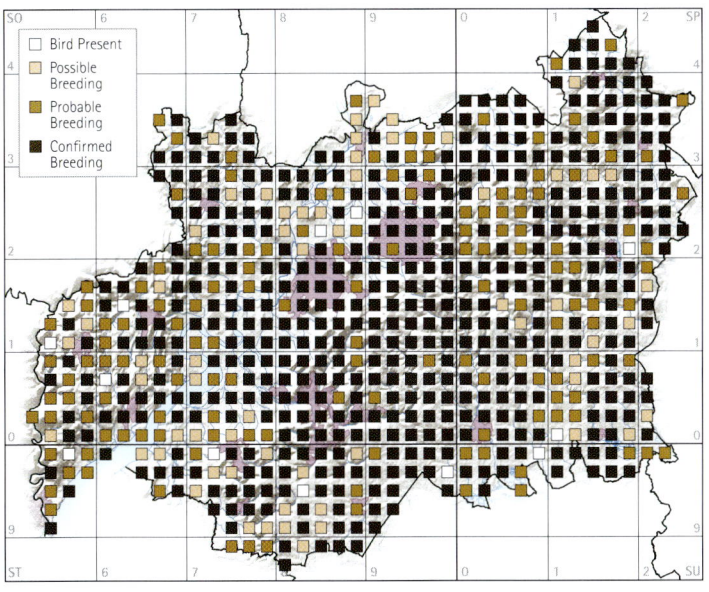

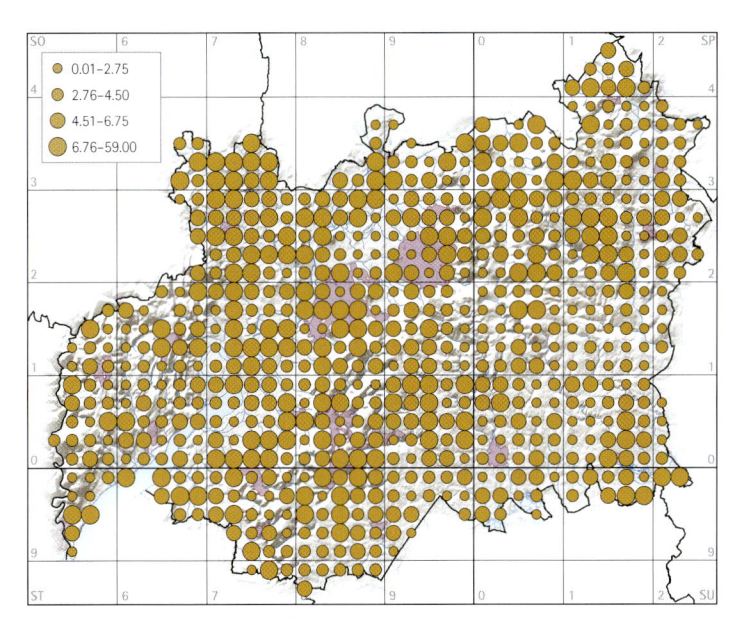

Breeding Distribution

Summer Abundance

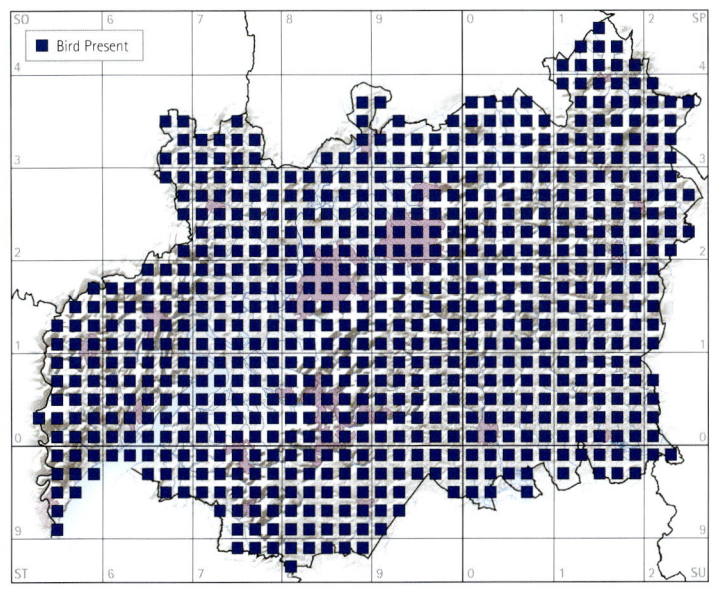

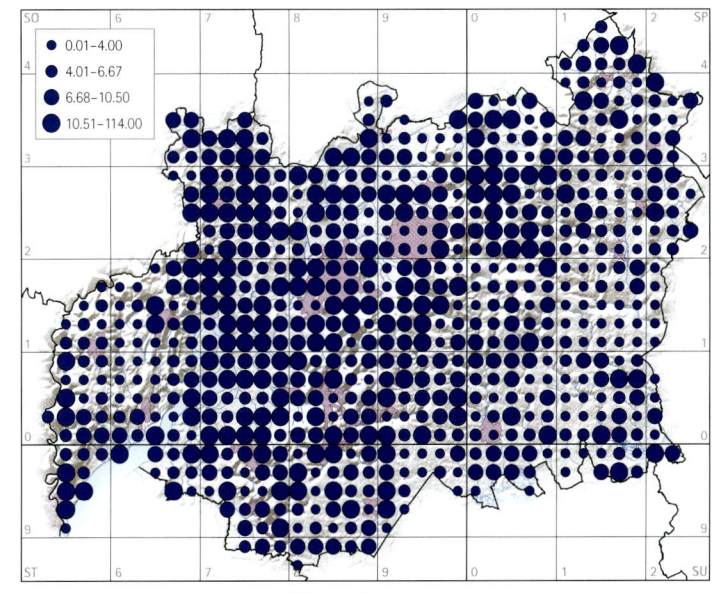

Winter Distribution

Winter Abundance

Raven (Northern Raven)
Corvus corax

The Raven is a very widespread species, extending over much of the Palearctic and Nearctic regions. They are 'so wide-ranging that the concept of habitat is hardly applicable' (BWP); they are found from sea level to high mountains and from the Arctic almost to the tropics, in practically all habitats apart from very extensive areas of dense forest. Ravens are often thought of as depending on carrion, but they are highly opportunistic feeders, taking a very wide range of foods, and will readily join flocks of gulls at landfill sites. They are mainly sedentary, but immatures in particular can undertake dispersive movements.

There has been an expansion of range in modern times over much of Europe, due largely to the relaxation of persecution pressure. In the British Isles they were formerly widespread; in the seventeenth century they foraged alongside Red Kites in London streets. During the nineteenth century however they were much reduced due to persecution by gamekeepers and others, and by the beginning of the twentieth century they were confined to parts of Scotland and Ireland, north and south-west England, and Wales. Persecution decreased during the twentieth century, but recovery in Britain was fairly slow and erratic up to the time of the 1988–91 Breeding Atlas. Since then however, the range has increased significantly and it now seems quite possible that Ravens may eventually spread across the whole of England, albeit probably remaining at low density in the predominantly arable farmland of the east.

Nesting pairs range over quite wide areas, and while the distinctive calls and aerial displays are good indications that breeding is taking place nearby, it can be difficult to pinpoint the exact site. There may therefore have been some degree of duplication of breeding records in neighbouring tetrads during the atlas fieldwork.

In Gloucestershire, the fortunes of the species have mirrored the national picture. It is doubtful whether any were still breeding in the county by 1880, but they were nesting again in the Dean and Wye Area from about 1952, and up to four pairs at least nested there almost annually up to 1980 (Swaine). Further east in the county they were still only being sighted occasionally at that time; a pair built a nest near North Nibley in 1972, but no young were seen. Since then there has been a noticeable increase in numbers and a quite dramatic spread across the county. In the Cotswolds Atlases area there were no records at all in 1983–87, but in 2003–07 they were found in 69 tetrads spread over all but one of the 13 10 km squares covered. In 1998, a nest 3 km east of Cheltenham was the easternmost breeding site in the county, but by 2007 there were breeding records in 24 Cotswold tetrads, scattered right across to the eastern county border.

The current distribution maps show records from all parts of the county and it is no longer unusual to see Ravens anywhere in Gloucestershire, although sightings are still rather less frequent in the Thames Area. The abundance maps show that the greatest densities are generally in the Forest of Dean and surrounding areas and in the higher parts of the Cotswolds, though this may well change in future if the current increase and spread continues.

In recent times there have been a number of records of gatherings of 50 or more Ravens in the county, which would have been almost unthinkable only 20 years ago. The maximum recent count was of 254 flying to roost at Walmore Common, near the traditional Forest of Dean stronghold, on May 31st 2007. However the maximum count during an atlas TTV was in the Cotswolds: 24 in SO91V, north-west of Cirencester in February 2010.

There are only three ringing recoveries of Ravens affecting the county. A nestling ringed near Longhope was found dead two months later, killed by 'pollution' very close to the ringing site, and another nestling ringed near Crickhowell in Powys was found dead 35 km to the east at Symonds Yat four years later. In addition, a chick colour-ringed near Ludlow, Shropshire on April 19th 1998 was seen at the Gloucester landfill site on many occasions between April 2003 and May 2008 (John Sanders).

Sponsored by John Coleman, Andy Jayne and Mike Metcalf, and in memory of Roger Tanner

Species accounts

	2007–11 Atlas fieldwork					Gloucestershire trends						UK population trends	
	Number of tetrads in which recorded (max 683)					*Occupied 10 km squares (max 26)*				*% of tetrads in which recorded (1st hour of TTV)*		*UK conservation status:* **Green**	
	Total	Confirmed	Probable	Possible	Present	1968–71	1981–84	1988–91	2007–11	1988–91	2008–11	Long term	Short term
Breeding	418	105	115	109	89	6		5	26	2.0	20.6	–	0
Winter	538						6		26			–	–

Breeding Distribution

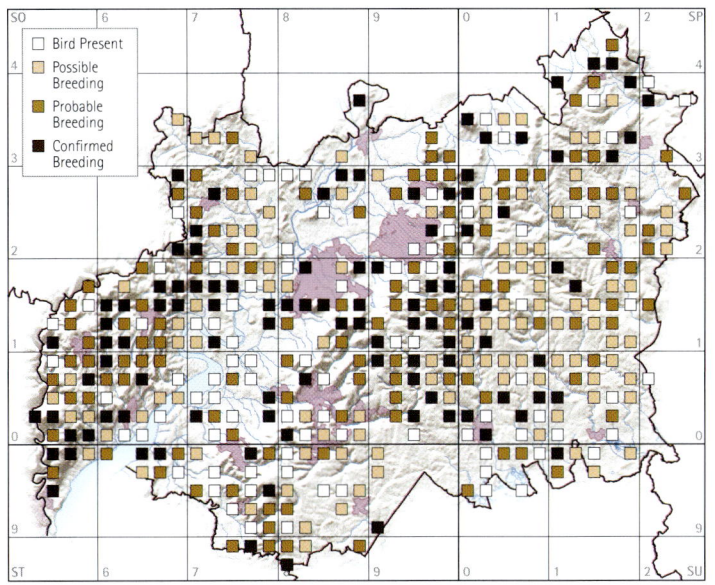

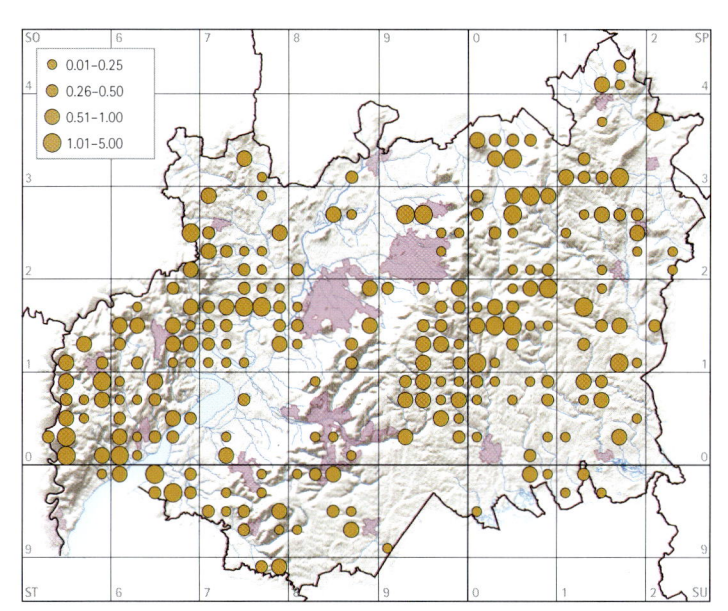

Summer Abundance

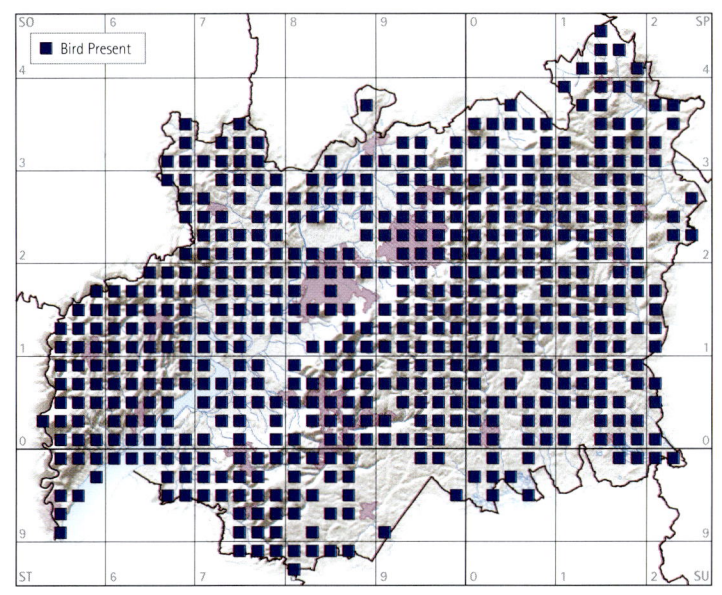

Winter Distribution

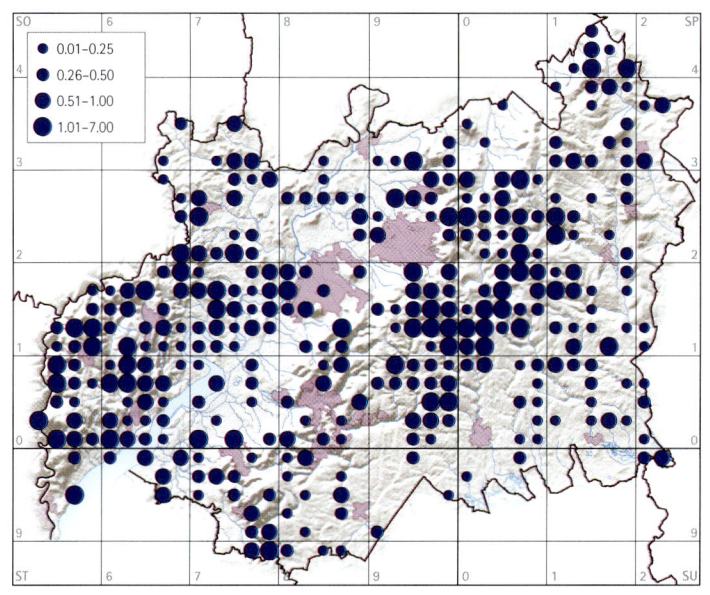

Winter Abundance

Goldcrest
Regulus regulus

Goldcrests breed across much of western and northern Europe and more discontinuously eastwards across Asia. In the breeding season they are strongly associated with conifer woods and plantations, but will breed in other woodland habitats, parks and gardens as long as some conifers are present (BWP). Goldcrests are notoriously vulnerable to hard winters, but because they can raise large broods (exceptionally laying as many as 12 eggs), numbers can recover quickly. Despite occasional sharp declines caused by cold weather, the national population appears to be fairly stable in the long term.

Although large numbers of Goldcrests are caught in the autumn at British coastal observatories, little is known about their migration patterns since few are ringed as nestlings, either in Britain or elsewhere. No doubt many of these autumn birds are from Fennoscandia, where the breeding areas are deserted in winter. On the other hand most British Goldcrests do not migrate and even the most inhospitable breeding sites in Britain are occupied throughout the year (Migration Atlas).

Many atlas surveyors will have found Goldcrests in the breeding season very soon after encountering conifers, but a few observers will have been unable to detect their very high-pitched song and calls. It is not easy to confirm breeding; in dense coniferous foliage it can be difficult to see young birds or to ascertain if adults are carrying food.

In Gloucestershire, the second Cotswolds Atlas reported a dramatic increase between 1987 and 2007, probably linked to a series of mild winters, whilst county BBS figures, despite some fairly wide year-to-year fluctuations, also indicate a generally increasing trend since 1994. The breeding season maps show that Goldcrests, as expected, tend to favour the areas of the county with the most woodland, namely the Forest of Dean and the Cotswold scarp. They are distributed widely over the Cotswolds, but not at such high densities, and are less common in the Severn Vale. The winter maps confirm that Goldcrests become much more widespread outside the breeding season, when they visit a greater range of habitat types including broad-leaved trees, hedgerows, open areas and even reed-beds. This no doubt reflects short-distance movements by some local birds but, in addition, three almost certain continental migrants, ringed in autumn in north-east England, were recovered in Gloucestershire later in the same season, and two ringed birds which moved between Gloucestershire and the Calf of Man may well also have originated from overseas.

Even over the short timescale of the atlas fieldwork, the winter data show a pattern of decline and recovery in response to winter temperatures (see graph). In the whole of the first winter period (2007–08) and the early part of the second (2008–09), the detection rate in TTVs was remarkably constant at around one Goldcrest per hour. Around Christmas 2008 and New Year 2009 there was a period of severely cold weather, and in the next survey period (January and February 2009), the detection rate fell by an amazing 70%. This lower rate of just 0.3 birds per hour was maintained in the whole of the following winter (2009–10) but, by the following year (2010–11), birds were once again being found at a rate close to one bird per hour. The population crash is confirmed by regional BBS figures for south-west England, which revealed a decrease of 47% in Goldcrest numbers between the 2008 and 2009 breeding seasons, but it is rare to be able to pin down such an event so precisely to a period of cold weather. The highest counts during TTVs came before the cold spell, with 32 birds in early 2008 in each of two adjacent tetrads in the Forest of Dean (SO60I and SO60J), and 30 in June 2008, also in SO60J.

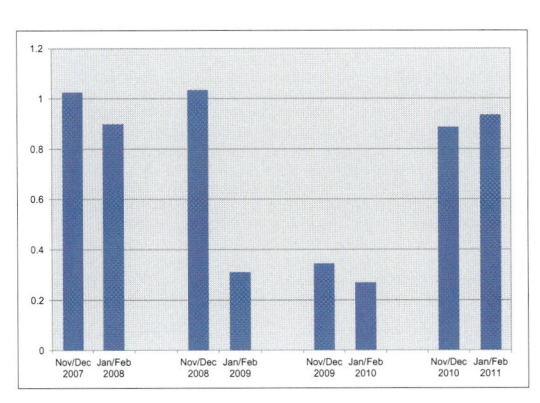

Goldcrests recorded per hour in winter TTVs during atlas fieldwork.

Sponsored by Shirley Hodges

Species accounts

2007–11 Atlas fieldwork				
Number of tetrads in which recorded (max 683)				
	Total	Confirmed	Probable	Possible	Present
Breeding	537	159	153	203	22
Winter	559				

Gloucestershire trends					
Occupied 10 km squares (max 26)				*% of tetrads in which recorded (1st hour of TTV)*	
1968–71	1981–84	1988–91	2007–11	1988–91	2008–11
26		26	26	45.6	41.6
	26		26		

UK population trends	
UK conservation status: **Green**	
Long term	Short term
−25%	−8%
–	–

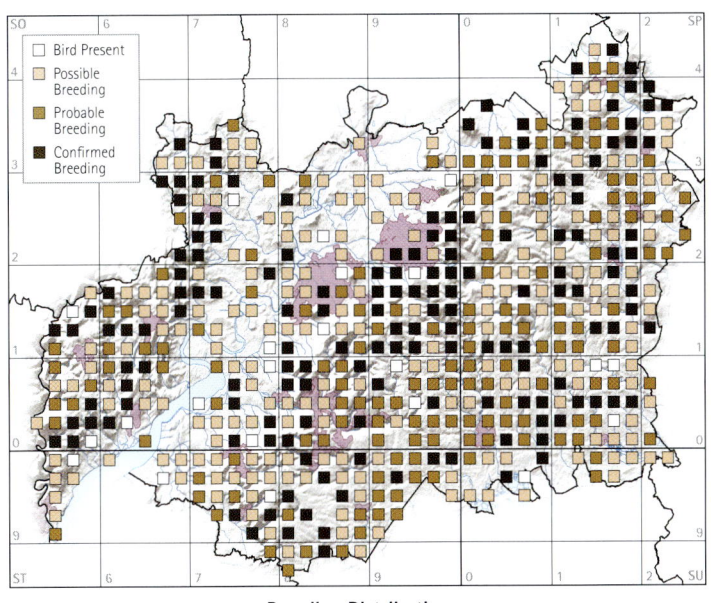

Breeding Distribution

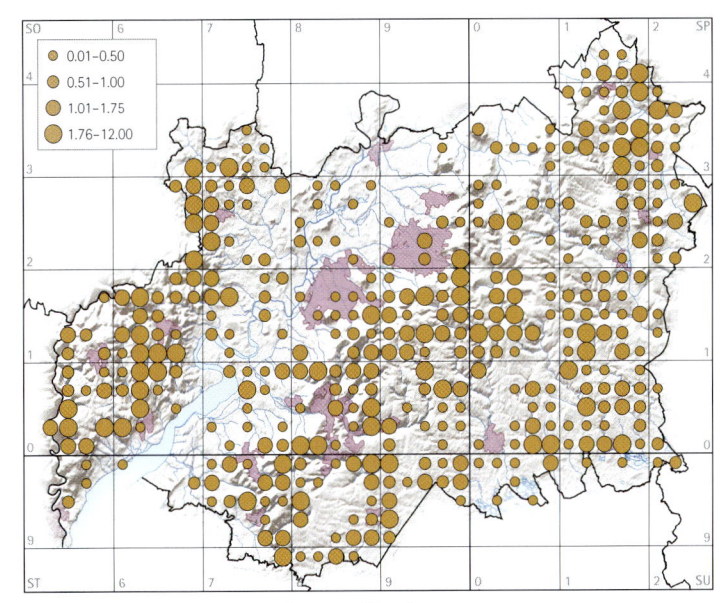

Summer Abundance

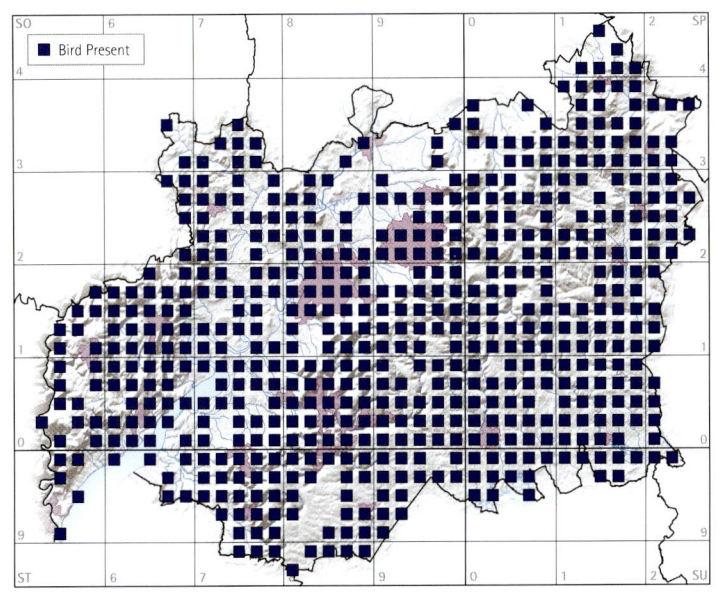

Winter Distribution

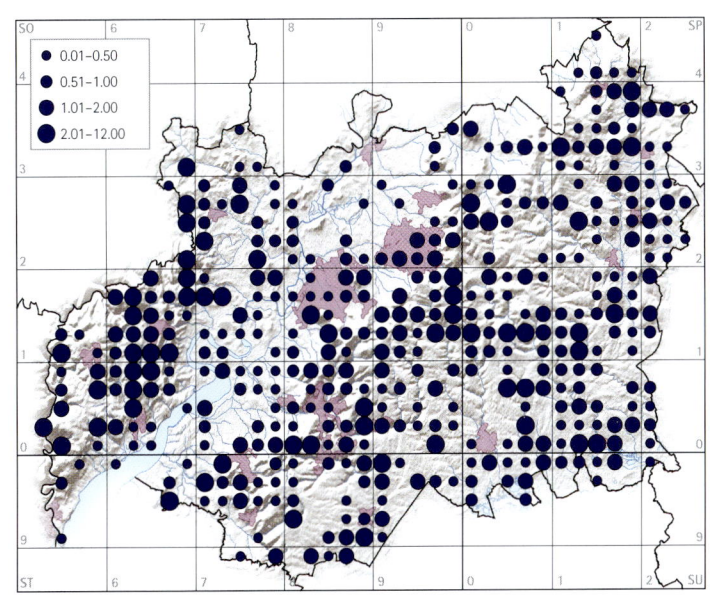

Winter Abundance

Firecrest (Common Firecrest)
Regulus ignicapilla

Firecrests are almost entirely confined to Europe, with scattered outlying populations in the North African mountains and the countries bordering the Black Sea. Those nesting in the north-east are migratory, wintering south to the southern limit of the breeding range, while southern populations are mainly resident. The nesting habitat is woodland, usually with at least some coniferous trees, but they are not as closely associated with conifers as Goldcrests.

Firecrest numbers have been stable or increasing in most countries in recent decades. They were first discovered nesting in Britain in 1962, and the 1968–72 and 1988–91 Breeding Atlases recorded a noticeable expansion of range between 1972 and 1991, although the vast majority of breeding records were south-east of a line between the Forest of Dean and the Wash. The national range has hardly changed since then and the British population was estimated to number about 800 territories in 2010. After breeding, most British birds leave their nesting areas to winter mainly close to the west and south coasts. Variable numbers of continental birds also pass through Britain on autumn passage and some remain here for the winter.

Firecrests are just as difficult to detect as Goldcrests. Their similarly high-pitched song and calls can be missed by observers with less than acute hearing, and they can be very unobtrusive,

Sponsored by the Cheltenham Bird Club

2007–11 Atlas fieldwork						Gloucestershire trends						UK population trends	
Number of tetrads in which recorded (max 683)					Occupied 10 km squares (max 26)				% of tetrads in which recorded (1st hour of TTV)		UK conservation status: Amber 6	
	Total	Confirmed	Probable	Possible	Present	1968–71	1981–84	1988–91	2007–11	1988–91	2008–11	Long term	Short term
Breeding	19	0	5	13	1	1		4	6	0.6	0	–	–
Winter	10						2		5			–	–

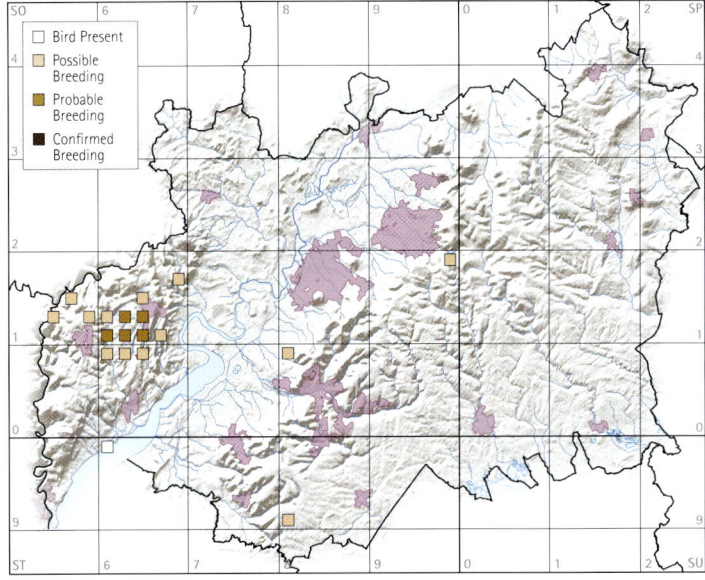

Breeding Distribution

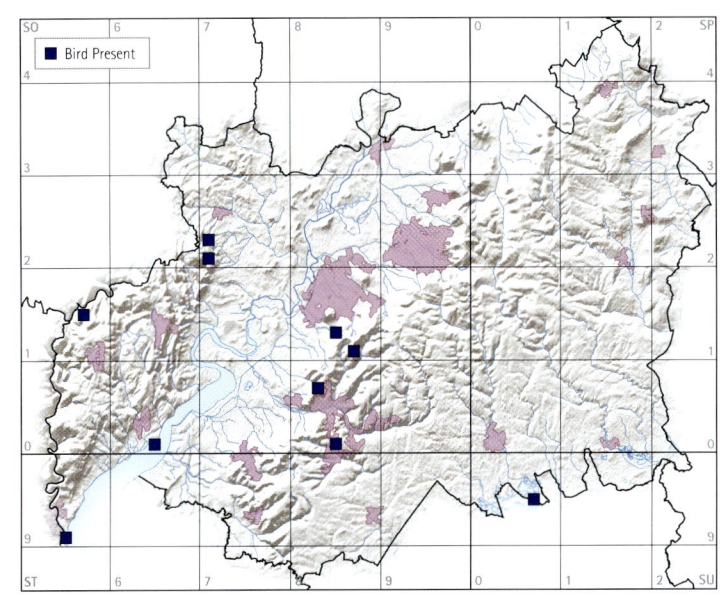

Winter Distribution

even skulking. In summer they may feed and sing in the tops of tall trees, but on the other hand they will sometimes feed in the open, apparently unconcerned by the presence of birdwatchers, and in general they are more easily found in winter, when they tend to move into lower trees and scrub.

There were a number of records in Gloucestershire during the nineteenth century (Mellersh and others) but details are lacking. Swaine reported instances of suspected breeding in the Forest of Dean at two sites in each of 1979 and 1980, and suggested that Firecrests might establish themselves in the county. This prediction was spectacularly fulfilled as early as 1982, when no fewer than 44 singing males were found in the Dean. However this impressive peak proved to be short-lived, with only ten pairs the following year. Since then, although breeding has been proved or suspected in all but a few years, the estimated number of pairs has usually varied between just one and five. The only exceptions were in 1989 when there may have been 15 to 20 pairs, 1995 when there were seven singing males, and 2007 when there may have been six pairs. It should be remembered that this is an easily overlooked species and the true numbers may well have been greater than those suggested by the figures. However, even during the fairly intensive atlas fieldwork there were no confirmed breeding records, although in all probability breeding did take place in many of the 15 Dean tetrads in which they were found. There have been occasional records of singing males elsewhere in Gloucestershire, but breeding has never been proved outside the Dean area.

The size of the population in nearby Wentwood (Monmouthshire/Newport) has been similarly variable following the first breeding record in 1974, with a peak of 21 singing males in 1989 (a year when numbers in the Dean were also quite high) but a decline after 1990 (Venables *et al.* 2008).

Swaine listed all the Gloucestershire winter records up to about 1980; at that time Firecrests were being seen in the county less than annually. These days there are usually two or three records between September and March each year, and at this season, as the winter distribution map indicates, they are just as likely to be seen in the Cotswolds or the Severn Vale as in the Dean.

Blue Tit (Eurasian Blue Tit)
Cyanistes caeruleus

The Blue Tit is one of the most familiar of British birds. The ancestral habitat was broad-leaved woodland, but they have adapted well to landscapes that have been modified by people and are now common on farmland and in gardens, even in inner cities, where they are familiar visitors to feeders. They breed widely wherever there are suitable holes for nesting, whether in trees, walls, nest-boxes or other artificial sites. The world range is almost completely confined to the Western Palearctic, extending from the Canary Islands to Norway and east almost to the Ural mountains, with outlying populations in south-west Asia. In the British Isles they occur everywhere except in treeless areas such as parts of the Scottish highlands. British populations are subject to short-term fluctuations, depending on the severity of winters and productivity during the breeding season, but appear to be stable in the long term.

Breeding Blue Tits are usually easy to find, especially around fledging time when the young are very noisy. The very high percentage of confirmed breeding records during the atlas survey reflects this, as well as their very common status.

Swaine described the Blue Tit as 'an abundant breeding species, occurring throughout the county', and this is still true today, with atlas records from virtually every tetrad at both seasons and no discernible changes in distribution, either in the county as a whole since the 1988–91 Breeding Atlas survey or in the area covered by the Cotswolds Atlases between 1987 and 2007. Blue Tits were recorded in 95–100% of county BBS squares every year between 1994 and 2010. However the abundance maps do indicate that, as might be expected, populations are not quite as dense in some less well-wooded areas, for example in the Severn Vale near Gloucester and Cheltenham and in some more extensive areas of arable farmland in parts of the Cotswolds. In winter Blue Tits often form flocks with other species which sometimes contain dozens of birds; the maximum number recorded in the county during a TTV was 72, in tetrad SO80W near Stroud in February 2011.

Blue Tits are essentially sedentary, although those in the northern and central parts of the world range sometimes undertake eruptive movements in response to high population density (BWP). A bird ringed on Helgoland off the German coast on October 3rd 2009, and found dead near Stonehouse on March 4th 2010, may well have undertaken such a movement. Fewer than six German-ringed birds have been found in the British Isles. British Blue Tits are even more sedentary than those from the Continent, and of the huge number of recoveries of British-ringed birds, 95% have been within 26 km of the ringing site. Movements of over 100 km within Britain are correspondingly rare, and there have only been five involving Gloucestershire: two ringed locally moved to Derbyshire and Dyfed, and birds ringed in London, Leicestershire and Somerset were found here.

Sponsored by Phil Davis

Species accounts

2007–11 Atlas fieldwork						Gloucestershire trends						UK population trends	
Number of tetrads in which recorded (max 683)						*Occupied 10 km squares (max 26)*				*% of tetrads in which recorded (1st hour of TTV)*		*UK conservation status:* **Green**	
	Total	Confirmed	Probable	Possible	Present	1968–71	1981–84	1988–91	2007–11	1988–91	2008–11	Long term	Short term
Breeding	682	640	30	10	2	26		26	26	97.0	97.8	+23%	+4%
Winter	681						26		26			–	–

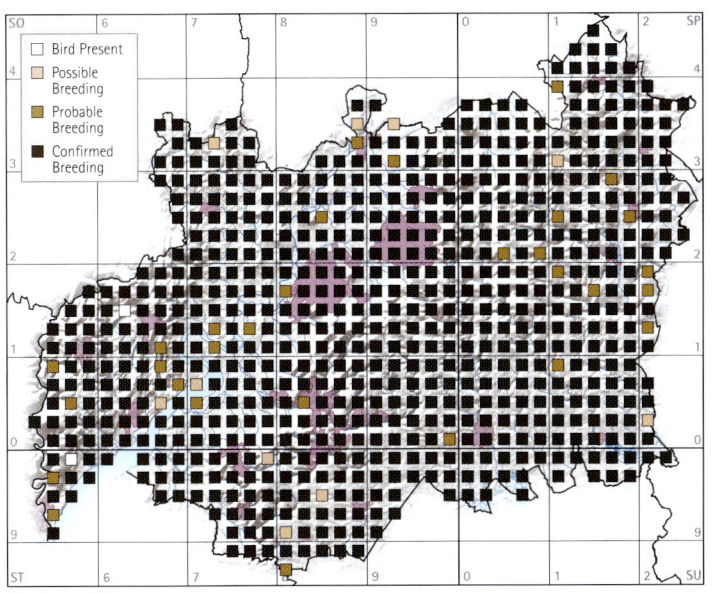

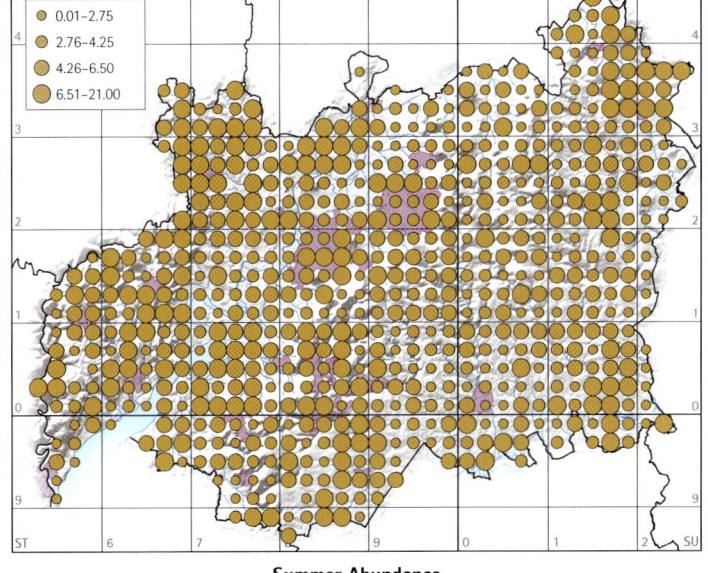

Breeding Distribution

Summer Abundance

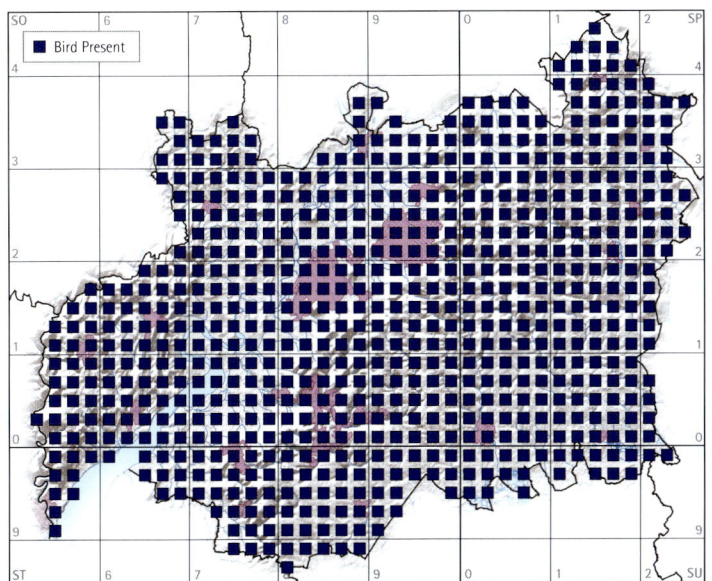

Winter Distribution

Winter Abundance

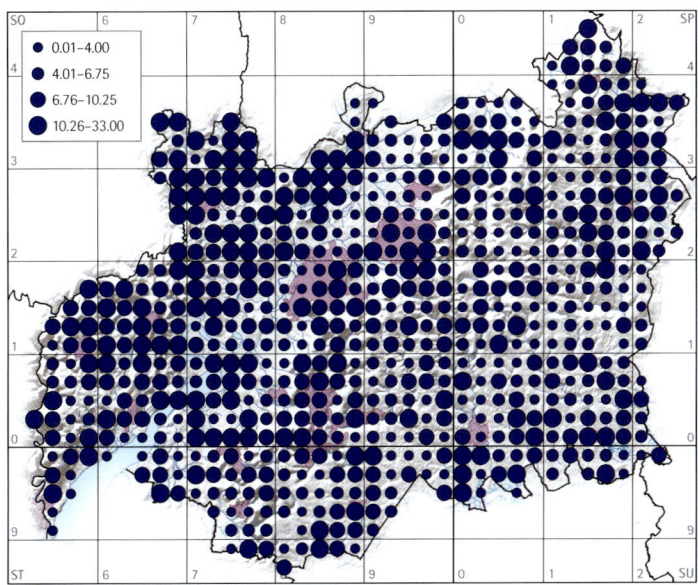

Great Tit
Parus major

Almost as familiar as the Blue Tit, the Great Tit is another originally woodland or woodland edge species that has adapted well to artificially modified landscapes. It is similarly a regular visitor to garden bird tables and will also take readily to nest-boxes. The world distribution is much more extensive than for Blue Tit, extending in the Western Palearctic from North Africa and the Levant to the far north of Norway and north-west Russia, and beyond that widely across Asia. There has been a northward extension of range in northern Europe in recent times, probably due to climate change and also (in Fennoscandia) the ability to survive the winter in and around towns and villages (BWP). In Scotland, this range expansion took place mainly in the first half of the twentieth century and, by the time of the 1988–91 Breeding Atlas, Great Tits were probably breeding in every 10 km square in mainland Britain. Population densities are however noticeably lower in regions with fewer trees and woodlands, such as parts of the Scottish highlands and, even in the most favoured habitats, numbers do not reach the levels attained by Blue Tits. More recently numbers have continued to increase, but there are year-to-year fluctuations in response to breeding success, winter weather, and especially winter food supplies in the form of tree seeds, particularly beechmast.

Swaine described Great Tits as common in Gloucestershire and widespread in a wide variety of habitats, and there has been no noticeable change in the last 30 years. They were recorded throughout the county both during fieldwork for the 1988–91 Breeding Atlas and in the present survey. The increase in the number of occupied tetrads (based on comparable TTV counts) between the two atlas periods could reflect a moderate increase in numbers, though a similar slight increase in the Cotswolds Atlas area between 1987 and 2007 was thought to be probably due to improved coverage. The abundance maps are similar to those for Blue Tit in that there are noticeable areas of lower density in less wooded districts, including parts of the Vales and the farmland of the Cotswolds. The maximum count during a winter TTV, of 66 in ST89P at Nailsworth in February 2008, was only just below the maximum of 72 for Blue Tit at that season. The comparable figures for the breeding season (45 for Great Tit and 65 for Blue Tit) correspond more closely to the two species' overall relative abundances.

During the nesting season, Great Tits are as easy to find as Blue Tits and their noisy young make proof of breeding easy to obtain, resulting in the very high levels of confirmed breeding during the current atlas fieldwork.

As with Blue Tits, Great Tits are essentially resident over their whole range, but birds from northern areas may undertake irruptive movements in some years in response to high population density and, presumably, pressure on food supplies. In Britain, there is a tendency for them to wander more widely in winters when there is no beech crop, but even so, the vast majority of ringing recoveries are far less than 20 km from the ringing site, and only a very small proportion of ringed birds have travelled more than 100 km. There have been five such long-distance recoveries involving our county: birds ringed locally have been found in Buckinghamshire, Kent and Powys, and Gloucestershire ringers have caught birds ringed in Cambridgeshire and Cheshire.

Sponsored by the Dursley Birdwatching and Preservation Society

Species accounts

2007–11 Atlas fieldwork					Gloucestershire trends						UK population trends	
Number of tetrads in which recorded (max 683)					Occupied 10 km squares (max 26)				% of tetrads in which recorded (1st hour of TTV)		UK conservation status: **Green**	
	Total	Confirmed	Probable	Possible	Present	1968–71	1981–84	1988–91	2007–11	1988–91	2008–11	Long term	Short term
Breeding	682	620	45	17	0	26		26	26	91.1	97.4	+91%	+45%
Winter	681						26		26			–	–

Breeding Distribution

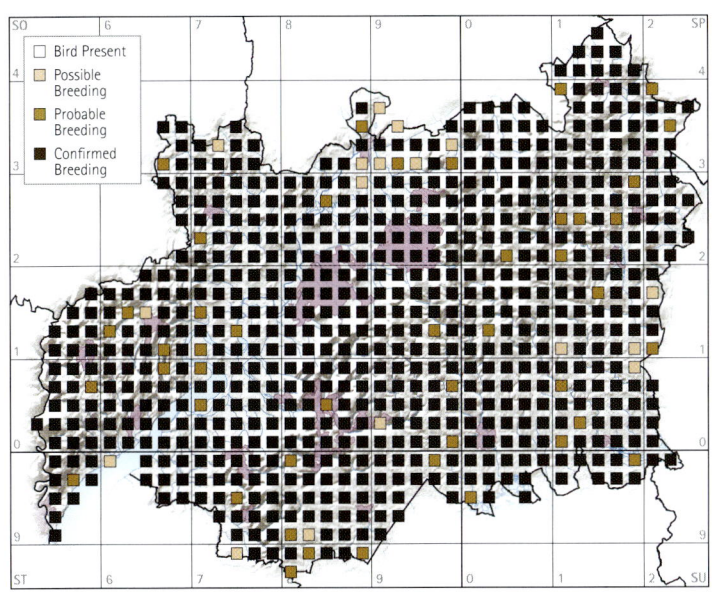

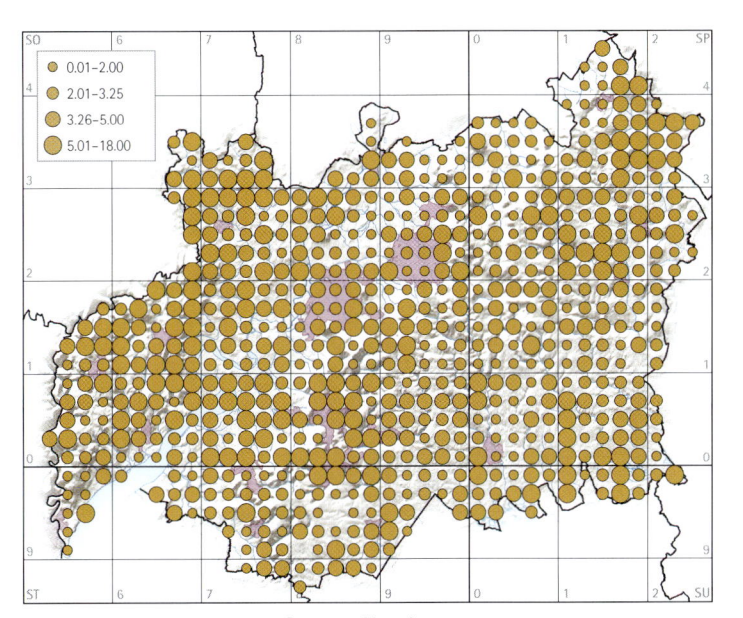

Summer Abundance

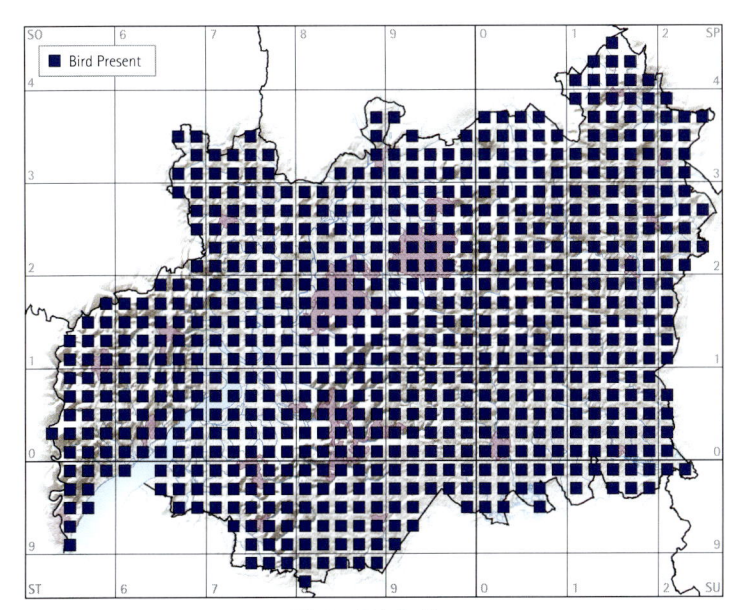

Winter Distribution

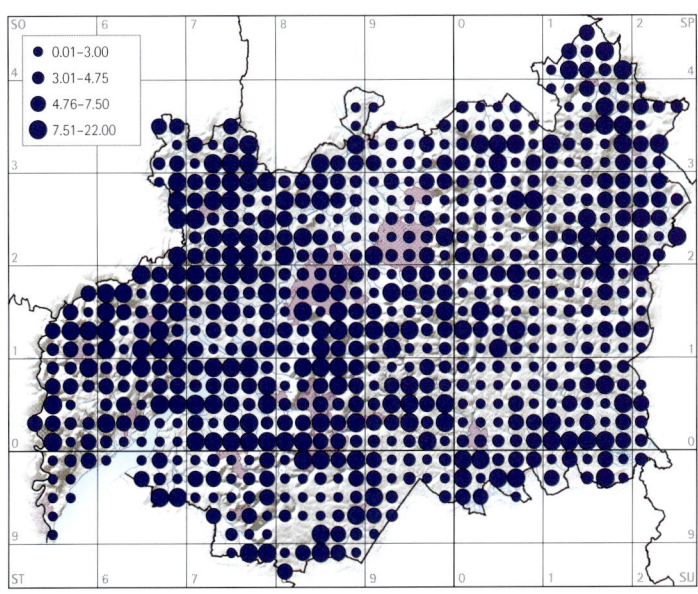

Winter Abundance

Coal Tit
Periparus ater

Unlike Great and Blue Tits, Coal Tits are mainly birds of coniferous rather than broad-leaved woodlands. They are also unlike most other tits in that they will nest just as readily on the ground, in a crevice or among tree roots, as in a hole in a tree. The world range extends over large areas of the Palearctic including much of western Europe, broadly corresponding with the distribution of coniferous woodland, although in some parts of the range beech and oak woods are the main habitat. There have recently been population increases and range expansions in parts of Europe, thought to be due to the planting of conifers and, in some places, the provision of nest-boxes (BWP).

Probably because of their preference for conifers, Coal Tits have taken less readily than the commoner tits to man-made habitats such as gardens and farmland. Nevertheless they are frequent visitors to bird tables, and they will breed in nest-boxes if they are not displaced by the more dominant Blue and Great Tits.

Coal Tits are found throughout the British Isles, again most commonly in areas with extensive conifer woodland or plantations. A steady increase in recent decades has quite possibly been driven by the continuing maturation of conifer plantations, and perhaps also by mild winters and an increasing tendency to visit bird tables, which could result in improved winter survival rates.

In Gloucestershire, Swaine described Coal Tits as 'not uncommon as a breeding species and found throughout the county', particularly in areas with conifers, and this is still the case today. The 2003–07 Cotswolds Atlas revealed a marked increase of 45% in tetrads with breeding records since 1983–87, though this may have been partly due to improved coverage. Similarly, county BBS figures were higher on average in 2003–10 than in 1994–2002, though with considerable year-to-year variation; clearly Coal Tits are more than holding their own here.

As might be expected, the maps reveal some fairly wide areas of absence or low density though the Severn Vale and parts of the Cotswolds and Thames NAs, where there is little suitable conifer habitat. The highest breeding densities are attained in the Forest of Dean, and also in parts of the Cotswolds where there is more extensive coniferous or mixed woodland, for example around Cirencester Park (SO90), Chedworth Woods (SP01) and the fairly well-wooded high wold and scarp in SO91. Coal Tits appear to have been slightly more wide-ranging in the county in winter, a season when they are not so completely reliant on conifers and when they will flock with other tits. The maximum winter TTV count of 33, in tetrad SO60H in the Lydney area of the Forest of Dean in January 2011, could well have included flocking birds. The very high maximum breeding season TTV count of 45 in SP13R near Moreton-in-Marsh on the rather late date of July 28th 2011 could have included juveniles.

Winter roaming apart, Coal Tits in the British Isles are essentially sedentary, although populations to the north and east are more dispersive or irruptive and continental birds reach Britain fairly frequently in autumn and winter. A first-winter bird ringed at Stroud in November 1969 and caught in Germany in 1971 was very likely to have been continental in origin. This was the first recorded movement of a British-ringed Coal Tit to Germany. Very few move as far as 100 km within the British Isles, so an immature ringed 103 km away in Hertfordshire in July 1971 and found dead in Gloucestershire later that year had made a fairly long journey.

Sponsored by Barbara Joy

Species accounts

	2007–11 Atlas fieldwork					Gloucestershire trends						UK population trends	
	Number of tetrads in which recorded (max 683)					Occupied 10 km squares (max 26)				% of tetrads in which recorded (1st hour of TTV)		UK conservation status: Green	
	Total	Confirmed	Probable	Possible	Present	1968–71	1981–84	1988–91	2007–11	1988–91	2008–11	Long term	Short term
Breeding	465	206	97	136	26	26		25	26	37.9	33.5	+30%	+12%
Winter	526						25		26			–	–

Breeding Distribution

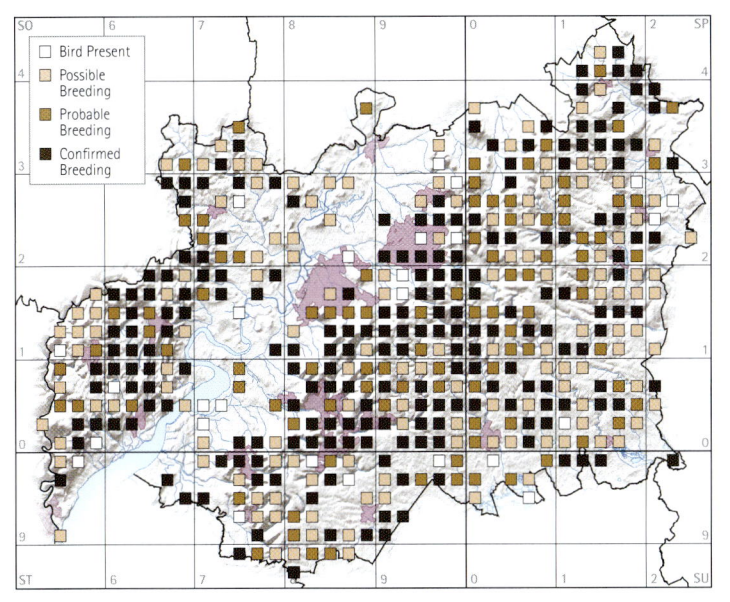

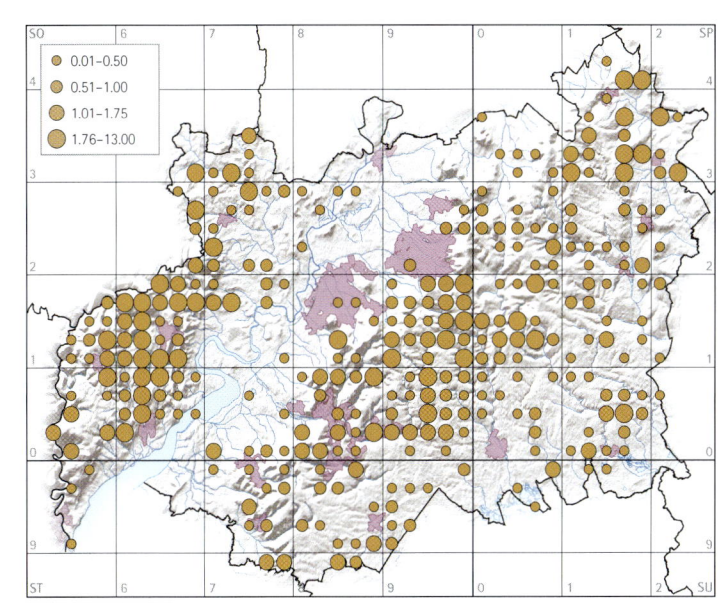

Summer Abundance

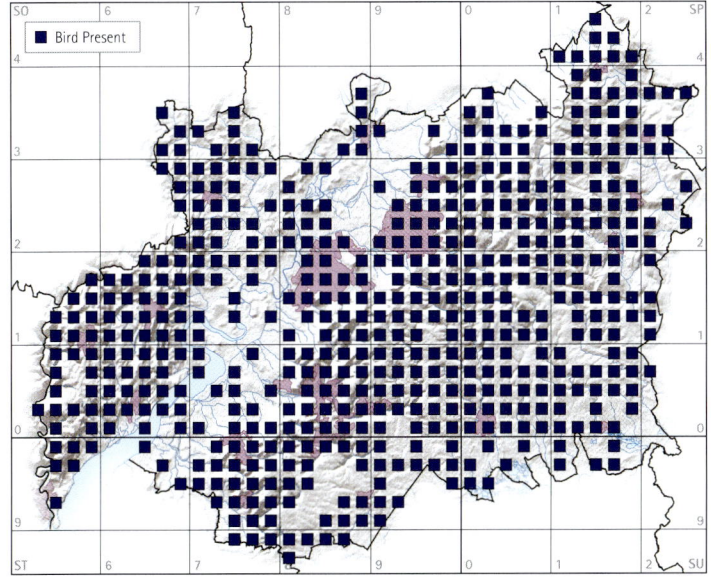

Winter Distribution

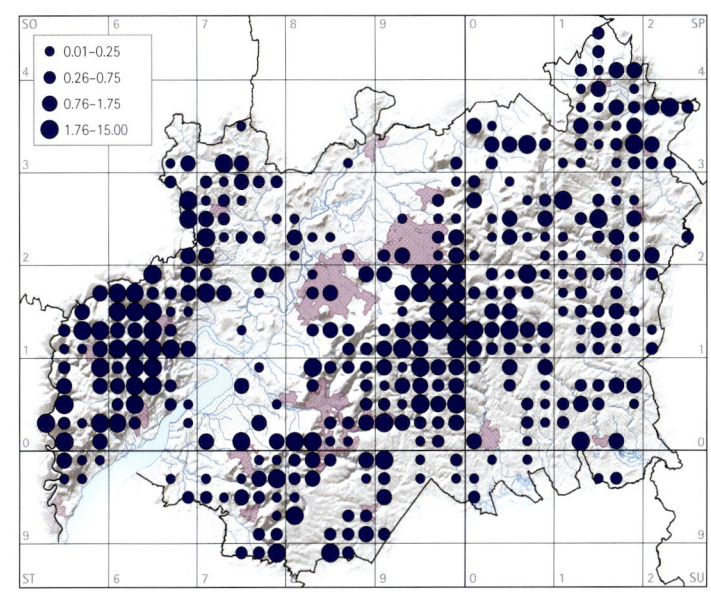

Winter Abundance

Willow Tit
Poecile montana

The breeding range of Willow Tits extends from Britain, France and Scandinavia across to the Far East. Although they range north to the edge of the tundra on the Continent, in Britain the distribution is distinctly southern, with few records north of the Forth–Clyde line, and they are extremely sedentary. They tend to prefer relatively small woods and stands of trees, often damp in character, and are unusual among tits in that they excavate their own nest cavities rather than making use of existing holes. They therefore require sufficient dead and decaying standing wood to provide nest sites. Willow Tits are very rarely seen in towns and cities, although in some parts of the country unmanaged, overgrown areas on the edges of conurbations may provide suitable habitat.

Willow Tits were only recognised as a distinct British breeding species as recently as 1900, owing to their similarity to Marsh Tits. Distinguishing between the two species in the field can be difficult, and it is possible that during the atlas fieldwork a small number of Willow Tits were misidentified as Marsh Tits, and vice versa. In addition, the usual Willow Tit call, a soft nasal buzzing, is more easily overlooked than the louder and more far-carrying calls of the other tits.

Although there have been increases in some parts of the European range, in Britain Willow Tits have undergone a catastrophic population crash in recent decades. There were an estimated 8,500 territories in the country in 2000, and the decline has continued since then, with the most recent estimates suggesting c.1,500 pairs in 2010. The reasons for this decrease are not yet clear but loss and fragmentation of habitats, no doubt exacerbated by the birds' very sedentary nature, is a strong possibility. Nest predation, perhaps by rapidly increasing numbers of Great Spotted Woodpeckers and/or grey squirrels, has also been suggested as a cause.

Their fortunes in Gloucestershire mirror the national picture. Swaine noted that 'though very thinly distributed', there were nevertheless 'records from widely scattered places in all major regions of the county'. The results from the current atlas survey confirm that there has been a severe and continuing decline throughout the county since then, and Willow Tits are now almost entirely confined to the Forest of Dean area, with no more than a few scattered sites in the Cotswolds and virtually none in the Vales. In the region covered by both Cotswolds Atlases, where there had already been a sharp decline between 1987 and 2007, there was a further decrease from 18 occupied tetrads to just 14 in the breeding season in the present survey.

Sponsored by Andy Lewis

Species accounts

2007–11 Atlas fieldwork						Gloucestershire trends						UK population trends	
Number of tetrads in which recorded (max 683)						Occupied 10 km squares (max 26)				% of tetrads in which recorded (1st hour of TTV)		UK conservation status: **Red 3**	
	Total	Confirmed	Probable	Possible	Present	1968-71	1981-84	1988-91	2007-11	1988-91	2008-11	Long term	Short term
Breeding	33	6	5	13	9	18		15	9	5.9	0.7	-92%	-76%
Winter	35						19		12			–	–

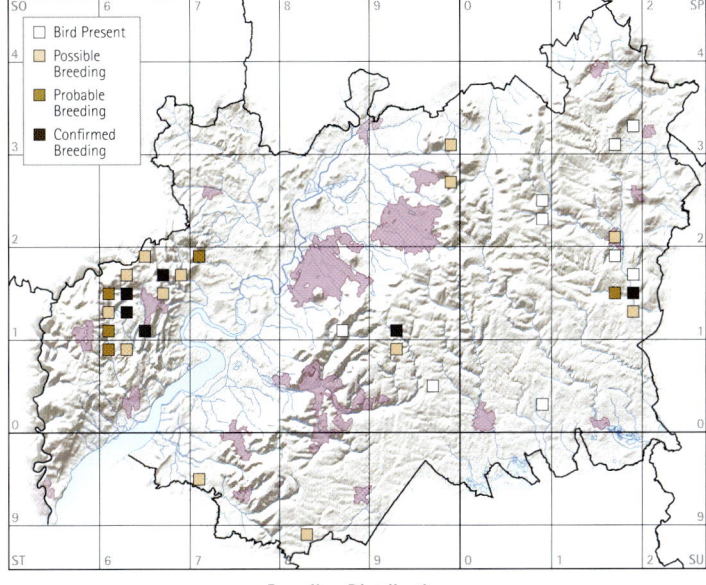

Breeding Distribution

A recent study of Willow Tits in the Forest of Dean (MacDonald 2011) confirmed the species' requirement here for the dense thickets, particularly including birch, which develop a few years after the clear-felling of stands of plantation trees. It appears that this habitat provides nesting sites that are relatively safe from predators. It also emerged that Willow Tits in the Dean require more open areas with tall trees, especially larch, which provide feeding habitat and probably song-posts. It is to be hoped that the forestry management in the Dean will continue to provide pockets of suitable habitat for them, although a follow-up survey in 2011 revealed only two pairs and two unpaired males in the whole of the Gloucestershire part of the Forest.

Outside the Dean and the more northern part of the Cotswolds, Willow Tits were found in the breeding season in the Westonbirt–Silk Wood area close to the Wiltshire border near Tetbury, and at Michaelwood in the Severn Vale, near the border with South Gloucestershire. It is very questionable whether these outlying records represent viable breeding populations.

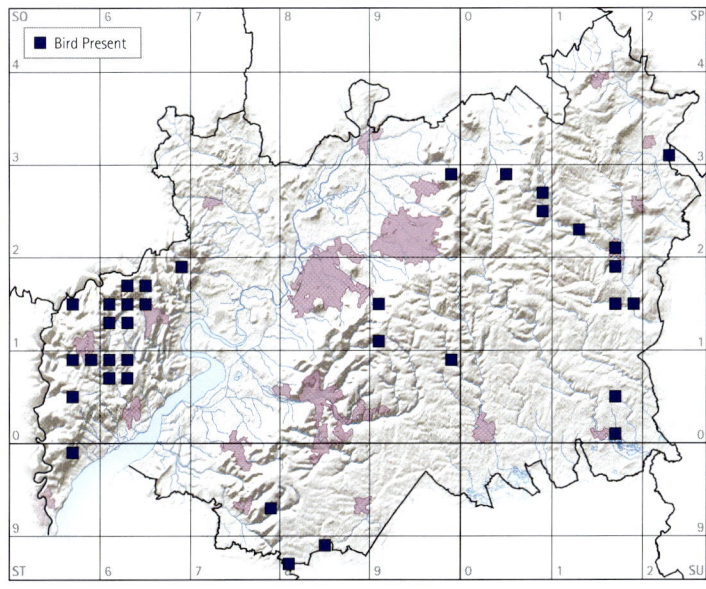

Winter Distribution

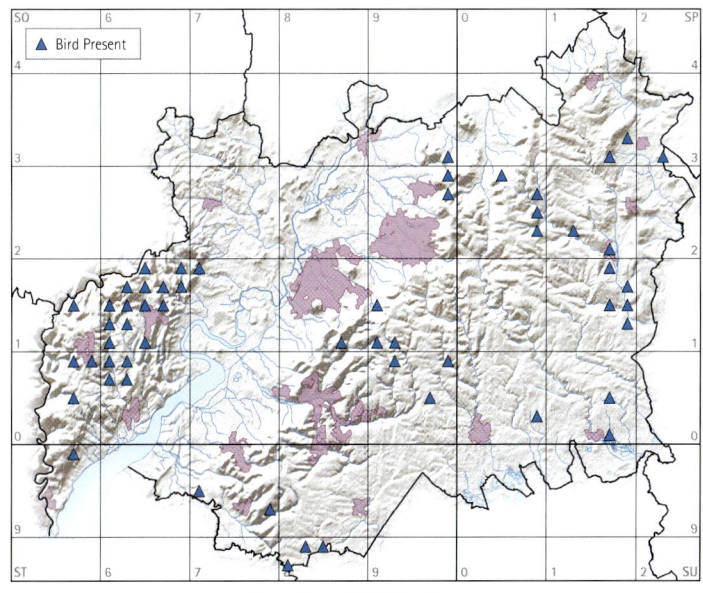

Year-Round Distribution

Marsh Tit
Poecile palustris

Marsh Tits have a very extensive world distribution, including wide areas of Europe and from central Asia east to China and Burma. In general they do not range as far north as the closely related Willow Tit. In Britain they are widespread in England and Wales, but only just extend over the border into south-east Scotland, where breeding was not proved until 1945 (BWP). The English name is a misnomer, at least in Britain, as the preferred habitat here is open broad-leaved woodland; they can also be found in parkland and well-wooded farmland. Unlike the commoner tits they rarely venture into heavily built-up areas, but they are frequent visitors to more rural gardens.

Distinguishing between Marsh and Willow Tits is not always easy, and it is possible that there may have been a few misidentifications during atlas fieldwork. However compared with Willow Tits, Marsh Tits are generally more easy to detect, with louder and more insistent calls and a more distinctive song.

In recent decades, decreases in numbers and range contractions have been reported for Marsh Tits from several European countries, including Britain. Between the 1968-72 and 1988-91 Breeding Atlases there was a 17% decrease in 10 km square occupancy over the country as a whole. The reasons for this decline are unclear, but habitat degradation and fragmentation, possibly exacerbated by predation, have been suggested.

Swaine described Marsh Tits as 'resident and moderately common' in Gloucestershire. They have evidently decreased since then, although more recently county BBS figures show no consistent trend between 1994 and 2009. The distribution maps shows that they are still fairly widespread, with records from nearly every 10 km square, although there is a large area of absence through the Severn Vale and some additional gaps in the more agricultural parts of the Cotswolds and Thames NAs. However at the tetrad level the situation looks much less healthy: as shown in the fact-box, there has apparently been a substantial decrease since the 1988-91 Breeding Atlas as measured by comparable TTV figures. In the area covered by the Cotswolds Atlases, a 21% increase in occupancy from 149 to 189 tetrads was recorded between 1987 and 2007, but this may have been due to more intense fieldwork in the second survey period; 'the feeling of some observers was that numbers had decreased' by 2007. There were records from 165 tetrads in the same area during the breeding season in the current survey.

The abundance maps show that Marsh Tits are commonest in the more heavily wooded areas of the Cotswolds, along the scarp and in parts of the higher wold. However they are never found in large numbers, and the maximum count on a TTV was ten, in SO91Y, above the Cotswold scarp south-east of Cheltenham, in February. (A count of 15 in SP13R on the late date of July 28th is very likely to have included some juveniles.) The great majority of TTVs recorded just one or two birds.

Marsh Tits are usually very sedentary, so records of ringed birds moving from Gloucestershire to Somerset and from Northamptonshire to Gloucestershire are rather unusual.

Sponsored by Jane Ford and David Harman

Species accounts

2007–11 Atlas fieldwork					Gloucestershire trends						UK population trends	
Number of tetrads in which recorded (max 683)					Occupied 10 km squares (max 26)				% of tetrads in which recorded (1st hour of TTV)		UK conservation status: **Red 3**	
	Total	Confirmed	Probable	Possible	Present	1968–71	1981–84	1988–91	2007–11	1988–91	2008–11	Long term	Short term
Breeding	281	115	65	83	18	26		26	24	32.7	14.5	–68%	–21%
Winter	352						26		26			–	–

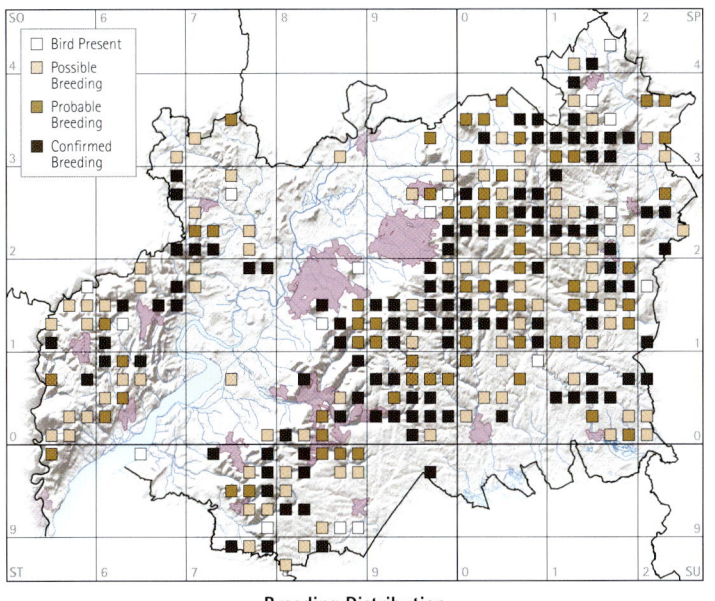

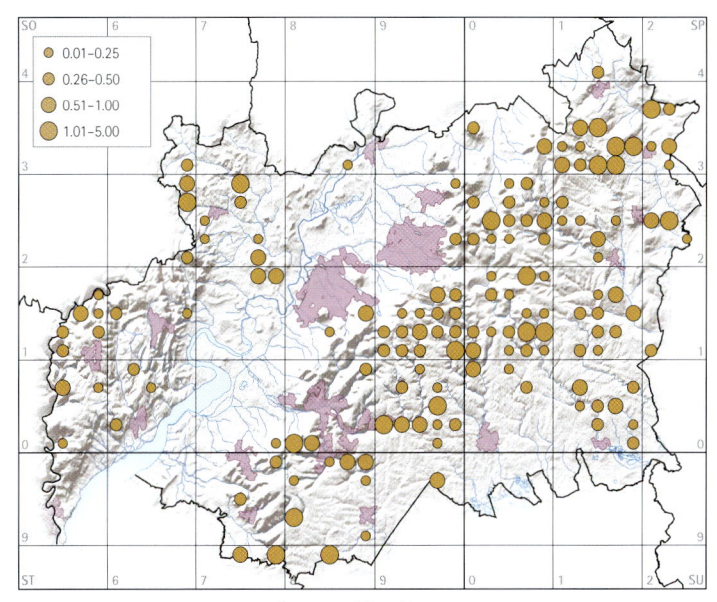

Breeding Distribution

Summer Abundance

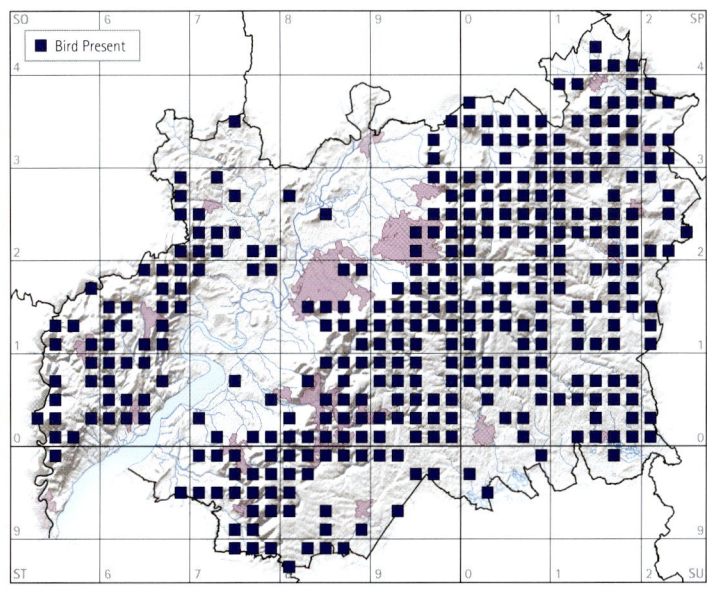

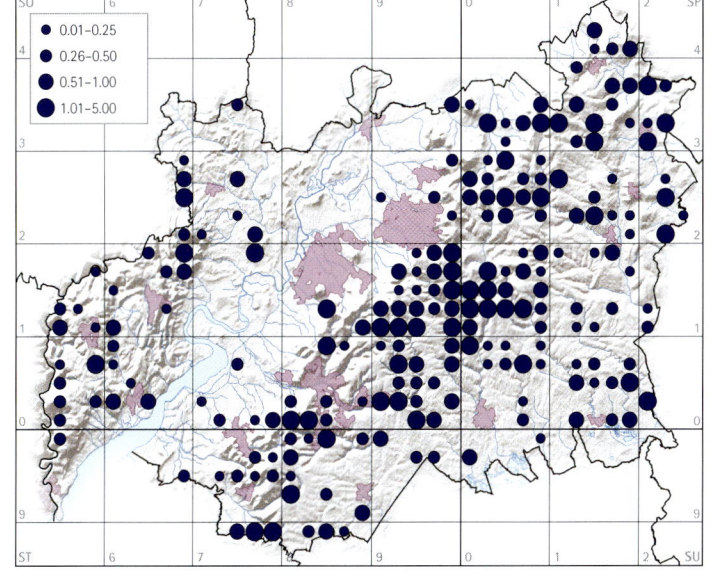

Winter Distribution

Winter Abundance

Bearded Tit (Bearded Reedling)
Panurus biarmicus

Bearded Tits are closely linked with large reed-beds, and are widely but very patchily distributed across Europe and from the Caspian Sea to north-east China. Numbers fluctuate considerably depending on winter mortality rates, but have tended to increase in Europe. In Britain only two known pairs remained after the cold winter of 1947 but since then they have greatly increased. They are generally residents or partial migrants, but are well known for their occasional eruptive movements.

Swaine mentioned several nineteenth-century reports from the Thames valley and near Gloucester; Mellersh stated that eggs were said to have been found in the county, but there is no evidence.

There were no county records in the twentieth century until winter 1959–60, when at least two were at Frampton sailing lake from November 1st until February 7th. There were then four arrivals associated with irruptions in the 1960s, all at Frampton. In 1960, 1965 and 1966, two to three birds arrived in October or November; on the first two occasions they remained until February, but the 1966 birds only stayed for a few weeks. Up to five were present from December 14th 1968 to March 23rd 1969.

Subsequently there have been arrivals in three years in the 1970s, two in the 1980s, none in the 1990s and three since 2000. Most birds stayed for only one day, the exceptions being two at Frampton from November 6th to 26th 1972 and one there from November 19th to 30th 2008. All post-1970 records have been of ones and twos except for 12 near Awre, across the Severn from Slimbridge, on October 16th 1972, and 11 at Walham Ponds, Gloucester on October 15th 1978. All but two arrivals were in October or November, and all were in the Frampton–Slimbridge area except for the Walham birds and two sightings at the Cotswold Water Park.

The total number of Bearded Tits seen in Gloucestershire since 1900 is only about 45 birds. Given this low total it might seem surprising that there is a ringing recovery involving the county: one of two birds caught at Frampton on November 6th 1966 proved to have been ringed 540 km away in the Netherlands on September 21st that year.

Shore Lark (Horned Lark)
Eremophila alpestris

Shore Larks of the Fennoscandian and Russian subspecies *E. a. flava* winter discontinuously in central Europe and along Baltic and North Sea coasts. In Britain, they have wintered regularly on the east coast since about 1870 (BWP) and have bred in Scotland on very rare occasions. There are three records for Gloucestershire:

1911: one at Robinswood Hill, Gloucester on October 20th.
1958: one on the foreshore near Frampton on November 1st.
1969: an adult in winter plumage by the estuary at Slimbridge on November 8th.

Mellersh refers to several Shore Larks shot in the county during the last 30 years of the nineteenth century, but these reports are unsubstantiated.

Woodlark
Lullula arborea

Largely confined to milder areas of the Western Palearctic, Woodlarks breed in various habitats but always need short grass or bare ground for feeding, longer vegetation for nesting, and scattered trees or bushes for song-posts. Birds from the north-eastern parts of the range are migratory, wintering around the Mediterranean, whilst British breeders are partial migrants. There has been a long-term contraction of their European range and a considerable decline in numbers.

In the nineteenth century Woodlarks were common across Wales and in England south of the Pennines (1875–1900 Atlas). There was a massive decline in the twentieth century, but in recent decades they have enjoyed something of a recovery here, though they are currently mainly confined to central southern England and East Anglia.

Mellersh described Woodlarks in 1902 as being distributed throughout the Forest of Dean, though 'localised by the denseness of the oak woods in some parts', and 'common in open glades' in the Cotswolds until about 1880. The picture for the first half of the twentieth century is somewhat mixed; it seems that Woodlarks were periodically fairly numerous, if local, but that they were sometimes affected by harsh winter weather, especially late frosts and snowfalls, to which they are particularly vulnerable because their breeding season begins very early. Swaine felt that there was some evidence of an increase between 1920 and the 1940s, and observers' notebooks from that period suggest that there may have been up to 300 pairs in the Dean area and perhaps 100 or more on the Cotswolds at times (Andrew Bluett). However, Swaine reported a drastic decline from around 1956; indeed the prolonged and bitterly cold winter of 1962–63 appears to have caused an abrupt and almost total disappearance of Woodlarks from the county, although some pairs continued to nest on spoil heaps and in young plantations in the Dean until about 1968, and the 1968–71 Breeding Atlas shows a confirmed record there, in 10 km square SO61.

Between 1968 and 1998 there were just six county records, four of which were outside the breeding season, but more recently there have been a number of sightings giving cause for hope that the delightful song of the Woodlark may again be regularly heard in Gloucestershire. In June 2004 a male sang on Cleeve Hill, and the following year a single bird flew over Sharpness on October 8th. In 2007 there were three autumn records, and in January 2008 six Woodlarks were found feeding in stubble near Lydney, which was probably the largest number seen in the county for 50 years. Later that year, a pair took up residence in suitable habitat during the nesting season, although breeding was not confirmed, and a single was also seen on October 29th in the Cotswold Water Park. Finally, in 2009, a pair raised chicks at a confidential site, the first confirmed breeding in the county for about 40 years. What was presumably the male from the same pair returned in spring 2010 and sang for two months, but evidently did not attract a mate.

Skylark
Alauda arvensis

Skylarks breed over most of the Western Palearctic and eastwards across Asia to Kamchatka and Japan. Breeding birds in the British Isles and other parts of western Europe are mainly resident, and are joined in winter by birds from migratory populations further to the north and east. Even in Britain, breeding grounds at higher altitudes are vacated in the winter, and Skylarks also undertake movements in response to cold weather.

Breeding habitat is provided by open countryside of various types, usually with grass, crops or other short vegetation. In the nesting season, Skylarks are almost invariably detected by their sustained and evocative song, often with several singing birds in earshot (even if not all are visible), enabling atlas fieldworkers to record 'possible' or 'probable' breeding with ease. On the other hand, obtaining proof of breeding is less easy and this species has a relatively low proportion of 'confirmed' records, although the patient and sharp-eyed will have seen adult birds carrying food. In the winter, characteristically restless flocks can be found especially in stubbles and ploughed fields.

Skylarks have suffered significant declines in the British Isles in the last 50 years, with numbers more than halved. One major cause is the increasing proportion of cereals that are sown in autumn or winter rather than in spring. Early sown crops have already grown fairly tall by the time the birds begin to nest, so they choose to build on or near the 'tram-lines' created by the tractor. As well as the obvious danger from farm machinery, this also leaves them much more vulnerable to predators such as foxes, because the nests are so much more visible. As a result, overall breeding success is lower than in spring-sown crops. There may be other causes linked to changes in farming practice, such as the reduced availability of seeds resulting from a decline in overwintered stubble.

Despite these ongoing national declines the Skylark is still a widespread and familiar bird in Gloucestershire, and the evidence from the current atlas fieldwork and the two Cotswolds Atlases is that the decline here has not been as steep as elsewhere. The TTV data actually show a slight increase in the number of tetrads in which Skylarks were found compared with 20 years ago, and the species even scraped into the 'top 20' most abundantly recorded birds during the atlas fieldwork (see p. 46), although this will partly reflect the fact that they are so easy to detect when they are singing.

Despite the intensification of crop production, it seems that the county still contains a sufficiently wide range of habitats to enable this species to hold its own. The abundance map clearly shows that their breeding stronghold is in the Cotswolds, where arable farming dominates and where there are also areas of semi-natural grassland, such as Cleeve Hill. However it is equally clear that they breed widely elsewhere in the county, and they are completely absent only from the heavily wooded Forest of Dean and the major conurbations. In winter, the Cotswolds are still favoured but there are also areas of greater density along the river Severn, presumably reflecting some movement away from high ground and/or arrivals of wintering birds from abroad.

The largest count during a TTV was 154 birds in tetrad ST88E near Didmarton in December 2009, but flocks of 500 by the sailing lake at Frampton and 410 at Clapton-on-the-Hill near Bourton-on-the-Water, both in December 2010, were the largest reported in the county during the atlas period. This was a particularly cold month, so these counts were probably a local reflection of a 'cold-weather movement'. In general over the last decade or so, it has been October when most Skylarks are usually recorded, and small flocks passing over on autumn migration are a familiar sight and sound, especially along the Cotswold scarp and other places where visible migration can be observed.

Sponsored by Andrew Cleaver and Andy Oliver, and in memory of John Bentley-Taylor

Species accounts

2007–11 Atlas fieldwork					Gloucestershire trends						UK population trends	
Number of tetrads in which recorded (max 683)					Occupied 10 km squares (max 26)				% of tetrads in which recorded (1st hour of TTV)		UK conservation status: **Red 3**	
	Total	Confirmed	Probable	Possible	Present	1968–71	1981–84	1988–91	2007–11	1988–91	2008–11	Long term	Short term
Breeding	574	166	262	134	12	26		26	26	59.2	65.1	−55%	−15%
Winter	518						26		26			–	–

Breeding Distribution

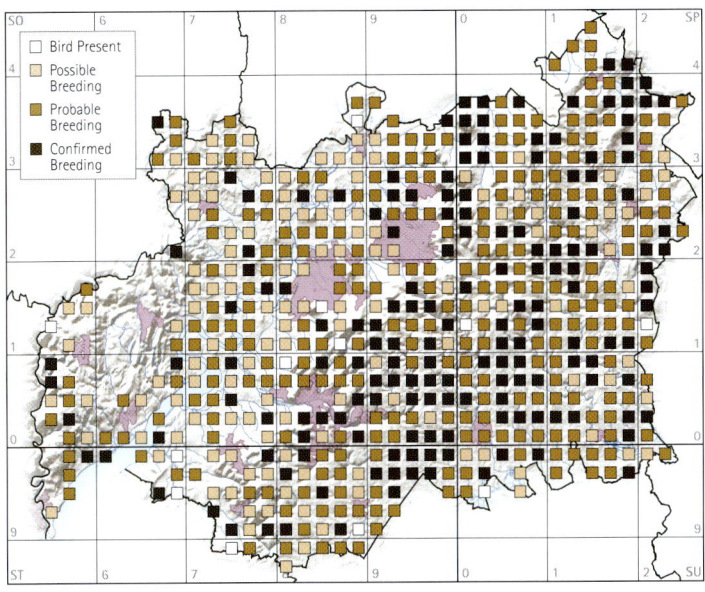

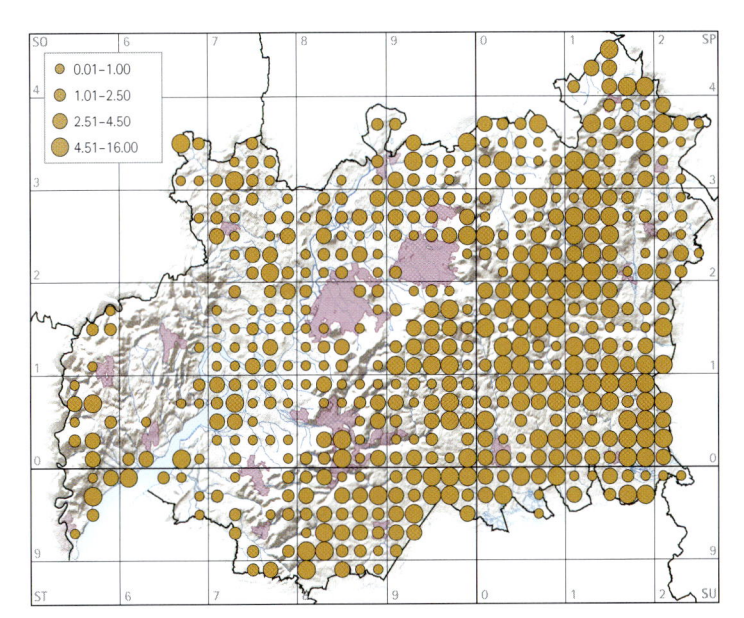

Summer Abundance

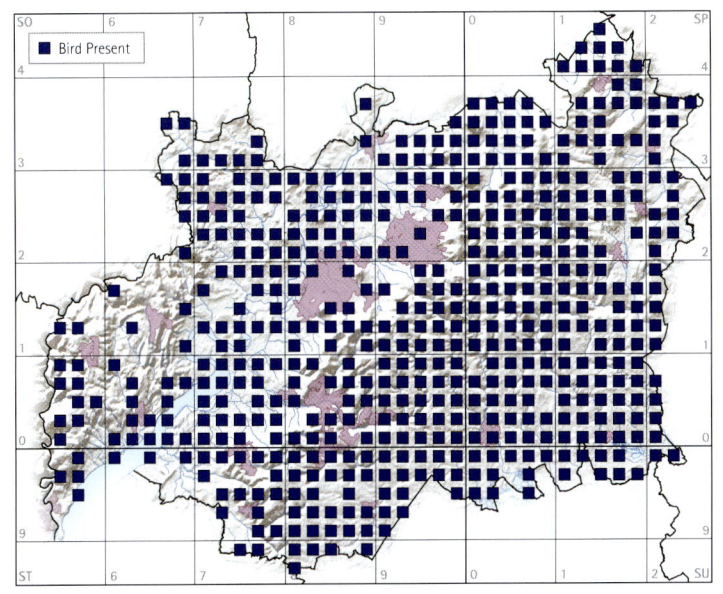

Winter Distribution

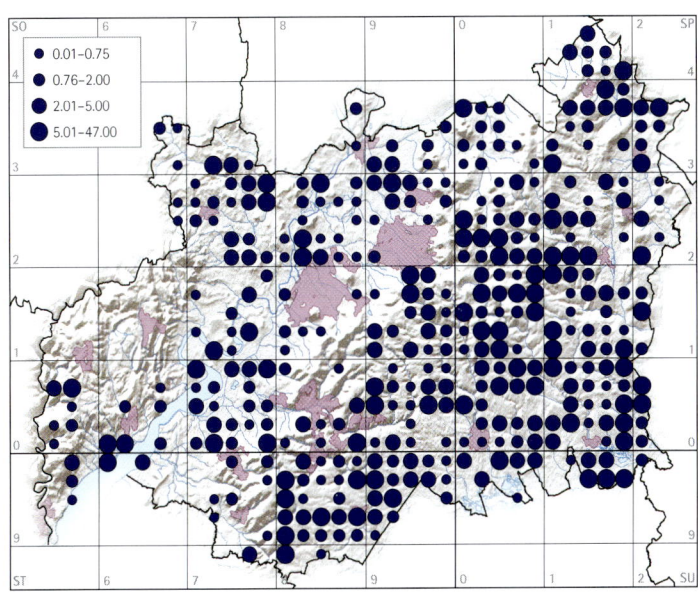

Winter Abundance

Sand Martin
Riparia riparia

Sand Martins breed across much of the northern hemisphere, and British and western European breeders winter just south of the Sahara in the Sahel region. Their natural breeding colonies are established in sandy river-banks and soft sea-cliffs, but in modern times they have flourished by exploiting suitable substrates in working gravel and sand extraction sites, where they (and the occasional Little Ringed Plover) often appear to be the only living things in a bleak landscape of bare ground and heavy machinery. Once a colony is found it is fairly easy to confirm breeding, as the birds can be observed entering nest-holes. However it is much more difficult to determine just how many holes are in use in a given season.

Sand Martin populations experience occasional catastrophic crashes caused by droughts in the Sahel, which may reduce the numbers of birds returning to breed by as much as two-thirds. It can take many years for numbers to recover from these slumps. There was one such population crash in 1968–69 and another in 1983–84, but subsequently the trends have been more positive, and Sand Martins seem to be more widespread than they were at the time of the 1988–91 Breeding Atlas, both nationally and in Gloucestershire.

This is one of the earliest migrants to return in spring, and the mean date of first arrival in Gloucestershire between 1977 and 2010 was March 14th; the earliest bird on record was at Slimbridge on

Sponsored by M G E Smith

2007–11 Atlas fieldwork					Gloucestershire trends						UK population trends	
Number of tetrads in which recorded (max 683)					Occupied 10 km squares (max 26)				% of tetrads in which recorded (1st hour of TTV)		UK conservation status: Amber 1	
	Total	Confirmed	Probable	Possible	Present	1968–71	1981–84	1988–91	2007–11	1988–91	2008–11	Long term	Short term
Breeding	80	17	4	8	51	17		7	8	2.6	3.5	+9%	+33%
Winter	0						0		0			–	–

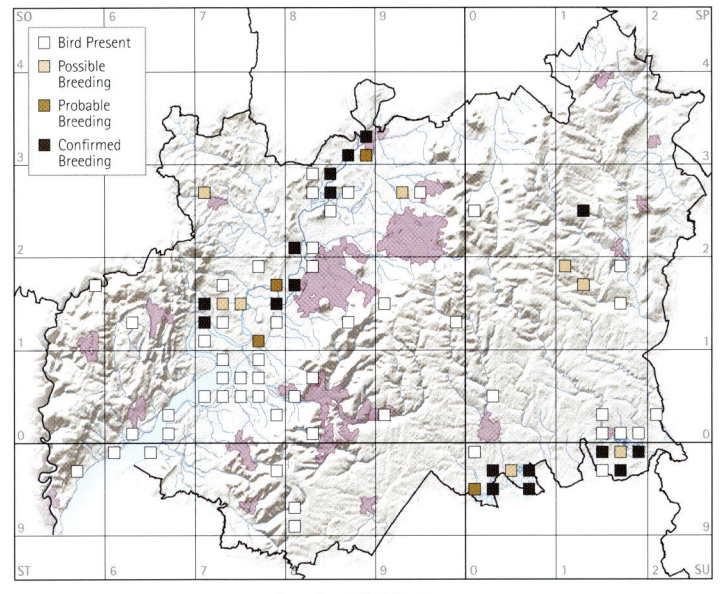

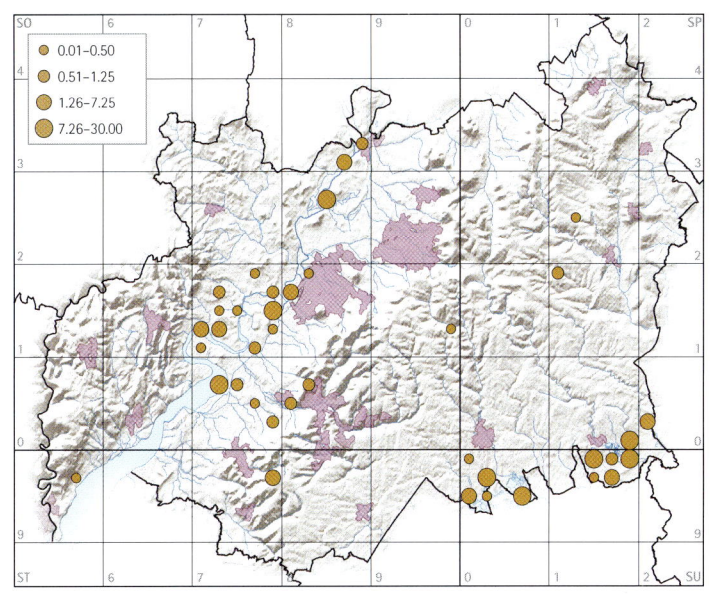

Breeding Distribution

Summer Abundance

February 22nd 2007. Sand Martins tend to leave earlier in autumn than House Martins and Swallows and the latest date for the county is October 28th 1996.

Swaine noted that many natural colonies in the county were small and temporary, and this still applies today. A few Sand Martins still nest here and there on the banks of the Wye and along the Severn and its tributaries, there is a colony in a Cotswold quarry and, during the fieldwork for the 2003–07 Cotswolds Atlas, breeding was strongly suspected at the Stoke Orchard landfill site. However these colonies are rather insignificant compared with the much greater numbers that use the Cotswold Water Park area, where considerable efforts are made by the mineral companies, with advice from the Cotswold Water Park Trust, to create suitable habitat each year. The colonies here are closely monitored and the birds' requirements are quite well understood. They prefer to use newly dug sand; Sand Martins are particularly vulnerable to parasites, which can build up in their nests and cause a reduction in breeding productivity if the same holes are used for more than one season, and even among pairs raising second broods during the first season (Gareth Harris). As individual sites are worked out they are restored, so they no longer contain suitable sandbanks, but further opportunities are provided by new workings and also by the creation of artificial banks.

Between 2004 and 2006 the number of nest holes found in the Water Park area was around 1,500. Despite the availability of many suitable banks, numbers fell to just over 1,000 in 2007 and to about 550 in 2008, and have remained around that level since (note that these figures refer to the whole of the Water Park, which straddles Gloucestershire and Wiltshire).

There have been a number of concerted Sand Martin ringing programmes in Britain at various times, and as a result there have been many recoveries involving Gloucestershire. Of some 300 movements between our county and elsewhere in the British Isles, the longest half-dozen reveal rapid southward movements of Scottish juveniles as early as July. In addition there have been about 30 recoveries between Gloucestershire other countries, including nine movements to and from Senegal, within the wintering area.

Swallow (Barn Swallow)
Hirundo rustica

The essence of summer for many people, Swallows breed throughout the northern hemisphere, up to the edge of the arctic tundra. Ringing recoveries have shown that birds nesting in particular regions spend the winter in very specific locations. For example, the British and Irish breeding populations migrate to South Africa and Namibia, an area they share with birds that breed in the former USSR near the borders between Europe and Asia (Migration Atlas).

Swallows associate closely with humans and nowadays they are almost entirely dependent on buildings for nesting. Both long and short-term population indicators for this species show a generally positive trend in the UK, although there are considerable regional variations. Surveying Swallows is generally straightforward, as they are conspicuous and approachable. Early in the season the observer can often deduce the location of nests by watching the birds enter buildings, and later the young birds can be seen being fed while perching on fences or wires near the breeding site. Hence there is a high proportion of 'confirmed' breeding records on the distribution map, many of them involving occupied nests.

In Gloucestershire, Swallows usually start to arrive towards the end of March; the average date of the first sighting from 1976 to 2010 was March 24th and the earliest was on March 9th in 1977. At the end of the season it is not unusual for stragglers to be recorded in the second half of October, but November records are more unusual and the latest on record was on November 30th 2003. The highest counts of Swallows in the county are often logged during the peak migration periods, especially by observers who count birds passing a particular point. Two thousand flying north over Slimbridge on April 20th 2008 was an unusually large number for spring passage, but movements of this order of magnitude are occasionally recorded in the autumn, especially after a successful breeding season. By far the highest count reported in recent times was the estimated 7,000–10,000 seen just before dusk at Frampton Pools on September 19th 1998. The observer noted that they possibly went to roost in a nearby maize field.

The Cotswolds Atlases detected little change in distribution in that area of the county between 1987 and 2007, and the data from the current atlas fieldwork confirm that Swallows are very widespread, being recorded in 99% of tetrads. In seems that almost every farm in Gloucestershire holds at least one breeding pair, and

Sponsored by Tony & Pam Perry

2007–11 Atlas fieldwork						Gloucestershire trends						UK population trends
Number of tetrads in which recorded (max 683)						Occupied 10 km squares (max 26)				% of tetrads in which recorded (1st hour of TTV)		UK conservation status: **Amber 1**
	Total	Confirmed	Probable	Possible	Present	1968–71	1981–84	1988–91	2007–11	1988–91	2008–11	Long term	Short term
Breeding	675	480	114	63	18	26		26	26	87.6	85.9	+21%	+34%
Winter	2						0		1			–	–

Breeding Distribution

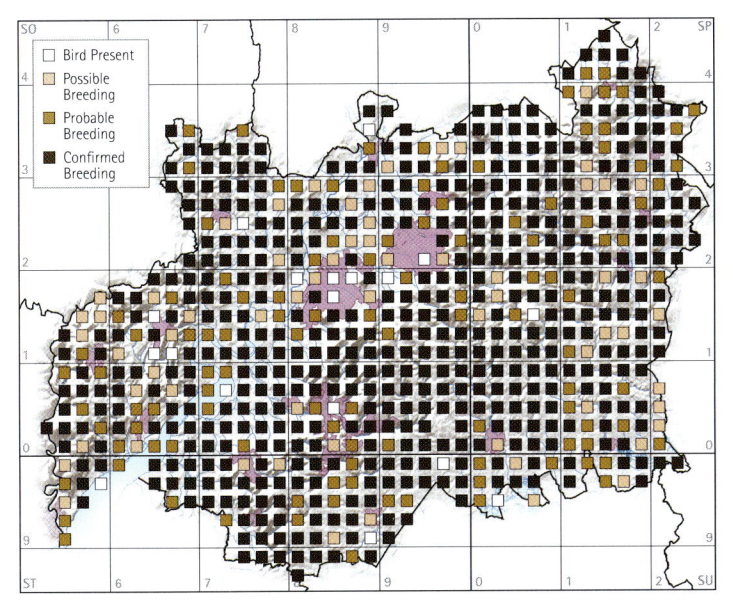

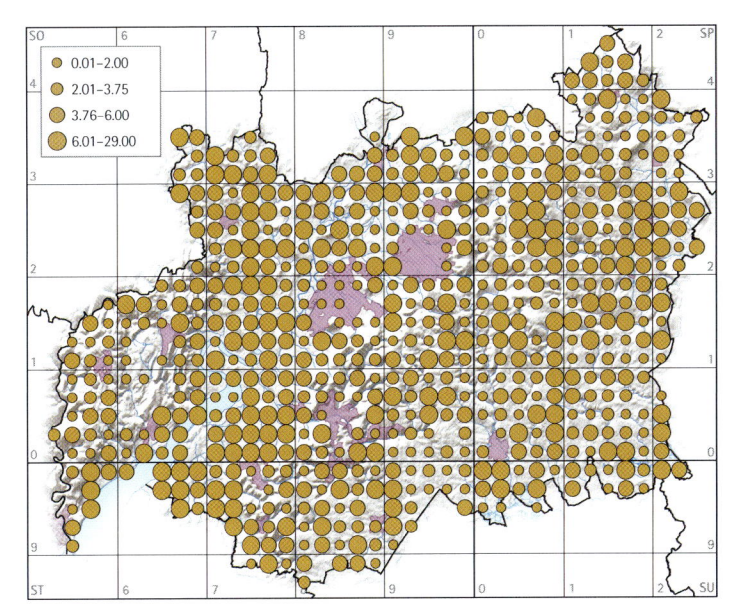

Summer Abundance

they are absent only from the most heavily built-up areas. However, the abundance map shows that they are more thinly distributed in the most densely wooded parts of the Forest of Dean and, to a lesser extent, in some parts of the higher Cotswolds where there are open areas of farmland with few suitable buildings for nest sites. This pattern is very similar to that described by Swaine.

Swallows can be caught and ringed in large numbers at roosts, and many nestlings are also easily accessible by ringers. As a result there had been about 100 recoveries of ringed birds involving Gloucestershire up to 2010. Fifty or so were between here and other counties in England and Wales, and there were 14 overseas movements of Gloucestershire-ringed birds, including two nestlings which migrated to Mozambique and South Africa.

House Martin (Common House Martin)
Delichon urbicum

House Martins breed across Europe and Asia but, unlike Swallows and Sand Martins, not in North America. European breeders winter in Africa south of the Sahara. In Britain they are widely distributed in both rural and urban areas and will readily establish new colonies on modern houses, building their conspicuous mud nests under the eaves or similar overhangs. Although they are usually very faithful to their nest sites from one year to the next, colonies do sometimes move, perhaps to new housing estates, which seem to attract House Martins very quickly. For example at the Lower Mill Estate in the Cotswold Water Park there were no nests in 2004 but 161 by 2011 (Gareth Harris). The long-term population trend for this species appears to be downward, both in Britain and in Europe as a whole, and there have been particularly steep declines in parts of England in recent years.

Breeding House Martins are generally easy to detect; they often reveal themselves by their 'double-click' calls, and they are active around their nests. During the atlas fieldwork most colonies should have been found during TTVs, and confirming breeding is particularly easy for this species as the young birds are often visible in the nest. The breeding season can be long, with juveniles from the first brood sometimes reported as helping to feed their younger siblings in the second (and in rare cases third) brood. In many years records are received of nests that are occupied long after most birds have left; the latest such record for Gloucestershire is a nest at Sharpness where young were still present on October 21st 1985.

The average date for the first arrival in the county is March 28th, although it is another month before they start to arrive in numbers. The earliest on record was on March 9th 2001. Autumn passage can produce large gatherings and flocks of several hundred are not unusual: 2,550 birds passed a site near Nailsworth over the course of 70 minutes on September 30th 2005, and about 1,000 perched on top of the grandstand at Cheltenham racecourse on September 9th 2000. There are occasional records of very late stragglers, the record being set in 1987, when birds were recorded in Leckhampton, Cheltenham until November 22nd. However there appears to have been a general tendency for most birds to leave earlier in recent years.

Mellersh, writing in 1902, felt that there had been a decrease in Gloucestershire, which he attributed to 'Hooligan' House Sparrows 'stealing' the nests of House Martins. Swaine quoted this opinion, but felt there was no convincing evidence of a decline. Indeed, the

Sponsored by the Cheltenham Bird Club

2007-11 Atlas fieldwork					Gloucestershire trends						UK population trends		
Number of tetrads in which recorded (max 683)					Occupied 10 km squares (max 26)				% of tetrads in which recorded (1st hour of TTV)		UK conservation status: Amber 1,3	
	Total	Confirmed	Probable	Possible	Present	1968-71	1981-84	1988-91	2007-11	1988-91	2008-11	Long term	Short term
Breeding	585	359	79	101	46	26		26	26	75.3	53.7	-45%	-4%
Winter	1							0	0			-	-

Breeding Distribution

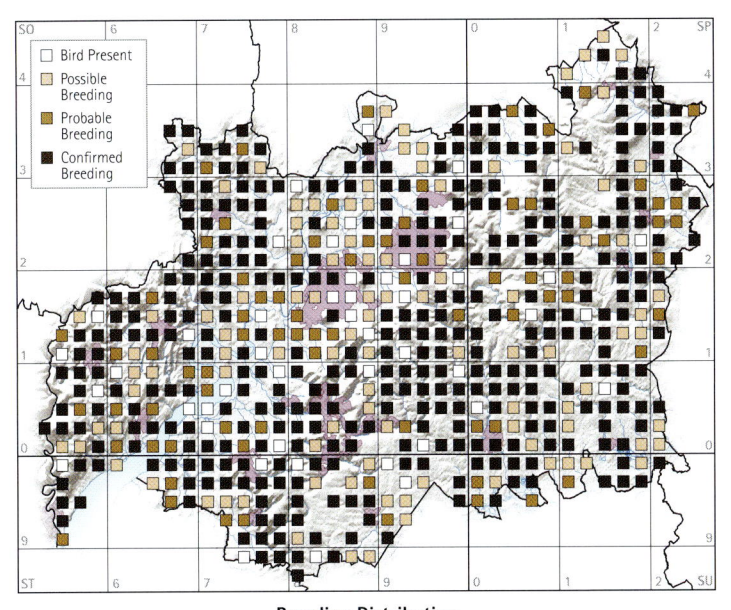

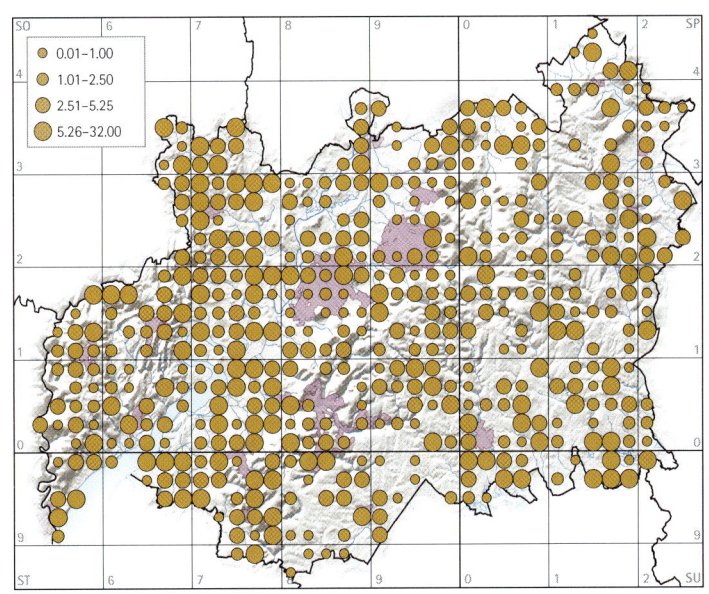

Summer Abundance

Cotswolds Atlases suggest a slight increase between 1983-87 and 2003-07, although this may be because of better coverage.

The distribution map shows that House Martins are very widespread in Gloucestershire. Swaine suggested that they were perhaps more numerous on the Cotswolds than in the lowland regions around 1980, but the abundance map indicates that at present densities are higher in the western half of the county. The 1988-91 Breeding Atlas suggested that three factors were needed for House Martins to thrive: suitable nest sites, warm, dry weather and plenty of insects. It could be that these conditions, particularly nest sites and food, are best satisfied in the west.

Swaine refers to older records of birds breeding on cliff faces and bridges in the Wye valley, but no such nest sites have been reported in the county in recent years.

A very unusual event was observed on August 10th 2007 at Longborough near Stow-on-the-Wold, when a small group of House Martins was seen to settle in an elder bush and feed on the berries (see photograph). This was only the second time this species had been recorded feeding on plant material (Brookes 2008).

Red-rumped Swallow
Cecropis daurica

Once a rare vagrant to Britain, the Red-rumped Swallow has been an annual visitor in small numbers since 1963, reflecting the northward expansion of its European breeding range. It was removed from the national rarities list in 2006. There have been two records in Gloucestershire:

2001: one at Slimbridge on April 5th.
2004: two at Harbour Road Lakes, Lydney, from April 28th to 30th, one remaining until May 5th.

Cetti's Warbler
Cettia cetti

The range of Cetti's Warbler includes much of southern Europe, north-west Africa, Asia Minor, the Middle East and south-west Asia. It was formerly much more restricted, but there was a gradual northward expansion during the twentieth century. It is mainly resident throughout much of its range, but birds breeding further to the east in Asia are migratory. The European population numbers up to 1.6 million pairs. In Britain it is typically found in dense undergrowth near water in lowland areas, but in southern Europe it also occurs in dry habitats and sometimes at fairly high altitude. It is a very skulking species, but its presence is often given away by its explosive calls and song, which can be heard throughout the year.

Cetti's Warbler was unknown in Britain until 1961 when the first record came from Hampshire. Following an influx in 1971, breeding was first confirmed in Kent in 1973 and southern England was rapidly colonised thereafter, albeit with occasional setbacks due to cold winters. The RBBP reported a total of 1,907 singing males or territories in Britain in 2010, over 97% of which were south of a line from Cardigan Bay to the Wash.

There were two unsubstantiated reports in Gloucestershire in 1981, but the first confirmed county record came in 1985 when a male found near Stroud on January 4th remained throughout the year. By June 6th it had attracted a female and the pair bred successfully, with two fledged young being seen on June 24th. Meanwhile a second male was found at another site on April 24th and was present throughout the summer. The first male remained on territory until February 21st 1986, but there were then no more county records until October 1990 when a single male was found at Purton Timber Ponds on the Gloucester and Sharpness Canal. Over the next few years a small population involving up to five singing males gradually became established at Purton, and then during the late 1990s regular reports came from the Slimbridge reserve and Frampton Pools and also the river Frome at Whitminster. The first report west of the Severn came in 2000 from Lydney Marsh, a small reed-bed on the outskirts of the town that is one of the few areas of suitable habitat on that side of the river. The next decade saw the species gradually colonise suitable habitat further up the Severn Vale, with sporadic records coming from sites such as Hempsted, Port Ham and Castlemeads near Gloucester, Coombe Hill Meadows, and the Mythe at Tewkesbury. The year 2002 was notable for the first records from the Cotswold Water Park, where a small population has subsequently become established, and also a sighting at Dowdeswell reservoir.

The maps clearly show the core areas at the Water Park and along the Severn. Latest figures put the county total at over 20 singing males. The summer and winter maps are very similar and demonstrate the rather sedentary nature of this species once birds are established in suitable habitat. However, immatures in particular will undertake dispersive movements, enabling new sites to be colonised, and there have been two fairly long-distance ringing recoveries involving Gloucestershire: an immature ringed at Slimbridge in August 2002 was caught by ringers 36 km away at the Water Park two years later, and one ringed at Chew Valley Lake, Somerset in October 2008 and caught by ringers at Slimbridge in August 2009 had moved 50 km.

Sponsored by the Dursley Birdwatching and Preservation Society

Species accounts 317

2007–11 Atlas fieldwork						Gloucestershire trends						UK population trends	
Number of tetrads in which recorded (max 683)					*Occupied 10 km squares (max 26)*				*% of tetrads in which recorded (1st hour of TTV)*		*UK conservation status:* **Green**	
	Total	Confirmed	Probable	Possible	Present	1968–71	1981–84	1988–91	2007–11	1988–91	2008–11	Long term	Short term
Breeding	28	3	8	15	2	0		0	8	0	1.5	–	–
Winter	20						0		7			–	–

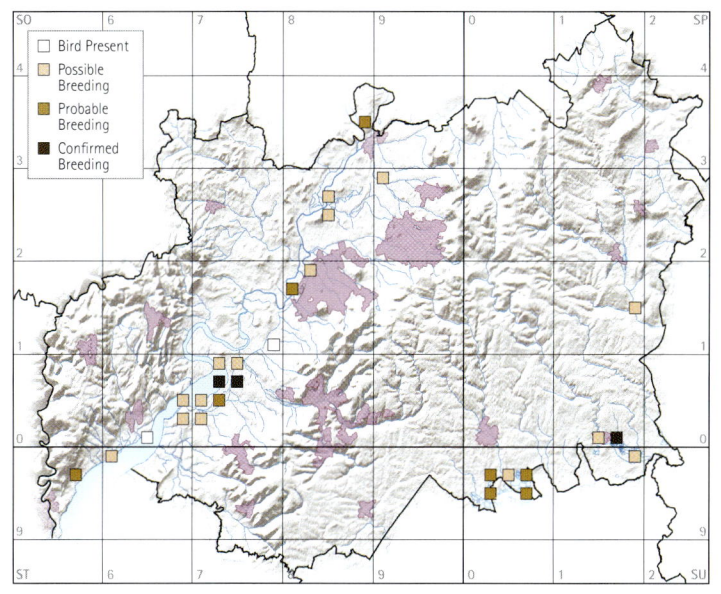

Breeding Distribution

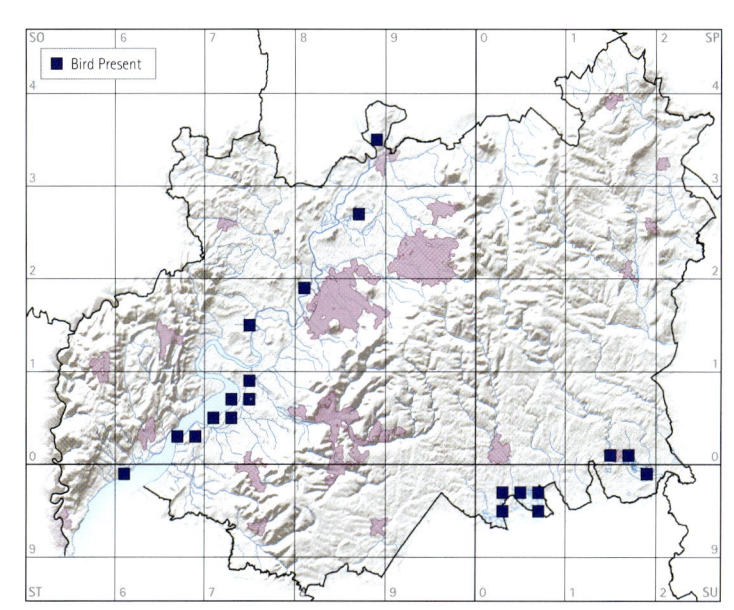

Winter Distribution

PETER PARTINGTON

Long-tailed Tit
Aegithalos caudatus

The breeding range of Long-tailed Tits extends in a broad band from the Atlantic seaboard of Europe east to Japan and Kamchatka, wherever their preferred habitat of deciduous woodland, scrub, hedges, orchards and other wooded landscapes occurs. They have an unusual co-operative breeding system, whereby if a pair's nesting attempt fails, each member of the pair will help another, related pair to raise their young, instead of trying to nest again as do most passerines. Outside the breeding season Long-tailed Tits are usually encountered in small flocks, normally consisting of 'extended family' groups, with ten or a dozen birds being usual but sometimes up to 20 or more. Such flocks also often include other species such as Blue and Great Tits, Goldcrests, Treecreepers and, in autumn, warblers. This flocking behaviour means that the distribution is 'clumped' rather than being spread uniformly through the habitat, and in theory this could lead to some flocks being completely missed during atlas fieldwork. On the other hand, the flocks are usually very vocal and mobile, increasing the chances of their being detected by a nearby observer. In the nesting season, Long-tailed Tits can be fairly unobtrusive until the chicks fledge, when they are noisy and conspicuous, and most confirmed breeding records were based on sightings of dependent fledged young.

In common with other small resident insectivorous birds, populations of Long-tailed Tits at the northern edge of the range, including in the British Isles, are very vulnerable to cold winters. They may gain some protection from such harsh conditions from their communal roosting behaviour (often huddling closely together to conserve heat overnight), and they may also have benefited from their fairly recently acquired habit of feeding at bird tables. Nevertheless, the size of the British breeding population does fluctuate according to winter weather. However, as they can raise so many young per season (often up to 12 per pair), they can recover quickly from low points, and the long-term national trend is one of wide fluctuations around a fairly stable overall level. There was little net change in distribution between the 1968–72 and 1988–91 Breeding Atlases.

Swaine described the Long-tailed Tit as a common breeding resident found in all parts of Gloucestershire, and this is still true today, as shown by the distribution maps. For a species so susceptible to short-term changes it is difficult to assess longer-term trends, but there has been a general feeling among birdwatchers that numbers have increased in the county since the early 1990s (2003–07 Cotswolds Atlas). The cold snap during winter 2008–09 resulted in quite a dramatic fall in county BBS figures, from about 60% of sites in 2008 to 37% in 2009. In 2010 however the cold weather early in the year apparently had no such ill-effects and in fact the BBS figure rose again to 68% that summer.

The abundance maps indicate that, as might be expected, densities are rather lower in areas of open countryside, for example in the higher parts of the Cotswolds and some areas of the Vale. The highest total recorded during a TTV was 60 in SO72Q, the tetrad including Highnam Woods RSPB reserve, in February 2008.

British and Irish Long-tailed Tits are mainly resident, and movements of over 100 km are unusual. Falling into this category are birds ringed in Somerset and Surrey and subsequently found in Gloucestershire.

Sponsored by Tricia Atkinson and Gerry Robbins, and in memory of Leonard Crew

Species accounts

	2007–11 Atlas fieldwork					Gloucestershire trends						UK population trends	
	Number of tetrads in which recorded (max 683)					Occupied 10 km squares (max 26)				% of tetrads in which recorded (1st hour of TTV)		UK conservation status: **Green**	
	Total	Confirmed	Probable	Possible	Present	1968-71	1981-84	1988-91	2007-11	1988-91	2008-11	Long term	Short term
Breeding	637	463	94	57	23	26		26	26	41.4	56.4	+109%	+24%
Winter	664						26		26			–	–

Breeding Distribution

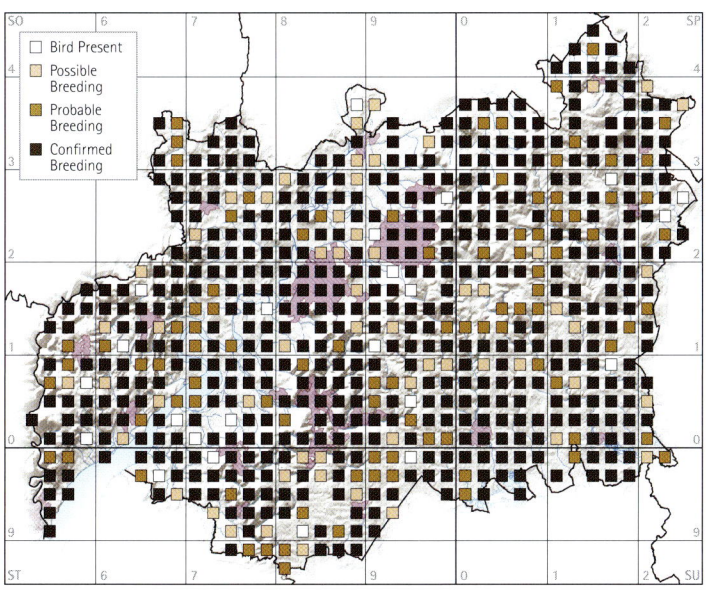

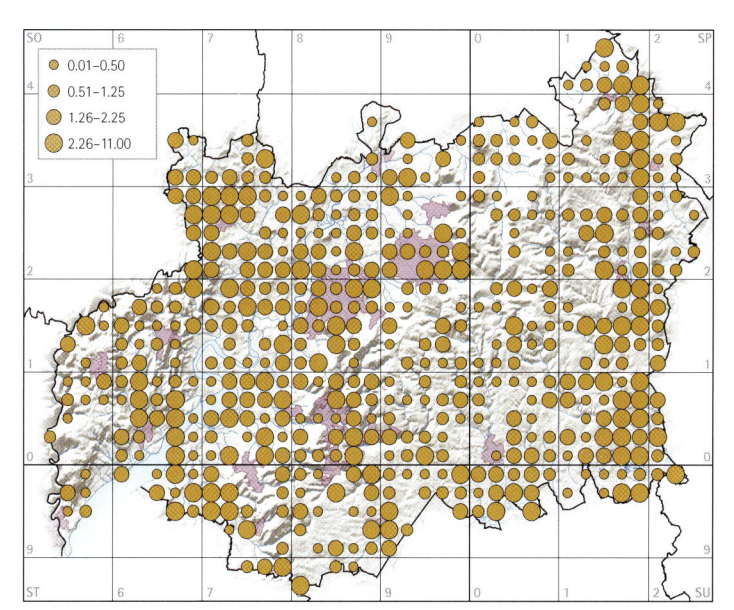

Summer Abundance

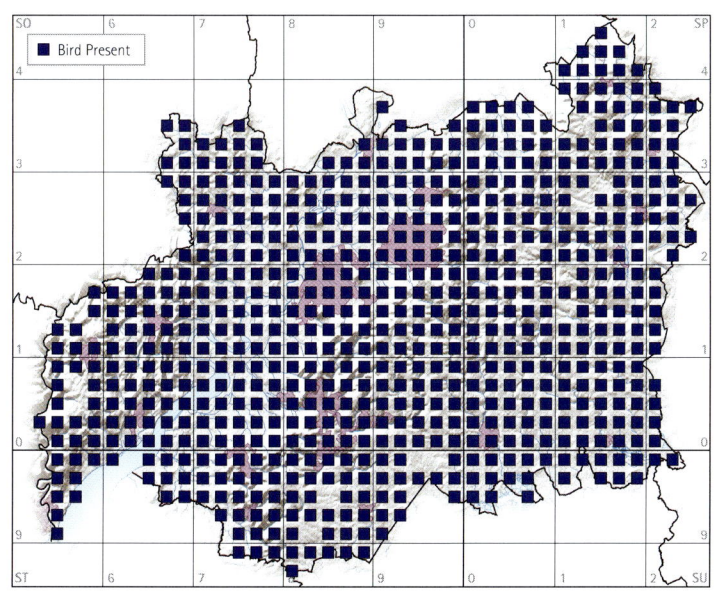

Winter Distribution

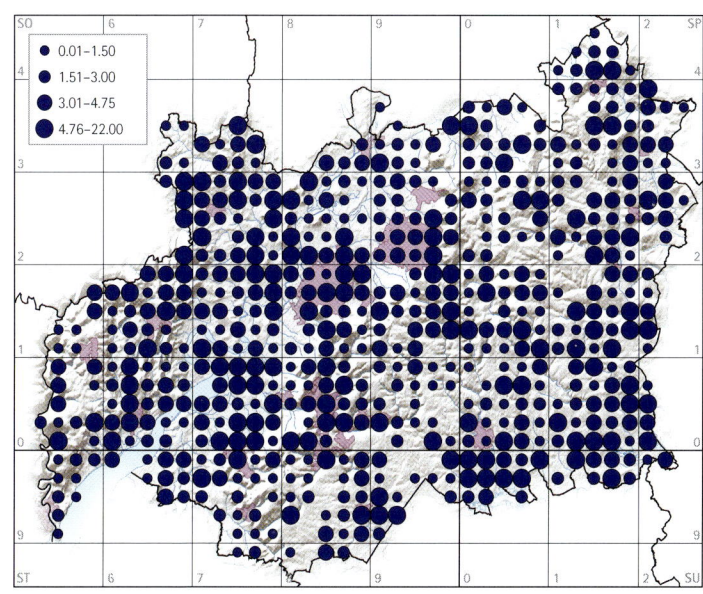

Winter Abundance

Wood Warbler
Phylloscopus sibilatrix

Wood Warblers breed in most European countries, with the notable exception of Iberia, and as far east as central Asia. A key breeding requirement is for closed-canopy woodland with little or no understorey and sparse ground cover. All Wood Warblers winter in Africa, where they are unusual among Palearctic migrants in that they can be found in the equatorial rainforest zone.

Numbers have declined all across Europe in recent decades. In the British Isles, they spread north in Scotland after the mid-nineteenth century, and although the small Irish population was increasing up to the 1988–91 Breeding Atlas, in England a decline had already set in by then, particularly in the south and east of the country. This decrease has accelerated subsequently, and in recent years has been little short of catastrophic. At the same time the national breeding range has tended to shrink back towards the upland and western areas which have always been the species' strongholds. Causes of this decrease may well include changes affecting the wintering areas, or even the regions through which the birds migrate, as well as the breeding range. The British population is currently about 17,000 males.

In Wales, the South-west Peninsula and elsewhere the preferred breeding habitat is usually upland oak woods, but in Gloucestershire suitable conditions are also provided by mature beech plantations. Swaine was still able to report that Wood Warblers nested 'in considerable numbers in the Forest of Dean and in outlying woods ... such as those near Symonds Yat, Newent and Highnam'. However there appeared to have been a recent decline in the small population in the beech woods along the Cotswolds scarp, and on the dip-slope there were only sporadic occurrences in small numbers, implying a decrease since Mellersh's day. There were 'few if any' in the low-lying Severn Vale and none in the Thames Area.

Since 1980 the decline has continued unabated. Between 1987 and 2007 the already severely depleted population in the area covered by the Cotswolds Atlases to all intents and purposes disappeared, and the current survey only managed to discover half a dozen birds in the whole of the Cotswolds over four seasons. Most or all of these were quite probably on passage, and the same is true of the sightings in the Vale. There were encouraging records from Highnam Woods (SO71U and SO72Q), and a scattering of observations in the Newent area, matching those reported by Swaine but, over the county as a whole, 36 of the 51 tetrads where Wood Warblers were recorded were located in the Forest of Dean, and 14 were in the single 10 km square SO61.

Even within the Dean the situation is far from healthy. In 1984 a survey by Ian Bullock, the Nagshead RSPB reserve warden at the time, revealed as many as 278 singing males in the Gloucestershire part of the Dean, and another 30 in the Wye Valley. There were still 46 singing males at Nagshead alone in 1990 ('a good year' according to the GBR), but only 22 in 2007, 15 in 2008 and 12 in both 2009 and 2010 (Hannah Morton). The most recorded during a TTV during the current survey was only four, in two Forest tetrads; males tend to sing less persistently once pairs are established, but on the other hand when they are singing they are audible from some distance, and two males per occupied tetrad could well be an optimistic overall figure. This would equate to a maximum of about 70 males in the whole of the Gloucestershire part of the Dean.

Sponsored by Andrew Bluett

Species accounts

2007–11 Atlas fieldwork						Gloucestershire trends					UK population trends	
Number of tetrads in which recorded (max 683)					*Occupied 10 km squares (max 26)*				*% of tetrads in which recorded (1st hour of TTV)*		*UK conservation status:* **Red 3**	
	Total	Confirmed	Probable	Possible	Present	1968–71	1981–84	1988–91	2007–11	1988–91	2008–11	Long term	Short term
Breeding	51	6	9	31	5	18		11	10	10.7	2.1	–	–63%
Winter	0						0		0			–	–

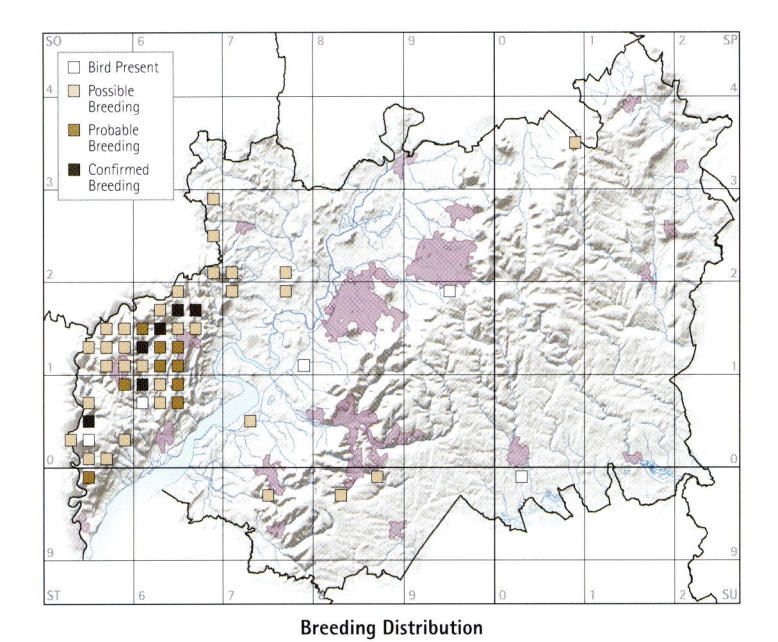

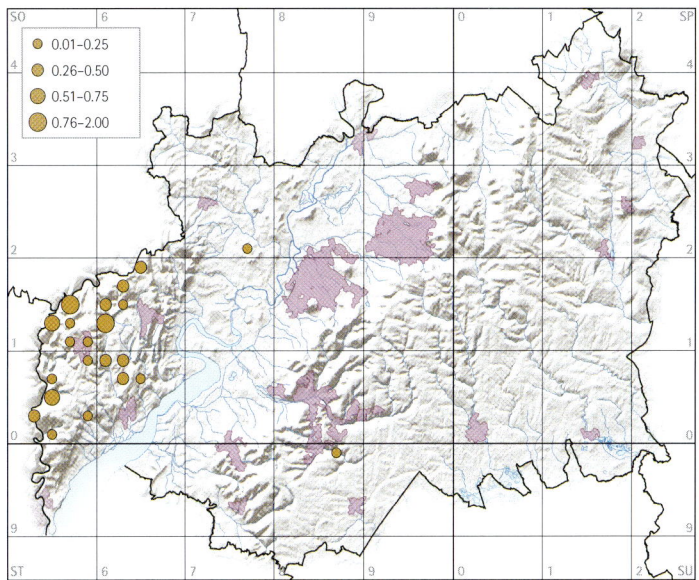

Breeding Distribution

Summer Abundance

On average, the first spring Wood Warblers arrive in the county around April 21st. The earliest on record, on April 7th 1997, might seem very unusual, but there have been first sightings only a few days later in a number of other years. Swaine said that they 'occur more widely on passage', but in recent years records of migrants have declined in line with the overall decrease. The vast majority leave the county by early August and the latest bird on record was on September 12th 2004. The sole ringing recovery involving Gloucestershire, of a Nagshead nestling ringed in 2001 and recovered in its first autumn at Titchfield Haven, Hampshire on July 25th, illustrates just how early they can depart.

Chiffchaff (Common Chiffchaff)
Phylloscopus collybita

Chiffchaffs breed from western Europe east to Lake Baikal and the north-west Himalayas. Over most of the breeding range all birds emigrate for the winter, those from the Western Palearctic moving as far as the northern Afrotropics. However some birds from western Europe, including the British Isles, remain all year round, and some birds from further afield move into Britain and Ireland for the winter. These winter birds are mainly of the local subspecies *P. c. collybita*, but they also include a few *P. c. abietinus* ('Scandinavian Chiffchaff'), and even fewer *P. c. tristis* ('Siberian Chiffchaff'). The plumages of the three subspecies intergrade and they can be difficult to separate even in the hand, although Siberian birds have a fairly distinctive call.

Although Chiffchaffs have been increasing in Britain over the past few decades, there have been both losses and gains in the northern half of the country. The favoured breeding habitat is open mature lowland woodland, but they will nest almost anywhere where there are some tall trees, including parkland, larger gardens, farmland spinneys and hedgerows. In winter, they prefer low-lying areas with bushes and scrub, often near water.

The very distinctive, repetitive song of the Chiffchaff is the first sign of spring for many birdwatchers in the British Isles. Wintering birds may start to sing in early March, and these days the first migrants arrive around the middle of the month. They sing continuously for much of the summer, making them easy to detect during atlas surveying. On the other hand, winter birds can be far more unobtrusive and easily overlooked.

Swaine described the Chiffchaff as a 'common summer visitor in all suitable areas' in Gloucestershire and this is still the case, with breeding records from throughout the county. The areas of greatest abundance are mostly in the Forest of Dean, Severn Vale and parts of the Cotswold scarp, with noticeably lower densities on the farmland of the Cotswold dip-slope, where suitable habitat is less widespread. Chiffchaffs have clearly become commoner as breeding birds in Gloucestershire, in line with the national trend: in the area covered by the Cotswolds Atlases there was a 28% increase in the number of occupied tetrads between 1987 and 2007, with an impressive 135% rise in the number of tetrads with confirmed breeding, though this may have been partly due to better coverage. County BBS figures also show a tendency to increase after 2000, though there have been some fairly wide fluctuations.

Swaine noted that Chiffchaffs had been recorded in winter 'from time to time in the past and almost annually since 1960', mainly in the Severn Vale but with some from the Cotswold Water Park and the Cotswolds. They have evidently become commoner here in winter more recently, as indicated by the reporting rates in the fact-box for the current atlas and the 1981–84 Wintering Atlas. The maps show that the favoured winter areas are still the same as described by Swaine, with noticeable concentrations in the low-lying Severn Vale and Thames NAs and far fewer in the Dean and the Cotswolds.

Swaine cited only three county records of eastern-race Chiffchaffs: one 'almost certainly' *abietinus* at Frampton in winter 1968–69, and two *tristis*, both in 1980: at Cheltenham from January to April and at Frampton in April. Since, then, despite the identification pitfalls, there have been increasing numbers of reports of birds showing the characteristics of these subspecies, with about eight identified as *tristis* and about 14 as *abietinus* since the turn of the twenty-first century.

Up to 2010, six Gloucestershire-ringed Chiffchaffs had been recovered on passage in France and Iberia. Four ringed here had been found in Morocco between January and March, and one in Senegal in November; these are well-documented wintering areas. More unusually, one ringed in Senegal in February 1974 was caught by ringers at Frampton in May the same year, and one ringed at Tarifa in southern Spain in November 2009 was caught at Pope's Hill near Littledean in October 2010. Comparatively few Chiffchaffs have been ringed in these countries, and recoveries in Britain are correspondingly unusual.

Sponsored by Robert Boon

Species accounts 323

	2007–11 Atlas fieldwork					Gloucestershire trends						UK population trends	
	Number of tetrads in which recorded (max 683)					*Occupied 10 km squares (max 26)*				*% of tetrads in which recorded (1st hour of TTV)*		*UK conservation status:* **Green**	
	Total	Confirmed	Probable	Possible	Present	1968–71	1981–84	1988–91	2007–11	1988–91	2008–11	Long term	Short term
Breeding	679	292	279	105	3	26		26	26	85.8	89.6	+49%	+52%
Winter	80						7		20			–	–

Breeding Distribution

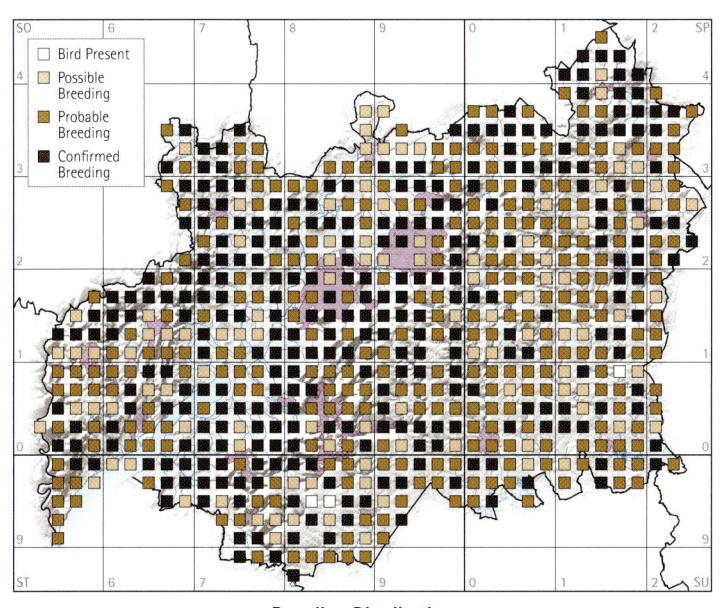

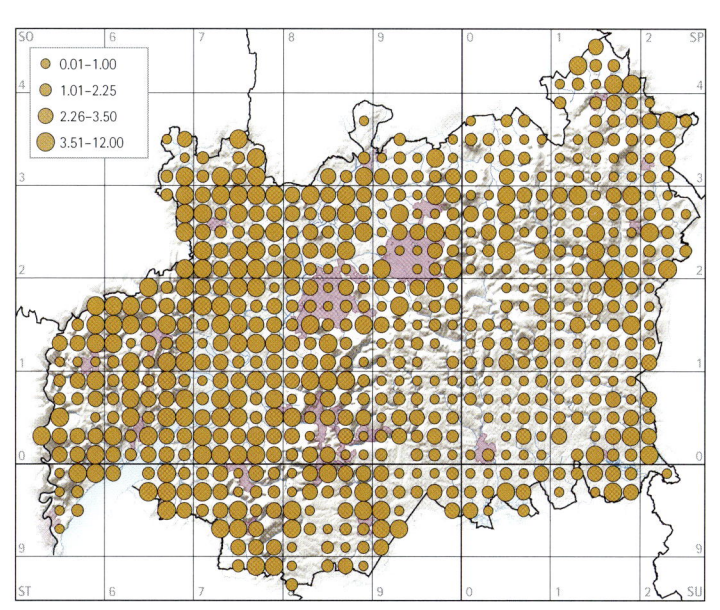

Summer Abundance

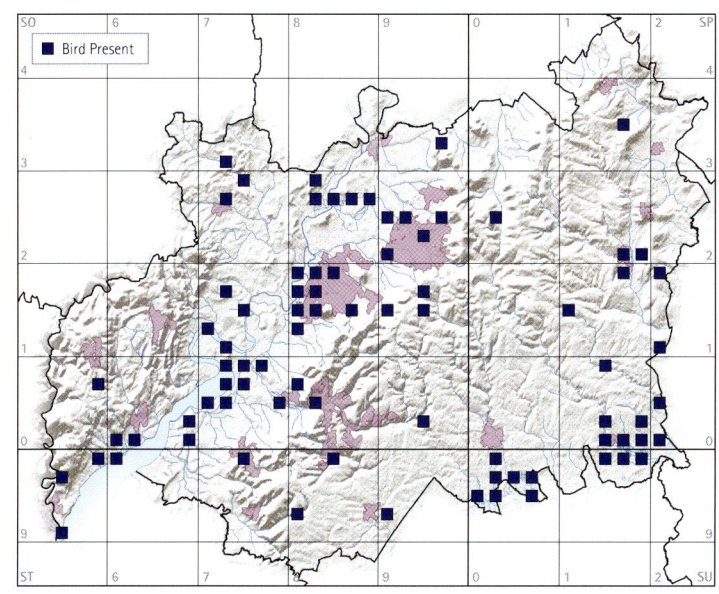

Winter Distribution

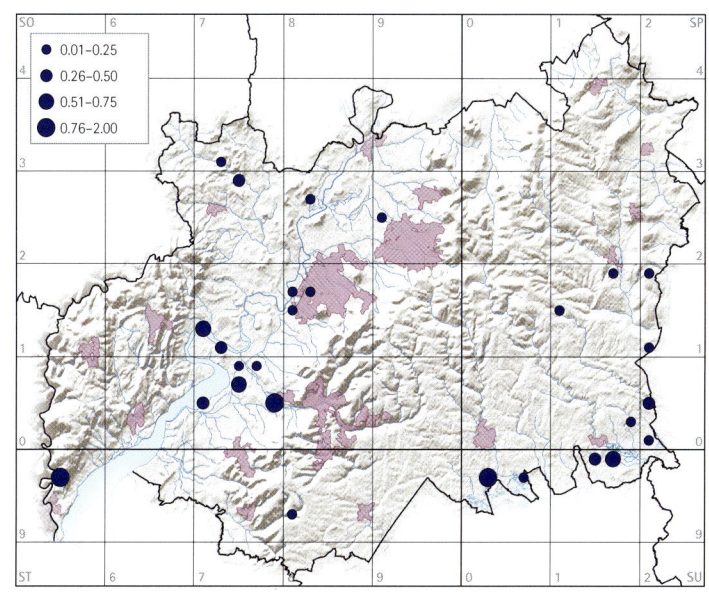

Winter Abundance

Willow Warbler
Phylloscopus trochilus

Willow Warblers breed very widely across the whole of northern Eurasia and winter in Africa south of the Sahara. In the breeding season they tend to avoid mature closed-canopy woodland and built-up areas, but can be found in many other habitats where there are trees or scrub with dense ground cover, such as young plantations, woodland edges, bushy valley bottoms and other uncultivated areas. They nest on or near the ground, especially in tangles at the bases of bushes.

Willow Warblers are probably the most numerous of summer visitors to Britain, but since the 1980s they have undergone a catastrophic decline in much of England and Wales, although at the same time numbers have increased in Scotland and Ireland (see Spotted Flycatcher, p. 366). There are some indications that even in the south the decline may have slowed or halted in the last few years.

One of the earliest summer visitors to arrive, the first Willow Warblers appear in Gloucestershire in the last few days of March (earliest record March 17th 1990). They are often first located by their sweet, fluid song, and for many birdwatchers this is still one of our most familiar songbirds. Like many other migrants they will sing while still on passage, so it is likely that some birds recorded during atlas fieldwork as singing (and therefore as possible breeders) were simply moving through. Observers were encouraged to confirm breeding by looking for adults carrying food, but success in this respect was evidently variable. Most have left by the end of August, with stragglers usually to the end of September (latest date October 23rd 1994).

The national decline has been equally noticeable in Gloucestershire, and although this is still a fairly common species here it no longer seems correct to describe it as 'an abundant and widespread summer visitor, breeding throughout the county', as Swaine did. In the area covered by the Cotswolds Atlases there was a substantial decrease between 1987 and 2007, both in the number of tetrads in which the species was recorded (from 278 down to 240) and in the number of confirmed breeding records. Willow Warblers had tended to disappear from less optimal habitats and to have become thinner on the ground even in more favoured areas. Elsewhere in the county the same pattern is evident. They seem to have abandoned the lower-lying ground of the Severn Vale and the edges of the Forest of Dean, and even at higher altitude numbers have fallen. For example at Slimbridge there were six singing males in June 2000, but only two pairs in 2002 and none by 2003.

Sponsored by John A S Green

2007–11 Atlas fieldwork						Gloucestershire trends					UK population trends	
Number of tetrads in which recorded (max 683)					Occupied 10 km squares (max 26)				% of tetrads in which recorded (1st hour of TTV)		UK conservation status: **Amber 3**	
	Total	Confirmed	Probable	Possible	Present	1968–71	1981–84	1988–91	2007–11	1988–91	2008–11	Long term	Short term
Breeding	534	78	168	268	20	26		26	26	86.0	41.6	–39%	–5%
Winter	1							0	0			–	–

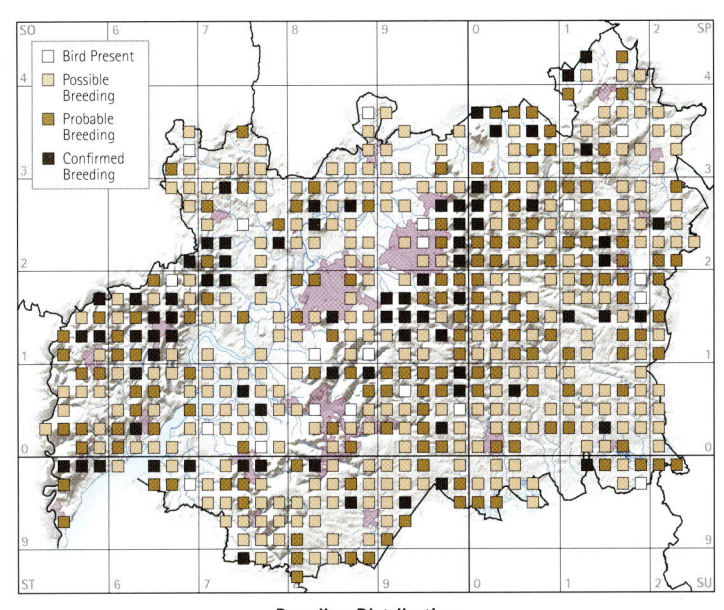

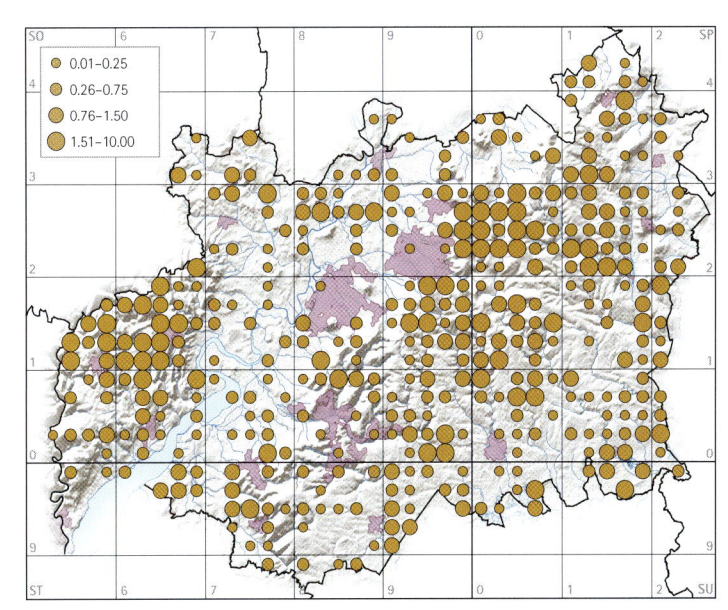

Breeding Distribution

Summer Abundance

Similarly there were as many as 112 pairs at Nagshead RSPB reserve in the Dean in 1989, decreasing to about 30 pairs in the mid-1990s and only 20 pairs by 2002. In the county as a whole, the BBS index declined fairly steadily from 67% of squares in 1994 to 31% in 2007.

In very recent years there has been a slight suggestion of a recovery, with the county BBS level up to 50% in 2010, the highest level for ten years, and Willow Warblers still fairly widely distributed in the county, as may be seen from the maps. During the current atlas period they were completely absent only from more open parts of the Vale, more continuously wooded areas of the Dean, and some of the very open farmland in the Cotswolds, where there has been a further thinning-out since 2007, more particularly in the east. The highest densities appear to be in parts of the Dean and some areas of the Cotswolds, particularly the scarp and high wold near Cheltenham. The maximum number recorded during a TTV was 34, on May 10th 2009 in SO92X, Cleeve Common.

It is to be hoped that the recent population crash in England has been no more than a temporary setback in the fortunes of this much-loved summer visitor.

Blackcap (Eurasian Blackcap)
Sylvia atricapilla

Blackcaps breed from the Cape Verde islands, the Azores and Norway eastwards across the Western Palearctic to west Siberia and Iran. Their habitat includes woods with a fairly sparse understorey, tall open scrub and large gardens. Their preference for taller trees means that they breed in suburbs and town centres more than other *Sylvia* warblers such as Whitethroats and Garden Warblers. Northern and eastern Blackcap populations are wholly migratory, wintering south to sub-Saharan Africa, while those breeding in the Mediterranean area are resident. Birds from intervening areas, including much of western Europe, are partial migrants; most, including British breeders, spend the winter in the Mediterranean countries. In recent decades there has been a spectacular increase in the number of Blackcaps wintering in the British Isles, from an average of only 22 records per year between 1945 and 1954 to over 3,000 birds at present (BWP). The evidence indicates that these birds are from continental European breeding populations. The increase has been linked with improved winter survival, possibly associated with the birds' increasing use of bird tables and feeders, where they will take a wide range of food.

Because of this sizeable wintering population, it is now difficult to decide in spring whether any individual Blackcap is an arriving migrant or a lingering winterer. The first migrants usually arrive in England about the end of March, with the main influx from mid-April. From late April Blackcaps' song can be confused with that of newly arrived Garden Warblers, but this is more likely to affect the atlas maps for Garden Warbler than for the more common and widespread Blackcap.

Blackcaps are 'possibly the most successful warblers in Britain and Ireland' (1988–91 Breeding Atlas) and their range and abundance have been increasing here since at least the mid-1950s. In the 20 years following the 1968–72 Breeding Atlas there was a noticeable spread west and north in Ireland and an extension of range in Scotland. This spread has continued, along with a substantial population increase.

In Gloucestershire, Swaine described Blackcaps as 'breeding throughout the county ... nowhere more plentiful than in the Forest of Dean'. Today they are practically ubiquitous here and all the indicators confirm that they have continued to increase. There must be hardly a kilometre square in the county that does not support a pair. They are particularly numerous in the west, in parts of the Severn Vale and the Forest of Dean, but there are also pockets of high density elsewhere, for example in the Thames Area in and around the Cotswold Water Park.

Mellersh only mentioned four reports of wintering in the county, and winter records remained unusual until about 1960. Between then and 1980 Swaine noted that 'up to 12 or more individuals were noted in each of several winters'. However a more detailed national survey (Leach 1981) revealed up to 120 in the county in early 1979. Swaine described this as 'surprising', but it would be unremarkable these days; indeed, ten were counted in a single TTV in February 2010 in tetrad ST69N, in the Severn Vale near Berkeley. However the distribution map shows that Blackcaps were largely absent in winter from wide areas of farmland in the Cotswolds and Thames NAs, and from the central parts of the Dean. The winter abundance map shows clusters of slightly higher density around some towns, notably Cheltenham and Gloucester. Blackcaps were apparently also fairly numerous in some rural areas in the Vale and in the north-west of the county, possibly reflecting their use of fruit remaining into winter in the orchards in these districts as well as their presence at village bird tables.

There have been a number of ringing recoveries of Blackcaps moving between Gloucestershire and countries as distant as Norway, Denmark, Algeria and Morocco, in line with their known or suspected wintering areas and migration routes. Rather more out of the ordinary was one ringed in Malta in November 1987 which was caught at Littleton-upon-Severn in South Gloucestershire in April 1989 and then found dead at Dursley in July 1990. Malta is apparently a rather unusual wintering area for British Blackcaps, and this one managed to elude the bird-catchers there.

Sponsored by John Phillips and Colin & Ingrid Twissell

Species accounts

2007–11 Atlas fieldwork					Gloucestershire trends						UK population trends		
Number of tetrads in which recorded (max 683)					Occupied 10 km squares (max 26)				% of tetrads in which recorded (1st hour of TTV)		UK conservation status: **Green**		
	Total	Confirmed	Probable	Possible	Present	1968–71	1981–84	1988–91	2007–11	1988–91	2008–11	Long term	Short term
Breeding	680	267	303	110	0	26		26	26	75.3	84.8	+175%	+73%
Winter	221						18		25			–	–

Breeding Distribution

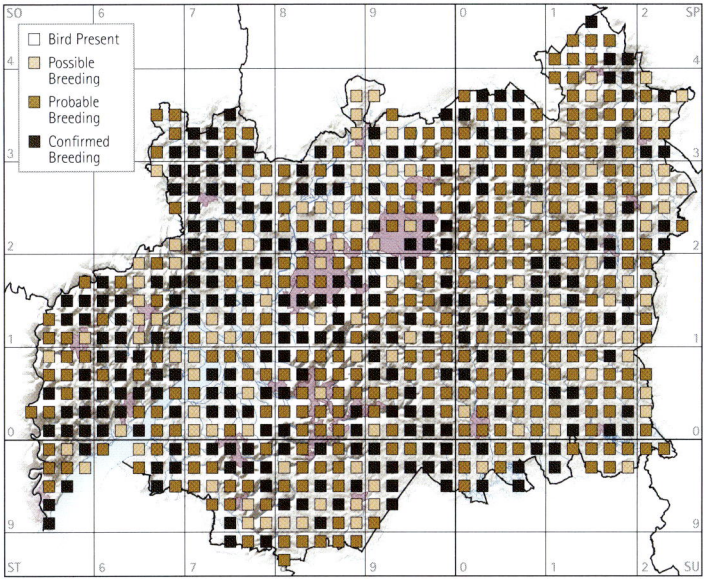

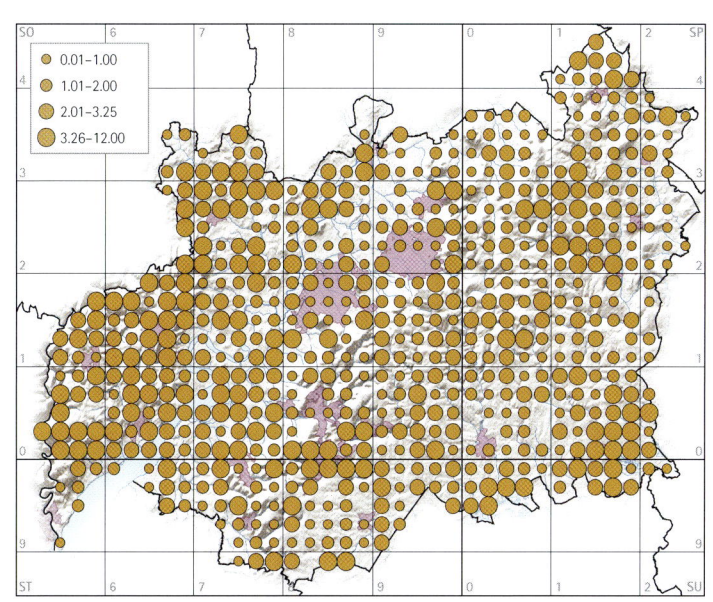

Summer Abundance

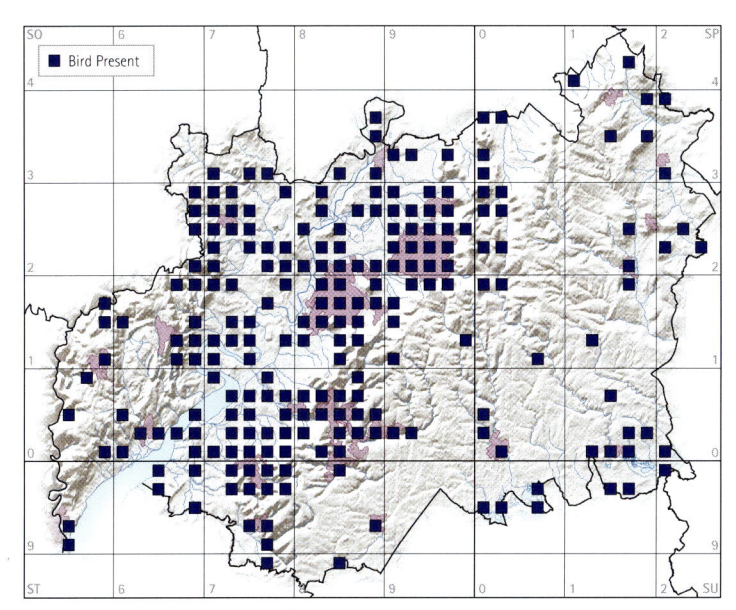

Winter Distribution

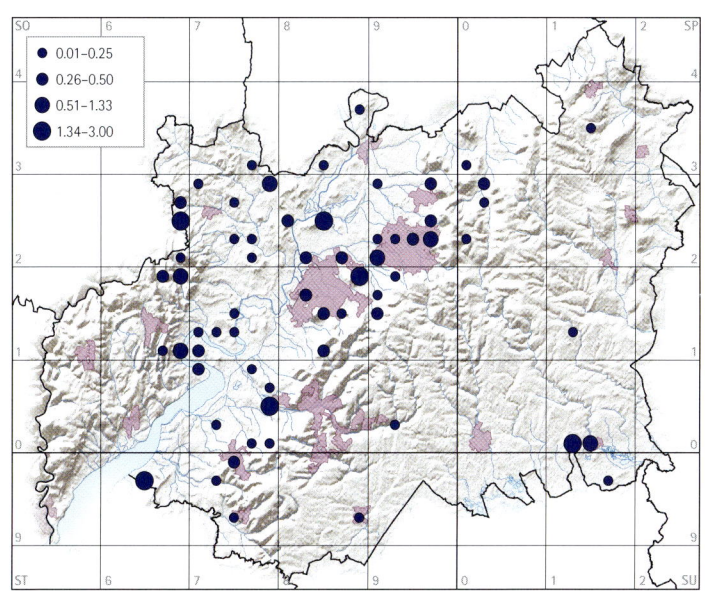

Winter Abundance

Garden Warbler
Sylvia borin

Garden Warblers tolerate cooler climates than other *Sylvia* warblers and they breed widely across Europe, thinning out towards the Mediterranean and north Scandinavia and extending eastwards through west Siberia. They winter widely in sub-Saharan Africa. The preferred nesting habitat is fairly dense scrub, less wooded than the sites preferred by Blackcap but taller and less open than typical Whitethroat habitat: woodland fringes and clearings, scrubby fields and bushy stream valleys.

In common with a number of other African migrants, Garden Warblers suffered a decline in the 1970s coinciding with drought in the Sahel region, immediately south of the Sahara. In the case of the Garden Warbler, which only migrates through the Sahel rather than wintering there, the crash was followed by a rapid recovery and increase in range up to the time of the 1988–91 Breeding Atlas, but the trend is now downwards again.

Garden Warblers are famously unobtrusive and nondescript, and in spring they are nearly always first detected by song; in fact very often the bird proves impossible to see even if it is singing quite close by. They can sound very similar to Blackcaps, and indeed the two species will mimic one another, so it is possible that some singing Garden Warblers were misidentified as Blackcaps, and vice versa, during atlas fieldwork. Their wary and retiring, even skulking habits resulted in a very low percentage of confirmed breeding records.

Swaine described the Garden Warbler as 'widespread and fairly common' in the county, though tending to avoid the higher, open parts of the Cotswolds where there is less suitable habitat. The Cotswolds Atlas surveys registered a 25% decrease in tetrad occupancy between 1987 and 2007, and it was thought that the decline could actually have been greater given the increased effort during the second survey. There has certainly been a decreasing trend in the county as a whole since the start of the new millennium, although this is complicated by some fairly wide short-term fluctuations: the Gloucestershire BBS index averaged 25% of surveyed squares between 1994 and 2002 but only 17% between 2003 and 2010, and the comparable TTV results indicate a decline between the 1988–91 Breeding Atlas and the latest survey, as shown in the fact-box. Nevertheless, the maps reveal that Garden Warblers are still fairly widely distributed over much of the county, though they are very thin on the ground in the Severn Vale and in more open parts of the Cotswolds. The highest densities occur in the west of the county (the Dean plateau and the area around Newent) and in the south-east (Thames Area, particularly the Cotswold Water Park). However they are also fairly abundant in parts of the Cotswolds where scrubby habitats are available.

In Gloucestershire, the earliest spring date on record is April 7th, in 1980; the average date of the first sighting is about April 20th. At the other end of the season, the latest recorded date for the county is October 18th, in 1990 and 1995. The first spring date has shown no long-term change since 1982, but the average date of the last sighting of the autumn advanced from September 25th between 1982 and 1997 to September 20th between 1998 and 2010. This change could be due to the recent decline in numbers, as observer effects would be expected to result in more late-lingering

	2007–11 Atlas fieldwork					Gloucestershire trends						UK population trends	
	Number of tetrads in which recorded (max 683)					Occupied 10 km squares (max 26)				% of tetrads in which recorded (1st hour of TTV)		UK conservation status: **Green**	
	Total	Confirmed	Probable	Possible	Present	1968–71	1981–84	1988–91	2007–11	1988–91	2008–11	Long term	Short term
Breeding	329	22	85	191	31	26		25	26	32.7	19.8	+6%	–10%
Winter	0						0		0			–	–

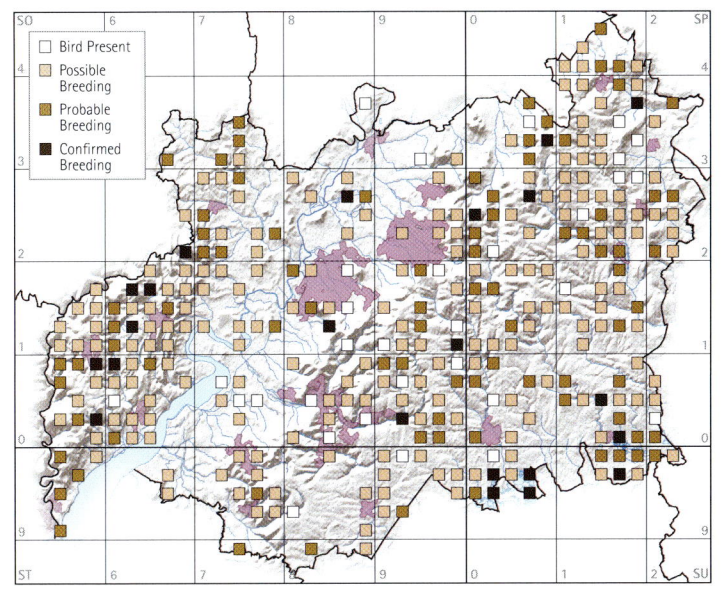

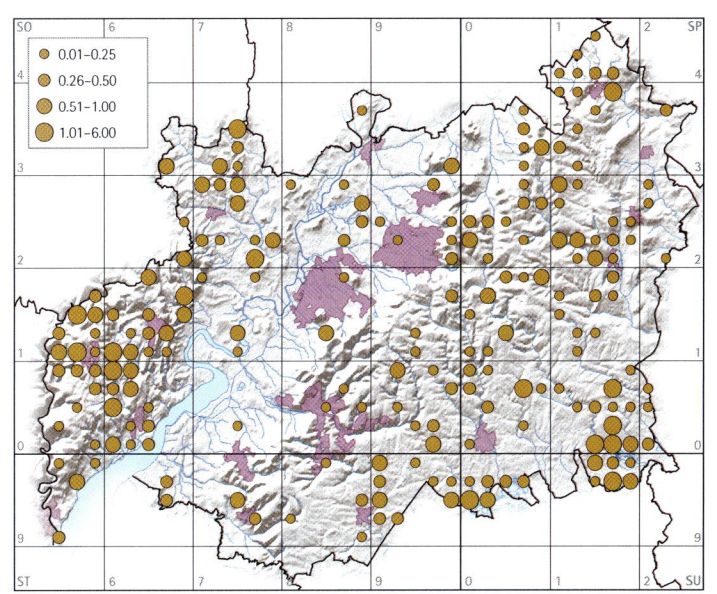

Breeding Distribution

Summer Abundance

individuals being detected, whereas such stragglers are less likely to be found when they are few in number. On the other hand, any tendency for extremely early spring birds to be overlooked because of declining numbers could be compensated for by a real advance in the arrival date associated with global warming.

There had only been six recoveries of ringed Garden Warblers involving Gloucestershire up to 2010. Four were within-Britain movements, to or from Sussex (two), Dorset and Shropshire. An immature ringed at Frampton in August 1964 was shot in southern Spain in 1965, and a male ringed near Tewkesbury in June 1984, probably breeding locally, was 'trapped' in Morocco on the rather late spring date of May 14th the following year.

Lesser Whitethroat
Sylvia curruca

Lesser Whitethroats breed over most of Europe (apart from northern Fennoscandia, the Mediterranean countries and western France) and eastwards to Pakistan and northern China. They have tended to increase and spread in Europe in recent decades, and they first bred in Ireland in 1990. There have also been moderate increases in numbers in Britain, although they are still most common in the south-east and are patchily distributed in northern and western England, Wales and southern Scotland. In these regions, where the species is on the edge of its range, numbers can fluctuate noticeably from year to year. They nest in bushes and scrub, choosing taller vegetation than Whitethroats but still avoiding continuous areas of mature woodland. Perhaps the most favoured habitat in the British Isles is farmland hedges, especially if they are allowed to grow tall and dense.

European breeding populations winter mostly in sub-Saharan Africa, mainly in the east of the continent. Lesser Whitethroats are unusual in that migrants from western Europe fly south-east in autumn and enter Africa via the eastern Mediterranean. There are occasional records in the British Isles in winter.

In spring, Lesser Whitethroats are often detected by their song, which is quite far-carrying and very distinctive once it is learned. However the song period is rather short and it can be missed if surveying does not coincide with such activity. They can be secretive, even skulking, especially when feeding young and, probably as a result, there was a fairly low percentage of confirmed breeding records during the atlas survey. In addition, as with many summer migrants, some singing males are no doubt moving through on passage.

Swaine described the Lesser Whitethroat as a summer visitor to most parts of the county. It was present 'sparingly' in the Forest of Dean, mainly in marginal land and more open areas, and was not uncommon in the Severn Vale and the north-west of the county, but at the same time was much more local in the Cotswolds, where it was most numerous in the major valleys. Small numbers also bred in the Thames Area.

In the area covered by the Cotswolds Atlases it was fairly widespread in 1983–87, especially in the north-east. Although there was a 40% increase in recorded tetrad occupancy between then and 2007, in accordance with national trends, it was felt that this was probably due to greater survey effort. The latest atlas results indicate that the distribution in the Cotswolds is broadly stable. The same is probably true of the county as a whole, although fluctuations continue: county BBS figures have varied between 5% and 29% of study squares between 1994 and 2010.

The maps show that Lesser Whitethroats are most common in the low-lying Severn Vale and Thames NAs, with another pocket of high density in the north-east around Chipping Campden. There are also fairly good numbers elsewhere in the Cotswolds, particularly in some of the more significant river valleys. In the Dean as a whole they can occur at quite high density but they are almost absent from the most heavily wooded central Forest. They are not as noticeably common in the Newent area in the north-west of the county now as was implied by Swaine.

Lesser Whitethroats arrive in Gloucestershire on average around April 20th, with a slight tendency towards earlier arrivals more recently. The earliest sighting on record was on April 7th 2009. The last lingering birds are usually seen in the second half of September; the latest migrant was on the very late date of November 3rd 2003. One on February 22nd 1992 at a feeding station in a Whitminster garden seems virtually certain to have wintered locally.

In accordance with the unusual migration route, the four foreign recoveries of Gloucestershire-ringed Lesser Whitethroats up to 2010 were in Italy (two), Albania and Egypt.

Sponsored by Iain & Jill Main

Species accounts

2007–11 Atlas fieldwork					Gloucestershire trends				UK population trends		
Number of tetrads in which recorded (max 683)					Occupied 10 km squares (max 26)				% of tetrads in which recorded (1st hour of TTV)		UK conservation status: **Green**	
	Total	Confirmed	Probable	Possible	Present	1968–71	1981–84	1988–91	2007–11	1988–91	2008–11	Long term	Short term
Breeding	373	56	82	219	16	25		23	26	25.2	20.1	+19%	+3%
Winter	0						0		0			–	–

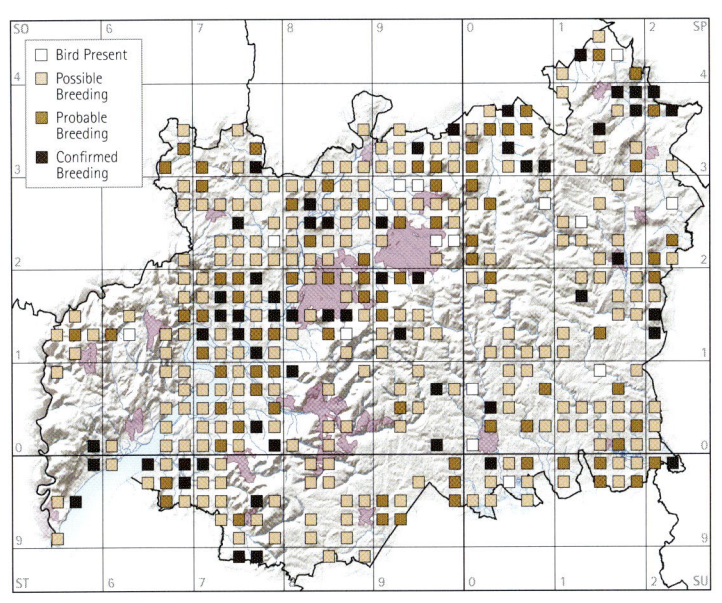

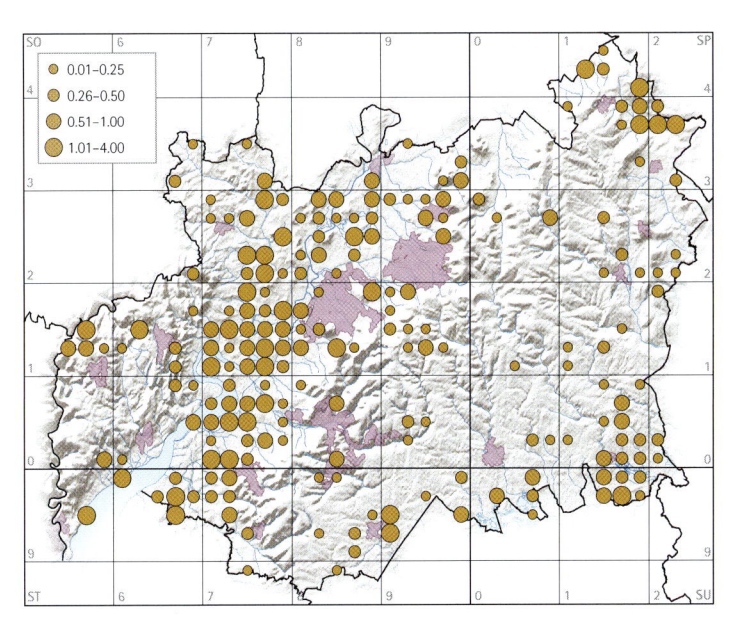

Breeding Distribution

Summer Abundance

PETER PARTINGTON

Whitethroat (Common Whitethroat)
Sylvia communis

Whitethroats breed in parts of North Africa, most of Europe (though not southern Iberia or northern Fennoscandia) and east to northern Iran and the Lake Baikal region of Siberia. All populations migrate to Africa, where they winter widely south of the Sahara. Their breeding habitat requirements fall at the 'scrubby' end of the spectrum shown by our common *Sylvia* warblers, from more developed woodland (Blackcap) to tall dense scrub (Garden Warbler, Lesser Whitethroat), to more open, lower vegetation lacking tall trees (Whitethroat). In Britain they can be found for example in hedgerows, in bushes around wetlands and on uncultivated land, and in woodland clearings.

Whitethroats are conspicuous when they arrive in spring, the males' loud, scratchy song and energetic display flights making them detectable at some distance. Even when feeding young they tend to make their presence felt with alarm calls and nervous posturing, enabling fairly high percentages of confirmed breeding records to be obtained by atlas fieldworkers.

The fortunes of the Whitethroat in Britain and Europe over the last half-century have been dominated by the massive population crashes of the 1960s and 1970s, resulting from severe droughts in the Sahel area of Africa. There have been a number of minor setbacks due to less severe droughts in more recent years and, to this day, numbers have not quite recovered to those pre-1960s levels.

Swaine described Whitethroats as being 'widespread and usually common … in all parts of the county', and noted that there had been a partial recovery over the ten years or so since the catastrophic crash of 1969. Since then the picture has been overwhelmingly positive, with all available indicators pointing to an ongoing, if at times faltering, recovery. In addition to the trends shown in the fact-box, there was 70% increase in the number of occupied tetrads in the area covered by the Cotswolds Atlases between 1987 and 2007, and the county BBS has shown a generally improving though rather erratic trend since 1994, with records in an average of 56% of survey squares between 1994 and 2002 and in 67% from 2003 to 2010.

The maps confirm that Whitethroats are very widespread in the county. They tend to avoid the major conurbations, although even here there are confirmed breeding records close to some town centres, presumably on overgrown 'brownfield sites' in some cases. The only other area of the county with rather fewer records is the more densely wooded central Forest of Dean.

The abundance map reveals areas of higher density in the Severn Vale, the Thames Area and parts of the Cotswolds. Whitethroats seem to be scarcer in some parts of the scarp and high wold, as well as, more predictably, on the more open parts of the dip-slope, where fields are large and the length of hedgerow correspondingly

Sponsored by Gordon & Jenny Kirk

Species accounts

2007–11 Atlas fieldwork					Gloucestershire trends					UK population trends	
Number of tetrads in which recorded (max 683)					Occupied 10 km squares (max 26)				% of tetrads in which recorded (1st hour of TTV)		UK conservation status: **Amber 3**	
	Total	Confirmed	Probable	Possible	Present	1968–71	1981–84	1988–91	2007–11	1988–91	2008–11	Long term	Short term
Breeding	643	301	209	122	11	26		26	26	47.5	61.1	+1%	+25%
Winter	0						0		0			–	–

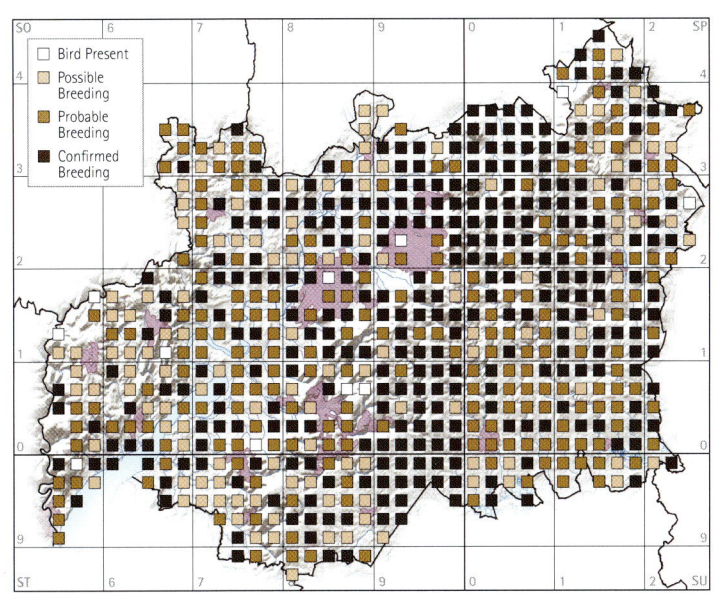

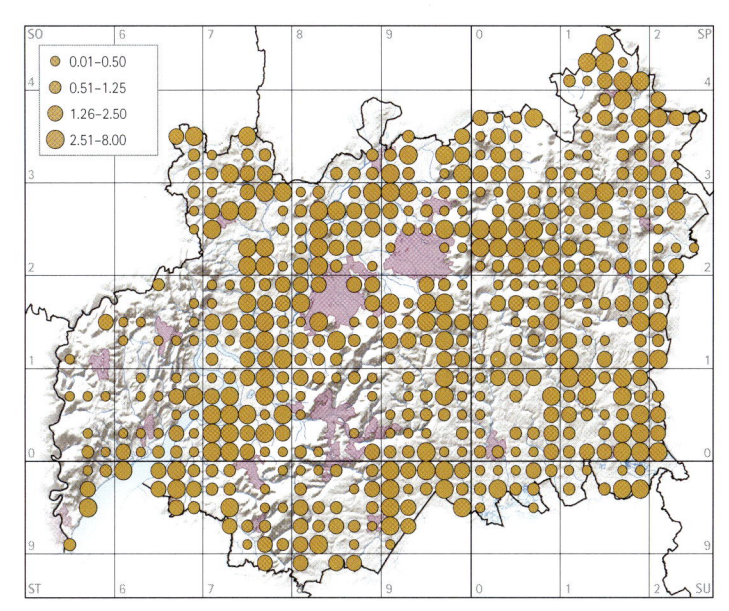

Breeding Distribution

Summer Abundance

small. They seem to be fairly tolerant of modern intensive hedge management, but even so they may tend to avoid areas where the majority of hedges are severely and repeatedly flailed.

On average the first Whitethroat of the year appears in Gloucestershire around April 15th, with a slight tendency to be earlier in more recent years; the earliest date on record is April 5th 2003. The last one is usually recorded towards the end of September, but October sightings have become increasingly frequent and there have been two later records: one on November 3rd 2003, and an exceptionally late bird at Hillesley, Wotton-under-Edge on November 26th 1998. In addition Swaine mentions one 'reported to have been seen' at Woodmancote near Cheltenham on December 17th 1967, but although winter records are not unheard of in Britain, this sighting cannot be considered to be confirmed.

There have been five recoveries of ringed Whitethroats between Gloucestershire and other English counties, and autumn movements of ringed birds from the county to north-east Portugal and the Atlantic coast of Morocco, in line with the known migration route of the British breeding population.

Grasshopper Warbler (Common Grasshopper Warbler)
Locustella naevia

Swaine described the species as widely but locally distributed over much of the county, with no mention of any decline, although it was 'of somewhat erratic occurrence in any particular locality'. There were 'moderate numbers' in young plantations and rough common land in the Dean Area, and rank marshy country near the river in the Severn Vale also provided breeding habitat. Bushy slopes with coarse grassland were preferred in the Cotswolds, and they were uncommon in the Thames Area.

Since then numbers have fallen steadily in line with national trends, and although there have been fluctuations from year to year, probably no more than ten pairs usually bred in the county during the first few years of the new millennium. Grasshopper Warblers have become very scarce as breeding birds in the Forest of Dean area and in recent years the stronghold, if such a word can be used, has been in the highest part of the county, in the Cleeve Hill area of the Cotswolds. In the 12 10 km squares covered by both Cotswolds

The breeding range of the Grasshopper Warbler extends from the British Isles and north Spain across central latitudes of Europe and east to central Asia. Western Palearctic birds are thought to winter in West Africa south of the Sahara. They breed mainly in dense but patchy low-growing vegetation, as provided for example by bramble patches, gorse-covered hillsides, dense bushes in stream valleys, and the early growth stages of new or regenerating plantations. These varied but at the same time rather sparsely distributed habitats result in a widespread but scattered breeding range in the British Isles.

Grasshopper Warblers have declined in numbers across much of Europe, especially since 1980. In Britain and Ireland, following increases in the 1960s, there was a severe population crash after 1971 and a 'general thinning out' over the whole of Britain between the 1968–72 and 1988–91 Breeding Atlases. The decrease was probably caused partly by losses or alterations to breeding habitats, but also by wider-ranging factors such as droughts in Africa. More recently there have been signs that the population has begun to recover.

Provided the observer's hearing has not become too insensitive to sound at the relevant frequency, the 'reeling' song of the Grasshopper Warbler is easy to detect, although it can be hard to pinpoint. However they are very skulking birds when nesting, and atlas fieldworkers are to be congratulated on obtaining proof of breeding at a number of Gloucestershire sites.

Sponsored by Ann M Smith-Covell

Species accounts

2007–11 Atlas fieldwork					Gloucestershire trends						UK population trends	
Number of tetrads in which recorded (max 683)					Occupied 10 km squares (max 26)				% of tetrads in which recorded (1st hour of TTV)		UK conservation status: **Red 3**	
	Total	Confirmed	Probable	Possible	Present	1968–71	1981–84	1988–91	2007–11	1988–91	2008–11	Long term	Short term
Breeding	55	4	8	34	9	25		14	17	3.2	0.9	–	+23%
Winter	0						0		0			–	–

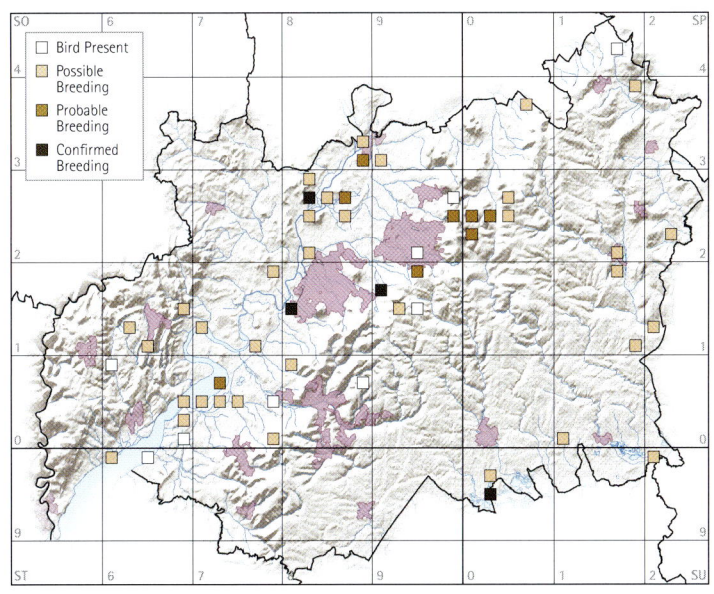

Breeding Distribution

Atlases they were already fairly sparsely distributed in 1983–87 but there had very probably been a further contraction by 2003–07.

In very recent years there has possibly been a slight reversal of the species' fortunes, again reflecting national trends. In the area covered by the second Cotswolds Atlas there was an increase from 14 to 20 occupied tetrads between 2007 and the present survey, and the map shows a scattering of occupied tetrads through the Vale, in addition to a slight concentration in the Cleeve Hill 'stronghold'. In 2010 up to 33 singing males were heard in the county as a whole, and whilst it should be borne in mind that many of these could have been passage migrants, there are nevertheless some grounds for cautious optimism concerning the future of this enigmatic bird in our county.

The average arrival date for Grasshopper Warblers in the Gloucestershire is around April 16th, with no evidence of any significant change; the earliest record was on April 2nd 1988. They become so unobtrusive after the nesting season that there are few autumn passage records: usually one or two stragglers are seen in September, and the latest sighting on record was on October 3rd 1998.

Sedge Warbler
Acrocephalus schoenobaenus

Tolerating colder climates than most warblers, Sedge Warblers breed over much of Europe (though not in the Mediterranean area) as far north as northern Norway, and east to central Siberia. They use a wider range of habitats than Reed Warblers, and while they are very often associated with wet or damp habitats they will also nest in dryer areas with low scrub and 'tangle', such as nettle beds, overgrown orchards, well-grown hedgerows, and even arable crops.

Sedge Warblers winter widely in sub-Saharan Africa, and the considerable fluctuations in numbers and range across Europe in recent decades have been shown to relate to the amount of rainfall in the Sahel region; in the British Isles there were steep declines due to droughts there in the 1960s and 1970s, with something of a recovery particularly since 1985.

The earliest spring arrival date for a Sedge Warbler in Gloucestershire is a very early March 18th, in 1990; the average first arrival date is around April 10th. They are nearly always first detected by their loud, babbling song, which makes them easy to find early in the season, and unlike Reed Warblers they sometimes sing from an exposed perch as well as from dense vegetation. However they can be rather skulking and wary when feeding young, so breeding can be difficult to confirm. The last birds to depart in autumn leave mainly during September, with a few stragglers to the end of the month in most years. There are a few October sightings, and the latest on record was one at Slimbridge on November 5th 2002.

Swaine stated that Sedge Warblers occurred 'in some numbers in suitable localities' in the county; they were uncommon in the Dean and Wye Area, bred along the river and by streams and ditches in the Severn Vale (though they had declined there 'in recent years'), and were very scarce visitors to most of the Cotswolds. A noticeable increase in the Thames Area was due to the development of the Cotswold Water Park.

This picture remains broadly the same today. Sedge Warblers are not very widespread in the county because of their habitat requirements, and even in optimum habitat they do not attain such high densities as Reed Warblers. The maximum count during a TTV was 30, in May 2008 in SU09I, in the western section of the Water Park – the same tetrad which produced the highest TTV count for Reed Warbler. There was evidently a contraction of range in the county between the 1968-72 and 1988-91 Breeding Atlases (between 1972 and 1991) but there has been no significant overall decline since then (see fact-box). The maps show that Sedge Warblers remain very much concentrated in the Vale and the Thames Area, but there are also a few breeding sites in the Cotswolds, particularly in the valley of the river Windrush including Bourton pits.

In common with Reed Warblers, Sedge Warblers have been ringed in large numbers at British wetland sites, generating many recoveries. Up to 2010 there were 60 movements of ringed birds between Gloucestershire and other English and Welsh counties. In addition 27 birds had travelled further, with 24 movements to and from France and the Channel Islands and three to Spain, all en route to and from their wintering areas in Africa.

Sponsored by Roy Bircher

Species accounts

2007–11 Atlas fieldwork					
Number of tetrads in which recorded (max 683)					
	Total	Confirmed	Probable	Possible	Present
Breeding	108	25	30	42	11
Winter	1				

Gloucestershire trends				
Occupied 10 km squares (max 26)				*% of tetrads in which recorded (1st hour of TTV)*	
1968–71	1981–84	1988–91	2007–11	1988–91	2008–11
19		15	21	7.1	6.5
		0	0		

UK population trends	
UK conservation status: **Green**	
Long term	Short term
–14%	+8%
–	–

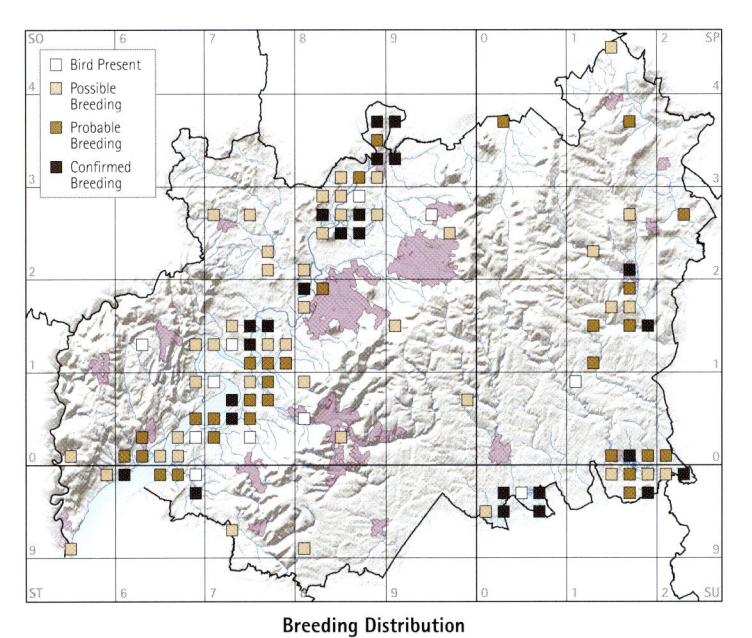

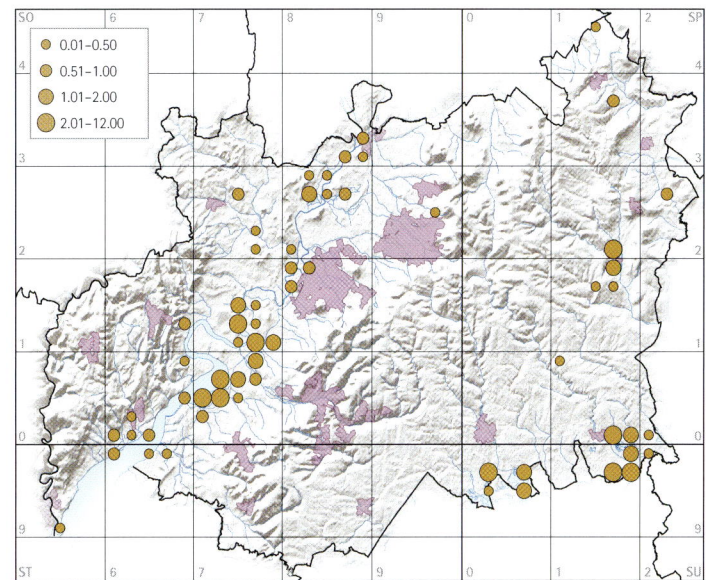

Breeding Distribution

Legend:
- Bird Present
- Possible Breeding
- Probable Breeding
- Confirmed Breeding

Summer Abundance

Legend:
- 0.01–0.50
- 0.51–1.00
- 1.01–2.00
- 2.01–12.00

Reed Warbler (Eurasian Reed Warbler)
Acrocephalus scirpaceus

Reed Warblers breed over much of Europe, as far north as Sweden and south Finland and less commonly in the southern countries. Further afield, they extend to east-central Asia and Iran. All populations winter in sub-Saharan Africa, south to Zambia. The breeding range has expanded considerably in Europe and the British Isles in recent decades, but in Britain they are still most common and widespread in the south and east, and very scarce in north and west Scotland; Ireland was colonised in 1980. In the British Isles as elsewhere they are strongly, though not exclusively, associated with *Phragmites* reed-beds, and they can nest successfully in very small patches of reed.

Breeding Reed Warblers very often draw attention to themselves with their loud, sustained songs. Their productive habitat can support a high density of pairs, and assessing the numbers present can be difficult. They often raise two broods in one season, and noisy fledged young can still be receiving food from their parents into September.

Swaine described Reed Warblers as nesting 'locally in small or moderate numbers' in the county, with breeding sites throughout the Severn Vale and also in the Thames Area (particularly the then relatively new Cotswold Water Park). Occurrences elsewhere in the Cotswolds were however 'exceptional'. Although the distribution map shows that the overall picture is still broadly the same today, all the available data confirm that there has been a considerable increase in numbers and range in the county since 1980. The highest densities occur where there are most reed-beds: in the lower Vale around Slimbridge and the Aylburton Warth area, and in and around the Water Park. Virtually every patch of reeds along the Severn, no matter how small or isolated, seems to hold at least one singing male, while the highest count during a TTV was an impressive 48, in June 2008 in tetrad SU09I, in the western section of the Water Park. In addition, there were a few breeding records in the Cotswolds, particularly in the Windrush valley but also in SP13 near Blockley, where Swaine stated that they 'used to breed'.

Simultaneously with the increase in numbers, there has been a distinct tendency towards earlier spring arrivals in Gloucestershire. From 1979 to 1994 the average first date in the county was April 23rd, while from 1995 to 2010 it was April 12th, a substantial advance. The earliest date on record is April 5th, in 1996. There also appears to have been a tendency for birds to remain in the county for longer in autumn: the average last date from 1979 to 1994 was September 19th, but from 1995 to 2010 it was October 5th; the latest bird to date was on October 23rd 2006. These changes could be partly due to increases

Sponsored by A H Eveleigh

Species accounts

	2007–11 Atlas fieldwork					Gloucestershire trends						UK population trends	
	Number of tetrads in which recorded (max 683)					Occupied 10 km squares (max 26)				% of tetrads in which recorded (1st hour of TTV)		UK conservation status: **Green**	
	Total	Confirmed	Probable	Possible	Present	1968–71	1981–84	1988–91	2007–11	1988–91	2008–11	Long term	Short term
Breeding	92	41	18	28	5	6		5	18	2.2	6.8	+135%	+30%
Winter	0							0	0			–	–

Breeding Distribution

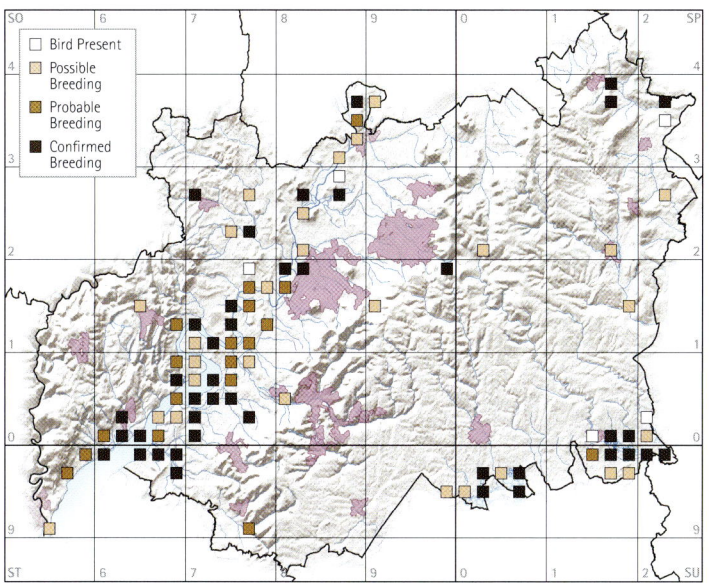

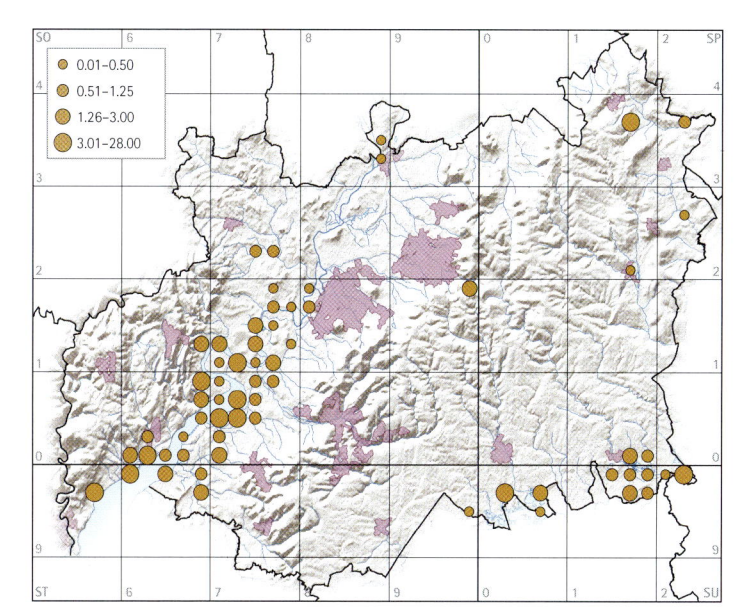

Summer Abundance

in the numbers of observers, making isolated individuals more likely to be detected, but this seems less likely to be true for Reed Warblers, which have a strong tendency to appear at traditionally well-watched reed-bed sites, than for more wide-ranging species.

Reed-beds are popular with British ringers, and ringing *Acrocephalus* warblers produces many recoveries of birds moving between wetlands. Up to 2010, there had been nearly 100 movements of ringed Reed Warblers between Gloucestershire and other English and Welsh counties. In addition there were 12 foreign recoveries, mostly involving birds moving along a fairly narrow corridor between the Channel Islands, western France and northern Spain, with two further recoveries on the Atlantic coast of Portugal. More spectacular was a juvenile ringed at Slimbridge in August 2001 and caught by ringers on the coast of Mauritania, West Africa, in October 2003.

A bird showing all the characters of the eastern (Asiatic) race *A. s. fuscus* ('Caspian Reed Warbler'), a rare visitor to Britain, was seen at Frampton on September 10th 2004. This record was accepted by the County Records Committee but was not submitted to the national Rarities Committee, which only assesses records of trapped and photographed individuals of this race.

Marsh Warbler
Acrocephalus palustris

Marsh Warblers breed mainly from eastern France to Russia, north to Sweden and south to Greece and Turkey, and they winter in south-east Africa. The breeding range has expanded north in recent decades. The species was not recognised until the turn of the nineteenth century, and the first British records came in the 1860s. By around 1910 Marsh Warblers were known to be breeding in about a dozen English counties, with the majority in Oxfordshire, Somerset, Gloucestershire and Worcestershire (1875–1900 Atlas). Currently this is a very rare breeding bird in Britain, with an average of just eight pairs per year between 2006 and 2010 (RBBP).

The first county record was in 1886 at Siddington, near Cirencester, and in 1902 Mellersh wrote that there were 'three or four' probable nesting places in the county, but this may have been an underestimate. In the following decades Gloucestershire became one of the strongholds of this species, with birds breeding in the rank vegetation in and around the osier or withy beds that were often established in worked-out claypits, excavated for the brick-making industry (see p. 15). Marsh Warblers used this habitat from Frampton in the south to Ashleworth in the north, and also up the Severn to Tewkesbury and beyond into Worcestershire. Three areas appear to have been particularly suitable: the Saul–Whitminster area, where two canals meet; an area to the north and west of Gloucester including Alney Island, Walham, Sandhurst and Ashleworth; and the area from Apperley north to Tewkesbury. There were also colonies elsewhere in the Severn Vale and occasionally in other locations, and it is estimated that between 65 and 85 pairs bred each year between the 1920s and the mid-1950s. From 1950 however the the brickworks had largely gone and agriculture was changing; drainage and canalisation caused water levels to fall and ponds to dry out, the riverside vegetation began to change its character, and the withies fell into decay and became overgrown. Along with these changes the Marsh Warbler population plummeted, with fewer and fewer birds being found through the late 1950s and 1960s; indeed by 1963 regular nesting in the sites to the west and south of Gloucester had ceased (Bluett 2007). In 1955 three pairs bred in the Thames Area (now the Cotswold Water Park), and singing males were recorded there in three subsequent years.

From the 1960s into the 1980s authenticated records and instances of breeding became ever less frequent and more scattered, in line with the national pattern. Breeding was still being confirmed annually from 1980 to 1984, and there was possibly a final breeding pair in 1985, but by 1986 the story was to all intents and purposes over, just 100 years after it began. Since then there have been just four records in the county: a male was trapped and ringed at Frampton Pools on June 5th 1987, one was on territory at the Cotswold Water Park for two weeks in June 1988, one sang at a site near Gloucester from May 31st to June 7th 1992, and a first-winter bird was at Slimbridge on September 10th 2009.

Yellow-browed Warbler
Phylloscopus inornatus

Yellow-browed Warblers were formerly considered to be very rare visitors to the British Isles, but the species was removed from the national rarities list as long ago as 1963. Since then the number of records per year has risen steadily, no doubt due partly to observer effects but also apparently to a genuine increase, which has also been noticed elsewhere in Europe. The Siberian breeding range barely extends into the Western Palearctic. The main wintering quarters are in south-east Asia, but evidently increasing numbers set off in a more or less westerly direction every autumn, producing annual totals in the British Isles in the low hundreds in recent years. Most are seen at the coast, particularly in eastern England and Scotland, but a number of inland counties have added this delightful little warbler to their lists in recent years. The first Gloucestershire record (and the third for Britain) was of one shot by the river Chelt near Cheltenham on October 11th 1867. The next sighting was not until 1986, when one spent from November 7th to 10th at Berkeley power station by the Severn Estuary; a second bird was present on 8th. The next was in 1995, at Slimbridge on October 12th and 13th, but since the year 2000 there have been no fewer than six sightings of single birds:

2002: Slimbridge on October 31st.
2003: Cotswold Water Park, west section, from December 29th to January 2nd 2004.
2006: Chipping Campden, in a garden on four occasions between February 18th and March 11th; and Slimbridge, from December 3rd to 6th.
2008: in a garden at Ruscombe near Stroud on October 22nd.
2011: mist-netted by ringers near Frampton on October 16th.

It is notable that while nationally records peak in late September and early October, a number of Gloucestershire birds have been in winter.

Pallas's Warbler (Pallas's Leaf Warbler)
Phylloscopus proregulus

These beautifully marked warblers breed in the Eastern Palearctic and winter mainly to the south-east of the breeding range. However in common with Yellow-browed Warblers, increasing numbers have been seen in western Europe in recent decades, especially since about 1985. In Britain usually about 50 to 100 are seen each year, mainly in late autumn and mostly on the east and south coasts, though inland records are becoming more frequent. The species was removed from the national rarities list in 1991. There have been two records in Gloucestershire:

1999: one in a garden at Blaize Bailey near Cinderford on November 8th, a record which has only recently been accepted.

2008: one in song at Frampton sailing lake from April 19th to 21st.

Dartford Warbler
Sylvia undata

The very sedentary Dartford Warbler is mainly a western Mediterranean species and in Britain, at the northern edge of its range, it is very vulnerable to the effects of cold winters. Even so, numbers in England and Wales have been rising steadily, reaching just over 3,000 pairs by 2006, so the increasing number of records in Gloucestershire in recent years is not unexpected:

1989: a male was on Leckhampton Hill, Cheltenham on November 19th.

2000: an adult male was found dead on Cleeve Hill on March 22nd.

2005: two were at Crabtree Hill in the Forest of Dean from August 31st to September 4th.

2006: a male was at Tidenham Chase, also in the Forest of Dean, from January 8th to 14th.

2008: one was found at Sharpness during an atlas TTV count on January 27th, and two singing males were at Crabtree Hill from May 3rd to 10th, with one remaining in the area until June 5th.

2010: a male was at Sherborne Water Meadows on April 17th.

In addition, Mellersh made an unsubstantiated assertion that the species once bred in Gloucestershire close to the border with Wiltshire.

Savi's Warbler
Locustella luscinioides

Savi's Warblers breed discontinuously in western Europe and more commonly further east, mainly in extensive marshes and reed-beds. They bred in Britain until the mid-nineteenth century and have done so again intermittently and in extremely low numbers in the south-east since 1960. There has been one record in Gloucestershire: a male in the north reed-bed at Frampton from May 20th to June 4th 2001.

Dusky Warbler
Phylloscopus fuscatus

The only county record of this Siberian warbler, which is an annual visitor to Britain in very small numbers, is of one at the marshes at Frampton on May 2nd 2004. Most British records are in autumn.

Barred Warbler
Sylvia nisoria

This east European species is a scarce but annual migrant in Britain, seen mainly on the east coast in autumn. The sole record in Gloucestershire is of an immature which was trapped and ringed at Minsterworth near Gloucester on August 26th 1979.

Icterine Warbler
Hippolais icterina

This Northern Palearctic warbler is a scarce annual passage migrant in Britain, mainly on the east and south coasts during autumn. The only Gloucestershire record is of a first-year male which was trapped and ringed at Churchdown Hill, Gloucester on September 23rd 1983.

Aquatic Warbler
Acrocephalus paludicola

The highly endangered Aquatic Warbler breeds very patchily from Poland eastwards into western Russia, having disappeared from western Europe along with much of its wetland habitat. It passes through southern Britain in variable numbers during the autumn, en route to its wintering grounds in sub-Saharan West Africa. It was removed from the national rarities list in 1983, largely because of an increase in records due to an upsurge in reed-bed ringing. There have been five Gloucestershire records. The first was an immature ringed at Frampton on August 12th 1979. This was followed by another immature, also caught for ringing, at Ashleworth Ham on September 14th 2003. The last three were all at Frampton, on September 10th 2004, August 18th to 20th 2006, and September 1st and 2nd 2010.

Great Reed Warbler
Acrocephalus arundinaceus

This large warbler with a voice to match breeds discontinuously through much of continental Europe and winters in Africa. There were a total of 244 British records to 2010 and it has been almost annual since 1958, though it remains on the national rarities list. There have been two county records:

1979: a male was singing in the eastern section of the Cotswold Water Park from June 23rd to 26th.

1981: a male was trapped and ringed at Frampton sailing lake on the last day of May and continued singing there until June 28th.

Waxwing (Bohemian Waxwing)
Bombycilla garrulus

Waxwings breed from northern Sweden eastwards across Siberia to the Pacific, and in parts of North America. In years when food is plentiful many overwinter within the breeding range, whilst in other years low food supplies send thousands of birds across the North Sea to Britain. Usually the majority only reach the north-eastern half of the country, but on occasion they will penetrate further south and west. Their favourite food is the fruit of rowans and related trees, which they often find in the incongruous surroundings of supermarket car parks and housing estates, where their confiding nature and delightful appearance attract both birders and non-birders alike.

The earliest written county record dates from as long ago as January 1683 (see p. 38), and there were sporadic reports during the nineteenth and early twentieth centuries. Swaine noted that records had become almost annual in Gloucestershire by 1980, albeit usually in very small numbers.

There were substantial immigrations into the county in winter 1965-66, winter 1970-71, January–March 1996, and the winters of 2004-05, 2008-09 and 2010-11, all coinciding with major irruptions on the national scale. Waxwings are highly mobile and it is impossible to assess total numbers with any confidence, but the largest flocks seen in 2004-05 (300 in Gloucester, January 29th and February 11th) and in 2010-11 (250 in Cinderford, December 12th), were far in excess of the maxima during the other major incursions, when no flocks of more than 30 birds were seen anywhere in the county.

The two most recent invasions coincided with the atlas survey period and the maps show that records were correspondingly widely distributed, though with a noticeable lack on the Cotswolds dip-slope where human settlements are few and far between. Waxwings are sometimes seen in non-invasion years, and in fact in the three decades since 1980 there have only been 13 years without a single sighting in Gloucestershire. Rarely are more than half a dozen seen together during such 'off-years'; the only exception was 17 in Cheltenham on January 16th 2008. The earliest-ever sighting in the county was on October 24th 1972, and the latest on May 4th 2003.

Sponsored by John Perrin

Species accounts 343

2007–11 Atlas fieldwork					Gloucestershire trends						UK population trends	
Number of tetrads in which recorded (max 683)					Occupied 10 km squares (max 26)				% of tetrads in which recorded (1st hour of TTV)		UK conservation status: **Green**	
	Total	Confirmed	Probable	Possible	Present	1968–71	1981–84	1988–91	2007–11	1988–91	2008–11	Long term	Short term
Breeding	1	0	0	0	1	0		0	0	0	0	–	–
Winter	91						0		21			–	–

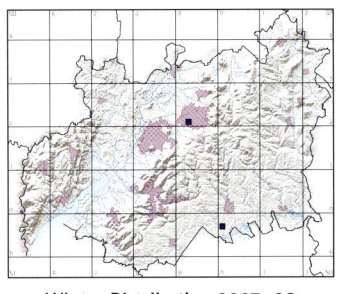

Winter Distribution 2007–08

Winter Distribution 2008–09

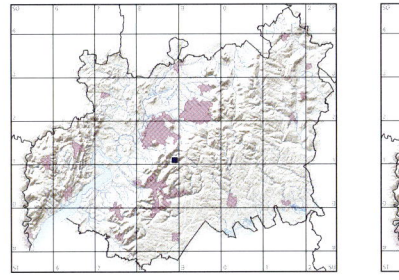

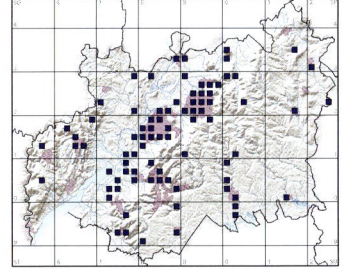

Winter Distribution 2009–10

Winter Distribution 2010–11

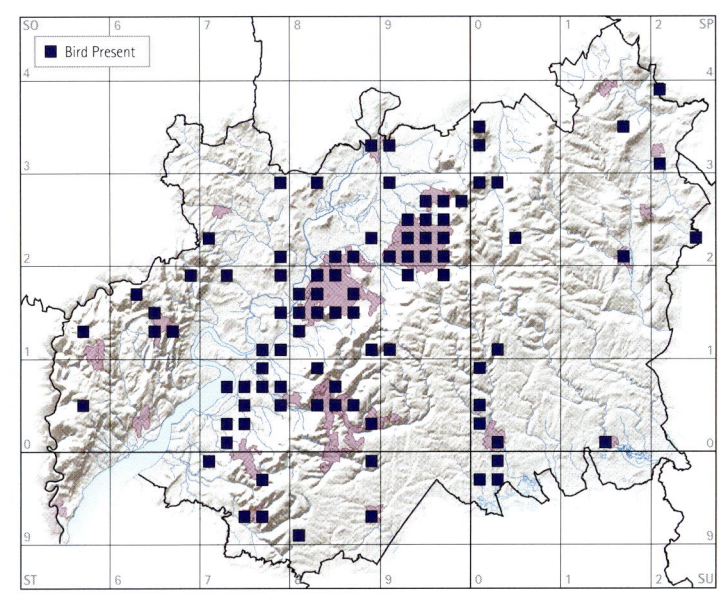

■ Bird Present

Winter Distribution 2007–11

GRAHAM WATSON

Nuthatch (Eurasian Nuthatch)
Sitta europaea

Nuthatches occur across most of Europe and much of Asia, including the Indian subcontinent. Their range is expanding, especially in northern Europe where they are moving northwards. In Britain they inhabit broad-leaved woodland, requiring mature or dead trees for nest sites, and are also found in less densely wooded areas such as parkland. Nuthatches are generally very sedentary and a pair will hold territory all year round, though continental birds sometimes undertake dispersive or eruptive movements.

This is a popular and engaging species. Their ability to move head-first down a tree trunk is unique among British birds, and their intolerance of other birds is particularly noticeable around garden feeders. Indeed, newly fledged Nuthatches even keep their distance from their siblings as soon as they have left the nest. In late winter and early spring adults are very vocal, and it seems likely that few birds will have eluded observers during those months. Later in the breeding season they are much quieter, making it more difficult to confirm breeding. If found, Nuthatch nests are easy to recognise as they always involve the use of mud, which the female uses either to reduce the size of the entrance to an existing hole (whether natural or previously excavated by woodpeckers), or to plaster more generally around the nest site (sealing the lid of a nest-box, for example). Nest sites may be used in successive years; the one in the photograph, in a garden in Ruscombe, near Stroud, was used in all four years of the atlas period.

National surveys have revealed an increase in numbers in Britain (they are absent from Ireland), along with an expansion of range: between the 1968–72 and 1988–91 Breeding Atlases the northern limit of their distribution moved north by about 100 miles, roughly to the England–Scotland border. Current atlas fieldwork shows that this trend has continued and Nuthatches can now be found in many parts of the Scottish lowlands. Numbers in Gloucestershire have reflected the national trend, with most surveys indicating increases over several decades. Swaine described the species as widely distributed in the county and referred to 'somewhat inconclusive' evidence of an increase since the earlier part of the twentieth century. In the area covered by the Cotswolds Atlases there was a substantial rise in the 20 years up to 2007, in both numbers of birds and numbers of tetrads in which they were recorded. Suitable habitat has probably not increased significantly in the county, suggesting that Nuthatches are increasing by exploiting previously unoccupied sites. Given their sedentary nature, it is reasonably safe to assume that they bred in almost all the locations in which they were recorded during atlas fieldwork, even if no breeding evidence was found.

The maps show that the highest densities occur in the Forest of Dean, followed by the Cotswold scarp, which is heavily wooded along much of its length. They are much more thinly spread in the Severn Vale and the Thames Area and on the Cotswold dip-slope, where there is less suitable habitat. Indeed this species shows one of the closest matches between distribution and landscape type, with the maps mirroring the county's wooded districts to a remarkable extent.

The highest number of Nuthatches reported during a winter TTV was an impressive 17, in tetrad SO61Z around Longhope in February 2008. A record of 25 during a late July TTV in SP13 could well have included some fledged young, and most observers encountered just one or two birds at either season.

Sponsored by Ginny James and Andy Oliver

Species accounts

	2007–11 Atlas fieldwork					Gloucestershire trends					UK population trends	
	Number of tetrads in which recorded (max 683)					Occupied 10 km squares (max 26)				% of tetrads in which recorded (1st hour of TTV)		UK conservation status: **Green**	
	Total	Confirmed	Probable	Possible	Present	1968–71	1981–84	1988–91	2007–11	1988–91	2008–11	Long term	Short term
Breeding	419	166	104	130	19	26		23	26	32.7	34.2	+203%	+66%
Winter	433						25		26			–	–

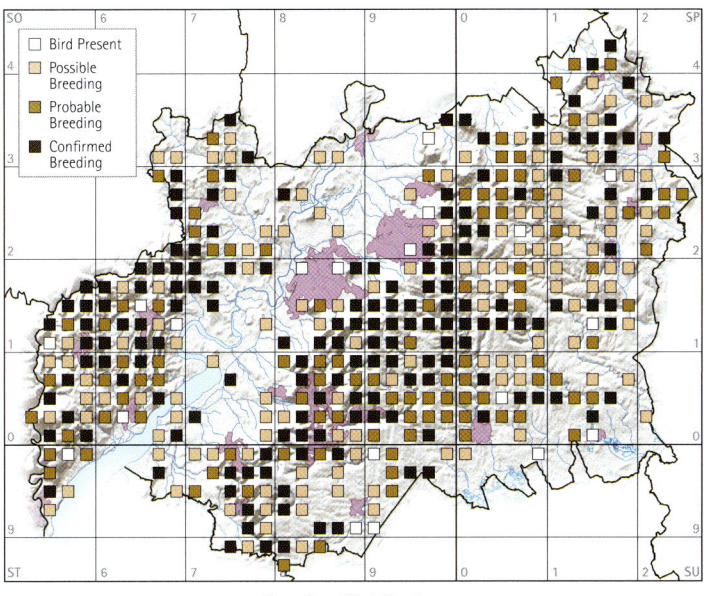

Breeding Distribution

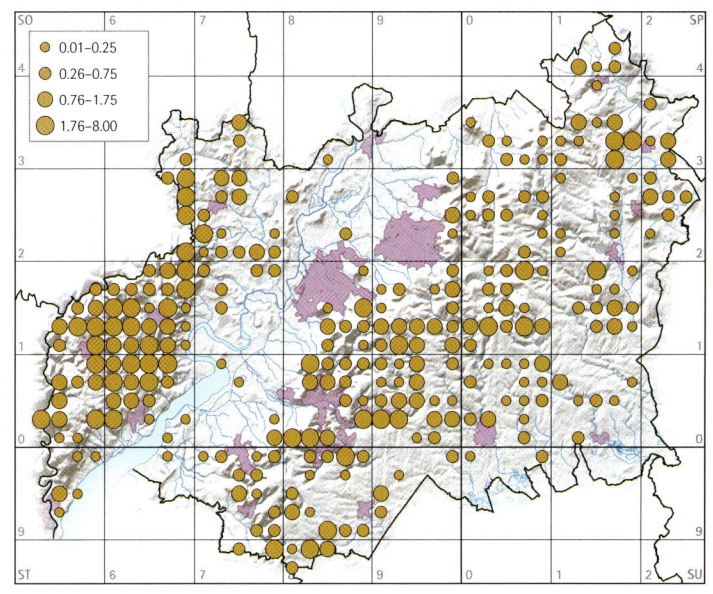

Summer Abundance

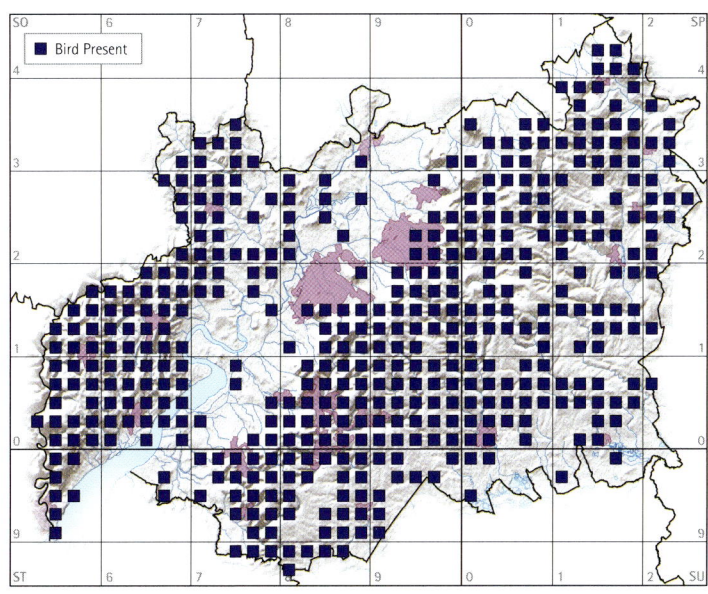

Winter Distribution

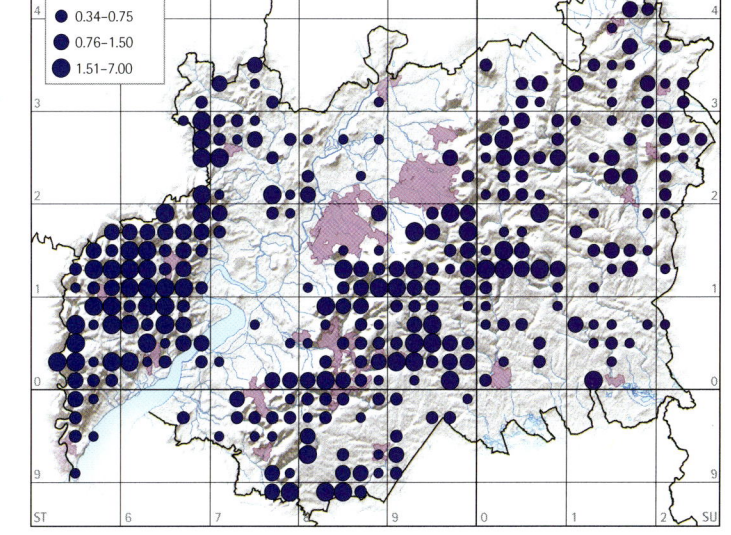

Winter Abundance

Treecreeper (Eurasian Treecreeper)
Certhia familiaris

Treecreepers breed across most of Europe and Asia. In wide areas of western Europe they are restricted to coniferous woods on higher ground and are replaced in the lowlands by the very similar Short-toed Treecreeper *Certhia brachydactyla*. However, in Fennoscandia and the British Isles (except for the Channel Islands), Short-toed does not occur and here Treecreepers occupy a wider range of habitats. In Britain and Ireland they are found wherever there are trees, especially mature broad-leaved species, not only in woodland but also in parks, gardens and farmland. They also use areas where there are smaller trees and bushes, as long as they can find a suitable nest site, which is usually behind a flap of loose bark in an ageing tree. In winter they are also found foraging in hedgerows.

With their unobtrusive habits and rather thin, quiet song that is easily 'drowned' by the calls and songs of other birds, Treecreepers can be overlooked, so the maps could well underestimate their range to some extent. They are very sedentary and generally solitary outside the breeding season; although they sometimes associate with flocks of tits and crests, usually only one Treecreeper is involved. Nests were rarely found during the atlas fieldwork and by far the commonest way of confirming breeding was by encountering family parties including young birds, which are speckled above rather like juvenile Robins.

Data from national surveys suggest that Treecreeper numbers have been fairly constant for many years, although they are vulnerable to cold winter weather, especially if tree trunks and branches are covered in frozen snow and ice. In the area covered by the Cotswolds Atlases an apparent increase in tetrad occupancy in the 20 years up to 2007 was attributed to greater observer effort rather than an actual rise in numbers. County BBS figures since 1994 have varied widely, with records from 12–34% of study squares each year, but with no clear long-term trend. The comparative TTV data in the fact-box seem to suggest something of a decrease since the 1988–91 Breeding Atlas.

The maps reflect the species' wholly arboreal nature, with the county's Treecreepers concentrated in the Forest of Dean and other well-wooded areas west of the Severn and also along the Cotswold scarp. They are scarce in (or absent from) the more intensively farmed treeless parts of the Cotswolds, and uncommon in much of the Severn Vale. Swaine noted that in winter they were more widely distributed and were 'sometimes seen in country not inhabited during the breeding season', but during the atlas fieldwork they were recorded in the same proportion of county tetrads (62%) in winter and in the breeding season, and any movements out of breeding habitat were evidently very short-range. There is no evidence in Britain of any altitudinal or other longer-range movements between seasons; indeed in ringing studies, adults are almost never found more than 500m from a previous capture site (Migration Atlas). However, an immature Treecreeper ringed in Gloucestershire in July 1978 was caught by a ringer 118 km away in Surrey in October of the same year. Movements of this length are extremely unusual: 'a movement of as much as 5 km is exceptional for a Treecreeper ... there are only five [British Isles] recoveries of more than 20 km' (Migration Atlas).

Sponsored by Lynne Garner, and in memory of Elizabeth John

Species accounts 347

2007–11 Atlas fieldwork						Gloucestershire trends						UK population trends	
Number of tetrads in which recorded (max 683)						*Occupied 10 km squares (max 26)*				*% of tetrads in which recorded (1st hour of TTV)*		*UK conservation status:* **Green**	
	Total	Confirmed	Probable	Possible	Present	1968–71	1981–84	1988–91	2007–11	1988–91	2008–11	Long term	Short term
Breeding	427	125	83	185	34	26		25	26	32.5	23.3	−22%	−6%
Winter	425						25		26			–	–

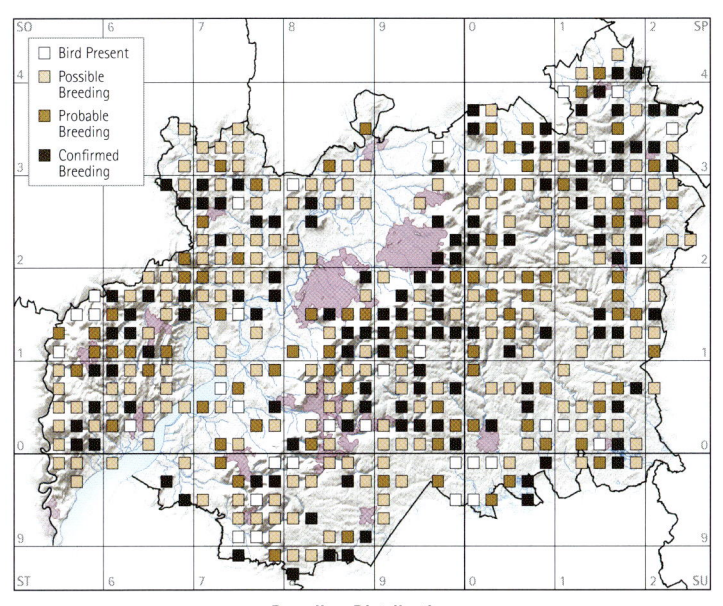

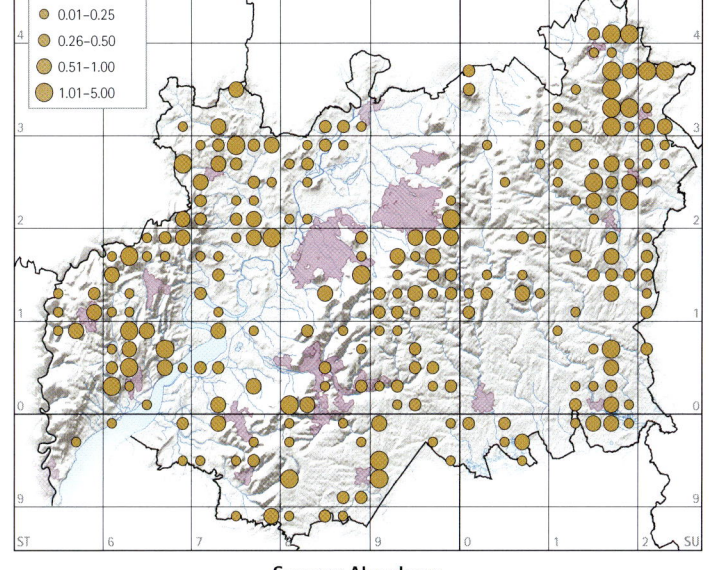

Breeding Distribution

Summer Abundance

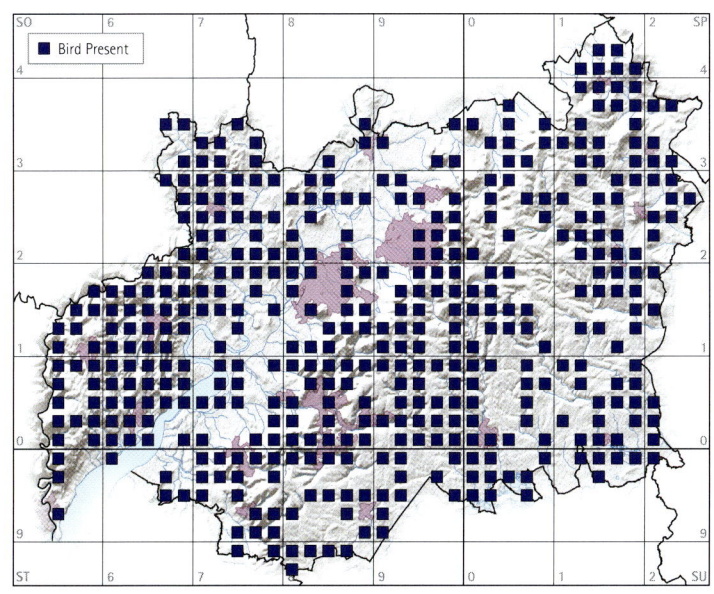

Winter Distribution

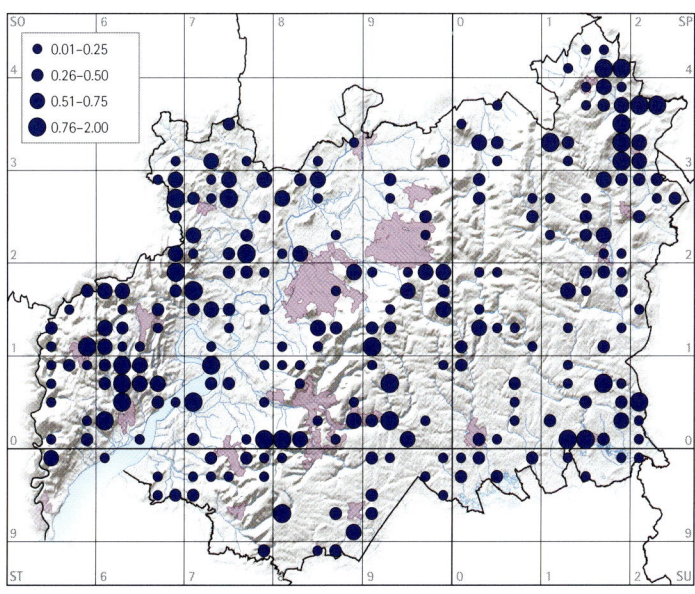

Winter Abundance

Wren (Winter Wren)
Troglodytes troglodytes

Tiny, nimble and easy to identify, the Wren is almost as much a British favourite as the Robin. The species has an extensive range from North Africa and Iceland through to European Russia and the Middle East, with separate populations in eastern Asia and North America. Within most of Europe the species is present all year round; northern and eastern birds are mainly migratory, whilst in the British Isles they are largely sedentary, although some birds move to the coast or to reed-beds in winter. Wrens live in a wide range of habitats: woods, scrub, farmland and gardens are all readily colonised.

Because of their small size and insectivorous diet, Wrens often suffer high mortality during hard winters. However, being double-brooded and laying large clutches, they can recover quickly and, as a result, populations vary widely from year to year: a recent estimate gave 21–36 million pairs in Europe in 2000, of which some 8 million were in Britain. Winter mortality notwithstanding, the Wren appears always to have been abundant and widespread here. The 1875–1900 Atlas describes it as a common or abundant breeder in all British and Irish counties in the nineteenth century. Witchell & Strugnell tell of bird-catchers paid twopence for a Wren's tail feathers, which were removed and used to make flies for fishing – the bird then being released.

The remarkably loud song often betrays its presence during the breeding season, and noisy families of fledglings are often conspicuous later on; in Gloucestershire during the current atlas fieldwork, singing or territorial display was recorded as the highest breeding criterion in 35% of tetrads, whilst in another 35% breeding was confirmed by the presence of fledged young.

Both Mellersh and Swaine described the species as common in Gloucestershire, and this is still true today. The maps show that Wrens are present in all areas of the county, although in both seasons they are apparently less abundant in some of the more open parts of the Cotswolds. All the local indicators, including the two Cotswolds Atlases, reveal a fairly stable county population. Between 1994 and 2010 Wrens always occurred in 94% to 100% of county BBS squares. There were declines in the cold winters of 1995–96 and especially 2008–09 but, after the former, numbers had recovered by the next winter, and after the latter, the BBS was up to 100% again by 2010.

Wrens are well known for forming communal roosts in cold weather. One such record came from the very severe winter of 1979, when dozens roosted in the eaves and loft of a cottage near Lydney, arriving nightly between January and March about half an hour before dark. The maximum count was an extraordinary 96 on February 15th (Haynes 1980). This may be compared with the highest winter TTV count during the current atlas survey: 51 in February 2009 in tetrad SU09J near Cirencester.

Most of the 30 movements of ringed Wrens involving Gloucestershire up to 2010 were short distance, in line with the generally sedentary nature of the English breeding population. However there have been five movements of over 100 km; the furthest travelled was by one ringed in Lancashire in April 1994 and killed by a cat 247 km away in Sevenhampton almost exactly a year later. In addition, a juvenile ringed at Slimbridge in August 1993 was found dead there after flying into a window in April 2000 – six years, eight months and 13 days later. This was the oldest known Wren in the British Isles up to 2010.

Sponsored by Gordon & Jenny Kirk, Linda Moore, and the Dursley Birdwatching and Preservation Society

Species accounts

	2007–11 Atlas fieldwork					Gloucestershire trends						UK population trends	
	Number of tetrads in which recorded (max 683)					Occupied 10 km squares (max 26)				% of tetrads in which recorded (1st hour of TTV)		UK conservation status: **Green**	
	Total	Confirmed	Probable	Possible	Present	1968–71	1981–84	1988–91	2007–11	1988–91	2008–11	Long term	Short term
Breeding	682	366	245	69	2	26		26	26	97.6	97.4	+44%	+12%
Winter	681						26		26			–	–

Breeding Distribution

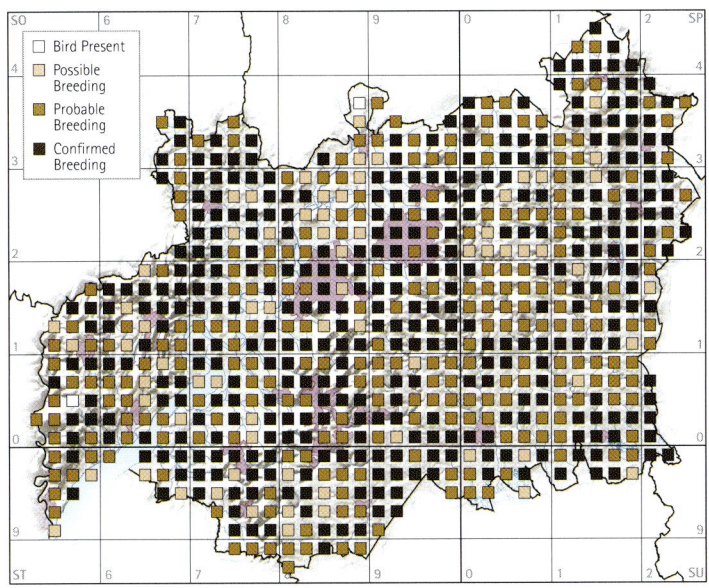

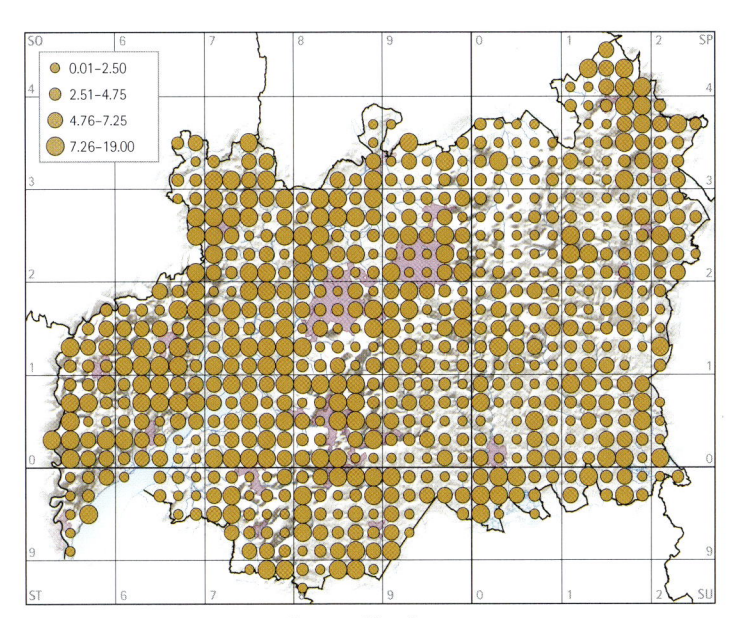

Summer Abundance

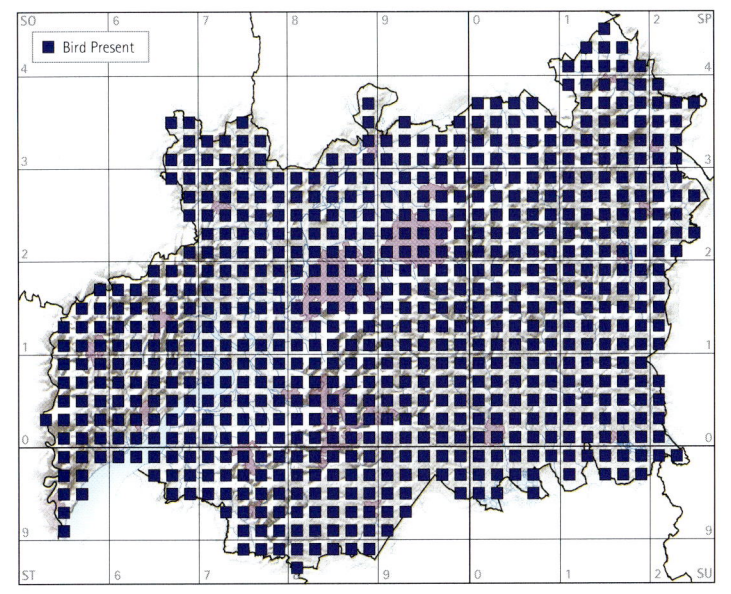

Winter Distribution

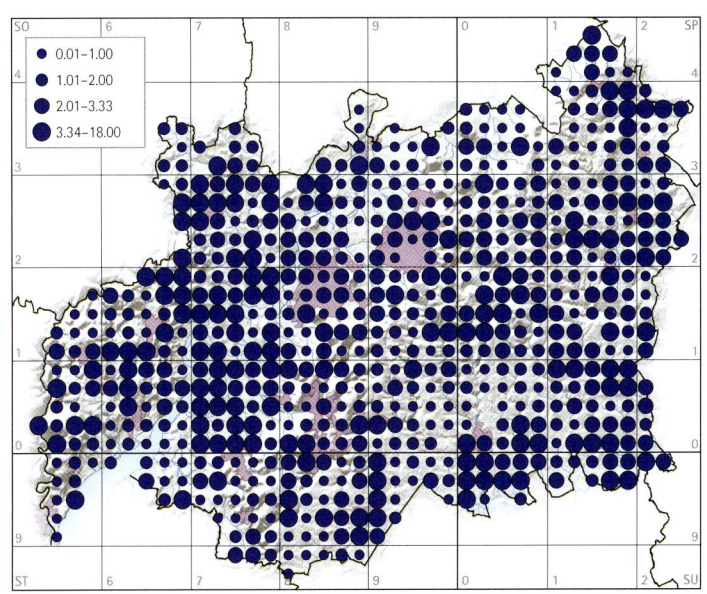

Winter Abundance

Starling (Common Starling)
Sturnus vulgaris

This very familiar, successful and globally widespread bird has benefited historically from the artificial transformation of landscapes over vast areas. Following a noticeable spread between the early nineteenth and mid-twentieth centuries it now breeds over most of Europe and large areas of Asia. There are also populations, descended from introduced birds, in North America, southern Africa and Australasia. More recently, declines have been reported from many European countries, although at the same time the breeding range has extended into Italy and northern Spain. Starlings are migratory over much of their range. British breeders are largely resident, but northern and eastern European birds move west and south to winter in western Europe and the Mediterranean basin.

In the British Isles there has been a severe and well-documented decline, beginning as long ago as the 1960s (BWP) and continuing today. The decrease is thought to be due to the widespread loss of unimproved grassland (the preferred foraging habitat being grazed permanent pasture), exacerbated by the replacement of hay with silage, the change to autumn rather than spring sowing of arable crops, and possibly also climate change, in particular perhaps an increased incidence of summer droughts, which make feeding difficult. However there was 'no indication of any contraction of range' (at the 10 km square scale) during the 20 years leading up to the 1988-91 Breeding Atlas.

In Gloucestershire, Swaine described the Starling as 'abundant, found throughout the county in all months', and made no mention of any recent decrease; it was less common on the high wold than elsewhere. By the time of the 2003-07 Cotswolds Atlas though, the decline was well under way with an 11% decrease in breeding records in that part of the county since 1987, despite improved coverage. Starlings appeared to have been lost from woodland and villages, i.e. areas where birds feed in farmland, more than from urban or suburban areas.

The current atlas results show that this is still a very widespread breeding bird in the county. However, all the indicators show that there has been a substantial decrease in both distribution and abundance, and Starlings can no longer be guaranteed to be seen on virtually every birdwatching excursion during the breeding season, as must surely have been the case 30 or 40 years ago. The breeding maps reveal some gaps in distribution in the Forest of Dean, where there is a lack of suitable habitat, and also in the Cotswolds, where there are widespread areas of low density in the more exclusively arable farmland of the dip-slope.

In winter, numbers of Starlings in the county are swollen by a big influx of immigrants from the Continent, and the maps confirm that they become more widespread than in the breeding season, with less extensive areas of low density. Mellersh reported a (winter) roost near Gloucester of perhaps a million birds around the turn of the twentieth century, though the sizes of these huge aggregations are notoriously hard to estimate. Swaine mentioned 'other large roosts', but nowadays it is unusual to see more than about 20,000 birds together. Roosts of 100,000 at Frampton in December 2005, and 'perhaps half a million' at Slimbridge in January 2003, are exceptional, and the largest flocks reported in the county in recent years have usually been in five figures. Away from roosts, some of the largest feeding flocks have been recorded at landfill sites, with 5,000 or more at the Gloucester landfill in 2006, for example. The highest count during a winter TTV in the current atlas survey was 4,500, in tetrad SO60F in mixed farmland by the Severn Estuary near Lydney in January 2009.

There have been about 140 recoveries of ringed Starlings moving between Gloucestershire and other English and Welsh counties, and nearly 40 foreign recoveries involving movements between Gloucestershire and 11 European countries, as distant as Lithuania, Belarus and western Russia.

Rose-coloured Starling (Rosy Starling)
Pastor roseus

Rose-coloured Starlings visit Britain from eastern Europe and beyond in variable numbers each year, depending on the fortunes of the widely fluctuating source populations. The species was removed from the national rarities list in 2002. There have been three Gloucestershire records:

1952: an adult was seen at close quarters on Cleeve Hill on March 30th.
1961: an adult in a Tewkesbury garden on July 17th.
1982: a juvenile by the M5 motorway at Haresfield near Gloucester on November 4th.

Mellersh mentioned five further records of single birds between 1855 and 1890. Swaine reported that one of these, at Colesbourne around 1875, was collected and the specimen was kept for some years at Cheltenham College Museum.

Sponsored by Phil Davis

Species accounts

2007–11 Atlas fieldwork						Gloucestershire trends						UK population trends	
Number of tetrads in which recorded (max 683)						*Occupied 10 km squares (max 26)*				*% of tetrads in which recorded (1st hour of TTV)*		*UK conservation status:* **Red 3**	
	Total	Confirmed	Probable	Possible	Present	1968–71	1981–84	1988–91	2007–11	1988–91	2008–11	Long term	Short term
Breeding	578	399	58	79	42	26		26	26	85.2	57.1	−78%	−45%
Winter	643						26		26			–	–

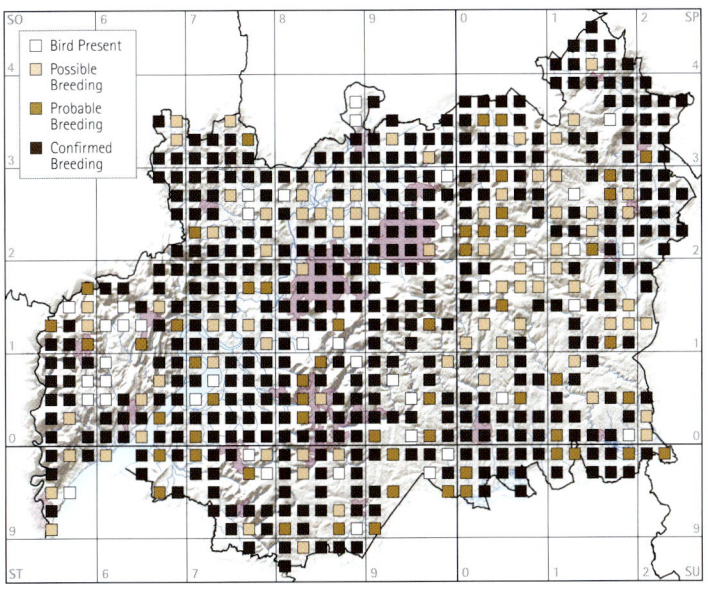

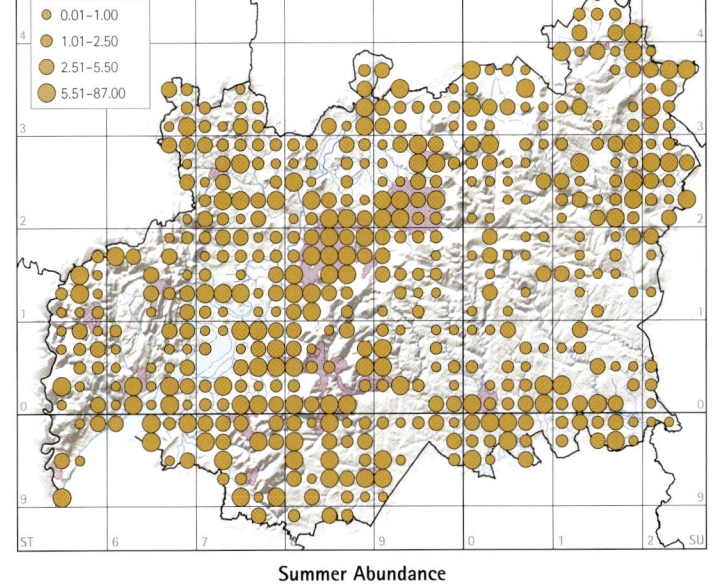

Breeding Distribution

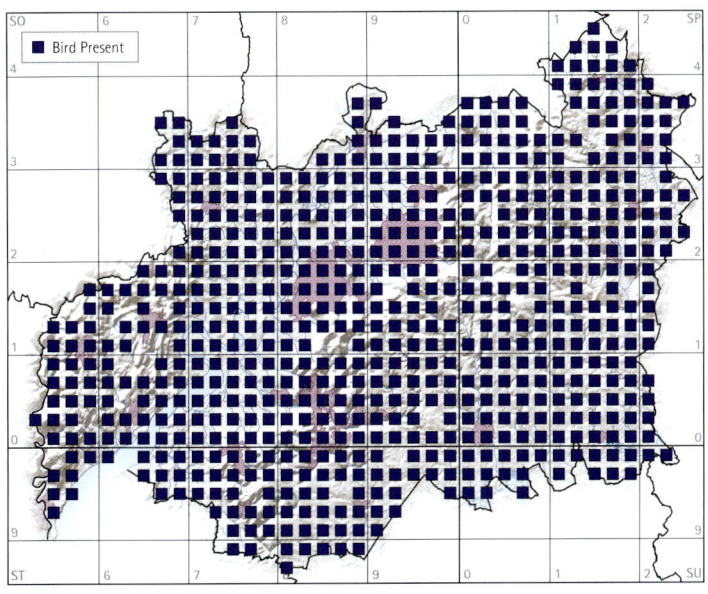

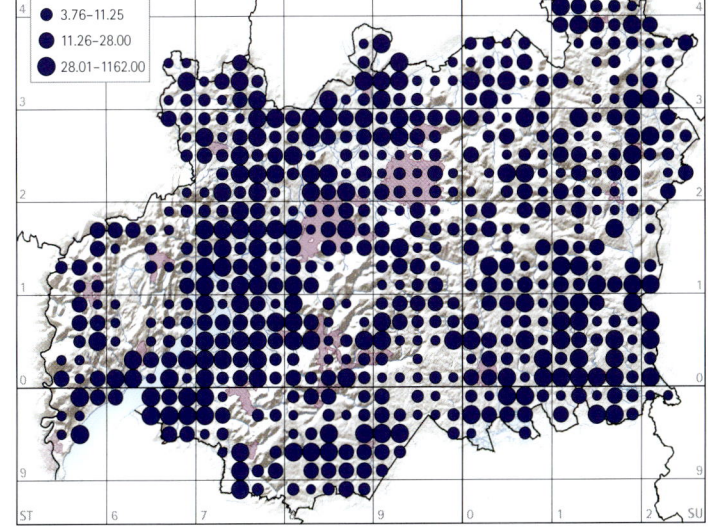

Summer Abundance

Winter Distribution

Winter Abundance

Dipper (White-throated Dipper)
Cinclus cinclus

The Dippers are a very unusual family of passerines, adapted to diving, swimming and even walking under water in search of their invertebrate prey, which in the British Isles is mainly the larvae of caddis-flies and mayflies. In mainland Britain suitable habitat lies mostly to the north and west of a line from Portland Bill in Dorset to Spurn Point in Yorkshire.

Dippers always nest near water, by fast-flowing upland streams and rivers and also on slower rivers as long as there are stretches of rapids produced by artificial features such as weirs or mill-races. They build their rounded, mossy and often conspicuous nests in natural cavities in rock-faces, tree roots or man-made structures. They are much scarcer in acidic waters, which hold fewer invertebrates and fish.

In Britain the breeding season can start early, with nest-building obvious from January and eggs laid from February, and in optimal habitat three broods may be raised in a single year. Although Dippers are rather shy, their loud calls are often audible above the sound of water and many birds will have been detected in this way during the atlas fieldwork. Predicting where they might be found is quite easy, so few birds will have been missed. They are most conspicuous when feeding young, and consequently the proportion of 'confirmed' breeding records is high.

National data show a decline in numbers, with various causes suggested: lower rates of water flow due to drought; silting-up resulting from the disturbance of stream edges by cattle; high populations of predators, notably mink; and acidification (caused by forestry and industry) and nitrification (due to the run-off of fertilisers), both of which have an adverse impact on insect prey.

Gloucestershire is on the very edge of the British range (there are no Dippers in England east of the Cotswolds), so any changes here might give an early warning of the fortunes of the population as a whole. In this respect the indicators are not encouraging. In the area covered by the Cotswolds Atlases there was a noticeable contraction in range and a 50% reduction in occupied tetrads between 1987 and 2007. This decline was especially severe in the east, where several river systems were completely deserted. The current atlas fieldwork confirms this contraction, albeit with the occasional positive feature such as the recolonisation of a stream in the 10 km square SP13. Comparison with previous national atlas data confirms a sharp decline in occupancy at the tetrad level within the county.

The maps show a noticeable concentration of Dippers in the streams of the Stroud valleys, including in Stroud itself where they breed very close to the town centre. These areas provide plenty of suitable nesting places in old mills, factories and even in the infrastructure of the disused canal. Dippers are also reasonably common in the Forest of Dean, where similar man-made features abound. Cheltenham still holds one or two pairs, as do a few traditional sites on the higher Cotswold streams such as the Churn and the Dikler, but these areas are looking increasingly like unsustainable outposts, given the general decline.

The winter map has slightly more dots, albeit in the same areas, suggesting that Dippers forage rather more widely outside the breeding season.

It is clear that Dippers are continuing to thrive where streams and rivers flow in valleys whose slopes are to a greater or lesser extent clothed in woodland, but have declined where they flow through terrain that is largely cultivated. Indeed it is rather ironic that Dippers are now most common in apparently 'industrialised' areas in the Stroud valleys. Perhaps these rivers are now cleaner than those flowing through farmland, where the gradual build-up of chemical contaminants is continuing. If the trends described here continue, it will not be long before this charismatic species disappears entirely from the higher Cotswold streams.

Dippers of the black-bellied northern European subspecies *C. c. cinclus* are recorded in Britain in most years, usually on the English east coast. There is just one Gloucestershire record, at South Cerney on December 17th 1972.

Sponsored by the Hon H J H Tollemanche and by the North Cotswold Ornithological Society, and in memory of Michael Catlin

Species accounts   353

	2007–11 Atlas fieldwork					Gloucestershire trends						UK population trends
	Number of tetrads in which recorded (max 683)					Occupied 10 km squares (max 26)				% of tetrads in which recorded (1st hour of TTV)		UK conservation status: **Green**
	Total	Confirmed	Probable	Possible	Present	1968–71	1981–84	1988–91	2007–11	1988–91	2008–11	Long term	Short term
Breeding	62	40	7	10	5	18		13	17	4.5	1.9	–32%	–35%
Winter	64							15	18			–	–

Breeding Distribution

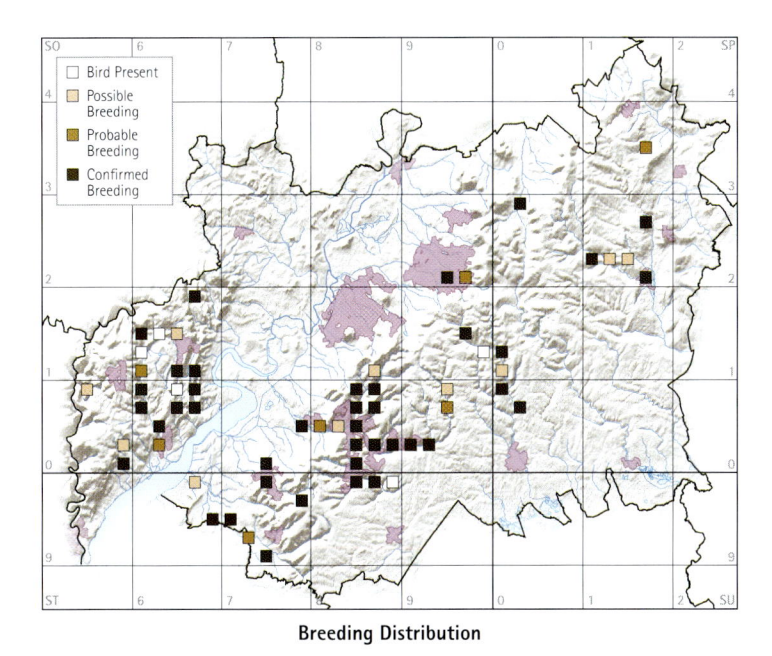

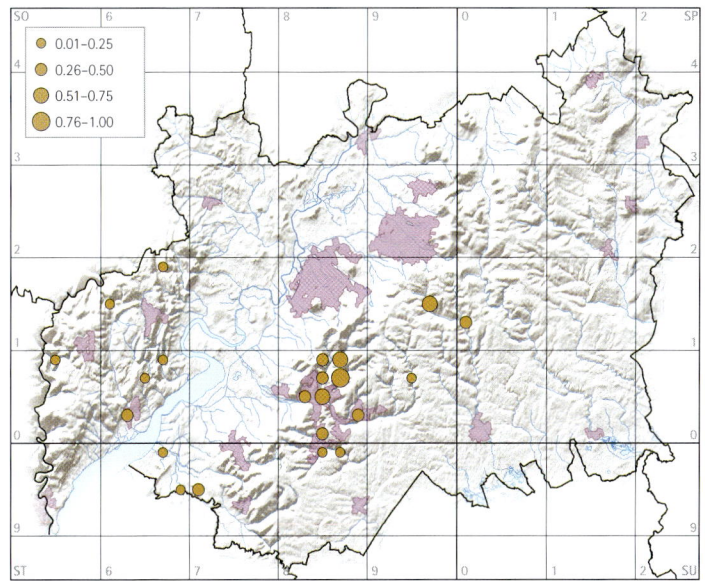

Summer Abundance

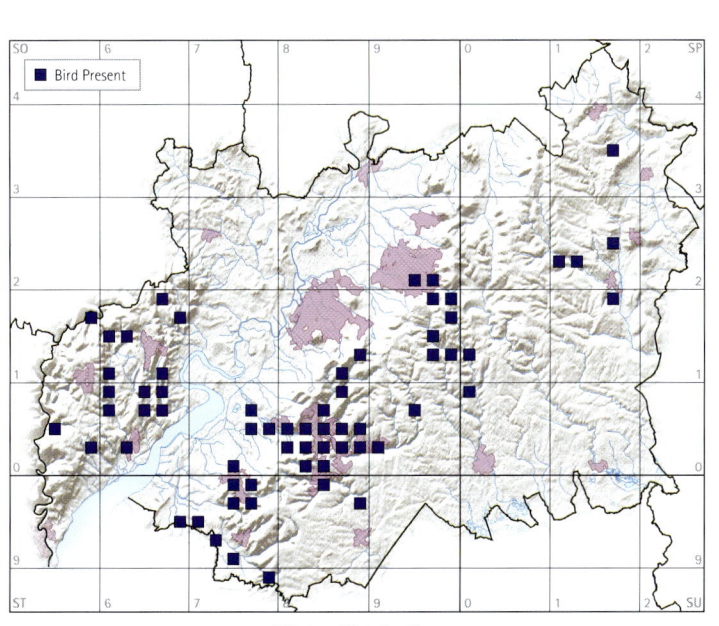

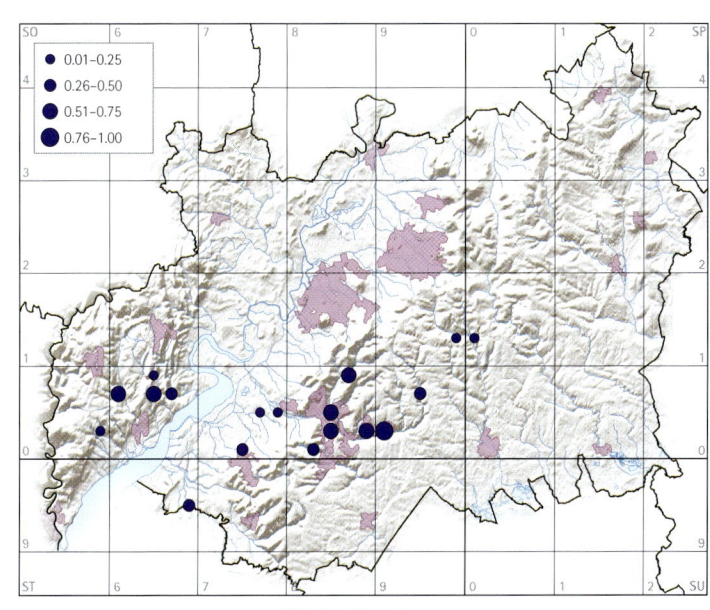

Winter Distribution

Winter Abundance

Ring Ouzel
Turdus torquatus

Ring Ouzels have a fragmented distribution in upland areas of Europe and eastwards to Turkmenistan. In Britain, where the declining population numbers about 7,000 pairs, they breed in moorland areas with crags, gullies or broken ground, although elsewhere they use more wooded habitat. British breeders winter in Iberia and north-west Africa.

Mellersh wrote that Ring Ouzels had bred regularly on the Cotswold scarp up to about 1885 but had been 'mercilessly shot' by collectors. Swaine quoted this, together with earlier references to breeding, but felt that first-hand evidence of actual breeding was lacking, summarising the position as 'former status uncertain, but now a passage migrant in small numbers, occurring chiefly in March–April and in October'.

Currently the nearest breeding areas are in Dartmoor, Wales and the Peak District, but migrants are still seen in Gloucestershire every year, with a roughly 5:1 ratio of spring to autumn sightings. Normally the first birds are seen in the last week of March, although the earliest bird recorded was on March 16th 2002, and in the autumn most are seen in October. British breeders start to arrive back on their territories as early as mid-March, so it is thought that most of the spring migrants recorded in Britain are Fennoscandian breeders, which have been drifted westwards from their more easterly migration route; this also accounts for the variable numbers recorded (Migration Atlas).

Probably more than any other migrant passerine, Ring Ouzels on passage in inland counties tend to be seen only at a few traditional sites. In Gloucestershire they are reliable at only one site and appropriately for an upland bird that is Cleeve Hill, the highest point in the county, which accounts for a large majority of records. The rough grassland cut by deep, scree-lined valleys clearly suits this species, one of the most wary of all our visitors; anyone lucky enough to encounter Ring Ouzels there will be left in no doubt that this is a bird of wild places. In good years, they are present there on most days in mid-April, and notable peak counts include 16 on April 17th 2007 and 19 on April 21st 2008. Such numbers are unusual though; the average peak spring count over the last 20 years is five or six.

Autumn records are far less frequent, perhaps because of different weather systems, and in most years involve single birds seen on one or two occasions. A notable exception was 2005 when, as part of a major influx into the country, much higher numbers than usual were seen in October, peaking with a remarkable 39 at Cleeve Hill on October 20th.

Sponsored by the North Cotswold Ornithological Society

White's Thrush (Scaly Thrush)
Zoothera dauma

White's Thrush breeds no closer to Britain than the Ural Mountains and the wintering areas are in south-east Asia, so it is perhaps surprising that by 2010 there had been 74 British records, 47 of them since 1950.

The only accepted Gloucestershire record of this skulking thrush was of one near Lechlade on October 30th 1966. An old report of one at at 'Campden' (presumably Chipping Campden) in September 1903, mentioned in Mellersh's manuscripts and quoted by Swaine, is not acceptable by modern standards.

Grey-cheeked Thrush
Catharus minimus

There has been one record in Gloucestershire of this North American thrush, which is an annual or near-annual autumn vagrant to the British Isles: an unfortunate bird killed itself by flying into a glass door at the WWT centre at Slimbridge on October 14th 1990.

Blackbird (Common Blackbird)
Turdus merula

Familiar to almost everyone in the British Isles from its presence in gardens, the Blackbird is also one of the most widespread and abundant birds in Europe, with perhaps 100 million breeding birds. During the twentieth century Blackbirds expanded into new areas, notably in Fennoscandia, and at present they occupy most of the Western Palearctic except the far north, as well as ranging widely further east across Asia. In western and central Europe they are largely resident, though some British breeders make short winter movements, either southwards within Britain or to Ireland; a very small proportion move as far as France and (rarely) northern Spain. However in winter numbers here are swollen to an estimated 20 million birds by migrants from the eastern half of the range, particularly Fennoscandia (1981–84 Wintering Atlas).

From the nineteenth century Blackbirds began to take advantage of man-made habitats in Britain (BWP), and the species spread out from its original woodland areas, eventually colonising suburban parks, gardens and the centres of cities. More recently the British population declined for a number of years from the 1970s, possibly due to colder winters. As a result the species was temporarily given amber conservation status, but this was revoked in 2001 following a slow recovery from the mid-1990s. There are currently estimated to be just under 5 million pairs of Blackbirds in Britain. The nesting season here extends at least from March to July and two or three broods are commonly raised. Breeding is easy to confirm when the distinctive fledged young are being fed in the open. In the current atlas survey, 91% of the county's tetrads had a confirmed breeding record and almost all of these cited fledged young or adults carrying food.

Both Mellersh and Swaine described Blackbirds as resident and numerous in Gloucestershire, and the current maps show that they are still present in numbers throughout the whole county. Indeed, in the current atlas fieldwork they were recorded in every tetrad during TTVs, winter and summer alike, the only species for which this was achieved. The species' status as the county's most widespread bird is confirmed by the local garden bird survey, which shows that Blackbirds visit 98% of Gloucestershire gardens in winter, in both rural and suburban areas – a higher percentage even than Blue Tit or Robin (2010 GBR; see also p. 50). Urban areas are also well represented on the maps, and the only region of the county where they are rather more sparsely distributed appears to be the arable farmland of parts of the Cotswold dip-slope. There is no evidence of any overall recent trends in numbers: the Cotswolds Atlases found no changes between 1987 and 2007, and Blackbirds have been recorded in every BBS square in the county each year since the survey began in 1994, a distinction shared only with Woodpigeons.

Swaine noted some large winter gatherings in the county, including 300 birds at Minsterworth in the Severn Vale in January 1979, and speculated that these could have included continental migrants. The maximum count during a winter TTV in the current survey was 134, in SO70Q in the Vale near Cam in December 2007. This compares with 65 in the breeding season, still an impressive total, in SO72N further north in the Vale near Newent in May 2008.

Blackbirds are ringed in fairly large numbers, and up to 2010 there had been 532 recoveries involving Gloucestershire. However 85% of these involved movements inside the county, and another 5% were to and from neighbouring counties. The longest movement within Britain was by one ringed 775 km away in Orkney on autumn passage and found dead near Dowdeswell in winter. There were also 39 recoveries of Blackbirds moving between Gloucestershire and ten northern European countries, as far away as Norway, Latvia and Poland.

TERENCE LAMBERT

Sponsored by E Golding, and in memory of Blackie

Species accounts

2007-11 Atlas fieldwork					Gloucestershire trends					UK population trends	
Number of tetrads in which recorded (max 683)					Occupied 10 km squares (max 26)				% of tetrads in which recorded (1st hour of TTV)		UK conservation status: Green	
	Total	Confirmed	Probable	Possible	Present	1968-71	1981-84	1988-91	2007-11	1988-91	2008-11	Long term	Short term
Breeding	682	624	43	15	0	26		26	26	100.0	100.0	-13%	+26%
Winter	682							26	26			-	-

Breeding Distribution

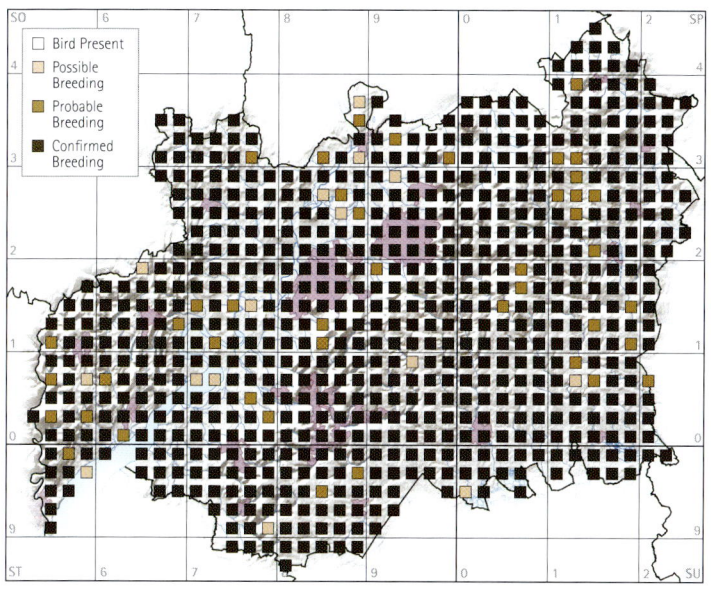

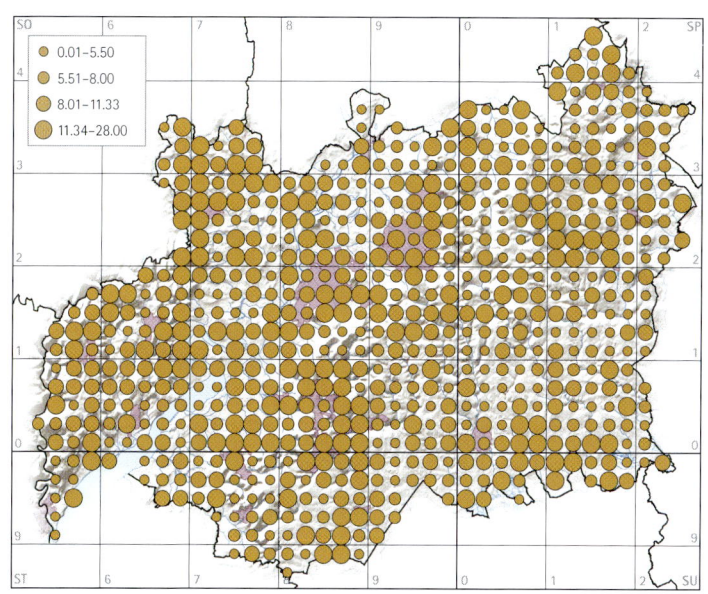

Summer Abundance

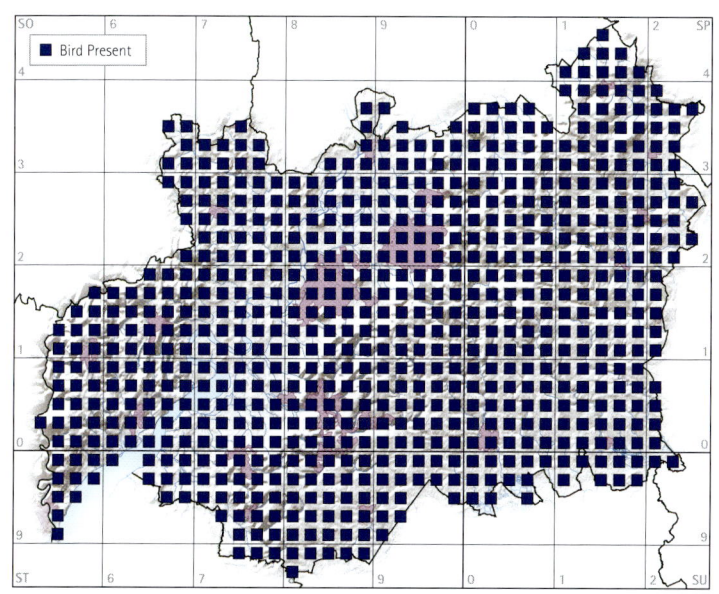

Winter Distribution

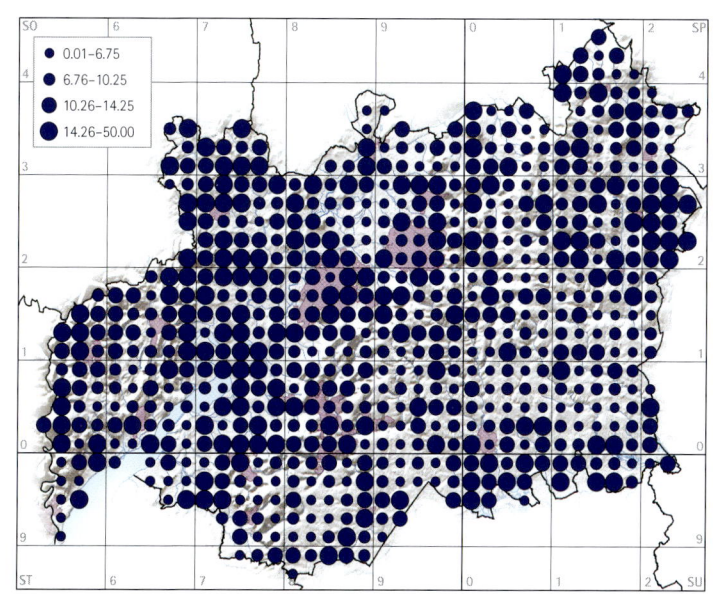

Winter Abundance

Fieldfare
Turdus pilaris

This familiar winter visitor is most commonly seen in flocks in farmland fields, hedges and orchards, searching for berries, fruits and invertebrates.

The Fieldfare has a very extensive breeding range, from Siberia in the east to central France in the west, with a stable population of up to 100 million. It has spread south-west though Europe over the last 100 years, and colonised much of France only in the last 50. Virtually the whole population migrates west or south-west in autumn, to winter south to the Mediterranean. These movements have a nomadic character, the direction and distance travelled depending on the availability and distribution of food at the end of the breeding season and during the winter. Ringing studies suggest that only 20% of birds return to the same site in successive winters. Those that visit the British Isles are mainly from Scandinavia, particularly Norway. A handful of birds remain to breed, almost all in the north-east.

In Gloucestershire, Fieldfares are passage migrants and winter visitors and there has never been any indication that they might breed here. There are almost always a few early arrivals in September, but the main influx takes place during October and numbers peak dramatically in November, as shown by the graph. The habitats that are used depend on weather conditions and on the size of the fruit and berry crops. If the ground is frozen they must seek food in hedgerows, gardens and orchards, and if no such alternatives are available they are obliged to migrate further. Swaine referred to movements away from the high ground of the Cotswolds with the onset of hard weather, and noted that autumn numbers there are rarely maintained after mid-December. This holds true today, with numbers tending to decline after the New Year, and the data for the last ten years suggest that this is because they move on out of the county altogether. The last winterers usually leave the county in the last ten days of April; the latest record since 2000 was of two at Great Barrington near the Oxfordshire border on May 12th 2002.

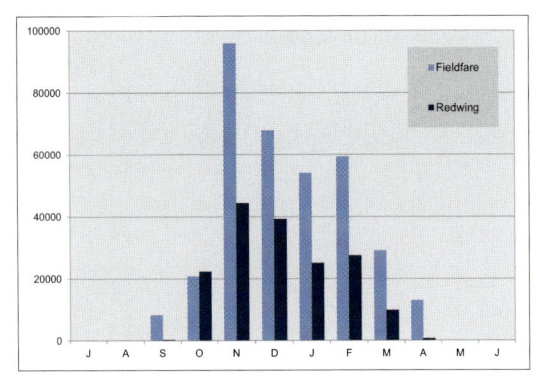

Fieldfare and Redwing numbers reported 2003-10, by month.

Although Fieldfares are seen almost everywhere in the county in winter, as confirmed by the distribution map, the abundance map shows that during the atlas fieldwork there were relatively few in the heavily wooded central part of the Forest of Dean and along parts of the Cotswold scarp, where feeding habitat is scarcer. Densities were also lower in the larger conurbations, although Fieldfares will move into gardens to feed during hard weather. Mellersh remarked on this behaviour at the beginning of the last century, but he made no mention of orchards as feeding habitat, although they were far more extensive in the county then than they are today. This could

Sponsored by the Rev & Mrs P van de Kasteele

Species accounts

2007–11 Atlas fieldwork					
Number of tetrads in which recorded (max 683)					
	Total	Confirmed	Probable	Possible	Present
Breeding	76	0	0	0	76
Winter	663				

Gloucestershire trends					
Occupied 10 km squares (max 26)				% of tetrads in which recorded (1st hour of TTV)	
1968–71	1981–84	1988–91	2007–11	1988–91	2008–11
0		0	0	0	0
		26	26		

UK population trends		
UK conservation status: **Red 3**		
Long term	Short term	
–	–	
–	–	

be because the fruit was a valuable crop at that time and was mostly harvested by the end of the autumn. In the modern Gloucestershire countryside, unharvested orchard fruits provide a significant food source for Fieldfares and other thrushes through the winter.

As might be expected from a mobile species which aggregates into large flocks, the numbers reported during atlas surveying varied widely. About one flock in 12 was at least 100 strong, and the maximum count in a TTV was 594, in tetrad SO72D near Newent in December 2007. Flocks containing 1,000 or more birds are unusual in Gloucestershire; the two largest on record, both estimated at 5,000, were at Slimbridge in November 1993 and November 2009. The NCOS winter survey indicates that numbers in the North Cotswolds have been broadly stable in recent decades, with averages of 36 birds per square kilometre between 1995 and 2003 and 38 from 2004 to 2010.

Fieldfares ringed in Gloucestershire in winter have been found in Sweden (two), Finland (two) and Norway (one), reflecting the known origins of the British wintering population.

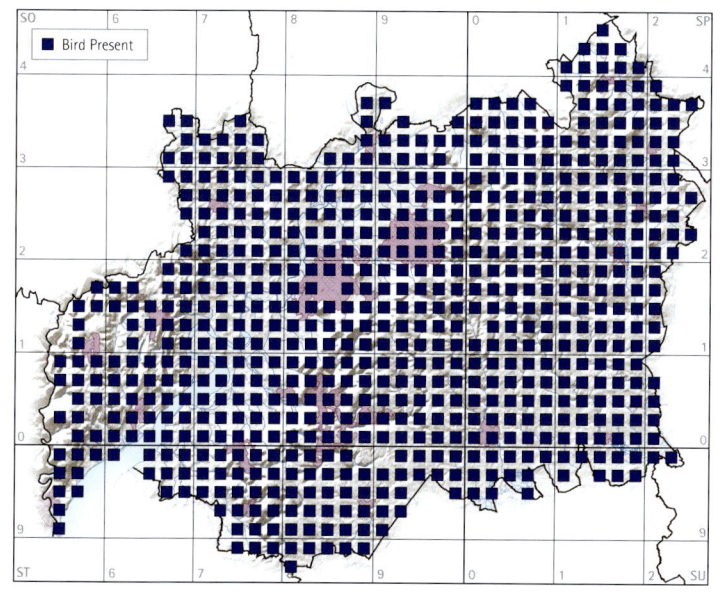

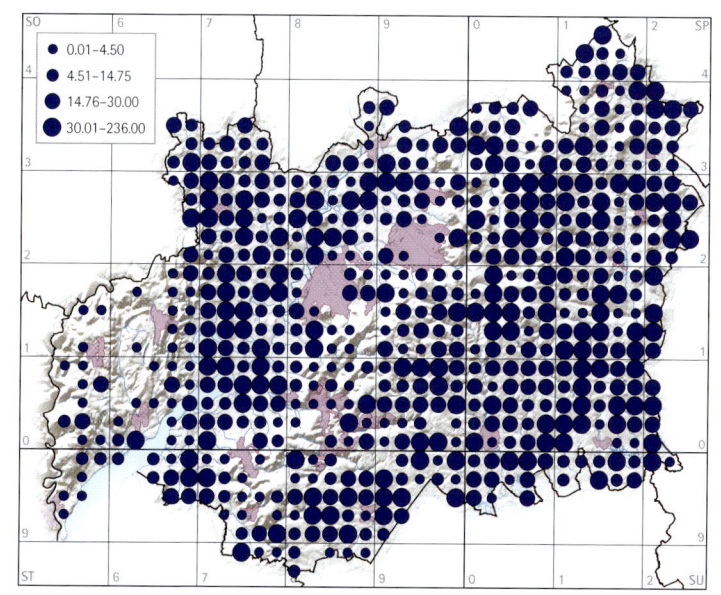

Winter Distribution

Winter Abundance

Song Thrush
Turdus philomelos

With its varied, repeated phrases, the Song Thrush has one of the most distinctive and well-known of all bird songs. Coupled with its penetrating voice, this makes the bird considerably easier to find than its well-concealed nest. In Gloucestershire during the current atlas project half the records where breeding status was given cited a singing male as evidence.

Song Thrushes breed throughout most of Europe and as far east as western Siberia. The European population is estimated to number between 14 and 26 million pairs, of which one million breed in Britain. The species was ancestrally a bird of woodlands, especially those with a dense understorey, but in modern times it has adapted well to more open habitats including farmland, parks and gardens, wherever there is cover in the form of shrubs or hedges.

Northern and eastern breeders are migratory, wintering in Iberia and the Mediterranean basin, while the more southern and western populations, including most British birds, are mainly resident. Some British breeders do move south and west, and Britain also receives winter visitors from the Low Countries. In addition, hard winters often cause Song Thrushes to undertake movements south and west; they are more sensitive to cold than other thrushes.

Formerly the species was abundant enough in Britain to be taken for granted, and early accounts are sketchy, but there was a well-documented severe decline during the two decades from the mid-1970s. Contributory factors included agricultural intensification and the increasing use of molluscicides in both farmland and gardens; snails are an important component of Song Thrushes' diet, meaning that they might find it difficult to cope with dry summers as well as cold winters. A recovery began in the mid-1990s and has continued, although populations are still only half of what they were 40 years ago.

Mellersh mentions the species only as a common Gloucestershire resident and a migrant. Swaine confirmed this assessment, although with the perceptive caveat that 'the overall trend at present seems to be towards decrease'. More recently, the national population decline and recent recovery have been reflected in the county. By 2003–07 the second Cotswolds Atlas survey was able to find Song Thrushes in nearly every tetrad in that region, a 20% increase in occupancy since the 1983–87 survey, although this could have been partly due to better coverage.

The maps show Song Thrushes to be currently present everywhere in the county at both seasons, although numbers are evidently lower on the higher parts of the Cotswolds, especially in winter; given the lack of trees and gardens there, this is not surprising. The breeding season abundance map shows higher densities in most well-wooded localities but also in some adjoining areas, perhaps suggesting that woodland is the preferred habitat from which birds spread out at times when numbers are high. The winter maps mirror the summer pattern to some extent but also seem to show a preference for lower altitudes. This could reflect movements of local birds in response to seasonal habitat changes or weather conditions, as well as influxes of winter visitors. The largest counts during atlas TTVs were in the north-west of the county at both seasons: 26 in May 2008 in tetrad SO72N (Upleadon, near Newent), and 24 in December 2009 in SO63X (on the Herefordshire border near Ledbury).

Of the 130 or so Song Thrush ringing recoveries involving Gloucestershire up to 2010, 66% related to movements within the county and another 15% to and from neighbouring counties, indicating that they are slightly more widely travelled than Blackbirds. Of the remaining 25 or so movements, all but two were within England and Wales, the longest being three birds which moved to west Cornwall and one ringed here in October and killed by a car in Suffolk the following spring. Further afield, a Gloucestershire nestling was found dead in Co. Cork, and one ringed on passage in October in north-west France was found dead at Fairford the following February. The movement to Ireland and two of those to Cornwall took place during the notoriously severe winter of 1962–63.

In memory of Kate Butters and of Peter Duddridge

Species accounts 361

	2007–11 Atlas fieldwork					Gloucestershire trends					UK population trends	
	Number of tetrads in which recorded (max 683)					Occupied 10 km squares (max 26)				% of tetrads in which recorded (1st hour of TTV)		UK conservation status: **Red 3**	
	Total	Confirmed	Probable	Possible	Present	1968–71	1981–84	1988–91	2007–11	1988–91	2008–11	Long term	Short term
Breeding	678	331	217	127	3	26		26	26	79.3	88.4	−49%	+24%
Winter	665						26		26			–	–

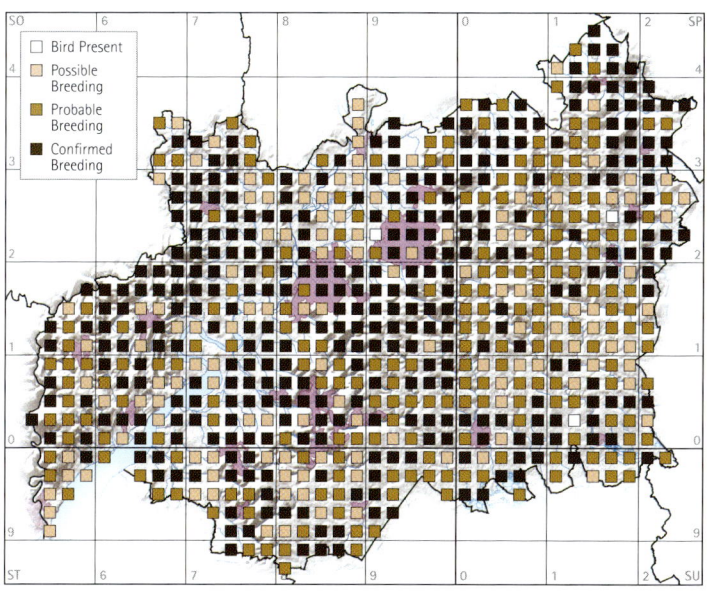

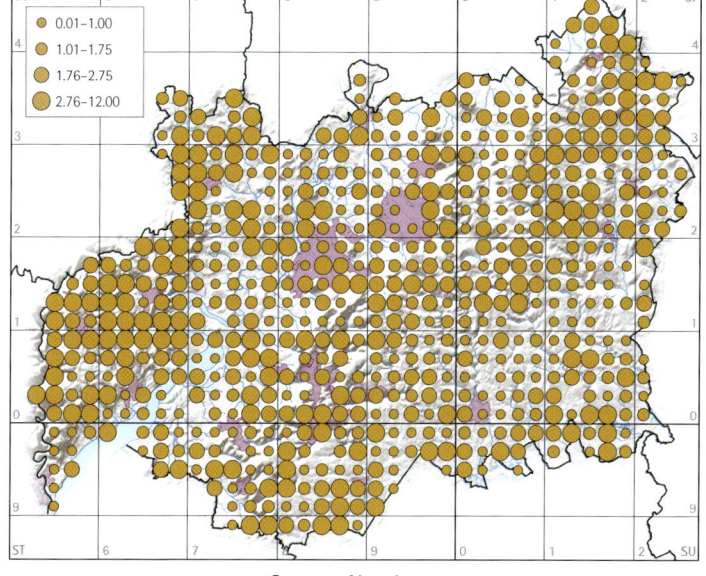

Breeding Distribution

Summer Abundance

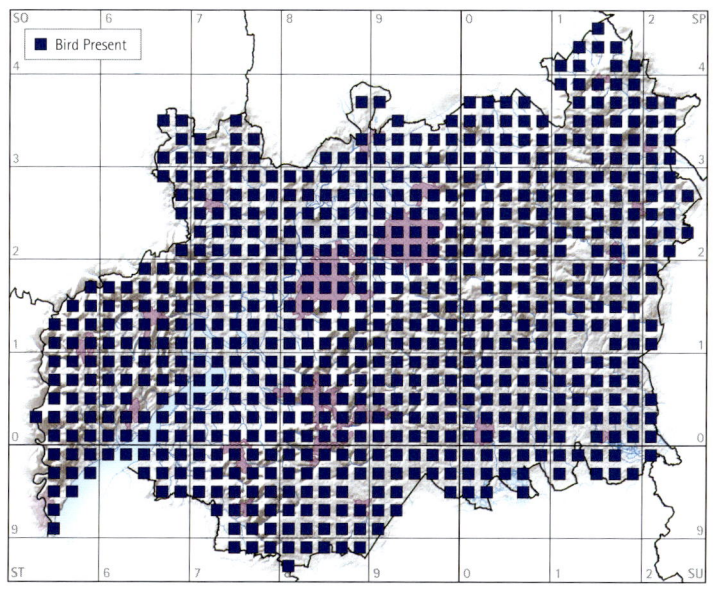

Winter Distribution

Winter Abundance

Redwing
Turdus iliacus

The Redwing is a regular winter visitor to the British Isles, occurring in large flocks often in the company of Fieldfares or Starlings. Its breeding range stretches across most of the Northern Palearctic, from Iceland to eastern Russia. The European population is estimated at between four and six million pairs, and appears to be stable. Redwings also breed in low numbers in Britain each year, mostly in the Scottish highlands. They have very occasionally bred in England, even as far south as Kent (Migration Atlas), but never in Gloucestershire.

Virtually the whole Redwing population moves south-west for the winter, many Western Palearctic birds migrating on a broad front to the British Isles and central and western Europe. Considerable numbers arrive in Britain every winter – something over a million birds in an average year – with more passage migrants continuing through to western France and Iberia. Redwings often migrate at night, when they are detectable by their thin, sibilant calls. The distance and direction of their migratory flights are determined by large-scale variations in weather and food supplies, and the same individual may spend successive winters in places thousands of kilometres apart.

In contrast to the breeding habitat of birch, pine and low scrubby thickets, wintering Redwings prefer open farmland with hedgerows and pastures, where they forage for berries and invertebrates, and like Fieldfares they visit orchards and even gardens to exploit fallen fruit, especially in hard weather.

In Gloucestershire the first few Redwings generally arrive in the last week of September and numbers build up rapidly through October, peaking in November as shown in the graph on p. 358. After that, they gradually drift away from the area over the course of the winter. The maps show that this thrush is widely distributed throughout the county, with a particularly strong presence in the Severn Vale. Areas where it is thinnest on the ground include the heavily wooded Forest of Dean, and also parts of the Cotswolds, for example around Tetbury and Aldsworth, where the fields are larger and hedges and copses fewer than on the higher wold. Mellersh went so far as to state that they 'greatly avoid the Cotswolds'. As Swaine pointed out, Redwings tend to desert the higher ground with the onset of hard winter weather. The maps also shows a sparse but significant presence in the major towns, reflecting the fact that they are more willing than Fieldfares to move into parks and gardens during freezing or snowy conditions.

Flocks of 1,000 to 2,000 Redwings were 'sometimes' noted in the Vale and the Cotswolds 30 years ago (Swaine), and 5,000 were seen at Slimbridge in December 1980. More recently, flocks of this size have been unusual: during the four years of the current atlas survey there were only three such counts, the maximum again being 5,000 at Slimbridge, in November 2008. The highest count during an atlas TTV was 710 in SP10R near Fairford in January 2008. The NCOS winter survey reveals no long-term changes in numbers in the North Cotswolds, with averages of 17 birds per square kilometre between 1995 and 2003 and also from 2004 to 2010.

In spring, Redwings leave the county a week or two earlier than Fieldfares and by the end of April there are usually only a few stragglers left. By this date the remaining birds are often very vocal, singing and chattering excitedly. The latest spring sighting since 2000 was at Ebworth on the Cotswold scarp on April 27th 2002.

There was a remarkable record in 2012 of a first-summer Redwing mist-netted by ringers at Frampton on the unprecedented date of July 21st. It was in an advanced state of moult and so was unlikely to have undertaken any recent long-distance flights, and it seems likely that it had failed to return to its natal area after winter 2011–12.

Of 11 Redwing ringing recoveries affecting Gloucestershire up to 2010, four involved movements of up to 260 km within Britain, a Belgian-ringed bird was found dead here, and Gloucestershire-ringed birds moved to France (three), Finland, Italy and Portugal. The variable, nomadic nature of their movements is demonstrated by the fact that birds caught wintering in Gloucestershire were found in France, Italy and Portugal in subsequent winters.

Sponsored by Terry Grant

Species accounts 363

2007–11 Atlas fieldwork					
Number of tetrads in which recorded (max 683)					
	Total	Confirmed	Probable	Possible	Present
Breeding	23	0	0	0	23
Winter	667				

Gloucestershire trends					
Occupied 10 km squares (max 26)				% of tetrads in which recorded (1st hour of TTV)	
1968–71	1981–84	1988–91	2007–11	1988–91	2008–11
0		0	0	0	0
	26		26		

UK population trends	
UK conservation status: **Red 3**	
Long term	Short term
–	–
–	–

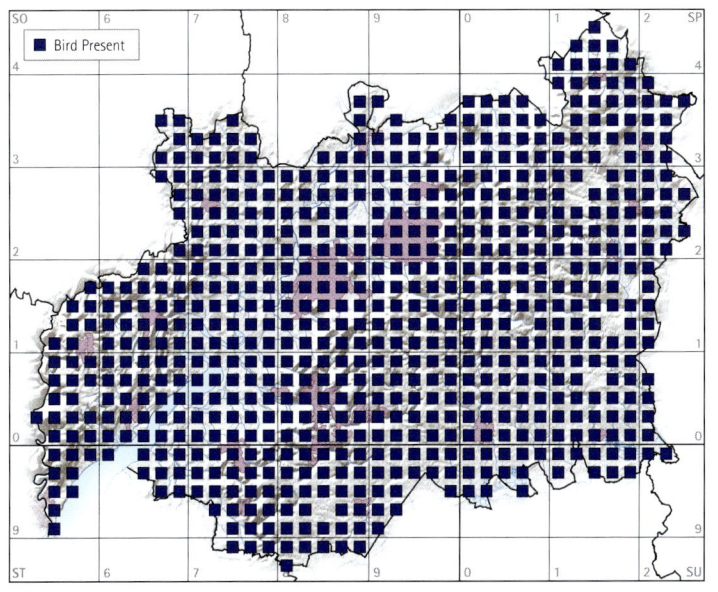

Winter Distribution

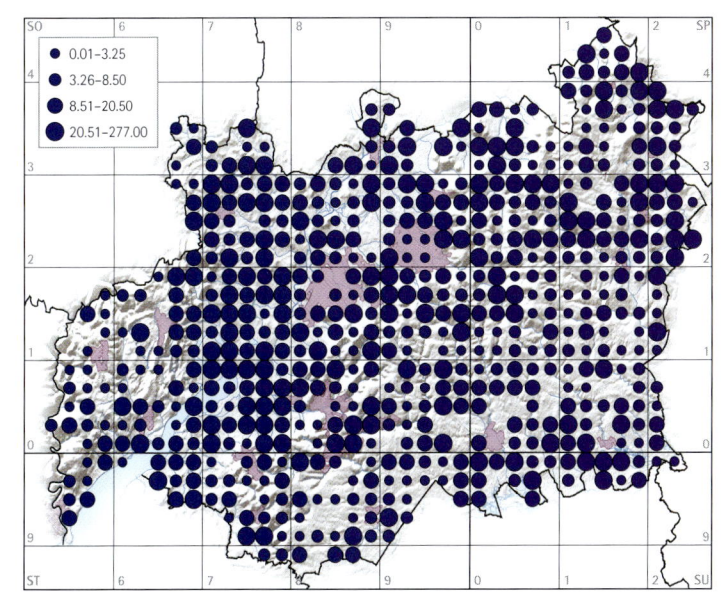

Winter Abundance

Mistle Thrush
Turdus viscivorus

With their far-carrying song and loud rattling calls, Mistle Thrushes are often heard before they are seen. They are birds of mature open woodland, wood pasture and, more recently, suburban parks and gardens. They need tall trees for nesting, and grassland and winter berries (notably mistletoe) to provide food.

Mistle Thrushes breeding in western Europe are mainly residents, but from Poland and Fennoscandia east to central Asia they are migrants, moving south-westwards into Europe for the winter. The European population is estimated to number between 2 and 4.4 million pairs and it is currently undergoing a moderate decline.

In the British Isles, Mistle Thrushes are widely but thinly distributed; their territories are large compared to other thrushes. They are mainly sedentary, though a small proportion migrate south to the Continent for the winter, and in late summer resident birds form post-breeding flocks which may move around locally. Later in the season these flocks break up and individuals vigorously defend winter food sources. A few Mistle Thrushes from continental Europe appear in Britain on passage and in winter, but in far lower numbers than for the other thrushes.

Mistle Thrushes expanded rapidly northwards in the early nineteenth century in both Britain and Europe, spreading out from their preferred upland woods. They were common in most counties by the start of the twentieth century, and continued to move into new habitats in suburban areas. Apart from fluctuations due to cold winters, numbers appeared steady through most of the twentieth century until a pronounced decline set in in the mid-1970s, which continues today. The reasons are unclear, but suggestions include a fall in annual survival rates (Siriwardena *et al.* 1998), possibly connected with the switch to autumn-sown cereal reducing the amount of open land available for spring foraging. The British population is currently estimated to be about 200,000 pairs.

There are few early records for Gloucestershire, although Mellersh mentioned that 'some scores of Mistle Thrushes will collect from all quarters, and busily tear up the turf after the cockchafer grubs that are to be found in the autumn months' in clearings in the Forest of Dean. Swaine noted that there had probably been an increase since that time despite hard winters, and described the bird as a common and widespread breeding species just as the national decline was starting to set in. The fact-box indicates a decline in occupied tetrads since the 1988-91 Breeding Atlas, but more recent local studies suggest that the Gloucestershire population may be stable, in contrast to some parts of the country. The proportion of county BBS squares where the species has been recorded has averaged around 52% since 1994, with no apparent trends, and the NCOS winter survey figures have also been 'remarkably stable' since 1995.

However Mistle Thrushes are much more sparsely distributed in the county than Song Thrushes or Blackbirds, as the fact-boxes and maps demonstrate. During the breeding season in particular they are less abundant where woodland is scarce, notably in the Severn Vale and some more open areas of the Cotswolds.

Swaine referred to flocks in excess of 60 birds being 'sometimes reported from August onward' and again this does not seem to have changed in more recent years; since the turn of the century the largest flock seen in the county each year has usually been between 30 and 40, with rather higher counts of 75 near Cranham on the Cotswolds scarp in August 2002 and 70 near Sherborne in the Windrush valley on August 30th 2004.

The Mistle Thrush is the most sedentary of our thrushes, with half of all British and Irish ringing recoveries showing movements of less than a kilometre (Migration Atlas). Fifteen of the 16 recoveries involving Gloucestershire up to 2010 related to movements within the county. The exception was a nestling ringed in Derbyshire in April 1981 and killed by a cat at Dursley in January 1982.

Sponsored by the Cheltenham Bird Club

Species accounts 365

2007–11 Atlas fieldwork					Gloucestershire trends						UK population trends		
Number of tetrads in which recorded (max 683)					Occupied 10 km squares (max 26)				% of tetrads in which recorded (1st hour of TTV)		UK conservation status: Amber 3		
	Total	Confirmed	Probable	Possible	Present	1968–71	1981–84	1988–91	2007–11	1988–91	2008–11	Long term	Short term
Breeding	578	229	157	157	35	26		26	26	58.0	43.9	−53%	−21%
Winter	633						26		26			–	–

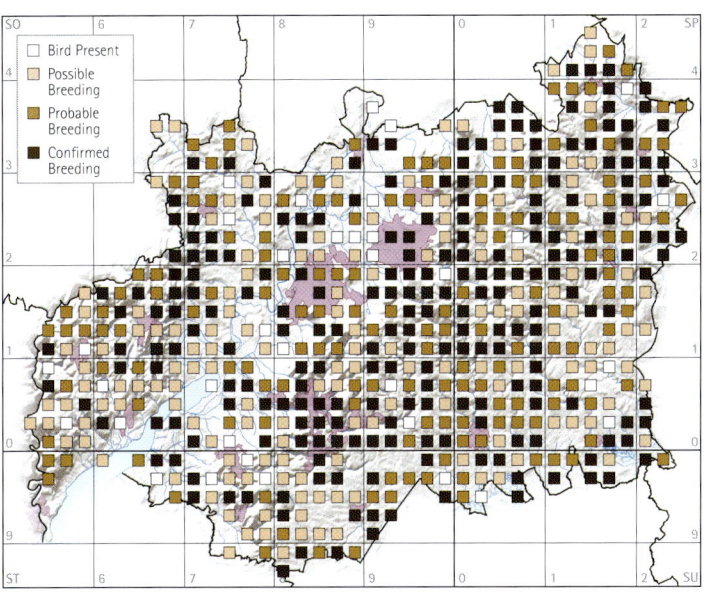

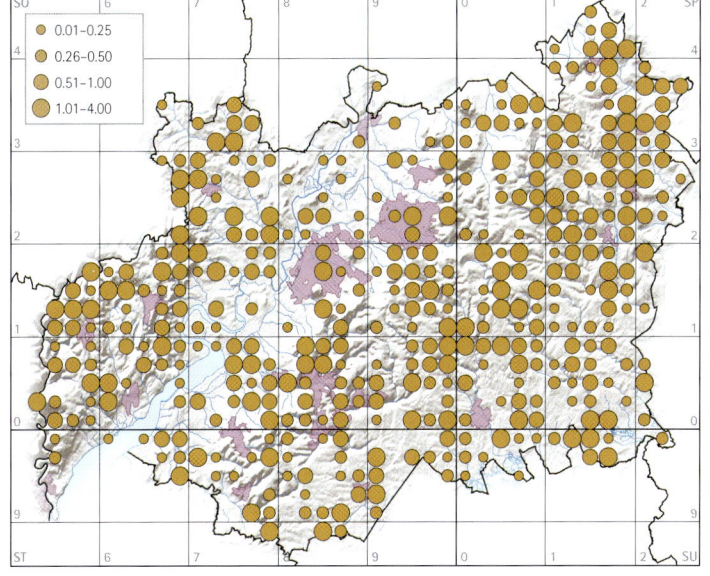

Breeding Distribution

Summer Abundance

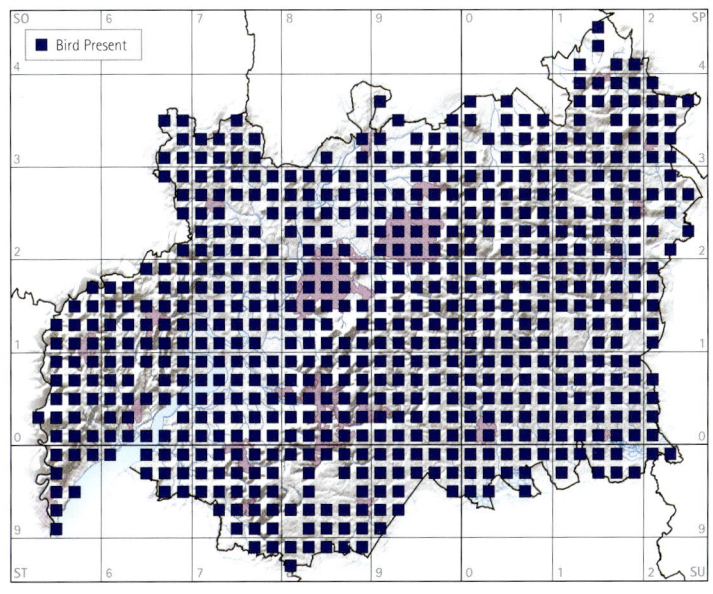

Winter Distribution

Winter Abundance

Spotted Flycatcher
Muscicapa striata

Spotted Flycatchers breed in a broad band from Morocco, Ireland and northern Norway east to the western Himalayas and winter in sub-Saharan Africa, some flying as far as South Africa. They nearly always choose areas with tall trees for breeding, but because they require exposed perches and clearings for foraging, dense continuous tree cover is avoided. They are therefore found in parkland and orchards as well as mature deciduous woodland, and in England they are traditionally birds of larger rural gardens, where they delight the human occupants with their confiding behaviour. They build their nests on flat branches or ledges and they quite often use buildings, especially creeper-covered walls.

Since the 1960s Spotted Flycatchers have undergone a catastrophic decline in numbers in several European countries, and by about 1990 the British population was only about a quarter of what it had been in 1960. The decline has continued unabated over the last 20 years, although in common with Willow Warblers and a few other summer visitors, the losses have been much more noticeable in the south and populations in Scotland have not suffered so much. The causes of this pattern are as yet unknown, although it has been suggested that climate change may be creating a wider mismatch between arrival date and spring phenology in the south, resulting in lower breeding success there, and/or that young birds arriving in Britain after their first winter abroad may be settling further north because the spring is too advanced by the time they reach their natal areas (Ockendon *et al.* 2012).

This is certainly one of the last spring migrants to arrive, with the first birds appearing in Gloucestershire on average about May 4th (earliest date April 22nd, in 1978). The undistinguished song, often given from a perch high in a tree, is easily overlooked, and the birds can be surprisingly difficult to see unless they are actively flycatching. On the other hand, at the end of the summer the food-begging calls of the young and the busy food-gathering of the parents mean that families can be very conspicuous. Second broods are not uncommon, and the last juveniles are often still being fed by their parents into late August. The average last sighting of the year in the county is about September 26th (latest October 14th 1984).

Swaine described the species as 'a common summer visitor, breeding throughout the county', commonest in the Dean, the Severn Vale, and in the Cotswolds along the scarp and the main dip-slope valleys. He made no mention of any decrease up to 1980, but in the area covered by the two Cotswolds Atlases the population 'certainly' declined between 1987 and 2007.

The current distribution map shows that Spotted Flycatchers remain fairly widespread in the county, and indeed they were

Sponsored by T & E Butler and Fraser Hart

2007–11 Atlas fieldwork						Gloucestershire trends						UK population trends	
Number of tetrads in which recorded (max 683)					Occupied 10 km squares (max 26)				% of tetrads in which recorded (1st hour of TTV)		UK conservation status: Red 3	
	Total	Confirmed	Probable	Possible	Present	1968–71	1981–84	1988–91	2007–11	1988–91	2008–11	Long term	Short term
Breeding	260	90	58	76	36	26		26	26	29.8	8.5	–87%	–47%
Winter	0						0		0			–	–

Breeding Distribution

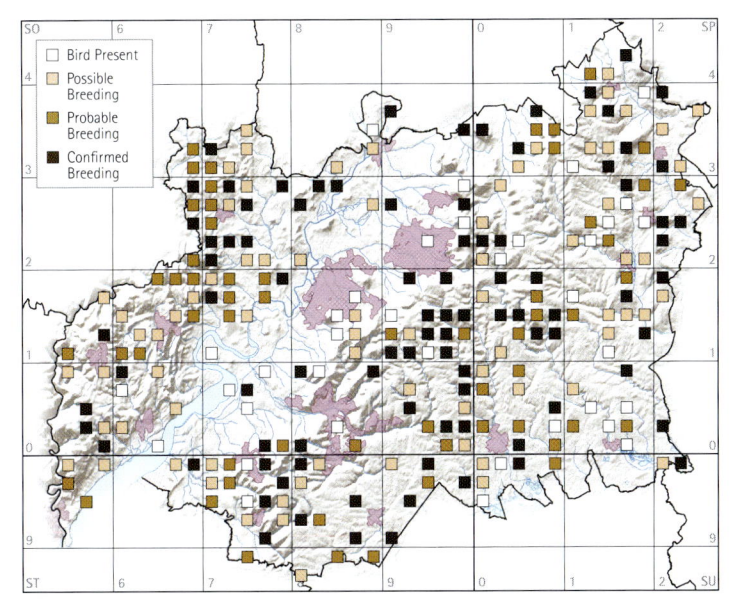

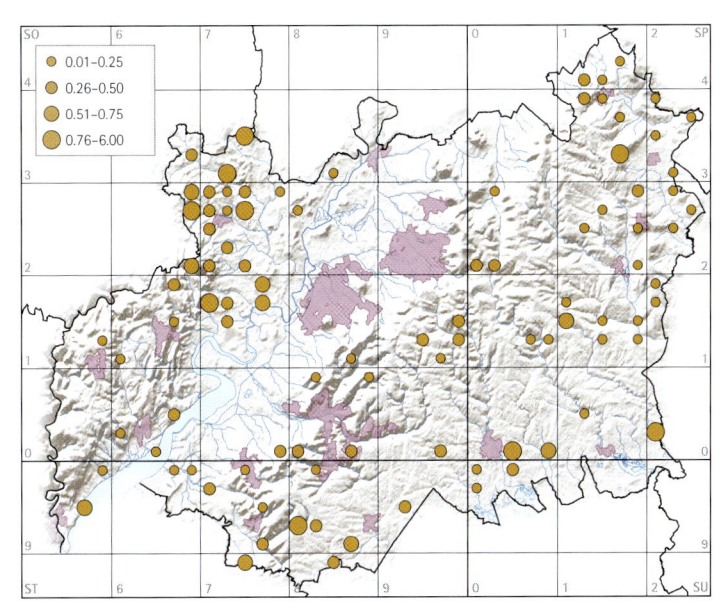

Summer Abundance

recorded in all 26 core 10 km squares. On a finer scale however, there were records in only 38% of tetrads in total during the atlas fieldwork, and the comparable TTV data in the fact-box reveal a severe decline since 1988–91, in line with the national picture. Also, although it is necessary to be cautious when interpreting the data for a fairly scarce species such as this, the pattern of relative abundance within the county appears to have changed slightly since Swaine was writing: Spotted Flycatchers now seem to be at their highest density in the 'orchard country' of the north-west, and there is a noticeable lack of records in the Vale in particular.

There have been three foreign recoveries of Gloucestershire-ringed Spotted Flycatchers. Two young birds ringed here in summer were recovered in autumn in north-east Portugal and on the Mediterranean coast of Morocco, in accordance with known migration routes. A nestling ringed in the county in July 1966 was shot in southern Spain on December 17th 1969, a late date for a Spotted Flycatcher to be so far north.

Robin (European Robin)
Erithacus rubecula

Britain's favourite bird is abundant and widespread throughout the British Isles, and on the Continent as well. Robins are found from the Atlantic coast all the way through to western Siberia, and from north Norway to the southern shores of the Mediterranean. The total European population is between 33 and 68 million pairs, of which about 5.5 million pairs are in Britain. In the western part of their range, including the British Isles, they are resident, but in Fennoscandia and from central Europe eastwards they are summer visitors, moving south or south-west in autumn to swell the winter population in France and the Mediterranean countries. Some Scandinavian birds travel down the east coast of Britain, producing 'falls' of hundreds in some autumns, but relatively few stay for the winter.

Robins breed in a wide variety of habitats including parks and gardens, hedgerows, coppices and thicker woodland. They seem only to require low scrub in which to nest and a more open area nearby for feeding. They mostly forage on the ground, taking small invertebrates, and the image of one accompanying a gardener digging over a patch of soil is almost a cliché. In winter they will switch to fruit when the ground is frozen or snow-covered and their preferred food is in short supply. Although they can suffer high mortality in hard winters the population recovers quickly, with pairs typically producing two or even three broods in a summer.

The Robin seems always to have been common in the British Isles and the 1875–1900 Atlas shows it as breeding abundantly in all counties. It seems largely to have avoided the attentions of bird-catchers who so plagued some of the finches, though Witchell & Strugnell noted that 'women will give a shilling apiece for robins, to be placed in their hats'. Parslow (1973) found no evidence of widespread change over the previous 100 years. Recent national increases, as indicated in the fact-box, are thought to be due partly to a period of mild winters, but also to increased breeding productivity.

In Gloucestershire, Mellersh and Swaine both described the species as common and widespread, and during the current survey Robins were found in all but one tetrad in the breeding season and all but two in winter. Breeding was confirmed in more than three-quarters of occupied tetrads, usually when newly fledged young were seen, and adults were seen feeding young in about a quarter of all tetrads. This is no surprise given how confiding Robins are, how familiar and vigorous their song is, and how different in appearance the juveniles are from the adults.

The two abundance maps show that Robins are found in quantity throughout Gloucestershire in both seasons, and while numbers in the open areas on top of the Cotswolds and down the dip-slope are lower than in the rest of the county, the 2003–07 Cotswolds Atlas noted that they are nevertheless very common there and possibly even increasing. The highest counts during TTVs were 48 in tetrad SO62X near Newent in the breeding season and 57 in SO50M at St Briavels, Forest of Dean, in winter.

Most British Robins are very sedentary, and about 90% of the 160 or so ringing recoveries involving Gloucestershire relate to movements within the county, or to and from adjoining counties. However there have also been recoveries here of birds ringed as far away as the Isle of Man, Cheshire, Derbyshire, Suffolk and Kent, while two ringed here in August moved to northern France. All indicate generally southward displacements in winter compared with the breeding season, and some were ringed as nestlings, demonstrating fairly long movements by definitely British birds. Swaine wrote that there was 'no ringing evidence of continental birds in the county' up to 1980, but immatures ringed in southern Norway in April 1980 and in Belgium in September 2009, and found dead here in the following winters, were surely continental birds.

TERENCE LAMBERT

In memory of Audrey Joyce Carman and of Peggy Saunders

Species accounts

2007–11 Atlas fieldwork					Gloucestershire trends						UK population trends		
Number of tetrads in which recorded (max 683)					*Occupied 10 km squares (max 26)*				*% of tetrads in which recorded (1st hour of TTV)*		UK conservation status: **Green**	
	Total	Confirmed	Probable	Possible	Present	1968–71	1981–84	1988–91	2007–11	1988–91	2008–11	Long term	Short term
Breeding	682	521	112	49	0	26		26	26	97.0	97.8	+49%	+19%
Winter	681						26		26			–	–

Breeding Distribution

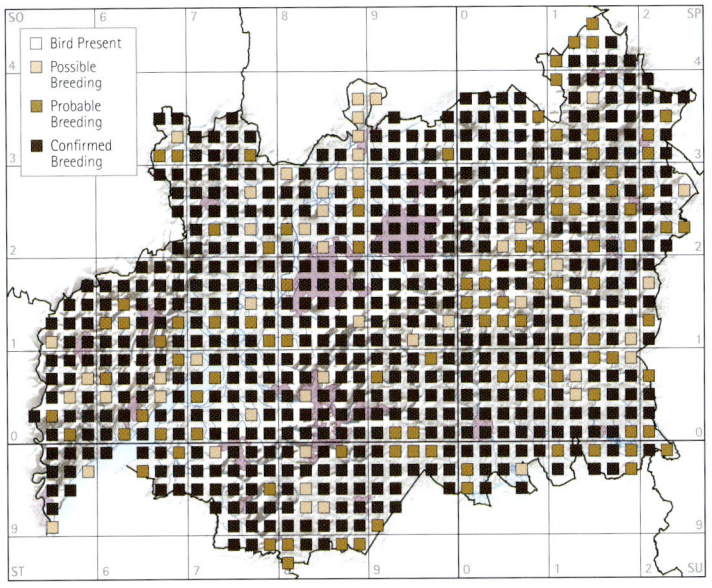

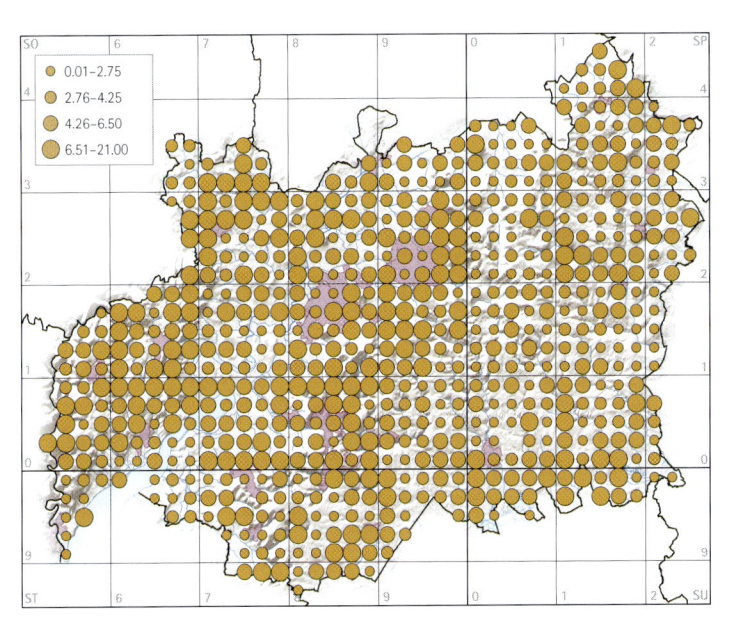

Summer Abundance

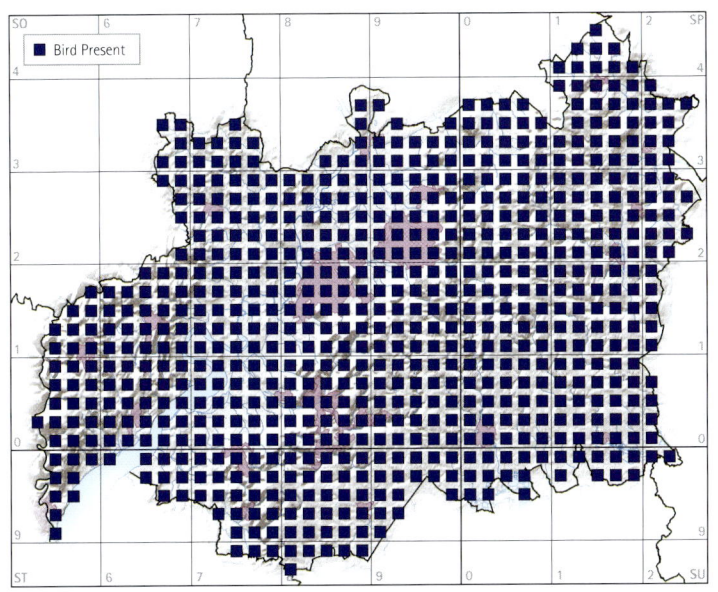

Winter Distribution

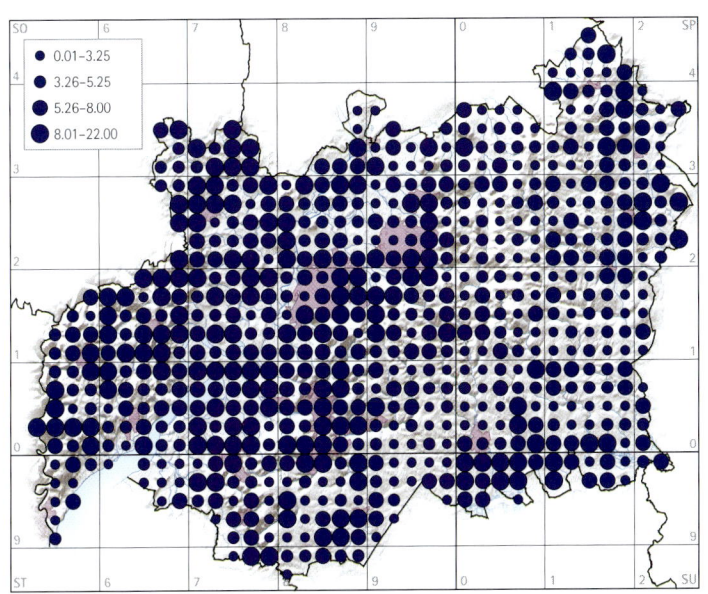

Winter Abundance

Nightingale (Common Nightingale)
Luscinia megarhynchos

Much talked of and written about but rarely encountered, Nightingales are welcome summer visitors to Britain, but sadly their beautiful song is no longer heard in many of their former haunts. They arrive here in April; the average first arrival in Gloucestershire is on April 14th, with possibly a slight tendency towards earlier dates in recent years, and the earliest date is April 6th, in 1998 and 2004. They raise a single brood of young and leave in August to winter in the savannah zone, south of the Sahara. Current studies are aiming to find the areas used by British birds in winter and on passage, and assess to what pressures they are subjected.

The world range extends from the Iberian peninsula and North Africa north to Germany, and as far east as Mongolia; Europe is thought to have a stable population of between 3.2 and 7 million breeding pairs. Britain lies on the limit of the breeding distribution and, as long ago as 1911, Ticehurst & Jourdain classified Gloucestershire as a county on the edge of the British range.

Nightingales favour dense, low-lying undergrowth for nesting, with areas of clear ground on which to forage for invertebrates. Coppiced woodland traditionally provided suitable habitat but, as coppicing diminished, favourable sites became fewer and nowadays woodland is also degraded by deer, which browse away the understorey. Scrubland and thickets, often in sheltered valleys or by disused gravel-pits and other workings, are now increasing in importance compared to woodland sites.

Until the early twentieth century the Nightingale appears to have been common in the south and east of England. Numbers fluctuated thereafter, but there was a sharp decline from the mid-1960s with a corresponding shrinkage in range, and the bird's heartland has contracted to a few south-eastern counties. The recent decrease is so severe that some argue for a change from amber to red listing (Holt *et al.* 2012). A targeted BTO survey in 1999 led to a national estimate of between 5,600 and 9,350 males (Wilson *et al.* 2002), while a repeat survey in 2012 is expected to confirm a continuing decline.

In Gloucestershire, Mellersh described the Nightingale as a scarce breeder, mainly in the damp, low-lying area between the Forest of Dean and Tewkesbury, and in the 'snug little valleys' that cut into the Cotswold scarp. Between 1927 and 1960 Nightingales were monitored in a block of woodland immediately adjacent to what is now Highnam Woods RSPB reserve (Philips Price 1961).

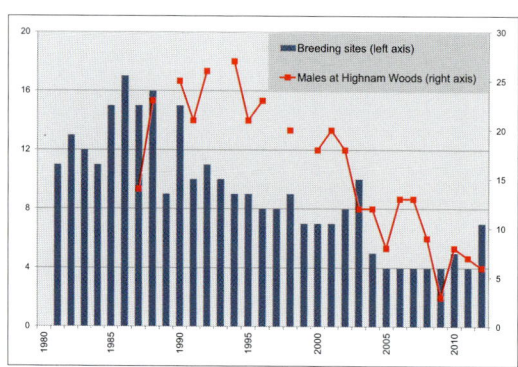

Nightingale breeding sites and males at Highnam Woods, 1981–2012.

Sponsored by Peter Ormerod

2007–11 Atlas fieldwork						Gloucestershire trends						UK population trends	
Number of tetrads in which recorded (max 683)					Occupied 10 km squares (max 26)				% of tetrads in which recorded (1st hour of TTV)		UK conservation status: **Amber 3**	
	Total	Confirmed	Probable	Possible	Present	1968-71	1981-84	1988-91	2007-11	1988-91	2008-11	Long term	Short term
Breeding	28	3	7	12	6	21		13	6	4.1	0.7	–	–60%
Winter	0						0		0			–	–

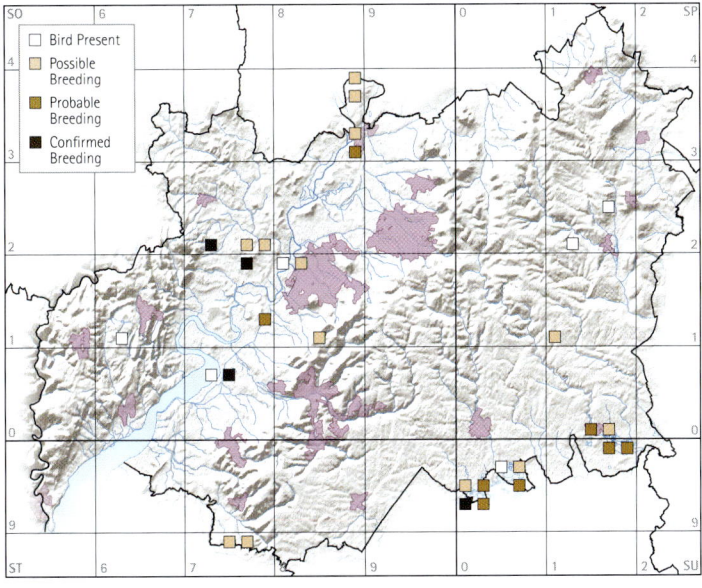

Breeding Distribution

males at seven sites in the county, with 12 in the western section of the Cotswold Water Park and six at Highnam Woods. The Water Park as a whole (Gloucestershire and Wiltshire) held 20 males, all but one in the western section. Studies there showed that although some new areas had been colonised, traditional sites are soon abandoned if scrub is removed or not managed (Gareth Harris, Cotswold Water Park Trust).

The graph shows changes in the number of sites in the county where Nightingales are likely to have bred, and the numbers of singing males at Highnam Woods. Neither the graph nor the distribution map, which confirms that they are clinging on in a handful of traditional sites, provide much cause for optimism.

Numbers there rose initially, probably due to an increase in brambles and ground vegetation when the rabbit population was low, but fell thereafter. The peak was in 1949, and although varying survey methods make it difficult to compare actual numbers then and now, it is noteworthy that around that time more Nightingales were recorded than Chiffchaffs, Blackcaps or Willow Warblers.

From the mid-1960s a new area of habitat began to appear around the gravel workings that became the Cotswold Water Park, and Swaine noted a population increase there and at other gravel-pits near Frampton. However, BTO surveys showed a decline in the county from 66 singing males in 1980 (Davis 1982) to 56 in 1999 (Wilson et al. 2002). Similarly the 2003–07 Cotswolds Atlas revealed a fall in occupancy from 28 tetrads in that part of the county in the mid-1980s to seven in the mid-2000s, with a formerly important site near Wormington village in 10 km square SP03 deserted since 2003, and it seems that Nightingales no longer breed in the Gloucestershire Cotswolds. The 2012 national census revealed just 25 territorial

Pied Flycatcher (Eurasian Pied Flycatcher)
Ficedula hypoleuca

Pied Flycatchers breed from Spain, the British Isles and Norway east to west-central Siberia, and winter in woodland habitats in West Africa south of the Sahara. In Britain they are mainly confined to western and northern areas, and 'it seems likely that the majority of British Pied Flycatchers now use nest-boxes rather than natural sites' (1988–91 Breeding Atlas). There was a slight expansion of range and increase in numbers between about 1970 and 1990 (Breeding Atlases), but more recently there has been a fairly severe decline.

Witchell & Strugnell and Mellersh referred to the species as being scarce in Gloucestershire, with occasional breeding records from the Severn Vale and elsewhere as well as in the Forest of Dean. Swaine described it as breeding in the Dean, and rarely east of the Severn. There were no suggestions of nesting in the area covered by the two Cotswolds Atlases, and the map shows that nearly all records during the current survey were in the Forest of Dean and the surrounding district; dots elsewhere almost certainly refer to passage migrants.

At what is now the RSPB reserve at Nagshead in the Dean, the Forestry Commission installed 84 nest-boxes in 1942 with the aim of encouraging more tits to nest; it was hoped that they would feed on the caterpillars of the winter moth, which were defoliating oak trees. It came as a surprise when 15 of the boxes were occupied by Pied Flycatchers. The population here has been monitored since 1948 and detailed, systematic studies began in in 1982. The numbers of birds breeding have fluctuated widely, as shown by the graph. The most important reason for these fluctuations, and particularly for the recent declines, may well be variations in the numbers of defoliating caterpillars, which are the flycatchers' preferred food. Formerly very abundant, these caterpillars have been almost absent in many recent years; the last year of heavy tree defoliation was 1987. The flycatchers are also vulnerable to poor weather (cold and wet) during the nestling period and when the young have recently fledged, and a number of recent summers have been marked by very unseasonal weather at just the wrong time. In addition, potential mammalian predators (stoats, weasels, wood mice and rarely dormice) have been discovered inside boxes, while grey squirrels and Great Spotted Woodpeckers may also take their toll. Despite all these factors, the mean fledging rate of 4.5 young per nesting attempt over the last ten years is fairly high, raising the possibility that habitat or climate changes in the wintering or migration areas may also be involved in the decline. Finally, despite the birds' protected status some nests were thought probably to have failed as a result of persistent disturbance from birdwatchers, particularly photographers. Flycatchers in a second breeding area in the Dean, which suffers less from disturbance, currently have higher fledging success. In any case, whatever the reasons for the overall decline, the Pied Flycatcher is clearly vulnerable in its Gloucestershire heartland.

The average first arrival in the county is about April 11th (earliest date on record April 4th 1995) and the last autumn sighting is usually towards the end of August (latest date September 28th 1999). Rather few migrants are seen away from the breeding sites.

The monitoring at Nagshead has added much to our knowledge of this species' breeding biology, notably the fairly frequent cases

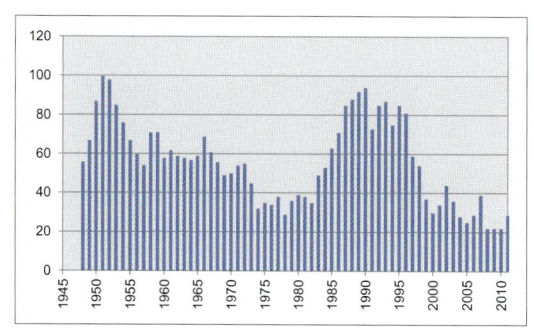

Pied Flycatcher pairs at Nagshead RSPB reserve, Forest of Dean, 1948–2011.

Sponsored by Frank & Liz Lander

Species accounts

2007–11 Atlas fieldwork				
Number of tetrads in which recorded (max 683)				
	Total	Confirmed	Probable	Possible	Present
Breeding	25	6	4	7	8
Winter	0				

Gloucestershire trends					
Occupied 10 km squares (max 26)				% of tetrads in which recorded (1st hour of TTV)	
1968–71	1981–84	1988–91	2007–11	1988–91	2008–11
4		7	5	4.5	0.3
		0	0		

UK population trends	
UK conservation status: **Amber 3**	
Long term	Short term
–	–51%
–	–

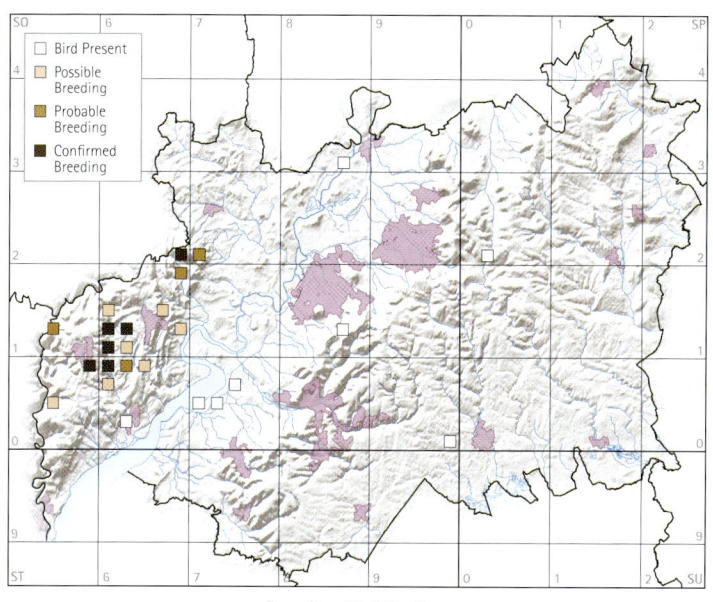

Breeding Distribution

of polygyny, and has given rise to many ringing recoveries. The three oldest known British Pied Flycatchers were all ringed and recaptured within this study area; the oldest was just over nine years old. There have been many interchanges of ringed birds between the Dean and other breeding areas, in particular in Gwent, Shropshire and 'Hereford & Worcester'. A 1994 nestling was killed by a car near Eastbourne in Sussex on August 5th that year, illustrating how early they may leave the country. There have also been a number of recoveries of Gloucestershire birds in the well-documented stopover area in northern Iberia, and six recoveries in Morocco, further along the migration corridor. Return migration tends to follow a more easterly route, and two spring recoveries in Algeria and Italy conform with this pattern.

Redstart (Common Redstart)
Phoenicurus phoenicurus

One of Britain's most handsome songbirds, the Redstart breeds throughout most of Europe, in parts of North Africa and the Middle East and eastwards to Lake Baikal in Siberia. It is a long-distance migrant, wintering in the Sahel savannah zone, south of the Sahara. Redstarts need cavities in trees or stone walls in which to nest, and scrub or low trees for feeding. They breed in a fairly wide range of habitats, particularly open, mature oak woodland but also including parkland, heath, well-wooded farmland and tree-lined river valleys. They feed on invertebrates, which they pick off the ground, catch in the tree canopy or even pluck out of the air like a flycatcher.

The European population is estimated to be between 2.1 and 4 million pairs. There was a marked decline in numbers on the Continent in the 1960s and 1970s, with the loss of mature woodland in its breeding range and degradation of its wintering habitat suggested as longer-term causes. The Redstart is also one of the species that has suffered worst from droughts in the Sahel, particularly the severe one in 1968. Since then there has been an overall moderate recovery.

In Britain, their distribution has undergone slow but significant changes since the end of the nineteenth century, when they bred in every county. There has been a major withdrawal from eastern, central and southern areas, while populations appear to be thriving in the more upland and western regions that have always been the species' heartland. There was a 20% decline in the number of occupied 10 km squares between the 1968–72 and 1988–91 Breeding Atlases, no doubt due at least in part to the 1968 Sahel drought, but more recently there has been an erratic recovery and there are now estimated to be about 100,000 pairs in the country.

Swaine noted that Redstarts bred 'throughout the county' and that the decline recorded in much of southern and eastern England prior to 1940 had not affected Gloucestershire until much later. However there appeared to have been a considerable decline in the Thames Area and possibly the Cotswolds just prior to 1980. The maps show that Redstarts were recorded quite widely in the county during the current atlas fieldwork, although breeding records were concentrated in the three very different areas that have been the strongholds here in recent years: the sheep-rearing country of the high wold east of the Cotswold scarp, with its stone walls and scattered bushes (2003–07 Cotswolds Atlas); the Forest of Dean with its mature oaks; and the floodplain of the Severn near Ashleworth with its willow pollards, where populations are probably at their highest density in the county albeit in a small area. Redstarts were present in some numbers in all three of these main areas during the current survey. In the area covered by the Cotswolds Atlases there was a moderate fall in tetrad occupancy between the mid-1980s and the mid-2000s, particularly noticeable in the Stour Valley in the north-east, but since then there has been a strong increase, from 58 tetrads with some form of breeding evidence in 2003–07 to 90 in the current survey. At present the prospects in our county for this delightful visitor appear to be good, although there is less cause for optimism elsewhere in this region of England.

The first Redstarts arrive in Gloucestershire fairly consistently in the first week in April (earliest date March 29th 1989), with few years seeing them more than a week earlier or later than average. Swaine

Sponsored by Simon Barker, Vic Polley, and the North Cotswold Ornithological Society

Species accounts

	2007–11 Atlas fieldwork					Gloucestershire trends						UK population trends		
	Number of tetrads in which recorded (max 683)					Occupied 10 km squares (max 26)				% of tetrads in which recorded (1st hour of TTV)		UK conservation status: **Amber 1**	
	Total	Confirmed	Probable	Possible	Present	1968–71	1981–84	1988–91	2007–11	1988–91	2008–11	Long term	Short term
Breeding	200	49	25	83	43	26		20	23	10.7	6.3	+27%	+7%
Winter	0							0	0			–	–

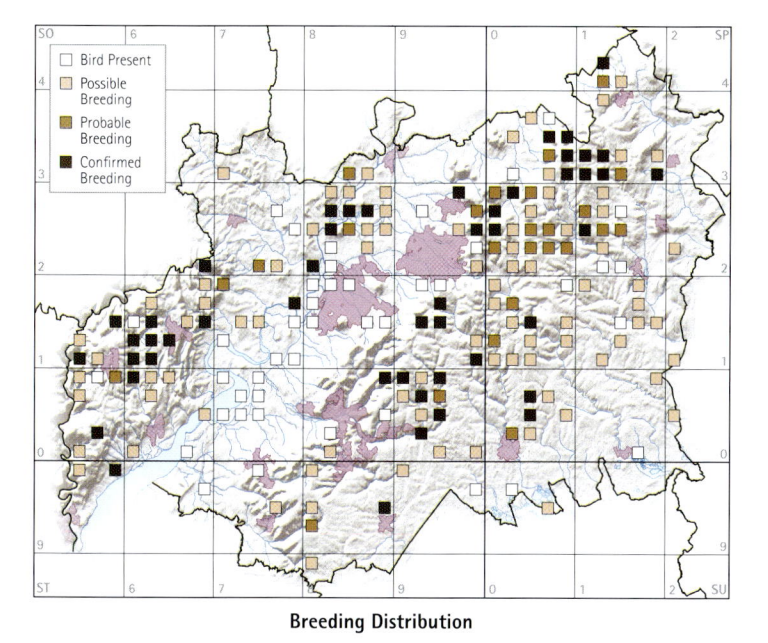

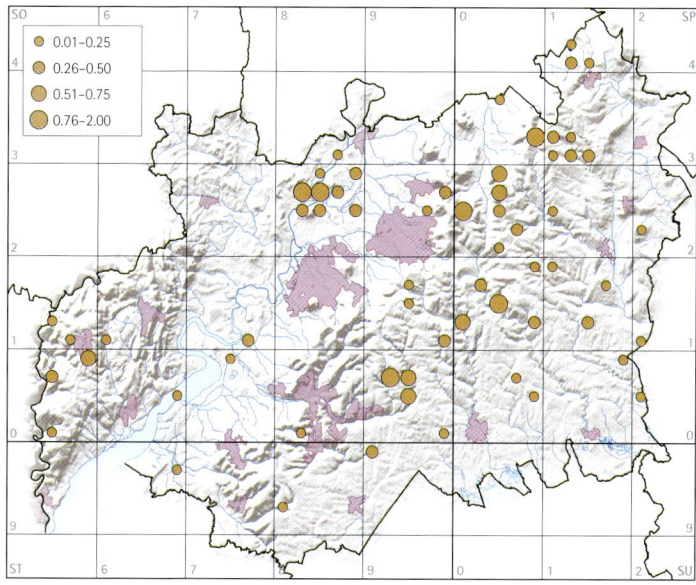

Breeding Distribution

Summer Abundance

noted that they appear almost simultaneously in the Cotswold Water Park and the Severn Vale, but take a few more days to be seen on the higher dip-slope. Autumn passage starts in early August and tends to peak around the Bank Holiday (possibly an observer effect!), and few are seen after mid-September; the latest one recorded in the county was on October 21st 1987. While eastern English counties sometimes receive falls of continental passage migrants, they do not reach Gloucestershire to any noticeable degree.

Redstarts ringed in Gloucestershire have been recovered on passage in France (four), Spain (four), Portugal and Morocco. Six of these ten recoveries were in south-west France and northern Iberia, areas where they are likely to pause to refuel on migration.

Black Redstart
Phoenicurus ochruros

Black Redstarts breed in the middle latitudes of the Western Palearctic and eastwards as far as central China. The European breeding range has undergone a long-term expansion to the north and north-west. Northern European birds are migratory, wintering mostly in the Mediterranean basin. In Britain, Black Redstarts occur mainly as passage migrants, but small numbers also winter, especially on the south and west coasts. In addition a few pairs nest in scattered British localities, with very few regular breeding areas; the average number of pairs over the period 2006–10 was 44.

Swaine wrote that in former years Black Redstarts had occurred irregularly though fairly frequently in Gloucestershire, with an increase in sightings from the 1950s reflecting the range expansion on the near Continent and the growth of the British breeding population at that time. Most records were in the Severn Vale, with some on the Cotswolds and fewer in the Thames Area. The majority were in March to May and October to December, with a peak in October. He also noted that singing males had been reported in four summers between 1958 and 1972.

Since 1980 the number of sightings seems to have increased, with about ten birds seen each year nowadays, though this may be due to observer effects to some extent. The graph shows that the peak is now in November, and there are perhaps more wintering birds than previously; certainly the buildings around Sharpness Docks and the former power station near Berkeley are now regular wintering sites. In general most records still come from the Vale, including the conurbations of Gloucester, Cheltenham and elsewhere. Almost all the other records are from the Cotswold scarp; they are infrequent on the dip-slope and in the Thames Area, and especially so in the Forest of Dean.

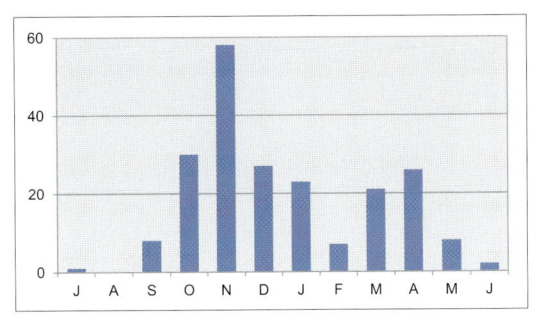

Black Redstart 1980–2010 by month of finding.

Gloucestershire is unusual among English counties in having no Black Redstart breeding records, although birds do occasionally occur in the breeding season, raising hopes that this attractive, alert species will one day nest in the county. Notably, in 2010 first-summer males were found singing in three different places between April 14th and June 14th.

Sponsored by the Dursley Birdwatching and Preservation Society

Whinchat
Saxicola rubetra

Whinchats breed widely across much of Europe and east to just beyond the Urals, although in general they occupy more northerly areas than the Stonechat and their distribution is more scattered in southern Europe. Birds from the entire range migrate to sub-Saharan Africa. Although the huge Russian population is thought to be secure, numbers further west, including in Britain, have declined significantly since the early twentieth century, and they no longer breed in many parts of southern and eastern England.

In Gloucestershire this was a widespread and locally common breeding bird in the nineteenth century. Mellersh stated that they favoured areas where the soil was poor and therefore uncultivated, and noted that 'the little open moorland' of May Hill was a stronghold; in summer 'there are over a hundred of these birds to be heard chatting [sic] from the tops of small bushes' there. They were also widespread in the Forest of Dean, in the riverside meadows of the Severn Vale, and on rough ground and lane-sides in the Cotswolds. Swaine wrote that a decline had started early in the twentieth century, and by the 1950s the Cotswolds were virtually deserted. The Severn Vale population too was sinking fast, with very few records after 1970, and the Forest of Dean stronghold was down to about 20 pairs by 1980, mainly in young plantations.

Sadly the Whinchat's demise in the county is now complete. Surveys in the Dean found around 35 pairs in several years in the 1980s, and 1990 was described as an excellent year, with up to 50 pairs possibly breeding there, but the subsequent decline was astonishingly rapid and by 1997 there were no summer records.

Breeding may have occurred at Ashleworth Ham in three years in the mid-1990s, and a female was seen apparently carrying food on Cleeve Hill on May 2nd 2005 (surely too early to be feeding young), but since then there has been no suggestion of nesting.

Whinchats continue to breed in more northern and western parts of Britain, and they still occur regularly on passage in our county, albeit in much smaller numbers than in the past. They are far more frequent in autumn than in spring, perhaps by a factor of five. They are one of the later spring migrants, with the first arrivals normally in the second half of April. Autumn passage is quite protracted, with occasional birds appearing as early as July; the main period is through August and September, and nowadays the peak week might produce up to 30 records. Almost all are seen in the Vale and on the higher Cotswolds.

Sponsored by Andy Jayne

Stonechat (Eurasian Stonechat)
Saxicola torquatus

The Stonechat is a bird of more or less rough, uncultivated land: low-grade pasture, moorland and coasts, especially where there is gorse or bracken. It feeds on invertebrates, and it may often be seen watching from a low vantage point before dropping down to the ground to catch its prey. Stonechats occur patchily in southern and western Europe and eastwards through Asia. Western birds are largely resident, but further east in Europe an increasing proportion of birds leave their breeding grounds to winter around the western Mediterranean and on the North African coast. European numbers are estimated to be between 1.8 and 4.6 million pairs, and the species is now thought to have stabilised after a severe decline in the 1970s and 1980s.

Stonechats were widespread in the British Isles at the end of the nineteenth century (1875–1900 Atlas) but suffered a decline from then on, especially in England. This was due partly to a series of cold winters, but more recently and more irreversibly to agricultural intensification (BWP). Nowadays they occur most commonly in coastal and upland areas, and in southern England they are concentrated in extensive areas of heath such as the New Forest. The British population numbers around 15,000 pairs, though there are wide fluctuations. National BBS results show a strong increase during the run of mild winters in the 1990s and early 2000s, but a sharp decline since 2006.

Most British Stonechats remain here over the winter, though from September onwards some migrate south to the western Mediterranean. Year-round residency is a risky strategy for an invertebrate feeder, and cold winters often cause high mortality and population crashes. The compensating advantage is an early start to breeding, with many resident pairs producing three or more broods; migrants, returning in February or March, tend to produce two (1988–91 Breeding Atlas).

In Gloucestershire, Swaine described the Stonechat as 'formerly a widespread and not uncommon resident ... now very much scarcer.' Following a marked decline from the 1920s onwards the remaining small population had been virtually exterminated by the harsh winters of 1940–41 and 1947–48, and breeding was not recorded again in the county until 1958. Since then there have never been more than a handful of successful pairs in any year, and sometimes there have been no reports of breeding for several years at a stretch.

With their habit of perching prominently and giving frequent contact calls, it is unlikely that many Stonechats were missed during the atlas fieldwork. The top graph shows the detection rates during TTVs throughout the survey period. It reveals not only the difference between the number of birds present in winter and summer, but also the immediate and dramatic impact of the bouts of very cold

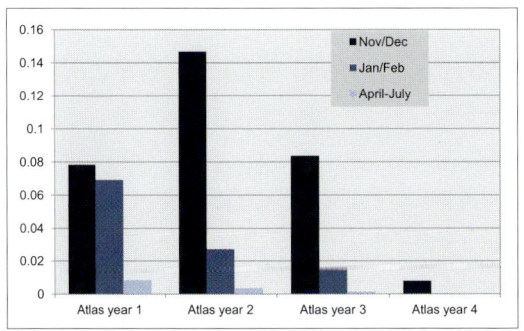

Stonechats recorded per hour in TTVs during atlas fieldwork.

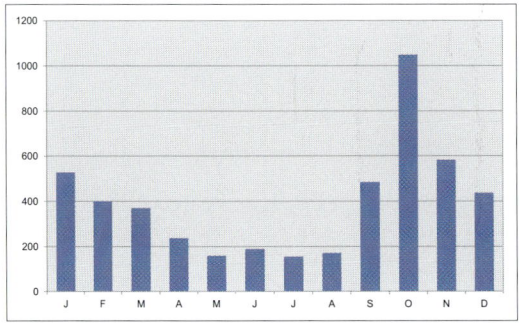

Stonechat numbers reported 2003–10, by month.

Sponsored by Arthur Ball, Miss Beatrice Gillam MBE, and the North Cotswold Ornithological Society

Species accounts

2007–11 Atlas fieldwork						Gloucestershire trends						UK population trends	
Number of tetrads in which recorded (max 683)					Occupied 10 km squares (max 26)				% of tetrads in which recorded (1st hour of TTV)		UK conservation status: Green	
	Total	Confirmed	Probable	Possible	Present	1968–71	1981–84	1988–91	2007–11	1988–91	2008–11	Long term	Short term
Breeding	30	7	3	8	12	3		1	6	0.2	0.9	–	+68%
Winter	196						5		26			–	–

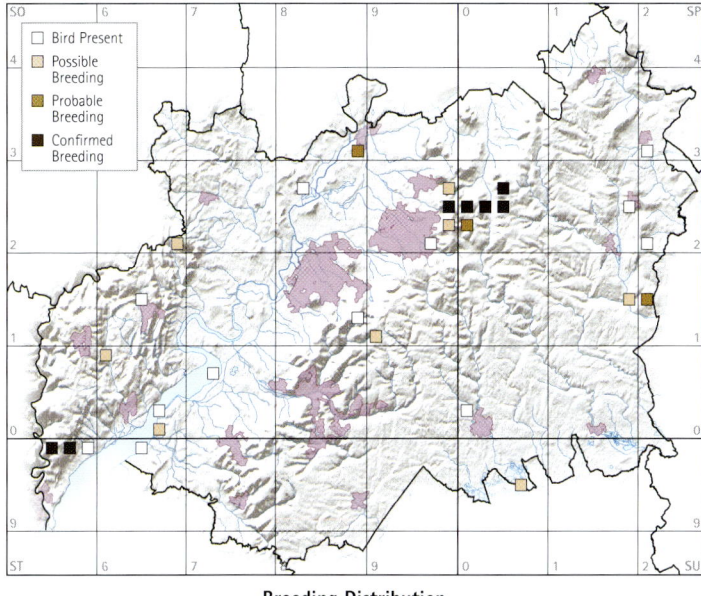

Breeding Distribution

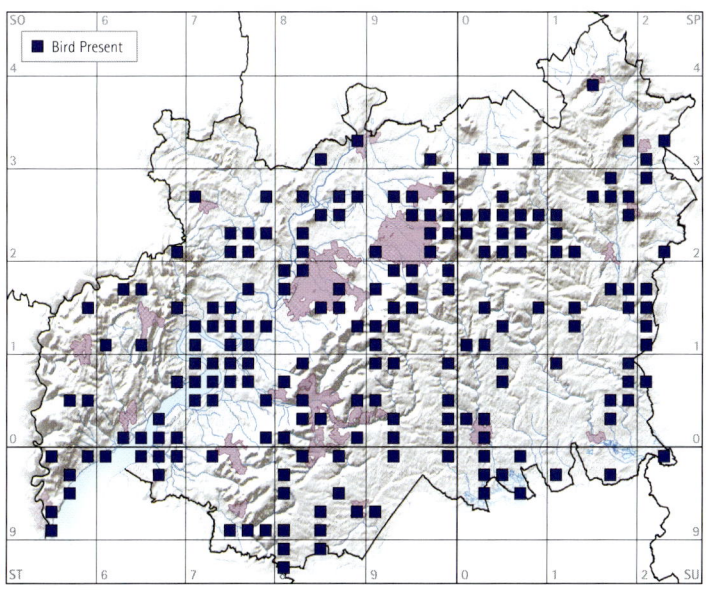

Winter Distribution

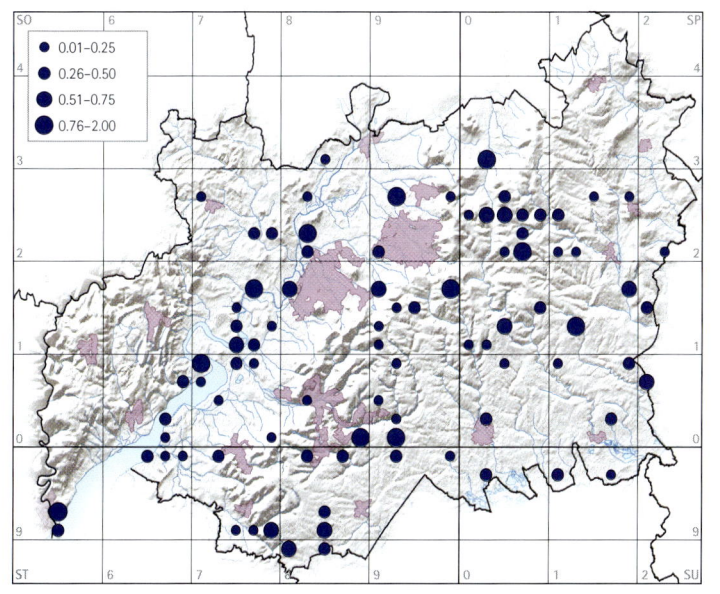

Winter Abundance

weather at the end of December 2008 and December 2009, which have resulted in the almost complete (though probably temporary) disappearance of the species from the county. Hence the great majority of sightings shown on the maps were recorded in the first 18 months of the four-year atlas period.

During the current survey breeding was confirmed at only two traditional sites in the county: Tidenham Chase in the Dean (ST59) and a more extensive area around Cleeve Common (SP02), where in the summer of 2011 a patient observer recorded a pair raising three broods. The young are estimated to have hatched in mid-April, June 6th and August 11th (Smith 2011).

There is a marked autumn passage through Gloucestershire, peaking in October (see bottom graph), with some birds remaining through the winter. The map shows a patchy but quite widespread distribution at this season, with nearly seven times as many tetrads occupied as in summer. There is a cluster of sightings along the Severn Vale, and there are also concentrations along some of the Cotswold river valleys. Cleeve Common also continues to be occupied in many winters, despite being so exposed.

Wheatear (Northern Wheatear)
Oenanthe oenanthe

Wheatears breed across most of Europe, much of northern and central Asia, and in Greenland and arctic North America. Virtually the entire world population winters in sub-Saharan Africa. Wheatears need rock crevices or burrows in which to nest close to insect-rich bare ground or short sward for foraging, and their breeding range includes a wide variety of open habitats such as tundra, moorland and more rocky upland areas. Marked population decreases in parts of western Europe, including southern England, are attributed to loss of habitat, mainly through cultivation and afforestation. British birds now mostly breed in the wilder north country, where they can occur at high densities, though they are still common on passage elsewhere.

According to Mellersh, Cotswold quarrymen drank 'an extra pint of beer all round' to celebrate the first Wheatear of spring, and they are still eagerly anticipated as (usually) the first spring migrant. In the nineteenth century they were common breeding birds in the Cotswolds, where the sheepwalks, stone walls and quarries provided the holes or burrows for nesting. In the Forest of Dean, quarries and mine-workings also held breeding pairs. A rapid decline appears to have started around the 1930s. At Cleeve Hill there were at least ten successful pairs in 1951, but by 1958 only a lone male was found (Andrew Bluett). By 1980 Swaine was describing Wheatears as mainly passage migrants in the county; a few pairs sometimes stayed to breed, but this was no longer an annual event. Since then, breeding has only occasionally been suspected and was last confirmed on Cleeve Hill in 2001.

Nevertheless this conspicuous bird is frequently recorded on spring and autumn passage from all parts of the county, and over the four years of the atlas period Wheatears were seen in nearly a quarter of all tetrads. They can turn up almost anywhere, but favoured habitats are well-grazed (or well-mown) grassland and bare arable land, so most are seen on the Cotswolds and also in the Severn Vale, where they tend to be found in fields adjacent to the river. Generally passage is more marked in spring, when groups of up to 20 birds can be seen and very occasionally more. The average first arrival date has advanced from March 15th in the 1980s to March 11th in the 2000s, which may well reflect a real change irrespective of any observer effects, while the earliest recorded date is February 25th, in 1994 and 2007. Autumn migration can begin as early as late July; a nestling ringed in Gwynedd on June 7th 1980 was killed by a cat 148 km to the south-east at Mitton, near Tewkesbury, on July 23rd that year. The last birds of the year are usually seen in early October and the latest date on record is November 15th 2009.

Sponsored by David Kennedy and Keith White

Bluethroat
Luscinia svecica

Bluethroats come in two forms (Red-spotted and White-spotted) and a complex assortment of subspecies. They have a rather patchy distribution in the more northerly parts of Eurasia and Alaska, with even a few Scottish breeding records. Some European birds winter in Iberia and the Mediterranean basin, while others migrate to sub-Saharan Africa. In Britain Bluethroats are scarce migrants at both seasons, mainly on the east coast and in the Northern Isles; inland records are unusual. Numbers here have declined since the 1970s, even though western European populations as a whole have tended to increase in recent decades. Swaine mentioned an authenticated Gloucestershire record from 1872 and an unsubstantiated one from 1875, and there were five more in the twentieth century:

- 1951: a male Red-spotted at Slimbridge on April 15th.
- 1975: another male Red-spotted in a garden at Brockworth (Gloucester) on May 23rd, which was caught and ringed.
- 1976: a female or immature at Slimbridge on October 30th.
- 1978: one, possibly two, at Frampton on April 22nd.
- 1993: a male White-spotted in a garden at Robinswood Hill, Gloucester, on April 29th.

In addition there was a report of one at a birdbath in Newent on May 15th 1976, but no details were submitted.

Red-breasted Flycatcher
Ficedula parva

This north Eurasian flycatcher is an annual passage migrant to Britain in small numbers, mostly during autumn. Inland records are very unusual. There have been two records in Gloucestershire:

- 1977: one on Churchdown Hill, Gloucester on September 25th.
- 1980: a female or first-winter at Slimbridge on September 19th.

The record of a pair at Fairford on August 21st 1935, mentioned by Swaine, is no longer considered to be acceptable.

Desert Wheatear
Oenanthe deserti

By the end of 2010 this wheatear of the arid regions of North Africa, the Middle East and central Asia had visited Britain 114 times. The bumper year of 1997 produced no fewer than 17 birds, including Gloucestershire's only record: a male at Bishop's Cleeve, Cheltenham on December 10th (Dymott 1997).

Dunnock
Prunella modularis

As a widespread and abundant bird with dull plumage and often secretive habits, this is not a species to inspire twitchers and it is often ignored except during organised surveys. However Dunnocks have attracted the attention of biologists for their very unusual mating system, involving complex variations on polygamy (Davies 1992). They are found throughout Europe from the Atlantic to the Urals. In western Europe they are resident; ringing has shown that only 5% of British birds move further than 5 km during their post-fledging dispersal. However in the north and east of their range they are summer visitors, moving south-westwards in autumn to winter amongst the residents of more temperate areas, or further south in the Mediterranean basin. Some from Scandinavia travel down the east coast of England in autumn, but few if any are thought to stay here.

Dunnocks in the British Isles prefer dense undergrowth, provided by scrub, hedgerows, coppice, or woodland with a shrub layer, in which to feed and nest. The species has been common throughout Britain at least since the nineteenth century (1875–1900 Atlas), and since 1945 it has been increasingly found in towns, possibly due to the proliferation of ornamental shrubs in suburban parks and gardens. From the mid-1970s to about 1990 there was a decline, which may have been due to woodland maturation and the negative impact of deer grazing (Fuller *et al.* 2005). Subsequently there has been a recovery and, although numbers are still at a lower level than prior to 1970, the British summer population was estimated at just over two million territories in 2000.

Dunnocks draw attention to themselves during the breeding season with frequent singing and conspicuous wing-flicking and chasing behaviour, and although they can be unobtrusive while feeding nestlings, the fledged young call fairly loudly and persistently. Singing and territorial behaviour were commonly recorded during the atlas fieldwork, and 'fledged young' was cited as proof of breeding in a third of all Gloucestershire tetrads where breeding behaviour was observed.

Swaine's impression was of a bird that was less common on the high, open wolds and also in the close, continuous woodland and plantations of the Forest of Dean. The present-day abundance maps certainly show a lower density on top of the Cotswolds at both seasons, and there are also some areas of lower abundance further down the dip-slope where fields are larger and hedgerows fewer. The heartland of the species in the county is perhaps the low-lying Severn Vale, including urban Gloucester. The highest TTV count during the atlas surveying was an impressive 44 birds in February 2009 in tetrad SO72I, on the edge of Newent.

In the area covered by the Cotswolds Atlases a slight increase in the number of tetrads where Dunnocks were found, from 270 to 300 between 1987 and 2007, was thought to be almost certainly due to better coverage. However BBS figures for Gloucestershire as a whole also suggest a slight increase, with records in about 80% of survey squares each year in the mid-1990s and about 90% more recently. The NCOS winter survey, confined to the Cotswolds, also indicates a very slight increase, from an average of 2.6 birds per square kilometre in 1995–2003 to 3.0 in 2004–10. The periods of severe winter weather during the survey period do not appear to have had a noticeable negative impact on Dunnocks in the county.

Ringing recovery data emphasise how sedentary Dunnocks are: there have been no recoveries outside the county of birds ringed in Gloucestershire, and only two ringed in other counties have been recovered here, from neighbouring 'Hereford & Worcester' and Wiltshire.

Sponsored by Julie Harper

Species accounts

2007–11 Atlas fieldwork						Gloucestershire trends						UK population trends		
Number of tetrads in which recorded (max 683)					*Occupied 10 km squares (max 26)*				*% of tetrads in which recorded (1st hour of TTV)*		*UK conservation status:* **Amber 3**	
	Total	Confirmed	Probable	Possible	Present	1968–71	1981–84	1988–91	2007–11	1988–91	2008–11	Long term	Short term
Breeding	680	356	222	100	2	26		26	26	82.8	92.2	−29%	+24%
Winter	676						26		26			–	–

Breeding Distribution

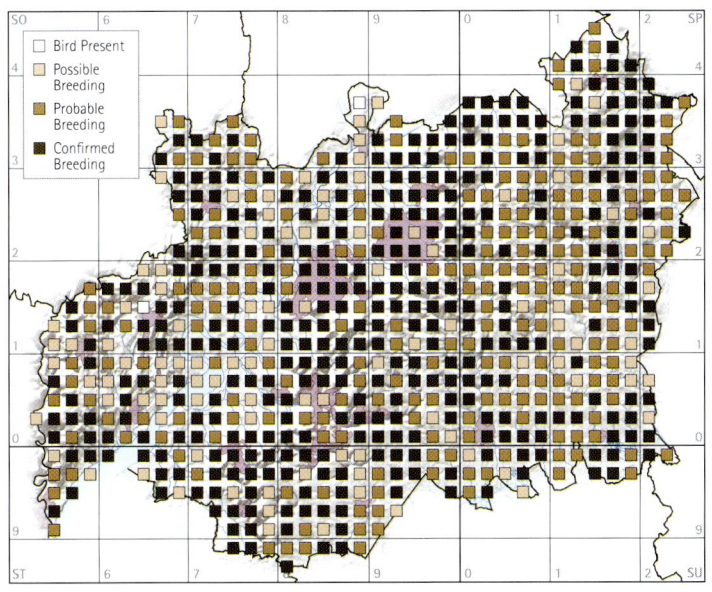

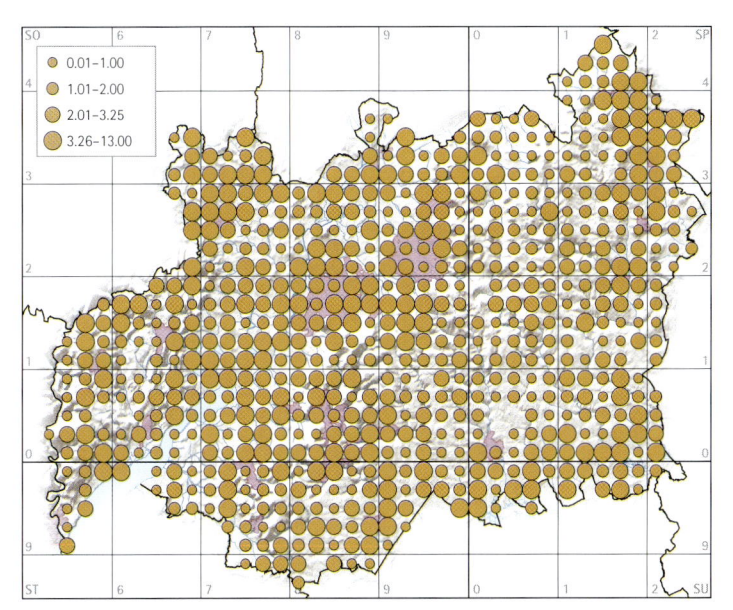

Summer Abundance

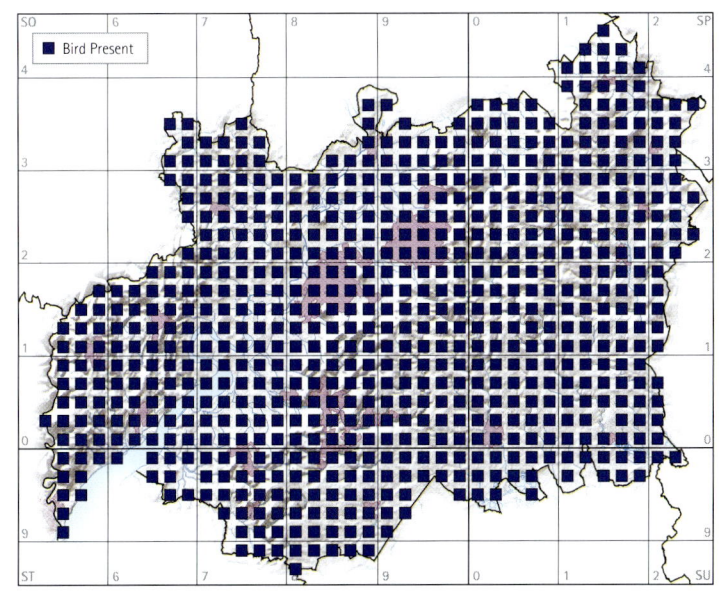

Winter Distribution

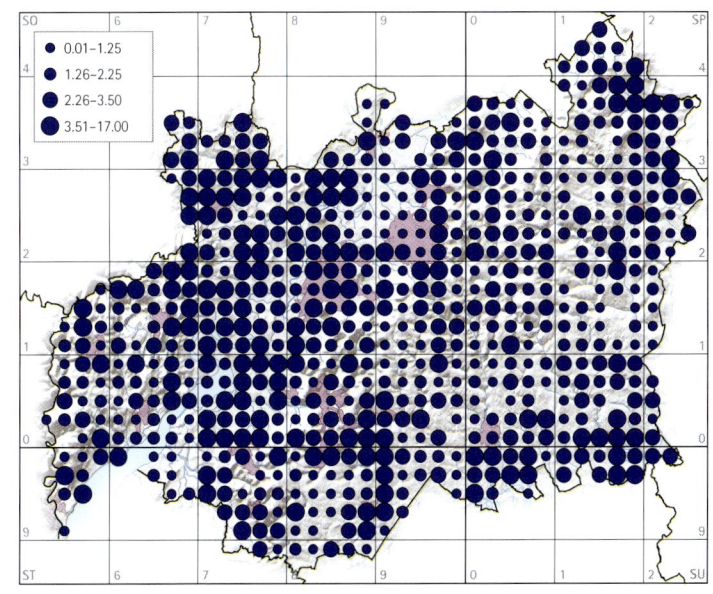

Winter Abundance

House Sparrow
Passer domesticus

One of the most abundant passerines in the world, House Sparrows are almost invariably associated with human settlements and demonstrate a remarkable capacity to adapt their feeding and nesting behaviour to benefit from whatever opportunities are available. They occur naturally across much of Eurasia, being absent from only the harshest environments and some small Atlantic islands. As a result of introductions, both deliberate and accidental, they are also well established in the Americas, Australasia, sub-Saharan Africa and many oceanic islands.

In Britain, House Sparrows were evidently extremely numerous at least from medieval times. They have long been regarded as a pest and a bounty was often paid for dead birds; sparrow pie was a common rural dish in Britain up to the time of the First World War and various trapping methods have been documented.

Mellersh described House Sparrows gathering in cornfields on the edges of towns in the Severn Vale in autumn, noting that 'on the borders of one large field of grain, no fewer than two thousand birds were killed, having been caught chiefly in basket-traps'. Such numbers are completely unknown now, but as recently as 1982 Swaine described the House Sparrow as a very common resident and stated that 'considerable flocks' were to be found in late summer and autumn. Indeed, in citing the above reference from Mellersh he commented simply that 'the species still does much damage to agriculture'.

Since then they have suffered a huge and well-publicised decrease in numbers, although the precise causes are not yet fully understood. The 1988–91 Breeding Atlas survey revealed that there had already been a fall of about 15% nationally since 1972, but this accelerated rapidly thereafter with estimated further declines of as much as two-thirds in some parts of the country. In Gloucestershire, although numbers have certainly fallen, neither the Cotswolds Atlas data nor the county results from the national atlas surveys imply a decline of such magnitude. The 2003–07 Cotswolds Atlas speculated that populations may have reached a low point in the mid to late 1990s (between the two local atlas periods), with something of a recovery since then. However the Gloucestershire Garden Bird Survey indicates a gradual but significant decrease since the late 1990s, though again there is the suggestion of a slight recovery in very recent years. Gloucestershire BBS data show no clear trends between 1994 and 2010, possibly because they are based only on presence or absence data rather than numbers of birds.

The maps show that despite the decreases House Sparrows are still widespread, and they were one of the most frequently encountered birds in atlas fieldwork; their familiar loud chirping calls make them easy to detect. They are still present in the most urban parts of the county as well as in many villages, and they are still a very familiar garden bird. On the Cotswolds and elsewhere they inhabit isolated farms and hamlets as well as larger villages, but the abundance maps show that the highest densities occur in the lower-lying parts of the county; they are less common on higher ground and they are not found in the densely wooded areas of the Forest of Dean. The largest number encountered during a TTV was 162 in June 2009 in tetrad SO92T in the Bishop's Cleeve area – a far cry from the thousands mentioned by Mellersh, but nonetheless a healthy number to find in the breeding season.

Sponsored by Viv Phillips

Species accounts

2007–11 Atlas fieldwork					Gloucestershire trends						UK population trends	
Number of tetrads in which recorded (max 683)					Occupied 10 km squares (max 26)				% of tetrads in which recorded (1st hour of TTV)		UK conservation status: **Red 3**	
	Total	Confirmed	Probable	Possible	Present	1968–71	1981–84	1988–91	2007–11	1988–91	2008–11	Long term	Short term
Breeding	614	495	72	37	10	26		26	26	76.5	69.9	−66%	−6%
Winter	611						26		26			–	–

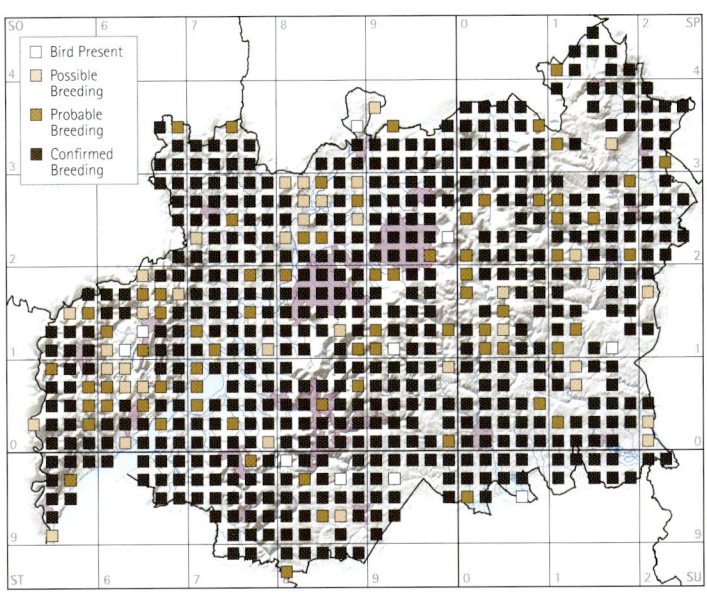

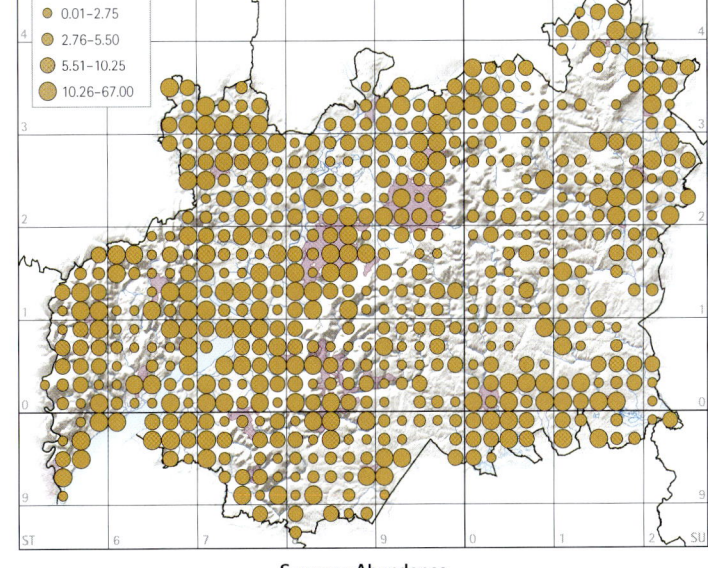

Breeding Distribution

Summer Abundance

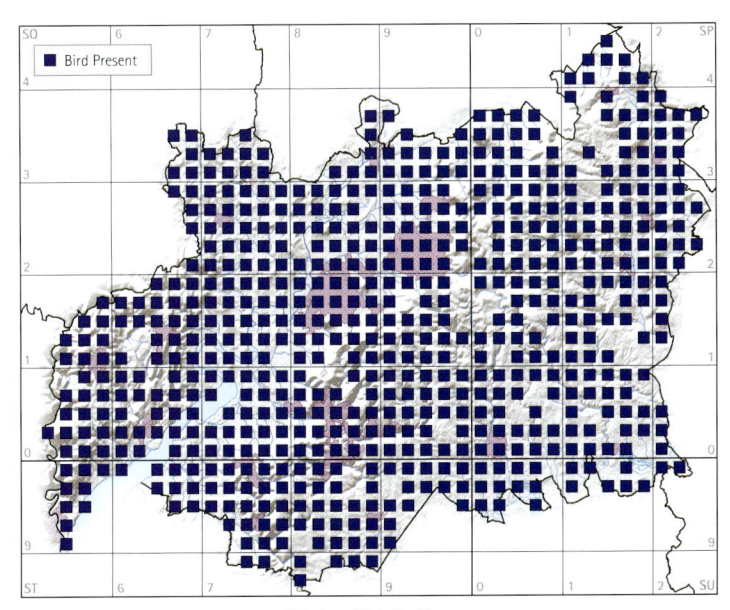

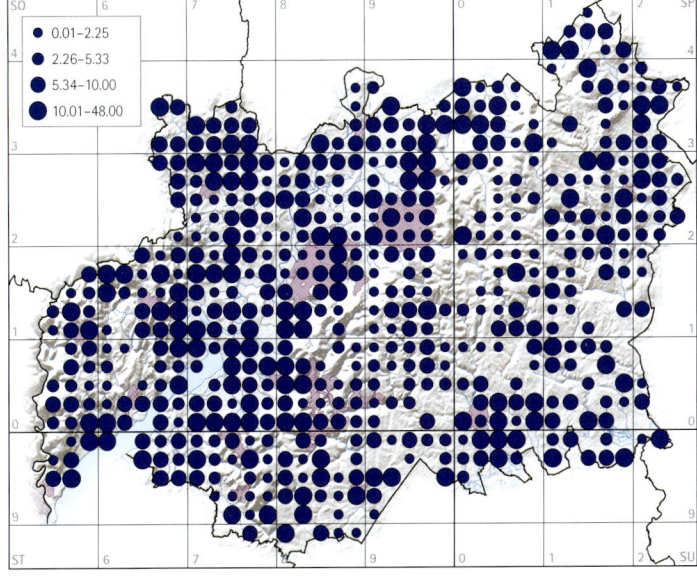

Winter Distribution

Winter Abundance

Tree Sparrow (Eurasian Tree Sparrow)
Passer montanus

Ranging over much of the Palearctic including most European countries, Tree Sparrows are mainly resident, although they sometimes undertake dispersive movements. Their preferred habitat is more or less wooded open country, including various types of farmland, in temperate or warm climates. They also require holes for nesting, usually but not always in trees. In Europe they are not usually found in towns, but in parts of the Far East they are common urban birds, filling a similar ecological niche to that occupied by House Sparrows in the west.

The history of the Tree Sparrow in the British Isles has been one of quite wide fluctuations in range and numbers (1988–91 Breeding Atlas). In general, populations were at high levels from the 1880s to the 1930s and again from about 1960 to 1978, with a low point around 1950 when they became temporarily extinct in Ireland and decreased considerably in Scotland. At the time of the 1968–72 Breeding Atlas they were still slowly extending their range, but from about 1978 onward a more noticeable and extended decline set in which has continued until very recently. However since about 1990 there has again been a modest recovery at the national level. The causes of these fluctuations are not well understood, but declines during the last 30 years or so are likely to be at least partly due to the intensification of farming; the more recent improvement could possibly be associated with the introduction of agri-environment schemes.

Writing around the beginning of the latest decline, Swaine stated that Tree Sparrows were 'more plentiful than is often realised, and distributed at least thinly in all parts' of Gloucestershire, with 'flocks of up to 300 birds' being reported from both the Severn Vale and the Cotswolds in winter. Since then numbers in the county have plummeted, as shown by the figures in the fact-box. Tree Sparrows are now completely absent from most districts, being virtually confined to parts of the Cotswolds and a very limited area of the Dean plateau. In the area covered by the Cotswolds Atlases there was a 27% decrease in occupancy from 59 to 43 tetrads in the 20 years up to 2007, and during the present survey they were only found in 19 tetrads in that part of the county during the breeding season. At the same time, there appears to have been a shift in the distribution's centre of gravity towards the south-east, where the Cotswold dip-slope borders the Thames Area. The colonisation of 10 km square SP23, which took place mainly between the two Cotswolds Atlas periods, was probably only temporary. On the Dean plateau, Tree Sparrows were found in just one tetrad during the breeding season, although in winter there were records from a few more tetrads around St Briavels and the situation in this part of the county might not be quite as dire as the breeding season map suggests. The very few records from tetrads outside the Cotswolds and the Dean at both seasons could possibly represent tiny breeding populations, but are more likely to be due to wandering individuals. The highest TTV count was of 12 birds in January 2008 in tetrad SP10R near Fairford.

In conclusion, Tree Sparrows have continued to decline at a near-catastrophic rate in Gloucestershire, and there is as yet no evidence that the recent improvement in the species' national status is being reflected here.

Sponsored by Fraser Hart

Species accounts

	2007–11 Atlas fieldwork					Gloucestershire trends						UK population trends	
	Number of tetrads in which recorded (max 683)					Occupied 10 km squares (max 26)				% of tetrads in which recorded (1st hour of TTV)		*UK conservation status:* **Red 3**	
	Total	Confirmed	Probable	Possible	Present	1968–71	1981–84	1988–91	2007–11	1988–91	2008–11	Long term	Short term
Breeding	28	8	7	7	6	26		20	8	7.5	1.0	–92%	+73%
Winter	37						26		13			–	–

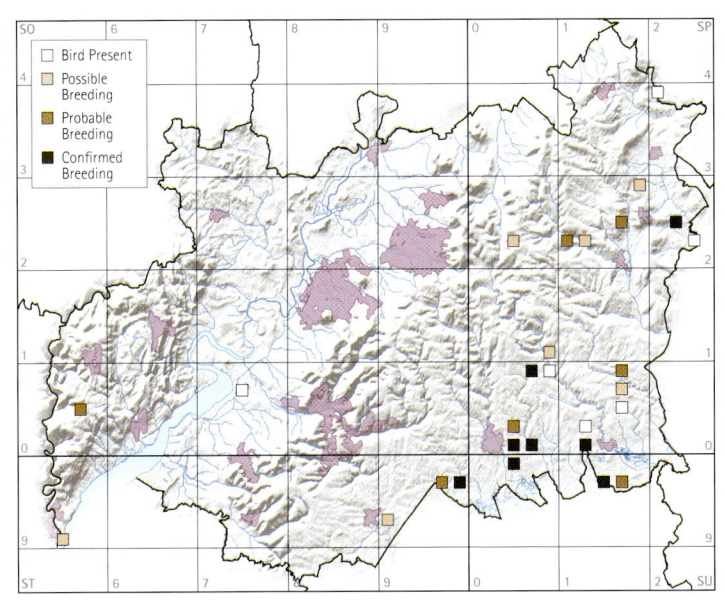

Breeding Distribution

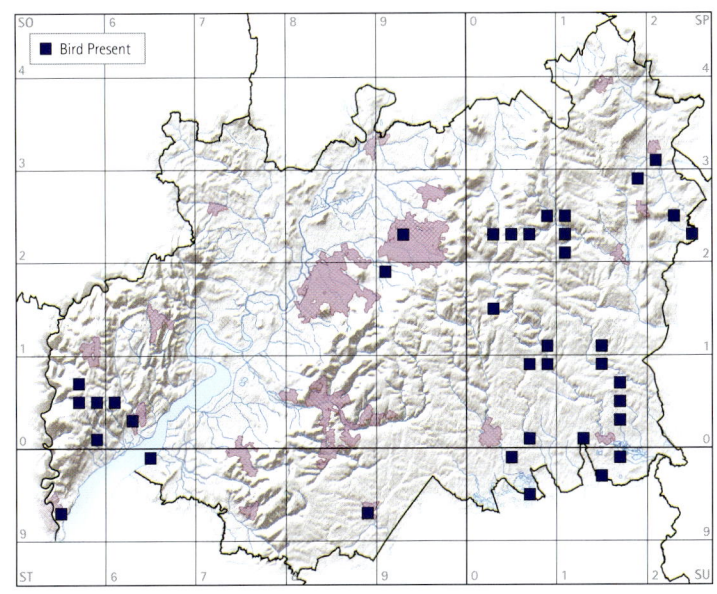

Winter Distribution

Yellow Wagtail (Western Yellow Wagtail)
Motacilla flava

Yellow Wagtails breed right across Europe and Asia, even extending into western Alaska. There are many subspecies, often with strikingly different head markings. Our local yellow-headed race *M. f. flavissima* breeds in England, eastern Wales and southern Scotland, and also on the coasts of Norway, Denmark and France. It sometimes hybridises with other subspecies, notably the more widespread Blue-headed Wagtail *M. f. flava*. Most Yellow Wagtails are long-distance migrants, and British birds winter in western Africa.

With bright plumage, a distinctive call and a tendency to perch on telegraph wires, Yellow Wagtails are conspicuous. Moreover they openly carry food to their young, resulting in a high proportion of confirmed and probable breeding records during the atlas survey. On the other hand, they often nest in large arable fields, distant from public rights of way, so some pairs will have been missed.

The 1968–72 Breeding Atlas described Yellow Wagtails as being 'almost invariably associated with water' using 'damp water meadows and marshy fields along river valleys and freshwater marshes on the coast'. The 1988–91 Breeding Atlas added that some pairs bred in cereal crops. By the late 1990s a study in eastern England found that arable crops, especially spring-sown potatoes and peas, were becoming particularly important habitats (Mason & Macdonald 2000), and Yellow Wagtails are now just as likely to be found nesting in cereals, legumes and other crops as in wet grassland.

This switch in habitat preference has occurred during a severe decline in the British population, with numbers falling by around three-quarters in just 40 years or so. The conservation status changed from green to amber and then to red in just eight years between 2001 and 2009.

In the late nineteenth century the lower Severn and Avon valleys were one of the national strongholds (1875–1900 Atlas) and in 1902 Mellersh described the Yellow Wagtail as one of the species 'whose chief haunts are in the Vale and not elsewhere in the county'. Swaine said 'breeding is largely restricted to riverside fields and marshes', adding that Yellow Wagtails were 'scarce or absent on the higher ground of the Cotswolds'. Not until the 1983–87 Cotswolds Atlas do we find any reference to nesting in legumes, but the 2003–07 Cotswolds Atlas described this as a 'distinct liking', noting a shift from river valleys to the higher arable farmland. Alongside these rapid changes in habitat preference, the local data also reveal a relentless decline in overall numbers.

As the maps show, Yellow Wagtails continue to breed in the Vale, but they are possibly more widespread on the high arable farmland of the Cotswolds, albeit rather thinly scattered and in small numbers. They will breed in cereals, but nowadays probably the best chance of discovering nesting Yellow Wagtails in Gloucestershire is to find a large field of broad beans or potatoes, preferably one crossed by telegraph wires.

They also occur as passage migrants in spring and autumn, especially by the Severn Estuary. The earliest date on record for the county is March 11th 1989, but they usually appear in the first week of April, with records in single figures throughout the month. Return migration produces the highest totals in late August or

Sponsored by Fraser Hart and by the North Cotswold Ornithological Society

Species accounts

2007–11 Atlas fieldwork					Gloucestershire trends				UK population trends	
Number of tetrads in which recorded (max 683)					Occupied 10 km squares (max 26)				UK conservation status: Red 3	
	Total	Confirmed	Probable	Possible	Present	1968–71	1981–84	1988–91	2007–11	1988–91	2008–11	Long term	Short term
Breeding	157	46	38	36	37	17		17	22	7.1	3.5	–75%	–55%
Winter	0							0		0		–	–

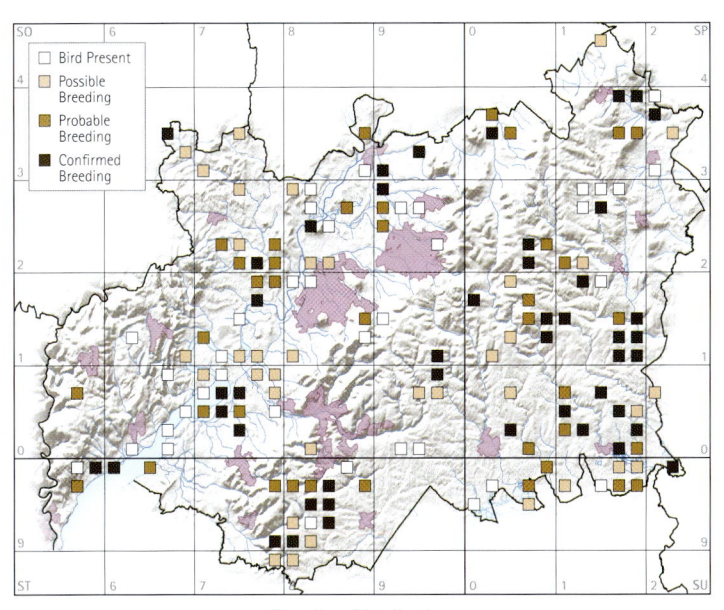

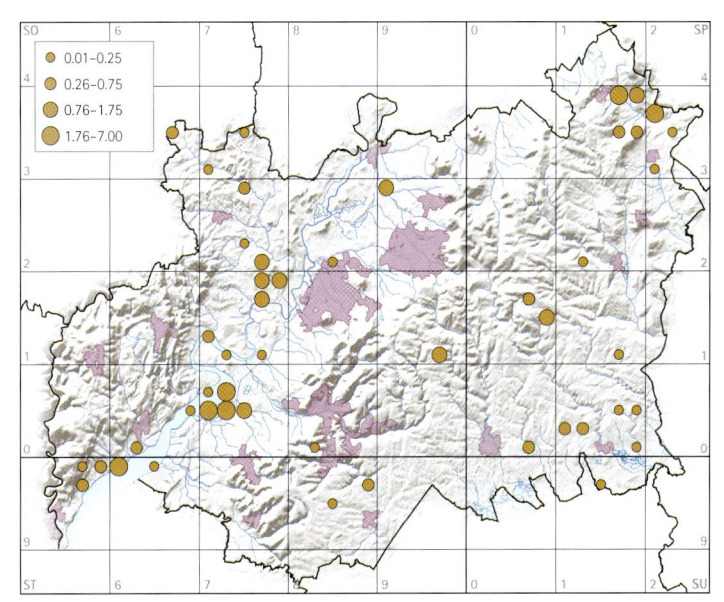

Breeding Distribution

Summer Abundance

early September, although inevitably numbers have declined in line with the national pattern and nowadays there are only a few dates each year when ten or more are seen. Notable recent maxima have included 30 at Lydney New Grounds on August 21st 2004 and 33 at Guscar Rocks on August 23rd 2009. The last birds of the year are normally recorded in early October; in 1995 one was seen on November 4th, and in 1981 an unusually late bird was caught for ringing in a Pied Wagtail roost on November 22nd.

Blue-headed Wagtails occur in the county in most springs, although numbers have been low recently, with no records in 2002, 2004, 2007 or 2008. Just one or two birds are normally seen, usually along the estuary. Mixed pairings with *flavissima* were recorded in the Thames Area in 1972, 1973, 1993 and 1994, and also suspected at Tiltups End near Nailsworth in 1994.

There are also two county records of Grey-headed Wagtails *M. f. thunbergi* from Fennoscandia, at Slimbridge on May 28th 1969 and at Frampton 100 Acre on May 10th 2001, and birds showing characteristics of the less distinctive central Asian subspecies *M. f. beema* (Sykes's Wagtail) were seen in 1982, 1996 and (possibly a hybrid) 1998.

Grey Wagtail
Motacilla cinerea

Grey Wagtails are more closely associated with water than the other wagtails, and in most parts of their breeding range these smart, active birds favour mountainous or hilly areas, inhabiting the same kind of shallow, fast-flowing streams that are used by Dippers. They occur very widely across the Palearctic where there is suitable habitat, including most of continental Europe and southern Scandinavia, and they are one of the few land-birds to breed in the Azores. They also breed on lowland watercourses, including canals, with man-made features such as weirs and locks (BWP). In Britain, Grey Wagtails are not shy and they often nest near humans, even in city centres. A much wider range of habitats is used in winter, notably sewage works and farmyards, especially those with slurry pits.

In many parts of their range they are wholly migratory, but in Britain they are partial migrants: birds from northern breeding areas migrate further south than their more southern counterparts, and some British breeders winter as far south as Iberia. In addition, birds nesting at high altitudes may make relatively short movements to winter lower down.

Grey Wagtails extended their European range significantly in the second half of the nineteenth century, perhaps because industrialisation provided habitat in new areas, and this expansion included the colonisation of lowland England (1875–1900 Atlas). Mellersh stated that Gloucestershire was on the extreme eastern edge of the species' range at that time, and they bred 'only exceptionally' on the Cotswolds. By Swaine's time though, they bred 'on suitable streams and rivers in most parts of the county, notably along the Wye Valley ... and along Cotswold rivers'.

In the current survey many atlas fieldworkers discovered that whatever the season, wherever you find suitable habitat you will find Grey Wagtails. In addition, they are usually conspicuous and vocal, and their distinctive calls and behaviour mean that few will have been overlooked. In the breeding season they can often be seen carrying food for their nestlings, and this is one of the species for which it was relatively easy to confirm breeding.

Like other insectivorous species, Grey Wagtails are vulnerable to hard winters, making it difficult to set baselines to monitor numbers. Anecdotal reports from atlas surveyors suggest that numbers in the third and fourth atlas breeding seasons were unusually low, following two hard winters, and this appears to be reflected in the data as a whole, which show an overall decline in the county since the last atlas period. However most national indicators, and the two Cotswolds Atlases, point to a general increase in recent times.

In the breeding season Grey Wagtails appear to be most numerous in the Forest of Dean and also along the Cotswold scarp, for example in the Stroud valleys where mills and old canal workings are used. On the high wold it is easy to match breeding records with the courses of the Cotswold streams. The winter maps show just how much more widespread this species is in winter and reveal the shift away from higher ground to the low-lying areas of the Severn Vale.

Overall, the month with the highest number of Grey Wagtail records in the county over the last ten years is October, suggesting that some migrating birds pass through. Certainly there is anecdotal evidence that garden ponds are most likely to be visited in the autumn. More unusual was a pair that regularly visited a garden bird table in Cheltenham in February 2003.

Of the six Grey Wagtail ringing recoveries involving Gloucestershire up to 2010, two showed movements of more than 100 km. An adult female ringed in the Forest of Dean in late July 2001 was found dead in Hampshire in December 2003, presumably having wintered there. More unexpectedly, another female ringed in the county in early August 1976 was found drowned 108 km away in Wiltshire in May the following year, suggesting a possible change of breeding area.

Sponsored by Peter Witchell, and in memory of John Tweedy

Species accounts 391

2007–11 Atlas fieldwork					Gloucestershire trends						UK population trends
Number of tetrads in which recorded (max 683)					Occupied 10 km squares (max 26)				% of tetrads in which recorded (1st hour of TTV)		UK conservation status: **Amber 3**
	Total	Confirmed	Probable	Possible	Present	1968–71	1981–84	1988–91	2007–11	1988–91	2008–11	Long term	Short term
Breeding	218	86	43	49	40	25		23	25	14.2	9.5	−35%	+15%
Winter	341						24		26			–	–

Breeding Distribution

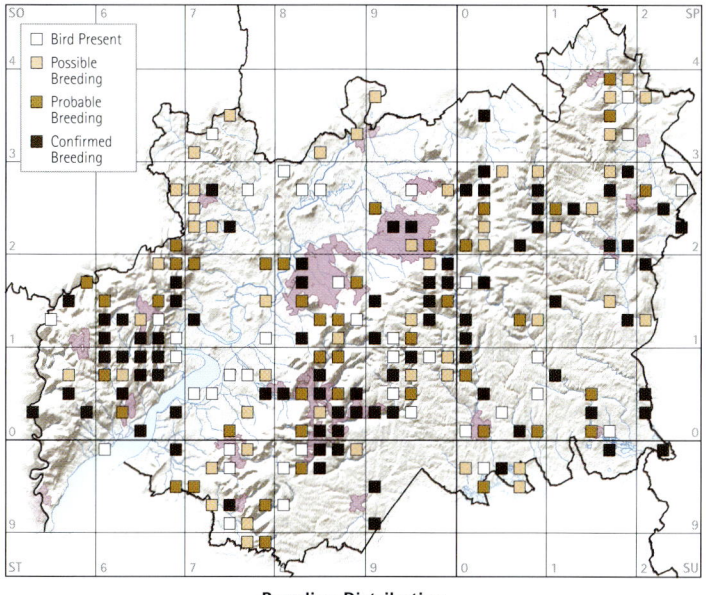

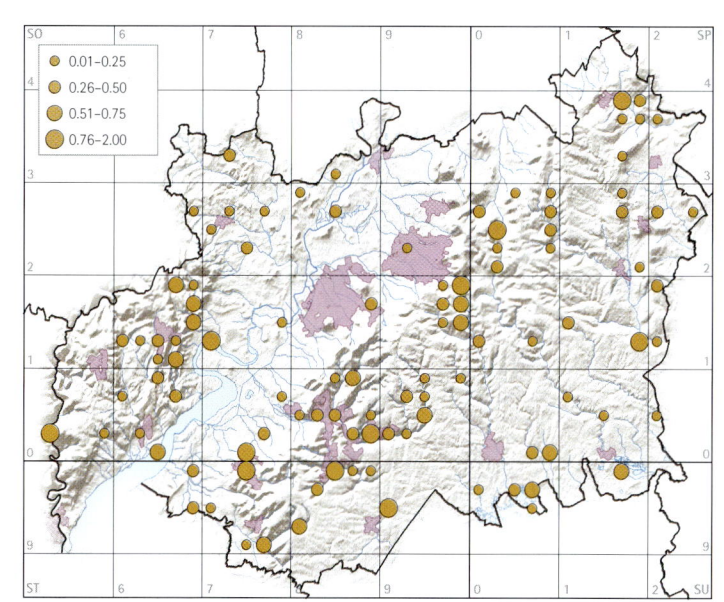

Summer Abundance

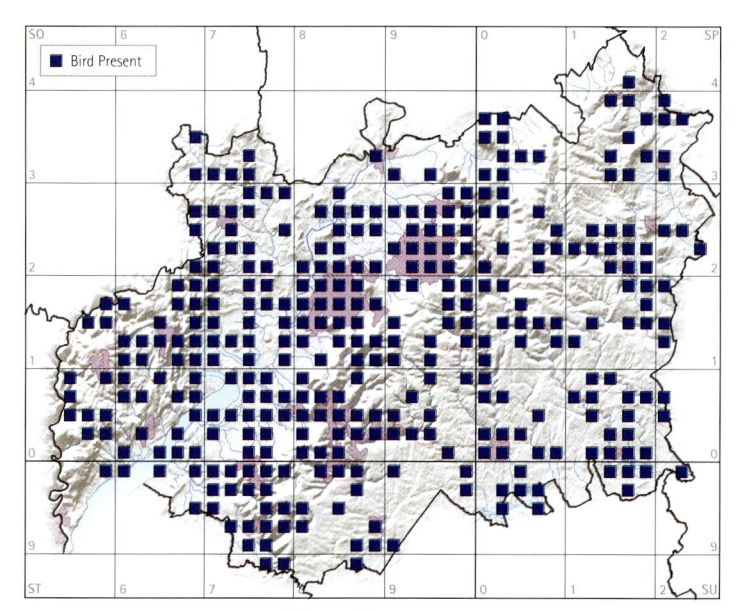

Winter Distribution

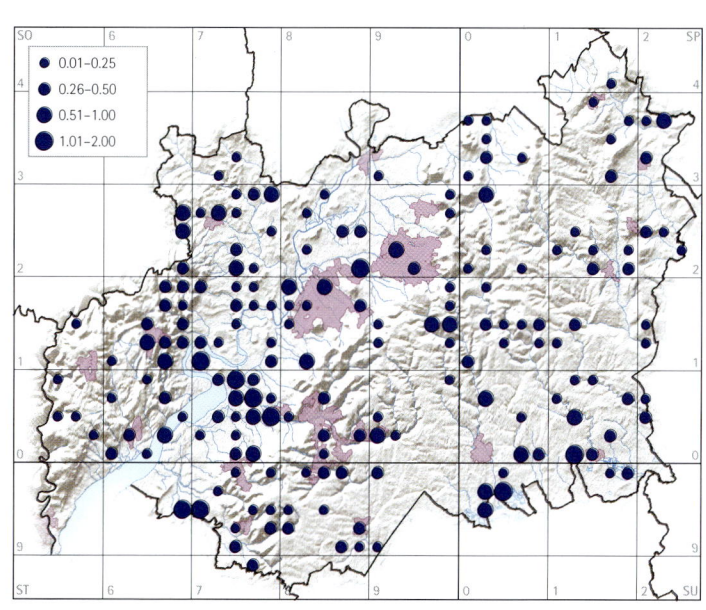

Winter Abundance

Pied and White Wagtail
Motacilla alba

There are about a dozen races in the White Wagtail complex, breeding from Greenland right across Eurasia to Alaska and as far south as Morocco, Asia Minor and Indo-China. The dark subspecies *M. a. yarrellii*, our familiar Pied Wagtail, is largely restricted to the British Isles, whereas *M. a. alba*, the White Wagtail, breeds across much of the rest of Europe, including Iceland and Fennoscandia, and very occasionally in Britain.

Over most of its range this species is migratory, and northern White Wagtails winter in the Mediterranean basin and tropical Africa. Some move through Britain on migration; indeed it is now recognised that in autumn roosts in Scotland, Whites may often outnumber Pieds (Forrester *et al.* 2007). Most northern British breeding birds winter in southern England or the western French coasts, while southern breeders are largely resident, although some move to Portugal and southern Spain. In all areas there is a withdrawal from higher altitude breeding grounds, where insect prey may be scarce in colder weather.

Pied Wagtails are found near human settlements year-round, perching conspicuously on the roofs of barns, houses and other buildings. Their bounding flight and their call are very recognisable, so this is a species which will often have revealed itself to atlas surveyors. In the breeding season adults are often easily seen carrying food to nests or young birds, so that confirming breeding was easier than for many other passerines. In winter, Pied Wagtails roost communally in large numbers, often in trees in well-lit areas such as town centres, supermarket car parks and motorway service stations; natural sites such as reed-beds are also used. However winter flocks feeding quietly on farmland are far less conspicuous, and some may have been overlooked.

In Britain, Pied Wagtails have increased in recent times and all indicators suggest that Gloucestershire is typical. The 2003–07 Cotswolds Atlas suggested a 'real and marked expansion' in that area, adding that most farmyards, stables, industrial or workshop sites, water treatment works and similar habitats supported breeding wagtails, often with more than one pair involved. Given that Swaine implied that there were few breeding pairs on the higher Cotswolds, it does seem that a genuine expansion has taken place.

The maps confirm that Pied Wagtails are widespread breeders in the county, and also indicate the markedly higher numbers in the low-lying areas in the Severn Vale in the winter, presumably reflecting migrants from further north. Reports sent to the county recorder reveal a definite peak in October, suggesting a significant passage through the county.

In the 1970s the ponds on the green in Frampton village held the largest winter roost, with 1,000–1,500 birds there in autumn 1978, but urban areas are now preferred. Trees in and around the Promenade, Cheltenham, held up to 1,150 in 1998–99, and a detailed study there revealed frequent movements between at least four different roost sites and, at one point, an almost complete switch to a previously unused fifth site (Michael Sutcliffe). Since 2002 the reported maxima have fallen and it may be that the birds are dispersed more widely, although the changing behaviour of observers could also be involved. Wagtail roosts are an aspect of county birdlife that would repay further study.

White Wagtails *M. a. alba* occur annually on passage at both seasons, although most sightings are in spring when birds are in more easily identifiable breeding plumage, and April alone has produced 60% of all records. In an average recent year there have been around ten reports in spring and five in autumn. Usually only one or two birds are involved, but higher numbers are not unknown. Most are seen in the Severn Vale and by the estuary, though this may reflect the distribution of observers.

Roosting Pied Wagtails are easily caught in mist-nets, and the resulting high British ringing totals had generated about 100 recoveries involving Gloucestershire by 2010. Fifty-five movements were within the county, and about 40 involved other British localities as far away as the Scottish highlands. Two locally ringed nestlings moved to north-west and south-west France in their first winters, and a juvenile ringed near Cheltenham in August 1961 was trapped in northern Spain the following January; this bird was more likely to have been a White Wagtail.

Sponsored by Graham Champken, Margaret Jennings and Mary Pegler

Species accounts   393

2007–11 Atlas fieldwork						Gloucestershire trends						UK population trends	
Number of tetrads in which recorded (max 683)						*Occupied 10 km squares (max 26)*				*% of tetrads in which recorded (1st hour of TTV)*		*UK conservation status:* **Green**	
	Total	Confirmed	Probable	Possible	Present	1968–71	1981–84	1988–91	2007–11	1988–91	2008–11	Long term	Short term
Breeding	590	280	91	170	49	26		26	26	35.9	41.3	–	–
Winter	612						26		26			–	–

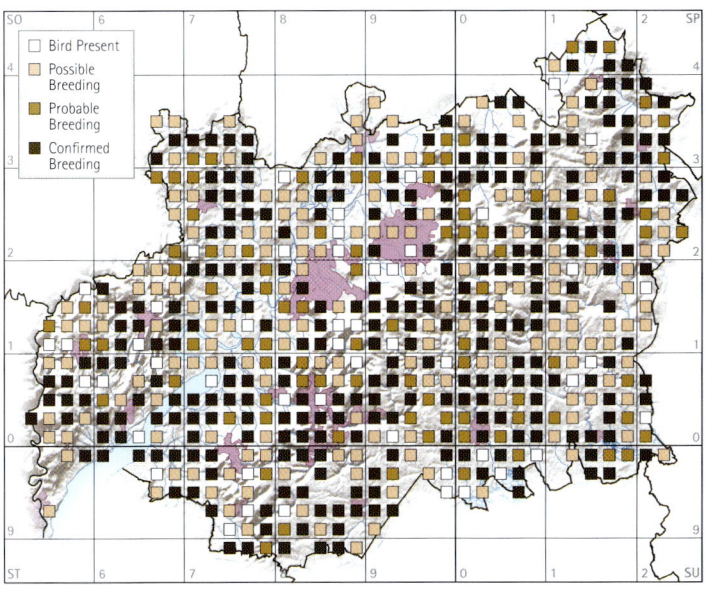

Breeding Distribution

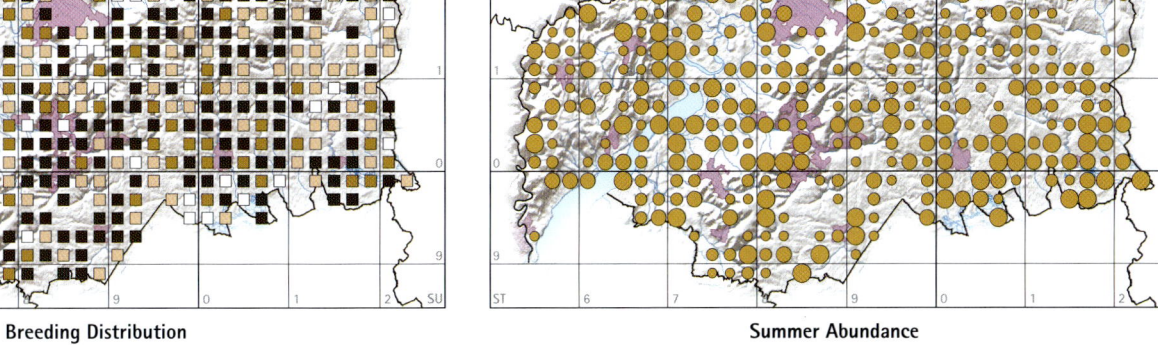

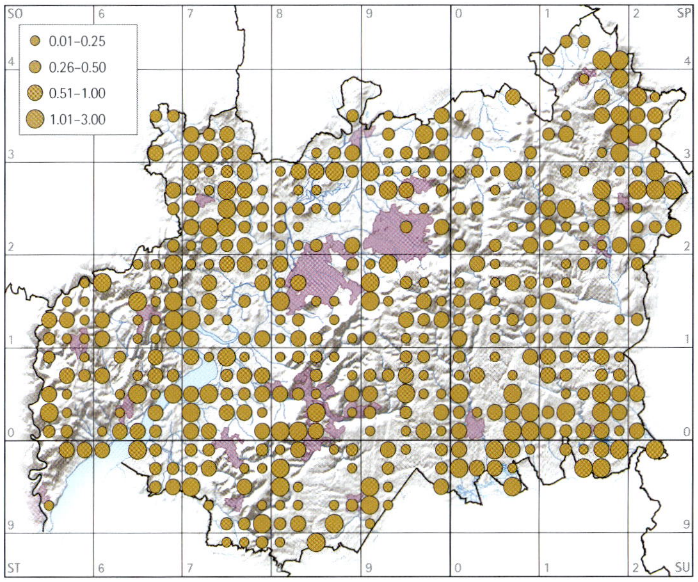

Summer Abundance

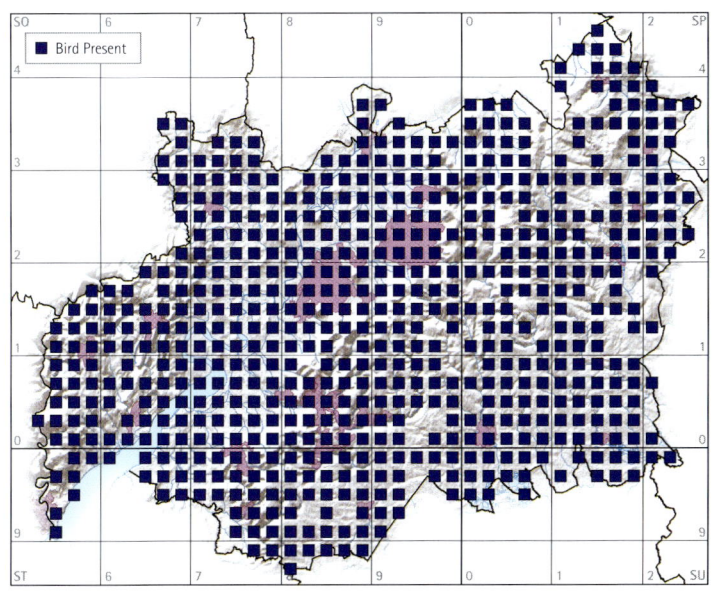

Winter Distribution

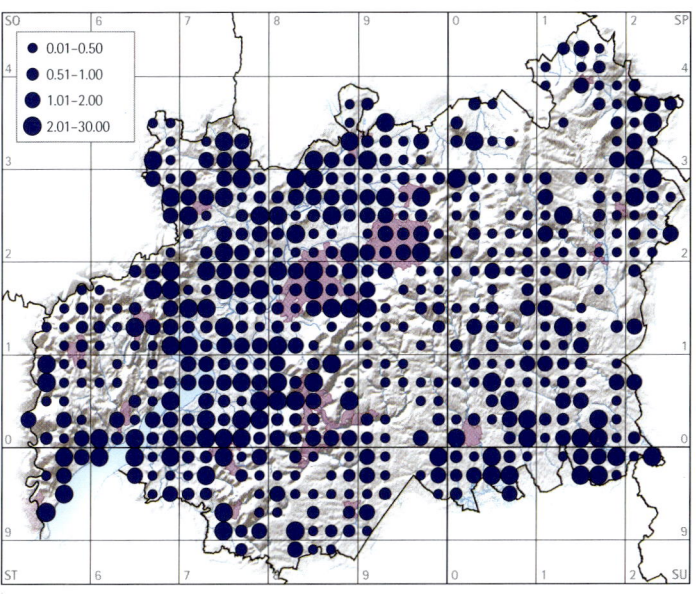

Winter Abundance

Tree Pipit
Anthus trivialis

Tree Pipits breed in most of continental Europe, eastwards across Siberia, and as far south as the Caspian Sea and the Himalayas. European breeders winter in Africa, south of the Sahara.

Uniquely among pipits and wagtails in the Western Palearctic, trees and bushes that can be used as song-posts and vantage points are just as important to this species as is the open ground that provides nest sites and suitable foraging terrain. The highest breeding densities are found in upland areas, and plantations in their first few years of growth are widely used.

In Britain, Tree Pipits significantly expanded their range northwards through Scotland in the first half of the twentieth century, but a decline in southern England started around 1930. Since then numbers have fallen dramatically, with a steeply negative long-term trend.

In Gloucestershire this is one of the earlier summer visitors to arrive and the first returning birds are usually reported in the first week of April (earliest March 21st 1990). Migrants on passage are reported fairly widely at sites away from the breeding areas, especially in autumn. The median last date in the county since 1980 is September 12th, and in only four years have there been any October records, the latest being on October 22nd 2000.

Although Tree Pipits are very similar in appearance to Meadow Pipits, their delightful song is distinctive and it is unlikely that many birds will have been overlooked during atlas fieldwork (see Meadow Pipit, p. 396, for more details).

Sponsored by the North Cotswold Ornithological Society

Species accounts

| | 2007–11 Atlas fieldwork ||||| Gloucestershire trends |||||| UK population trends ||
| | Number of tetrads in which recorded (max 683) ||||| Occupied 10 km squares (max 26) |||| % of tetrads in which recorded (1st hour of TTV) || UK conservation status: **Red 3** ||
	Total	Confirmed	Probable	Possible	Present	1968–71	1981–84	1988–91	2007–11	1988–91	2008–11	Long term	Short term
Breeding	97	24	31	31	11	24		18	17	15.2	4.4	–75%	–13%
Winter	0							0	0			–	–

Breeding Distribution

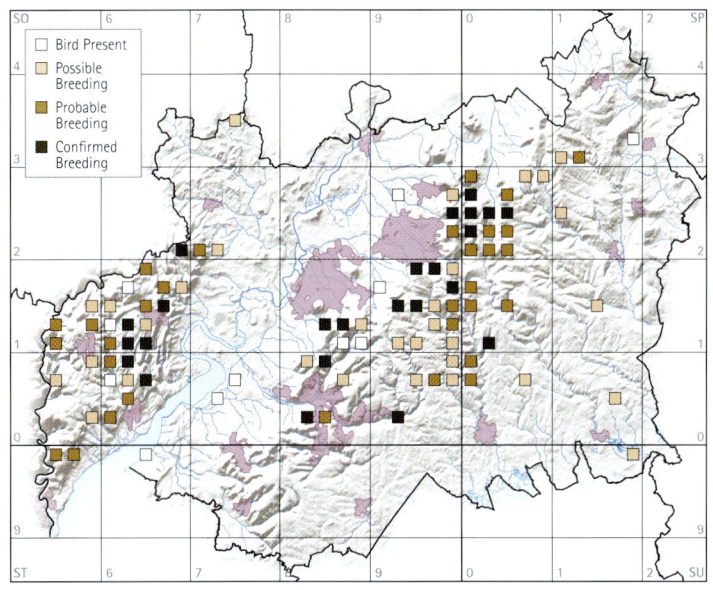

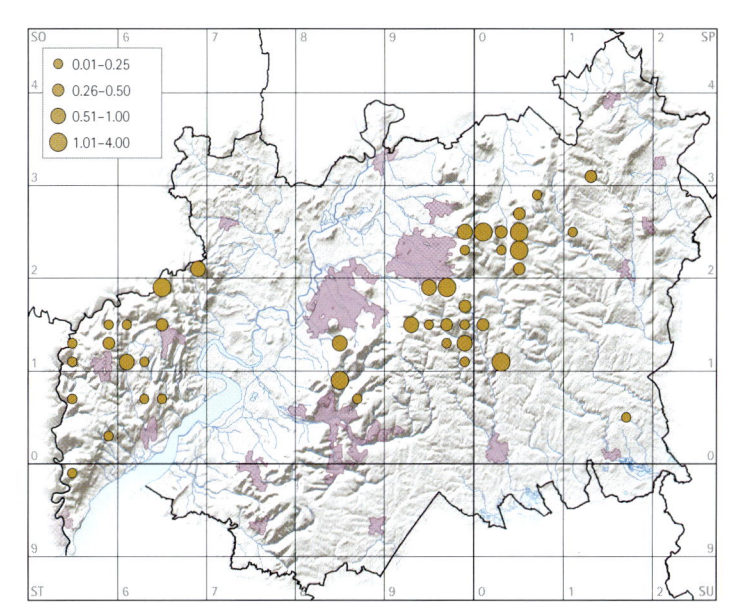

Summer Abundance

It is difficult to assess the historical status of Tree Pipits in Gloucestershire. Witchell & Strugnell's correspondents referred to them as 'common', 'fairly common' and 'common on the hills', and Mellersh mentioned the species only in the list at the end of his book, a status it shares with species such as Dunnock, Blue Tit and Wren, suggesting that it was too common to warrant specific comment. Swaine described Tree Pipits as 'widespread but somewhat local', but the long-term national decline has been reflected in the county and as the distribution map shows, they are now confined to the Forest of Dean, a rather small area on the highest parts of the Cotswold scarp, where the main breeding habitat is low-density natural woodland with rough grassland, plus a few plantations on the scarp and the dip-slope. The occupation rate at the tetrad level has fallen severely, with a reduction of almost three-quarters since 1988–91 (see fact-box). This is broadly in line with the 'more than 60%' decline between 1987 and 2007 reported in the second Cotswolds Atlas, which revealed that many sites in the Cotswolds had been abandoned, especially those involving new plantations or clear-felled woodland: it was noted that the population had largely retreated to uncultivated scarp slopes. The speed of this decline suggests that Gloucestershire's Tree Pipits are in crisis. Nowhere in the county can they be described as abundant; the largest number seen during an atlas TTV was ten, in June 2009 in tetrad SP02C which includes the plantations just east of Cleeve Common, but in half of the tetrads in which Tree Pipits were found just one bird was recorded. Even at the Nagshead RSPB reserve, which is an area of prime habitat, the number of breeding pairs fell from 19 in 1980 to nine in 2010.

Another worrying aspect revealed by the atlas fieldwork is that there was a rather low rate of 'confirmed' breeding records. Like the wagtails, Tree Pipits carry food to their young very conspicuously, so this suggests that they may be failing to raise offspring, as suggested in the second Cotswolds Atlas. Certainly this species' prospects in the county do not appear to be promising.

Meadow Pipit
Anthus pratensis

Meadow Pipits are very much a northern species, extending as far as south-east Greenland, Iceland and western Siberia; very few breed south of central France. Over most of their range they are migratory, although the distance they move south in winter is variable, depending on weather conditions. In most years the British Isles are included in their wintering areas, albeit at the northern limit; indeed Britain and nearby parts of the Continent are the only areas where Meadow Pipits can be found all year round. Ringing recoveries have shown that most British breeders migrate (many to the Iberian peninsula), but some do stay for the winter. Meadow Pipits are diurnal migrants and overflying flocks are a feature of both spring and autumn.

Even within Britain Meadow Pipits breed more commonly in the north, favouring moors and bogs on higher ground. They are also found in many other open grassy habitats with scattered bushes and trees, and are quite common in some coastal areas. In winter their high altitude breeding grounds are abandoned but they become much more widespread, using a broader range of habitats.

Their distinctive display flight and rather repetitive song (almost always delivered during ascent) make Meadow Pipits fairly easy to identify during spring and summer fieldwork, though some care is needed to separate them from Tree Pipits (which have a more varied song, usually delivered during descent), especially as the two species are sometimes found together. Wintering Meadow Pipits might be overlooked if feeding quietly in long vegetation, but as soon as they take off they reveal themselves as they call repeatedly, even on the shortest flights.

Across Europe, Meadow Pipit populations are in long-term decline, with decreases of around 50% since 1980 (PECBMS 2011) and the situation in Britain is broadly similar. Gloucestershire is also following the same pattern, with all available data showing noticeable declines that appear to be part of a much longer-term trend, linked to changes in land use. Thus Mellersh described Meadow Pipits as 'common in the summer' on the Cotswold downs, whereas Swaine said that they bred only 'locally' on the Cotswolds and, by the time of the 2003–07 Cotswolds Atlas, they had more or less disappeared as a breeding bird from the high wold. The decline has evidently continued since then, and in the current atlas survey the species was not recorded at all in nine of the 26 core 10 km squares during the breeding season. In fact, as the distribution map shows, breeding is now confined to relatively few places: some areas of rough grassland on the top of the Cotswold scarp, such as Cleeve Hill and the Stroud commons; some wetter lowland grassy areas near the Severn Estuary; and a few other scattered locations. Meadow Pipits do not generally use cultivated land for breeding, which might explain why they seem to be doing so much worse than the Skylark in our county.

The winter maps reveal a very different picture: Meadow Pipits are widespread in Gloucestershire at that season. This species is somewhat unusual in its ability to exploit both pasture and arable fields in winter, so suitable habitat is available throughout the county. The Severn Vale clearly holds the highest winter densities, although there appear to be fairly well-populated areas elsewhere, notably lower-lying parts of the Cotswolds. The maximum count during an atlas TTV was 122 in November 2010 in SP11V in the Cotswolds near the Oxfordshire border, and winter flocks of up to 300 birds were noted during the atlas period on several occasions. Many of these birds will have come from further north and east, perhaps Scotland or Fennoscandia. Individuals ringed in North Yorkshire in September and Suffolk in October, and caught by ringers in Gloucestershire in subsequent autumns, are likely to have been continental migrants.

Sponsored by Rosalind John

Species accounts 397

	2007–11 Atlas fieldwork					Gloucestershire trends						UK population trends	
	Number of tetrads in which recorded (max 683)					Occupied 10 km squares (max 26)				% of tetrads in which recorded (1st hour of TTV)		UK conservation status: **Amber 3**	
	Total	Confirmed	Probable	Possible	Present	1968–71	1981–84	1988–91	2007–11	1988–91	2008–11	Long term	Short term
Breeding	122	25	16	27	54	21		19	17	10.5	6.0	–44%	–21%
Winter	450						24		26			–	–

Breeding Distribution

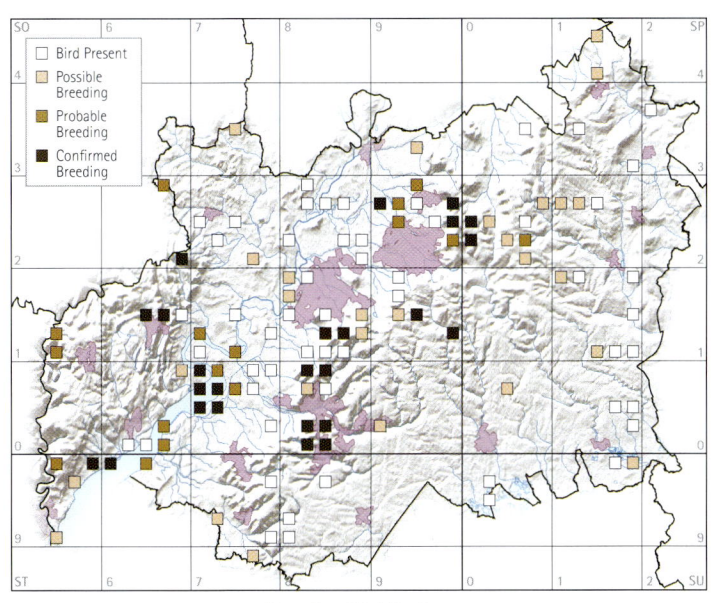

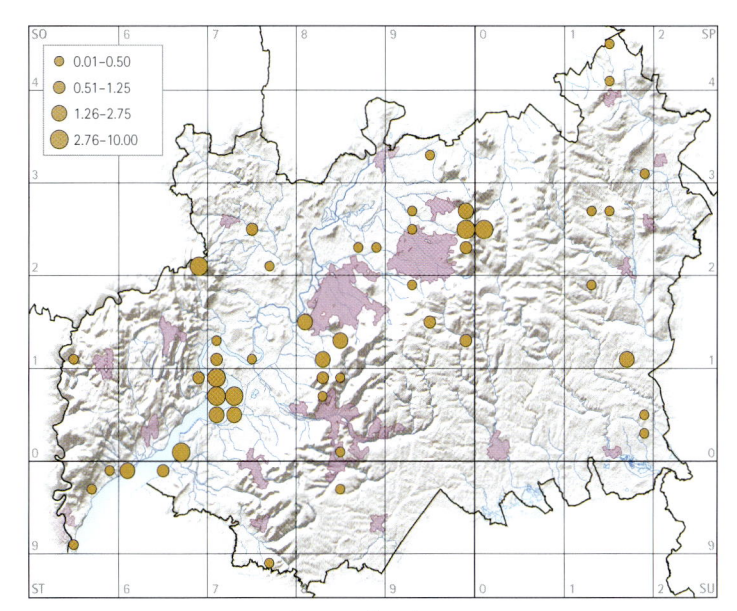

Summer Abundance

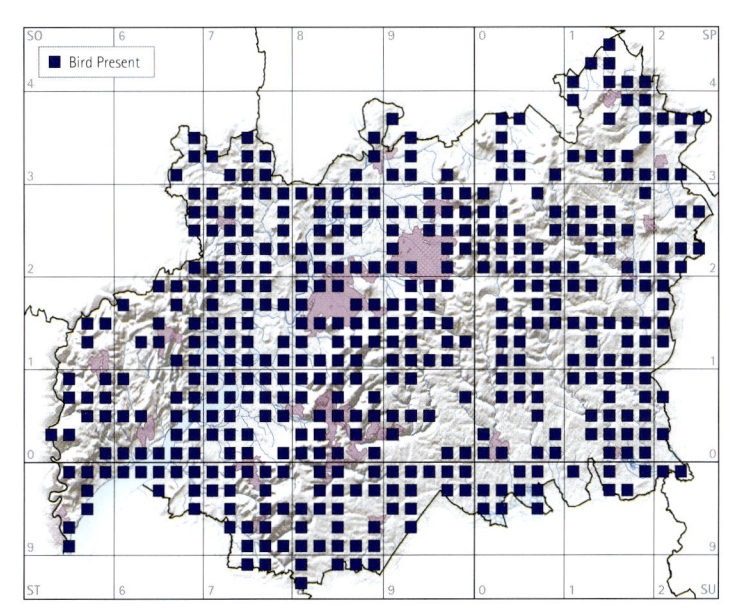

Winter Distribution

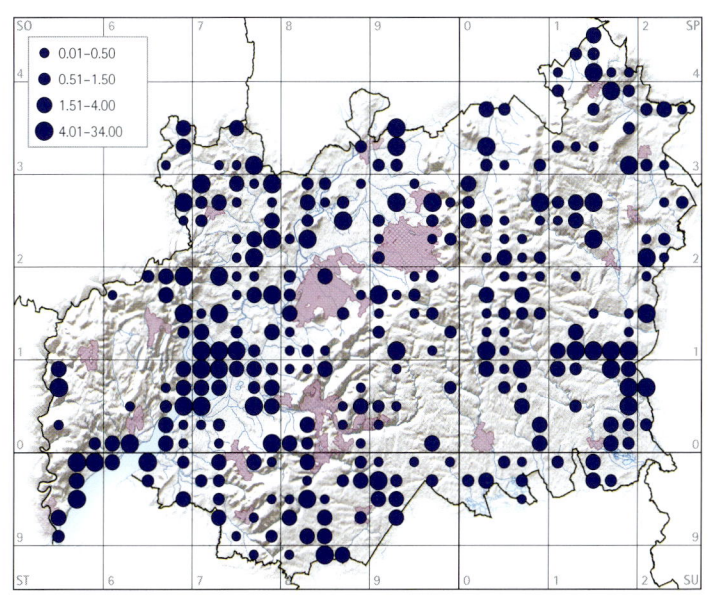

Winter Abundance

Rock Pipit (Eurasian Rock Pipit)
Anthus petrosus

Endemic to the coasts of north-west Europe, Rock Pipits are generally found within sight of the sea, breeding on cliffs and rocky shores. Most of the coastline around the British Isles provides suitable habitat, the main exceptions being parts of south-east and north-west England. The majority of British and Irish birds are resident, but Rock Pipits from more northern populations leave their breeding areas entirely and move south for the winter; birds of the Scandinavian race *A. p. littoralis* winter regularly in Britain, especially on the south and east coasts of England (Migration Atlas).

This is a scarce bird in Gloucestershire, recorded annually but in low numbers. Most records are in winter from more or less rocky areas along both shores of the lower Severn, mainly from Awre and Frampton downriver as far as the county boundary. Away from the Severn Estuary, sightings are very unusual. Most records are of one or two birds, and the highest count at any site in any particular year is usually between five and ten, although higher numbers are occasionally reported. Recent maxima are 15 roosting at Sharpness in December 2003, 12 at Berkeley Pill in 2004 and 13 in the same area in 2006.

There is just one confirmed breeding record in the county: a pair nested successfully at Beachley Point in 1995. However, Mellersh describes the species as a breeding bird in the 'Lower Wye valley', so it is possible that this 1995 record was not an absolute 'first'.

In winter it is very difficult to distinguish between birds from the two different races, *petrosus* and *littoralis*, so in the absence of any ringing records it is hard to say how many Scandinavian birds reach the shores of the Severn. In breeding plumage they are easier to identify, and there is one record of a bird from this race at Berkeley Shore on April 17th 2009.

	2007–11 Atlas fieldwork					Gloucestershire trends					UK population trends	
	Number of tetrads in which recorded (max 683)					Occupied 10 km squares (max 26)				% of tetrads in which recorded (1st hour of TTV)		UK conservation status: **Green**	
	Total	Confirmed	Probable	Possible	Present	1968–71	1981–84	1988–91	2007–11	1988–91	2008–11	Long term	Short term
Breeding	1	0	0	1	0	0		0	0	0	0	–	–
Winter	15						0		3			–	–

Richard's Pipit
Anthus richardi

Migratory Richard's Pipits breed in central and eastern Asia and most winter from Pakistan to Malaysia. However they are regular though uncommon passage migrants in Europe, and wintering birds are now seen regularly in southern Spain and North Africa; few other species share this migration pattern (Migration Atlas). They are fairly regular in Britain in autumn, mostly on the east coast, Scilly and Shetland, and there are a few in spring as well. Sightings have increased noticeably in recent decades, as has the proportion of spring records, and the species was removed from the national rarities list in 1983.

Swaine noted that Mellersh had referred to a report from the county in 1888, but no identification details were given. There was apparently only one other record up to 1980, of a bird 'caught by a dog' at Moreton Valence near Gloucester on December 14th 1931. However since 1980 there have been sightings in ten years, involving two records in the 1980s, three in the 1990s and six since 2000. All have been between mid-October and early December in the Severn Vale, apart from a single near Winchcombe on January 9th 1994, and all have been singles apart from two in the Frampton–Slimbridge area in November 2009 and a remarkable record of three together at Frampton breakwater between October 25th and 29th 1985.

Water Pipit
Anthus spinoletta

Regarded as being conspecific with Rock Pipits until 1986, Water Pipits breed high in the mountains of central and southern Europe, and discontinuously eastwards as far as north-west China. European breeders winter at lower altitudes across much of Europe and, unusually, some migrate north or north-west from their breeding grounds. Some of these birds reach Britain, and small numbers are regular visitors in winter in parts of southern England, as well as occurring on passage. Unlike Rock Pipits they prefer fresh water, so are found in habitats such as watercress beds and freshwater marshes, though they also use brackish coastal wetlands and estuaries. Some birds have been shown to return to the same wintering area in successive years (Migration Atlas).

Swaine noted three or four records from the Severn Vale between 1950 and 1980, and several from the Cotswold Water Park from 1972 to 1980: in total about nine birds, all in March or April.

Since then Water Pipits have been recorded in five years in the 1980s, six in the 1990s and seven since 2000. There have been ten or fewer records in each month from October to May, apart from a sharp peak of 30 in March. All the October records except one were in 2007, when up to four birds were seen with Meadow Pipits over several weeks at Ashleworth Ham and Coombe Hill reserves. Almost all post-1980 sightings are from the Vale, the only exceptions being at the Water Park in 1984, 1986, 1987 and 2010, and a very unusual record of three birds at Hatherop, near Fairford on January 27th 2007. Within the Vale, there are regular records as might be expected from well-watched sites such as the Frampton–Slimbridge area and the Severn Hams, but it is Aylburton Warth, downriver from Lydney, that stands out as by far the most reliable site in the county, with records there in most years since 1995.

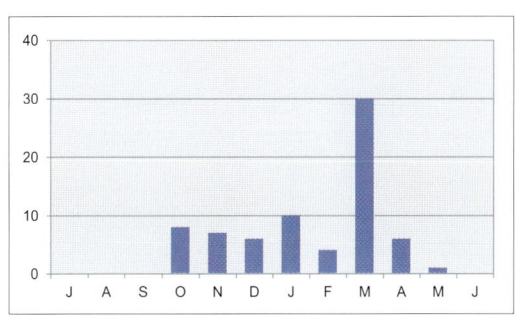

Water Pipit 1980–2010 by month of finding.

Tawny Pipit
Anthus campestris

Breeding across middle latitudes of the Palearctic from Spain and North Africa to Mongolia, Tawny Pipits are annual visitors to Britain with up to about 30 records per year, mainly on southern and East Anglian coasts. The species was removed from the national rarities list in 1983. There have been two records in Gloucestershire:

1995: one on the foreshore at Frampton on May 1st.
2002: one by the Severn at the Awre peninsula near Blakeney on April 24th.

Red-throated Pipit
Anthus cervinus

This tundra species which winters mainly in Africa and south-east Asia is a scarce but annual visitor to Britain during both passage periods, mostly on the east and south coasts. It was removed from the national rarities list in 2006. There have been two records in Gloucestershire:

1980: an adult in summer plumage at the Frampton marshes from April 18th to May 7th.
2006: one at Ashleworth Ham on November 4th.

Chaffinch (Common Chaffinch)
Fringilla coelebs

The Chaffinch is a familiar and abundant bird throughout the British Isles at all times of the year. Its breeding range extends from North Africa through the whole of Europe up to the Arctic Circle, and east to the Lake Baikal region. Recent population estimates suggest somewhere in the region of 100 million pairs in Europe, and about 5.6 million territories in Britain. One reason for its success is its versatility: it breeds readily in both rural and urban settings, in woodland, copses, hedges and gardens; it eats a wide range of seeds and feeds its young on a variety of invertebrates. British birds are largely resident, but during the winter the population here is approximately doubled by immigrants, mainly from Fennoscandia where they are nearly all summer visitors.

Unsurprisingly the species is of least conservation concern, although the smaller and brighter British and Irish subspecies *F. c. gengleri* is amber listed. A decline in the 1950s and 1960s probably caused by toxic seed dressings has been made good, and numbers have continued to increase in recent decades. However since 2005, Chaffinches in this country and Fennoscandia have been affected by the trichomonosis parasite, though the impact has been less dramatic than for Greenfinches.

In Gloucestershire, Swaine described the species as 'an abundant resident ... throughout the county, and a winter visitor ... in all areas'; winter flocks of 400 to 500 were 'not rare.' This status has essentially been maintained over the last three decades. The very widespread breeding distribution in the Cotswolds was unchanged between 1997 and 2007, and county BBS figures since 1994 show only a slight recent decline, from 100% of survey squares up to 2000 to 94% from 2008, perhaps associated with the effects of trichomonosis.

It is relatively easy to obtain proof of breeding for Chaffinches, as shown by the preponderance of 'probable' and 'confirmed' squares on the summer distribution map. In reality they probably bred in virtually every kilometre square in the county during the atlas period. The summer abundance map shows something of an east–west split, with more birds encountered per hour in the Cotswolds, presumably because the habitat in this part of the county is closer to the optimum. The maximum number found in a breeding season TTV was on the Cotswold dip-slope: 56 in tetrad SP01Y near Northleach in April 2010.

There is a steady influx of migrants into the county from October, with numbers peaking in January and February. During the atlas period Chaffinches were as widespread in winter as they were in the breeding season. The winter abundance map indicates that numbers are again generally higher in the Cotswolds, probably reflecting the presence of beech woods with their supply of seeds, and arable land with stubble and ploughed fields.

The winter atlas data is complemented by two local studies: during its 16-year history the NCOS winter survey has recorded an average of between 15 and 22 birds per square kilometre, while the Gloucestershire Garden Bird Survey shows a decline of a few per cent over the 18 winters of the study. Since the year 2000 the largest winter flock reported in the county each year has ranged between 250 and 600 birds, while the highest count during a winter TTV was of 360 birds in SP13N near Chipping Campden in November 2010.

Ringing recoveries highlight the sedentary behaviour of the native Chaffinch. Of the 128 birds ringed in Gloucestershire and recovered up to 2010, 96 had remained within the county. The furthest movement within the British Isles was by a male ringed in Newent Woods in autumn and found dead in Northumberland in late May three years later, a date that suggests it was probably a British breeder. Similarly, only 16 Chaffinches ringed in the British Isles outside Gloucestershire have been recovered here, mostly from fairly nearby but one from as far away as Co. Clare, Ireland. The 25 interchanges of ringed birds between Gloucestershire and other countries show the origins and route of the winter influx, with a preponderance in the Low Countries and a few in Germany, Denmark, Norway and Sweden.

Sponsored by Phil Davis

Species accounts

	2007–11 Atlas fieldwork					Gloucestershire trends					UK population trends	
	Number of tetrads in which recorded (max 683)					Occupied 10 km squares (max 26)				% of tetrads in which recorded (1st hour of TTV)		UK conservation status: **Green**	
	Total	Confirmed	Probable	Possible	Present	1968–71	1981–84	1988–91	2007–11	1988–91	2008–11	Long term	Short term
Breeding	682	411	199	69	3	26		26	26	99.2	98.5	+36%	+11%
Winter	681						26		26			–	–

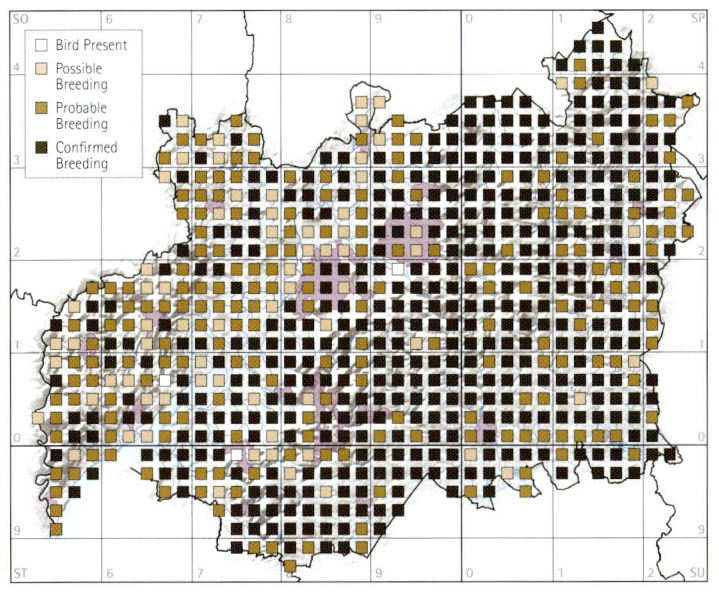

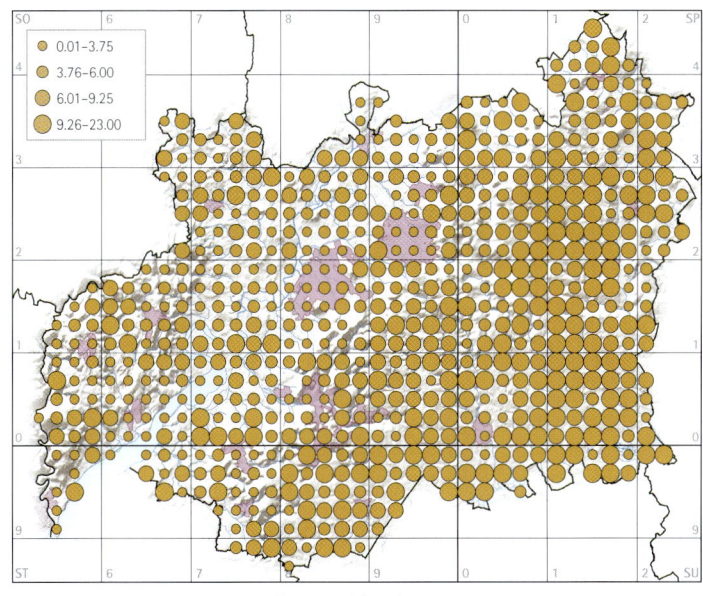

Breeding Distribution

Summer Abundance

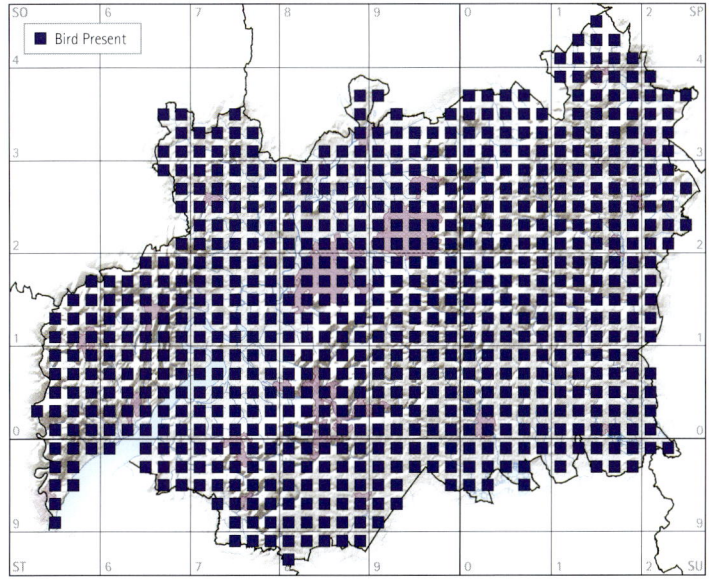

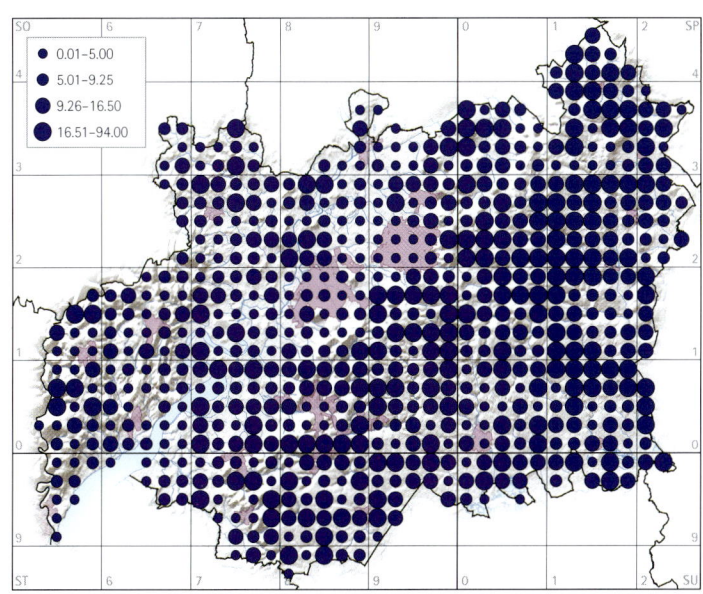

Winter Distribution

Winter Abundance

Brambling
Fringilla montifringilla

The Brambling is almost exclusively a winter visitor to Britain although a few pairs sometimes nest here, mostly in Scotland. It breeds in open woodland up to the Arctic Circle, from Norway eastwards across Russia. In winter the breeding areas are completely vacated; Western Palearctic birds migrate south and west from Fennoscandia and Russia to central and western Europe, including the British Isles, where they forage in flocks often in company with Chaffinches. These movements have a nomadic or irruptive character and are governed by the availability of their preferred winter food, beechmast. Variations in the size and distribution of this seed crop give rise to wide year-to-year fluctuations in the numbers using any given wintering area: BWP gives a range of between 50,000 and 2,000,000 birds in Britain. When supplies of beechmast are exhausted, Bramblings will join Chaffinches and other seed-eaters on arable farmland, and they may also move into gardens; the BTO's Garden BirdWatch registers peak numbers in March, when natural food is running low.

Swaine described Bramblings as winter visitors to Gloucestershire in very variable numbers, and this remains true today. They usually arrive here in October (September records are rare), and numbers tend to build up to a January peak and decline gradually through to April, with a handful of May records. Swaine reported a flock of over 1,000 in a flax field near the Worcestershire border in January 1955, and hinted that such large flocks may have been rather more frequent in the nineteenth century. However in more recent decades maxima of 100–200 have been nearer the norm, and the flock of 1,000 feeding in a field of sunflowers at Aylburton Warth in December 2007 was by far the largest reported in the county during the current atlas fieldwork. The most seen during a TTV was 480, in tetrad ST99B near Tetbury in January 2008.

Over the four-year atlas period as a whole Bramblings were very widespread in the county, as shown by the maps and the figures in the fact-box, but the extent of the variation between years is shown by the separate maps and TTV figures for each winter, which reveal 2007–08 to have been a true 'Brambling winter'.

The abundance map shows distinct concentrations in the beech woods along the Cotswold scarp, while numbers of Bramblings reported from the Forest of Dean have tended to decrease in recent years. Both Mellersh and Swaine referred to hundred-strong flocks there, and during the 1990s and early 2000s flocks of over 100 were fairly regular but, more recently, 50 birds together would be noteworthy. There has been some felling of mature beech in the Dean in recent years, which could be a contributory factor, but

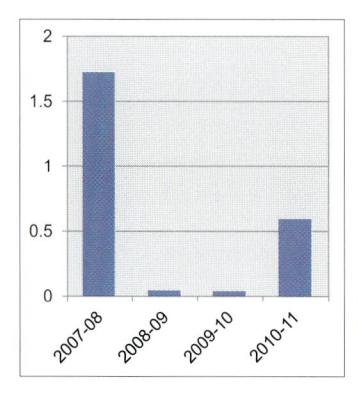

Bramblings recorded per hour in winter TTVs during atlas fieldwork.

In memory of Bill & Mary Fenton

| | 2007–11 Atlas fieldwork ||||| Gloucestershire trends |||||| UK population trends ||
| | Number of tetrads in which recorded (max 683) ||||| Occupied 10 km squares (max 26) |||| % of tetrads in which recorded (1st hour of TTV) || UK conservation status: Green ||
	Total	Confirmed	Probable	Possible	Present	1968–71	1981–84	1988–91	2007–11	1988–91	2008–11	Long term	Short term
Breeding	45	0	0	0	45	0		0	0	0	0	–	–
Winter	325						24		26			–	–

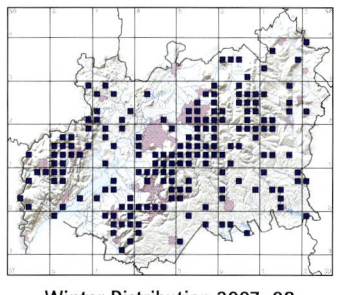

Winter Distribution 2007–08

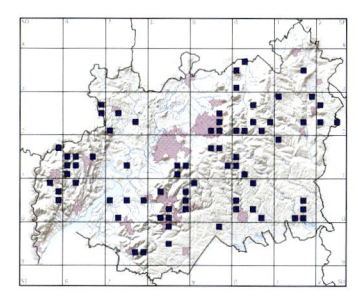

Winter Distribution 2008–09

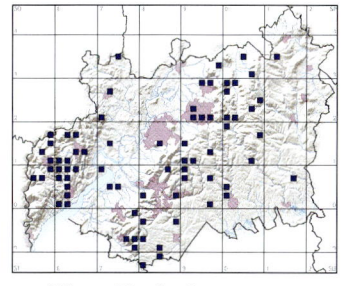

Winter Distribution 2009–10

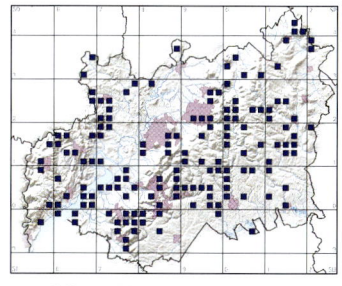

Winter Distribution 2010–11

observer effects may also be involved: Bramblings and birdwatchers do not necessarily always favour the same areas of the Forest.

National ringing recoveries suggest that Bramblings wintering in Britain arrive from Fennoscandia in a wide swathe along the whole east coast after a direct crossing of the North Sea; this contrasts with migrating Chaffinches, which largely choose a shorter English Channel route. Up to 2010 there had been 11 recoveries of ringed Bramblings involving Gloucestershire. Of five movements within Britain, the two longest were by birds ringed at the bird observatories on Bardsey (Gwynedd) and the Isle of May (Fife) in autumn and found here later in the same season, reflecting this more diffuse migration route. Further afield, there were interchanges between the county and Belgium (three), Denmark, France and Norway.

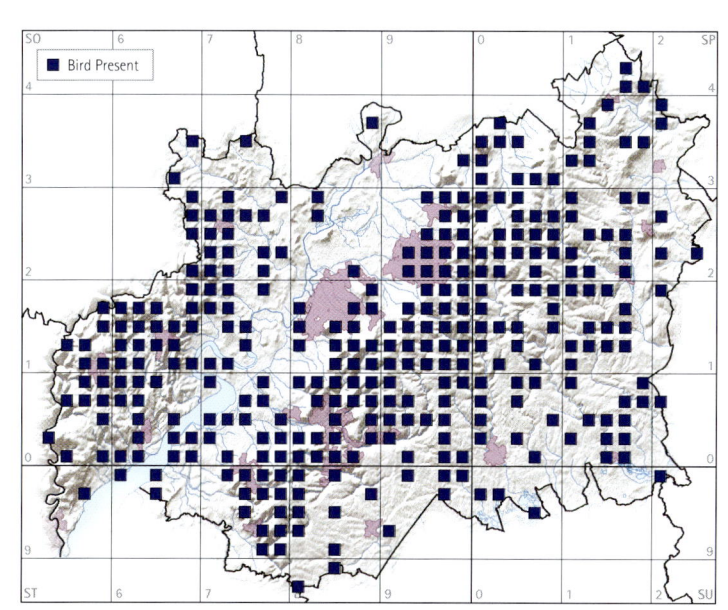

Winter Distribution 2007–11

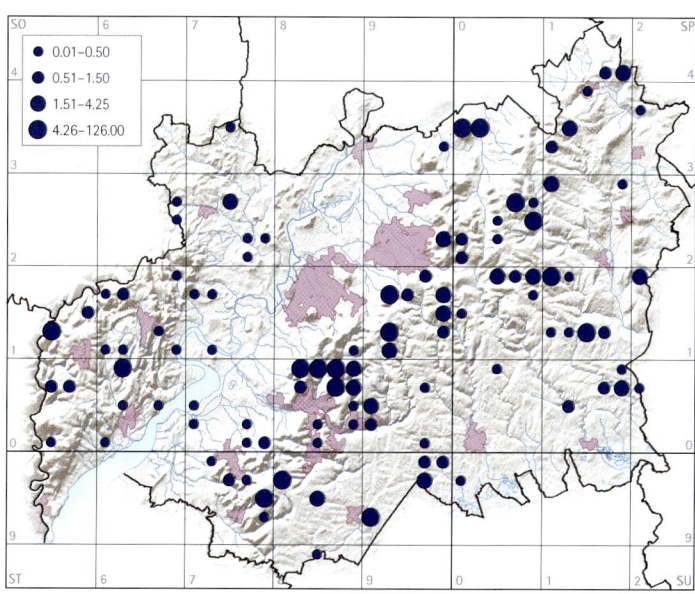

Winter Abundance 2007–11

Greenfinch (European Greenfinch)
Chloris chloris

Greenfinches are nowadays a familiar sight in British parks and gardens, where they nest in trees and taller shrubs. Their range extends across the Western Palearctic below the Arctic Circle from the Atlantic to the Urals, and also to central Asia, parts of North Africa and Asia Minor. There are estimated to be about 700,000 breeding pairs in Britain and some 20 million pairs in Europe.

They are partial migrants within this range, with some winter movement from Norway to northern Scotland and from the near Continent to south-east England. British and Irish birds largely stay within their breeding range and the majority make no seasonal movements at all, although they have apparently become more mobile in recent years (BWP), due perhaps to the decreasing availability of food on farmland in winter.

The Greenfinch is very largely a seed-eater (even the young have a high proportion in their diet), and up to the middle of the twentieth century it was essentially a farmland bird, dependent on weed seeds and spilt grain. Numbers fell in the early 1960s due to toxic seed dressings, but in more recent decades they have recovered strongly and at the same time have become much more numerous in towns and villages, where they benefit from the increased popularity of garden bird-feeding. One negative aspect of this change is that since 2005 Greenfinches in many areas of the British Isles have suffered from trichomonosis, a disease which can be passed on through food and water provided in gardens (Robinson *et al.* 2010).

With their loud, distinctive song and conspicuous display flights, Greenfinches are readily detectable in the breeding season. Parents often bring their newly fledged young to garden feeding stations, and during the atlas fieldwork the presence of fledglings was given as the criterion in over 80% of cases of confirmed breeding in Gloucestershire.

Mellersh considered the Greenfinch to be the commonest species of seed-eating bird in the Cotswolds, though by the end of the nineteenth century it had been overtaken by the Chaffinch. Swaine described it as 'a common and widespread resident ... in autumn and winter ... their numbers may be augmented from elsewhere.' Nowadays flocks of 100 or more in Gloucestershire are worthy of comment. During the atlas survey the highest count during a winter TTV was 92, in tetrad SO80T near Stroud in November 2007; the highest breeding season count was 31, in SO70Q not far from Slimbridge in July 2008. These figures are a far cry from the 450 'on a number of occasions' and the 2,500 seen in a flax field in January 1955, reported by Swaine.

In the area covered by the Cotswolds Atlases there was thought to have been a 'moderate expansion' between 1987 and 2007, and the current distribution maps show Greenfinches to be very widespread within the county at both seasons. They have been recorded in 77–88% of BBS squares since 1994, with a slight tendency to increase in recent years despite the impact of trichomonosis (but see p. 51 for the fortunes of those visiting gardens). The abundance maps for both seasons reveal patchy variations in density across the county, which may be linked with the availability of breeding and feeding habitat as well as, possibly, the chances of observers encountering localised flocks. Gardens are clearly attractive in winter, while in recent records where food in the wider countryside has been noted, about a fifth have mentioned game cover strips. What is evident is that the overall pattern of variation in abundance across the county was broadly similar in winter and in the breeding season, even including an apparent preference for Gloucester over Cheltenham; our Greenfinches evidently do not move far. Indeed, the rather sedentary nature of British Greenfinches in general is reflected in the ringing recoveries involving the county: of a total of 522 movements up to 2010, about 80% were either within Gloucestershire or to and from neighbouring counties. A handful flew over 300 km, to Northumberland, Durham and North Yorkshire; these were mostly ringed here in winter and recovered in the breeding season. Finally, two birds ringed here in winter were recovered in early spring in Belgium and France, where they would presumably have bred.

Sponsored by Iain & Jill Main

Species accounts 405

2007–11 Atlas fieldwork					Gloucestershire trends					UK population trends	
Number of tetrads in which recorded (max 683)					Occupied 10 km squares (max 26)				% of tetrads in which recorded (1st hour of TTV)		UK conservation status: Green	
	Total	Confirmed	Probable	Possible	Present	1968–71	1981–84	1988–91	2007–11	1988–91	2008–11	Long term	Short term
Breeding	671	277	265	121	8	26		26	26	77.9	81.9	0	+2%
Winter	645						26	26				–	–

Breeding Distribution

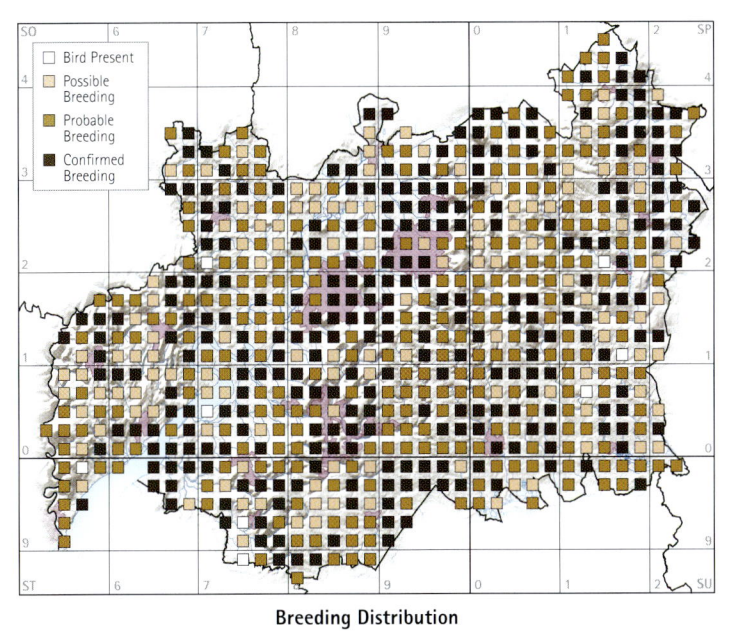

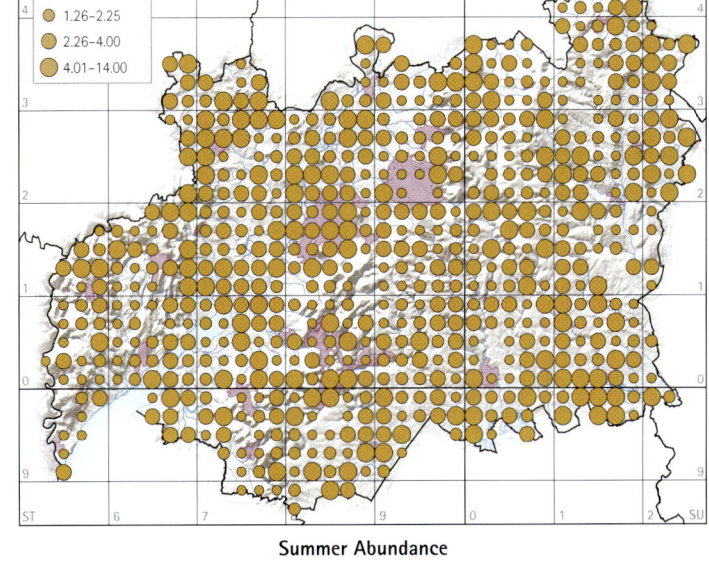

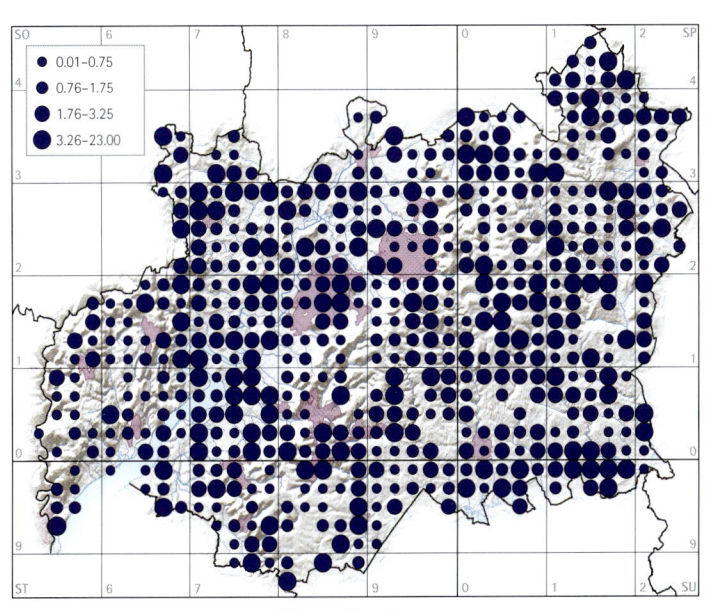

Summer Abundance

Winter Distribution

Winter Abundance

Goldfinch (European Goldfinch)
Carduelis carduelis

Possibly the most spectacularly colourful of British songbirds, the Goldfinch has become a popular visitor to garden feeders in recent years. Its breeding range extends over much of the southern and middle latitudes of the Western Palearctic and eastwards to the Himalayas. There are some 20 million pairs in Europe, including about 300,000 in the British Isles. Goldfinches are partial migrants, with varying numbers each year moving south or south-west to the southern part of the breeding range. It has been estimated that up to 80% of British breeders leave the country, with most wintering in Spain (Migration Atlas). The preferred nesting habitat – woodland edge, scrub, parks and orchards – overlaps with that of the Greenfinch, but outside the breeding season Goldfinches concentrate more on seeds of the *Compositae* family (thistles, sunflowers etc.). Mellersh noted that the Goldfinch 'proves itself of great service since it feeds itself as much as possible on thistles.'

The British Goldfinch population has undergone considerable fluctuations in the last 200 years, largely because of human activities. Clearly they were very abundant indeed in places in the early nineteenth century: William Cobbett estimated that he saw about 10,000 on thistles along half a mile of roadside on the Gloucestershire–Wiltshire border during one of his 'Rural Rides' on September 11th 1826. The cage-bird trade contributed to drastic declines later in the nineteenth century, but protective legislation and an increase in overgrown, untended land during the early twentieth-century agricultural depression allowed a recovery to take place. Since the 1970s populations have continued to fluctuate quite widely, with a general tendency to increase and to extend northwards more recently, helped perhaps by milder winters, agri-environment measures and increased garden feeding.

In Gloucestershire, Witchell & Strugnell cited frequent reports of flocks of 500 or 600 Goldfinches in the nineteenth century, and Mellersh described how 'bird-catchers netted from five to fourteen dozen birds in a day'. Swaine described the species as 'widespread, breeding in moderate numbers in suitable localities throughout the county'. He considered flocks of 50 birds to be 'now quite usual' and highlighted flocks of 400 (Thames Area, 1958) and 200 (Forest of Dean, 1965).

All the available information points to a steady increase in the county in more recent decades. In various surveys between 1987 and 2010, tetrad occupancy in the Cotswolds increased from 60% to 98%, the proportion of gardens visited by Goldfinches in winter doubled to 43%, and the proportion of occupied BBS squares tripled to 88%. During the current atlas fieldwork the species was found in nearly every tetrad in the county at both seasons. Goldfinches appear to have become more adaptable in recent years, dispersing to exploit a wider range of habitats than in the past, so huge concentrations like that described by Cobbett may never be seen again; indeed flocks of 50 or more are now quite noteworthy in the county. The maximum winter TTV count during atlas fieldwork was 64, in tetrad ST79D in the Vale near Berkeley in November 2008.

The breeding season abundance map indicates rather lower densities in the core of the Forest of Dean and in some more treeless areas of farmland in the Cotswolds, as might be expected. The equivalent map for winter appears rather more patchy, with some parts of the Vale also seemingly less favoured, although this may be partly because flocking birds such as this are more likely to be completely missed by surveyors at this season.

Up to 2010 there had been 17 ringing recoveries revealing movements of Goldfinches between Gloucestershire and other counties in the British Isles, tending to show displacement towards the south in winter compared with the breeding season. The longest movement in this category was by one ringed here in winter and recovered in Co. Kildare, Irish Republic, in spring. There were also seven recoveries of Gloucestershire-ringed birds in Spain and one in northern France, reflecting the winter exodus of British breeders.

Sponsored by John Moseley

Species accounts

2007–11 Atlas fieldwork					Gloucestershire trends					UK population trends	
Number of tetrads in which recorded (max 683)					Occupied 10 km squares (max 26)				% of tetrads in which recorded (1st hour of TTV)		UK conservation status: **Green**	
	Total	Confirmed	Probable	Possible	Present	1968–71	1981–84	1988–91	2007–11	1988–91	2008–11	Long term	Short term
Breeding	676	380	214	78	4	26		26	26	60.6	84.4	+103%	+73%
Winter	668						26		26			–	–

Breeding Distribution

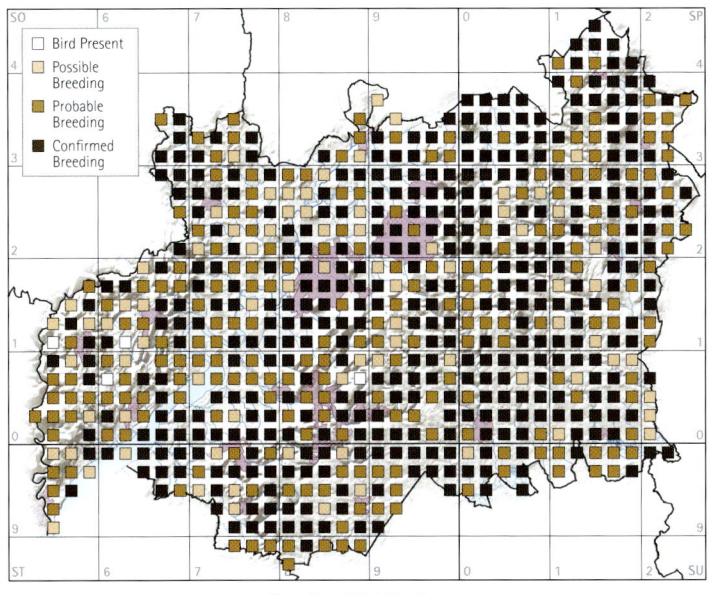

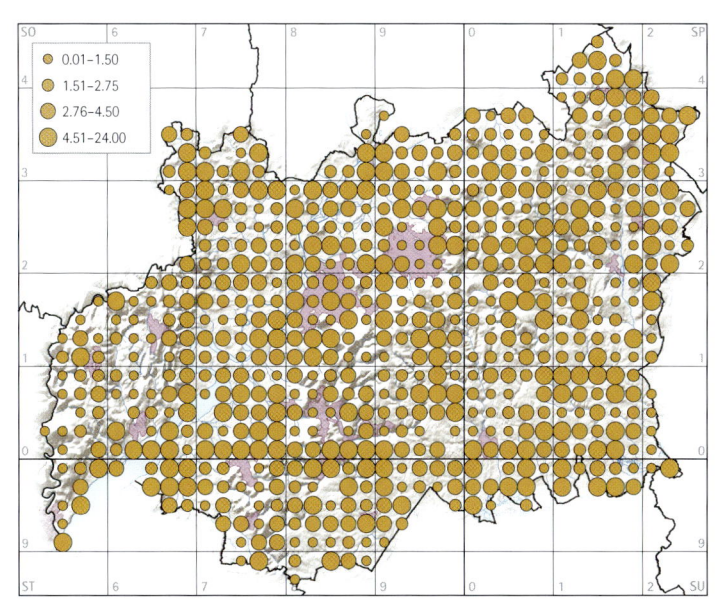

Summer Abundance

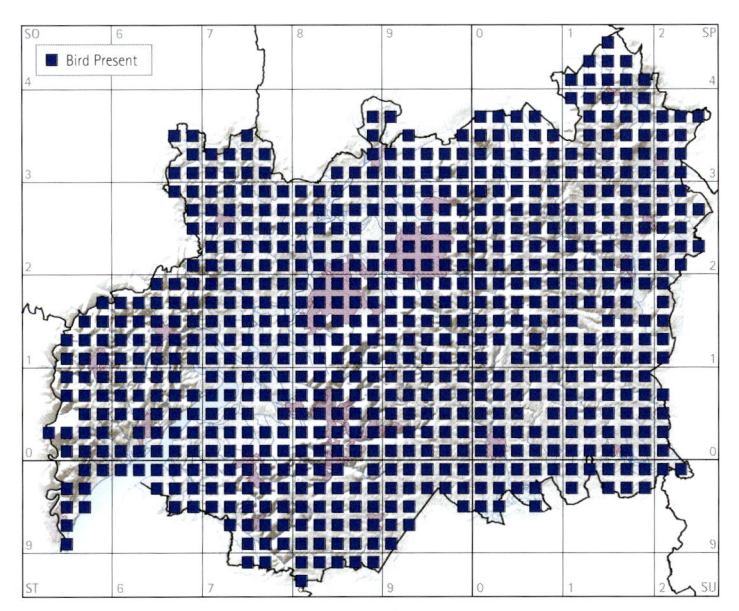

Winter Distribution

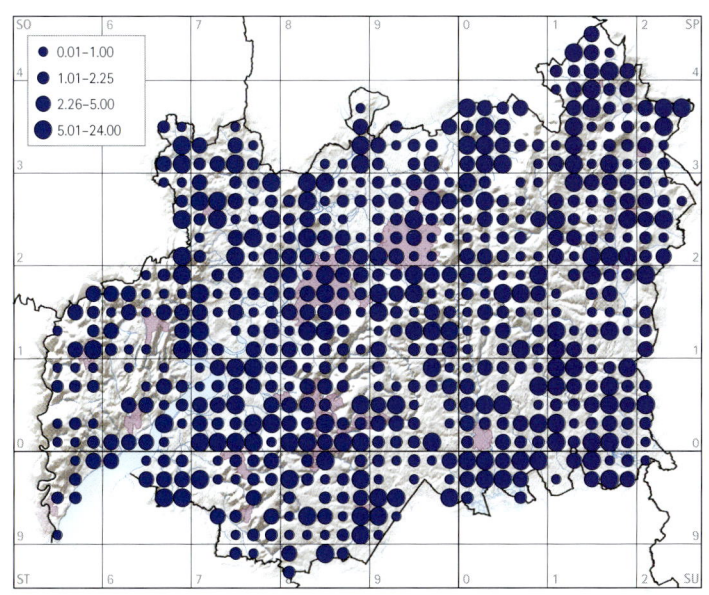

Winter Abundance

Siskin (Eurasian Siskin)
Carduelis spinus

In common with the crossbills, the life history of this small, elegant finch is intimately bound up with variations in the amount of seed produced by a single tree species. In the Siskin's case it is spruce that is crucial, although they will also feed on pine seeds in the breeding season, and in winter they turn to alder and birch. In addition, since the 1960s Siskins have increasingly visited garden feeders, especially in late winter when their natural food sources are depleted.

The vast majority of Western Palearctic Siskins breed in Fennoscandia and Russia, where they are summer visitors; there are also less migratory populations in other parts of Europe. The European breeding population is estimated at between 10 and 18 million pairs while in Britain, following substantial increases since the early twentieth century due to the maturing of conifer plantations, there are now about 350,000 pairs, more than there have ever been before. They now breed across most of the country, although they are still thinly distributed in much of lowland England. In winter the population is augmented by influxes of migrants sweeping south-west from Scandinavia and beyond, arriving on the east coast usually from mid-September. At the same time some British breeding birds move south to continental Europe for the winter.

Siskins have a distinctive song and a conspicuous song-flight, but they usually build their small, camouflaged nests near the tops of tall trees, making proof of breeding difficult to obtain unless fledged young are seen being fed.

Swaine reported occasional breeding in the Forest of Dean, as did the 1968–72 Breeding Atlas. By the start of the 1990s there was a substantial summer population there, although breeding was rarely confirmed. From then to the present sightings have increased, as have confirmed breeding records. Outside the Dean however Siskins are still scarce breeders, reflecting the lack of suitable habitat, as may be seen from the maps. In the area covered by the Cotswolds Atlases breeding was considered unlikely to have taken place in 1983-87 and there was only a single possible breeding record in 2003-07. The scattering of probable and confirmed records in the Cotswolds during the current survey could indicate an extension of the breeding range, but may also reflect better coverage.

In winter, sightings come from all parts of the county; during the atlas period they were recorded in nearly four times as many tetrads as in the breeding season. The main concentrations were still in the Dean but there were also considerable numbers also along the Cotswold scarp. Numbers do not start to build up until October, and the peak is generally in February or March. The maximum count during a TTV was 172, in tetrad SO71D near Blaisdon in February 2011.

As with other birds dependent on tree seeds, there are autumns when the food supply in Scandinavia is too low to support them and Siskins irrupt into Britain. If they reach Gloucestershire it is the areas outside the Forest of Dean that show the biggest increase. Since 2000, these winters have been 2002–03, 2005–06 and 2007–08. Flocks of up to 100 birds are seen fairly frequently in the county in such irruption years; the largest recorded since 2000 was 300 in the Vale near Westbury-on-Severn at the end of December 2007. They are frequently seen in the company of Lesser Redpolls, feeding on the seeds of stream-side alders.

Because they come so readily to artificial feeders Siskins are easily caught by ringers, and the many hundreds ringed in Gloucestershire have generated a correspondingly large number of recoveries. Of 159 within-Britain interchanges involving Gloucestershire up to 2010, only 16 birds were both ringed and recovered within the county. The remaining 143 revealed movements to and from all parts of Britain, with noticeable concentrations in Highland Region (35 recoveries) and Strathclyde (14). In addition there had been 22 movements to and from nine foreign countries, as far away as Scandinavia, Lithuania, Poland and the Czech Republic.

Sponsored by Gordon & Jenny Kirk

Species accounts

2007–11 Atlas fieldwork					Gloucestershire trends					UK population trends	
Number of tetrads in which recorded (max 683)					Occupied 10 km squares (max 26)				% of tetrads in which recorded (1st hour of TTV)		UK conservation status: Green	
	Total	Confirmed	Probable	Possible	Present	1968–71	1981–84	1988–91	2007–11	1988–91	2008–11	Long term	Short term
Breeding	95	22	18	26	29	4		5	13	2.0	2.5	–	+38%
Winter	344						24		26			–	–

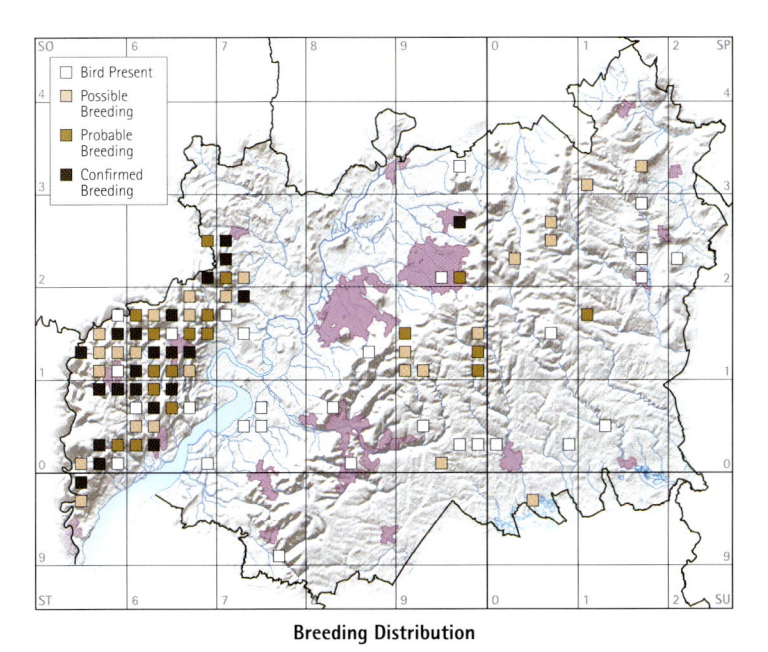

Breeding Distribution

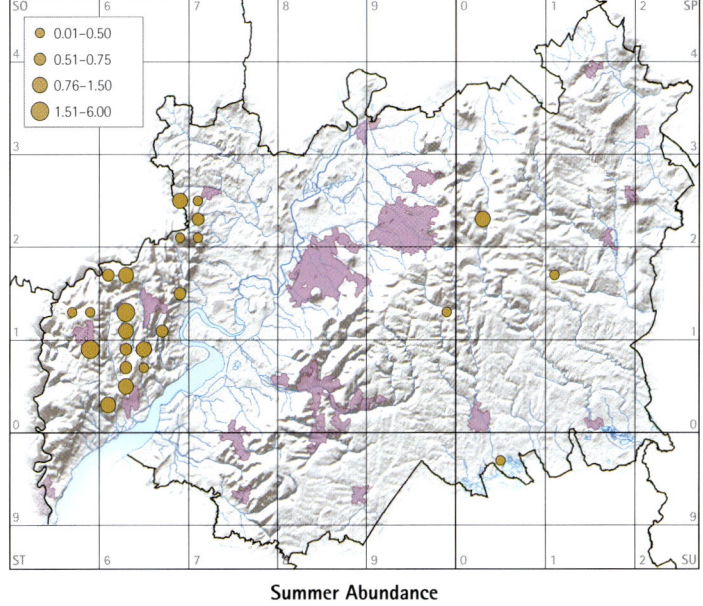

Summer Abundance

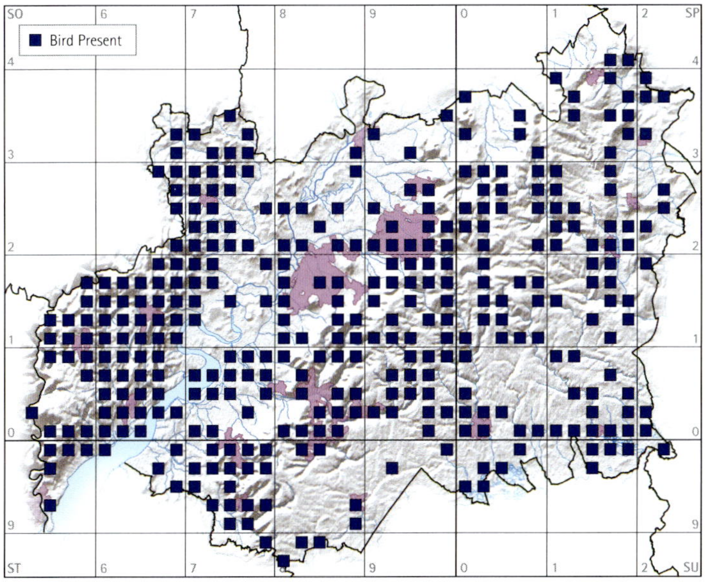

Winter Distribution

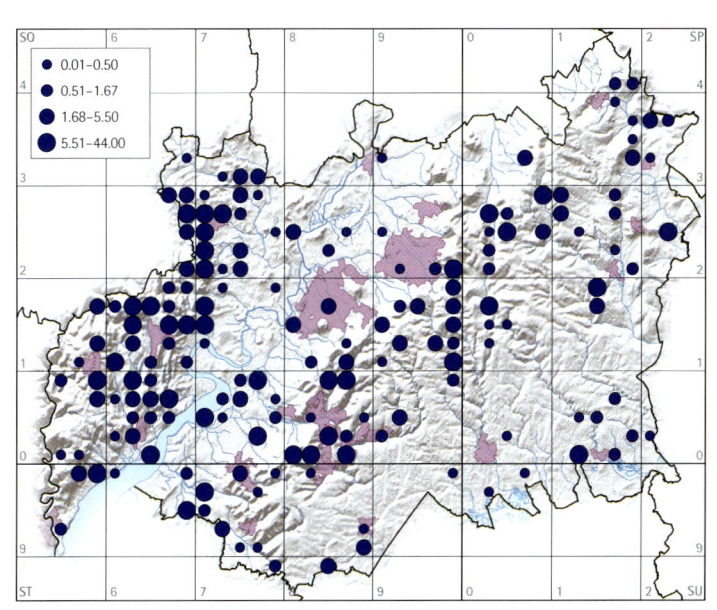

Winter Abundance

Linnet (Common Linnet)
Carduelis cannabina

The Linnet is a specialised seed-eater which even feeds its young on seeds rather than invertebrates. The English and scientific names recall its association with flax (linseed) and hemp, in the days when these crops were widely grown. It nests in hedgerows and bushes in farmland and uncultivated places alike, where its subdued but tuneful song evokes warm spring days in the countryside.

Linnets breed from North Africa and western Europe across to central Asia. Northern and eastern populations are migratory, wintering in the south of the breeding range, and even in milder parts of the range higher ground may be vacated in winter; some birds from the British Isles winter in Spain and western France.

Like Goldfinches, Linnets were trapped in thousands in the past for the cage-bird trade, a practice that was only outlawed in England and Wales as recently as 1953. More significantly, like many other seed-eaters they have been negatively affected by changing agricultural practices. During the nineteenth century the enclosure of common land and its subsequent ploughing resulted in some losses of nesting habitat, though Linnets were still 'common' up to the beginning of the twentieth century (1875–1900 Atlas). From about the mid-1960s onwards, toxic agricultural chemicals followed by other forms of farming intensification brought a drastic decline in populations. In more recent years, with the introduction of agri-environment measures and the increased sowing of oil-seed rape, which provides a widely used food source, there are signs that the declines may have been halted and that in some areas the trend may now be slightly upwards. However unlike Goldfinches, Linnets rarely feed in gardens so they have not benefited from feeding stations. The British population was estimated at about half a million territories in 2000.

In Gloucestershire, Swaine wrote that the Linnet was still a 'common and widespread bird' and this remains essentially true today. Indeed, the Cotswolds Atlases revealed a dramatic increase in distribution from 153 to 280 tetrads in that part of the county between 1987 and 2007, and it was suggested that the Linnet may be 'one of the few species to have benefited from ... set-aside'. The breeding season maps reveal that Linnets are still very widespread, in the Cotswolds and in the county in general, although as might be expected there are noticeable gaps in the Forest of Dean and in the larger conurbations. The breeding season abundance map emphasises their preference for Cotswold farmland, even including areas on the dip-slope where the arable fields are larger and there are fewer bushes and scrub for nesting. County BBS figures have fluctuated considerably since 1994, but there are no indications of any consistent trends: Linnets were found in an average of 60% of study squares per year up to 2002, and 56% since then.

The winter maps show Linnets to be less widespread than during the breeding season, as is the case with some other flocking species. There is a noticeable concentration of records in the Cotswolds, where most of the large flocks were found, and in the more southern part of the Vale. Winter flocks of over 100 birds have become more common in the last decade, and counts of 1,000 or more are not unknown: a huge flock of 5,000 was recorded feeding in abandoned mustard fields near Edgeworth, by the upper Frome valley north-west of Cirencester, throughout February 1991. There were two counts of 250 during winter TTVs in the current survey, both in the Cotswolds: in SO91Q, north-west of Cirencester and not very far from Edgeworth, and in SP11G near Northleach.

The origins of Linnets wintering in Gloucestershire are uncertain, but the few ringing recoveries involving the county offer some hints: singles moved here from Greater Manchester, the West Midlands and West Yorkshire. In addition four ringed here as nestlings or juveniles were recovered in south-west France in autumn; these movements were in the 1930s and 1960s and in three cases the recovery details specify 'freshly dead (trapped)' – in other words presumably taken for food. There is also one movement in the opposite direction: a bird ringed in south-west France in December 1968 was found dead at Longhope in June the following year.

Sponsored by Tony & Pam Perry

Species accounts

	2007–11 Atlas fieldwork					Gloucestershire trends						UK population trends		
	Number of tetrads in which recorded (max 683)					Occupied 10 km squares (max 26)				% of tetrads in which recorded (1st hour of TTV)		UK conservation status: **Red 3**	
	Total	Confirmed	Probable	Possible	Present	1968–71	1981–84	1988–91	2007–11	1988–91	2008–11	Long term	Short term
Breeding	597	203	280	96	18	26		26	26	53.1	47.6	−56%	−23%
Winter	358						24		26			–	–

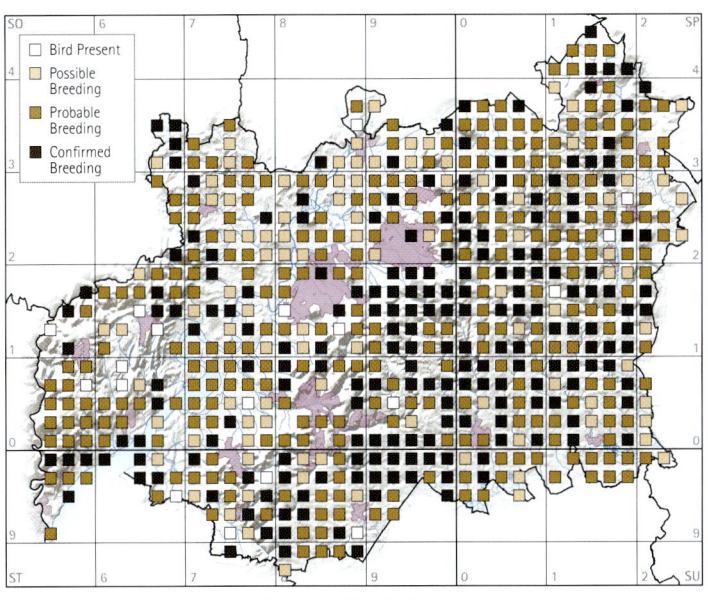

Breeding Distribution

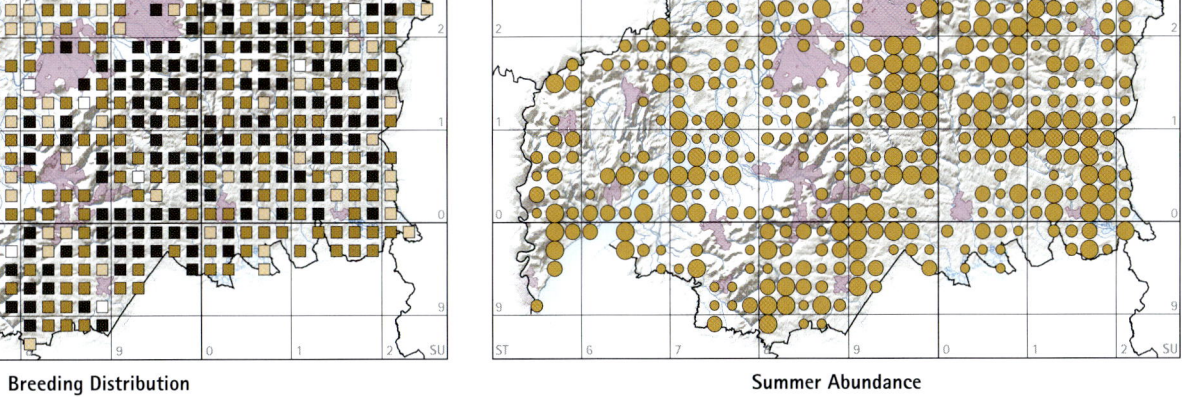

Summer Abundance

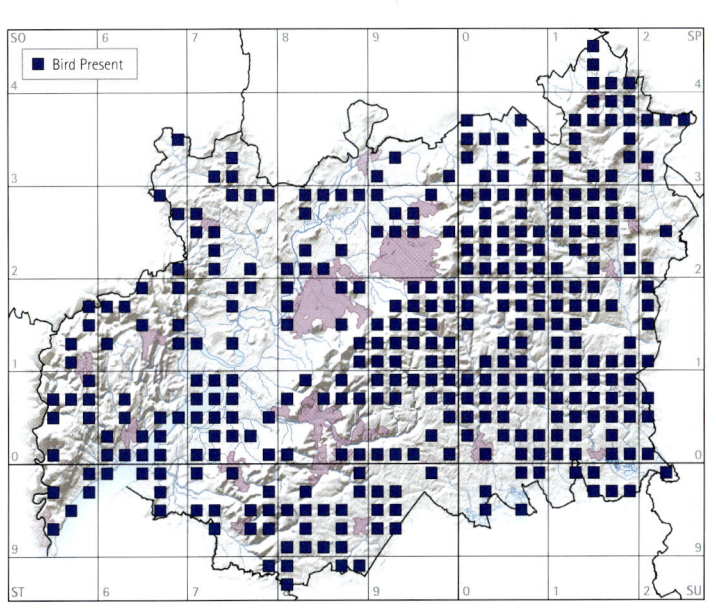

Winter Distribution

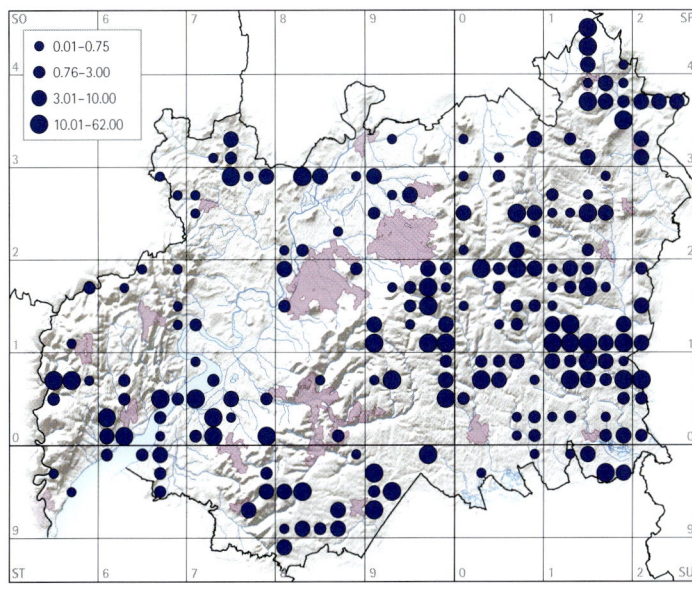

Winter Abundance

Lesser Redpoll
Carduelis cabaret

Until 2001 the Lesser Redpoll was treated as conspecific with the Mealy (also known as Common) Redpoll. It inhabits warmer climates than its cousins: the British Isles supports a high proportion of the population, but the breeding range extends to the Low Countries, Denmark, southern Scandinavia and central Europe. Many British birds, especially from further north, move south-eastwards across the Channel to winter in north Germany and France, although some get no further than southern England. In addition variable numbers of continental birds move into Britain to winter. The movements tend to be eruptive rather than regular seasonal migrations: the numbers of birds involved and the distances travelled depend on food supplies.

Lesser Redpolls breed in woods and plantations, where they feed on small tree seeds, particularly birch and alder. They will also take a wide range of other small seeds including those of arable weeds, and have shown an increasing tendency to visit garden feeders in recent years, especially towards the end of the winter when natural food is running short.

Their dependence on birches in particular underlies the Lesser Redpoll's recent fortunes in Britain. There was a decline in the 1920s, but numbers increased during the 1950s following the creation of new conifer plantations, where birch trees readily establish themselves, after the Second World War (1968-72 Breeding Atlas). The population peaked in the early 1970s but then declined drastically again to the mid-1990s, probably because the birches were being progressively shaded out as plantations matured; the general intensification of agriculture over the same period may also have played a part (1988-91 Breeding Atlas). The total British breeding population was estimated at 25,000 pairs in 2000, and the species has moved rapidly along the conservation scale from green, to amber (2002), to red listed (2008), though this has also been influenced by the taxonomic reclassification.

Writing in 1902 Mellersh described Lesser Redpolls, which he treated separately from Mealy, as 'resident breeder and wintering', and noted that they nested in several locations including Cheltenham. Swaine reported small numbers breeding in the Forest of Dean between 1976 and 1980, also noting that there had been no other confirmed breeding since the early 1900s. Subsequent county bird reports have simply noted that a few pairs attempt to breed each year. In the area covered by the Cotswolds Atlases, just one singing bird was found in 1983-87 and none in 2003-07. In the current survey breeding was not confirmed anywhere in the county; the distribution map reveals just a small nucleus of probable breeders in the Forest of Dean and a scattering of records elsewhere, particularly along the Cotswold scarp. However confirming breeding can be difficult, as nests are often high and foraging adults range widely.

It is as a winter visitor that Lesser Redpolls are most familiar among Gloucestershire birdwatchers, and the winter maps show that numbers are far higher and the distribution is much more widespread at this season, with records widely scattered across the Cotswolds and the Vale in addition to the Dean. The winter abundance map suggests that the distribution is rather clumped, with larger groups scattered across the county, and apparently showing no preference for the Dean. Winter numbers vary considerably from year to year

Sponsored by Vic Polley

Species accounts

2007–11 Atlas fieldwork						Gloucestershire trends						UK population trends	
Number of tetrads in which recorded (max 683)					Occupied 10 km squares (max 26)				% of tetrads in which recorded (1st hour of TTV)		UK conservation status: **Red 3**	
	Total	Confirmed	Probable	Possible	Present	1968–71	1981–84	1988–91	2007–11	1988–91	2008–11	Long term	Short term
Breeding	42	0	4	12	26	8		6	8	1.6	0.3	–88%	+16%
Winter	212							21	26			–	–

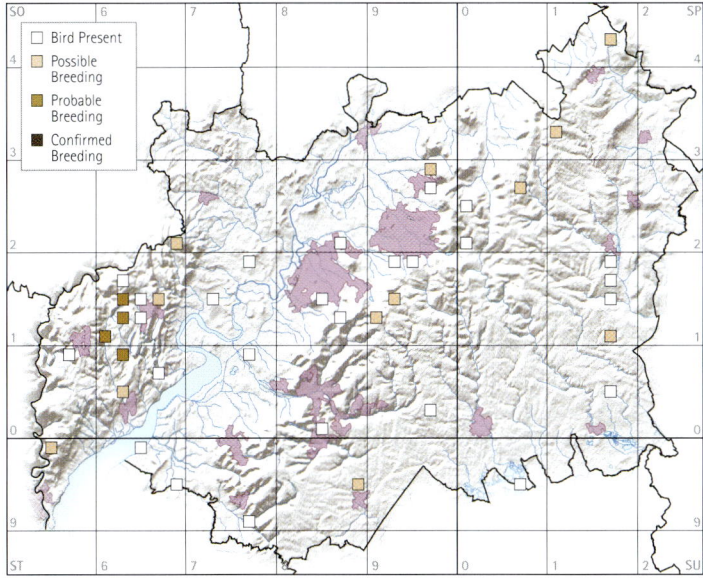

Breeding Distribution

but in general have tended to be lower more recently; while Swaine described flocks of 30 as being common, the majority of sightings in recent years have been in single figures. However the largest winter flock seen during the atlas fieldwork was of 100 birds in SO61G near the Speech House in the Forest of Dean in December 2007, while the highest count during a winter TTV was 50, in SP12U by Longborough in December 2008. Most double-figure flocks came from the Forest of Dean.

Up to 2010 there had been 20 ringing recoveries revealing movements of Lesser Redpolls between Gloucestershire and other English counties. The four longest movements were of 270–80 km, between here and North Yorkshire, Humberside and Kent (two). Three of these involved coastal localities, suggesting that birds were leaving or entering the country. All suggest broadly southerly displacements in winter compared with earlier in the year.

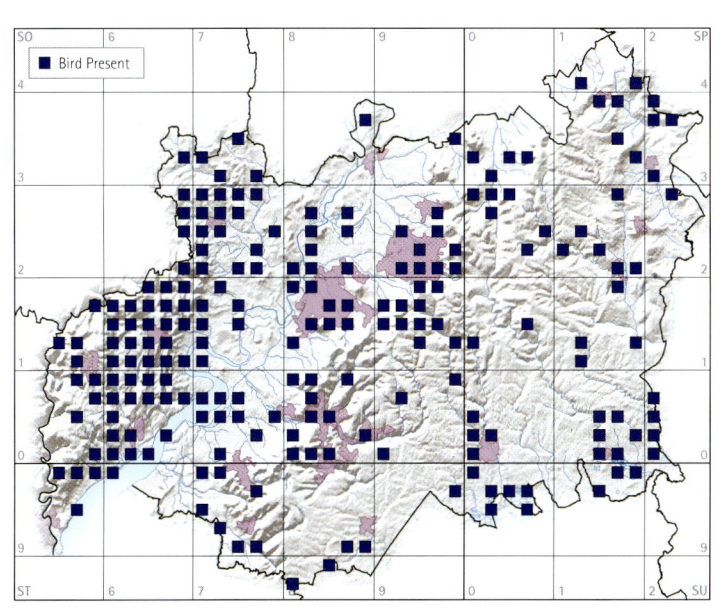

Winter Distribution

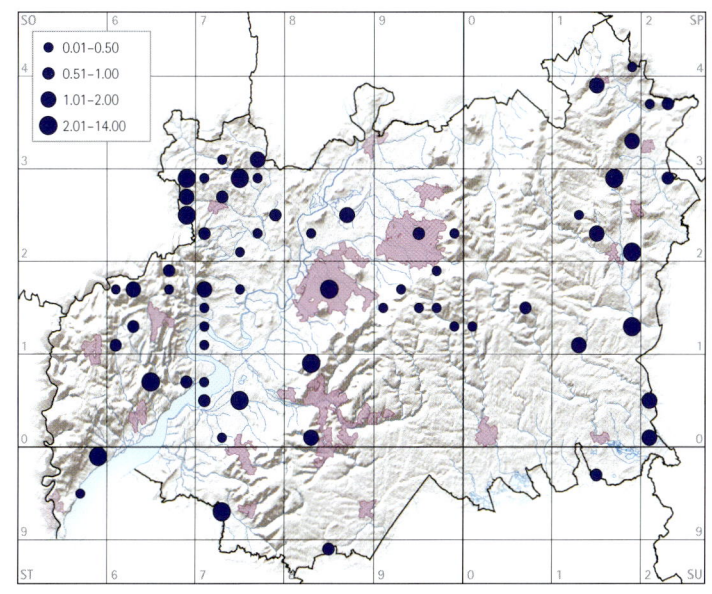

Winter Abundance

Common Crossbill (Red Crossbill)
Loxia curvirostra

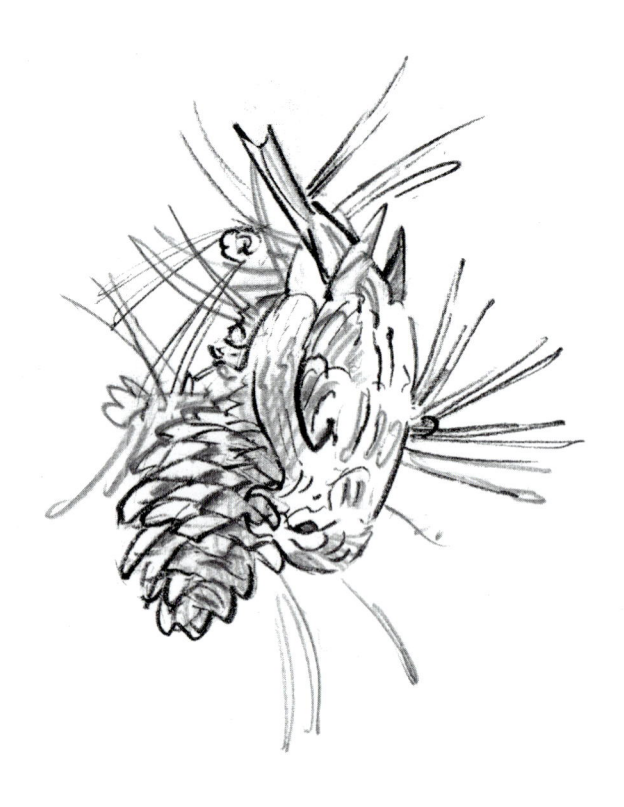

Crossbills feed on conifer seeds, which are prised out of the cones with their specialised bills. The taxonomy of the various species and races has been subject to much recent revision.

The Common Crossbill that occurs in Britain, *L. c. curvirostra*, feeds mainly on Norway spruce and inhabits vast areas of temperate and northern conifer forests, from western Europe through Asia to the Pacific coast. The amount of spruce seed produced varies considerably between years, and parties of birds range around locally to find supplies. In years when the seed crop is poor, large flocks of Crossbills move south and west from Fennoscandia and Russia into western Europe and Britain, boosting the breeding populations there sometimes by a factor of hundreds. Unsurprisingly given these irruptions, estimates of the bird's numbers vary widely: BirdLife International gives 6 to 13 million pairs in Europe, while the British population between 1968 and 1990 was estimated at 1,000 to 20,000 pairs. However, fluctuations notwithstanding, the average numbers breeding in England and Wales increased dramatically during the late twentieth century as conifer plantations matured, as correctly predicted in the 1968–72 Breeding Atlas.

The Crossbill's breeding season is mainly between November and March, following the maturation of the seed crop, though breeding behaviour has been noted in every month of the year in Britain (1981–84 Wintering Atlas). This resulted in some uncertainty in assessing breeding status and also numbers of breeding birds during the current atlas project, as some young may have fledged by the time the spring fieldwork began and juveniles and adults can only be distinguished in the field if reasonable views are obtained. The majority of Gloucestershire atlas records that were assigned a breeding status merely involved birds in suitable habitat, while six out of the only seven records of confirmed breeding were of fledged young; even these should be treated with caution given the dispersal that can occur soon after fledging.

In Gloucestershire the majority of Crossbill sightings, including nearly all breeding records, come from the Forest of Dean. Mellersh recorded it as a rare resident which had extended its range into the county when stands of 'firs' and larches were planted, and which bred in small numbers in the Forest. He referred to 'great invasions' in 1868 and 1899, with some birds in 1899 being 'killed with catapults by boys, who tried to make a few pence by selling them as rarities.' By the time Swaine was writing, conifer plantations had become much more widespread, and he described Crossbills as occurring here almost annually, with a number of confirmed breeding records. He also mentioned an irruption in 1929, with 'thousands' overwintering in (unusually) the Cotswolds. Another immigration in the summer of 1962 saw up to 500 remaining through the following hard winter.

The 2003–07 Cotswolds Atlas described Crossbills as uncommon and irregular breeders there, due to the lack of mature coniferous woodland. The latest survey maps confirm this, with a small breeding heartland in the Dean and only scattered sightings on the higher Cotswolds and a few in the Severn Vale. However despite this restricted distribution there has been a tendency for the number of records to increase in succeeding atlas projects (see fact-box).

As might be expected for such a specialised feeder, the distribution within the county does not vary greatly between winter and summer. However, the graph illustrates the difficulties in drawing conclusions about this erratic species, which appears to have been present in some numbers in the summer of 2008, but was hardly recorded at all in 2009 until an apparent influx in July of that year, followed by widespread records in the winter of 2009–10. The highest count during an atlas TTV was 20, in tetrad SO51R in the Dean near Coleford in December 2009. In the survey as a whole, the largest number encountered was 90 in flight at Saul Warth near Slimbridge on July 25th 2009.

Overall the county's small population of Crossbills appears to be fairly stable, although the species' continuing presence here no doubt depends on repeated influxes from elsewhere.

Sponsored by the Dursley Birdwatching and Preservation Society

Species accounts

2007–11 Atlas fieldwork					Gloucestershire trends					UK population trends	
Number of tetrads in which recorded (max 683)					*Occupied 10 km squares (max 26)*				*% of tetrads in which recorded (1st hour of TTV)*		*UK conservation status:* **Green**	
	Total	Confirmed	Probable	Possible	Present	1968–71	1981–84	1988–91	2007–11	1988–91	2008–11	Long term	Short term
Breeding	56	7	10	11	28	3		4	9	0.6	1.2	–	+10%
Winter	41							6	13			–	–

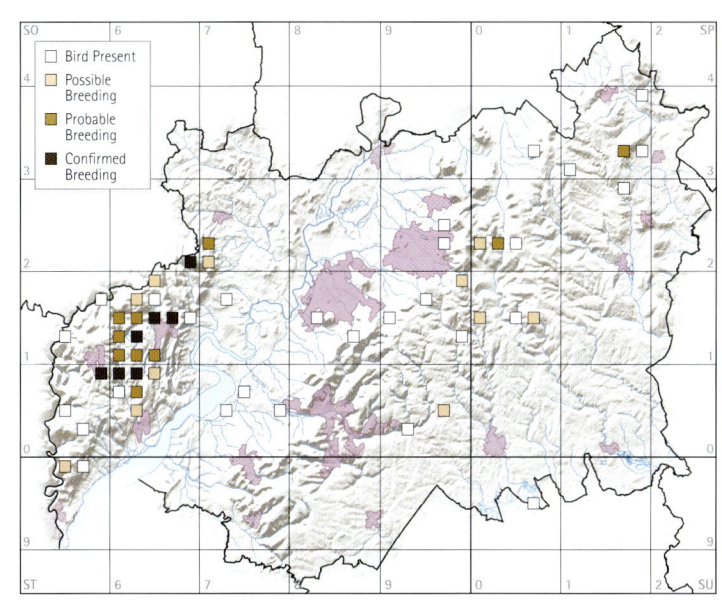

Breeding Distribution

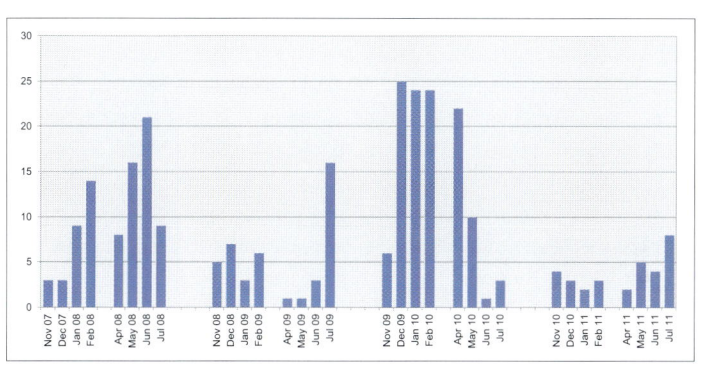

Crossbill: number of tetrads in which recorded in each month of atlas fieldwork.

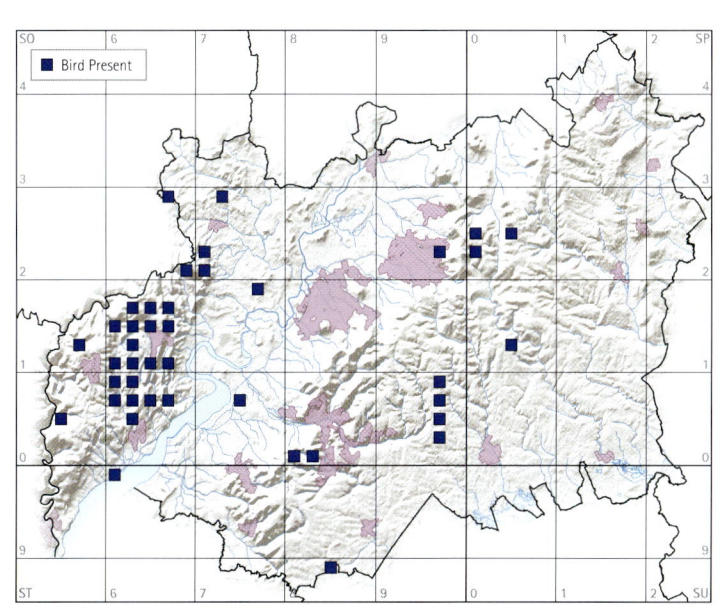

Winter Distribution

LEWIS THOMSON

Bullfinch (Eurasian Bullfinch)
Pyrrhula pyrrhula

Bullfinches breed across the temperate parts of Europe and Asia, from Portugal to Kamchatka and Japan. Globally the species is of least conservation concern, with between three and six million pairs in Europe alone. They are mainly resident, although large, bright northern European birds sometimes undertake eruptive movements which take them as far as northern and eastern Britain. They are versatile plant-feeders, taking buds, fruit and seeds from a variety of trees and shrubs, and they prefer to nest in deciduous woodland and scrub.

With their quiet calls, unobtrusive behaviour and liking for dense vegetation, Bullfinches are easily overlooked. Of the 800 or so county atlas records where a breeding code was provided, only 12% were 'confirmed', and of these the vast majority related to fledged young. On the other hand, Bullfinches are rarely seen alone, and 40% of these records were of pairs, implying 'probable' breeding, by far the highest proportion of pairs recorded among passerines.

Bullfinches have been widely regarded as pests in regions with orchards because they will feed on the buds of fruit trees and bushes. Throughout the nineteenth century they were trapped and killed in large numbers by orchard proprietors and also by rural householders, who grew much of their own fruit and vegetables. There was also some trapping for the cage-bird trade, though far less than with Linnets or Goldfinches. With all these pressures the Bullfinch declined at least until the Wild Bird Protection Acts of the 1890s. There was then a recovery through the first half of the twentieth century, but from the 1960s the trend reversed, possibly due to agricultural intensification (particularly the removal of hedgerows) and perhaps the loss of traditional orchards. From the 1970s to the 1990s numbers decreased so much that the species was red-listed, but in the last ten years the population has stabilised, with an estimated 158,000 territories in 2000.

Despite the national decline Swaine was able to report that Bullfinches were still widespread within Gloucestershire around 1980, and to note that they had increased since Mellersh's time. In the area covered by the Cotswolds Atlases there was an increase in the proportion of occupied tetrads from 63% to 81% between 1987 and 2007, although this was thought to be largely due to greater survey effort. The more recent of these figures is very similar to that found for the whole county during the breeding season in the current survey, although comparative TTV counts suggest a decline since the late 1980s (see fact-box). Gloucestershire BBS data show some marked year-to-year fluctuations but no clear trends since the mid-1990s.

Mellersh knew of no records of breeding Bullfinches from the Severn Vale around 1900, and Swaine considered them to be absent or scarce as breeding birds on the higher open Cotswolds. The breeding season maps show that there are still gaps in the distribution running up through the Vale and out to the Newent area, and that densities are still noticeably lower in the arable 'prairies' of the Cotswold dip-slope. The areas with highest abundance appear to be a broad band along the Cotswold scarp and high wold, and also along the southern border of the county in the Thames Area, where hedgerows tend to be less intensively managed than in the Vale farmlands. The winter maps reveal a rather wider distribution than in the breeding season, though they are still less common in the Vale.

Nowadays Bullfinches are rarely found in groups of ten or more. The highest count during an atlas TTV was 18, in December 2009 in SU19T near the south-east county border.

Of the 44 ringing recoveries of Bullfinches involving Gloucestershire up to 2010, 38 related to movements within the county. Four of the remaining six were to and from neighbouring counties, but the other two birds undertook rather long movements for this basically sedentary species: both ringed as immatures in November 1964, in different parts of the county, one was 'trapped' in Kent almost exactly a year later (perhaps in an orchard) and the other was killed by a cat in Harrow, Greater London, in May 1966.

Sponsored by M J Bradley and Margaret Headon

Species accounts

	2007–11 Atlas fieldwork					Gloucestershire trends						UK population trends	
	Number of tetrads in which recorded (max 683)					Occupied 10 km squares (max 26)				% of tetrads in which recorded (1st hour of TTV)		UK conservation status: **Amber 3**	
	Total	Confirmed	Probable	Possible	Present	1968–71	1981–84	1988–91	2007–11	1988–91	2008–11	Long term	Short term
Breeding	561	141	284	113	23	26		26	26	50.9	36.3	–47%	–4%
Winter	606						26		26			–	–

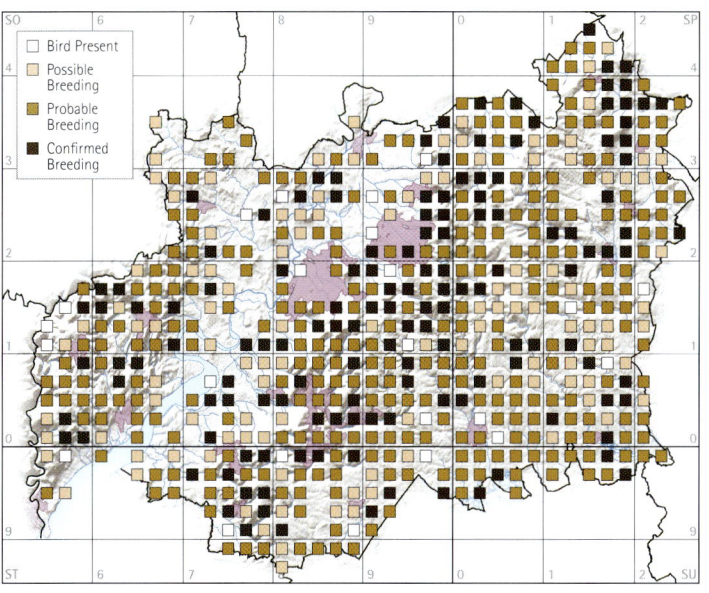

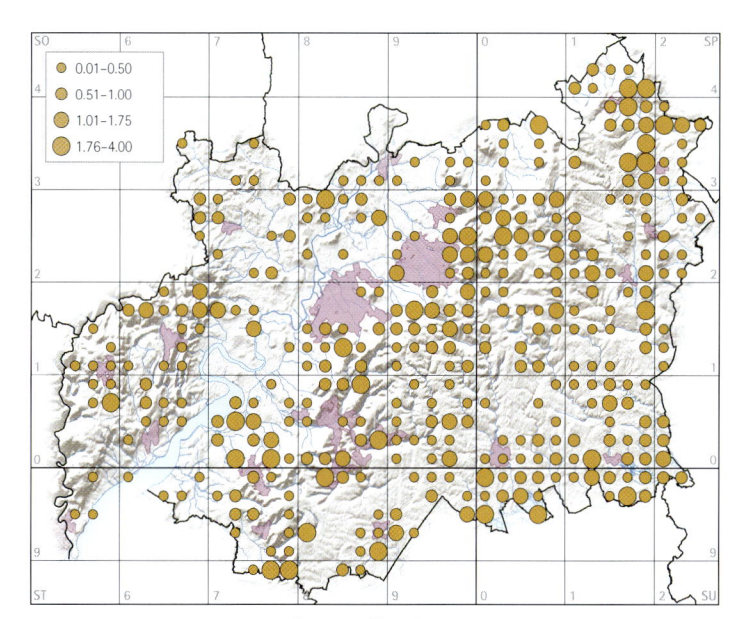

Breeding Distribution

Summer Abundance

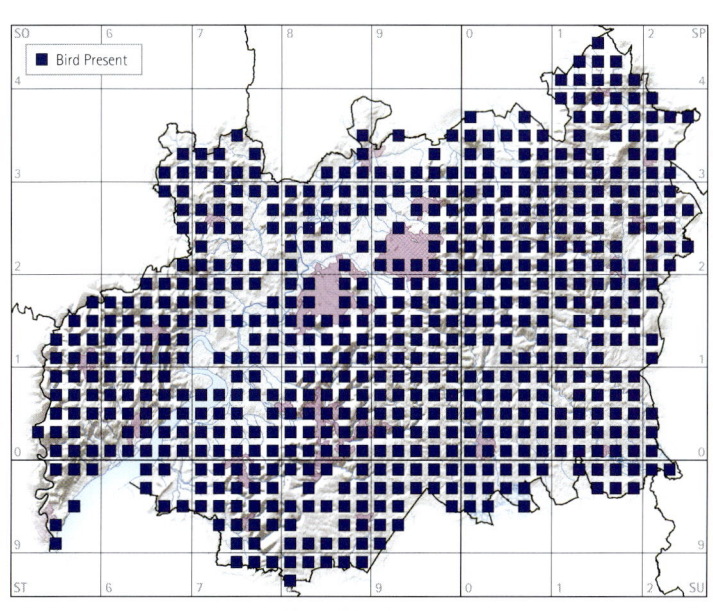

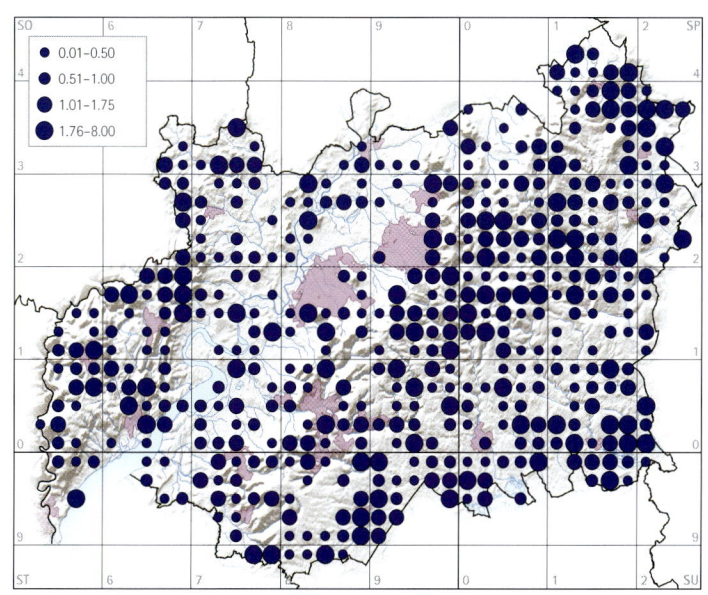

Winter Distribution

Winter Abundance

Hawfinch
Coccothraustes coccothraustes

Hawfinches breed across the Palearctic from Britain to Japan, mainly in broad-leaved woodlands. Their distribution is ultimately determined by the presence of the trees whose hard fruits provide their favoured food: beech, hornbeam, yew, wild cherry, sycamore, hawthorn and wych elm (Hagemeijer & Blair 1997). Elm seeds in particular are a valuable food source in the early spring, when other seeds are becoming depleted. Hawfinches are essentially woodland birds, but where they are common they also use cherry and plum orchards, well-wooded gardens and parks. Northern populations are partly migratory but British birds are basically resident, though they may become more widespread in winter.

There have been increases over most of Europe during the last 25 years or so (Hagemeijer & Blair 1997), but in Britain the range has contracted: between the 1968–72 and 1988–91 Breeding Atlases the number of occupied 10 km squares decreased from 459 to 315. It has been suggested that this decline could be a result of woodland fragmentation and/or the loss of elms due to Dutch elm disease. The British distribution is now very patchy, and is mainly confined to a handful of discrete pockets in the south and west.

Although Hawfinches are shy and elusive birds, their loud, distinctive calls can bring favoured woodlands alive in the late winter and early spring, when courtship and territorial activity reaches its peak. Their large-headed, short-tailed silhouette makes them unmistakeable when flying overhead.

In Gloucestershire, Mellersh described the species as 'not uncommon anywhere' at the beginning of the twentieth century. Swaine noted that they had been reported 'widely, but only in very small numbers, from the Cotswolds, Severn Vale and ... Forest of Dean' between 1950 and 1980. In the area covered by the Cotswolds Atlases, they were breeding in very small numbers in the Stow-on-the-Wold and Moreton-in-Marsh area in 1983–87, but this small colony had died out by the early 1990s. Most breeding season records during the current atlas survey came from a single core 10 km square (SO61, in the heart of the Forest of Dean), with only a few nesting records from neighbouring squares. However the two sightings in suitable habitat in the Cotswolds are encouraging.

The British breeding population has previously been estimated on a basis of 10–20 pairs per occupied 10 km square (1988–91 Breeding Atlas). However, given that they will nest semi-colonially in prime habitat, ten pairs per occupied tetrad seems more realistic for the heavily wooded Forest of Dean, suggesting a county population of some 150–200 pairs.

During the current atlas period Hawfinches were much more widespread in winter than during the breeding season, with records scattered across the county. The winter range here was apparently wider than during the 1981–84 Wintering Atlas, with sightings in almost twice as many 10 km squares (see fact-box). This could reflect an increasing presence of continental migrants, although in

Sponsored by Mr Ron Beddis

Species accounts

2007–11 Atlas fieldwork						Gloucestershire trends						UK population trends	
Number of tetrads in which recorded (max 683)						Occupied 10 km squares (max 26)				% of tetrads in which recorded (1st hour of TTV)		UK conservation status: Red 3	
	Total	Confirmed	Probable	Possible	Present	1968–71	1981–84	1988–91	2007–11	1988–91	2008–11	Long term	Short term
Breeding	27	5	8	10	4	10		6	7	1.4	0.1	–	–
Winter	62							10	18			–	–

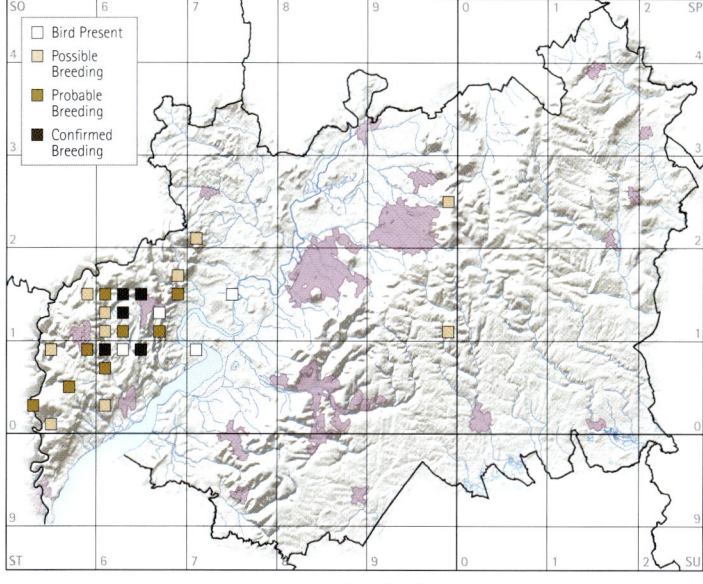

Breeding Distribution

winter 2009–10, when presumed continental birds were present in the Forest of Dean, numbers of records were not particularly high elsewhere in the county.

The Forestry Commission has established feeding areas for Hawfinches in the Dean in recent years, and since 2001 some 260 birds have been ringed there. Together with a similar number in the Gwent part of the lower Wye Valley, the total represents some 25% of all Hawfinches ever ringed in Britain.

The ringing has revealed that movements between the Dean and the Wye Valley are so frequent that birds in this whole area must be considered as a single population, and this region is now one of the species' main pockets of abundance in Britain.

Relatively few Hawfinches having been ringed in total, there are correspondingly few recoveries. However a handful of foreign-ringed birds, mainly from southern Norway, have been recovered in Britain, suggesting a possibly regular influx of northern birds during the winter. Although most of these movements have been to northern Britain, a Norwegian-ringed bird was caught in the Dean in March 2010 and a Swedish-ringed bird was caught there in March 2012.

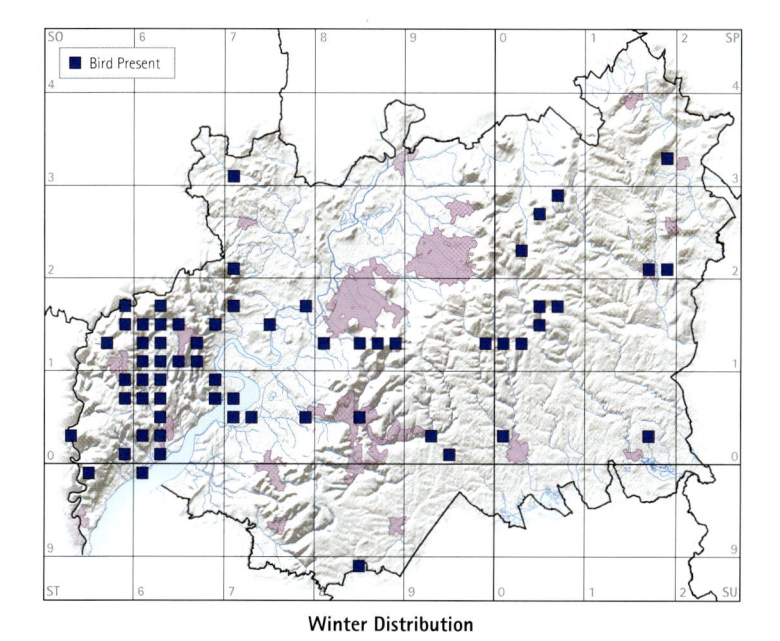

Winter Distribution

PETER PARTINGTON

Serin (European Serin)
Serinus serinus

Following a marked northward range expansion from the early nineteenth century onwards, the Serin now breeds over most of continental Europe. There are very occasional nesting records in southern England, but the Serin is known here mainly as a very scarce spring and autumn migrant. It was removed from the national rarities list in 1983. There have been three records in Gloucestershire:

1961: one fed on thistles in the enclosures at Slimbridge from July 13th to 16th.
1968: one flew over Slimbridge calling on April 6th.
1979: a male near Sandhurst, Gloucester on September 7th.

Twite
Carduelis flavirostris

Twite breed in upland regions of the British Isles and Fennoscandia, and also in south-central Asia. Norway holds the bulk of the European population. In the British Isles, breeding numbers are plummeting; the 1988–91 Breeding Atlas gave an estimate of 62,000 pairs, but this had decreased to just 10,000 pairs by the end of the century (Langston *et al.* 2006). Twite tend to move to lower ground, particularly coastal salt-marsh, in the winter.

The Gloucestershire records reflect the long-term decline. Mellersh's manuscripts suggest that flocks of Twite could be found on Cleeve Hill on occasions in the 1880s, and a comment in Witchell & Strugnell referred to the species as 'common'. By 1902, Mellersh regarded the Twite as a winter visitor, 'less frequent than formerly' and chiefly to the higher Cotswolds. The only Cotswold record since then however was a single bird at Bourton-on-the-Water in January and February 1932. Ones and twos were reported in the Frampton–Slimbridge area on five occasions between 1966 and 1980, and a remarkable flock of 25 was at the Cotswold Water Park on November 23rd 1980. There were nine by the estuary at Frampton on March 4th 1984, two remaining until April 5th, and the most recent county record was of a male at Beachley Point on January 17th 1987.

Mealy Redpoll (Common Redpoll)
Carduelis flammea

Until 2001 regarded as conspecific with the Lesser Redpoll *C. cabaret*, this species has a circumpolar distribution in high latitudes, and in Europe it breeds in Fennoscandia. European Mealy Redpolls generally migrate south-east from their breeding grounds, but in some years some head south-west and winter in the British Isles, usually in the company of Lesser Redpolls. Swaine notes that this species was seen 'from time to time' in Gloucestershire, and this is still the case. Nowadays they are recorded in most years in very small numbers, the largest recent group being five near Littledean in winter 2005–06. In the last ten years there has been an increase in the number of birds reported, but this may well be because observers are taking more interest in the difficult task of distinguishing between Mealy and Lesser Redpolls since the species were separated.

Arctic Redpoll
Carduelis hornemanni

Arctic Redpolls breed on the tundra of Eurasia and North America. Most British records for which the race is determined relate to Coues's Redpoll *C. h. exilipes*, which was removed from the national rarities list following an influx of 431 birds in winter 1995–96 that more than doubled the previous total; however it has become much rarer again in Britain since 2005. It was in 1996 during the major invasion that the only Gloucestershire sighting was recorded: a male in Highnam Woods between February 16th and 21st and again on March 20th and 21st (Avery & Jayne 1996).

Two-barred Crossbill
Loxia leucoptera

The Old World subspecies of the Two-barred Crossbill breeds in the larch forests of northern Eurasia, from where it makes irregular dispersive or eruptive southward movements. There were 173 British records between 1950 and 2010, including 23 birds in both 1987 and 1990, and 59 in 2008. Most records coincide with Common Crossbill invasions and are concentrated in the east.

The only record in Gloucestershire relates to a female at New Fancy View in the Forest of Dean from February 15th to March 16th 1998 (Heaven 1998).

Parrot Crossbill
Loxia pytyopsittacus

The Parrot Crossbill breeds across northern Eurasia and sometimes irrupts into western and central Europe. It has bred rarely in East Anglia since 1984 and a survey in 2008 (Summers & Buckland 2010) found about 100 birds breeding in the Scottish highlands.

There is one record for Gloucestershire. Of three 'Crossbills' killed near Cheltenham in late November 1861, two preserved specimens were identified by H. F. Witherby in 1935 as Parrot Crossbills. This stood for over 100 years as the only 'multiple' record of the species in Britain.

Common Rosefinch
Carpodacus erythrinus

This bright-coloured (in the male) but surprisingly unobtrusive finch has extended its range westwards into Europe over the last two centuries. The wintering areas are in southern Asia from Pakistan to China, but increasing numbers have been seen in Britain in recent decades and it was removed from the national rarities list in 1983.

There has been just one record in Gloucestershire: a male sang from willows at Ashleworth Ham from May 31st to June 3rd 2009 (Smart 2009).

Snow Bunting
Plectrophenax nivalis

Snow Buntings have a circumpolar breeding distribution, extending further north into the Arctic than Lapland Buntings, but also with a small population in the Scottish mountains. They migrate south for the winter, European birds regularly reaching the Black Sea. In Britain they are commonest in winter along the east coast, but they are also regularly seen elsewhere, including inland.

Swaine described the Snow Bunting as an irregular winter visitor to the county, occurring singly or in parties of fewer than ten birds. Since 1950 there have been about 70 county records involving some 130 birds. Approximate numbers of records and birds per decade, and the number of records per month, are shown in the graphs. Swaine listed additional records from April 1951 and May 1958, but these are no longer considered to be acceptable.

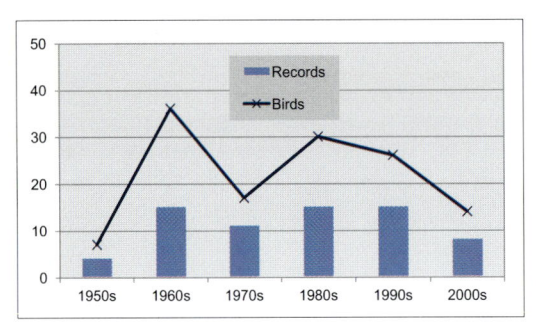

Snow Bunting records by decade, 1950-2009.

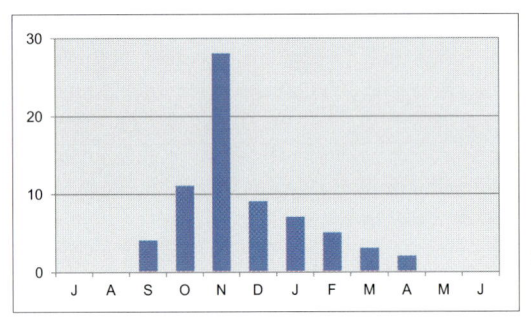

Snow Bunting 1950-2010 by month of finding.

Of post-1950 records about 80% were singles, 16% involved groups of two to nine birds, and there have been two double-figure flocks: ten flying south over Frampton Pools on October 21st 1984, and a flock by the Severn Estuary at Slimbridge from December 1996 to February 1997 which peaked at 12 on January 14th. About 80% of autumn records (September to November) were one-day sightings, compared with 50% in winter (December to February); evidently autumn birds here are more likely to be passing straight through en route to winter quarters elsewhere. Only ten of the 70 records involved birds remaining for more than ten days.

The earliest sighting in the county was one at Slimbridge on September 20th 1963, and the latest was at Coombe Hill Meadows on April 4th 1959. Although Mellersh stated that prior to 1900 most were seen in the Cotswolds, records nowadays come mainly from the estuary, especially the well-watched Slimbridge area.

Lapland Bunting (Lapland Longspur)
Calcarius lapponicus

Lapland Buntings breed all round the circumpolar arctic and boreal regions. Western Palearctic birds winter mostly in southern Russia and Ukraine, but some Fennoscandian breeders also winter in north-west Europe, including the British Isles, where they are joined by some from Greenland.

A few pairs have bred in Scotland in recent decades but it is as passage migrants and winter visitors that they are best known in Britain. Most winter at or near the east coast of England, but there are fairly frequent records elsewhere, including some inland.

The earliest report in Gloucestershire was of one 'found alive in a shed housing canaries and other caged birds' at Wotton-under-Edge in October 1956 (Swaine); however this record does not satisfy modern criteria for acceptance and the first authenticated sighting was at Slimbridge on November 20th 1967.

There have now been 15 county records: two in the 1960s, three in the 1970s, one in 1985, two in the 1990s and a remarkable seven since the year 2000. Apart from two at Slimbridge on December 12th 1977, all were single birds. Ten were found between September 21st and November 20th, one each in January and February, and two in early April. Nearly all were by the Severn Estuary at Slimbridge, the exceptions being further downriver at Lydney New Grounds on October 2nd 1998 and Aylburton Warth on November 17th 2011, and at the western section of the Cotswold Water Park on April 8th 1985. Very few have stayed longer than one day, but one remained at Slimbridge from January 25th to March 28th 2004, and sightings there on February 16th and April 1st 2011 could conceivably have related to a long-staying individual.

Yellowhammer
Emberiza citrinella

The breeding range of the Yellowhammer extends over all but the most northern and southern parts of the Western Palearctic and eastwards into Siberia. Those breeding in the north and east move south and west for the winter, but western European birds are sedentary. Populations have declined across parts of Europe since about 1980.

This is still a widespread and fairly familiar bird in much of the British Isles, but populations here have also decreased markedly since the mid-1980s. It thrives on arable farmland and in some places on scrubby uncultivated land, avoiding built-up areas and most woodland. The species was still green-listed in 1996, although there had already been some noticeable declines in parts of northern Scotland, Ireland, Wales and south-west England between the 1968–72 and 1988–91 Breeding Atlases. However it was red-listed in 2002 because of accelerating declines, thought to be due largely to the conversion of arable farmland to pasture, exacerbated by the switch from spring to autumn sowing and the consequent losses of winter stubble.

The Yellowhammer's distinctive song and conspicuous perching make it fairly easy to find in summer, and parents are often seen carrying food for their young, allowing breeding to be confirmed. However some late breeding successes may have been missed during atlas surveying as they can be feeding young into August. Winter flocks, particularly smaller groups, can be hard to find as the birds blend in surprisingly well with the background on ploughed land or in stubble.

In Gloucestershire, Mellersh reported that Yellowhammers had already ceased to breed in the Severn Vale by the end of the nineteenth century, due to the replacement of cereals by pasture. However Swaine implied that this was no longer true, noting that they were widespread and 'found quite commonly in all the main regions of the county ... probably most numerous on the dip-slope.' In the Forest of Dean they were confined to 'marginal ground' and young plantations, and winter flocks of 100–200 were 'sometimes' encountered in the Vale, the Cotswolds and the Thames Area.

The maps reveal a noticeable contrast between the Cotswolds and the rest of the county at both seasons, with a clear demarcation closely following the line of the scarp. Sightings were noticeably sparse in the Vale, conforming with Mellersh's remarks of more than 100 years ago, although some Yellowhammers do still breed there. In much of the Dean Area the habitat is not optimal, and a decrease, with local extinctions, has continued here into recent years; nevertheless, there are still a few pairs on the arable farmland of the Dean plateau.

In their Cotswolds stronghold however Yellowhammers remain very widespread and relatively common. The 2003–07 Cotswolds Atlas reported 'no evidence of a decline' between 1987 and 2007, and the current maps again show no convincing signs of the decrease that has affected other parts of the county and wide areas of the British Isles. The substantial decline in comparable TTV figures for the whole of Gloucestershire between the 1988–91 Breeding Atlas and the current survey (see fact-box), therefore implies a very considerable decrease away from the more stable Cotswolds area.

The winter maps reveal broadly the same distribution as in summer, but Yellowhammers were found in 12% fewer tetrads. This is probably because sources of winter food are more localised, causing birds to aggregate at fewer sites. Yellowhammers prefer cereal grain and other large grass seeds in winter, and these can be difficult to find in modern landscapes. Since 1990 the largest reported winter flocks have usually been between 100 and 200 birds, with no indication of any trends in maximum flock size over this period. A flock of about 500 at Dumbleton near Tewkesbury on January 28th 1996 seems to have been the largest on record in the county, and another 'enormous flock' of 300 was counted on set-aside near Birdlip on January 23rd 2003. The highest count during an atlas winter TTV was 135, in November 2010 in SP13N near Chipping Campden.

Sponsored by Krysia Kolodziejek and by the North Cotswold Ornithological Society

Species accounts

2007–11 Atlas fieldwork					Gloucestershire trends						UK population trends	
Number of tetrads in which recorded (max 683)					Occupied 10 km squares (max 26)				% of tetrads in which recorded (1st hour of TTV)		UK conservation status: **Red 3**	
	Total	Confirmed	Probable	Possible	Present	1968–71	1981–84	1988–91	2007–11	1988–91	2008–11	Long term	Short term
Breeding	532	225	171	123	13	26		26	26	76.5	55.1	–56%	–17%
Winter	463						26		26			–	–

Breeding Distribution

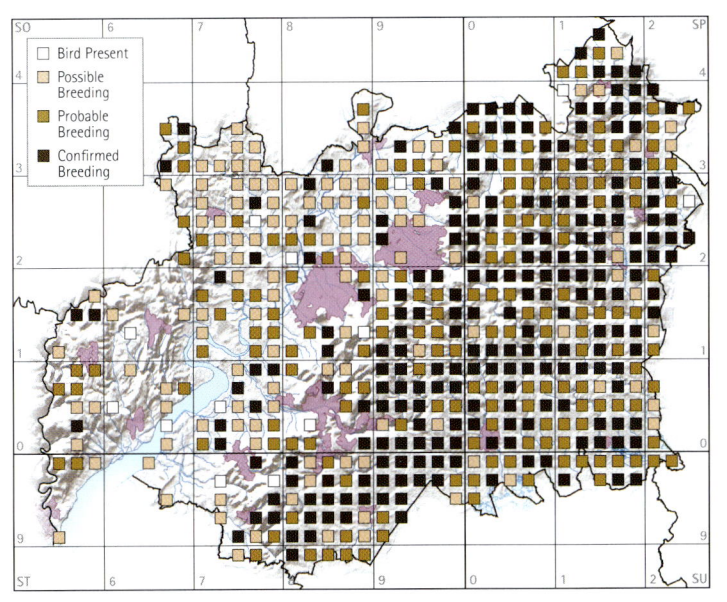

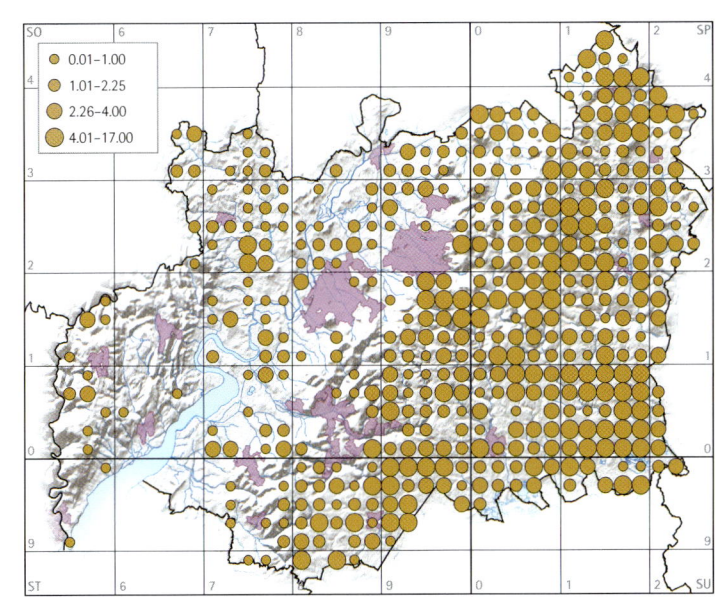

Summer Abundance

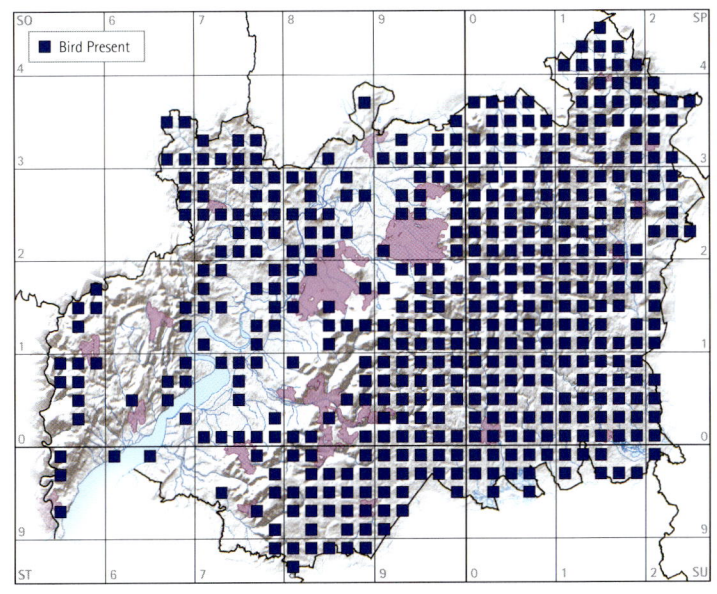

Winter Distribution

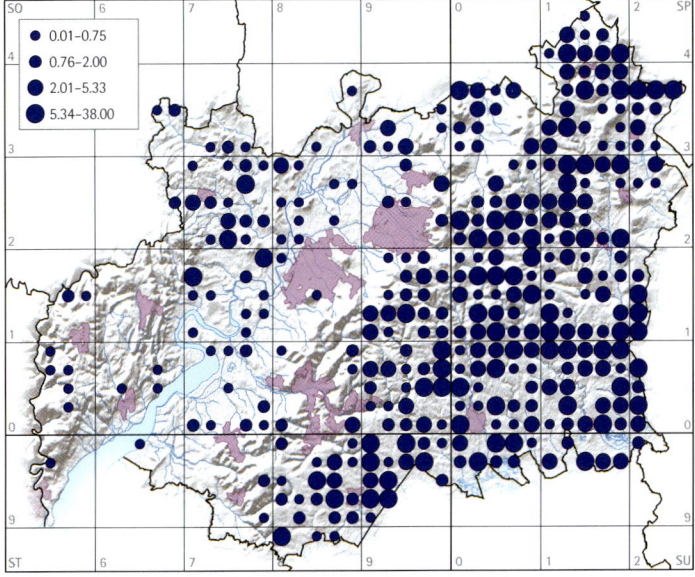

Winter Abundance

Reed Bunting (Common Reed Bunting)
Emberiza schoeniclus

Reed Buntings breed over practically all of the Western Palearctic apart from most of the Mediterranean basin, and eastwards across wide areas of northern Asia. They are mainly resident in the south-west, but many birds leave northern and eastern Europe for the winter, moving as far as the southern shores of the Mediterranean. Most British Isles breeders are sedentary but a minority, especially in the north, move to milder areas to winter; a few reach continental Europe. In addition a few Fennoscandian breeders winter here.

Although wetlands are their preferred breeding habitat, Reed Buntings will 'spill over' into drier areas such as young forestry plantations and farmland (particularly oil-seed rape), and in winter they are more wide-ranging, foraging on seeds with other buntings and finches.

British populations decreased sharply after the mid-1970s, almost certainly due to a decline in the availability of winter seeds as a result of agricultural intensification (Migration Atlas). However numbers subsequently stabilised and have shown signs of a recovery in recent years, perhaps partly helped by the increased use of rape fields.

In Gloucestershire, Swaine noted that Reed Buntings were 'present at all seasons and not uncommon in suitable habitats ... more widespread in autumn and winter and flocks of 30–40 birds, occasionally more, have been noted'. The breeding season maps show that, as might be expected, Reed Buntings are most common in the Severn Vale and the extensive wetlands of the Cotswold Water Park, and are much more thinly scattered on the Cotswolds and in the Forest of Dean. This has always been a fairly scarce species in the Cotswolds because of a scarcity of suitable habitat but, in the area covered by the two Cotswolds Atlases, an 80% increase in tetrad occupancy was registered between 1987 and 2007, though this may have been partly due to better coverage. In any case, it seems that the range in that area has declined again since the 2003–07 atlas, with reports from 51 tetrads in the current survey compared with 60 at that time. Over the county as a whole there has been no significant change since the 1988–91 Breeding Atlas (see fact-box). The highest densities in the breeding season during the current survey were around the eastern section of the Water Park, where TTV counts of 15 were recorded in tetrads SU19P and SU19Y.

Reed Buntings are more widespread outside the breeding season, as noted by Swaine and as shown by the winter maps, even though some breeding sites may be deserted. They were found in all 10 km squares in the county in winter during the current survey. This is something of an increase since the 1981–84 Wintering Atlas, although it could partly result from unusual movements during the cold weather of winters 2008–09 and 2009–10.

Since 1990 the largest winter feeding flocks reported each year have usually ranged between 30 and 40 birds, similar to the numbers given by Swaine; a flock of 100 at Slimbridge in early 1999 was 'exceptional'. Reed Buntings form communal reed-bed roosts in winter which can support higher concentrations of birds; for example over 200 were counted arriving at such a roost near Tewkesbury in January 2007. On the other hand the highest count during a winter TTV was only 11, in December 2008 in tetrad SO71A in the Vale at Arlingham.

Although it is difficult to be certain about changes in the fortunes of this sparsely distributed species, it would seem that in Gloucestershire it is maintaining itself in fairly stable numbers but has not returned to its higher, pre-1970 population levels.

There have been 33 Reed Bunting ringing recoveries involving Gloucestershire, about two-thirds of which were within the county or to and from adjacent counties. Of the remaining 13, the furthest movements within Britain were by birds that moved from Cheshire to Gloucestershire and from here to Cornwall. More unusually, one ringed at Frampton in March 1966 died after flying into a window-pane 1,500 km away in northern Sweden in May the same year. This was the first recovery of a British-ringed Reed Bunting in that region.

Sponsored by M J & J Bridge

Species accounts

2007–11 Atlas fieldwork					Gloucestershire trends						UK population trends	
Number of tetrads in which recorded (max 683)					Occupied 10 km squares (max 26)				% of tetrads in which recorded (1st hour of TTV)		UK conservation status: **Amber 3**	
	Total	Confirmed	Probable	Possible	Present	1968–71	1981–84	1988–91	2007–11	1988–91	2008–11	Long term	Short term
Breeding	169	51	40	67	11	19		21	22	11.2	10.4	−33%	+30%
Winter	199						21		26			–	–

Breeding Distribution

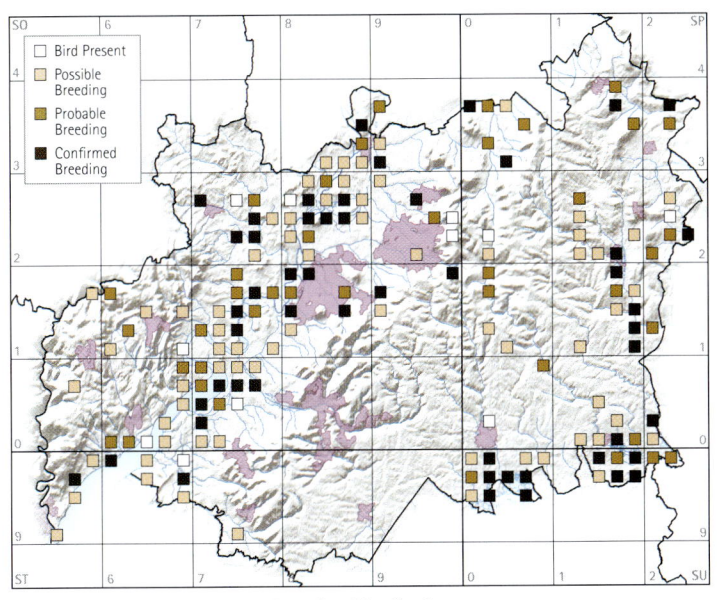

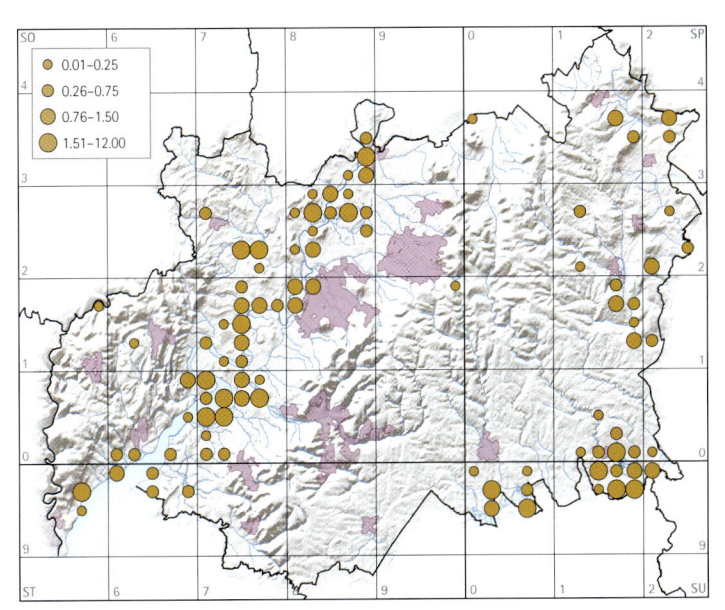

Summer Abundance

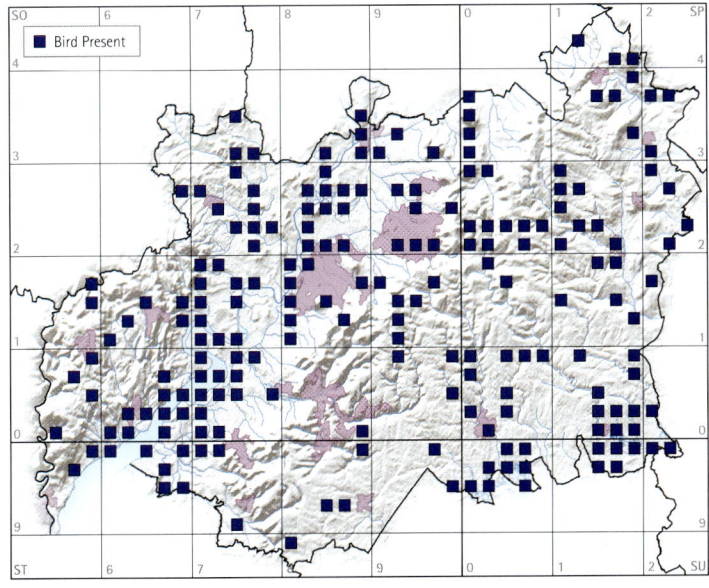

Winter Distribution

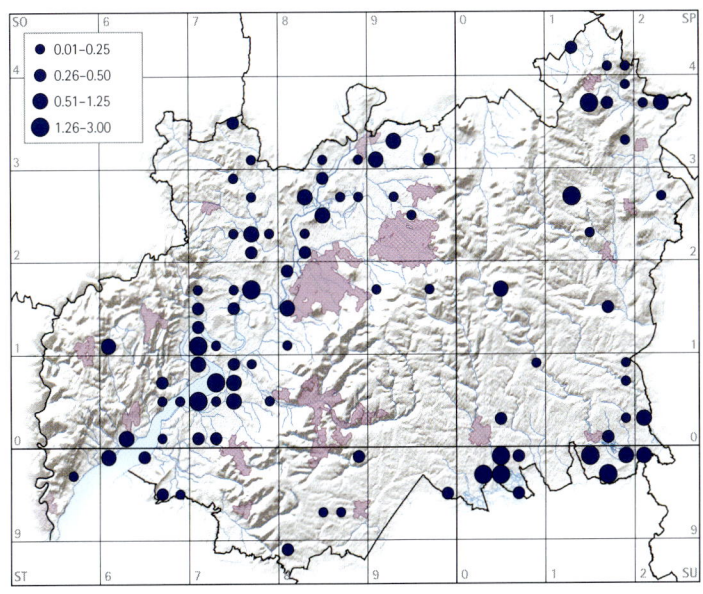

Winter Abundance

Corn Bunting
Emberiza calandra

Corn Buntings have suffered particularly badly from the intensification of farming since the mid-twentieth century. They need a reliable supply of seeds over winter (formerly readily available in cereal stubbles) and they often nest in cereal or grass fields, where they are vulnerable to farm machinery. The 1988–91 Breeding Atlas suggested that they might have suffered from declines in insect food during the breeding season, while a long-term study in Scotland (Perkins *et al.* 2012) points to a decrease in the abundance of weeds among arable crops as a significant factor.

Formerly widespread across the British Isles, Corn Buntings have now been completely lost from Ireland (Taylor & O'Halloran 2002) and almost completely from Wales, and there have also been severe losses in Scotland and England. An estimate in 2000 put the British population at about 10,000 territories. The world range extends from North Africa and Britain across middle and lower Palearctic latitudes to north-west China. European populations are mainly resident and many have been in decline since about 1980.

With a far-carrying and distinctive song, Corn Buntings are fairly easy to detect during the breeding season, but nests are hard to find and as they are late breeders some fledged birds may have been missed during atlas fieldwork. In winter their unobtrusive behaviour and drab plumage, combined with their liking for large stubble fields, means that flocks can be overlooked.

In Gloucestershire, Mellersh reported that Corn Buntings were 'scarcer in the Cotswolds than in the Vale grain districts'. By about 1980 this pattern had been reversed and they were becoming increasingly restricted to the Cotswolds, although Swaine noted that there were still small numbers in the Severn Vale, from the Tewkesbury area east to the foot of the Cotswolds and south towards Gloucester, and between Arlingham and Slimbridge. They were widespread in the Cotswolds but much scarcer in the Thames Area.

Since then the range has contracted further and the Corn Bunting is now very much a bird of the Cotswolds. In the northern part of the Vale there are only occasional reports of pairs near Tewkesbury, in the Wormington area nearer the foot of the Cotswolds, and north-west of Cheltenham. Records are very unusual lower down the Vale and the population near Arlingham has disappeared.

The Cotswolds Atlases recorded a contraction from 80 to 54 occupied tetrads between 1987 and 2007; losses were most severe in the north around Chipping Campden and in the area south of Cheltenham. During the current survey Corn Buntings were found during the breeding season in about 70 tetrads in the same area, perhaps indicating a slight recovery. Over the Cotswolds as a whole, the breeding distribution map reveals that the species is mostly confined to two areas of open country very much dominated by arable farming: a fairly wide region east of a line through Cheltenham and Cirencester, and a smaller nucleus west of Tetbury. The presence of the sizeable population in this second area was only confirmed as a result of the atlas fieldwork. There are also fairly frequent records east and north-east of Fairford, where numbers have however tended to decline in recent years, and on the southern border of the county east of Tetbury, on the borders of the Cotswolds and the Thames Area. The general feeling among local birdwatchers in recent years is that Corn Buntings appear to be reasonably stable in the core areas.

One of the most remarkable finds of the winter atlas fieldwork was an impressive 300 Corn Buntings near Naunton in November 2010. As part of a Higher Level Stewardship scheme, wheat along the boundary of a field had been left uncut and had evidently attracted birds from some distance. A flock of at least 225 had been seen on ploughed land in the same area in February 2008. Other large flocks since 1980 were 120 near Ebworth, east of Painswick, in early 1984 and 110 near Naunton in February 2006. The highest count during an atlas TTV was 62 in tetrad ST88E, south-west of Tetbury, in February 2010. Swaine remarked that in winter 'occasionally up to 50 birds' were seen. It is possible that winter feeding areas have become scarcer in recent years, causing more birds to accumulate at the few remaining sites.

Sponsored by the North Cotswold Ornithological Society

Species accounts

2007–11 Atlas fieldwork						Gloucestershire trends					UK population trends	
Number of tetrads in which recorded (max 683)					Occupied 10 km squares (max 26)				% of tetrads in which recorded (1st hour of TTV)		UK conservation status: **Red 2,3**	
	Total	Confirmed	Probable	Possible	Present	1968–71	1981–84	1988–91	2007–11	1988–91	2008–11	Long term	Short term
Breeding	94	21	37	29	7	17		17	14	8.1	3.8	−90%	−33%
Winter	43						17		10			−	−

Breeding Distribution

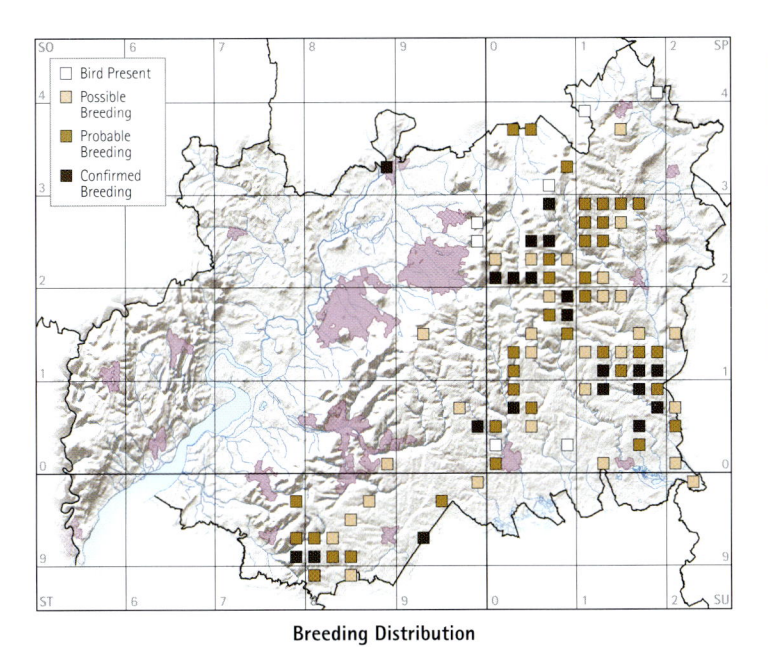

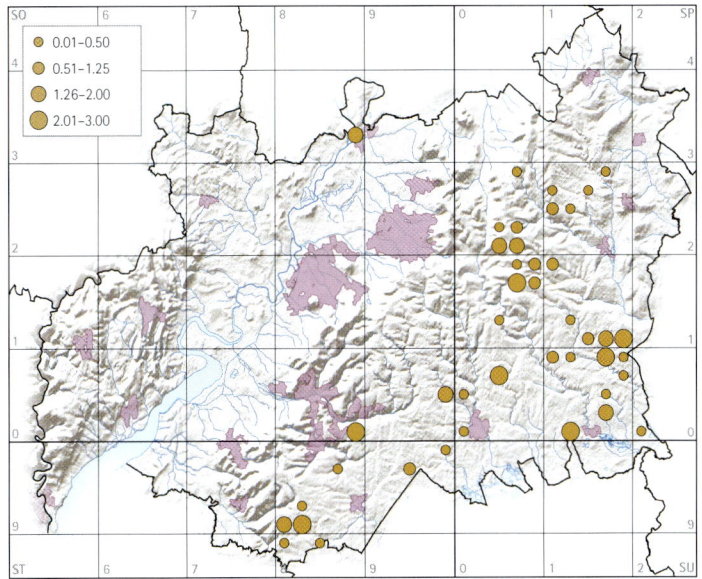

Summer Abundance

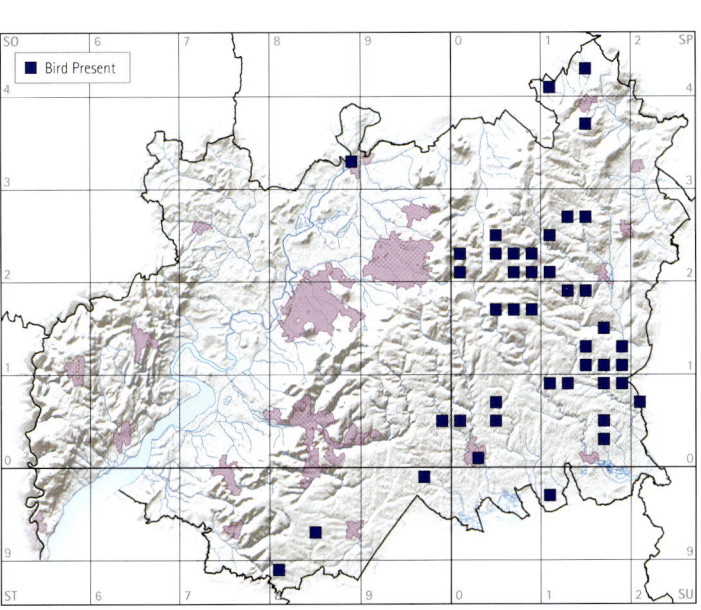

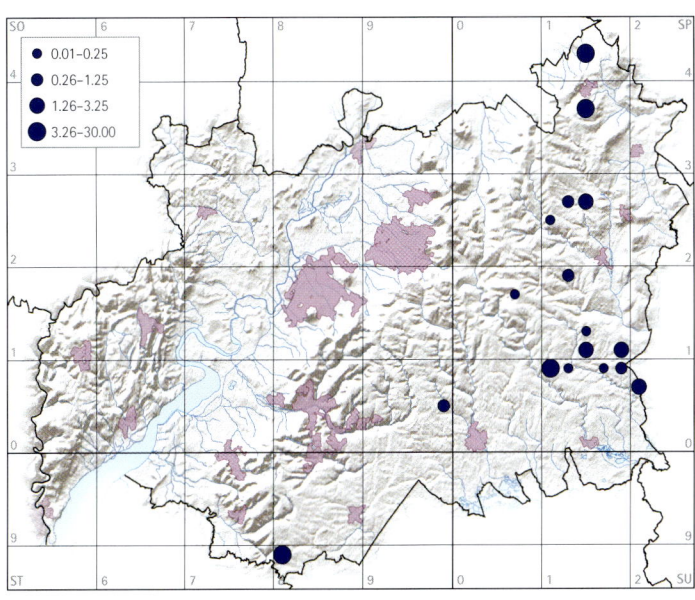

Winter Distribution

Winter Abundance

Cirl Bunting
Emberiza cirlus

With fairly exacting requirements in terms of climate and habitat, Cirl Buntings are found only in the warmer countries of western and southern Europe, Turkey and north-west Africa. They are mostly resident except in colder parts of the range, where many birds move away for the winter. Both range and numbers have suffered a long-term decline in the north-west, including in Britain, but they have spread in the south and east, and indeed the European population in general has enjoyed a 'moderate increase' in recent times (Hagemeijer & Blair 1997). They were first recorded breeding in Britain in 1800, in south Devon (BWP), and subsequently spread over wide areas of England and Wales. Numbers peaked in the 1930s, but by 1938 there was already evidence of a decline in the north and west; Witherby *et al.* (1938–41) described them as 'widely, but locally distributed'. Over the next few decades there was a precipitous decline and, by the time of the 1988–91 Breeding Atlas, Cirl Buntings had more or less withdrawn to south Devon, which remains their stronghold. Intensive conservation measures since then have brought about an increase in numbers in this core area, and a new population has recently been artificially established in Cornwall, but there are no indications of further expansion.

The historical information about Cirl Buntings in Gloucestershire is rather confusing, as the various sources give different opinions as to their status. In 1892 Witchell & Strugnell described them as 'generally distributed, but nowhere abundant', and in 1902 Mellersh, referring to the Severn Vale, stated that they were 'fairly common' and nested 'throughout the district'. This almost certainly reflects a very patchy distribution (most authors were confining their accounts to a small area) so the status of Cirl Buntings in Gloucestershire from about 1850 to 1950 is perhaps best described as 'resident, but local and not common'. The evidence suggests that they favoured lower-lying areas in the Vale and possibly along the lower slopes of the Cotswold scarp, but were absent or at best very uncommon in the higher wolds. This is certainly in keeping with their intolerance of lower temperatures and their requirements for areas with small fields, large hedgerows and tall trees. The county bird reports, which started in 1947, include confirmed breeding records from Apperley, Moreton Valence, Highnam, Lassington, Taynton and Minsterworth (all in the Severn Vale) up to the mid-1950s, but these reflect the last remnants of a disappearing population. There are a few further records up to 1960 of both singing males and wintering birds, but these were probably wanderers from a relict population in Worcestershire (Lord *et al.* 1970; Harrison *et al.* 1982). Since 1960 there has been just one record: two males feeding in a garden at Frocester near Stonehouse in September 1981.

Little Bunting
Emberiza pusilla

This Northern Palearctic species is a scarce annual migrant to Britain, having been removed from the national rarities list in 1994. Three-quarters of records have been in autumn, and over half in October alone, suggesting that both Gloucestershire birds had arrived some time before they were found:

- 2002: one at Tidenham Chase in the Forest of Dean from November 28th to February 22nd 2003.
- 2006: one was found in Cam, near Dursley, during an RSPB Garden Birdwatch on January 29th, and was seen daily until April 29th.

Dark-eyed Junco
Junco hyemalis

The nominate subspecies, 'Slate-coloured Junco', to which these records refer, breeds in the north and east of North America and is a partial migrant. It is a rare vagrant to the Western Palearctic and there had been 36 British records by the end of 2010, mostly during spring. Few years produce more than one individual, so it is intriguing that six occurred in 2007 and four in 2008. Quite remarkably for a Nearctic landbird, there have been two records in Gloucestershire:

- 1975: a male at Haresfield near Stroud from April 1st to 12th.
- 2010: a first-year male near Witcombe from January 8th until April 7th.

Exotics and escapes

Many birds that are kept in captivity in Britain escape or are released. Some establish self-sustaining populations, become recognised as part of the country's avifauna and are admitted to Category C of the British List: examples are Canada Goose, Mandarin, Ruddy Duck, Pheasant, Red-legged Partridge and Little Owl. All such species are treated in the main species accounts, as are Red Kite, Great Bustard and Crane, which are currently the subjects of reintroduction schemes in or around Gloucestershire.

The status of originally alien or 'exotic' species at a particular time and in a specific area of the country may depend on how long they have been present in Britain and where they were introduced. Thus for example there are well-established feral breeding populations of Barnacle Geese and Red-crested Pochards in Gloucestershire, so we have included them in the main species accounts, but we still regard Ring-necked Parakeets and Black Swans as 'exotics' here, even though the former has been admitted to Category C on the basis of the large, self-sustaining population in the Home Counties and the latter may also be in the process of establishing itself in the country.

There is little information on this topic in previous Gloucestershire bird books; Swaine mentions species that 'are establishing self-maintaining breeding populations' but makes no reference to other escapes. The information below summarises all known county records from 1980 to 2010, although systematic recording of exotics in the GBR did not start until 1994. Rather than putting all species in a single list, we feel it is more informative to group them according to the circumstances in which they are generally kept in captivity. The figures in brackets refer to the numbers of records of each species since 1980, which provide an approximate guide to how common or otherwise these birds are, but readers should bear in mind that individual birds are often seen several times in different places, and conversely many birdwatchers still do not report sightings of 'exotics' and common 'tame' species such as domestic breeds of Mallard.

In general, species that have been recorded in Gloucestershire as wild birds (and which therefore have their own species accounts) are not included here, even though captive individuals of some of these species, particularly wildfowl, have also occurred in the county.

Wildfowl

Swans, geese and ducks are often kept in collections, and Slimbridge has one of the largest in the world, so it is no surprise that this group has most species, with records as follows:

Black Swan *Cygnus atratus* (281). This originally Australasian species has been recorded almost every year since 1980, with some long-staying birds and at least two successful breeding attempts. They tend to breed during the southern summer and territorial birds can be very aggressive towards Bewick's and Whooper Swans, so they are not particularly welcome on these species' wintering grounds.

Ruddy Shelduck *Tadorna ferruginea* (41) plus hybrid Ruddy Shelduck x Shelduck (one). Ruddy Shelducks are common in wildfowl collections and sightings are usually assumed to be of escaped birds, even though there are wild populations as close as eastern Europe and genuine migrants are believed to have occurred very infrequently in Britain. Escaped birds have occasionally bred in the country.

Bar-headed Goose *Anser indicus* (80) plus hybrid Bar-headed Goose x Greylag Goose (10).

Muscovy Duck *Cairina moschata* (69).

Chiloe Wigeon *Anas sibilatrix* (14).

Wood Duck *Aix sponsa* (12).

Ringed Teal *Callonetta leucophrys* (seven).

White-cheeked (Bahama) Pintail *Anas bahamensis* (two).

There are single records of Fulvous Whistling Duck *Dendrocygna bicolor*, Emperor Goose *Chen canagica*, Ross's Goose *Anser rossii*, Australian Shelduck *Tadorna tadornoides* (plus hybrid Australian Shelduck x Paradise Shelduck *Tadorna variegata* and another unknown hybrid involving this species), Cinnamon Teal *Anas cyanoptera*, Speckled (Yellow-billed) Teal *Anas flavirostris*

(= *A. andium*), Cape Teal *Anas capensis* and Hooded Merganser *Lophodytes cucullatus*.

In this group there are also numerous records of hybrids between various *Aythya* ducks, many of which involve escaped birds.

Gamebirds

This group consists mainly of pheasants, which are often kept in captivity. Some of these species have established small breeding populations in other parts of Britain.

Helmeted Guineafowl *Numida meleagris* (12).

Golden Pheasant *Chrysolophus pictus* (10).

Indian Peafowl *Pavo cristatus* (six).

Reeves's Pheasant *Syrmaticus reevesii* (three).

Lady Amherst's Pheasant *Chrysolophus amherstiae* (two).

Silver Pheasant *Lophura nycthemera* (one).

Blue-eared Pheasant *Crossoptilon auritum* (one).

Raptors and owls

These will have escaped from 'birds of prey' collections or from individual falconers.

Eagle Owl *Bubo bubo* (three).

Bengal Eagle Owl *Bubo bengalensis* (two).

Lanner *Falco biarmicus* (two).

Gyr Falcon *Falco rusticolus* (two) (note that this species *has* occurred as a wild bird (see p. 149), but two records are believed to have been falconers' birds).

Bald Eagle *Haliaeetus leucocephalus* (one).

Harris's Hawk *Parabuteo unicinctus* (one).

Also in this group are various hybrids between Peregrine, Lanner, Saker *Falco cherrug* and probably other falcons.

Cage-birds and pets

Some of the parrots and related species are capable of surviving for some time in the wild in Britain – the Blue-and-yellow Macaw mentioned here frequented the Robinswood Hill area of Gloucester from at least August 2005 to February 2010. This group also includes Ring-necked Parakeet, which now breeds commonly in the Home Counties and is still spreading.

Ring-necked Parakeet (Rose-ringed Parakeet) *Psittacula krameri* (23).

Cockatiel *Nymphicus hollandicus* (four).

Budgerigar *Melopsittacus undulatus* (two).

Blue-and-yellow Macaw *Ara ararauna* (two).

Diamond Dove *Geopelia cuneata* (two).

Zebra Finch *Taeniopygia guttata* (two).

There are also single records of Alexandrine Parakeet *Psittacula eupatria*, Peach-faced (Rosy-faced) Lovebird *Agapornis roseicollis*, Barbary Dove *Streptopelia risoria*, Black-naped Oriole *Oriolus chinensis*, White-collared Yuhina *Yuhina diademata*, White-throated Laughingthrush *Garrulax albogularis*, Greater Necklaced Laughingthrush *Garrulax pectoralis*, Amethyst (Violet-backed) Starling *Cinnyricinclus leucogaster*, Canary *Serinus canaria*, Red-billed Quelea *Quelea quelea*, Village Weaver *Ploceus cucullatus* and Superb Starling *Lamprotornis superbus* (this bird was recorded in the GBR for 2000 as a 'Superb Spireo *Spireo supurbus*' [sic], and is assumed to be this species, as the former scientific name was *Spreo superbus*).

There are about 20 other records of unknown or unidentified parrot and parakeet species.

Finally there are single records of a few miscellaneous waterbirds known to be kept in collections: Flamingo *Phoenicopterus* sp(p)., White Stork *Ciconia ciconia* (wild individuals of which have also been seen), White Pelican *Pelecanus onocrotalus* and Grey-headed Gull *Chroicocephalus cirrocephalus*.

Appendix 1: Square stewards and fieldworkers

Atlas square stewards

'Core' squares stewards

SO50	Ivan Proctor	SO82	Mike Smart	SP11	Andy Lewis		
SO51	John Phillips	SO90	Martin Wright	SP12	Rob Brookes, then		
SO60	Barry Embling	SO91	Terry Fenton		Andy Lewis		
SO61	John Phillips	SO92	Beryl Smith	SP13	Andy Warren		
SO70	Neil Smart	SP00	Tony Perry	SP22	Terry Barratt		
SO71	Andrew Jayne	SP01	Dave Pearce	ST69	Roy Jellings		
SO72	Mervyn Greening	SP02	Steve Owen	ST79	Vic Polley		
SO80	Gordon Kirk	SP03	Tim Hutton	ST89	Philip Boobyer		
SO81	Paul Masters	SP10	Ian Ralphs	ST99	Philip Pope		

Border squares stewards

SO62/63/73	Juliet Bailey
SO83/93	Mike Smart
ST78/88 and SU09/19/29	Gordon Kirk
SP14/20/21	Andy Lewis
SP23	Terry Barratt
ST59	John Phillips

Atlas observers

This list contains the names of everyone who submitted Gloucestershire records to the BTO for the atlas fieldwork or to BirdTrack during the atlas period. Names are shown in the format in which they were submitted to the BTO.

Duncan Michael Abbott
David Ackland
Debbie Adams
Nick Adams
Jonathan Adey
Mike Alexander
Colin Allen
Elizabeth Allen
Sherry Allen-Pearson
David Anderson
S E Andrews
Shaun Ankers
Diane Aps
Mike Archer
John Arnfield
Sue Arnold

John Arrowsmith
David Ashdown
Simon Ashley
Peter Atkey
Paul Aubrey
V J Austin
M I Avery
Richard Baatsen
Claire Backshall
Geoffrey Bailey
Juliet Bailey
Colin Baker
Philip Baker
Arthur Ball
Kay Ball
Ann Banks

S R J Barker
P Barlow
Dave Barnes
Prunella Barnes
Martin Barnsley
T I Barratt
Michael Barrett
Christopher Bartlett
Alan Baxter
Sam Bayley
John Bayliss
J Beal
Sarah Beall
Ron Beddis
Alison Bennett
Val Bentley

Andrew Bevan
Gerry Bilbao
Robert Billingsley
Alastair Binham
Richard Birch
Roger Birch
R K Bircher
John Birkett
G Bishton
Lesley Bizley
Gavin Black
Austin Blackburn
Paul Blackburn
James Blair
Richard Bland
Robert Bloor

Andrew Bluett
William Blumsom
Catherine Blundell
Trevor Blythe
Mervyn Bonham
Philip Boobyer
Robert Boon
Christopher Booth
Peter Robert Brash
Andy Bray
Kane Brides
M J Bridge
Christopher Britton
Dru Brooke-Taylor
Colin Brooks
Ruth Brown
Janet Bryan
Sylvia Bryan
L W Buchanan
Frances Buckel
M A Bullen
Graham Bullivant
Bob Bullock
Nicky Bullock
Kelvin Bulpin
Tom Burditt
David Burns
Jeff Butcher
A J Butler
Dick Butling
Brian Caffrey
Mike Caiden
Bruce Calder
George Candelin
Peter Capsey
Steven Carey
V Carnell
Ben Carpenter
Helena Carter
P E Castle
Barry Catlin
R C Catlin
F B Caudwell
R Chadburn
David Chadwick
Martin Chadwick
Graham Champken
Andrew Chapman
Jim Chapman
Neil Chapman
W R Chapman
Angela Charles
Clare Charlton
Dave Chown
Bill Church
Frank Charles Clark

Joanne Clark
J Clarke
Graham Clarkson
John Clements
Barbara Mary Clifton
Robert Coatsworth
Tony Coatsworth
Andrew Cobley
Richard Cockroft
John Coleman
Mark Collier
Steve Coney
Micheal Conneely
Allan Cook
Norman Cooke
Michael Cooksley
Andrew Cooper
Hannah Cooper
Christopher Coppock
Les Cornwell
Lyn Corrie
David Cosh
Ian Cox
Helen Crabtree
D J Cramp
Peter Cranswick
P M Crawshaw
Robert Crompton
Michelle Cross
Andrew Crutchley
Ken Cservenka
G C Cundale
Rob Curtis
Kenneth Cypher
Chris Dale
Paul Darby
Roger Darsley
Ian Davies
Keith Davies
Richard Davies
Steve Davies
Phil Davis
Lana Deacon
Sian Defferary
Brenda Dendy
Bob Dennison
K J Derrett
David Dewsbury
Fergus Dignan
Duncan Dine
Tom Dingwall
George Ditchburn
Julie Dix
Stewart Dobson
Nicholas John Donnithorne
FLS FRES

Amy Doore
John Dowding
Elton Patrick Drew
Ed Drewitt
Jane Elizabeth Druett
Peter Dryburgh
Robert Dunn
Brian Dyke
P E Dykes
Anthony Edwards
Stephen Edwards
I M Elphick
Joy Elworthy
Barry Embling
David Emery
Stephen England
Clare Evans
David Evans
Glynne Evans
Jessica Evans
John Evans
Michael Evans
Terry Evans
Tony Eveleigh
Richard Facey
Malcolm Fairley
Charles Farrell
Bridget Farrer
Paul Fawcett
Teresa Fenn
Terry Fenton
Roger Ferguson
David Fernleigh
Sue Finn
Terence Flanagan
Alastair Flannagan
K Fleming
M R Fletcher
B Flitcroft
Paul Floyd
John Flynn
Phil Flynn
Joe Foley
Jane Ford
Sam Forest
Jill Forshaw
Derek Foster
Oliver Fox
William Francis
Ben Fraser
David Freeman
Christopher Furley
Roy Fussell
Steven Gale
Bee Choo Gallivan
Brian Garland

Graeme Garner
Lynne Garner
Roger Gaunt
Robert Gaze
Jonathan Patrick Phillips Gilder
Andrew Godden
Nicholas James Godwin
Martin Gomer
N G Goodship
Bev Goodwin
J Gould
Terry Grant
Vaughan Grantham
Brian Gray
Richard Gray
Yvonne Grech
Harry Green
Iain Green
Colin Greenfield
M Greening
R Greer
Stuart Greer
Gillian Margaret Gregory
Paul Gregory
Sheila Gregory
Helen Jane Griffiths
Robin Griffiths
Jonathan Groom
R D Gross
Anthony Gutteridge
William Haines
Richard Hale
Allan Hall
R M Halliwell
Claire Halpin
Sheelagh Halsey
Peter Hancocks
Stewart Hares
Anthony Harris
Gareth Harris
Joe Harris
Andrew Harrison
Elizabeth Harrison
G R Harrison
Sophie Harrison
Ian Hartley
Eddie Harwood
Janet Hawes
Clive Hawkins
Bill Haynes
Margaret Hayter
William Hayward
P J Hazelwood
Richard Hearn
Brian Hedley
Martin Henderson

Appendix 1: Square stewards and fieldworkers

Anthony Paul Herbert
Ken Heron
Roger Hewitt
Rupert Higgins
Christopher Hill
John Hingley
Mark Paul Hobson
Debbie Hodges
John Holder
David Holland
R Homan
Christine Horsley
Tim Hounsome
Alexander Howard
A Hughes
Susan Hughes
Trevor Hughes
Richard Humphrey
Richard Humphreys
D J Humphries
Catherine Hunt
M S Hunt
Kathryn Hunter
Robin Husbands
Edward Hutchings
J V P Hutchins
Eric Hutchinson
A Hutchison
T C Hutton
Colin Hyde
Colin Isted
David Jackson
Virginia James
Andrew Jayne
M Jeeves
Roy Jellings
Rosalind John
Laura Johns
Tana Johnson
Michael Johnstone
Ceri Jones
Dyfed Wyn Jones
Elizabeth Jones
Ennis Jones
Graham Jones
Keith Jones
Ken Jones
Meurig Giles Morgan Jones
P H Jones
Tim Jones
Carole Jordan
Derek Julian
Norman Kaduck
John Kedward
Alistair Keen
David Kennett

David King
J King
Mike King
Paul King
Wilfred King
Kevin Kingscott
Melvyn Kirby
Gordon Kirk
Krystyna Kolodziejek
Gehardt Kruckow
Margaret Janet Kyffin
D A Lane
Mark Lang
Charles Lankester
Anthony Lansdown
Richard Lansdown
David Lathbury
Helen Layton
Vincent Lea
Mary Leathwood
David Lee
Kenneth Lee
Jonathon Lees
Andy Lewis
Jerry Lewis
Mike Lewis
Red Liford
Cris Little
Gavin Rhys Lloyd
Thomas Howard Lloyd
Andy Lodge
Garth Lowe
Clare Lyddon
Lorna Lythgoe
Ben Macdonald
Georgie Mackie-Forrest
Paul Madgett
Peter Maguire
Iain Main
Simon Mair
Michal Maniakowski
Hugh Manistre
Lynn Mann
Graham Christopher Maples
A R Marfell
Nick Marriner
Fen Marshall
Paul Marshall
Stephen Keith Marshall
Graham Martin
James Martin
Jeff Martin
John Martin
Robert Martin
Ruth Martin
Paul Masters

Carol Mathews
Emily Matthews
Richard May
Lynne Mayers
Dave Mayfield
Trevor Maynard
John McCaig
Tracy McCarthy
Ian McCulloch
Andrew Raymond McDermid
Stuart McFarlane
Martin John McGill
Katy McGilvray
Graeme McLaren
Jon McLeod
E K McMahon
Alexander McNeil
Peter McQuail
Kathy Meakin
John Melling
Catherine Constantsia Mendez
J H Mercer
George Merry
J E Middleton
John Miles
Mark Miles
H J Miller
Barrie Mills
John Milner
Kim Milsom
James Milton
Christopher Moore
Sarah Moore
Mary Morgan
Colin Morris
Jenny Morrison
Robert Moss
Geoff Moyser
Philip Mugridge
D A Murdoch
John Murray
Steve Mynard
Richard Nash
Mervyn Needham
Kevin New
M A H Newman
S P Newman
Lesley Nickell
Peter John Norfolk
A Nuttall
Darren Oakley-Martin
Steve Oates
J O'Hanlon
Chris Oldershaw
Andrew Oliver
J C C Oliver

Padraig O'Meachair
Peter Ormerod
Eric Osbaldeston
J Osborne
Mark O'Sullivan
Steve Owen
W M Oxbury
R B Palmer
Rob Palmer
Stephen Palmer
G R Parker
Colin Parkes
Zoe Parrott
David Paynter
Darren Michael Pearce
David Pearce
Joanna Pearce
Roger Peart
Stuart Pedley
Chris Pendleton
Gavin Peplow
W F Peplow
Anthony Perry
Doreen Pettitt
Bob Phelps
Christine Phelps
Annette Phillips
N J Phillips
Roy Phillips
Viv Phillips
Malcolm Pick
Verity Picken
R H Pickering
Bekki Pierce
Lawrence Pierce
Trevor Michael Pinchen
Claire Piper
David Piper
Bryn Pitcher
Michael Pittaway
Neil Graham Pleasance
Michael Plumley
M J Pollard
Martin Polley
Bob Pomfret
Philip Pope
Robert Pople
Christopher Porter
Anne Potter
S E Powell
Tony Powell
Geoffrey Pratt
Richard Prentice
Kevan Price
David Priddis
John Prince

435

David Pritchard
Ivan Proctor
Brian Prudden
Neil Pryce-Jones
J R Pullen
R Purveur
John Putley
Richard Pye
William Quantrill
Sue Ralph
Ian Ralphs
Alan Ramsell
Neil Rawlings
Robert Ready
Eleanor Reast
Craig Reed
Jan Rees
Susan Reeves
Erwyn Rentzenbrink
Tom Reynolds
Alex Rhodes
Edward Rice
M J Ridley
Peter Ridout
Renton Righelato
Edna Riley
Gerry Robbins
Diana Roberts
Simon Roberts
Derek Robertson
M F Robinson
Peter Robinson
Ian Roe
D I Rogers
Margaret Rogers
Tony Rogers
David Rolfe
Alan Roman
Chris Ross
Nigel Ross
Nick Rossiter
Sue Rowe
Stephen Rudge
David Rugg
Jim Rushforth
Louise Russell
Kevin Rylands
W J Ryman
Michael John Saffery
D G Salmon
Alan Salter
J R Samuel

Ric Sandifer
S P Satterthwaite
Martin Saunders
Tony Scott
David Scott-Langley
Paul Seligman
Alasdair Shaw
Marc Shaw
Amanda Shipton
Beryl Simmonds
Karen Sarah Simpson
Peter Sketch
Frank Skinner
Ken Slater
Michael Smart
Neil Smart
Richard Smart
Beryl Smith
Camilla Smith
Francis Smith
Geoffrey Smith
Jonathan Smith
Julia Smith
Marcus Smith
P A Smith
Peter Smith
Wayne Brian Smith
Wilfred L Smith
Christine Smyth
B Snell
Pat Sory
Ian Speechley
I A Stachnicki
R Steer
Ann Sterry
Anne Sterry
Edward Stevens
Gavin Stewart
Dave Stoddard
Christopher Stott
Ashley Stow
Peter Strangeman
Tamasine Stretton
Martin Sullivan
John Sumner
Michael Sutcliffe
Paul Sutton
Robert Swift
Ann Swindale
Bruce Taggart
Celia Tanner
Giles Tarbuck

Amanda Tarren
Jane Taverner
A Taylor
A J Taylor
Howard Taylor
J Taylor
Paul Taylor
Valerie Anne Taylor
George Tedbury
Michael Edward Teesdale
Claire Temple
Carmel Ann Terry
Roger Theobald
Andrew Thomas
J M Thomas
Lewis Thomson
Stuart Thomson
John Tilt
Colin Titcombe
Vicky Todd
Alan Tompsett
Darren Tonge
Lyn Townsend
Sue Townsend
Mike Trew
Paul Tubb
John Tucker
Simon Tucker
Christopher Tudge
Jack Turner
R Turner
Sash Tusa
Ingrid Twissell
Annette Twyman
S J Tyler
Graham Uney
Ewan Urquhart
James Vale
Rob Vaughan
J Vickers
G F Waite
Robert Wakelam
I R Walker
David Wall
Michele Wall
Thomas Wall
Steve Wallace
Peter Walters
Robin Ward
Roger Ward
A Wardell
Kathy Warden

David William A Warner
Andy Warren
Paul Alexander Watkins
David Watson
Graham Watson
Michael Watson
Peter Watson
D Wawman
Joy Way
Alan Wearmouth
Andrew Webb
Carolyn Webb
Toby Webb
Tom Wells
Gemma Western
J Wheeler
Mike Wheeler
Mark Whitaker
Keith White
Ken White
Richard White
Chris Whitfield
J P Widgery
Barbara Wilden
A Wilkie
Colin Wilkinson
David Wilkinson
Brian Willder
Alan Williams
Elspeth Williams
Philip Williams
Robert Williams
C S Williamson
P Willis
Hazel Muriel Willmott
I J Wilton
Isabel Winstanley
Patrick Wise
Chris Withers
Adrian Wood
Barbara Wood
Shaun Woodcock
Helen Woodman
A E L Woods
M W C Woodward
Francis Workman
Jean Worthington
M R Wright
Neville Wright
D W Yalden
John Young
Susanne Zamze

Appendix 2: Scientific names of non-bird species

Alder   *Alnus* spp.
Ash   *Fraxinus excelsior*
Beech   *Fagus sylvatica*
Bilberry   *Vaccinium myrtillus*
Birch   *Betula* spp.
Black Poplar   *Populus nigra*
Bracken   *Pteridium aquilinum*
Bramble   *Rubus fruticosus*
Caddis-flies   *Trichoptera*
Crack Willow   *Salix fragilis*
Dormouse   *Muscardinus avellanarius*
Dragonflies   *Odonata*
Eel (European Eel)   *Anguilla anguilla*
Elder   *Sambucus nigra*
English Elm   *Ulmus procera*
Fallow Deer   *Dama dama*
Fox (Red Fox)   *Vulpes vulpes*
Gorse   *Ulex* spp.
Grey Squirrel   *Sciurus carolinensis*
Hawthorn   *Crataegus monogyna*
Heather   *Calluna vulgaris*
Hornbeam   *Carpinus betulus*
Larch   *Larix* spp.
Mayflies   *Ephemeroptera*
Mistletoe   *Viscum album*
Muntjac Deer (Reeves's Muntjac)   *Muntiacus reevesi*
Norway Lemming   *Lemmus lemmus*
Norway Spruce   *Picea abies*
Oak   *Quercus* spp.
Painted Lady   *Vanessa cardui*
Pine   *Pinus* spp.
Plum   *Prunus domestica*
Rabbit   *Oryctolagus cuniculus*
Reed   *Phragmites australis*
Roe Deer   *Capreolus capreolus*
Rowan   *Sorbus aucuparia*
Salmon (Atlantic Salmon)   *Salmo salar*
Scots Pine   *Pinus sylvestris*
Sessile Oak   *Quercus petraea*
Signal Crayfish   *Pacifastacus leniusculus*
Spruce   *Picea* spp.
Stoat   *Mustela erminea*
Sycamore   *Acer pseudoplatanus*
Voles   *Microtus* spp.
Weasel   *Mustela nivalis*
Wild Boar   *Sus scrofa*
Wild Cherry   *Prunus avium*
Wild Daffodil   *Narcissus pseudonarcissus*
Willow   *Salix* spp.
Winter Moth   *Operophtera brumata*
Wood Mouse   *Apodemus sylvaticus*
Wych Elm   *Ulmus glabra*
Yew   *Taxus baccata*
Zebra Mussel   *Dreissena polymorpha*

Appendix 3: A checklist of the birds of Gloucestershire

Mute Swan   *Cygnus olor*
Bewick's Swan   *Cygnus columbianus*
Whooper Swan   *Cygnus cygnus*
Bean Goose   *Anser fabalis*
Pink-footed Goose   *Anser brachyrhynchus*
White-fronted Goose   *Anser albifrons*
Lesser White-fronted Goose   *Anser erythropus*
Greylag Goose   *Anser anser*
Snow Goose   *Anser caerulescens*
Canada Goose   *Branta canadensis*
Barnacle Goose   *Branta leucopsis*
Brent Goose   *Branta bernicla*
Red-breasted Goose   *Branta ruficollis*
Egyptian Goose   *Alopochen aegyptiaca*
Shelduck   *Tadorna tadorna*
Mandarin Duck   *Aix galericulata*
Wigeon   *Anas penelope*
American Wigeon   *Anas americana*
Gadwall   *Anas strepera*
Teal   *Anas crecca*
Green-winged Teal   *Anas carolinensis*
Mallard   *Anas platyrhynchos*
Pintail   *Anas acuta*
Garganey   *Anas querquedula*
Blue-winged Teal   *Anas discors*
Shoveler   *Anas clypeata*
Red-crested Pochard   *Netta rufina*
Pochard   *Aythya ferina*
Ring-necked Duck   *Aythya collaris*
Ferruginous Duck   *Aythya nyroca*
Tufted Duck   *Aythya fuligula*
Scaup   *Aythya marila*
Lesser Scaup   *Aythya affinis*
Eider   *Somateria mollissima*
Long-tailed Duck   *Clangula hyemalis*

Common Scoter   *Melanitta nigra*
Velvet Scoter   *Melanitta fusca*
Goldeneye   *Bucephala clangula*
Smew   *Mergellus albellus*
Red-breasted Merganser   *Mergus serrator*
Goosander   *Mergus merganser*
Ruddy Duck   *Oxyura jamaicensis*
Black Grouse   *Tetrao tetrix*
Quail   *Coturnix coturnix*
Red-legged Partridge   *Alectoris rufa*
Grey Partridge   *Perdix perdix*
Pheasant   *Phasianus colchicus*
Red-throated Diver   *Gavia stellata*
Black-throated Diver   *Gavia arctica*
Pacific Diver   *Gavia pacifica*
Great Northern Diver   *Gavia immer*
Fulmar   *Fulmarus glacialis*
Manx Shearwater   *Puffinus puffinus*
Storm Petrel   *Hydrobates pelagicus*
Leach's Petrel   *Oceanodroma leucorhoa*
Gannet   *Morus bassanus*
Cormorant   *Phalacrocorax carbo*
Shag   *Phalacrocorax aristotelis*
Bittern   *Botaurus stellaris*
Little Bittern   *Ixobrychus minutus*
Night-heron   *Nycticorax nycticorax*
Squacco Heron   *Ardeola ralloides*
Cattle Egret   *Bubulcus ibis*
Little Egret   *Egretta garzetta*
Great White Egret   *Ardea alba*
Grey Heron   *Ardea cinerea*
Purple Heron   *Ardea purpurea*
Black Stork   *Ciconia nigra*
White Stork   *Ciconia ciconia*
Glossy Ibis   *Plegadis falcinellus*

Appendix 3: A checklist of the birds of Gloucestershire

Spoonbill   *Platalea leucorodia*
Little Grebe   *Tachybaptus ruficollis*
Great Crested Grebe   *Podiceps cristatus*
Red-necked Grebe   *Podiceps grisegena*
Slavonian Grebe   *Podiceps auritus*
Black-necked Grebe   *Podiceps nigricollis*
Honey-buzzard   *Pernis apivorus*
Black Kite   *Milvus migrans*
Red Kite   *Milvus milvus*
Marsh Harrier   *Circus aeruginosus*
Hen Harrier   *Circus cyaneus*
Montagu's Harrier   *Circus pygargus*
Goshawk   *Accipiter gentilis*
Sparrowhawk   *Accipiter nisus*
Buzzard   *Buteo buteo*
Rough-legged Buzzard   *Buteo lagopus*
Golden Eagle   *Aquila chrysaetos*
Osprey   *Pandion haliaetus*
Kestrel   *Falco tinnunculus*
Red-footed Falcon   *Falco vespertinus*
Merlin   *Falco columbarius*
Hobby   *Falco subbuteo*
Gyr Falcon   *Falco rusticolus*
Peregrine   *Falco peregrinus*
Water Rail   *Rallus aquaticus*
Spotted Crake   *Porzana porzana*
Little Crake   *Porzana parva*
Baillon's Crake   *Porzana pusilla*
Corncrake   *Crex crex*
Moorhen   *Gallinula chloropus*
Coot   *Fulica atra*
Crane   *Grus grus*
Little Bustard   *Tetrax tetrax*
Great Bustard   *Otis tarda*
Stone-curlew   *Burhinus oedicnemus*
Black-winged Stilt   *Himantopus himantopus*
Avocet   *Recurvirostra avosetta*
Oystercatcher   *Haematopus ostralegus*
American Golden Plover   *Pluvialis dominica*
Golden Plover   *Pluvialis apricaria*
Grey Plover   *Pluvialis squatarola*
White-tailed Plover   *Vanellus leucurus*
Lapwing   *Vanellus vanellus*
Little Ringed Plover   *Charadrius dubius*
Ringed Plover   *Charadrius hiaticula*
Kentish Plover   *Charadrius alexandrinus*
Dotterel   *Charadrius morinellus*
Whimbrel   *Numenius phaeopus*
Curlew   *Numenius arquata*
Black-tailed Godwit   *Limosa limosa*
Bar-tailed Godwit   *Limosa lapponica*
Turnstone   *Arenaria interpres*
Knot   *Calidris canutus*
Ruff   *Philomachus pugnax*
Broad-billed Sandpiper   *Limicola falcinellus*
Curlew Sandpiper   *Calidris ferruginea*

Stilt Sandpiper   *Calidris himantopus*
Temminck's Stint   *Calidris temminckii*
Sanderling   *Calidris alba*
Dunlin   *Calidris alpina*
Purple Sandpiper   *Calidris maritima*
Baird's Sandpiper   *Calidris bairdii*
Little Stint   *Calidris minuta*
White-rumped Sandpiper   *Calidris fuscicollis*
Buff-breasted Sandpiper   *Tryngites subruficollis*
Pectoral Sandpiper   *Calidris melanotos*
Semipalmated Sandpiper   *Calidris pusilla*
Wilson's Phalarope   *Phalaropus tricolor*
Red-necked Phalarope   *Phalaropus lobatus*
Grey Phalarope   *Phalaropus fulicarius*
Common Sandpiper   *Actitis hypoleucos*
Spotted Sandpiper   *Actitis macularius*
Green Sandpiper   *Tringa ochropus*
Spotted Redshank   *Tringa erythropus*
Greenshank   *Tringa nebularia*
Lesser Yellowlegs   *Tringa flavipes*
Wood Sandpiper   *Tringa glareola*
Redshank   *Tringa totanus*
Jack Snipe   *Lymnocryptes minimus*
Woodcock   *Scolopax rusticola*
Long-billed Dowitcher   *Limnodromus scolopaceus*
Snipe   *Gallinago gallinago*
Great Snipe   *Gallinago media*
Collared Pratincole   *Glareola pratincola*
Pomarine Skua   *Stercorarius pomarinus*
Arctic Skua   *Stercorarius parasiticus*
Long-tailed Skua   *Stercorarius longicaudus*
Great Skua   *Stercorarius skua*
Puffin   *Fratercula arctica*
Razorbill   *Alca torda*
Little Auk   *Alle alle*
Guillemot   *Uria aalge*
Little Tern   *Sternula albifrons*
Gull-billed Tern   *Gelochelidon nilotica*
Caspian Tern   *Hydroprogne caspia*
Whiskered Tern   *Chlidonias hybrida*
Black Tern   *Chlidonias niger*
White-winged Black Tern   *Chlidonias leucopterus*
Sandwich Tern   *Sterna sandvicensis*
Common Tern   *Sterna hirundo*
Roseate Tern   *Sterna dougallii*
Arctic Tern   *Sterna paradisaea*
Ivory Gull   *Pagophila eburnea*
Sabine's Gull   *Xema sabini*
Kittiwake   *Rissa tridactyla*
Bonaparte's Gull   *Chroicocephalus philadelphia*
Black-headed Gull   *Chroicocephalus ridibundus*
Little Gull   *Hydrocoloeus minutus*
Ross's Gull   *Rhodostethia rosea*
Laughing Gull   *Larus atricilla*
Franklin's Gull   *Larus pipixcan*
Mediterranean Gull   *Larus melanocephalus*

Common Gull   *Larus canus*
Ring-billed Gull   *Larus delawarensis*
Lesser Black-backed Gull   *Larus fuscus*
Herring Gull   *Larus argentatus*
Yellow-legged Gull   *Larus michahellis*
Caspian Gull   *Larus cachinnans*
American Herring Gull   *Larus smithsonianus*
Iceland Gull   *Larus glaucoides*
Glaucous-winged Gull   *Larus glaucescens*
Glaucous Gull   *Larus hyperboreus*
Great Black-backed Gull   *Larus marinus*
Pallas's Sandgrouse   *Syrrhaptes paradoxus*
Rock Dove/Feral Pigeon   *Columba livia*
Stock Dove   *Columba oenas*
Woodpigeon   *Columba palumbus*
Collared Dove   *Streptopelia decaocto*
Turtle Dove   *Streptopelia turtur*
Cuckoo   *Cuculus canorus*
Barn Owl   *Tyto alba*
Little Owl   *Athene noctua*
Tawny Owl   *Strix aluco*
Long-eared Owl   *Asio otus*
Short-eared Owl   *Asio flammeus*
Nightjar   *Caprimulgus europaeus*
Swift   *Apus apus*
Alpine Swift   *Apus melba*
Kingfisher   *Alcedo atthis*
Bee-eater   *Merops apiaster*
Hoopoe   *Upupa epops*
Wryneck   *Jynx torquilla*
Green Woodpecker   *Picus viridis*
Great Spotted Woodpecker   *Dendrocopos major*
Lesser Spotted Woodpecker   *Dendrocopos minor*
Golden Oriole   *Oriolus oriolus*
Isabelline Shrike   *Lanius isabellinus*
Red-backed Shrike   *Lanius collurio*
Great Grey Shrike   *Lanius excubitor*
Woodchat Shrike   *Lanius senator*
Magpie   *Pica pica*
Jay   *Garrulus glandarius*
Nutcracker   *Nucifraga caryocatactes*
Jackdaw   *Corvus monedula*
Rook   *Corvus frugilegus*
Carrion Crow   *Corvus corone*
Hooded Crow   *Corvus cornix*
Raven   *Corvus corax*
Goldcrest   *Regulus regulus*
Firecrest   *Regulus ignicapilla*
Blue Tit   *Cyanistes caeruleus*
Great Tit   *Parus major*
Coal Tit   *Periparus ater*
Willow Tit   *Poecile montana*
Marsh Tit   *Poecile palustris*
Bearded Tit   *Panurus biarmicus*
Woodlark   *Lullula arborea*
Skylark   *Alauda arvensis*

Shore Lark   *Eremophila alpestris*
Sand Martin   *Riparia riparia*
Swallow   *Hirundo rustica*
House Martin   *Delichon urbicum*
Red-rumped Swallow   *Cecropis daurica*
Cetti's Warbler   *Cettia cetti*
Long-tailed Tit   *Aegithalos caudatus*
Pallas's Warbler   *Phylloscopus proregulus*
Yellow-browed Warbler   *Phylloscopus inornatus*
Dusky Warbler   *Phylloscopus fuscatus*
Wood Warbler   *Phylloscopus sibilatrix*
Chiffchaff   *Phylloscopus collybita*
Willow Warbler   *Phylloscopus trochilus*
Blackcap   *Sylvia atricapilla*
Garden Warbler   *Sylvia borin*
Barred Warbler   *Sylvia nisoria*
Lesser Whitethroat   *Sylvia curruca*
Whitethroat   *Sylvia communis*
Dartford Warbler   *Sylvia undata*
Grasshopper Warbler   *Locustella naevia*
Savi's Warbler   *Locustella luscinioides*
Icterine Warbler   *Hippolais icterina*
Aquatic Warbler   *Acrocephalus paludicola*
Sedge Warbler   *Acrocephalus schoenobaenus*
Marsh Warbler   *Acrocephalus palustris*
Reed Warbler   *Acrocephalus scirpaceus*
Great Reed Warbler   *Acrocephalus arundinaceus*
Waxwing   *Bombycilla garrulus*
Nuthatch   *Sitta europaea*
Treecreeper   *Certhia familiaris*
Wren   *Troglodytes troglodytes*
Starling   *Sturnus vulgaris*
Rose-coloured Starling   *Pastor roseus*
Dipper   *Cinclus cinclus*
White's Thrush   *Zoothera dauma*
Grey-cheeked Thrush   *Catharus minimus*
Ring Ouzel   *Turdus torquatus*
Blackbird   *Turdus merula*
Fieldfare   *Turdus pilaris*
Song Thrush   *Turdus philomelos*
Redwing   *Turdus iliacus*
Mistle Thrush   *Turdus viscivorus*
Spotted Flycatcher   *Muscicapa striata*
Robin   *Erithacus rubecula*
Nightingale   *Luscinia megarhynchos*
Bluethroat   *Luscinia svecica*
Red-breasted Flycatcher   *Ficedula parva*
Pied Flycatcher   *Ficedula hypoleuca*
Black Redstart   *Phoenicurus ochruros*
Redstart   *Phoenicurus phoenicurus*
Whinchat   *Saxicola rubetra*
Stonechat   *Saxicola torquatus*
Wheatear   *Oenanthe oenanthe*
Desert Wheatear   *Oenanthe deserti*
Dunnock   *Prunella modularis*
House Sparrow   *Passer domesticus*

Appendix 3: A checklist of the birds of Gloucestershire

Tree Sparrow   *Passer montanus*
Yellow Wagtail   *Motacilla flava*
Grey Wagtail   *Motacilla cinerea*
Pied Wagtail   *Motacilla alba*
Richard's Pipit   *Anthus richardi*
Tawny Pipit   *Anthus campestris*
Tree Pipit   *Anthus trivialis*
Meadow Pipit   *Anthus pratensis*
Red-throated Pipit   *Anthus cervinus*
Rock Pipit   *Anthus petrosus*
Water Pipit   *Anthus spinoletta*
Chaffinch   *Fringilla coelebs*
Brambling   *Fringilla montifringilla*
Greenfinch   *Chloris chloris*
Serin   *Serinus serinus*
Goldfinch   *Carduelis carduelis*
Siskin   *Carduelis spinus*
Linnet   *Carduelis cannabina*
Twite   *Carduelis flavirostris*
Lesser Redpoll   *Carduelis cabaret*
Mealy/Common Redpoll   *Carduelis flammea*
Arctic Redpoll   *Carduelis hornemanni*
Two-barred Crossbill   *Loxia leucoptera*
Common Crossbill   *Loxia curvirostra*
Parrot Crossbill   *Loxia pytyopsittacus*
Common Rosefinch   *Carpodacus erythrinus*
Bullfinch   *Pyrrhula pyrrhula*
Hawfinch   *Coccothraustes coccothraustes*
Snow Bunting   *Plectrophenax nivalis*
Lapland Bunting   *Calcarius lapponicus*
Dark-eyed Junco   *Junco hyemalis*
Yellowhammer   *Emberiza citrinella*
Cirl Bunting   *Emberiza cirlus*
Little Bunting   *Emberiza pusilla*
Reed Bunting   *Emberiza schoeniclus*
Corn Bunting   *Emberiza calandra*

References

Alexander, H. G. 1914. A report of the Land-Rail Inquiry. *British Birds* 8: 82–92.

Anon. 1989. Goshawk Breeding Habitat in Lowland Britain. *British Birds* 82: 56–67.

——. 1990. Breeding Biology of Goshawk in Lowland Britain. *British Birds* 83: 527–40.

Austin, G. E. & Rehfisch, M. M. 2005. Shifting nonbreeding distributions of migratory fauna in relation to climate change. *Global Change Biology* 11: 31–38.

Avery, G. R. & Jayne, A. 1996. Arctic Redpoll at Highnam Woods. GBR 1996: 85.

Baillie, S. R., Marchant, J. H., Leech, D. I., Renwick, A. R., Joys, A. C., Noble, D. G., Barimore, C., Conway, G. J., Downie, I. S., Risely, K. & Robinson, R. A. 2010. *Breeding Birds in the Wider Countryside: their conservation status 2010*. BTO Research Report No. 565. BTO, Thetford.

——, Marchant, J. H., Leech, D. I., Renwick, A. R., Eglington, S. M., Joys, A. C., Noble, D. G., Barimore, C., Conway, G. J., Downie, I. S., Risely, K. & Robinson, R. A. 2012. *Breeding Birds in the Wider Countryside*. BTO Research Report No. 609. BTO, Thetford.

Baker, H., Stroud, D. A., Aebischer, N. J., Cranswick, P. A., Gregory, R. D., McSorley, C. A., Noble, D. G. & Rehfisch, M. M. 2006. Population estimates of birds in Great Britain and the United Kingdom. *British Birds* 99: 25–44.

Balmer, D., Gillings, S., Caffrey, B., Swann, B., Downie, I. & Fuller, R. 2013. *Bird Atlas 2007–11: The Breeding and Wintering Birds of Britain and Ireland*. BTO, Thetford.

Bannerman, D. A. 1958. *The Birds of the British Isles*. Vol. 7. Edinburgh, Oliver & Boyd.

Barnes, J. A. G. 1952. The Status of the Lesser Black-backed Gull. *British Birds* 45: 3–17.

Bluett, A. 2007. The Marsh Warbler – A Gloucestershire Retrospective. *The Gloucestershire Naturalist* 18: 73–94.

——. 2012. A History of Ornithology, Ornithological Records and Contributions of the Natural History Societies in Gloucestershire. *The Gloucestershire Naturalist* 23: 4–41.

Bowler, J. M. 1996. Feeding strategies of Bewick's Swans in winter. PhD Thesis, University of Bristol.

—— & Rees, E. C. 1998. Bewick's Swans in Gloucestershire. *The Gloucestershire Naturalist* 11: 63–71.

Bowly E. 1860. List of Birds seen in Siddington, Gloucestershire (1856). *Proceedings of the Cotteswold Naturalists' Club* 2: xiv–xvi.

Brookes, R. 2008. House Martins eating elderberries. *British Birds* 101: 384.

Brown, A., Gilbert, G. & Wotton, S. 2012. Bitterns and Bittern Conservation in the UK. *British Birds* 105: 58–87.

Bullen, M. 1993. *Forty Years On*. DPBS, Dursley.

——. 1998. Severn Estuary Gull Count. *The Gloucestershire Naturalist* 11: 11–17.

Burfield, I. & van Bommel, F. 2004. *Birds in Europe*. BirdLife International, Cambridge.

Callaghan, D. A. & Green, A. J. 1993. Wildfowl at Risk. *Wildfowl* 44: 149–69.

Christian, J. 1999a. The Corncrake in the Vale. *The Gloucestershire Naturalist* 12: 1–11.

——. 1999b. *Sketches of Dean Birds*. Newnham, Gloucestershire, Magpie Publishing.

Clements, R. J. & Everett, C. M. 2012. Densities and dispersion of breeding Eurasian Hobbies *Falco subbuteo* in southeast England. *Bird Study* 59: 74–82.

Cobbett, W. [1830] 1985. *Rural Rides*. Penguin Books, London.

Cramp, S., Simmons, K. E. L. & Perrins, C. M. (Eds). 1977–94. *Handbook of the birds of Europe, the Middle East and North Africa: the birds of the Western Palearctic*. 9 vols. Oxford University Press, Oxford.

Davies, N. B. 1992. *Dunnock Behaviour and Social Evolution*. Oxford University Press, Oxford.

Davis, P. G. 1982. Nightingales in Britain in 1980. *Bird Study* 29: 73–79.

Delany, S., Scott, D., Dodman, T. & Stroud, D. (Eds.). 2009. *An Atlas of Wader Populations in Africa and Western Eurasia*. Wetlands International, Wageningen, The Netherlands.

Dobson, A. D. M., Clarke, M., Kjellen, N. & Clarke, R. 2012. The size and migratory origins of the population of Hen Harriers *Circus cyaneus* wintering in England. *Bird Study* 59: 218–27.

Durham, M. E. 1990. The Severn Estuary Gull Group Report 1990. GBR 1990: 88–92.

Dymott, P. 1997. Desert Wheatear at Bishop's Cleeve. GBR 1997: 93.

Eaton, M. A., Brown, A. F., Noble, D. G., Musgrove, A. J., Hearn, R., Aebischer, N. J., Gibbons, D. W., Evans, A. & Gregory, R. D. 2009. Birds of Conservation Concern 3: the population status of birds in the United Kingdom, Channel Islands and the Isle of Man. *British Birds* 102: 296–341.

——, Balmer, D. E., Cuthbert, R., Grise, P. V., Hall, J., Hearn, R. D., Holt, C. A., Musgrove, A. J., Noble, D. G., Parsons, M., Risely, K., Stroud, D. A. & Wotton, S. 2011. *The state of the UK's birds 2011*. RSPB, BTO, WWT, CCW, JNCC, NE, NIEA and SNH, Sandy, Bedfordshire.

Evans, E. 1880. The Birds of Gloucestershire. *Transactions of the Stroud Natural History and Philosophical Society* 1880: 116–32.

Faber, M., Betleja, J., Gwiazda, R. & Malczyk, P. 2001. Mixed colonies of large white-headed gulls in southern Poland. *British Birds* 94: 529-34.

Ferns, P. N., Green, G. H. & Round, P. D. 1979. Significance of the Somerset and Gwent Levels in Britain as feeding areas for migrant Whimbrels *Numenius phaeopus*. *Biological Conservation* 16: 7-22.

Forrester, R. W., Andrews, I. J., McInerny, C. J., Murray, R. D., McGowan, R. Y., Zonfrillo, B., Betts, M. W., Jardine, D. C. & Grundy, D. S. (Eds.). 2007. *The Birds of Scotland*. 2 vols. Scottish Ornithologists' Club, Aberlady.

Fuller, R. J., Noble, D. G., Smith, K. W. & Vanhinsbergh, D. 2005. Recent declines in populations of woodland birds in Britain: a review of possible causes. *British Birds* 98: 116-43.

Gibbons, D. W., Reid, J. B. & Chapman, R. A. 1993. *The New Atlas of Breeding Birds in Britain and Ireland: 1988-1991*. T. & A. D. Poyser, London.

Gill, F. & Donsker, D. (Eds.). 2012. IOC World Bird Names (Version 2.11). http://www.worldbirdnames.org/.

Hagemeijer, W. J. M. & Blair, M. J. (Eds.). 1997. *The EBBC Atlas of European Breeding Birds, their distribution and abundance*. T. & A. D. Poyser, London.

Harrison, G. R., Dean, A. R., Richards, A. J. & Smallshire, D. 1982. *The Birds of the West Midlands*. West Midland Bird Club, Birmingham.

Harrop, A. H. J. 2011. The Wiltshire Hawk Owl and criteria for accepting historical records. *British Birds* 104: 162-63.

Haynes, V. 1980. Communal Roosting by Wrens. *British Birds* 73: 104-05.

Hearn, R. 2005. Gloucestershire Ringing Report 2005. GBR 2005: 134-46.

Heaven, A. 1998. Two-barred Crossbill in the Forest of Dean. GBR 1998: 153-54.

Holling, M. & RBBP. 2009. Rare breeding birds in the United Kingdom in 2006. *British Birds* 99: 158-203.

Holloway, S. 1996. *The Historical Atlas of Breeding Birds in Britain and Ireland, 1875-1900*. T. & A. D. Poyser, London.

Holt, C. H., Hewson, C. M. & Fuller, R. J. 2012. The Nightingale in Britain: status, ecology and conservation needs. *British Birds* 105: 172-87.

Inglis, I. R., Isaacson, A. J., Thearle, R. J. P. & Westwood, N. J. 1990. The effects of changing agricultural practice on Woodpigeon *Columba palumbus* numbers. *Ibis* 132: 262-72.

Jönsson, O. 2011. Great Black-backed Gulls breeding at Khniffis Lagoon, Morocco and the status of Cape Gull in the Western Palearctic. *Birding World* 24: 68-76.

Kershaw, M. & Cranswick, P. A. 2003. Numbers of wintering waterbirds in Great Britain, 1994/5-1998/9. *Biological Conservation* 111: 91-104.

Lack, P. 1986. *The Atlas of Wintering Birds in Britain and Ireland*. T. & A. D. Poyser, England.

Langston, R. H. W., Smith, T., Brown, A. F. & Gregory, R. D. 2006. Status of breeding Twite *Carduelis flavirostris* in the UK. *Bird Study* 53: 55-63.

Leach, I. H. 1981. Wintering Blackcaps in Britain and Ireland. *Bird Study* 28: 5-14.

Lees, J. 2006. American vagrants at Slimbridge WWT: September 2006. GBR 2006: 160-62.

——, 2009. Pacific Diver at WWT Slimbridge: November 2009. GBR 2009: 176-77.

Lord, J., Munns, D. J., Beck, T. K. & Richards, A. J. 1970. *Atlas of breeding birds of the West Midlands*. Collins, London.

Macdonald, B. 2011. Survey of the Willow Tit in the Forest of Dean, Gloucestershire. *The Gloucestershire Naturalist* 22: 20-27.

Main, I., Pearce, D. & Hutton, T. 2009. *Birds of the Cotswolds: a new breeding atlas*. Liverpool University Press, Liverpool.

Malling Olsen, K. & Larsson, H. 2004. *Gulls of Europe, Asia and North America*. Christopher Helm, London.

Mason, C. F. & Macdonald, S. M. 2000. Influence of landscape and land-use on the distribution of breeding birds in farmland in eastern England. *Journal of Zoology* 251: 339-48.

Mellersh, W. L. 1902. *A Treatise on the Birds of Gloucestershire*. John Bellows, Gloucester.

Mikkola, H. 1983. *Owls of Europe*. T. & A. D. Poyser, Calton.

Mitchell, C., Hearn, R. & Stroud, D. 2012. The merging populations of Greylag Geese breeding in Britain. *British Birds* 105: 498-505.

Mudge, G. P. & Ferns, P. N. 1980. *A census of breeding gulls in the inner Bristol Channel*. Unpublished report.

Musgrove, A. J., Austin, G. E., Hearn, R. D., Holt, C. A., Stroud, D. A. & Wotton, S. R. 2011. Overwinter population estimates of British waterbirds. *British Birds* 104: 364-97.

Nicholls, H. G. 1858. *The Forest of Dean*. John Murray, London.

Niles, J. R. A. & Cooper, S. 1969. *Birds of the Dean Forest Park*. Forest of Dean Newspapers Ltd, Coleford.

Norris, C. A. 1945. Summary of a report on the distribution and status of the Corn-Crake (*Crex crex*). *British Birds* 38: 142-48.

Ockendon, N., Hewson, C. M., Johnston, A. & Atkinson, P. W. 2012. Declines in British-breeding populations of Afro-Palearctic migrants are linked to bioclimatic wintering zone in Africa, possibly via constraints on arrival time advancement. *Bird Study* 59: 111-25.

Parslow, J. 1973. *Breeding Birds of Britain and Ireland*. T. & A. D. Poyser, Berkhamsted.

PECBMS [Pan-European Common Bird Monitoring Scheme]. 2011. *Population Trends of Common European Breeding Birds 2011*. CSO, Prague.

Perkins, A. J., Watson, A., Maggs, H. E. & Wilson, J. D. 2012. Conservation insights from changing associations between habitat, territory distribution and mating system of Corn Buntings *Emberiza calandra* over a 20-year population decline. *Ibis* 154: 601-15.

Petty, S. J. 1996. *Reducing disturbance to goshawks during the breeding season*. Research Information Note 267. Forestry Commission, Edinburgh.

Philips Price, M. 1961. Warbler fluctuations in oak woodland in the Severn Valley. *British Birds* 54: 100–06.

Phillips, J. & Phillips, V. 2011. Spotted Sandpiper at Lydney New Grounds. GBR 2011: 173–74.

Pitches, A. 2012. News and Comment. *British Birds* 105: 423–24.

Potts, G. R. 1989. The impact of releasing hybrid partridges on wild Red-legged Partridge populations. *Game Conservancy Annual Review* 20: 81–85.

Quinn, J. L. 1995. *Severn Vale Breeding Wader Survey 1995*. RSPB, Sandy.

Robinson, H. W. 1914. Avocets in Gloucestershire. *British Birds* 7: 235.

Robinson, R. A., Lawson, B., Toms, M. P., Peck, K. M., Kirkwood, J. K., Chantrey, J., Clatworthy, I. R., Evans, A. D., Hughes, L. A., Hutchinson, O. C., John, S. K., Pennycott, T. W., Perkins, M. W., Rowley, P. S., Simpson, V. R., Tyler, K. M. & Cunningham, A. A. 2010. Emerging Infectious Disease Leads to Rapid Population Declines of Common British Birds. *PLoS ONE* 5(8): e12215. doi:10.1371/journal.pone.0012215.

Rock, P. 2004. A study of the effects of deterring gulls from Gloucester Landfill for a period of two weeks in March 2004. Unpublished report to Gloucestershire Gull Action Group.

——. 2005. Urban Gulls: problems and solutions. *British Birds* 98: 338–55.

——. 2006. A study to discover the overwintering rate of urban Lesser Black-backed Gulls within a radius of circa 100 km of Bristol. Unpublished report to various sponsors.

——. 2009. *Roof-nesting Gulls in Gloucester*. Unpublished report for Gloucester City Council.

Sanders, J. D. 1996. Franklin's Gull at Gloucester Landfill Site. GBR 1996: 84.

——. 2006. Glaucous-winged Gull, a species new to Europe. GBR 2006: 165–70.

——. 2007a. The Glaucous-winged Gull in Gloucestershire – a new British bird. *Birding World* 20: 13–19.

——. 2007b. Baltic Gull at Gloucester Landfill Site. GBR 2007: 155–58.

——. 2010. Glaucous-winged Gull in Gloucestershire: new to Britain. *British Birds* 103: 53–59.

——. 2011. Gull Scaring at Landfill Sites. *Gloucester Naturalists' Society News*, December 2011: 6–7.

Sangster, G., Collinson, J. M., Helbig, A. J., Knox, A. G. & Parkin, D. T. 2005. Taxonomic recommendations for British birds: third report. *Ibis* 147: 821–26.

——, Collinson, J. M., Knox, A. G., Parkin, D. T. & Svensson, L. 2007. Taxonomic recommendations for British birds: fourth report. *Ibis* 149: 853–57.

Sellers, R. M. 1979. The Changing Status of the Cormorant in Gloucestershire. GBR 1979: 56–61.

Sharpe, C. M. 2007. *Manx Bird Atlas*. Liverpool University Press, Liverpool.

Sharrock, J. T. R. 1976. *The Atlas of Breeding Birds in Britain and Ireland*. BTO, Thetford.

Shawyer, C. R. 1998. *The Barn Owl*. Arlequin, Chelmsford.

Siriwardena, G. M., Baillie, S. R. & Wilson, J. D. 1998. Variation in the survival rates of British farmland passerines with respect to their population trends. *Bird Study* 45: 276–92.

Skov, H., Heinänen, S., Žydelis, R., Bellebaum, J., Bzoma, S., Dagys, M., Durinck, J., Garthe, S., Grishanov, G., Hario, M., Kieckbusch, J. K., Kube, J., Kuresoo, A., Larsson, K., Luigujoe, L., Meissner, W., Nehls, H. W., Nilsson, L., Petersen, I. K., Roos, M. M., Pihl, S., Sonntag, N., Stock, A. & Stipniece, A. 2011. *Waterbird Populations and Pressures in the Baltic Sea*. Nordic Council of Ministers, Copenhagen.

Smart, S. 2009. Common Rosefinch at Ashleworth. GBR 2009: 178–79.

Smith, G. A. 2011. Pair of Stonechats. *Newsletter of the North Cotswold Ornithological Society*, November 2011: 9–10.

Smith, K. W. & Charman, E. C. 2012. The ecology and conservation of the Lesser Spotted Woodpecker. *British Birds* 105: 294–307.

Snow, D. W. & Perrins, C. M. 1998. *The Birds of the Western Palearctic, Concise Edition*. 2 vols. Oxford University Press, Oxford.

Stanbury, A. 2011. The changing status of the Common Crane in the UK. *British Birds* 104: 432–47.

——. & Sills, N. Common Crane habitats in Britain. *British Wildlife* 23: 381–90.

Stewart, P. F. 1997. A summary of ringing activities 1986–1996. *First Progress Report*. SEGG, Gloucester.

Summers, R. W. & Buckland, S. T. 2010. A first survey of the global population size and distribution of the Scottish Crossbill *Loxia scotica*. *Bird Conservation International* 21: 186–98.

Sutcliffe, M. 2010. Garden Bird Survey 2010. GBR 2010: 166–73.

Swaine, C. M. 1982. *Birds of Gloucestershire*. Alan Sutton, Gloucester.

Taylor, A. J. & O'Halloran, J. 2002. The decline of the Corn Bunting *Miliaria calandra* in the Republic of Ireland. *Biology and Environment: Proceedings of the Royal Irish Academy* 102: 165–75.

Taylor, M. & Marchant, J. H. 2011. *The Norfolk Bird Atlas 1999–2007*. BTO, Thetford.

Ticehurst, N. F. & Jourdain, F. C. R. 1911. On the distribution of the Nightingale in the breeding season in Great Britain. *British Birds* 5: 2–21.

Venables, W. A., Clarke, R. M., Jones, C., Lewis, J. M. S., Tyler, S. J., Walker, I. R. & Williams, R. A. 2008. *The Birds of Gwent*. Christopher Helm, London.

Voous, K. H. 1960. *Atlas of European Birds*. Nelson, London.

Walkden, P. 2009. *The Wild Geese of the New Grounds*. Friends of WWT Slimbridge, Slimbridge.

Webster B., & Wood, G. 1976. *A Guide to Birds in Gloucestershire with Part of Avon*. Heart of England Countryside Tours, Northampton.

Wernham, C. V., Toms, M. P., Marchant, J. H., Clark, J. A., Siriwardena, G. M. & Baillie, S. R. (Eds.). 2002. *The Migration Atlas: movements of the birds of Britain and Ireland*. T. & A. D. Poyser, London.

Wiktander, U., Olsson, O. & Nilsson, S. G. 2001. Seasonal variation in home-range size and habitat area requirement of the Lesser Spotted Woodpecker (*Dendrocopos minor*) in south Sweden. *Biological Conservation* 100: 387–95.

Wilson, A. M., Henderson, A. C. B. & Fuller, R. J. 2002. Status of the Nightingale *Luscinia megarhynchos* in Britain at the end of the 20th century with particular reference to climate change. *Bird Study* 49: 193–204.

Wiltshire Ornithological Society. 2007. *Birds of Wiltshire.* Wiltshire Ornithological Society, Devizes.

Witchell, C. A. & Strugnell, W. B. 1892. *The Flora and Fauna of Gloucestershire.* Stroud Press, Stroud.

Witherby, H. F., Jourdain, F. C. R., Ticehurst, N. F. & Tucker, B. W. 1938–41. *The Handbook of British Birds.* 5 vols. Witherby, London.

Wood, J. D. 1952. Review. *British Birds* 45: 10–111.

Wright, M. R., Williams, M. F., Alexander, K. N. A., Dymott, P. H., Hookway, R. C., Owen, S. M., Robinson, M. F., Ralphs, I. L. & Stainton, M. S. 1990. *An Atlas of Cotswold Breeding Birds.* Drinkwater, Shipston-on-Stour.

Zöckler, C. & Lysenko, I. 2000. *Water birds on the edge. First circumpolar assessment of climate change impact on arctic breeding water birds.* World Conservation Press, Cambridge.

Index to scientific names of birds

Page numbers in **bold** refer to the main species accounts.

Accipiter gentilis   **142**
Accipiter nisus   **144**
Acrocephalus arundinaceus   **341**
Acrocephalus paludicola   **341**
Acrocephalus palustris   **340**
Acrocephalus schoenobaenus   **336**
Acrocephalus scirpaceus   **338**
Actitis hypoleucos   **197**
Actitis macularius   **209**
Aegithalos caudatus   **318**
Agapornis roseicollis   432
Aix galericulata   **76**
Aix sponsa   431
Alauda arvensis   **308**
Alca torda   **242**
Alcedo atthis   **268**
Alectoris chukar   **108**
Alectoris rufa   **108**
Alle alle   **243**
Alopochen aegyptiaca   **73**
Anas acuta   **86**
Anas americana   **91**
Anas andium   432
Anas bahamensis   431
Anas capensis   432
Anas carolinensis   **91**
Anas clypeata   **88**
Anas crecca   **82**
Anas cyanoptera   432
Anas discors   **91**
Anas flavirostris   432
Anas penelope   **78**
Anas platyrhynchos   **84**
Anas querquedula   **90**
Anas sibilatrix   431
Anas strepera   **80**
Anser albifrons   **64**
Anser anser   **66**
Anser brachyrhynchus   **63**
Anser caerulescens   **73**
Anser erythropus   **72**
Anser fabalis   **63**
Anser indicus   431
Anser rossii   431
Anthus campestris   **399**

Anthus cervinus   **399**
Anthus petrosus   **398**
Anthus pratensis   **396**
Anthus richardi   **398**
Anthus spinoletta   **399**
Anthus trivialis   **394**
Apus apus   **266**
Apus melba   **270**
Apus pallidus   **266**
Aquila chrysaetos   **149**
Ara ararauna   432
Ardea alba   **129**
Ardea cinerea   **126**
Ardea purpurea   **130**
Ardeola ralloides   **128**
Arenaria interpres   **204**
Asio flammeus   **263**
Asio otus   **262**
Athene noctua   **258**
Aythya affinis   **99**
Aythya collaris   **99**
Aythya ferina   **94**
Aythya fuligula   **96**
Aythya marila   **98**
Aythya nyroca   **99**

Bombycilla garrulus   **342**
Botaurus stellaris   **123**
Branta bernicla   **71**
Branta canadensis   **68**
Branta leucopsis   **70**
Branta ruficollis   **73**
Bubo bengalensis   432
Bubo bubo   432
Bubulcus ibis   **129**
Bucephala clangula   **102**
Burhinus oedicnemus   **177**
Buteo buteo   **146**
Buteo lagopus   **149**

Cairina moschata   431
Calcarius lapponicus   **423**
Calidris alba   **181**
Calidris alpina   **184**
Calidris bairdii   **208**
Calidris canutus   **180**

Calidris ferruginea   **183**
Calidris fuscicollis   **208**
Calidris himantopus   **208**
Calidris maritima   **206**
Calidris melanotos   **208**
Calidris minuta   **182**
Calidris pusilla   **207**
Calidris temminckii   **206**
Callonetta leucophrys   431
Caprimulgus europaeus   **264**
Carduelis cabaret   **412**
Carduelis cannabina   **410**
Carduelis carduelis   **406**
Carduelis flammea   **420**
Carduelis flavirostris   **420**
Carduelis hornemanni   **421**
Carduelis spinus   11, **408**
Carpodacus erythrinus   **421**
Catharus minumus   **355**
Cecropsis daurica   **315**
Certhia familiaris   **346**
Cettia cetti   **316**
Charadrius alexandrinus   **173**
Charadrius dubius   **170**
Charadrius hiaticula   **172**
Charadrius morinellus   **173**
Chen canagica   431
Chlidonias hybrida   **241**
Chlidonias leucopterus   **241**
Chlidonias niger   **240**
Chloris chloris   **404**
Chroicocephalus cirrocephalus   432
Chroicocephalus philadelphia   **232**
Chroicocephalus ridibundus   **214**
Chrysolophus amherstiae   432
Chrysolophus pictus   432
Ciconia ciconia   **130**, 432
Ciconia nigra   **130**
Cinclus cinclus   **352**
Cinnyricinclus leucogaster   432
Circus aeruginosus   **140**
Circus cyaneus   **141**
Circus pygargus   **149**
Clangula hyemalis   **101**
Coccothraustes coccothraustes   **418**

Index to scientific names of birds

Columba livia **244**
Columba oenas **246**
Columba palumbus **248**
Corvus corax **290**
Corvus cornix **288**
Corvus corone **288**
Corvus frugilegus **286**
Corvus monedula **284**
Coturnix coturnix **114**
Coturnix japonica 114
Crex crex **160**
Crossoptilon auritum 432
Cuculus canorus **254**
Cyanistes caeruleus **296**
Cygnus atratus 431
Cygnus columbianus **60**
Cygnus cygnus **62**
Cygnus olor **58**

Delichon urbicum **314**
Dendrocopos major **274**
Dendrocopos minor **276**
Dendrocygna bicolor 431

Egretta garzetta **124**
Emberiza calandra **428**
Emberiza cirlus **430**
Emberiza citrinella **424**
Emberiza pusilla **430**
Emberiza schoeniclus **426**
Eremophila alpestris **306**
Erithacus rubecula **368**

Falco biarmicus 432
Falco cherrug 432
Falco columbarius **152**
Falco peregrinus **156**
Falco rusticolus **149**, 432
Falco subbuteo **154**
Falco tinnunculus **150**
Falco vespertinus **149**
Ficedula hypoleuca **372**
Ficedula parva **381**
Fratercula arctica **243**
Fringilla coelebs **400**
Fringilla montifringilla **402**
Fulica atra **164**
Fulmarus glacialis **117**

Gallinago gallinago **188**
Gallinago media **206**
Gallinula chloropus **162**
Garrulax albogularis 432
Garrulax pectoralis 432
Garrulus glandarius **282**
Gavia arctica **116**
Gavia immer **116**
Gavia pacifica **116**

Gavia stellata **116**
Gelochelidon nilotica **235**
Geopelia cuneata 432
Glareola pratincola **177**
Grus grus **166**

Haematopus ostralegus **168**
Haliaeetus leucocephalus 432
Himantopus himantopus **177**
Hippolais icterina **341**
Hirundo rustica **312**
Hydrobates pelagicus **118**
Hydrocoloeus minutus **216**
Hydroprogne caspia **235**

Ixobrychus minutus **128**

Junco hyemalis **430**
Jynx torquilla **271**

Lamprotornis superbus 432
Lanius collurio **278**
Lanius excubitor **278**
Lanius isabellinus **279**
Lanius senator **279**
Larus argentatus **222**
Larus atricilla **232**
Larus cachinnans **227**
Larus canus **218**
Larus delawarensis **233**
Larus fuscus **220**
Larus glaucescens **233**
Larus glaucoides **228**
Larus hyperboreus **229**
Larus marinus **230**
Larus melanocephalus **217**
Larus michahellis **227**
Larus pipixcan **233**
Larus smithsonianus **233**
Larus thayeri 228
Limicola falcinellus **206**
Limnodromus scolopaceus **209**
Limosa lapponica **193**
Limosa limosa **192**
Locustella luscinioides **341**
Locustella naevia **334**
Lophodytes cucullatus 432
Lophophanes cristatus 53
Lophura nycthemera 432
Loxia curvirostra **414**
Loxia leucoptera **421**
Loxia pytyopsittacus **421**
Lullula arborea **307**
Luscinia megarhynchos **370**
Luscinia svecica **381**
Lymnocryptes minimus **187**

Melanitta fusca **101**
Melanitta nigra **100**

Melopsittacus undulatus 432
Mergellus albellus **104**
Mergus merganser **106**
Mergus serrator **105**
Merops apiaster **270**
Milvus migrans **149**
Milvus milvus **138**
Morus bassanus **119**
Motacilla alba **392**
Motacilla cinerea **390**
Motacilla flava **388**
Muscicapa striata **366**

Netta rufina **92**
Nucifraga caryocatactes **279**
Numenius arquata **194**
Numenius phaeopus **196**
Numida meleagris 432
Nycticorax nycticorax **128**
Nymphicus hollandicus 432

Oceanodroma leucorhoa **118**
Oenanthe deserti **381**
Oenanthe oenanthe **380**
Oriolus chinensis 432
Oriolus oriolus **279**
Otis tarda **166**
Oxyura jamaicensis **107**
Oxyura leucocephala 107

Pagophila eburnea **232**
Pandion haliaetus **148**
Panurus biarmicus **306**
Parabuteo unicinctus 432
Parus major **298**
Passer domesticus **384**
Passer montanus **386**
Pastor roseus **350**
Pavo cristatus 432
Pelecanus onocrotalus 432
Perdix perdix **110**
Periparus ater **300**
Pernis apivorus **139**
Phalacrocorax aristotelis **122**
Phalacrocorax carbo **120**
Phalaropus fulicarius **205**
Phalaropus lobatus **205**
Phalaropus tricolor **209**
Phasianus colchicus **112**
Philomachus pugnax **186**
Phoenicopterus sp(p). 432
Phoenicurus ochruros **376**
Phoenicurus phoenicurus **374**
Phylloscopus collybita **322**
Phylloscopus fuscatus **341**
Phylloscopus inornatus **340**
Phylloscopus proregulus **341**
Phylloscopus sibilatrix **320**

Phylloscopus trochilus 324
Pica pica 280
Picus viridis 272
Platalea leucorodia 131
Plectrophenax nivalis 422
Plegadis falcinellus 130
Ploceus cucullatus 432
Pluvialis apricaria 174
Pluvialis dominica 207
Pluvialis squatarola 176
Podiceps auritus 136
Podiceps cristatus 134
Podiceps grisegena 136
Podiceps nigricollis 137
Poecile montana 302
Poecile palustris 304
Porzana parva 161
Porzana porzana 161
Porzana pusilla 161
Prunella collaris 53
Prunella modularis 382
Psittacula eupatria 432
Psittacula krameri 432
Puffinus puffinus 117
Pyrrhula pyrrhula 416

Quelea quelea 432

Rallus aquaticus 158
Recurvirostra avosetta 167
Regulus ignicapilla 294
Regulus regulus 292
Rhodostethia rosea 232

Riparia riparia 310
Rissa tridactyla 213

Saxicola rubetra 377
Saxicola torquatus 378
Scolopax rusticola 190
Serinus canaria 432
Serinus serinus 420
Sitta europaea 344
Somateria mollissima 101
Spreo superbus 432
Stercorarius longicaudus 212
Stercorarius parasiticus 210
Stercorarius pomarinus 212
Stercorarius skua 211
Sterna dougallii 235
Sterna hirundo 238
Sterna paradisaea 237
Sterna sandvicensis 236
Sternula albifrons 234
Streptopelia decaocto 250
Streptopelia risoria 432
Streptopelia turtur 252
Strix aluco 260
Sturnus vulgaris 350
Sylvia atricapilla 326
Sylvia borin 328
Sylvia communis 332
Sylvia curruca 330
Sylvia nisoria 341
Sylvia undata 341
Syrmaticus reevesii 432
Syrrhaptes paradoxus 115

Tachybaptus ruficollis 132
Tadorna ferruginea 431
Tadorna tadorna 74
Tadorna tadornoides 431
Tadorna variegata 431
Taeniopygia guttata 432
Tetrao tetrix 115
Tetrax tetrax 166
Tringa erythropus 199
Tringa flavipes 209
Tringa glareola 201
Tringa nebularia 200
Tringa ochropus 198
Tringa totanus 202
Troglodytes troglodytes 348
Tryngites subruficollis 208
Turdus iliacus 362
Turdus merula 356
Turdus philomelos 360
Turdus pilaris 358
Turdus torquatus 354
Turdus viscivorus 364
Tyto alba 256

Upupa epops 270
Uria aalge 242

Vanellus leucurus 205
Vanellus vanellus 178

Xema sabini 232

Yuhina diademata 432

Zoothera dauma 355

Index to English names of birds

All references to names in common, everyday use (see p. 53) are included. The 'official' IOC names are referenced only when they differ substantially from these names, i.e. they are not included when they are modified only by the addition of the prefix 'Common', 'Eurasian', 'European', Northern' or 'Western'. (Note that some names in everyday use are prefixed by 'Common', such as Common Gull and Common Scoter, and in these cases they are included.) In addition, the IOC name is not included where it and the everyday name differ only in the form of words (for example Gyr Falcon/Gyrfalcon). Page numbers in **bold** refer to the main species accounts.

Alexandrine Parakeet   432
Alpine Accentor   53
Alpine Swift   **270**
American Golden Plover   **207**
American Herring Gull   **233**
American Wigeon   **91**
Amethyst Starling   432
Aquatic Warbler   **341**
Arctic Redpoll   **421**
Arctic Skua   23, **210**, 211, 212
Arctic Tern   23, **237**, 238
Atlantic Puffin   **243**
Australian Shelduck   431
Avocet   **167**
Azorean Gull   **227**

Bahama Pintail   431
Baillon's Crake   **161**
Baird's Sandpiper   **208**
Bald Eagle   432
Baltic Gull   220
Barbary Dove   432
Bar-headed Goose   431
Barnacle Goose   39, **70**
Barn Owl   15, 37, **256**, 258
Barn Swallow   **312**
Barred Warbler   **341**
Bar-tailed Godwit   19, 23, **193**
Bean Goose   39, **63**
Bearded Reedling   **306**
Bearded Tit   **306**
Bee-eater   **270**
Bengal Eagle Owl   432
Bewick's Swan   15, 37, **60**, 62, 162
Bittern   **123**
Blackbird   50, **356**, 360, 364
Black Brant   71
Blackcap   **326**, 328, 332, 371
Black-crowned Night Heron   **128**
Black Grouse   **115**
Black-headed Gull   36, **214**, 218
Black Kite   **149**

Black-legged Kittiwake   **213**
Black-naped Oriole   432
Black-necked Grebe   **137**
Black Redstart   **376**
Black Stork   128, **130**
Black Swan   431
Black-tailed Godwit   **192**
Black Tern   15, 54, **240**, 241
Black-throated Diver   **116**
Black-throated Loon   **116**
Black-winged Stilt   **177**
Blue-and-yellow Macaw   432
Blue-eared Pheasant   432
Blue-headed Wagtail   388, 389
Bluethroat   **381**
Blue Tit   50, **296**, 300, 318, 356, 395
Blue-winged Teal   **91**
Bohemian Waxwing   **342**
Bonaparte's Gull   **232**
Brambling   **402**
Brant Goose   **71**
Brent Goose   39, **71**
Broad-billed Sandpiper   **206**
Budgerigar   432
Buff-breasted Sandpiper   207, **208**
Bullfinch   **416**
Buzzard   5, 26, **146**, 150

Canada Goose   11, **68**, 70, 431
Canary   423, 432
Cape Teal   432
Carrion Crow   154, 262, **288**
Caspian Gull   **227**
Caspian Tern   **235**
Cattle Egret   128, **129**
Cetti's Warbler   **316**
Chaffinch   51, **400**, 402, 403, 404
Chiffchaff   **322**, 371
Chiloe Wigeon   431
Chukar   108
Cinnamon Teal   432
Cirl Bunting   **430**

Coal Tit   **300**
Cockatiel   432
Collared Dove   **250**, 253
Collared Pratincole   **177**
Common Gull   31, 214, **218**
Common Merganser   **106**
Common Murre   **242**
Common Redpoll   **420**
Common Rosefinch   **421**
Common Sandpiper   **197**, 209
Common Scoter   **100**, 101
Common Tern   36, 237, **238**
Coot   11, 36, 80, **164**
Cormorant   5, **120**, 122, 124
Corn Bunting   15, 31, **428**
Corncrake   114, **160**
Coues's Redpoll   421
Crane   **166**
Crested Tit   53
Crossbill (Common)   11, 31, **414**, 421
Cuckoo   **254**
Curlew   11, 15, 22, 37, **194**
Curlew Sandpiper   54, 182, **183**, 208

Dark-eyed Junco   **430**
Dartford Warbler   **341**
Desert Wheatear   **381**
Diamond Dove   432
Dipper   11, 26, 31, **352**, 390
Dotterel   **173**
Dunlin   22, 23, **184**, 206
Dunnock   254, **382**, 395
Dusky Warbler   **341**

Eagle Owl   432
Egyptian Goose   **73**
Eider   **101**
Emperor Goose   431

Feral Pigeon   **244**
Ferruginous Duck   **99**
Fieldfare   **358**, 362
Firecrest   11, **294**

Flamingo 432
Franklin's Gull **233**
Fulmar 23, **117**
Fulvous Whistling Duck 431

Gadwall 36, **80**
Gannet 23, **119**
Garden Warbler 326, **328**, 332
Garganey **90**
Glaucous Gull 22, 228, **229**
Glaucous-winged Gull **233**
Glossy Ibis 128, **130**
Goldcrest **292**, 294, 318
Golden Eagle **149**
Goldeneye 80, **102**
Golden Oriole **279**
Golden Pheasant 432
Golden Plover 31, **174**, 178
Goldfinch 51, **406**, 410, 416
Goosander 5, 105, **106**
Goshawk 11, 31, 44, **142**, 144
Grasshopper Warbler 27, **334**
Great Black-backed Gull **230**
Great Bustard **166**
Great Cormorant **120**
Great Crested Grebe 36, 132, **134**
Great Egret **129**
Greater Necklaced Laughingthrush 432
Greater Scaup **98**
Greater White-fronted Goose **64**
Great Grey Shrike 46, 156, **278**
Great Northern Diver **116**
Great Northern Loon **116**
Great Reed Warbler **341**
Great Skua 23, **211**
Great Snipe **206**
Great Spotted Woodpecker 156, 272, **274**, 276, 302, 372
Great Tit **298**, 300, 318
Great White Egret **129**
Greenfinch 51, 400, **404**, 406
Green Sandpiper **198**
Greenshank **200**
Green-winged Teal **91**
Green Woodpecker 144, **272**
Grey-cheeked Thrush **355**
Grey-headed Gull 432
Grey-headed Wagtail **389**
Grey Heron 124, **126**, 171
Greylag Goose 11, 39, **66**, 431
Grey Partridge 15, 31, 108, **110**
Grey Phalarope **205**
Grey Plover 23, **176**
Grey Wagtail 5, 37, **390**
Guillemot **242**
Gull-billed Tern **235**
Gyr Falcon **149**, 432

Harris's Hawk 432
Hawfinch 11, 15, 31, **418**
Helmeted Guineafowl 432
Hen Harrier 31, **141**
Herring Gull 220, **222**, 224, 225, 227, 229, 230, 233
Hobby 36, **154**
Honey-buzzard **139**
Hooded Crow **288**
Hooded Merganser 432
Hoopoe **270**, 271
Horned Grebe **136**
Horned Lark **306**
House Martin 46, 266, 311, **314**
House Sparrow 50, 314, **384**, 386

Iceland Gull 22, **228**
Icterine Warbler **341**
Indian Peafowl 432
Isabelline Shrike **279**
Ivory Gull **232**

Jackdaw 11, 246, **284**
Jack Snipe 144, **187**
Japanese Quail 114
Jay **282**

Kentish Plover **173**
Kestrel 11, 31, **150**, 246
Kingfisher 5, 37, **268**
Kittiwake 23, **213**
Knot 19, **180**
Kumlien's Gull 228

Lady Amherst's Pheasant 432
Lanner 432
Lapland Bunting 422, **423**
Lapland Longspur **423**
Lapwing 11, 15, 31, **178**, 202
Laughing Gull **232**
Leach's Petrel 23, **118**, 210, 211
Leach's Storm Petrel **118**
Lesser Black-backed Gull 37, 41, **220**, 222, 224, 225, 226, 227, 230
Lesser Redpoll 408, **412**
Lesser Scaup **99**
Lesser Spotted Woodpecker 11, 15, **276**
Lesser White-fronted Goose 39, **72**
Lesser Whitethroat **330**, 332
Lesser Yellowlegs **209**
Linnet 11, 49, **410**, 416
Little Auk 242, **243**
Little Bittern **128**
Little Bunting **430**
Little Bustard **166**
Little Crake **161**
Little Egret **124**, 129, 211
Little Grebe **132**

Little Gull 15, **216**, 232
Little Owl 257, **258**, 431
Little Ringed Plover 36, **170**, 310
Little Stint 144, **182**
Little Tern **234**
Long-billed Dowitcher **209**
Long-eared Owl **262**
Long-tailed Duck **101**
Long-tailed Jaeger **212**
Long-tailed Skua **212**
Long-tailed Tit **318**

Magpie **280**, 288
Mallard 11, 37, **84**, 102, 431
Mandarin Duck 11, **76**, 431
Manx Shearwater **117**, 156
Marsh Harrier **140**
Marsh Tit 302, **304**
Marsh Warbler 15, 254, **340**
Meadow Pipit 27, 254, **396**, 399
Mealy Redpoll 412, **420**
Mediterranean Gull **217**
Merlin **152**
Mew Gull **218**
Mistle Thrush **364**
Montagu's Harrier **149**
Moorhen 11, 37, **162**, 164, 171
Muscovy Duck 431
Mute Swan 11, 36, 37, **58**

Night-heron **128**
Nightingale 15, 36, 39, 254, **370**
Nightjar 11, **264**
Nutcracker **279**
Nuthatch **344**

Osprey **148**
Oystercatcher 15, 36, **168**

Pacific Diver **116**
Pacific Loon **116**
Pallas's Leaf Warbler **341**
Pallas's Sandgrouse **115**
Pallas's Warbler **341**
Pallid Swift 266
Paradise Shelduck 431
Parasitic Jaeger **210**
Parrot Crossbill **421**
Peach-faced Lovebird 432
Pectoral Sandpiper 207, **208**, 209
Peregrine 5, 73, 117, 148, **156**, 226, 239, 242, 243, 244, 279, 432
Peregrine Falcon **156**
Pheasant 110, **112**, 143, 431
Pied Avocet **167**
Pied Flycatcher 11, 41, 254, **372**
Pied Wagtail 389, **392**
Pink-footed Goose 39, **63**

Index to English names of birds

Pintail **86**
Pochard 36, 80, **94**, 107
Pomarine Skua **212**
Puffin 242, **243**
Purple Heron **130**
Purple Sandpiper **206**

Quail 15, 31, **114**

Raven 5, 26, 156, 238, **290**
Razorbill **242**
Red-backed Shrike **278**
Red-billed Quelea 432
Red-breasted Flycatcher **381**
Red-breasted Goose **73**
Red-breasted Merganser **105**
Red-crested Pochard 36, 80, **92**
Red Crossbill **414**
Red-footed Falcon **149**
Red Kite 31, **138**, 290
Red Knot **180**
Red-legged Partridge **108**, 110, 431
Red-necked Grebe **136**
Red-necked Phalarope 144, **205**
Red Phalarope **205**
Red-rumped Swallow **315**
Redshank 15, 36, 37, 178, **202**
Redstart 11, 27, **374**
Red-throated Diver **116**
Red-throated Loon **116**
Red-throated Pipit **399**
Redwing **362**
Reed Bunting 15, 36, 37, 254, **426**
Reed Warbler 15, 36, 37, 254, 336, **338**
Reeves's Pheasant 432
Richard's Pipit **398**
Ring-billed Gull **233**
Ringed Plover 23, **172**
Ringed Teal 431
Ring-necked Duck **99**
Ring-necked Parakeet 431, 432
Ring Ouzel 27, **354**
Robin 50, 348, 356, **368**
Rock Dove **244**
Rock Pipit **398**, 399
Rook 164, **286**, 288
Roseate Tern **235**
Rose-coloured Starling **350**
Rose-ringed Parakeet 432
Ross's Goose 431
Ross's Gull **232**
Rosy-faced Lovebird 432
Rosy Starling **350**
Rough-legged Buzzard **149**
Ruddy Duck **107**, 431
Ruddy Shelduck 431

Ruddy Turnstone **204**
Ruff **186**

Sabine's Gull 23, **232**
Saker 432
Sanderling 23, **181**
Sand Martin 5, 36, **310**, 314
Sandwich Tern **236**
Savi's Warbler **341**
Scaly Thrush **355**
Scaup 80, **98**
Sedge Warbler 36, 46, **336**
Semipalmated Sandpiper **207**
Serin **420**
Shag **122**
Shelduck 22, 36, **74**, 211, 431
Shore Lark **306**
Short-eared Owl 31, **263**
Shoveler 36, **88**
Silver Pheasant 432
Siskin 11, **408**
Skylark 27, 31, 49, 153, **308**, 396
Slate-coloured Junco 430
Slavonian Grebe **136**, 137
Smew 36, **104**
Snipe 15, 156, 187, **188**
Snow Bunting **422**
Snow Goose **73**
Song Thrush **360**, 364
Sparrowhawk **144**, 205
Speckled Teal 432
Spoonbill **131**
Spotted Crake **161**
Spotted Flycatcher 254, **366**
Spotted Nutcracker **279**
Spotted Redshank **199**
Spotted Sandpiper **209**
Squacco Heron **128**
Starling 51, 144, **350**, 362
Stilt Sandpiper **208**
Stock Dove 11, 31, 244, **246**
Stonechat 11, 27, 377, **378**
Stone-curlew **177**
Storm Petrel 23, **118**
Superb Starling 432
Swallow 311, **312**, 314
Swift 15, **266**
Sykes's Wagtail 389

Tawny Owl 76, 256, 258, **260**, 262
Tawny Pipit **399**
Teal 37, **82**, 90, 102, 156
Temminck's Stint **206**
Thayer's Gull 228
Treecreeper 318, **346**
Tree Pipit 11, 27, **394**, 396
Tree Sparrow 11, 15, 31, 37, **386**

Tufted Duck 36, **96**, 99, 102, 107
Tundra Swan **60**
Turnstone 23, **204**
Turtle Dove 11, **252**
Twite **420**
Two-barred Crossbill **421**

Velvet Scoter **101**
Village Weaver 432
Violet-backed Starling 432

Water Pipit **399**
Water Rail **158**
Waxwing 38, 46, **342**
Wheatear **380**
Whimbrel 23, **196**
Whinchat **377**
Whiskered Tern **241**
White-cheeked Pintail 431
White-collared Yuhina 432
White-fronted Goose 15, 39, 63, **64**, 70, 72, 73, 211
White-headed Duck 107
White Pelican 432
White-rumped Sandpiper 207, **208**
White's Thrush **355**
White Stork 128, **130**, 432
White-tailed Lapwing **205**
White-tailed Plover **205**
Whitethroat 11, 326, 328, 330, **332**
White-throated Dipper **352**
White-throated Laughingthrush 432
White Wagtail **392**
White-winged Black Tern **241**
White-winged Tern **241**
Whooper Swan 37, 60, **62**
Wigeon 37, **78**, 100, 102
Willow Tit 11, 274, **302**, 304
Willow Warbler 11, **324**, 366, 371
Wilson's Phalarope **209**
Winter Wren **348**
Woodchat Shrike **279**
Woodcock **190**
Wood Duck 431
Woodlark **307**
Woodpigeon 47, 51, **248**, 356
Wood Sandpiper **201**
Wood Warbler 11, **320**
Wren 51, 254, **348**, 395
Wryneck 270, **271**

Yellow-billed Teal 432
Yellow-browed Warbler **340**
Yellowhammer 11, 31, 44, 49, **424**
Yellow-legged Gull **227**
Yellow Wagtail 15, 31, 37, **388**

Zebra Finch 432

Gloucestershire Ornithological Co-ordinating Committee brings together the various bird clubs and natural history organisations in Gloucestershire to collaborate on bird recording and conservation efforts. It oversees and supports the work of the county bird recorder and the production of the annual county bird report.